Why Do You Need this New Edition?

Technological innovations in communication, transportation, and various information tools have helped to create the greatest mixing of cultures that the world has ever seen. In order for you to function well in your private and public lives today, you will need to be competent in intercultural communication. Our goal in this book is to give you the knowledge, motivation, and skills to accomplish that objective. Considerable progress has been made by scholars and practitioners of intercultural communication over the past several years, and this edition accurately reflects their progress. Updates throughout the book provide you with the most contemporary scholarship and applications available to help prepare you to be a successful intercultural communicator in a variety of contexts.

Here are 6 good reasons why you should buy this new edition of *Intercultural Competence*:

1 **Substantial revisions of the material on cultural patterns** update the frameworks used to understand the range of cultural differences and similarities.

2 **Updated Culture Connections boxes** provide emotional connections and illustrate the lived experiences of intercultural communicators. Nearly half of the Culture Connections boxes are new to this edition, and were chosen carefully to provide the opportunity for you to "feel" relevant aspects of intercultural competence.

3 Throughout, an **expanded focus on the new information technologies and their effects on intercultural communication** will prepare you to overcome today's challenges to intercultural competence.

4 Chapter 9 has been substantially revised to reflect current ideas about contrastive rhetoric and the pragmatics of language use. **Cultural differences in both organizational preferences and in the preferred styles of persuasion** have been reorganized and updated.

5 Chapter 11 has been revised and updated to reflect **current ideas related to the health care, education, and business contexts.**

6 The discussions of "race" and "biology" have been updated to reflect current scientific and social scientific knowledge on these topics.

PEARSON

INTERCULTURAL COMPETENCE

Interpersonal Communication across Cultures

Sixth Edition

Myron W. Lustig
San Diego State University

Jolene Koester
California State University, Northridge

Allyn & Bacon

Boston   New York   San Francisco
Mexico City   Montreal   Toronto   London   Madrid   Munich   Paris
Hong Kong   Singapore   Tokyo   Cape Town   Sydney

Editor-in-Chief: *Karon Bowers*
Acquisitions Editor: *Jeanne Zalesky*
Editorial Assistant: *Megan Lentz*
Marketing Manager: *Suzan Czajkowski*
Production Supervisor: *Liz Napolitano*

Editorial Production Service: *Elm Street Publishing Services*
Manufacturing Buyer: *JoAnne Sweeney*
Electronic Composition: *Integra Software Services, Pvt. Ltd.*
Photo Researcher: *Rachel Lucas, Jessica Riu*
Cover Designer: *Kristina Mose-Libon*

Library of Congress Cataloging-in-Publication Data

Lustig, Myron W.
    Intercultural competence : interpersonal communication across cultures / Myron W. Lustig, Jolene Koester. — 6th ed.
      p. cm.
    Includes bibliographical references and index.
    ISBN 0-205-59575-8 (alk. paper)
      1. Intercultural communication.   2. Communicative competence—United States.   3. Interpersonal communication—United States.   I. Koester, Jolene.   II. Title.

    HM1211.L87 2010
    303.48'2—dc22

2008046304

10 9 8 7 6 5 4 3 EBA 13 12 11 10

Allyn & Bacon
is an imprint of

www.pearsonhighered.com

ISBN-10:   0-205-59575-8
ISBN-13: 978-0-205-59575-4

Contents

PART TWO Cultural Differences in Communication

PART THREE Coding Intercultural Communication

7 Verbal Intercultural Communication 165

8 Nonverbal Intercultural Communication 197

9 The Effects of Code Usage in Intercultural Communication 223

Preface

Nothing in all the world is more dangerous than sincere ignorance and conscientious stupidity.

—Martin Luther King, Jr.

As we complete this first decade of the twenty-first century, the world is vastly different from what it was a generation ago, or a decade ago, or even a few years ago. Technological innovations—in communication, transportation, and various information tools—have helped to create the greatest mixing of cultures the world has ever seen. More than ever before, competence in intercultural communication is required for you to function well in your private and public lives; there is a very strong imperative for you to learn to communicate with people whose cultural heritage makes them very different from you. Our goal in this book is to give you the knowledge, motivation, and skills to accomplish that objective.

New to This Edition

Considerable progress has been made by scholars and practitioners of intercultural communication and related disciplines, and this edition reflects those changes. Many of the substantial changes may not be obvious to the casual reader, nor should they be. For instance, there is an extensive update of the research citations that undergird the presentation of information and ideas. These changes help the book remain contemporary. They appear at the back in the Notes Section, where they are available to the interested reader without intruding on the flow of the text. Similar changes occur in the end-of-chapter materials, where the "For Discussion" questions and the "For Further Reading" suggestions have been updated substantially.

Among the major changes are the following:

■ Substantial revision of the material on cultural patterns (Chapters 4 and 5), which includes major updates and additions to these ideas. Geert Hofstede has added two dimensions to his landmark research on cultural dimensions, and a new taxonomy from the GLOBE researchers offers an innovative and sophisticated framework with which to understand the range of cultural differences and similarities.

■ Throughout, many examples have been updated or added, and many new ideas are explicated in detail. Similarly, we have heightened our emphasis on the use of current technologies that affect intercultural communication.

■ Chapter 9 has been substantially revised to reflect current ideas about contrastive rhetoric and the pragmatics of language use. Cultural differences in both organizational preferences and in the preferred styles of persuasion have been reorganized and updated.

■ Chapter 11 has been revised and updated to reflect current ideas related to the health care, education, and business contexts.

■ The sections in Chapter 2 that discuss "race" and "biology" have been updated to reflect current scientific and social scientific knowledge on these topics.

■ About half of the "Culture Connections" boxes are new, as are about half of the photographs. We have selected and placed these elements very carefully, to underscore more clearly the conceptual issues being discussed.

■ The book's graphic elements have been improved significantly to support reader interest and involvement; new to this edition is the use of color to "catch the eye" and direct attention to the various ideas that we include.

Additional changes to this addition are too numerous to enumerate completely, but among them we have:

■ Updated statistics in Chapter 1 and added the Interpersonal Imperative to connect these ideas more closely to the overall theme of the text.

- Rearranged several topics—including the material about intercultural contacts—for increased coherence and "flow" of ideas.
- Refined our discussion of cultural patterns, the significance of social practices, and the defining attributes of intercultural competence.
- Updated the lists of intercultural films and online resources, which can be used to provide access to a wide variety of cultures and cultural patterns.

Unchanged in This Edition

Some things have not changed, nor should they. Our students and colleagues have helped to guide the creation of this sixth edition of *Intercultural Competence*. They have affirmed for us the critical features in this book that provide the reader with a satisfying experience and are useful for learning and teaching about intercultural communication. These features include:

- **An easy-to-read conversational style.** Students have repeatedly praised the clear and readable qualities of the text. We have tried, in this and previous editions, to assure that students have an "easy read" as they access the book's ideas.
- **A healthy blend of the practical and the theoretical, of the concrete and the abstract.** We believe strongly that a textbook on intercultural communication needs to include both a thorough grounding in the conceptual ideas and an applied orientation that makes those ideas tangible.
- **Culture Connections boxes that provide emotional connections.** The Culture Connections boxes exemplify and integrate important concepts while providing access to the affective dimension of intercultural competence. These boxes also illustrate the lived experiences of intercultural communicators. About half of the Culture Connections boxes are new to this edition, and we chose each selection carefully to provide the opportunity for students to "feel" some aspect of intercultural competence.
- **A strong grounding in theory and research.** Intercultural communication theories and their supporting research provide powerful ways of viewing and understanding intercultural communication phenomena. We also link the presentation of theories to numerous illustrative examples. These conceptual underpinnings to intercultural communication have been updated, and we have incorporated ideas from literally hundreds of new sources across a wide spectrum of inquiry. These sources form a solid bibliography for those interested in pursuing specific topics in greater depth. As we have done in the past, however, we have chosen to maintain the text's readability by placing the citations at the end of the book, where they appear in detailed endnotes that are unobtrusive but available to interested readers.
- **A focus on the significance and importance of cultural patterns.** Cultural patterns provide the underlying set of assumptions for cultural and intercultural communication. The focus on cultural patterns as the lens through which all interactions are interpreted is thoroughly explored in Chapters 4 and 5, and the themes of these two chapters permeate the concepts developed in all subsequent chapters.
- **Attention to the impact of technology on intercultural communication.** From Chapter 1, where we describe the technological imperative for intercultural communication that challenges us to be interculturally competent, to Chapter 12, where we analyze the perils and possibilities for living in an intercultural world, and throughout each of the intervening chapters, this edition is focused on the new information technologies and their effects on intercultural communication.
- **A consideration of topics not normally emphasized in intercultural communication textbooks.** Although it is standard fare for most books to consider verbal and nonverbal code systems, we provide a careful elaboration of the nature of differing logical systems, or preferred reasoning patterns, as well as a discussion of the consequences for intercultural communication when the expectations for the language-in-use are not widely shared. Similarly, drawing heavily on the available information about interpersonal communication, we explore the dynamic processes of establishing and developing relationships between culturally different individuals, including an elaboration of issues related to "face" in interpersonal relationships.
- **Pedagogical features that enhance student retention and involvement.** Concluding each chapter are For Discussion questions; they can be used to guide in-class conversations, or they may serve as the basis for short, focused assignments. Similarly, the For Further Reading suggestions can be readily understood by the beginning student and provide additional entry into that chapter's ideas.

Acknowledgment of Cultural Ancestry

At various points in our writing, we were amazed at how subtly but thoroughly our own cultural experiences had permeated the text. Lest anyone believe that our presentation of relevant theories, examples, and practical suggestions is without the distortion of culture, we would like to describe our own cultural heritage. That heritage shapes our understanding of intercultural communication, and it affects what we know, how we feel, and what we do when we communicate with others.

Our cultural ancestry is European, and our own cultural experiences are predominantly those that we refer to in this book as European American. Both of our family backgrounds and the communities in which we were raised have influenced and reinforced our cultural perspectives. The European American cultural experience is the one we know best, simply because it is who we are. Many of our ideas and examples about intercultural communication, therefore, draw on our own cultural experiences.

We have tried, however, to increase the number and range of other cultural voices through the ideas and examples that we provide. These voices and the lessons and illustrations they offer represent our colleagues, our friends, and, most important, our students.

Importance of Voices from Other Cultures

Although we have attempted to include a wide range of domestic and international cultural groups, inevitably we have shortchanged some simply because we do not have sufficient knowledge, either through direct experience or through secondary accounts, of all cultures. Our errors and omissions are not meant to exclude or discount. Rather, they represent the limits of our own intercultural communication experiences. We hope that you, as a reader with a cultural voice of your own, will participate with us in a dialogue that allows us to improve this text over a period of time. Readers of previous editions were generous with their suggestions for improvement, and we are very grateful to them for these comments. We ask that you continue this dialogue by providing us with your feedback and responses. Send us examples that illustrate the principles discussed in the text. Be willing to provide a cultural perspective that differs from our own and from those of our colleagues, friends, and students. Our commitment now and in future editions of this book is to describe a variety of cultural voices with accuracy and sensitivity. We ask for your help in accomplishing that objective.

Issues in the Use of Cultural Examples

Some of the examples in the following pages may include references to a culture to which you belong or with which you have had substantial experiences, and our examples may not match your personal knowledge. As you will discover in the opening chapters of this book, both your own experiences and the examples we recount could be accurate. One of the tensions we felt in writing this book was in making statements that are broad enough to provide reasonably accurate generalizations but specific and tentative enough to avoid false claims of universal applicability to all individuals in a given culture.

We have struggled as well with issues of fairness, sensitivity, representativeness, and inclusiveness. Indeed, we have had innumerable discussions with our colleagues across the country—colleagues who, like ourselves, are committed to making the United States and its colleges and universities into truly multicultural institutions—and we have sought their advice about appropriate ways to reflect the value of cultural diversity in our writing. We have responded to their suggestions, and we appreciate the added measure of quality that these cultural voices supply.

Text Organization

Our goal in this book is to provide ideas and information that can help you achieve competence in intercultural communication. Part One, Communication and Intercultural Competence, orients you to the central ideas that underlie this book. Chapter 1 begins with a discussion of five imperatives for attaining intercultural competence. We also define and discuss the nature of communication generally and interpersonal communication specifically. In Chapter 2, we introduce the notion of culture and explain why cultures differ. Our focus then turns to intercultural communication, and we distinguish that form of communication from others. As our concern in this book is with interpersonal communication among people from different cultures, an understanding of these key concepts is critical. Chapter 3 begins with a focus on the United States as an intercultural community, as we address the delicate but important issue of how to characterize its cultural mix and the members of its cultural groups. We then lay the groundwork for our continuing discussion of intercultural competence by explaining what competence is, what its components are, and how people can achieve it when they communicate with others. The chapter also focuses on two communication tools that could help people to improve their intercultural competence.

Part Two, Cultural Differences in Communication, is devoted to an analysis of the fundamental ways that cultures vary. Chapter 4 provides a general overview of the ways in which cultures differ, and it emphasizes the importance of cultural patterns in differentiating among communication styles. This chapter also examines the structural features that are similar across all cultures. Chapter 5 offers three taxonomies that can be used to understand systematic differences in the ways in which people from various cultures think and communicate. Chapter 6 underscores the importance of cultural identity and the consequences of biases within intercultural communication.

In Part Three, Coding Intercultural Communication, we turn our attention to verbal and nonverbal messages, which are central to the communication process. Chapter 7 examines the coding of verbal languages and the influences of linguistic and cultural differences on attempts to communicate interculturally. Chapter 8 discusses the effects of cultural differences on nonverbal codes, as the accurate coding and decoding of nonverbal symbols is vital in intercultural communication. Chapter 9 investigates the effects or consequences of cultural differences in coding systems on face-to-face intercultural interactions. Of particular interest are those experiences involving participants who were taught to use different languages and organizational schemes.

Part Four, Communication in Intercultural Relationships, emphasizes the associations that form among people as a result of their shared communication experiences. Chapter 10 looks at the all-important issues related to the development and maintenance of interpersonal relationships among people from different cultures. Chapter 11 highlights the processes by which communication events are grouped into episodes and interpreted within such contexts as health care, education, and business. Finally, Chapter 12 emphasizes intercultural contacts and highlights the ethical choices individuals must face when engaged in interpersonal communication across cultures. The chapter concludes with some remarks about the problems, possibilities, and opportunities for life in our contemporary intercultural world.

A Note to Instructors

Accompanying the text is an Instructor's Manual and a Test Bank, which are available to instructors who adopt the text for their courses. They provide pedagogical suggestions and instructional activities to enhance students' learning of course materials. Also available is our companion reader, *AmongUS: Essays on Identity, Belonging, and Intercultural Competence* (Second Edition). We have revised *AmongUS* extensively, so that it now functions more closely as a companion to this text. Please contact your Pearson representative for these materials.

Teaching a course in intercultural communication is one of the most exciting assignments available. It is difficult to convey in writing the level of involvement, commitment, and interest displayed by typical students in such courses. These students are the reason that teaching intercultural communication is, quite simply, so exhilarating and rewarding.

Acknowledgments

Many people have assisted us, and we would like to thank them for their help. Literally thousands of students and faculty have now reviewed this text and graciously shared their ideas for improvements. A substantial portion of those ideas and insightful criticisms has been incorporated into the current edition, and we continue to be grateful for the helpful comments and suggestions that have spurred vital improvements. The following reviewers contributed detailed comments for this edition: Daren C. Brabham, University of Utah; Laura A. MacLemale, Monroe Community College; Robert N. St. Clair, University of Louisville; and Dr. Karl V. Winton, Marshall University. We are indebted to the students and faculty at our respective institutions, to our colleagues in the communication discipline, and to many people throughout higher education who have willingly shared their ideas and cultural voices with us.

We continue to be very grateful that the study of intercultural communication has become an increasingly vital and essential component of many universities' curricula. While we harbor no illusions that our influence was anything but minor, it is nevertheless gratifying to have been a "strong voice in the chorus" for these positive changes. Finally, we would like to acknowledge each other's encouragement and support throughout the writing of this book. It has truly been a collaborative effort.

Myron W. Lustig
Jolene Koester

CHAPTER 1

Introduction to Intercultural Competence

In this second decade of the twenty-first century, culture, cultural differences, and intercultural communication are among the central ingredients of your life. As inhabitants of this post-millennium world, you no longer have a choice about whether to live and communicate with people from many cultures. Your only choice is whether you will learn to do it well.

The world has changed dramatically from what it was even a generation ago. Across the globe and throughout the United States, there is now a heightened emphasis on culture. Similarly, there is a corresponding interplay of forces that both encourage and discourage accommodation and understanding among people who differ from one another. This emphasis on culture is accompanied by numerous opportunities for experiences with people who come from vastly different cultural backgrounds. Intercultural encounters are now ubiquitous; they occur within neighborhoods, across national borders, in face-to-face interactions, through mediated channels, in business, in personal relationships, in tourist travel, and in politics. In virtually every facet of life—in work, play, entertainment, school, family, community, and even in the media that you encounter daily—your experiences necessarily involve intercultural communication.

What does this great cultural mixing mean as you strive for success, satisfaction, well-being, and feelings of involvement and attachment to families, communities, organizations, and nations? It means that the forces that bring people from other cultures into your life are dynamic, potent, and ever present. It also means that competent intercultural communication has become essential.

Our purpose in writing this book is to provide you with the conceptual tools for understanding how cultural differences can affect your interpersonal communication. We also offer some practical suggestions concerning the adjustments necessary to achieve competence when dealing with these cultural differences. We begin by examining the forces that create the need for increased attention to intercultural communication competence.

■ These U.S. American tourists plot a day's sightseeing in Amsterdam. Tourism is a major international industry, bringing people from many cultures into contact with one another.

Imperatives for Intercultural Competence

The need to understand the role of culture in interpersonal communication is growing. Because of demographic, technological, economic, peace, and interpersonal concerns, intercultural competence is now more vital than ever.

The Demographic Imperative for Intercultural Competence

The United States—and the world as a whole—is currently in the midst of what is perhaps the largest and most extensive wave of cultural mixing in recorded history. Recent census figures provide a glimpse into the shape of the changing demographics of the U.S. population.

The U.S. population is now more than 300 million, of which 66.8 percent are European American, 14.8 percent are Latino, 12.8 percent are African American, 4.6 percent are Asian American, and 1.0 percent are Native American.[1] Although all U.S. cultural groups are expected to increase in size over the next forty years, the average 0.8 percent annual rate of U.S. population growth, while modest, is not likely to be uniform. If current trends continue, by 2050, the U.S. population of about 429 million is expected to be about 49 percent European American, 27 percent Latino, 14 percent African American, 9 percent Asian American, and 1 percent Native American.[2] As William A. Henry says of these changes, "the browning of America will alter everything in society, from politics and education to industry, values, and culture."[3]

Census figures indicate that cultural diversity is a nationwide phenomenon. Half of the states in the United States have at least 50,000 Native American residents, half have at least 100,000 Asian American residents, and 40 percent of the states exceed these numbers

■ The United States is a nation comprised of many cultural groups. These immigrants are becoming new citizens of the United States.

for both cultural groups. Latinos make up nearly a third of the populations of California and Texas, and they constitute at least 20 percent of the people in Arizona, Florida, Nevada, and New Mexico. Eighteen states have African American populations that exceed a million;[4] African Americans constitute more than 57 percent of the District of Columbia's population, and they comprise at least a fifth of the populations in nine states including Alabama, Delaware, Maryland, and Louisiana. There already are "minority-majorities"—populations of African Americans, Native Americans, Pacific Islanders, Latinos, and Asian Americans that, when combined, outnumber the European American population—in California, Hawaii, New Mexico, and Texas, as well as in such cities as Atlanta, Baltimore, Birmingham, Chicago, Cleveland, Dallas, Detroit, Fresno, Gary, Houston, Laredo, Los Angeles, Memphis, Miami, New York, Oakland, San Antonio, San Francisco, San Jose, and Washington.

Much of the U.S. population shift can be attributed to immigration.[5] In 2006, about 37.5 million people—or about 12.5 percent of the U.S. population—were immigrants. This is the highest percentage of immigrants since 1930, but it is about 50 percent lower than the peak immigration years of 1890 through 1910[6] and about the same as it was in 1850, the first year the Census Bureau asked people for their place of birth.[7] What distinguishes the current wave of immigrants from those of the early 1900s, however, is the country of origin. In 1900, the proportion of European immigrants to the United States was 86 percent; by 1970, Europeans still comprised 62 percent of the immigrant population. By 2004, however, only 13.6 percent of immigrants to the United States were European.[8] Conversely, in 1970 only 19 percent of the foreign-born U.S. population was from Latin America, and 9 percent was from Asia. In 2004, more than half of the immigrants to the United States came from Latin America, and a quarter came from Asia.[9]

CULTURE connections

If the world was a village of 1,000 people,

There would be:

- 565 Asians
- 143 Africans
- 121 Europeans
- 86 Latin Americans (Central Americans and South Americans)
- 51 North Americans
- 29 Middle Easterners
- 5 Australians/Oceanians

There would be:

- 333 Christians
- 210 Muslims
- 133 Hindus
- 58 Buddhists
- 4 Sikhs
- 2 Jews
- 1 Baha'i
- 118 People practicing other religions
- 141 Atheists or nonreligious

—*Bureau of the Census, 2008; www.adherents.com; and www.about.com*

Recent data clearly show that the United States is now a multicultural society. About 18 percent of the people in the United States speak a language other than English at home.[10] Of children in urban public schools, one-third speak a first language other than English. There are more Muslims, Hindus, and Buddhists in the United States than there are Lutherans or Episcopalians. However, the "typical" foreign-born resident in the United States is actually quite different from what many people suppose. She or he has lived in the United States for about 20 years. Of those over age 25, more than two-thirds have a high school diploma, and more than a quarter are college graduates. This latter figure is identical to the college graduation rate of the native-born U.S. population.[11] Foreign-born adults in the United States are likely to be employed, married, and living with their spouse and with one or two children.[12] As Antonia Pantoja and Wilhelmina Perry note about the U.S. demographics,

> The complete picture is one of change where large numbers of non-European immigrants from Africa, Asia, South and Central America, and the Caribbean will constitute majorities in many major cities. These immigrants will contribute to existing social movements. Many of these new immigrants are skilled workers and professionals, and these qualities will be highly valued in a changing United States economy. They come from countries with a history of democratic civil struggles and political revolutions. They arrive with a strong sense of cultural and ethnic identity within their intact family and social networks and strong ties to their home countries. At the same time they have a strong determination to achieve their goals, and they do not intend to abandon or relinquish their culture as the price for their success.[13]

The consequences of this "browning of America" can be seen in every major cultural and social institution. Many U.S. schools can now be characterized as "Classrooms of Babel."[14] In New York City public schools, for example, more than 160 different languages are spoken.[15] In the city of Los Angeles, more than 100 different languages are spoken.[16]

■ U.S. Americans are as varied as the landscape. Here, a group of colleagues, who represent several different cultures, have a friendly conversation.

Institutions of higher education are certainly not exempt from the forces that have transformed the United States into a multicultural society.[17] The enrollment of "minority-group" college students is increasing annually. Additionally, there are about 2.5 million international students in higher education. Of these, about 583,000 international students—22 percent of the total—are enrolled in U.S. universities. The U.S. enrollment is an increase of nearly 10 percent from the previous year and just 3,000 fewer than the record enrollment set before the 2001 terrorist attacks and subsequent visa restrictions.[18] Similarly, the number of U.S. students studying abroad was nearly a quarter of a million in 2006, an increase of 8.5 percent from the previous year and 150 percent more than a decade ago. [19]

The United States is not alone in the worldwide transformation into multicultural societies. Throughout Europe, Asia, Africa, South America, and the Middle East, there is an increasing pattern of cross-border movements that is both changing the distribution of people around the globe and intensifying the political and social tensions that accompany such population shifts. This demographic imperative requires a heightened emphasis on intercultural competence.

The Technological Imperative for Intercultural Competence

Marshall McLuhan coined the term global village to describe the consequences of the mass media's ability to bring events from the far reaches of the globe into people's homes, thus shrinking the world.[20] Today, the "global village" is an image that is used to describe the worldwide web of interconnections that modern technologies have created. Communications media such as the Internet, communication satellites, and cell phones now make it possible to establish virtually instantaneous links to people who are thousands of miles away. In the past fifteen years, international telephone traffic has more than tripled. At the same time, the number of cell phone users has grown from virtually zero to more than a billion people—about a sixth the world's population—and Internet users also exceed a billion people.[21]

Modern transportation systems contribute to the creation of the global village. A visit to major cities such as New York, Los Angeles, Mexico City, London, Nairobi, Istanbul, Hong Kong, or Tokyo, with their multicultural populations, demonstrates that the movement of people from one country and culture to another has become commonplace. "There I was," said Richard W. Fisher, president of the Federal Reserve Bank of Dallas, "in the middle of a South American jungle, thumbing out an e-mail [on my BlackBerry] so work could get done thousands of miles away… Technology, capital, labor, and ideas, now able to move at unprecedented speed across national boundaries, have integrated the world to an unprecedented degree."[22]

Modern information technologies allow people in the United States and throughout the world to participate in the events and lives of people in other places. Many world events are experienced almost instantaneously and are no longer separated from us in time and space. Scenes of a flood in New Orleans or Iowa, of an earthquake in China, or of a typhoon in Myanmar are viewed worldwide on local television stations; immigrants and expatriates maintain their cultural ties by participating in Internet chat groups; the Travel Channel and similar fare provide insights into distant cultures; and a grandmother in India uses a webcam to interact with her granddaughter in New York. As blogger and entrepreneur Vinnie Mirchandani concludes,

CULTURE connections

Flushing [New York] is a sea. A baptismal sea that churns out New Americans. It admits a constant influx of new people, not so much from other parts of America as from the rest of the world, people who come from other continents across seas and deserts and rivers and over mountains. You see them everywhere in Flushing. On the subway. On the street. At stores. The new people. You can always tell them right away from the way they dress or wear their hair; or from the language they speak or the subtle scents they carry; or from other such myriads of small things. Some carry their villages in their walk, and others wear the terrain they come from on their faces. As unmistakable as their hard-to-erase accents.

It never ceases to amaze me that they all find their way and manage to build a new life here. It seems a miracle that they all somehow survive. Some of them come here with nothing. Nothing but memories and a dream and a will. Some smuggled in as stowaways on a ship. So awfully unprepared. But even they manage. Most of them, anyway. They find places to live. They find work. They put food on the table for their families. They buy their first TV set. Their first dining-room table. Their first car. Their first apartment or house. And their children start school, and are on their way to becoming Americans. It's nothing special. Really. As they say, people do it every day. And so many people have done it before them. And so many will do it, long, long after them. And after all, we did that. There's no mystery at all, Remember? Once we were that new people on the street, shopping for our first whatever, and once we were the kids on the street in our fresh-off-the-boat clothes. But I don't remember how we did it. It was our parents' responsibility to put food on the table, to buy that first TV set and the first house.

—*Mia Yun*

When I travel around the world, I see grandmas with headsets speaking on Skype to their loved ones at the other end of world. I see people crowding in Internet cafes. I see teenagers furiously texting each other. I hear unusual phrases like "I left you a missed call." I see people using their mobile phones to buy from vending machines.[23]

These increased contacts, which are facilitated by recent technological developments, underscore the significant interdependencies that now link people to those from other cultures. Intercultural links are reinforced by the ease with which people can now travel to other places. Nearly 64 million U.S. residents travel abroad annually.[24] Likewise, citizens of other countries are also visiting the United States in record-setting numbers.

Technology allows and facilitates human interactions across the globe and in real time. Such instantaneous communication has the potential to increase the amount of communication that occurs among people from different cultures, and this expansion will necessarily add to the need for greater intercultural competence. "The world is flat," as Thomas Friedman so aptly suggests, because the convergence of technologies is creating an unprecedented degree of global competitiveness based on equal opportunities and access to the marketplace.[25] Similarly, consider YouTube, which has encouraged the widespread dissemination of visual and auditory ideas by anyone with access to an inexpensive digital video camera. Unlike the more restrictive and more expensive television stations, which require access to

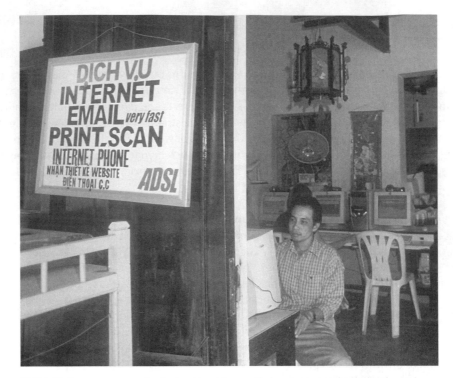

■ This Vietnamese man, who is checking his e-mail, demonstrates the technological imperative for intercultural communication.

sophisticated equipment and distribution networks, such Internet-based social networking sites as MySpace, Facebook, and YouTube, as well as such "simulated worlds" as Second Life, are used by an extraordinarily large number of people to connect with others whom they have never met—and will never meet—in face-to-face interactions.

The technological imperative has increased the urgency for intercultural competence. Because of the widespread availability of technologies and long-distance transportation systems, intercultural competence is now as important as it has ever been.

The Economic Imperative for Intercultural Competence

The economic success of the United States in the global arena increasingly depends on individual and collective abilities to communicate competently with people from other cultures. Clearly, U.S. economic relationships require global interdependence and intercultural competence. For instance, U.S. international trade has more than doubled every decade since 1960, and it now exceeds $2.9 trillion annually, or more than fifty times what it was just forty years ago.[26] U.S. trade as a percentage of gross world product has risen from 15 percent in 1986 to nearly 27 percent in 2006.[27] Consequently, the economic health of the United States is now inextricably linked to world business partners.

Corporations can also move people from one country to another, so within the work-force of most nations, there are representatives from cultures throughout the world.

■ The economic imperative for intercultural communication is exemplified by these western and Middle Eastern businessmen, and their interpreter, who are developing their interpersonal relationships.

However, even if one's work is within the national boundaries of the United States, intercultural competence is imperative. The citizenry of the United States includes many individuals who are strongly identified with a particular culture. Thus, it is no longer safe to assume that clients, customers, business partners, and coworkers will have similar cultural views about what is important and appropriate.

The U.S. workplace reflects the increasing cultural diversity that comprises the nation as a whole. For example, the number of businesses opened by Asian Americans grew 24 percent between 1997 and 2002, increasing at twice the national average. These businesses generate more than $326 billion in revenues annually.[28] The number of African American businesses also continue to grow; more than a million small businesses are now owned by African Americans.[29] Similarly, Latinos and Latinas are opening businesses at a faster pace now than ever before. By 2012, there will likely be 3.2 million Latino-owned businesses that generate more than $465 billion in annual gross receipts.[30] In sum, the economic imperative for intercultural competence is powerful, pervasive, and likely to increase in the coming years.

The Peace Imperative for Intercultural Competence

The vision of interdependence among cultural groups throughout the world and in the United States has led Robert Shuter to declare that "culture is the single most important global communication issue" that humans face.[31] The need to understand and appreciate

■ The peace imperative for intercultural communication is exemplified by the goals and experiences of the athletes and fans of the Olympics.

those who differ from ourselves has never been more important. As the President's Commission on Foreign Languages and International Studies has said,

> Nothing less is at stake than the nation's security. At a time when the resurgent forces of nationalism and of ethnic and linguistic consciousness so directly affect global realities, the United States requires far more reliable capabilities to communicate with its allies, analyze the behaviors of potential adversaries, and earn the trust and sympathies of the uncommitted. Yet, there is a widening gap between these needs and the American competence to understand and deal successfully in a world in flux.[32]

Witness the recent problems in Darfur, Chechnya, Zimbabwe, Central Asia, Indonesia, the Middle East, Afghanistan, Venezuela, and in Iraq; in each instance, cultures have clashed over the right to control resources and ideologies. But such animosities do not just occur outside the borders of the United States. Consider the proliferation of such groups as the neo-Nazis, white nationalists, racist skinheads, and those with links to the Ku Klux Klan. The Southern Poverty Law Center has estimated that, in 2007, there were nearly nine hundred "hate groups," an increase of more than 40 percent in just seven years.[33] Likewise, the frequency of hate crimes is increasing dramatically. In 2002, there were almost four thousand hate crimes committed against individuals because of their race, culture, religion, or social group membership.[34] In 2006, that number had doubled to almost eight thousand, and it was up about 8 percent from just the year before.[35] Often, such crimes are directed against Latinos,[36] African Americans,[37] Jews,[38] Muslims,[39] Asian Americans,[40] and members of various other cultural and social groups. As Catharine R. Stimpson has said of these "culture clashes," the refusal to live peaceably in pluralistic societies [has been] one of the bloodiest problems—nationally and internationally—of the 20th century. No wizard, no fairy godmother is going to make this problem disappear. And I retain a pluralist's stubborn, utopian hope that people can talk about, through, across, and around their differences and that these exchanges will help us live together justly.[41]

The Interpersonal Imperative for Intercultural Competence

The demographic, technological, economic, and peace imperatives all combine to create a world in which human interactions are dominated by culture, cultural differences, and the ability of humans to understand and interact within multiple cultural frameworks. In short, the quality of your daily life—from work to play to family to community interactions—will increasingly depend upon your ability to communicate competently with people from other cultures. Your neighbors may speak different first languages, have different values, and celebrate different customs. Your family members may include individuals from cultural backgrounds other than yours. Your colleagues at work may belong to various cultures, and you may be expected to participate in intercultural and cross-national teams with them; a team leader in Chicago might have a supervisor in Switzerland and team members located in New York, San Francisco, Buenos Aires, Melbourne, Johannesburg, and Shanghai.

There are some obvious consequences to maintaining competent interpersonal relationships in an intercultural world. Such relationships will inevitably introduce doubt about others' expectations and will reduce the certainty that specific behaviors, routines, and rituals mean the same things to everyone. Cultural mixing implies that people will not always feel completely comfortable as they attempt to communicate in another language or as they try to talk with individuals who are not proficient in theirs. Their sense of "rights" and "wrongs" will be threatened when challenged by the actions of those with an alternative cultural framework. Many people will need to live in two or more cultures concurrently, shifting from one to another as they go from home to school, from work to play, and from the neighborhood to the shopping mall. The tensions inherent in creating successful intercultural communities are obvious as well. Examples abound that underscore how difficult it is for groups of culturally different individuals to live, work, play, and communicate harmoniously. The consequences of failing to create a harmonious intercultural society are also obvious—human suffering, hatred passed on from one generation to another, disruptions in people's lives, and unnecessary conflicts that sap people's creative talents and energies and that siphon off scarce resources from other important societal needs.

CULTURE connections

"I knew we differed culturally, but different isn't wrong; different is merely different. Basically we're all human."

—*Deon Meyer*

■ The challenge of communicating in an intercultural world occurs in our families, homes, work settings, schools, and neighborhoods.

The challenge of the twenty-first century—and our challenge to you in this book—is to understand and to appreciate cultural differences and to translate that understanding into competent interpersonal communication.

Communication

To understand intercultural communication events, you must first study the more general processes involved in all human communication transactions. All communication events, including intercultural ones, are made up of a set of basic characteristics. Once these characteristics are known, they can be applied to intercultural interactions in order to analyze the unique ways in which intercultural communication differs from other forms of communication.

Defining Communication

The term communication has been used in many ways for varied, and often inconsistent, purposes.[42] For example, Frank Dance identified 15 different conceptual components for the term,[43] and Dance and Carl Larson listed 126 different definitions for *communication*.[44] Like all terms or ideas, we chose our specific definition because of its usefulness in explaining the thoughts and ideas we wish to convey. Consequently, our definition is not the "right" one, nor is it somehow "more correct" than the others. Indeed, as you might expect, our definition is actually very similar to many others with which you may be familiar. However, the definition we have selected is most useful for our purpose of helping you to achieve interpersonal competence when communicating in the intercultural setting.

> *Communication is a symbolic, interpretive, transactional, contextual process in which people create shared meanings.*

To understand what this definition means, we will explore its implications for the study of intercultural communication.

Characteristics of Communication

Six characteristics of our definition of communication require further elaboration. Our definition asserts that communication is symbolic, interpretive, transactional, contextual, and a process, and it involves shared meanings. Let's examine each of these characteristics more closely.

Communication Is Symbolic   Symbols are central to the communication process because they represent the shared meanings that are communicated. A symbol is a word, action, or object that stands for or represents a unit of meaning. Meaning, in turn, is a perception, thought, or feeling that a person experiences and might want to communicate to others. These meaning-full experiences could include sensations resulting from a room's temperature, thoughts about a teacher in a particular course, or feelings of happiness or anger because of what someone said. However, the private meanings within a person cannot be shared directly with others. They can become shared and understood only when they are interpreted as a message. A message, then, refers to the "package" of symbols used to create shared meanings. For example, the words in this book are symbols that, taken together, form the message that we, the authors, want to communicate to you.

People's behaviors are frequently interpreted symbolically, as an external representation of feelings, emotions, and internal states. To many people in the United States, for example, raising an arm with the hand extended and moving the hand and arm up and down symbolizes saying good-bye. Flags can symbolize a country, and most of the world's religions have symbols that are associated with their beliefs.

There is an important characteristic of symbols that might not be obvious to you but that nevertheless affects your ability to be a competent participant in intercultural communication: Symbols vary in their degree of arbitrariness. That is, the relationships between symbols and their referents can vary in the extent to which they are fixed or arbitrary.

Some symbol systems, such as verbal languages and a special class of nonverbal symbols called *emblems*, are completely unrelated to their referents except by common agreement among a group of people to refer to things in a particular way. (Emblems are discussed more fully in Chapter 8.) There is nothing peacelike, for instance, in the peace symbol, which is a nonverbal emblem that can be displayed by extending the index and middle fingers upward from a clenched fist. The same symbol was used by Winston Churchill to indicate victory, and to many people in South American countries it is regarded as an obscene gesture. Similarly, there is nothing booklike in the object you are holding as you read these words. We call the object a book not because there is anything inherent in the object that suggests "book" but simply because, by common agreement among users of English, we have agreed to do so. Those who speak other languages have other symbols, which are equally arbitrary, to refer to the same referents.

It is quite possible for a community of language users to agree to refer to some objects by using symbols that differ from the common ones. For example, the people in a class (perhaps even your class) could decide to change the symbols and refer to the teacher as a *door,* the students as *cows,* the blackboard as a *pancake,* the classroom as a *bar,* and the desks as *pineapples.* A description of the classroom with these new and arbitrarily assigned symbols might read as follows: "When the cows entered the bar, they sat down at their pineapples, and the door began to write on the pancake." Although the sentence sounds strange (and perhaps quite humorous), if everyone consistently referred to the objects in the same way, the meaning that would be created in using these symbols would soon become widely shared.

For many symbol systems, such as most nonverbal and visual ones, the relationship between the symbols and their referents is much less arbitrary than that of verbal languages. Such symbols as a growling stomach when hungry, a child's tears when sad, or a portrait that details a person's facial features are all so intrinsically associated with their referents that the range of expected meanings is very restricted. However, these types of symbols are useful precisely because much less knowledge of a specific language and culture is required to understand them. Thus, international traffic symbols, which consist of easily understood pictures, are frequently used in place of words to instruct drivers who might otherwise be a major hazard. Yet even with these traffic symbols, which are designed specifically to be understood easily, it cannot be assumed that everyone will automatically interpret the symbols in an identical fashion.

Communication Is Interpretive   Messages do not have to be consciously or purposefully created with the specific intention of communicating a certain set of meanings for others to be able to make sense of the symbols forming the message. Rather, communication is always an interpretive process. Whenever people communicate, they must interpret the symbolic behaviors of others and assign significance to some of those behaviors in order to create a meaningful account of the others' actions. This idea suggests that each person in a communication transaction may not necessarily interpret the messages in exactly the same way. Indeed, during episodes involving intercultural communication, the likelihood is high that people will interpret the meaning of messages differently.

Many people incorrectly use the word *communication* to represent an acceptable level of similarity or agreement in their conversations. They might use the phrase "I really could communicate with her" when they have had a very pleasant conversation in which the other person expressed a similar point of view, or they might say "I just can't communicate with him anymore" when disagreements exist. These errors confuse two very different outcomes of the communication process.

The first outcome of communication is understanding what the others are trying to communicate. Understanding means that the participants have imposed similar or shared interpretations about what the messages actually mean. Indeed, without some degree of understanding between the participants, it would be inaccurate to claim that communication has even occurred. Thus, failed attempts at communication, such as when an accident victim calls for help and no one is nearby to hear, are not actually communication.

CULTURE connections

I love traveling. Being a outsider in so many places makes me very aware of my own beliefs, values, and assumptions about the world. Traveling in places so different from my own experience vividly engages my mind and body, and everything seems fascinating. One very interesting thing I have noticed as a Latina visiting other countries is that I have a tendency to identify myself as a Texan, a Tejana, rather than an American. When I talked about this to a girlfriend, I realized why. I say I am *Tejana* because, in Texas, there are many women like me – minorities who are sandwiched between the Mexican and American cultures. To me, Texas represents that netherworld of "not American/not Mexican" citizenry. It's a place where there are a lot of people like me, living in the borderlands between two cultures, not fully one or the other.

—*Laurie L. Lopez Charlés*

The second outcome is reaching agreement on the particular issues that have been discussed. Agreement means that each participant not only understands the other's interpretations but also holds a view that is similar. However, although understanding is a necessary ingredient to say that communication has occurred, agreement is not a requirement of communication. It is possible, and often quite likely, that people will understand one another's position or ideas yet not agree with them. For instance, two people who differ in their basic beliefs about religion or politics can still communicate about their personal preferences in a meaningful and fulfilling way without necessarily expecting the other person to agree.

It should be obvious that complete accuracy in interpreting the meanings that are shared by people is rare, if not impossible. Such a level of accuracy would require symbols to be understood by the participants in *exactly* the same way. Further, even if complete understanding was possible in a given instance, it would be impossible to verify that the meanings that were created for the symbols were identical in the minds of all participants.

Our stipulation that communication requires understanding does not imply that because completely accurate interpretations are impossible, communication is also impossible. Rather, we need to recognize that there are different levels or degrees of understanding. Communication requires a degree of understanding sufficient to accomplish the purposes of the participants, which can vary from one experience to another. For example, it may or may not be communication if a man, who is dressed in unfamiliar clothes and who is obviously from another culture, walks up to you and, after bowing, utters some sounds that seem like they could be language but whose meaning is unknown to you. If his purpose is merely to provide you with a ritualistic greeting and, recognizing this, you return his bow, then, relative to the purposes of the participants, we would say that the two of you have created shared meanings for your behaviors, and, consequently, communication has occurred. However, if he is asking you for directions and you merely return his bow without even recognizing his intended goal, then shared meanings do not exist, and communication has not occurred relative to the task at hand.

Communication Is Transactional   To suggest that communication is transactional implies that all participants in the communication process work together to create and sustain the meanings that develop. A transactional view holds that communicators are simultaneously sending and receiving messages at every instant that they are involved in conversations.

The earliest views of the communication process were *actional*. An actional view held that communication was a linear, one-way flow of ideas and information and that the focus of this view was primarily on information transmission, or what the sender should do to structure a message that would achieve a desired result. As Figure 1.1 indicates, the earliest actional models did not even include the receivers of the messages. Later actional models added a receiver at the end of the message arrow, but those who held this view were still not very concerned with the receiver's characteristics.[45]

Actional views of the communication process are not very useful in the study of intercultural communication for two very important reasons. First, the underlying assumption of the actional view is that the sender's goal is to persuade the receiver. The sender is not really interested in understanding others, being sensitive to cultural differences, or developing better interpersonal relationships; rather, the focus is on telling and selling. Second, actional views of communication assume that the receivers of messages are somehow inferior to the senders, with little ability to become involved in or to influence the communication process. In this view, those who create the messages should merely manipulate the receivers.

The limitations of the actional view led to the development of the *interactional* view of the communication process. Whereas the former emphasizes transmission of the message, the latter emphasizes interpretation. The interactional view explicitly includes the receiver in the communication process, and it recognizes that the receivers provide the senders with ongoing responses, called feedback, about how the messages are received.[46] As Figure 1.2 indicates, the focus of this view is still primarily sender-oriented. The model merely recognizes that senders must continually adapt their messages to the changing perceptions of the receivers to be most effective in influencing them. The implied goal of the interactional view of communication is to influence and control the receiver.

Like actional views, interactional views of the communication process are not very useful in the study of intercultural communication. The goal of the sender is still one of influencing others rather than being culturally sensitive and thereby improving intercultural relationships. The receivers, in the interactional view, need to be understood only insofar as that understanding is necessary to manipulate them more effectively. A final criticism of the interactional view is that it is not really a model of true interaction. Rather, it suggests a sequence of action–reaction behaviors in which messages are exchanged between a sender and a receiver, who perhaps alternate in these roles. Absent from the interactional view is any sense that the participants co-produce and co-interpret the messages that are communicated.

The limitations of the actional and interactional views have led to the development of the *transactional* view, which emphasizes the construction or shared creation

FIGURE 1.1   An actional view of communication.

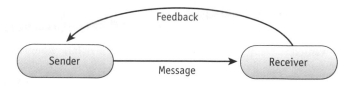

FIGURE 1.2 **An interactional view of communication.**

of messages and meanings. The transactional view differs from the earlier views in two ways. First, it recognizes that the goal of communication is not merely to influence and persuade others but also to improve one's knowledge, to seek understanding, to develop agreements, and to negotiate shared meanings. Second, it recognizes that, at any given instant, no one is just sending or just receiving messages; therefore, there are no such entities as pure senders or pure receivers. Nor does it make sense to describe a single message as being the exclusive one at any selected moment. Rather, all participants are simultaneously interpreting multiple messages at all moments. These messages include not only the meaning of the words that are said but also the meaning conveyed by the tone of voice, the types of gestures, the frequency of body movements, the motion of the eyes, the distances between people, the formality of the language, the seating arrangements, the clothing worn, the length of pauses, the words unsaid, and much more. Thus, as Figure 1.3 indicates, in the transactional view, it is impossible to describe one person as exclusively the sender and the other as exclusively the receiver.

Communication Is Contextual   All communication takes place within a setting or situation called a context. By context, we mean the place where people meet, the social purpose for being together, and the nature of the relationship. Thus, the context includes the physical, social, and interpersonal settings within which messages are exchanged.

The Physical Context   The physical context includes the actual location of the interactants: indoors or outdoors, crowded or quiet, public or private, close together or far apart, warm or cold, bright or dark. The physical context influences the communication process in many obvious ways. Dean Barnlund captures its importance: "The streets of Calcutta, the avenues of Brazilia, the Left Bank of Paris, the gardens of Kyoto, the slums of Chicago, and the canyons of lower Manhattan provide dramatically different backgrounds for human interaction."[47] An afternoon conversation at a crowded sidewalk café and an evening of candlelight dining in a private salon will differ in the kinds of topics that are covered and in the interpretations that are made about the meanings of certain phrases or glances. As Donald Klopf so poignantly

FIGURE 1.3 **A transactional view of communication.**

illustrates, knowledge of the physical context often provides important information about the meanings that are intended and the kinds of communication that are possible:

> I wanted to see her one more time before leaving Hong Kong. So I called her at work and she agreed to lunch. Near her office was a traditional *dim sum* restaurant. Sounded good to me; *dim sum* literally means "to touch the heart" and she had done that to me. What a mistake! Noisy?! The place was bedlam. The waitresses shouted out their wares—some sixty to seventy *dim sum* choices. We shared a table with a couple of tourists who griped about the food, and everything else. Crowded, every steno around must have decided on a *yam cha* meal today. Words of endearment didn't seem appropriate there. "Let's go next door to the Lau Ling Bar," I suggested, "for our black tea." Quiet and refined, it was the proper site to touch the heart, and I think I did.[48]

The Social Context The social context refers to the widely shared expectations people have about the kinds of interactions that normally should occur given different kinds of social events. Of course we realize that communication at funerals differs from that at a party; the social context of a classroom makes us expect certain forms of communication that differ from those at a soccer game. However, there is often a great deal of difficulty in understanding the social contexts for communication events that involve other cultures, as the common expectations about what behaviors are preferred or prohibited may be very different. For instance, before a funeral in Ireland, an all-night celebration called a wake is sometimes held. Such festive behaviors, which are appropriate to the social context of an Irish funeral, would be completely inappropriate where the social context dictates that alternative behaviors are more fitting.

CULTURE connections

My grandmother speaks Gujarati and grew up in Bombay and Jamnagar, a small city in the north-western state of Gujarat, though in those years (and even into my father's youth) India was not yet an independent country and Jamnagar was a princely kingdom ruled by the wealthy family of one of my grandfather's childhood playmates. My grandmother speaks some Marathi and Hindi as well as Gujarati, but no English, and since all my life I have spoken only English, for nearly thirty-five years she and I have never talked to one another without the aid of intermediaries. This is an awkward way to converse with a grandparent, especially one I've seen as frequently as my grandmother, but for a long time I wasn't aware of it. On the contrary, what seemed presumptively normal and natural when I was young was the notion that events around me, however slight or large, took place in a few different Indian languages, and that like instruments they often had to be restrung in different alphabets and sounds. It seemed an ordinary matter of fact that conversations were complicated not just by who was present but by how they listened and what language they heard, and I got used to the idea that I was often privy to only part of a conversation, half an understanding. As a result, it came to seem inevitable that conversations either had to be accepted with all their ungainly, opaque areas, or else gradually deciphered.

—Nina Mehta

The Interpersonal Context   The interpersonal context refers to the expectations people have about the behaviors of others as a result of differences in the relationships between them. Communication between teachers and students, even outside the classroom context, differs from communication between close friends. Communication among friends differs from communication among acquaintances, coworkers, or family members. As people get to know each other and develop shared experiences, the nature of their interpersonal relationships is altered. This change in the interpersonal context is accompanied by alterations in the kinds of messages created and in the interpretations made about the meanings of the messages exchanged. As we suggested about physical and social contexts, people behave differently from one interpersonal context to another. The meanings assigned to particular behaviors can differ dramatically as different definitions of the context are imposed. As John Condon has said about differences in male–female relationships in the United States and Mexico,

> There are meanings to be read into settings and situations which must be learned if one is to avoid misunderstandings and even unpleasant experiences. A boss who invites his secretary out for a drink after work may or may not have ulterior motives in either country. However, the assumption that this was a romantic overture would be far more common in Mexico City than in New York or Los Angeles.[49]

Communication Is a Process   People, relationships, activities, objects, and experiences can be described either in static terms or as part of a dynamic process. Viewing communication in static terms suggests that it is fixed and unchanging, whereas viewing it as a process implies that things are changing, moving, developing, and evolving. A process is a sequence of many distinct but interrelated steps. To understand communication as a process, it is necessary to know how it can change over time.

Like the adage "You can't stand in the same stream twice," communication events are unique, as seemingly identical experiences can take on vastly different meanings at different stages of the process. This stream of events, which involves both past experiences and future expectations, is always moving and changing. Thus, the very same message may be interpreted very differently when said at different stages of the communication process.

Communication Involves Shared Meanings   The interpretive and transactional nature of communication suggests that correct meanings are not just "out there" to be discovered. Rather, meanings are created and shared by groups of people as they participate in the ordinary and everyday activities that form the context for common interpretations. The focus, therefore, must be on the ways that people attempt to "make sense" of their common experiences in the world.

Interpersonal Communication

Definitions, as we have said, are chosen because they are useful for conveying the thoughts, ideas, and distinctions that one wishes to explain.

> *Interpersonal communication is a form of communication that involves a small number of individuals who are interacting exclusively with one another and who therefore have the ability both to adapt their messages specifically for those others and to obtain immediate interpretations from them.*

Each of the four characteristics of this definition will now be discussed.

A Small Number of People   To a certain degree, all communication could be called interpersonal, as it occurs between (*inter*) two or more people. However, we think it useful and practical to differentiate those relationships that involve a relatively small number of people—such as couples, families, friends, work groups, and even classroom groups—from those involving much larger numbers of people—such as public rallies or massive television audiences. Unlike other forms of communication, interpersonal communication involves person-to-person interactions. In addition, the perception that a social bond has developed between the interactants, however tenuous and temporary it may seem, is also much more likely.

People Interacting Exclusively with One Another   Unlike public speaking or mass media communication events, in which messages are sent to large, undifferentiated, and heterogeneous audiences, interpersonal communication typically involves clearly identified participants who are able to select those with whom they interact. In addition, when people interact directly with one another, they may use many sensory channels to convey information. Such details as looks, grunts, touches, postures, nods, smells, voice changes, and other specific behaviors are all available for observation and interpretation. Interestingly, given the ease with which people worldwide can use telephones and the Internet—for e-mail, list serves, chatrooms, and instant messaging—interpersonal communication can now occur across global distances, and interpersonal relationships now can be built and sustained with these non–face-to-face channels.

CULTURE connections

… Ashley Edelhart Hall knows where I'm coming from. She is the biracial daughter of a white man and a black woman who openly acknowledges her blended heritage. In fact, she made a point of asking that I include her maiden name—Edelhart—in honor of her father. Yet she considers herself black and says she cannot remember a time when she identified otherwise, despite her outward appearance.

She spoke with me over the phone from her home in Southern California. "I look like whoever I'm standing next to," said Ashley. "If I'm standing in a group of Italian girls, people will think I'm a white Italian. If I'm standing next to Latina girls, they'll think I'm Latina. If I'm standing next to Middle Eastern girls, they'll think I'm Middle Eastern. No one ever thinks I'm black, though. I have to be with New Orleans Creole girls for them to think that I'm black," she explained, providing further evidence that the Chameleon Effect isn't just something I made up.

"People would always say stupid stuff to me when they'd find out that I was black," she said. "I've had people say, 'Oh, but you're so beautiful. Why would you say that you're black? Just don't say anything.' And I'm thinking, do you even know how ignorant you sound saying something like that? You are talking to a black person."

—*Elliott Lewis*

CULTURE connections

We may have all come on different ships, but we're in the same boat now.

—*Attributed to Martin Luther King, Jr.*

Adapted to Specific Others   Because interpersonal communication involves a small number of people who can speak exclusively to one another, it is possible for the participants to assess what is being understood and how the messages are being interpreted. Because many of the messages are designed to evoke a particular effect in other people, the messages can be adapted to fit the specific people for whom they are intended.

Immediate Interpretations   In interpersonal communication, in contrast to books or newspapers, the interpretation of messages can occur essentially simultaneously with their creation. The swift and instantaneous adaptations that people can make as a consequence of these immediate interpretations can permit a subtle and ongoing adjustment to the setting and the other participants.

The Challenge of Communicating in an Intercultural World

There are no simple prescriptions or pat answers that can guarantee competent interpersonal communication among people from different cultures, nor has anyone discovered how to eliminate the destructive consequences of prejudice and racism. The importance of maintaining one's cultural identity—and therefore the need to preserve, protect, and defend one's culturally shared values—often creates a rising tide of emotion that promotes fear and distrust while encouraging cultural autonomy and independence. This emotional tide, whose beneficial elements increase people's sense of pride and help to anchor a people in time and place, can also be a furious and unbridled force of destruction.

Nevertheless, the joys and benefits of embracing an intercultural world are many. As the world is transformed into a place where cultural boundaries cease to be impenetrable barriers, differences among people become reasons to celebrate and share rather than to fear and harm. As Richard Rodriguez puts it,

> We are at one of the great moments of civilization. Nothing as audacious as what we are trying to achieve has been attempted in human history, where you have the Iranian living next door to the Pakistani, living next door to the Cambodian, living next door to the Irishman, living next door to the Mexican. There is just no country that has ever tried this at the level at which we're trying it.[50]

In sum, the opportunities to understand, experience, and benefit from unfamiliar ways are unprecedented. You are—we are all—twenty-first century pioneers on an incredible voyage, a new kind of pilgrim on a new frontier.

CULTURE connections

For the truth is, I think that we are always plural. Not either this *or* that, but this *and* that. And we always embody in our multiple shifting consciousnesses a convergence of traditions, cultures, histories coming together in this time and this place and moving like rivers through us. And I know now that the point is to look back with insight and without judgment, and I know now that it is of the nature of being in this place, this place of convergence of histories, cultures, ways of thought, that there will always be new ways to understand what we are living through, and that I will never come to a point of rest or of finality in my understanding.

—*Leila Ahmad*

Summary

The chapter began with descriptions of five imperatives for achieving intercultural communication competence: the economic, technological, demographic, peace, and interpersonal imperatives. Intercultural competence is now more important than it has ever been.

Next, the chapter provided a general analysis of the human communication process and discussed the topics of communication and interpersonal communication. These topics are of central importance to an understanding of intercultural communication, as they form the foundation for all of our subsequent ideas about the nature of intercultural transactions.

We defined communication as a symbolic, interpretive, transactional, contextual process in which people create shared meanings. Each of the characteristics of communication included in the definition was considered in turn. The role of symbols, which are the words, actions, or objects that stand for or represent units of meaning, was discussed. The consequences of the interpretation of symbols by both senders and receivers of messages on the outcomes of communication were explored. We also described the transactional nature of communication as involving the mutual influence of all individuals on communicative outcomes, so that every person simultaneously creates and interprets meanings and messages. The physical, social, and interpersonal contexts that bound each message were explained. Finally, we described communication as a process, an always-changing flow of interpretations.

We then narrowed our focus to the study of interpersonal communication, which we defined as a form of communication that involves a small number of people who can interact exclusively with one another and who therefore have the ability both to adapt their messages specifically for those others and to obtain immediate interpretations from them. Again, each of the important characteristics of interpersonal communication contained in this definition was considered.

Living in an intercultural world provides numerous challenges and opportunities, as your success and well-being increasingly depend on your ability to behave competently in intercultural encounters. In Chapter 2, we consider two concepts that are central to this book: culture and intercultural communication.

For Discussion

1. What are some of the implications for a United States in which, within your lifetime, European Americans will no longer comprise a majority of the population?
2. Identify some of the ways in which your life is influenced by the presence of individuals from cultures that differ from your own.
3. Which of the imperatives for intercultural competence—demographic, technological, economic,

peace, or interpersonal—is the most powerful motivator for you to improve your intercultural competence?
4. Communication has been defined as "a symbolic, interpretive, transactional, contextual process in which people create shared meanings." What do each of the elements in this definition mean? In your view, which is/are the most important?

For Further Reading

Isa Engleberg and Diana R. Wynn, *The Challenge of Communicating: Guiding Principles and Practices* (Boston: Allyn & Bacon, 2008). Excellent background for students who have not previously studied the human communication process.

Thomas L. Friedman, *The World Is Flat: A Brief History of the Twenty-First Century*, further updated and expanded ed. (New York: Picador, 2007). Globalization—the integration of capital, technology, and information across national borders—is creating both a global market and a global village. This book underscores the tensions between the forces toward globalization and the forces of culture, geography, tradition, and community.

Shelley D. Lane, *Interpersonal Communication: Competence and Contexts* (Boston: Pearson/Allyn & Bacon, 2008). Provides insights into the special characteristics that influence interpersonal communication. This approach to interpersonal communication focuses on competence and fits well with the general approach of this book.

Vincent N. Parrillo, *Strangers to These Shores: Race and Ethnic Relations in the United States*, 9th ed. (Boston: Allyn & Bacon, 2009). Redefines the United States from a nation with only a European American history to one that, from its very beginning, has been a racially and culturally diverse country.

Sarah Trenholm, *Thinking through Communication: An Introduction to the Study of Human Communication*, 5th ed. (Boston: Allyn & Bacon, 2008). Another excellent introduction to the study of human communication that will be particularly useful to the beginning student of communication.

U.S. Census Bureau, www.census.gov. This Web site is a veritable treasure trove of statistical information about the multicultural character of the population of the United States of America.

For additional information about intercultural films and about Web sites for researching specific cultures, please turn to the Resources section at the back of this book.

CHAPTER 2

Culture and Intercultural Communication

This book is about interpersonal communication among people from different cultures. Our goal is to explain how you can achieve interpersonal competence in interactions that involve intercultural communication. This chapter provides a general understanding of culture and intercultural communication. It also includes a discussion about why one culture differs from another. Chapter 3 will continue the discussion by exploring the nature of intercultural communication competence.

Culture

Definitions of *culture* are numerous. In 1952, Alfred L. Kroeber and Clyde Kluckhohn published a book with more than 200 pages devoted to different definitions of the term.[1] Since then, many other scholars have offered additional definitions and approaches.

Our concern in this book is with the link between culture and communication. Consequently, our definition of *culture* is one that allows us to investigate how culture contributes to human symbolic processes.

Defining Culture for the Study of Communication

Our goal in presenting a particular definition of culture is to explain the important link between culture and communication. However, we emphasize that the way we define culture is not the "right" or "best" way. Rather, it is a definition that is useful for our purpose of helping you to understand the crucial link between culture and communication as you set out to improve your intercultural competence.

> *Culture is a learned set of shared interpretations about beliefs, values, norms, and social practices, which affect the behaviors of a relatively large group of people.*

Culture Is Learned   Humans are not born with the genetic imprint of a particular culture. Instead, people learn about their culture through interactions with parents, other family members, friends, and even strangers who are part of the culture. Later in this chapter we explain why some cultures are so different from others. For now, we want to describe the general process by which people learn their culture.

Culture is learned from the people you interact with as you are socialized. Watching how adults react and talk to new babies is an excellent way to see the actual symbolic transmission of culture among people. Two babies born at exactly the same time in two parts of the globe may be taught to respond to physical and social stimuli in very different ways. For example, some babies are taught to smile at strangers, whereas others are taught to smile only in very specific circumstances. In the United States, most children are asked from a very early age to make decisions about what they want to do and what they prefer; in many other cultures, a parent would never ask a child what she or he wants to do but would simply tell the child what to do.

Culture is also taught by the explanations people receive for the natural and human events around them. Parents tell children that a certain person is a good boy because _____. People from different cultures would complete the blank in contrasting ways. The people with whom the children interact will praise and encourage particular kinds of behaviors (such as crying or not crying, being quiet or being talkative). Certainly there are variations in what a child is taught from family to family in any given culture. However, our interest is not in these variations but in the similarities across most or all families that form the basis of a culture. Because our specific interest is in the relationship between culture and interpersonal communication, we focus on how cultures provide their members with a set of interpretations that they then use as filters to make sense of messages and experiences.

CULTURE connections

Culture's Core

I recall now, so very clearly,
as evening clings like tapestry,
a distant time when I was small
and loved to creep along the wall
toward the circle cast by light
where elders talked, among themselves, into the night.

They filled the room with stirring tales, as I—
in my pajamas with the little feet—would lie
behind the outsized chair, hair pressed to rug,
listening invisibly, 'til wakened by the hug
of arms that cradled me 'round knee and head
and placed me back in sagging bed.

They told their stories,
one by one, of hardships suffered, and of glories—
times endured, evils feared,
stunning triumphs engineered
by luck, effort, patience, cunning,
and those who saved themselves by running.

I remember, too, the sagas told
about the turning points in growing old
amidst the tempests once withstood,
and tender details of first kisses, which were good
for waves of jokes and laughter
that I scarcely understood 'til after
I had aged, and learned of love affairs,
and private things that people do in pairs.

So now, like sages who have been and done,
who've told their tales of favors lost and won,
I primp my heirs with stories from my youth
of the vainglorious pursuits of truth,
justice, and the 'Merican way,
'til a still small voice can guide, I pray,
the journey forth where only they may go,
toward a promised land, which I will never know.

Thus repeats the simple lore
of passion, pleasure, pain, and pride
that marks us all, deep down inside,
as humans with a common core.

—Myron W. Lustig

Culture Is a Set of Shared Interpretations   Shared interpretations establish the very important link between communication and culture. Cultures exist in the minds of people, not just in external or tangible objects or behaviors. Integral to our discussion of communication is an emphasis on symbols as the means by which all communication takes place. The meanings of symbols exist in the minds of the individual communicators; when those symbolic ideas are shared with others, they form the basis for culture. Not all of an individual's symbolic ideas are necessarily shared with other people, and some symbols will be shared only with a few. A culture can form only if symbolic ideas are shared with a relatively large group of people.

Culture Involves Beliefs, Values, Norms, and Social Practices   The shared symbol systems that form the basis of culture represent ideas about beliefs, values, norms, and social practices. Because of their importance in understanding the ways in which cultures vary and their role in improving intercultural communication competence, the first section of Chapter 4 is devoted to their detailed explanation. For now, it is enough to know that beliefs refer to the basic understanding of a group of people about what the world is like or what is true or false. Values refer to what a group of people defines as good and bad or what it regards as important. Norms refer to rules for appropriate behavior, which provide the expectations people have of one another and of themselves. Social practices are the predictable behavior patterns that members of a culture typically follow. Taken together, the shared beliefs, values, norms, and social practices provide a "way of life" for the members of a culture.

■ The beliefs, values, norms, and social practices of one's culture are learned. This Malaysian family's dinner to celebrate the end of Ramadan provides an important setting in which cultural patterns are acquired.

CULTURE connections

Sometimes the worst things are not what people say to your face or what they say at all, it is the things that are assumed. I am in line at the grocery store, studying at a café, on a plane flying somewhere.

"Her English is excellent, she must have grown up here," I hear a lady whisper. "But why on earth does she wear that thing on her head?"

"Oh that's not her fault," someone replies, "her father probably forces her to wear that."

I am still searching for a profound thirty-second sound byte to use when I hear comments like that. The trouble is that things like that never take thirty seconds to say. So I say nothing, but silence does not belong there. I want to grasp their hands and usher them home with me. Come, meet my father. Don't look at the wrinkles, don't look at the scars, don't mind the hearing aid, or the thick accent. Don't look at the world's effect on him; look at his effect on the world. Come to my childhood and hear the lullabies, the warm hand on your shoulder on worst of days, the silly jokes on the mundane afternoons. Come meet the woman he has loved and respected his whole life, witness the confidence he has nurtured in his three daughters. Stay the night; hear his footsteps come in at midnight after a long day's work. That thumping is his head bowing in prayer although he is exhausted. Granted, the wealth is gone and the legacy unknown, but look at what the bombs did not destroy. Now tell me, am I really oppressed? The question alone makes me laugh. Now tell me, is he really the oppressor? The question alone makes me cry.

—*Waheeda Samady*

Culture Affects Behavior   If culture were located solely in the minds of people, we could only speculate about what a culture is, since it is impossible for one person to see into the mind of another. However, these shared interpretations about beliefs, values, and norms affect the **behaviors** of large groups of people. In other words, the social practices that characterize a culture give people guidelines about what things mean, what is important, and what should or should not be done. Thus, culture establishes predictability in human interactions. Cultural differences are evident in the varying ways in which people conduct their everyday activities, as people "perform" their culture in their behavioral routines.

Within a given geographical area, people who interact with one another will, over time, form social bonds that help to stabilize their interactions and patterns of behavior. These social practices become the basis for making predictions and forming expectations about others. However, no one is entirely "typical" of the culture to which she or he belongs; each person differs, in unique ways, from the general cultural tendency to think and to behave in a particular way. Nor is "culture" the complete explanation for why people behave as they do: differences in age, gender, social status, and many other factors also affect the likelihood that people will enact specific behaviors. Thus, "culture" is an important, but not the only, explanation for people's conduct.

■ By teaching and explaining to their children, parents help them develop a common set of meanings and expectations.

Culture Involves Large Groups of People   We differentiate between smaller groups of individuals, who may engage in interpersonal communication, and larger groups of people more traditionally associated with cultures. For example, if you work every day with the same group of people and you regularly see and talk to them, you will undoubtedly begin to develop shared perceptions and experiences that will affect the way you communicate. Although some people might want to use the term *culture* to refer to the bonds that develop among the people in a small group, we prefer to distinguish between the broad-based, culturally shared beliefs, values, norms, and social practices that people bring to their interactions and the unique expectations and experiences that arise as a result of particular interpersonal relationships that develop. Consequently, we will restrict the use of the term *culture* to much larger, societal levels of organization.

Culture is also often used to refer to other types of large groups of people. Mary Jane Collier and Milt Thomas, for example, assert that the term "can refer to ethnicity, gender, profession, or any other symbol system that is bounded and salient to individuals."[2] Our definition does not exclude groups such as women, the deaf, gays and lesbians, and others identified by Collier and Thomas. However, our emphasis is primarily on culture in its more traditional forms, which Collier and Thomas refer to as *ethnicity*.

Culture and Related Terms

Terms such as *nation, race,* and *ethnic group* are often used synonymously with the term *culture. Subculture* and *co-culture* are other terms that are sometimes used in talking about groups of people. There are important distinctions, however, between these terms and the groups of people to which tshey might refer.

Nation   In everyday language, people commonly treat *culture* and *nation* as equivalent terms. They are not. Nation is a political term referring to a government and a set of formal and legal mechanisms that regulate the political behavior of its people. These regulations often encompass such aspects of a people as how leaders are chosen, by what rules the leaders must govern, the laws of banking and currency, the means to establish military groups, and the rules by which a legal system is conducted. Foreign policies, for instance, are determined by a nation and not by a culture. The culture, or cultures, that exist within the boundaries of a nation-state certainly influence the regulations that a nation develops, but the term *culture* is not synonymous with *nation*. Although one cultural group predominates in some nations, most nations contain multiple cultures within their boundaries.

The United States is an excellent example of a nation that has several major cultural groups living within its geographical boundaries; European Americans, African Americans, Native Americans, Latinos, and various Asian American cultures are all repre-sented in the United States. All the members of these different cultural groups are citizens of the nation of the United States.

Even the nation of Japan, often regarded as so homogeneous that the word *Japanese* is commonly used to refer both to the nation and to the culture, is actually multicultural. Though the Yamato Japanese culture overwhelmingly predominates within the nation of Japan, there are other cultures living there. These groups include the Ainu, an indigenous group with their own culture, religion, and language; other cultures that have lived in Japan for many generations and originate mainly from Okinawa, Korea, and China; and more recent immigrants also living there.[3]

Race   Race commonly refers to certain physical similarities, such as skin color or eye shape, that are shared by a group of people and are used to mark or separate them from others. Contrary to popular notions, however, race is not primarily a biological term; it is a political and societal one that was invented to justify economic and social distinctions. In the United States, for example, various non–Anglo-Saxon and non-Nordic cultural groups that would now be regarded as predominantly "white"—European Jews and

CULTURE connections

Why do you talk like that? Where are you from? Is that string in your hair? Newness is easy to detect, especially with immigrants. Everything about you is a dead giveaway. And people constantly watch and stare through the scrutinizing lens of curiosity. That was a foreign thing for me, being questioned, being eyed. From top to bottom, the eyes would travel. From top to bottom, taking a silent inventory of the perceived differences: the way I wore my hair wrapped with thread as thick as an undiluted accent, or in small braids intricately woven like a basket atop my head; my clothing, a swirl of bright, festive colors dyed on fabric much too thin for the shivery East Coast climate.

—*Meri Nana-Ama Danquah*

people from such places as Ireland, Italy, Poland, and other eastern and southern European locales—were initially derided as being racial "mongrels" and therefore nonwhite.[4] Conversely, Latinos who were classified as "white" through the 1960 census are now regarded by the United States as "not-quite whites, as in Hispanic whites."[5] Similarly, the U.S. Census Bureau has changed the racial classification of various Asian American groups from white to Asian. Thus, one's "race" is best understood as a social and legal construction.[6]

Although racial categories are inexact as a classification system, it is generally agreed that race is a more all-encompassing term than either *culture* or *nation.* Whereas many western European countries principally include people from the Caucasian race, not all Caucasian people are part of the same culture or nation. Consider the cultural differences among the primarily Caucasian countries of Great Britain, Norway, Germany, and Italy to understand the distinction between culture and race.

Sometimes race and culture do seem to work hand in hand to create visible and important distinctions among groups within a larger society; and sometimes race plays a part in establishing separate cultural groups. An excellent example of the interplay of culture and race is in the history of African American people in the United States. Although race may have been used initially to set African Americans apart from Caucasian U.S. Americans, African American culture provides a strong and unique source of identity to members of the black race in the United States. Scholars now acknowledge that African American culture, with its roots in traditional African cultures, is separate and unique and has developed its own set of cultural patterns. Although a person from Nigeria and an African American are both from the same race, they are from distinct cultures. Similarly, not all black U.S. Americans are part of the African American culture, since many have a primary cultural identification with cultures in the Caribbean, South America, or Africa.

Race can, however, form the basis for prejudicial communication that can be a major obstacle to intercultural communication. Categorization of people by race in

CULTURE connections

It could be, perhaps, because I am neither engineer nor musician. Because I'm neither gringa nor Latina. Because I'm not any one thing. The reality is I am a mongrel. I live on bridges; I've earned my place on them, stand comfortably when I'm on one, content with betwixt and between.

I've spent a lifetime contemplating my mother and father, studying their differences. I count both their cultures as my own. But I'm happy to be who I am, strung between identities, shuttling from one to another, switching from brain to brain. I am the product of people who launched from one land to another, who slipped into other skins, lived by other rules—yet never put their cultures behind them.

—*Marie Arana*

the United States, for example, has been the basis of systematic discrimination and oppression of people of color. We will explore the impact of racism more fully in Chapter 6.

Ethnicity *Ethnic group* is another term often used interchangeably with culture. Ethnicity is actually a term that is used to refer to a wide variety of groups who might share a language, historical origins, religion, nation-state, or cultural system. The nature of the relationship of a group's ethnicity to its culture will vary greatly depending on a number of other important characteristics. For example, many people in the United States still maintain an allegiance to the ethnic group of their ancestors who emigrated from other nations and cultures. It is quite common for people to say they are German or Greek or Armenian when the ethnicity indicated by the label refers to ancestry and perhaps some customs and practices that originated with the named ethnic group. Realistically, many of these individuals now are typical members of the European American culture. In other cases, the identification of ethnicity may coincide more completely with culture. In the former Yugoslavia, for example, there are at least three major ethnic groups—Slovenians, Croatians, and Serbians—each with its own language and distinct culture, who were forced into one nation-state following World War II. It is also possible for members of an ethnic group to be part of many different cultures and/or nations. For instance, Jewish people share a common ethnic identification, even though they belong to widely varying cultures and are citizens of many different nations.

Subculture and Co-culture Subculture is also a term sometimes used to refer to racial and ethnic minority groups that share both a common nation-state with other cultures and some aspects of the larger culture. Often, for example, African Americans, Arab Americans, Asian Americans, Native Americans, Latinos, and other groups are referred to as subcultures within the United States. The term, however, has connotations that we find problematic, because it suggests subordination to the larger European American culture. Similarly, the term co-culture has become more commonly used in an effort to avoid the implication of a hierarchical relationship between the European American culture and these other important cultural groups

CULTURE connections

What I understand by manners is a culture's hum and buzz of implication. I mean the whole evanescent context in which its explicit statements are made. It is that part of a culture which is made up of half-uttered or unuttered or unutterable expressions of value. They are hinted at by small actions, sometimes by…tone, gesture, emphasis, or rhythm, sometimes by the words that are used with a special frequency or a special meaning.

—*Lionel Trilling*

that form the mosaic of the United States. This term, too, is problematic and should be avoided. *Co-culture* suggests, for instance, that there is a single overarching culture in the United States, thus giving undue prominence to the European American cultural group and implicitly suggesting, as Thierry Devos and Mahzarin Banaji note, that "American equals White."[7] We view the United States as a nation within which there are many cultures, and we regard African Americans, Arab Americans, Chinese Americans, Native Americans, Latinos, and similar groups of people as cultures in their own right.[8] When used to refer to cultural groups within a nation, therefore, the term *co-culture* strikes us as redundant. When used to refer to one's identity as a member of various groups based on occupation, hobbies, interests, and the like, *co-culture* seems less precise than such alternative terms as *lifestyle* or *social group*. Chapter 6 elaborates on this distinction between one's cultural and social identities.

Why Cultures Differ

Cultures look, think, and communicate as they do for very practical reasons: to have a common frame of reference that provides a widely shared understanding of the world and of their identities within it; to organize and coordinate their actions, activities, and social relationships; and to accommodate and adapt to the pressures and forces that influence the culture as a whole.

Members of a culture seldom notice these motives because they usually exert a steady and continuous effect of everyone. Few people pay attention to the subtleties of commonplace events and circumstances. Instead, they remain oblivious to the powerful forces that create and maintain cultural differences. This tendency has led Gustav Ichheiser to declare that "nothing evades our attention as persistently as that which is taken for granted."[9]

In this section, we ask you to explore with us the taken-for-granted forces that create and maintain cultural differences. Our goal is to explain *why* one culture differs from another. As you read, consider your own culture and compare it to one that is very different or foreign to you. Why are they different? Why aren't all cultures alike? Why do cultures develop certain characteristics? Why do cultures communicate as they do? Why are they changing?

Forces That Maintain Cultural Differences

Cultural differences are created and sustained by a complex set of the forces that are deeply embedded within the culture's members. We have selected six forces that help to generate cultural differences, including a culture's history, ecology, technology, biology, institutional networks, and interpersonal communication patterns. Of course, this list is by no means exhaustive. Consider these forces as representing factors with the potential to influence the ways in which cultures develop and maintain their differences yet change over time.

History The unique experiences that have become part of a culture's collective wisdom constitute its history. Wars, inheritance rules, religious practices, economic consequences, prior events, legislative acts, and the allocation of power to specific individuals are all historical developments that contribute to cultural differences.

As one of literally thousands of possible examples of the effects of historical forces on the development and maintenance of a culture, let us briefly consider a set of events that occurred in Europe during the late fourteenth century. The experience of bubonic plague, commonly known as the Black Death, was widely shared throughout most of Europe as well as in portions of Africa and Asia. It affected subsequent beliefs and behaviors for many generations.

In 1347, a trading ship traveling to Europe from the Black Sea carried an inadvertent cargo—a horrible disease known as the Black Death. It was spread rapidly by infected fleas carried by rats, and within two years it had traveled from the southern tip of Italy across the entire European continent, killing between one-third and one-half of the European population. There were recurring outbreaks about every decade until the early eighteenth century. Unlike famine, the Black Death attacked every level and social class. When the initial wave of the epidemic was over, the survivors began a reckless spending spree, fueled in large measure by the newly acquired wealth left by the dead and by a sense of anarchy. The diminished availability of workers meant that labor, now a scarce commodity, was in demand. Workers throughout Europe organized to bargain for economic and political parity, and revolts against religious and political institutions were commonplace over the next several centuries. Often, however, workers' demands for retribution were either unrealistic or unrelated to the actual causes of the unrest, and the targets of the revolts were frequently foreigners or other helpless victims who were used as scapegoats for political purposes.

Although the Black Death was not the only historical force behind European cultural change, and indeed is insufficient by itself as an explanation for the changes in modern Europe, it was certainly a crucial experience that was recounted across the generations and influenced the development of European cultures. For instance, although the Black Death can now be controlled with modern-day antibiotics, a recent outbreak of bubonic plague in India caused mass panic and widespread evacuations to other cities, thus inadvertently spreading the disease to uninfected areas before it was contained. One important consequence of the Black Death was the unchallenged expectation that all population increases were desirable, as new births would replace those who had died and would thereby lead to increased standards of living. This belief

■ The Great Wall of China symbolizes the importance and centrality of historical events on modern Chinese cultures.

CULTURE connections

He looked at her now, the smile lighting her narrow eyes, eyes sometimes hazel, sometimes a light brown, sometimes verging on a mossy green. He'd never been close enough for long enough to figure out which was the one true color. Her hair was thick and black and as shiny as a raven's wing, and had once hung to her belt in a neat French braid. Now it was cropped short, brushed straight back from a broad brow, falling into a natural part over her right temple, the ends apt to curl into inky commas around her ears. Her cheekbones were high and flat and just beginning to take on that bronze tint he had noticed during previous summers, all gifts of her Aleut heritage, although the high bridge of her nose was all Anglo and the jut of her chin as Athabascan as it got.

—*Dana Stabenow*

predominated for more than 400 years, leading people to ignore the evidence that over-crowding in some cities was the cause of disease and famine. In 1798, Thomas Malthus challenged this belief, arguing that human populations might be limited by their available food supply.

Recent examples of the influence of historical events are abundant. In the United States, for instance, consider the economic depression of 1929 and the fear of hyperinflation in 1979; the lessons learned in the "Cold War" with the Soviet Union and in "hot" wars with Germany, Japan, Korea, Vietnam, Somalia, Afghanistan, and Iraq; bread lines and gas lines; the proliferation of AIDS, cancer, and drugs; and the deaths of John F. Kennedy, Martin Luther King, Jr., John Lennon, Ronald Reagan, the astronauts aboard the *Challenger*, and the firefighters at the World Trade Center on September 11, 2001. All of these events have had profound effects on the ways in which U.S. Americans view themselves and their country. You have undoubtedly heard parents or other elders describe historical events as significantly influencing them and the lives of everyone in their generation. Descriptions of these events are transmitted across generations and form the shared knowledge that guides a culture's collective actions. As David McCullough says of such events and experiences, "You have to know what people have been through to understand what people want and what they don't want. That's the nub of it. And what people have been through is what we call history."[10]

Ecology   The external environment in which the culture lives is the culture's ecology. It includes such physical forces as the overall climate, the changing weather patterns, the prevailing land and water formations, and the availability or unavailability of certain foods and other raw materials.

There is a considerable amount of evidence to demonstrate that ecological conditions affect a culture's formation and functioning in many important and often subtle ways. Often, the effects of the culture's ecology remain hidden to the members of a culture because the climate and environment are a pervasive and constant force. For example, the development and survival of cultures living in cold-weather climates demand an adaptation that often takes the form of an increased need for technology, industry, urbanization, tolerance for ambiguity, and social mobility.[11] High levels of involvement and closer physical distances in communication characterize cultures that develop in warm climates. High-contact cultures tend to be located in such warm-weather climates as the Middle East, the Mediterranean region, Indonesia, and Latin America, whereas low-contact cultures are found in cooler climates such as Scandinavia, northern Europe, England, portions of North America, and Japan.[12]

In the United States, differences in climate are related to variations in self-perceptions and interaction patterns. Compared with residents in the warmer areas of the South, for instance, those living in the colder areas of the northern United States tend to be less verbally dramatic, less socially isolated, less authoritarian in their communication style, more tolerant of ambiguity, more likely to avoid touching others in social situations, and lower in feelings of self-importance or self-worth.[13] Surviving a harsh cold-weather climate apparently requires that people act in a more constrained and organized fashion, maintain flexibility to deal with an ambiguous and unpredictable environment, cooperate with others to stave off the wind and the weather, and recognize how puny humans are when compared to such powerful forces as ice storms and snow drifts.

Another important aspect of the ecological environment is the predominant geographical and geological features. For instance, an abundant water supply shapes the economy of a region and certainly influences the day-to-day lifestyles of people. If water is a scarce commodity, a culture must give a major portion of its efforts to locating and providing an item that is essential to human life. Energy expended to maintain a water supply is not available for other forms of accomplishment. Likewise, the shape and contour of the land, along with the strategic location of a culture in relation to other people and places, can alter the mobility, outlook, and frequency of contact with others. Natural resources such as coal, tin, wood, ivory, silver, gold, spices, precious stones, agricultural products, and domesticated animals all contribute to the ecological forces that help to create differences among cultures.

■ Global warming and its corresponding climate changes, including melting of the Perito Moreno glacier field in southern Argentina, requires cultures throughout the world to adapt in order to survive.

Technology The inventions that a culture has created or borrowed are the culture's technology, which includes such items as tools, microchips, hydraulic techniques, navigational aids, paper clips, barbed wire, stirrups, and weapons. Changes in the available technology can radically alter the balance of forces that maintain a culture. For instance, the invention of barbed wire allowed the U.S. American West to be fenced in, causing range wars and, ultimately, the end of free-roaming herds of cattle.[14] Similarly, stirrups permitted the Mongols to sweep across Asia, because they allowed riders to control their horses while fighting with their hands.

You have undoubtedly experienced the relationship of technology to culture. Most likely, you have always lived in a home with a microwave oven, though this technology was less common a generation ago. Two generations before microwave ovens became common, most homes also did not have refrigerators and freezers, relying instead on daily trips to the butcher and the baker and on regular visits from the milkman and the iceman to keep foods from spoiling. Think about how a family's food preparation has changed in the United States. Grocery stores now stock very different food products because of the prevalence of refrigerators and microwave ovens; entirely new industries have developed as well (as shown by the many freezer-to-microwave dishes).

Other examples of technological changes with even greater consequences are microprocessors and nanotechnologies, which have encouraged artificial intelligence, stronger and lighter materials, wireless communications, Internet search engines, iPods and other mp3 players, and "smart" machines that are capable of adapting to changing circumstances. The corresponding revolution in the storage, processing, production, and transmission of printed words (such as this textbook), spoken words and other sounds, and visual images is leading to a world in which there is access to an abundance of information.

One special form of technology that has had a major influence on cultures around the world is the media. Media are any technologies that extend the ability to communicate

■ Harnessing the energy of animals has been a major labor-saving technology throughout the world. This Amish man uses horses to harvest his corn crop.

beyond the limits to face-to-face encounters. The media allow humans to extend their sensory capabilities, to communicate across time and long distances, and to duplicate messages with ease. Traditional media, such as books, newspapers, magazines, telegraph, telephone, photography, radio, phonograph, and television, have had a major influence in shaping cultures. New media technologies such as satellites, DVDs, high-definition TVs, iPod players, "smart" mobile phones with 3G wireless capabilities, computers, streaming videos, and the Internet with its chat rooms, instant messaging, blogs, and email, further extend the capabilities of the traditional media to influence cultures.

The Internet alone has radically transformed the way in which people are able to interact with one another. Email, in the form of text-based messages, was the first widely used Internet tool; it allowed family members, friends, and coworkers who were widely dispersed to maintain contact easily. Now one's photos, videos, and other visual images can also move almost instantaneously across cyberspace, allowing people to share their key experiences with others. Similarly, Internet-based phone services allow people to talk just as if they were on a landline telephone and for little or no extra cost beyond that of the Internet connection. MySpace, Facebook, and other rapidly developing social networking sites create other Internet-based mechanisms for people—regardless of geographic location—to stay in touch. Thus the Internet helps people to sustain their culture's beliefs, values, norms, and social practices. For example, cyber-worshippers who are unable to take part in a *puja* (Hindu prayer ceremony) in India's holy city of Varanasi can now participate via cyberspace.[15] A counterpoint to these beneficial consequences of the Internet is its availability for introducing new ideas and images into cultures, which may speed up and change the nature of the culture itself.

Media can be responsible for minimizing the effects of geographic distance by increasing the speed, volume, and opportunities with which ideas can be introduced from one culture to another in a matter of seconds. The latest designs from a Paris fashion show can be captured digitally and instantly transmitted to Hong Kong manufacturers within minutes of their display in France, and accurate copies of the clothing can be ready for sale in the United States within a very short time.

Especially relevant is the way in which media technologies influence people's perceptions about other cultures. How do *Seinfeld* reruns, beamed by satellite to Rio de Janeiro, influence the way Brazilians try to communicate with someone from the United States?[16] In what ways do U.S. action-adventure films, in which many of the characters commit acts of violence to resolve interpersonal disagreements, affect the expectations of people from Egypt when they visit the United States? To what extent do media programs accurately reflect a culture and its members? With the ready availability of television programs, music, and movies from multiple cultures, what are the consequences to

■ Technology is now an everyday part of people's lives. Here a new father balances work and family responsibilities.

specific cultures that these different ways of behaving and living have? As George A. Barnett and Meihua Lee have suggested:

> Throughout the world, many cultures depend heavily on imported television programs, primarily from the United States, Western Europe, or Japan. Most are entertainment and sports programs. Since the early 1980's, along with the emergence of a genuinely global commercial media market, the newly developing global media system has been dominated by three or four dozen large, transnational corporations, with fewer than 10 mostly U.S.-based conglomerates towering over the global market.[17]

So what are people learning from these pervasive media messages? In a comprehensive study of U.S. prime-time television shows, James W. Chesebro concludes that the messages are clear and consistent: the values portrayed include individuality and authority.[18]

> Marine major J. D. "Mac" MacGillis on *Major Dad,* Jack Taylor of *The Family Man,* Murphy Brown, Nash Bridges, Commander Harmon "Harm" Rabb, Jr. on *Jag,* and Detective John Munch and Lieutenant Al Giardello on *Homicide: Life on the Streets,* all are individuals, but they also wield authority, authority directed toward a liberal end. For the last twenty-five years on American television, such leader-centered figures have accounted for 35 percent of all primetime television series. . .
>
> The vast majority of [U.S.] primetime television entertainment—some 70 percent of all series—has promoted the same two values—individuality and authority—during the last twenty-five years. The repetition of these same values from season to season and from series to series—particularly when placed in the elegantly produced settings and as enacted by actors and actresses who have already captured the public's imagination—is likely to leave its influence, if not overtly change the attitudes, beliefs, and actions of viewers.[19]

Thus, media-generated stereotypes, and technology in general, have important consequences for the processes and outcomes of intercultural communication.

Biology   The inherited characteristics that cultural members share are the result of biology, as people with a common ancestry have similar genetic compositions. These hereditary differences often arise as an adaptation to environmental forces, and they are evident in the biological attributes often referred to as *race.* Depending on how finely you wish to make distinctions, there are anywhere from three to hundreds of human races. Biologists are quick to point out, however, that there is far more genetic diversity within each race than there is among races, as humans have had both the means and the motives to mate with others across the entire spectrum of human genetic differences. This makes race an arbitrary but sometimes useful term.[20]

Although it is undeniable that genetic variations among humans exist, it is equally clear that biology cannot explain all or even most of the differences among cultures. For example, the evidence from studies that have been conducted in the United States on differences in intelligence suggests that most of the variation in intelligence quotient (IQ) scores is unrelated to cultural differences. Studies of interracial adoption, for instance, reveal that educational and economic advantages, along with the prebirth intrauterine environment, are the critical factors in determining children's IQ scores.[21] The data therefore suggest that, although hereditary differences certainly exist, most of the distinctions among human groups result from cultural learning or environmental causes rather than from genetic or biological forces. As Michael Winkelman suggests, "biology provides the basis for acquiring capacities, while culture provides those specific skills as related to specific tasks and behaviors."[22]

Readily observable biological differences among groups of people have been amply documented, particularly for external features such as body shape, skin color, and other physical attributes. These visible differences among cultures are often used to define racial boundaries, although they can be affected by climate and other external constraints and are therefore not reliable measures of racial makeup. Better indicants of genetic group distinctions, according to scientists who study their origins and changes, are the inherited single-gene characteristics such as differences in blood types, earwax, and the prevalence of wisdom teeth. Type B blood, for instance, is common among Asian and African races, whereas Rh-negative blood is relatively common among Europeans but rare among other races; Africans and Europeans have soft, sticky ear wax, whereas Japanese and many Native American groups have dry, crumbly earwax; and many Asians lack the third molars, or wisdom teeth, whereas about 15 percent of Europeans and almost all West Africans have them.[23] Of course, racial distinctions such as these are not what is intended by those who differentiate among individuals based on their physical or "racial" characteristics.

A complicating factor in making racial distinctions is that virtually all human populations have the same genetic origins. One theory about human biological differences holds that all humans descended from common ancestors who lived in northeast Africa, just south of what is now the Red Sea, more than 100,000 years ago.[24] By 50,000 years ago, they were living in various tribes and spoke a common language. Migrations of small groups of these ancestral humans began and continued incrementally in a slow expansion by successive generations, through the Middle East, India, Asia, Europe, and across Ice Age land-bridges to Australia, the Americas, and the rest of the world.[25]

In 1950 the United Nations declared that *race* was not a biological term, and scholars have generally agreed that there is no scientific basis for *race*.[26] However, research on the study of human genomes (the hereditary information in one's DNA) has reintroduced the notion that *race* may be biologically based. These studies have been propelled by pharmaceutical companies that want to target race-based health differences and by crime scene investigators who want to narrow their search for suspects.[27] Luigi Cavalli-Sforza

CULTURE connections

Then a foreign concept to the Middle East, the nation-state is still an idea with which the entire region struggles. Many Kurds have never really accepted the West's imposed borders, which in some places severed tribes and even families in half. "A thousand sighs, a thousand tears, a thousand revolts, a thousand hopes," goes an old Kurdish poem about the Kurds' determination to be masters of their own lands.

—*Christiane Bird*

agrees that clustering individuals based on biological similarities may be helpful for many types of medical investigations, but he argues that basing those groupings on current notions of *race* are not very useful.[28] Dismissing the "one-per-continent" view of common conceptions of *race*, Cavalli-Sforza offers the following illustration:

> The remarkable differences in genetic pathologies found among Ashkenazim and Sephardim (Jews of northern-European and Mediterranean origin) populations indicate that genetic clusters of individuals of medical interest may have to be small to be really useful; even a relatively small group like Jews has to be split into subclusters for medical genetics research. If the size of these groups should be an example of the size of useful genetic clusters from a medical point of view, then one would need on the order of a thousand genetic clusters for the whole species.[29]

Such a shift in viewpoint would eliminate, from a biological perspective, the need for racial groupings and would instead encourage alignment by human genome variability.[30]

The lack of a substantial biological basis for racial distinctions does not mean that race is unimportant. Rather, *race* should be understood as a social, political, and personal term that is used to refer to those who are believed by themselves or by others to constitute a group of people who share common physical attributes.[31]

Racial differences are often used politically to define those features that are used to include some individuals in a particular group while excluding others. Thus race can form the basis for prejudicial communication that can be a major obstacle to competent intercultural communication. Categorization of people by race in the United States, for example, has been the source of systematic discrimination and oppression of many people of color. Consequently, race-based distinctions have left a substantial legacy of harmful social and political consequences. As Audrey Smedley and Brian D. Smedley aptly suggest about this legacy, "race as biology is fiction, racism as a social problem is real."[32] We will explore the impact of racism more fully in Chapter 6.

Institutional Networks   Institutional networks are the formal organizations in societies that structure activities for large numbers of people. These include government, education, religion, work, professional associations, and even social organizations. With the new media that have recently become available, institutional networks can be created and sustained more readily through the power provided by information technologies.

The importance of government as an organizing force is acknowledged by the emphasis placed in secondary schools on the different types of government systems around the globe. Because their form of government influences how people think about the world, this institutional network plays an important role in shaping culture.

The importance of institutional networks is also illustrated by the variability in the ways that people have developed to display spirituality, practice religion, and confront their common mortality. Indeed, religious practices are probably as old as humankind. Even 50,000 years ago, Neanderthal tribes in western Asia buried their dead with food, weapons, and fire charcoal, which were to be used in the next life.

Religion is an important institutional network that binds people to one another and helps to maintain cultural bonds. However, the manner in which various

■ Buddhists pray together at a temple. The practice of religion provides important institutional networks in most cultures.

religions organize and connect people differs widely. In countries that practice Christianity or Judaism, people who are deeply involved in the practice of a religion usually belong to a church or synagogue. The congregation is the primary means of affiliation, and religious services are attended at the same place each time. As people become more involved in religious practices, they meet others and join organizations in the congregation, such as men's and women's clubs, Bible study, youth organizations, and Sunday school. Through the institutional network of the church or synagogue, religious beliefs connect people to one another and reinforce the ideas that initially led them to join.

Religious organizations in non-Christian cultures are defined very differently, and the ways they organize and connect people to one another are also very different. In India, for example, Hindu temples are seemingly everywhere. Some are very small and simple, whereas others are grand and elaborate. The idea of a stable congregation holding regularly scheduled services, as is done in the religious practices of Christianity and Judaism, is unknown. People may develop a level of comfort and affiliation with a particular temple, but they don't "join the congregation" and attend prayer meetings. They simply worship in whatever temple and at whatever time they deem appropriate.

Interpersonal Communication Patterns The face-to-face verbal and nonverbal coding systems that cultures develop to convey meanings and intentions are called

CULTURE connections

Being a good host, being a good guest, proving one's generosity, and putting kinship above all—these are the central preoccupations of an Afghan. And I think I know where the values come from. Before technology, in our hard, dry land, we lived on the edge. We didn't have the luxury of considering each individual as a sovereign state and every social relationship as voluntary. We couldn't think in terms of leveling the playing field and giving everyone an equal chance in the competition of all against all—a fundamental premise of democracy in a modern Western state. Living like that could have killed us.

Instead, we developed a culture that said, No one is ever on their own. Everyone belongs to a big group. The prosperity and survival of the group comes first. And no, everyone is not equal. Some are patriachs, and some are poor relations; that's life. But generosity is the value that makes it all work.

—*Tamim Ansaray*

interpersonal communication patterns. These patterns include links among parents, siblings, peers, teachers, relatives, neighbors, employers, authority figures, and other social contacts.

Differences in interpersonal communication patterns both cause and result from cultural differences. Verbal communication systems, or languages, give each culture a common set of categories and distinctions with which to organize perceptions. These common categories are used to sort objects and ideas and to give meaning to shared experiences. Nonverbal communication systems provide information about the meanings associated with the use of space, time, touch, and gestures. They help to define the boundaries between members and nonmembers of a culture.

Interpersonal communication patterns are also important in maintaining the structure of a culture because they are the means through which a culture transmits its beliefs and practices from one generation to another. The primary agents for conveying these basic tenets are usually parents, but the entire network of interpersonal relationships provides unrelenting messages about the preferred ways of thinking, feeling, perceiving, and acting in relation to problems with which the culture must cope. For instance, when a major storm causes death and the destruction of valuable property, the explanations given can shape the future of the culture. An explanation that says "God is punishing the people because they have disobeyed" shapes a different perception of the relationship among humans, nature, and spirituality than an explanation that says "Disasters such as this one happen because of tornadoes and storms that are unrelated to human actions."

Cultures organize and assign a level of importance to their interpersonal communication patterns in various ways, and the level of importance assigned in turn influences other aspects of the culture. Ideas concerning such basic interpersonal relationships as *family* and *friend* often differ because of unique cultural expectations about the obligations and privileges that should be granted to a particular network of people. In the

United States, for instance, college students consider it appropriate to live hundreds of miles from home if doing so will allow them to pursue the best education. Many Mexican college students, however, have refused similar educational opportunities because, in Mexico, one's family relationships are often more important than individual achievement. In the Republic of Korea, family members are so closely tied to one another in a hierarchy based on age and gender that the oldest male relative often has the final say on such important matters as where to attend school, what profession to pursue, and whom to marry.

Because an understanding of cultural differences in interpersonal communication patterns is so crucial to becoming interculturally competent, it is a central feature of this book. Subsequent chapters will focus specifically on the importance of interpersonal communication patterns and will consider more general issues about the nature of interpersonal communication among cultures.

The Interrelatedness of Cultural Forces

Although we have discussed the forces that influence the creation and development of cultural patterns as if each operated independently of all the others, we do wish to emphasize that they are all interrelated. Each force affects and is affected by all of the others. Each works in conjunction with the others by pushing and pulling on the members of a culture to create a series of constraints that alter the cultural patterns.

As an example of the interrelationship among these powerful forces, consider the effects of population, religion, resource availability, and life expectancy on the formation of certain cultural values and practices in Ireland and India during the late nineteenth century.[33] In Ireland, the population was large relative to the available food, and severe food shortages were common. Therefore, there was a pressing need to reduce the size of the population. Because the Irish were predominantly Catholic, artificial methods of birth control were unacceptable. Given the negative cultural value associated with birth control and the problems of overpopulation and lack of food, a cultural practice evolved that women did not marry before the age of about thirty. The population was reduced, of course, by the delay in marriages. India, at about that same time, also had harsh economic conditions, but the average life expectancy was about twenty-eight years, and nearly half of the children died before age five. Given that reality, a cultural value evolved that the preferred age for an Indian woman to marry was around twelve or thirteen. That way, all childbearing years were available for procreation, thus increasing the chances for the survival of the culture.

Cultural adaptations and accommodations, however extreme, are rarely made consciously. Rather, cultures attempt to adjust to their unique configuration of forces by altering the shared and often unquestioned cultural assumptions that guide their thoughts and actions. Thus, changes in a culture's institutions or traditions cause its members to alter their behaviors in some important ways. These alterations, in turn, foster additional adjustments to the institutions or traditions in a continual process of adaptation and accommodation.

Jared Diamond has suggested that it is the interrelationship of these cultural forces that explains the European conquest of the Americas.[34] Why, Diamond asks, were western Europeans able to conquer the indigenous cultures that were living in the Americas, rather than the other way around? Why didn't the native cultures of North and South America conquer Europe? Why, in other words, did the European cultures become disproportionately powerful? In a thorough and well-reasoned argument, Diamond concludes very convincingly that the answers to his questions are unrelated to any biological differences that might have existed; cultural differences in intellect, initiative, ingenuity, and cognitive adaptability have been minor, and the variability of these mental attributes within each culture has been so much greater than their variations across cultures. Rather, the explanation for who-conquered-whom begins with two important environmental or ecological advantages that western Europeans had over the native peoples of the Americas, which lead to institutional, technological, and biological advantages.

The first ecological advantage of the Europeans was the availability of a large number of wild species that had the potential to be domesticated. The variety of these domesticated plants and large animals provided food, transportation, mechanical power, carrying ability, and military advantages. By happenstance, an enormous range of possibilities for domestication was available to the Europeans but not to the cultures living in the Americas. Both massive varieties of plants (grains, fruits, vegetables) and the ready availability of many types of large animals (sheep, goats, cows, pigs, and horses) provided the Europeans with many opportunities for domestication that their counterparts in the Americas simply did not have.

The second ecological advantage of the Europeans was the shape and topography of Europe. Unlike the Americas, Europe has an east-west axis. Axis orientation affects the likelihood that domesticated crops will be able to spread, since locales that are east and west of each other, and therefore at about the same latitude, share the same day length and its seasonable variations. Seeds that are genetically programmed to germinate and grow in specific climatic conditions will likely be able to produce food to the east or the west of their initial locations, but typically they will not grow if planted far to the north or south.

These ecological advantages led to the production and storage of large quantities of food, which in turn encouraged the growth of larger communities. This is so because an acre of land can feed more herders and farmers—often, up to a hundred times more—than it can hunter-gatherers. Domesticated plants and animals provided not just food but also the raw materials for making many other useful items: clothing, blankets, tools, weapons, machinery, and much more.

As populations grew, so too did two additional forces: an increased complexity in the institutional networks, and biological changes in the form of resistance to infectious diseases. First, large population densities must pay much more attention to issues of social control. Rulers, bureaucracies, complex political units, hierarchical organizational structures, and the concentration of wealth are all required to accomplish large public projects and to sustain armies for defense and conquest. Domestication of plants and animals also meant that some people who were not needed for food production could become the specialists who managed the bureaucracies or who developed and manufactured useful products.

Second, there is a powerful biological relationship among population density, the availability of domesticated animals, and the spread of infectious diseases. Most of the major epidemics—smallpox, tuberculosis, malaria, plague, measles, influenza, cholera, typhus, diphtheria, mumps, pertussis, yellow fever, syphilis, gonorrhea, AIDS, and many more—originally jumped to humans from diseases that were carried by animals. Epidemics end when those who are available to be infected either die or become immune. Because many generations of Europeans had been exposed to the infectious diseases that initially came from their domesticated animals, they were able to survive the epidemics that they subsequently spread to the Americas (inadvertently or otherwise) with devastating consequences. (The number of native peoples in the Americas, estimated at about 20 million when Columbus arrived, was down to about 1 million two centuries later.) In sum, Diamond asserts,

> Plant and animal domestication meant much more food and hence much denser human populations. The resulting food surpluses, and (in some areas) the animal-based means of transporting those surpluses, were a prerequisite for the development of settled, politically centralized, socially stratified, economically complex, technologically innovative societies. Hence the availability of domestic plants and animals ultimately explains why empires, literacy, and steel weapons developed earliest in Eurasia and later, or not at all, on other continents. The military uses of horses and camels, and the killing-power of animal derived germs, complete the list of major links between food production and conquest.[35]

Intercultural Communication

A simple way to define the term *intercultural communication* is to use the definition of *communication* that was provided in the previous chapter and insert the phrase "from different cultures." This addition would yield the following definition:

> *Intercultural communication is a symbolic, interpretive, transactional, contextual process in which people from different cultures create shared meanings.*

This definition, although accurate, is difficult to apply. In the following examples, we describe several situations and ask you to analyze them with this definition in mind. Our intention in the discussion that follows is to give you a more sophisticated understanding of the term *intercultural communication* by exploring more fully the meaning of the phrase "people from different cultures."

Examples of Intercultural Interactions

Read the description of each interaction and think carefully about the questions that follow. Decide whether you think the communication between the people involved is or is not intercultural. Our answers to these questions are provided in the subsequent discussion.

Example 1

Dele is from Nigeria, and Anibal is from Argentina. Both young men completed secondary education in their own countries and then came to the United States to study. They studied at the same university, lived in the same dormitory their first year on campus, and chose agriculture as their major. Eventually, they became roommates, participated in many of the same activities for international students, and had many classes together. After completing their bachelor's degrees, they enrolled in the same graduate program. After four more years in the United States, each returned to his home country and took a position in the country's Agricultural Ministry. In emails, phone calls, and the occasional visit with each other, both comment on the difficulties that they are experiencing in working with farmers and the larger agribusiness interests within their own country.

Questions for Example 1

■ When they first begin their studies in the United States, is the communication between Dele and Anibal intercultural communication?

■ When they complete their studies in the United States, is the communication between Dele and Anibal intercultural communication?

■ After they return to their home countries, is the communication between each man and the agricultural business managers with whom they work intercultural communication?

Example 2

Janet grew up in a small town of about 3,500 people in western Massachusetts. She is surrounded by her immediate family, many other relatives, and lots of friends. Her parents grew up in this same town, but Janet is determined to have experiences away from her family and away from the small portion of New England that has formed the boundaries of her existence. Despite parental concerns, Janet goes to one of Colorado's major public universities, and she begins her life in the West. Janet is at first excited and thrilled to be living in Colorado, but within a very short period of time, she begins to feel very isolated. She is assigned to live in a coeducational dormitory, and she finds it disconcerting to be meeting male students as she walks down the hallway in her bathrobe. Although her fellow students seem friendly, her overtures for coffee or movies or even studying together are usually met with a smile and a statement that "It would be great, but...." The superficial friendliness of most of the people she meets starts to annoy her, and Janet becomes bad-tempered and irritable.

Questions for Example 2

■ Is the culture of Massachusetts sufficiently different from that of Colorado to characterize Janet's communication with her fellow students as intercultural?

■ Would Janet have had the same kinds of feelings and reactions if she had moved into a coeducational dormitory at a public university in Massachusetts?

Example 3

Even though Hamid's parents immigrated to the United States from Iran (Persia) before he was born, they speak Persian at home and expect Hamid to behave according to Persian family values and norms. Because Hamid is the eldest child, his parents have additional expectations for him. Hamid loves his parents very much, but he finds their expectations difficult to fulfill. He thinks he speaks respectfully to his mother and father when he tells them that he is going out with friends rather than staying for a celebration to which his extended family has been invited, but his parents tell him that he is being disrespectful. The family reaches a major crisis when Hamid announces that he is going to go to a college that has a good studio arts program, rather than pursue the business degree that his parents want him to earn in preparation for taking over the family business.

Question for Example 3

- Is Hamid's communication with his parents intercultural, either because Hamid is very U.S. American and his parents are Persian or because parents and children have different cultures?

Example 4

Jane Martin works for a U.S. company that has a major branch in South Korea. Although Jane is fairly young, her boss has asked her to travel to Seoul to teach her Korean counterparts a new internal auditing system. Despite Jane's lack of linguistic skill in Korean (she speaks no Korean) and little experience in another country (she has spent a week in London and a week in Paris on holiday), she is confident that she will be successful in teaching the Korean employees the new system. She has won high praise for her training skills in the United States, and the company promises to provide her with a good interpreter. "After all," Jane thinks, "we're all part of the same company—we do the same kinds of work with the same kinds of corporate regulations and expectations. Besides, Koreans are probably familiar with U.S. Americans."

Questions for Example 4

- Is Jane's communication with South Koreans intercultural, or does working for the same corporation mean that Jane and her South Korean counterparts share a common culture?
- Is Jane's age and gender a factor in communication with her Korean counterparts?
- Would you answer the previous questions any differently if Jane's company were sending her to the branch office in England rather than to the one in South Korea?

Example 5

Jody has been fascinated with South Asian cultures since she was a child, when her family lived next door to one from India and her best friend was a girl named Priya. As Jody got older, she began to read about India. More importantly, she became "hooked" on movies from or about India. Because she lived in a large urban area, "Bollywood" films were regularly available, and she often went to a theater to see them. Jody has also rented many DVDs that are directed by and populated with people from India, and she has watched them carefully as well. Though many of these films are in Hindi or another Indian language that Jody doesn't speak, she is confident that she understands them. Jody is now a third-year student at her state university, and recently she was offered an opportunity to study in India for a semester. She is very excited about this chance to live with an Indian family and take classes at an Indian university. She is very familiar with Indian food, dress, and films, and she really regards herself as very knowledgeable about and comfortable with Indian culture. Jody believes that she will have no trouble adjusting to life in India.

Questions for Example 5

- How accurate is Jody's assessment that she understands Indian culture from her reading and extensive exposure to Indian films?
- Can intercultural communication take place even when people do not share a common language?
- Will Jody's communication with her Indian host family be less intercultural because of her familiarity with Indian films?

Example 6

John has worked for the same company, based in Minneapolis, Minnesota, for the six years since his graduation from college. A recent promotion means that John has to move to his company's branch office in Milwaukee, Wisconsin. John faces difficulties almost immediately after beginning work in Milwaukee. His boss has a much different management style than the one with which John is familiar. His new job responsibilities require some knowledge and sophistication in areas in which John is not an expert. After several months on the job, John is feeling fairly beleaguered and is beginning to lose confidence in his abilities.

Question for Example 6

- Is John's communication with his boss intercultural communication?

Example 7

When he was eight years old, Jorge's family immigrated to Texas from Mexico. At first, Jorge did not know English, but, as he progressed through school, he gradually became a fluent English speaker. The language spoken at home, however, was always

Spanish. Jorge felt proud to have a family that celebrated its Mexican cultural heritage; his parents had made great sacrifices to move to the United States, but their hopes for a better life for their children motivated them to immigrate. Jorge was an excellent student in college, ultimately received an MBA, and landed a challenging job in a well-known company. One day Jorge learned that his company was going to expand its operations to Chile and, because Jorge was one of the few Spanish-speaking managers in the company, he was going to be sent to Chile to manage the business there. His bosses presumed that because Jorge knows Spanish, he will be the ideal person for this important work. Jorge, on the other hand, is nervous and tries to explain that, while knowing the Spanish language is important, the culture in Chile is a very different from that of Mexico. Even the spoken and written forms of Spanish are quite different in the two cultures.

Questions for Example 7

■ Is Jorge correct that Mexican and Chilean cultures are sufficiently different to make his communication with Chileans intercultural?
■ How important is it to know how to speak a language in intercultural communication?

Each of these examples represents a likely communication event in today's world. It is very probable that two people from different countries will spend an extended period of time in a third country, as Dele and Anibal have. It is also very likely that these two people will, over time, form relationships that create a shared set of experiences. Moving from one part of a country to another is a commonplace occurrence, whether the goal is to attend a university, as Janet did, or to advance professionally, as John did. Immigration of people from one country to another also occurs frequently, producing communication problems typical of those experienced by U.S.-born-and-raised Hamid with his Persian-born-and-identified parents. The significance of the global marketplace means that work often takes people to countries around the world, as companies like Jane's and Jorge's become increasingly multinational. With the advent of modern communication technologies, many more people will be able to select television programs, films, music, radio shows, and computerized messages that are arranged in verbal and nonverbal codes different from their own. Jody's experience with the Indian films will be repeatable almost everywhere. But are these examples, all of which involve communication, also examples of intercultural communication? Do any of them clearly *not* involve intercultural communication? In the next sections, we attempt to provide answers to these questions.

Similarities and Differences between Communicators

By applying the definition of intercultural communication given at the beginning of the chapter, it would be relatively simple to categorize each example. You would go through the examples and make a bipolar choice—either yes or no—based on whether the people in the examples were from different cultures. Thus, you would probably decide that the communication between Anibal and Dele was intercultural when they arrived in the United States. It would be much more difficult to judge their communication after they completed their studies. Perhaps you would decide that their communication with people from their own country following their return home was not intercultural, or perhaps you would say that it was. Similarly, you might be convinced that Colorado is indeed a different culture from Massachusetts, or you might argue vehemently that it is not. Most likely you would decide that Jane's communication with her Korean counterparts was intercultural, even though they undoubtedly did share some common expectations about work performance because the same company employed them. Had her company decided to send Jane to England instead of to Korea, her communication with her English coworkers would have been similarly intercultural. Yet you might feel a bit uncomfortable, as we are, with the idea of putting U.S.–Korean communication into the same category as U.S.–English communication. Similarly, Jorge has language skills and some cultural knowledge, which makes him a better choice for the Chilean assignment than his European American colleagues who speak only English and know little about the cultures in Latin America, but his communication in Chile will certainly be more challenged than it would be if his assignment had been to Mexico City.

The difficulties encountered in a simple yes-or-no decision lead us to suggest an alternative way of thinking about intercultural communication. What is missing is an answer to three questions that emerge from the preceding examples:

1. What differences among groups of people constitute cultural differences?
2. How extensive are those differences?
3. How does extended communication change the effects of cultural differences?

This last question suggests the possibility that initially one's interactions could be very intercultural, but subsequent communication events could make the relationship far less intercultural.

To demonstrate the importance of these questions, we would like you to take the examples presented earlier and arrange them in order from most intercultural to least intercultural.[36] Use a continuum like the one shown in Figure 2.1.

Most   **Least**
intercultural   **intercultural**

FIGURE 2.1 **A continuum of interculturalness.**

Thus, you will be identifying the degree of interculturalness in each interaction and, in effect, you will be creating an "interculturalness" scale. It should even be possible to make distinctions among those communication situations that are placed in the middle, with some closer and some farther from the most intercultural end. When you place the examples on a continuum, they might look something like Figure 2.2.

We suspect that the continuum you have created is very similar to ours. Where we might disagree is on how we ordered the examples placed near the middle.

The next important issue for understanding the definition of intercultural communication concerns the characteristics present in the encounters. What is it about the people, the communication, the situation, or some combination of those factors that increases the likelihood that the communication will be intercultural?

What varies and changes across the examples is the degree of similarity or the amount of difference between the interactants. For instance, Anibal (from Argentina) and Dele (from Nigeria) are very different when they first come to study in the United States. Each speaks English but as a second language to Spanish and Yoruba, respectively; their facility with

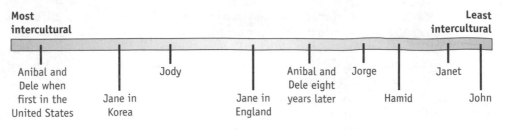

FIGURE 2.2   A continuum of interculturalness, with examples.

English is initially weak, and they are uncomfortable with it. In addition, their values, social customs, gestures, perceptions of attractiveness, and expectations about personal space and how friendships are established differ. Initially, Anibal and Dele are culturally very different, or heterogeneous, and their communication should certainly be placed near the "most intercultural" end of the continuum. However, after eight years in the United States, having studied the same academic subjects, shared many of the same friends, and participated in many common experiences, their communication with each other does not have the same degree of interculturalness as it did initially. Certainly, each still retains part of his own cultural heritage and point of view, but the two men have also created an important set of common understandings between themselves that is not grounded in their respective cultural frameworks.

Janet, in contrast, was placed near the "least intercultural" end of the continuum because of the degree of similarity, or homogeneity, she shares with Coloradans. They speak the same language, and their values, gestures, social perceptions, and expectations about relationships are all similar. Certainly, Coloradans use slang and jargon with which Janet is not familiar, but they speak, read, and study in English. And certainly, Coloradans, particularly urban Coloradans, seem to place importance on different things than Janet does. She also thinks it unusual and a bit uncomfortable to be sharing a living space with men she does not even know. Nevertheless, the magnitude of these differences is relatively small.

There are learned differences among groups of people that are associated with their culture, such as cultural patterns, verbal and nonverbal codes, relationship rules and roles, and social perceptions. When such important differences are relatively large, they lead to dissimilar interpretations about the meanings of the messages that are created, and they therefore indicate that people are from different cultures. Thus,

> *People are from different cultures whenever the degree of difference between them is sufficiently large and important that it creates dissimilar interpretations and expectations about what are regarded as competent communication behaviors.*

Definition of Intercultural Communication

Previous definitions have described the central terms *communication* and *culture*. By combining the meanings of these terms with the ideas suggested in our discussion about the degrees of difference that can occur among people from dissimilar cultures, we offer the following definition of intercultural communication:

> *Intercultural communication occurs when large and important cultural differences create dissimilar interpretations and expectations about how to communicate competently.*

CULTURE connections

My parents didn't want their daughter to be Korean, but they don't want her fully American, either. Children of immigrants are living paradoxes. We are the first generation and the last. We are in this country for its opportunities, yet filial duty binds us. When my parents boarded the plane, they knew they were embarking on a rough trip. I don't think they imagined the rocks in the path of their daughter.

—*Caroline Hwang*

The degree to which individuals differ is the degree to which there is interculturalness in a given instance of communication. Situations in which the individuals are very different from one another are most intercultural, whereas those in which the individuals are very similar to one another are least intercultural.

Intercultural Communication and Related Terms

The relationship between culture and communication is important to many disciplines. Consequently, many terms have been used to describe the various ways in which the study of culture and communication intersect: *cross-cultural communication, international communication, intracultural communication, interethnic communication,* and *interracial communication.* The differences among these terms can be confusing, so we would like to relate them to the focus of study in this book.[37]

Intracultural Communication   The term intercultural, used to describe one end point of the continuum, denotes the presence of at least two individuals who are culturally different from each other on such important attributes as their value orientations, preferred communication codes, role expectations, and perceived rules of social relationships. We would now like to relabel the "least intercultural" end of the continuum, which is used to refer to communication between culturally similar individuals, as intracultural. John's communication with his new boss in Milwaukee is intracultural. Janet's communication with her fellow students in Colorado is more intracultural than intercultural. Both *intercultural* and *intracultural* are comparative terms. That is, each refers to differences in the magnitude and importance of expectations that people have about what constitutes competent communication behaviors.

Interethnic and Interracial Communication   Just as *race* and *ethnic group* are terms commonly used to refer to cultures, *interethnic* and *interracial communication* are two labels commonly used as substitutes for *intercultural communication.* Usually, these terms are used to explain differences in communication between members of racial and ethnic groups who are all members of the same nation-state. For example, communication between African Americans and European Americans is often referred to as interracial communication. The large numbers of people of Latino origin who work and live with people of European ancestry produce communication characterized as interethnic. Sometimes the terms are also used to

■ Intercultural communication occurs when large and important cultural differences create dissimilar interpretations and expectations about how to communicate competently.

refer to communication between people from various ethnic or racial groups who are not part of the same nation but live in specific geographic areas. Although it may be useful in some circumstances to use the terms *interethnic* and *interracial,* we believe these types of communication are most usefully categorized as subsets of intercultural communication.

Both ethnicity and race contribute to the perceived effects of cultural differences on communication, which moves that communication toward the "most intercultural" end of the continuum. We will therefore rely on the broader term of *intercultural communication* when discussing, explaining, and offering suggestions for increasing your degree of competence in interactions that involve people from other races and ethnic groups. In Chapter 6, however, when considering particular cultural biases, we will give special attention to the painful and negative consequences of racism.

Cross-Cultural Communication   The term cross-cultural is typically used to refer to the study of a particular idea or concept within many cultures. The goal of such investigations is to conduct a series of intracultural analyses in order to compare one culture with another on the attributes of interest. For example, someone interested in studying the marriage rituals in many cultures would be considered a cross-cultural researcher. Scholars who study self-disclosure patterns, child-rearing practices, or educational methods as they exist in many different cultures are doing cross-cultural comparisons. Whereas intercultural communication involves interactions among people from different cultures, cross-cultural communication involves a comparison of

CULTURE connections

You're general, but you're also specific. A citizen and a person, and the person you are is like nobody else on the planet. Nobody has the exact memory that you have. What is now known is not all that you are capable of knowing. You are your own stories and therefore free to imagine and experience what it means to be human without wealth. What it feels like to be human without domination over others, without reckless arrogance, without fear of others unlike you, without rotating, rehearsing and reinventing the hatreds you learned in the sandbox. And although you don't have complete control over the narrative (no author does, I can tell you), you could nevertheless create it.

—*Toni Morrison*

interactions among people from the same culture to those from another culture. Although cross-cultural comparisons are very useful for understanding cultural differences, our principle interest is in using these cross-cultural comparisons to understand intercultural communication competence.

International Communication   International communication refers to interactions among people from different nations. Scholars who compare and analyze nations' media usage also use this term. Certainly, communication among people from different countries is likely to be intercultural communication, but that is not always true, as illustrated by the example of Anibal and Dele after eight years together in the United States. As we suggested with the terms *interracial* and *interethnic communication*, we prefer to focus on *intercultural communication*.

Summary

Our goal in this chapter has been to provide an understanding of some of the key concepts underlying the study of intercultural competence. We began with a discussion of the concept of culture. From the many available approaches to defining culture, we selected one that emphasizes the close relationship between culture and communication. We defined *culture* as a learned set of shared interpretations about beliefs, values, norms, and social practices, which affect the behaviors of a relatively large group of people. We emphasized that people are not born with a culture but learn it through their interactions with others. Our definition located culture in the minds of people, and in the shared ideas that can be understood by their effects on behavior. We distinguished between culture and other groups to which people belong by suggesting that culture occurs only

when beliefs, values, norms, and social practices affect large groups of people. We next made some important distinctions among terms such as *culture, nation, race, ethnic group,* and *subculture*.

We also explored some of the reasons that cultures differ. The shared experiences remembered by cultural members, or a culture's history, were considered first. In the United States, for instance, the lesson of the country's historical experiences affects U.S. Americans' views of their government's relationships with other countries. The ways in which a culture's unique ecology profoundly alters the collective actions of its people were then illustrated. Next, we discussed the biological or genetic forces affecting cultures. Genetic variations among people are only a small source of cultural differences. We also explained the role of the formal organizations of a culture, the institutional networks such as government, religion, work organizations, and other social organizations. These institutional networks organize groups of individuals and provide the regulations by which the culture functions as a collective. The undisputed effects of technology on a culture were explored next. Technological differences promote vast changes in the ways cultures choose to function. Finally, interpersonal communication patterns, the means by which cultural patterns are transmitted from one generation to another, were considered. These interpersonal communication patterns include the links a culture emphasizes among parents, siblings, peers, teachers, relatives, neighbors, authority figures, and other social contacts. The reciprocal relationship among these forces suggests the inevitability

and constancy of accommodations and changes that characterize all cultures.

The chapter concludes with a discussion of a topic that is central to this book: intercultural communication. We began with several examples, which were followed by an exploration of issues related to similarities and differences among communicators that produce intercultural communication. Finally, after providing our definition of intercultural communication, we differentiated between that term and related terms, including *intracultural, interethnic, interracial, cross-cultural,* and *international* communication. In Chapter 3, we consider an additional concept that is the focal point of this book—intercultural communication competence.

For Discussion

1. What differences are there between the view that "people are born into a culture" versus the opinion that "one becomes a member of a culture through a process of learning"?
2. In the United States, how are the terms *nation, race, culture,* and *co-culture* used inaccurately?
3. How do you think the ever-present cell phone, as a medium to communicate with others, is changing

interpersonal relationships within the cultures of the United States?
4. What is implied by the statement that "race as biology is fiction, racism as a social problem is real"? Do you agree or disagree with this statement?
5. What links are there between intercultural communication and interpersonal communication?

For Further Reading

William B. Gudykunst, *Theorizing about Intercultural Communication* (Thousand Oaks, CA: Sage, 2005). A lucid and insightful guide to theories and theorizing about intercultural communication phenomena.

Myron W. Lustig and Jolene Koester (eds.), *AmongUS: Essays on Identity, Belonging, and Intercultural Competence,* 2nd ed. (Boston: Allyn & Bacon, 2006). This collection includes many essays, written in the first person, that document the emotions and experiences of people living in a multicultural world.

Joseph Shaules, *Deep Culture: The Hidden Challenges of Global Living* (Buffalo: Multilingual Matters, 2007). A comprehensive discussion about how people can understand, adjust to, and live in other cultures.

Ronald Takaki (ed.), *Debating Diversity: Clashing Perspectives on Race and Ethnicity in America,* 3rd ed. (New York: Oxford University Press, 2002). Essays in this volume look at the differences and similarities in the experiences of various racial and ethnic groups that make up the "pattern" of race and ethnicity in the United States.

Nicholas Wade, *Before the Dawn: Recovering the Lost History of Our Ancestors* (New York: Penguin, 2006). A "good read" that describes the history, biology, and language development of the earliest humans.

For additional information about intercultural films and about Web sites for researching specific cultures, please turn to the Resources section at the back of this book.

CHAPTER 3

Intercultural Communication Competence

■ **The United States as an Intercultural Community**
Metaphors of U.S. Cultural Diversity
What Do You Call Someone from the United States of America?
Cultural Groups in the United States
■ **Competence and Intercultural Communication**
Intercultural Communication Competence

The Components of Intercultural Competence
■ **Basic Tools for Improving Intercultural Competence**
The BASICs of Intercultural Competence
Description, Interpretation, and Evaluation
■ **Summary**

When does communication become intercultural communication? What distinguishes intercultural communication from communication that is not intercultural? What does it mean to be a competent intercultural communicator? In Chapters 1 and 2, we defined the terms *communication, culture,* and *intercultural communication.* In this chapter, we first discuss the multicultural nature of the United States, where intercultural competence is essential. Then we focus our attention on the components and characteristics of intercultural communication competence. Our purpose is to establish boundaries and common understandings about this central idea.

The United States as an Intercultural Community

A set of complicated issues underlies our discussion in Chapter 1 about the imperatives for intercultural communication. Stated most simply, these issues focus on what it means to be an American and on decisions about how to refer to the various cultural groups that reside within the borders of the United States. In the following sections, we first examine the implications of four metaphors that have been used to describe U.S. cultural diversity. Next, we analyze the question of what to call someone from the United States. Finally, we describe the difficult choices we faced in selecting labels to refer to the domestic cultures within the United States.

CULTURE connections

When I was a kid, I didn't know my father had an accent. I knew that he had come to America from Baghdad before I was born, that he was an Arab, that he had grown up speaking Arabic before he learned English. But to me, he was as American as my American mother. The fact that my father was from another country was an interesting novelty to me, but it was part of some distant past that had nothing to do with our lives.

I learned that my father had an accent when I was in my early teens. A friend of mine mentioned it, and I told him he was crazy. I told my mother about this and she said, "Of course your father has an accent, don't you hear it?" It was after this that I listened closely to my father speak, and for the first time heard his accent.

What I knew of my father was that he was a good dad. He played catch with me in the backyard after he got home from work. He took us fishing. He loved sports. He also loved literature, and occasionally he read the Koran in Arabic. He sang Arab songs in the shower. He loved to cook. He loved his family.

My father, Ismail Mohamad al-Samarrai, came to this country in 1953 at the age of 24 to study physical education. He had been a teacher in his country. He came with a suitcase, a suit, "a toothbrush, and $60." He also came with a scholarship. He met my mother in Springfield, Mass., where he went to college. She was charmed by his accent. He was "such a gentleman," she said.

In photos of his early years here, he is slim and a bit handsome. He had dark, alert eyes, black hair, a happy appearance. His nickname was "Smiles." He adopted the name "Al."

"I came to America with an open mind," he said. "Almost as soon as I arrived, I felt like I was born here. I liked the people, the food, the movies, the freedom. I could dance with a girl."

He did miss his culture. He said he particularly missed sitting in coffeehouses reading and discussing Arab literature. He had wanted to be a writer, and had written some articles and short stories for newspapers and magazines in Iraq. A few of these pieces were read on the BBC. But he and other writers could not write freely there.

"You could not say honestly what you wanted to say," he said. "I thought I would write once I got to America. But I didn't."

(continued)

He was a typical young "radical" in Iraq. He protested against the government, a monarchy-dictatorship that predated Saddam Hussein. He once saw a police officer shoot a protester. The angry crowd reacted by mauling the cop. Dad spent brief periods in jail and was once whipped by police.

"When I left Iraq, I knew in the back of my mind I would not go back," he said. Before long, he moved to Miami because he couldn't tolerate the cold New England winter. My mother, who to him at the time was just someone he'd dated, "followed" him down, he said.

"I didn't follow him," Mother said. "I thought Miami was the most beautiful place in the world."

They married, had me, and my father lost his scholarship and dropped out of college so he could work. They had two more children. My father never went back to college or to Iraq. He spent his life working at jobs he didn't care for.

But his children earned college degrees.

They raised us as Christians, in my mother's religion. Dad played an active role in this, attending church with us. He even served as an usher.

"Why didn't you raise us as Muslims?" I asked him much later.

"I wanted you to fit in with your own people," he said. "You are Americans."

I was 6 when my father became an American citizen. I remember him pulling into our driveway with a big smile on his face, waving a little American flag. "I'm an American now," he said.

I looked at him closely. "You still look the same," I said, apparently dismayed that some visual transformation had not occurred.

I can only guess at the adjustments my father must have made during his life here as he became fluent in English and accepted a new culture and a new life.

"What are you?" I once asked him. "An Arab, an American, or an Arab-American?"

"I would not put a hyphen in a description of me," he said. "I am an American with an Arab heritage. I am proud of and fond of my culture. But if I must have a hyphen,"—he chuckled—"then I am an American-American."

—*Fariss Samarrai*

Metaphors of U.S. Cultural Diversity

Many cultural groups live within the borders of the United States. When people talk about the blend of U.S. cultural groups, their ideas are often condensed into a few key words or phrases. These summary images, called metaphors, imply both descriptions of what is and, less obviously, prescriptions of what should be. Although we will have much more to say in subsequent chapters about the effects of language and labeling on the intercultural communication process, we would like to focus now on four metaphors that have been used to describe the cultural mix within the United States: a melting pot, a set of tributaries, a tapestry, and a garden salad.

The Melting Pot Metaphor   Perhaps the oldest metaphor for describing multiple cultures in the United States is the melting pot.[1] America, according to this image, is like a huge crucible, a container that can withstand extremely high temperatures and can therefore be used to melt, mix, and ultimately fuse together metals or other substances. This image was the dominant way to represent the ideal blending of cultural groups at a time when the hardened steel that was forged in the great blast furnaces of Pittsburgh helped to make the United States into an industrial power. According to this view, immigrants from many cultures came to the United States to work, live, mix, and blend together into one great assimilated culture that is stronger and better than the unique individual cultures of which it is composed.

Dynamic as the melting pot metaphor has been in the United States, it has never been an accurate description. The tendency for diverse cultures to melt together and assimilate their unique heritages into a single cultural entity has never really existed. Rather, the many cultural groups within the United States have continuously adapted to one another as they accommodated and perhaps adopted some of the practices and preferences of other groups while maintaining their own unique and distinctive heritages.

The Tributaries Metaphor   A currently popular metaphor for describing the mix of cultures in the United States is that of tributaries or tributary streams. America, according to this image, is like a huge cultural watershed, providing numerous paths in which the many tributary cultures can flow. The tributaries maintain their unique identities as they surge toward their common destination. This view is useful and compelling. Unlike the melting pot metaphor, which implies that all cultures in the United States ought to be blended to overcome their individual weaknesses, the tributary image seems to suggest that it is acceptable and desirable for cultural groups to maintain their unique identities. However,

■ Intercultural communication occurs when there are significant differences among the communicators. What do you suppose are the consequences of these differences for the people shown here?

when the metaphor of tributaries is examined closely, there are objections to some of its implications.

Tributary streams are small, secondary creeks that ultimately flow into a common stream, where they combine to form a major river. Our difficulty with this notion rests in the hidden assumption that the cultural groups will ultimately and inevitably blend together into a single, common current. Indeed, there are far fewer examples of cultures that have totally assimilated into mainstream U.S. culture than there are instances of cultures that have remained unique. Further, the idea of tributaries blending together to form one main stream suggests that the tributaries are somehow subordinate to or less important than the mighty river into which they flow.

The Tapestry Metaphor   A tapestry is a decorative cloth made up of many strands of thread. The threads are woven together into an artistic design that may be pleasing to some but not to others. Each thread is akin to a person, and groups of similar threads are analogous to a culture. Of course, the types of threads differ in many ways; their thickness, smoothness, color, texture, and strength may vary. The threads can range from gossamer strands to inch-thick yarn, from soft silk to coarse burlap, from pastel hues to fluorescent radiance, and from fragile spider webs to steel cables. The weaving process itself can vary from one location to another within the overall tapestry. Here, a wide swatch of a single type of thread may be used; there, many threads might be interwoven with many others, so no single thread is distinguished; and elsewhere, the threads may have been grouped together into small but distinguishable clumps.

Although the metaphor of a tapestry has much to commend it, the image is not flawless. After all, a tapestry is rather static and unchangeable. One does not typically unstring a bolt of cloth, for instance, only to reassemble the threads elsewhere in a different configuration. Cultural groups in the United States are more fluid than the tapestry metaphor might imply; migrations, immigrations, and mortality patterns all alter the cultural landscape. Despite its limitations, however, we find this metaphor preferable to the previous two.

The Garden Salad Metaphor   Like a garden salad made up of many distinct ingredients that are being tossed continuously, some see the United States as made up of a complex array of distinct cultures that are blended into a unique, and one hopes tasteful, mixture. Substitute one ingredient for another, or even change how much of each ingredient is present, and the entire flavor of the salad may be changed. Mix the salad differently and the look and feel will also differ. A salad contains a blend of ingredients, and it provides a unique combination of tints, textures, and tastes that tempt the palate.

Like the other metaphors, the garden salad is not without its flaws. In contrast to the tapestry image, which implies that the United States is too fixed and unchanging, a garden salad suggests an absence of firmness and stability. A typical garden salad has no fixed arrangement; it is always in a state of flux. Cultural groups in the United States, however, are not always moving, mixing, and mingling with the speed and alacrity that the metaphor would suggest. Nevertheless, we recommend this metaphor, and that of the tapestry, as the two images that are likely to be most useful in characterizing the diversity of cultural groups in the United States. In addition, we encourage you to invent your own metaphors.

What Do You Call Someone from the United States of America?

Many people who live in the United States of America prefer to call themselves American. However, people from Brazil, Argentina, Guatemala, Mexico, and many other Central and South American countries also consider themselves American, as they are all part of the continents known collectively as the Americas. Indeed, people from these countries consider the choice of *American* for those from the United States to be imperialistic and insulting. They resent the implication that they are less central or less important.

An alternative choice for a name, which is frequently selected by those who are trying to be more sensitive to cultural differences, is *North American*. *North American* is the English translation of the Spanish label that is commonly used by people from many Central and South American countries to refer to people from the United States, and the name is widely regarded as far less insulting and imperialistic. However, this label still has the potential for creating friction and causing misunderstanding. *North American* refers to an entire continent, and people from Mexico and Canada are, strictly speaking, also North Americans. Indeed, conversations with Canadians and Mexicans have confirmed for us that *North American* is not the ideal term.

One possibility that is often overlooked is to refer to people from the United States as *United Statians* or *United Staters*. These labels have the obvious advantage of being unambiguous, as they specifically identify people from a single country. Realistically, however, these are not labels that citizens of the United States would regard as comfortable and appropriate, and we agree that they are artificial and unlikely to be widely used.

CULTURE connections

"Where's Brighton Beach?" I asked. "In England," my mother said, searching the kitchen cabinets for something she'd misplaced. "I mean the one in New York." "Near Coney Island, I think." "How far is Coney Island?" "Maybe half an hour." "Driving or walking?" "You can take the subway." "How many stops?" "I don't know. Why are you so interested in Brighton Beach?" "I have a friend there. His name is Misha and he's Russian," I said with admiration. "Just Russian?" my mother asked from inside the cabinet under the kitchen sink. "What do you mean, *just* Russian?" She stood up and turned to me. "Nothing," she said, looking at me with the expression she sometimes gets when she's just thought of something amazingly fascinating. "It's just that you, for example, are one-quarter Russian, one-quarter Hungarian, one-quarter Polish, and one-quarter German." I didn't say anything. She opened a drawer, then closed it. "Actually," she said, "you could say you're three-quarters Polish and one-quarter Hungarian, since Bubbe's parents were from Poland before they moved to Nuremberg, and Grandma Sasha's town was originally in Belarus, or White Russia, before it became part of Poland." She opened another cabinet stuffed with plastic bags and started rooting around in it. I turned to go. "Now that I'm thinking about it," she said, "I suppose you could also say you're three-quarters Polish and one-quarter Czech, because the town Zeyde came from was in Hungary before 1918, and in Czechoslovakia after, although the Hungarians continued to consider themselves Hungarian, and briefly even became Hungarian again during the Second World War. Of course, you could always just say you're half Polish, one-quarter Hungarian, and one-quarter English, since Grandpa Simon left Poland and moved to London when he was nine."

—*Nicole Krauss*

Our preference is the label U.S. Americans. This referent retains the word *American* but narrows its scope to refer only to those from the United States. The term retains the advantages of a name that is specific enough to be accurate, yet it does not resort to a form of address that people would be unlikely to use and would regard as odd.

Cultural Groups in the United States

It is also important to select terms that adequately and sensitively identify the variety of cultural groups that make up the U.S. citizenry. As the population of the United States becomes increasingly more varied culturally, it is extremely urgent that we find ways to refer to these cultures with terms that accurately express their differences but avoid negative connotations and evaluations.

Some of the terms used in the past have negative associations, and we, as authors, have struggled to find more appropriate alternatives. For example, earlier writings about intercultural communication often referred to the culture associated with white U.S. Americans as either the "dominant" culture or the "majority" culture. The term *dominant* usually suggested the economic and political power of white U.S. America, referring to the control of important sources of institutional and economic power. The term often conveyed a negative meaning to members of other cultural groups, as it suggested that white U.S. Americans were somehow better or superior. It also implied that people from nondominant cultures were somehow subordinate or inferior to the dominant group. As more and more cultural groups have gained political and economic power in the United States, *dominant* no longer accurately reflects the current reality.

An alternative label for white U.S. Americans was *majority culture*. This term was intended to reflect a numerical statement that the majority of U.S. Americans are from a particular cultural group. *Majority* was often coupled with the term *minority*, which also had negative connotations for many members of other cultural groups: it suggested to some people that they were not regarded as important or significant as members of the majority. In addition, as previously suggested, nonwhite cultural groups now make up a sufficient proportion of the total population, so white U.S. Americans no longer constitute an absolute majority in many places. Thus, we prefer to avoid such emotionally charged words as *majority, minority, dominant, nondominant,* and *subordinate* when we discuss the cultural groups residing in the United States.

We have also elected not to use the term *white* or *Caucasian* in all subsequent discussions about a specific cultural group of U.S. Americans. *White* and *Caucasian* refer to a particular race. As suggested in Chapter 2, a racial category does not necessarily identify and distinguish a particular culture. Although many members of this group prefer to use the term *white*,[2] we think it is less useful in this book on inter*cultural* communication to refer to a cultural group in the United States by a term that denotes race. Consequently, because their common cultural heritage is predominantly European, we have chosen to describe white U.S. cultural members as *European Americans*.

Many black Americans prefer to be identified by a term that distinguishes them by their common cultural characteristics rather than by their racial attributes. *African American* recognizes the effects of traditional African cultural patterns on U.S. Americans of African heritage, and it acknowledges that African American cultural patterns are distinct from those of European Americans. Because it denotes a cultural rather than a racial distinction, we will use the term *African American* in this book.

Another set of terms is usually applied to those residents of the United States whose surname is Spanish. *Hispanic, Chicano, Mexican American,* and *Latino* are often used interchangeably, but the distinctions between the terms can be quite important.[3] *Hispanic* derives from the dominant influences of Spain and the Spanish language, but many shy away from this term because it tends to homogenize all groups of people who have Spanish surnames and who use the Spanish language. *Chicano* (or *Chicana*) refers to the "multiple-heritage experience of Mexicans in the United States" and speaks to a political and social consciousness of the Mexican American.[4] Specific terms such as *Mexican American* or *Cuban American* are preferred by those who wish to acknowledge their cultural roots in a particular national heritage while simultaneously emphasizing their pride in being U.S. Americans.[5] Finally, *Latino* (or *Latina*) is a cultural and linguistic term that includes "all groups in the Americas that share the Spanish language, culture, and traditions."[6] As Earl Shorris notes, "Language defines the group, provides it with history and home; language should also determine its name—Latino."[7] Because *Latino* and *Latina* suggest cultural distinctions, we will use them in this book.

Terms routinely used to describe members of other cultural groups include *Native American, Arab American, Asian American,* and *Pacific Islander.* Each of these labels, as well as those previously described, obscures the rich variety of cultures that the single term represents. For instance, many tribal nations can be included under the term *Native American,* and members of those groups prefer a specific reference to their culture (e.g., Chippewa, Sioux, Navajo, Choctaw, Cherokee, and Inuit). Similarly, *Asian American* is a global term that can refer to Japanese Americans, Chinese Americans, Malaysian Americans, Korean Americans, and people from many other cultures that geographically originated in the part of the world loosely referred to as Asia. Even *European American* obscures differences among those whose heritage may be English, French, Italian, or German. Our use of these overly broad terms is not meant to deny the importance of cultural distinctions but to allow for an economy of words. We will use the broader, more inclusive, and less precise terms when making a generalization that describes a commonality among these cultures. When using examples that are limited to a particular culture, we will use the more specific nomenclature.

CULTURE connections

Increasingly, one meets children who really don't know how to say what they are. They simply are too many things. I met a young girl in San Diego at a convention of mixed-race children, among whom the common habit is to define one parent over the other—black over white, for example. But this girl said that her mother was Mexican and her father was African. The girl said "Blaxican." By reinventing language, she is reinventing America.

—*Richard Rodriguez*

Notice that there are some inherent difficulties in our choices of cultural terms to refer to U.S. Americans. If precision were our only criterion, we would want to make many further distinctions. But we are also aware of the need for economy and the force of common usage. Although it is not our intent to advocate terms that ignore or harm particular cultural groups, we do prefer a vocabulary that is easily understood, commonly used, and positively regarded. Please remember, however, that the term preferred by specific individuals is an important reflection of the way they perceive themselves. Michael Hecht and Sidney Ribeau, for example, found differences in the expressed identities of individuals who defined themselves as "black" versus "black American."[8] Similarly, a "Chicana" defines herself differently from someone who labels herself a "Mexican American."

Competence and Intercultural Communication

Competent interpersonal communication is a worthy and often elusive goal. Interpersonal competence in intercultural interactions is an even more difficult objective to achieve, because cultural differences create dissimilar meanings and expectations that require even greater levels of communication skill. We base our understanding of intercultural competence on the work of scholars who have studied communicative competence from a primarily intracultural perspective and on the conclusions of other scholars who have studied intercultural competence.

The study of intercultural competence has been motivated primarily by practical concerns. Businesses, government agencies, and educational institutions want to select people for intercultural assignments who will be successful. Lack of intercultural competence means failed business ventures, government projects that have not achieved their objectives, and unsuccessful learning experiences for students.

Intercultural Communication Competence

Although there is still some disagreement among communication scholars about how best to conceptualize and measure communication competence, there is increasing agreement about certain of its fundamental characteristics.[9] In our discussion, we draw heavily on the work of Brian Spitzberg and his colleagues. The following definition of communication competence illustrates the key components of their approach:

> Competent communication is interaction that is perceived as effective in fulfilling certain rewarding objectives in a way that is also appropriate to the context in which the interaction occurs.[10]

This definition provides guidance for understanding communicative and intercultural competence in several ways. A key word is *perceived* because it means that competence is best determined by the people who are interacting with each other. In other words, communicative competence is a social judgment about how well a person interacts with others. That competence involves a social perception suggests that it will always be specific to the context and interpersonal relationship within which it occurs. Therefore, whereas judgments of competence are influenced by an

■ In this Oktoberfest celebration, German Americans celebrate their cultural traditions.

assessment of an individual's personal characteristics, they cannot be wholly determined by them, because competence involves an interaction between people.

Competent interpersonal communication results in behaviors that are regarded as appropriate. That is, the actions of the communicators fit the expectations and demands of the situation. Appropriate communication means that people use the symbols they are expected to use in a given context.

Competent interpersonal communication also results in behaviors that are *effective* in achieving desired personal outcomes. Satisfaction in a relationship or the accomplishment of a specific task-related goal is an example of an outcome people might want to achieve through their communication with others.

Thus, communication competence is a social judgment that people make about others. The judgment depends on the context, the relationship between the interactants, the goals or objectives that the interactants want to achieve, and the specific verbal and nonverbal messages that are used to accomplish those goals.

The Components of Intercultural Competence

Our central concern in this book is improving your intercultural competence, and the ideas presented here are the key to doing so. In the remaining chapters, we will return to the concepts that follow to suggest ways to improve your ability.

A word of caution is necessary before we begin, however. We cannot write a prescription guaranteed to ensure competence in intercultural communication. The complexity of human communication in general, and intercultural communication in particular, denies the possibility of a quick fix. There is not necessarily only one way to be competent in your intercultural interactions. Even within the context of a specific person and specific setting, there may be several paths to competent interaction. The goal here is to understand the many ways that a person can behave in an interculturally competent manner.

The remaining portion of this chapter provides a description of the characteristics of people, what they bring to the intercultural communication situation, and the nature of the communication itself, all of which increase the possibility of competence in intercultural communication. Subsequent chapters build on this discussion by offering guidelines for achieving competence. The summary of previous research suggests that competent intercultural communication is contextual; it produces behaviors that are both appropriate and effective, and it requires sufficient knowledge, suitable motivations, and skilled actions. Let's examine each of these components.

Context   Intercultural competence is contextual. An impression or judgment that a person is interculturally competent is made with respect to both a specific relational context and a particular situational context. Competence is not independent of the relationships and situations within which communication occurs.

Thus, competence is not an individual attribute; rather, it is a characteristic of the association between individuals.[11] It is possible, therefore, for someone to be perceived as highly competent in one set of intercultural interactions and only moderately competent in another. For example, a Canadian woman living with a family in India might establish competent relationships with the female family members but be unable to relate well to the male members.

Judgments of intercultural competence also depend on cultural expectations about the permitted behaviors that characterize the settings or situations within which people communicate. The settings help to define and limit the range of behaviors that are regarded as acceptable. Consequently, the same set of behaviors may be perceived as very competent in one cultural setting and much less competent in another. As an obvious example that competence is situationally determined, consider what might happen when two people who come from very different cultural backgrounds are involved in a close business relationship. Whereas one person might want to use highly personalized nicknames and touching behaviors in public, the other person might regard such visible displays as unwarranted and therefore incompetent.

Many previous attempts to describe intercultural competence have erroneously focused on the traits or individual characteristics that make a person competent. Thus, in the past, individuals have been selected for particular intercultural assignments based solely on such personality attributes as authoritarianism, empathy, self-esteem, and world-mindedness. Because intercultural competence is contextual, these trait approaches have been unsuccessful in identifying competent intercultural communicators. Although specific personality traits might allow a person to be more or less competent on particular occasions, there is no prescriptive set of characteristics that inevitably guarantees competence in all intercultural relationships and situations.

Appropriateness and Effectiveness   Both interpersonal competence and intercultural competence require behaviors that are appropriate and effective. By appropriate we mean those behaviors that are regarded as proper and suitable given the expectations generated by a given culture, the constraints of the specific situation, and the nature of the relationship between the interactants. By effective we mean those behaviors that lead to the achievement of desired outcomes. The following example illustrates this important distinction between appropriateness and effectiveness.

Brian Holtz is a U.S. businessperson assigned by his company to manage its office in Thailand. Mr. Thani, a valued assistant manager in the Bangkok office, has recently been arriving late for work. Holtz has to decide what to do about this problem. After carefully thinking about his options, he decides there are four possible strategies:

1. Go privately to Mr. Thani, ask him why he has been arriving late, and tell him that he needs to come to work on time.
2. Ignore the problem.
3. Publicly reprimand Mr. Thani the next time he is late.
4. In a private discussion, suggest that he is seeking Mr. Thani's assistance in dealing with employees in the company who regularly arrive late for work, and solicit his suggestions about what should be done.

Holtz's first strategy would be effective, as it would probably accomplish his objective of getting Mr. Thani to arrive at work more promptly. However, given the expectations of the Thai culture, which are that one person never directly criticizes another, such behavior would be very inappropriate. Conversely, Holtz's second strategy would be appropriate but not effective, as there would probably be no change in Mr. Thani's behavior. The third option would be neither appropriate nor effective because public humiliation might force Mr. Thani, a valuable employee, to resign. The fourth option, which is the best choice, is both appropriate and effective. By using an indirect means to communicate his concerns, Mr. Thani will be able to "save face" while Holtz accomplishes his strategic goals.

Knowledge, Motivations, and Actions   Intercultural competence requires sufficient knowledge, suitable motivations, and skilled actions. Each of these components alone is insufficient to achieve intercultural competence.

Knowledge   Knowledge refers to the cognitive information you need to have about the people, the context, and the norms of appropriateness that operate in a specific culture. Without such knowledge, it is unlikely that you will interpret correctly the meanings of

CULTURE connections

The first week I lived in Dhaka, Bangladesh I was not sure I could ever find life there normal. I moved to Bangladesh to teach in a private English-language university and, although comfortable in my office and apartment, I felt disoriented when I walked in the crowded streets. Before I left home I did not think of any of the difficulties of living in Dhaka because all of my friends and family did that for me. No one wanted me to go because they were all worried that I would die of something—diarrhea, floods, arsenic poisoning. In order to convince them that I would be all right I focused entirely on the positives—my job, learning Bengali, the people I would meet, and places I would visit. In my attempt to make Bangladesh seem desirable to those who did not want me to go, I had lost sight of the potential difficulties of life there.

At first, everything intimidated me: I was afraid of riding in a rickshaw. I was stared at whenever I left my house. I didn't know if I could tolerate eating curry once or twice a day, let alone eating it with my hands. I was assaulted by beggars. I had an allergic reaction to the dust.

—*Kate Baldus*

■ At an official ceremony in New Zealand, then president Bill Clinton receives a *hongi* from a Maori tribal elder, which is a traditional greeting in which the participants press their noses together. Intercultural competence requires an understanding of the appropriate and effective communication behaviors that are expected in a given setting.

other people's messages, nor will you be able to select behaviors that are appropriate and that allow you to achieve your objectives. Consequently, you will not be able to determine what the appropriate and effective behaviors are in a particular context.

The kinds of knowledge that are important include culture-general and culture-specific information. Culture-general information provides insights into the intercultural communication process abstractly and can therefore be a very powerful tool in making sense of cultural practices, regardless of the cultures involved. For example, the knowledge that cultures differ widely in their preferred patterns (or rules) of interaction should help to sensitize you to the need to be aware of these important differences. This book is an excellent example of a source for culture-general knowledge. Knowledge about interpersonal communication and the many ways in which culture influences the communication process is very useful in understanding actual intercultural interactions.

Intercultural competence also depends on culture-specific information, which is used to understand a particular culture. Such knowledge should include information about the forces that maintain the culture's uniqueness (see Chapter 2) and facts about the cultural patterns that predominate (see Chapters 4 and 5). The type of intercultural encounter will also suggest other kinds of culture-specific information that might be useful. Exchange students might want to seek out information about the educational system in the host country. Businesspeople may need essential information about the cultural dynamics of doing business in a specific country or with people from their own country who are members of different cultural groups. Tourists would benefit from guidebooks that provide information about obtaining lodging, transportation, food, shopping, and entertainment.

An additional—and crucial—form of culture-specific knowledge involves information about the specific customs that govern interpersonal communication in the culture. For example, before traveling to Southeast Asia, it would be very useful to know that many Southeast Asian cultures regard a display of the soles of the feet as very offensive. This small bit of information can be filed away for later recall when travelers visit temples and attempt to remove their shoes. The imperative to learn about other cultures is equally strong for those cultures with which you interact on a daily basis. Culture-specific knowledge about the rules and customs of the multiple cultures that make up the cultural landscape of the United States is essential information if you are to be interculturally competent.

Often overlooked is knowledge of one's own cultural system. Yet the ability to attain intercultural competence may be very closely linked to this kind of knowledge. Knowledge about your own culture will help you to understand another culture. Fathi Yousef has even suggested that the best way to train businesspeople who must deal with cultural differences might be to teach them about the characteristics of their own culture rather than those of others.[12] The idea behind this admonition is that, if people are able to understand how and why they interpret events and experiences, it is more likely that they would be able to select alternative interpretations and behaviors that are more appropriate and effective when interacting in another culture.

Motivations   Motivations include the overall set of emotional associations that people have as they anticipate and actually communicate interculturally. As with knowledge, different aspects of the emotional terrain contribute to the achievement of intercultural competence. Human emotional reactions include both feelings and intentions.

Feelings refer to the emotional or affective states that you experience when communicating with someone from a different culture. Feelings are not thoughts, though people often confuse the two; rather, feelings are your emotional and physiological reactions to thoughts and experiences. Feelings of happiness, sadness, eagerness, anger, tension, surprise, confusion, relaxation, and joy are among the many emotions that can accompany the intercultural communication experience. Feelings involve your general sensitivity to other cultures and your attitudes toward the specific culture and individuals with whom you must interact. How would you characterize your general motivation toward other cultures? Are you excited by the thought of talking with someone from a culture that is different from yours? Or are you anxious at the prospect? Do you think your culture is superior to other cultures? Are you even willing to entertain the idea that another culture's ways of doing various life activities might be as good as, or even better than, your culture's ways? Some people simply do not want to be confronted with things that differ from what they are used to. The different sights, sounds, and smells of another culture are often enough to send them running back to the safety of a hotel room. Eagerness and a willingness to experience some uncertainty is a necessary part of your motivation to achieve intercultural competence.

Intentions are what guide your choices in a particular intercultural interaction. Your intentions are the goals, plans, objectives, and desires that focus and direct your behavior. Intentions are often affected by the stereotypes you have of people from other cultures because stereotypes reduce the number of choices and interpretations you are willing to consider. For instance, if you begin an intercultural interaction having already formed a negative judgment of the other person's culture, it will be very difficult for you to develop accurate interpretations of the behaviors that you observe. Intentions toward the specific interaction partner also must be positive. If your intentions are positive, accurate, and reciprocated by the people with whom you are interacting, your intercultural competence will likely be enhanced.

Actions   Finally, actions refer to the actual performance of those behaviors that are regarded as appropriate and effective. Thus, you can have the necessary information, be motivated by the appropriate feelings and intentions, and still lack the behavioral skills necessary to achieve competence. For example, students from other cultures who enroll in basic public speaking classes often have an excellent understanding of the theory of speech construction. In addition, they have a positive attitude toward learning U.S. speaking skills; they want to do well and are willing to work hard in preparation. Unfortunately, their speaking skills sometimes make it difficult for them to execute the delivery of a speech with the level of skill and precision that they would like.[13]

CULTURE connections

The other students call her "white girl."

Justine Steele is a senior at Independence High School in San Jose, a sprawling campus of 4,054 students where 8 percent are Caucasian.

"Look around," she says. There are Indians and Vietnamese, Mexicans and Filipinos.

Here, a girl with blonde hair and blue eyes stands out.

"During multicultural rallies, when there are Indian dancers and Chinese dancers, it's a little strange to not have something, or someone, representing me," says Justine, 17....

It's a delicate situation, and Justine knows it. She's a minority on campus who's otherwise in the majority nationwide....

But her campus mirrors a demographic shift that is taking place in many parts of the United States. Census figures show that whites as the minority will soon be the reality in many regions of the country. So in discussions outside and inside the classroom, when the words "diversity" and "multiculturalism" are tossed around, there are those like Justine who wonder—either loudly or quietly—where they fit in.

"That's the million dollar question. It's come up among people who think about a truly multicultural society and what that looks like," says Anthony Lising Antonio, associate professor of education at Stanford University....

"The fact is, we still don't understand what 'whiteness' is," says Antonio.

"It's been such a norm that we haven't defined it, and I think white students might feel like they're in a cultural vacuum, whereas other folks—the Asians and the Latinos, for example—have something tangible to call their culture." ...

Some white students assimilate, which in high school-speak translates to "acting black" or "acting Asian" or "acting Latino."

Some, like Justine, consciously or unconsciously self-segregate.

—*Jose Antonio Vargas*

Basic Tools for Improving Intercultural Competence

In the preceding section, we suggested that intercultural competence means using your knowledge, motivation, and skills to deal appropriately and effectively with cultural differences. We now offer two tools to assist you in becoming more interculturally competent. These tools can help you improve your interpersonal interactions and will facilitate the development of intercultural relationships.

The BASICs of Intercultural Competence

The Behavioral Assessment Scale for Intercultural Competence (BASIC), developed by Jolene Koester and Margaret Olebe,[14] is based on work done originally by Brent Ruben and his colleagues.[15] A very simple idea provides the key to understanding how to use these BASIC skills: what you actually do, rather than your internalized attitudes or your projections of what you might do, is what others use to determine whether you are interculturally competent. The BASIC skills are a tool for examining people's communication behaviors—yourself included—and in so doing provides a guide to the very basics of intercultural competence.

Eight categories of communication behavior are described in the BASIC instrument, each of which contributes to the achievement of intercultural competence. As each of the categories is described, mentally assess your own ability to communicate. Do you display the behaviors necessary to achieve intercultural competence? From what you now know about intercultural communication, what kinds of changes might make your behavior more appropriate and effective?

Before we describe each of the BASIC skills, we would like to emphasize that the BASIC descriptions of behaviors are culture-general. That is, most cultures use the types of behaviors that are described to make judgments of competence about themselves and others. But within each culture there may be, and in all likelihood will be, different ways of exhibiting these behaviors. For example, actions that show respect for others, and the ability to maintain conversations and manage communicative interactions, are necessary in all cultures for someone to be judged as competent. However, the way each culture teaches its members to exhibit these actions is culture-specific. Even among the various cultural groups that live in the United States, the rules for taking turns in a conversation vary widely. The eight types of communication behaviors are each discussed and are summarized in Figure 3.1.

Display of Respect   Although the need to display respect for others is a culture-general concept, within every culture there are specific ways to show respect and specific expectations about those to whom respect should be shown. What constitutes respect in one culture, then, will not necessarily be so regarded in another culture.

Respect is shown through both verbal and nonverbal symbols. Language that can be interpreted as expressing concern, interest, and an understanding of others will often convey respect, as will formality in language, including the use of titles, the absence of jargon, and an increased attention to politeness rituals. Nonverbal displays of respect include showing attentiveness through the position of the body, facial expressions, and the use of eye contact in prescribed ways. A tone of voice that conveys interest in the other

Display of Respect	The ability to show respect and positive regard for another person
Orientation to Knowledge	The terms people use to explain themselves and the world around them
Empathy	The capacity to behave as though you understand the world as others do
Interaction Management	Skill in regulating conversations
Task Role Behavior	Behaviors that involve the initiation of ideas related to group problem-solving activities
Relational Role Behavior	Behaviors associated with interpersonal harmony and mediation
Tolerance for Ambiguity	The ability to react to new and ambiguous situations with little visible discomfort
Interaction Posture	The ability to respond to others in descriptive, nonevaluative, and nonjudgmental ways

FIGURE 3.1   BASIC dimensions of intercultural competence.

person is another vehicle by which respect is shown. The action of displaying respect increases the likelihood of a judgment of competence.

Orientation to Knowledge   Orientation to knowledge refers to the terms people use to explain themselves and the world around them. A competent orientation to knowledge occurs when people's actions demonstrate that all experiences and interpretations are individual and personal rather than universally shared by others.

Many actions exhibit people's orientation to knowledge, including the specific words that are used. Among European Americans, for instance, declarative statements that express personal attitudes or opinions as if they were facts and an absence of qualifiers or modifiers would show an ineffective orientation to knowledge:

- "New Yorkers must be crazy to live in that city."
- "Parisians are rude and unfriendly."
- "The custom of arranged marriages is barbaric."
- "Every person wants to succeed—it's human nature."

In contrast, a competent intercultural communicator acknowledges a personal orientation to knowledge, as illustrated in the following examples:

- "I find New York a very difficult place to visit and would not want to live there."
- "Many of the people I interacted with when visiting Paris were not friendly or courteous to me."
- "I would not want my parents to arrange my marriage for me."
- "I want to succeed at what I do, and I think most people do."

At least some of the time, all people have an orientation to knowledge that is not conducive to intercultural competence. In learning a culture, people develop beliefs about the "rightness" of a particular way of seeing events, behaviors, and people. It is actually very natural to think, and then to behave, as if your personal knowledge and experiences are universal. Intercultural competence, however, requires an ability to move beyond the perspective of your cultural framework.

Empathy   Empathy is the ability of individuals to communicate an awareness of another person's thoughts, feelings, and experiences, and such individuals are regarded as more competent in intercultural interactions. Alternatively, those who lack empathy, and who therefore indicate little or no awareness of even the most obvious feelings and thoughts of others, will not be perceived as competent. Empathetic behaviors include verbal statements that identify the experiences of others and nonverbal codes that are complementary to the moods and thoughts of others.

It is necessary to make an important distinction here. Empathy does not mean "putting yourself in the shoes of another." It is both physically and psychologically impossible to do so. However, it is possible for people to be sufficiently interested and aware of others that they appear to be putting themselves in others' shoes. The skill we are describing here is the capacity to *behave as if one understands the world as others do*. Of course, empathy is not just responding to the tears and smiles of others, which may, in fact, mean something very different than your cultural interpretations would suggest. Although empathy does involve responding to the emotional context of another person's experiences, tears and smiles are often poor indicators of emotional states.

Interaction Management   Some individuals are skilled at starting and ending interactions among participants and at taking turns and maintaining a discussion. These interaction

CULTURE connections

I imagined what I might be doing in a few weeks' time back in San Francisco, among family and friends. It was a scene that held no surprises. Everything there was familiar, and although not predictable it was all within parameters I was comfortable with. I didn't have any complaints about my life in the States, really, but it lacked something I couldn't identify. Maybe it was that it was too comfortable. Haiti was anything but. My thoughts drifted to what it would be like to stay in Haiti longer, to actually identify myself as living there rather than just visiting for a finite period. I had just spent three tough months adjusting to a country I had barely known, learning a new language, adapting to the cultural differences and trying not to be swallowed in the political upheaval. Somehow I'd jumped the hurdles and was still standing. That was a good feeling, one I was proud of. It made me realize that I had skills and talent and even ambition and curiosity I hadn't explored, and I wanted more.

—*Kathie Klarreich*

management skills are important because, through them, all participants in an interaction are able to speak and contribute appropriately. In contrast, dominating a conversation or being nonresponsive to the interaction is detrimental to competence. Continuing to engage people in conversation long after they have begun to display signs of disinterest and boredom or ending conversations abruptly may also pose problems. Interaction management skills require knowing how to indicate turn taking both verbally and nonverbally.

Task Role Behavior   Because intercultural communication often takes place where individuals are focused on work-related purposes, appropriate task-related role behaviors are very important. Task role behaviors are those that contribute to the group's problem-solving activities—for example, initiating new ideas, requesting further information or facts, seeking clarification of group tasks, evaluating the suggestions of others, and keeping a group on task. The difficulty in this important category is the display of culturally appropriate behaviors. The key is to recognize the strong link to a culture's underlying patterns and to be willing to acknowledge that tasks are accomplished by cultures in multiple ways. Task behaviors are so intimately entwined with cultural expectations about activity and work that it is often difficult to respond appropriately to task expectations that differ from one's own. What one culture defines as a social activity, another may define as a task. For example, socializing at a restaurant or a bar may be seen as a necessary prelude to conducting a business negotiation. Sometimes that socializing is expected to occur over many hours or days, which surprises and dismays many European Americans, who believe that "doing business" is separate from socializing.

Relational Role Behavior   Relational role behaviors concern efforts to build or maintain personal relationships with group members. These behaviors may include

■ Learning about other cultures is a necessary prerequisite to achieving intercultural competence.

verbal and nonverbal messages that demonstrate support for others and that help to solidify feelings of participation. Examples of competent relational role behaviors include harmonizing and mediating conflicts between group members, encouraging participation from others, general displays of interest, and a willingness to compromise one's position for the sake of others.

Tolerance for Ambiguity   Tolerance for ambiguity concerns a person's responses to new, uncertain, and unpredictable intercultural encounters. Some people react to new situations with greater comfort than do others. Some are extremely nervous, highly frustrated, or even hostile toward the new situations and those who may be present in them. Those who do not tolerate ambiguity well may respond to new and unpredictable situations with hostility, anger, shouting, sarcasm, withdrawal, or abruptness.

Others view new situations as a challenge; they seem to do well whenever the unexpected or unpredictable occurs, and they quickly adapt to the demands of changing environments. Competent intercultural communicators are able to cope with the nervousness and frustrations that accompany new or unclear situations, and they are able to adapt quickly to changing demands.

Interaction Posture   Interaction posture refers to the ability to respond to others in a way that is descriptive, nonevaluative, and nonjudgmental. Although the specific verbal and nonverbal messages that express judgments and evaluations can vary from culture to culture, the importance of selecting messages that do not convey evaluative judgments is paramount. Statements based on clear judgments of rights and wrongs indicate a closed or predetermined framework of attitudes, beliefs, and values, and they are used by the evaluative, and less competent, intercultural communicator. Nonevaluative and nonjudgmental actions are characterized by verbal and nonverbal messages based on descriptions rather than on interpretations or evaluations.

Description, Interpretation, and Evaluation

We have approached the study of intercultural competence by looking at the elements of culture that affect interpersonal communication. There is, however, a tool that allows people to control the meanings they attribute to the verbal and nonverbal

CULTURE connections

"The legal system can force open doors and, sometimes, even knock down walls. But it cannot build bridges. That job belongs to you and me.... We can run from each other, but we cannot escape each other. We will only attain freedom if we learn to appreciate what is different and muster the courage to discover what is fundamentally the same.... Take a chance, won't you? Knock down the fences that divide. Tear apart the walls that imprison. Reach out; freedom lies just on the other side."

—*Thurgood Marshall, former U.S. Supreme Court justice, July 4, 1992, at Independence Hall in Philadelphia, where Marshall received the Philadelphia Liberty Medal* symbols used by others. The tool is based on the differences in how people think about, and then verbally speak about, the people with whom they interact and the events in which they participate.

The interaction tool is called description, interpretation, and evaluation (D-I-E). It starts with the assumption that, when most people process the information around them, they use a kind of mental shorthand. Because people are taught what symbols mean, they are not very aware of the information they use to form their interpretations. In other words, when people see, hear, and in other ways receive information from the world around them, they generally form interpretations and evaluations of it without being aware of the specific sensory information they have perceived. For example, students and teachers alike often comment about the sterile, institutional character of many of the classrooms at universities. Rarely do these conversations detail the specific perceptual information on which that interpretation is based. Rarely does someone say, for instance, "This room is about twenty by forty feet in size, the walls are painted a cream color, there is no artwork on the walls, it is lit by eight fluorescent bulbs, and the floors are cream-colored tiles with multiple pieces of dirt." Yet when students and professors say that their classroom is "sterile, institutional-looking, and unattractive," most people who have spent a great deal of time in such rooms have a fairly accurate image of the classroom. Similarly, if a friend is walking toward you, you might say, "Hi! What's wrong? You look really tired and upset." That kind of comment is considered normal, but if you said instead, "Hi! Your shoulders are drooping, you're not standing up straight, and you are walking much slower than usual," it would be considered strange. In both examples, the statements considered to be normal are really interpretations and evaluations of sensory information the individual has processed.

The skill we are introducing trains you to distinguish among statements of description, interpretation, and evaluation. These statements can be made about all characteristics, events, persons, or objects. A statement of description details the specific perceptual cues and information a person has received, without judgments or interpretations—in other words, without being distorted by opinion. A statement of interpretation provides a conjecture or hypothesis about what the perceptual information might mean. A statement of evaluation indicates an emotional or affective judgment about the information.

Often, the interpretations people make of perceptual information are very closely linked to their personal evaluation of that information. Any description can have many different interpretations, but because most people think in a mental shorthand, they are generally aware of only the interpretation that immediately comes to mind, which they use to explain the event. For example, teachers occasionally have students who arrive late to class. A statement of description about a particular student engaging in this behavior might be as follows:

- Kathryn arrived ten minutes after the start of the class.
- Kathryn also arrived late each of the previous times the class has met.

Statements of interpretation, which are designed to explain Kathryn's behavior, might include some of the following:

- Kathryn doesn't care very much about this particular class.
- Kathryn is always late for everything.

CULTURE connections

Alternative communication began early, on our Beijing-bound flight. A stout Chinese man in a navy-blue suit was the last to board. He plopped down in the aisle seat next to my travel mate, Aaron, and threw his seat belt across his lap.

Neither Aaron nor I had yet learned how to say as much as "hello" in Chinese. We caught the blue-suited man's attention and greeted him with a silent nod and smile.

He turned away with a look of slight disgust, which we interpreted as a message to cease efforts at socialization. We were discouraged by the hostility of this first encounter, but we were determined to improve our pathetic capacity.

We opened our China travel book and started in on the "Useful Phrases" section. As we practiced counting from 1 to 10 quietly, we were startled to hear the third resident of our row chime in to correct our pronunciation of the number 2, ("aarrr," not "rrr").

We overeagerly corrected ourselves, thanked him generously, and went on counting, making it clear that constructive criticism was welcome. For the remainder of the flight, Mr. Wang leaned over our book and pointed out our mistakes. We shared a few laughs.

It did not matter that much of what Mr. Wang taught us was forgotten or misunderstood. What mattered was that his image of us as happily ignorant was dispelled, as was our image of him as hostile. We communicated.

—*Jessica Adler*

- Kathryn has a job on the other side of campus and is scheduled to work until ten minutes before this class. The person who should relieve her has been late, thus not allowing Kathryn to leave to be on time for class.
- Kathryn is new on campus this semester and is misinformed about the starting time for the class.

For each interpretation, the evaluation can vary. If the interpretation is "Kathryn doesn't care very much about this class," different professors will have differing evaluations:

- I am really offended by that attitude.
- I like a student who chooses to be enthusiastic only about classes she really likes.

The interpretation a person selects to explain something like Kathryn's behavior influences the evaluation that is made of that behavior. In people's everyday interactions, distinctions are rarely made among description, interpretation, and evaluation. Consequently, people deal with their interpretations and evaluations as if these were actually what they saw, heard, and experienced.

The purpose of making descriptive statements when you are communicating inter-culturally is that they allow you to identify the sensory information that forms the basis of your interpretations and evaluations. Descriptive statements also allow you to consider alternative hypotheses or interpretations. Interpretations, although highly personal, are very much affected by underlying cultural patterns. Sometimes when you engage in intercultural communication with specific persons or groups of people for an extended period of time, you will be able to test the various interpretations of behavior that you are considering. By testing the alternative interpretations, it is also possible to forestall the evaluations that can negatively affect your interactions. Consider the following situation, and notice how differences among description, interpretation, and evaluation affect John's intercultural competence:

> John Richardson has been sent by his U.S.-based insurance company to discuss, and possibly to sell, his company's products with an Argentinean company that has expressed great interest in them. His secretary has set up four appointments with key company officials. John arrives promptly at his first appointment, identifies himself to the receptionist, and is asked to be seated. Some thirty minutes later he is ushered into the office of the company official, who has one of his employees in the office with whom he is discussing another issue. John is brought into the office of his second appointment within a shorter period of time, but the conversation is constantly disrupted by telephone calls and drop-in visits from others. At the end of the day, John is very discouraged; he calls the home office and says, "This is a waste of time; these guys aren't interested in our products at all! I was left cooling my heels in their waiting rooms. They couldn't even give me their attention when I got in to see them. There were constant interruptions. I really tried to control myself, but I've had it. I'm getting on a plane and coming back tomorrow."

John would be better off if he approached this culturally puzzling behavior by separating his descriptions, interpretations, and evaluations. By doing so, he might choose very different actions for himself. Descriptive statements might include the following:

- My appointments started anywhere from fifteen to thirty minutes later than the time I scheduled them.
- The people with whom I had appointments also talked to other company employees when I was in their offices.
- The people with whom I had appointments accepted telephone calls when I was in their offices.

Interpretations of this sensory information might include the following:

- Company officials were not interested in talking with me or in buying my company's products.
- Company officials had rescheduled my appointments for a different time, but they neglected to tell my secretary about the change.
- In Argentina, attitudes toward time are very different from those in the United States; although appointments are scheduled for particular times, no one expects that people will be available at precisely that time.
- In Argentina, it is an accepted norm of interaction between people who have appointments with each other to allow others to come into the room, either in person or by telephone, to ask their questions or to make their comments.

These interpretations suggest very different evaluations of John's experiences. His frustration with the lack of punctuality and the lack of exclusive focus on him and his ideas may still be a problem even if he selects the correct cultural interpretation, which is that in Argentina, time is structured and valued very differently than it is in the United

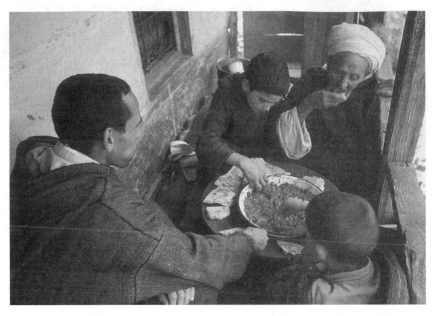

■ Contrast the difference between your own culture and the culture of those in this picture. Use the skills of Description, Interpretation, and Evaluation to understand this Algerian family eating their meal of bread and lentils. How difficult would it be for you to communicate competently in this setting?

States. But by considering other interpretations, John's evaluations and his actions will be more functional, as he might say the following:

■ I don't like waiting around and not meeting according to the schedule I had set, but maybe I can still make this important sale.

■ Some of the people here arc sure interesting and I am enjoying meeting so many more people than just the four with whom I had scheduled appointments.

The tool of description, interpretation, and evaluation increases your choices for understanding, responding positively to, and behaving appropriately with people from different cultures. The simplicity of the tool makes it available in any set of circumstances and may allow the intercultural communicator to suspend judgment long enough to understand the symbols used by the culture involved.

Summary

The United States is an intercultural community, and four metaphors—melting pots, tributaries, tapestries, and garden salads—were introduced to describe its diversity. We suggested that the term *U.S. American* should be used to characterize someone from the United States but noted that a variety of terms are used to refer to the nation's cultural groups. The goal is to find ways to refer to cultural groups that reflect their differences accurately while avoiding negative connotations and evaluations.

This chapter next focused on intercultural communication competence. We began by explaining *intra*cultural communication competence, which was followed by an examination of *inter*cultural competence. Three components of intercultural competence were discussed, including the interpersonal and situational contexts within which the communication occurs; the degree of appropriateness and effectiveness in the interaction; and the importance of knowledge, motivations, and actions.

Two tools were provided to improve intercultural competence. The first is the culture-general Behavioral Assessment Scale for Intercultural Competence (BASIC), which includes the ability to display respect, a recognition that knowledge is personal rather than universal, an empathic sense about the experiences of others that results in behaviors appropriate to those experiences, the ability to manage interactions with others, skills in enacting appropriate task and relational role behaviors, the capacity to tolerate uncertainty without anxiety, and a nonevaluative posture toward the beliefs and actions of others. Within each culture there will be culturally specific ways of behaving that are used to demonstrate these competencies. The second tool is the ability to distinguish among the techniques of description, interpretation, and evaluation. This tool encourages communicators to describe the sensory information they receive and then to construct alternative evaluations about their perceptions by making correspondingly different interpretations.

For Discussion

1. What do you think about using the terms *United Statians, United Staters, North Americans,* or *U.S. Americans* to refer to people in the United States? What alternative phrases might accurately and sensitively be used to refer to people from the United States?
2. What do we lose, and what do we gain, by using general terms such as *Asian American* and *Native American* when referring to cultural groups in the United States?
3. What does it mean to say that communication competence is a social judgment that people make about others? Would people from different cultures likely judge the same kinds of communication behaviors as competent? Why or why not?
4. Why is it impossible to "put yourself in someone else's shoes"?
5. What three BASIC skills would you argue are most important for developing intercultural communication competence?
6. How would you describe your own interaction posture?

For Further Reading

Khaled Hosseini, *The Kite Runner* (New York: Riverhead Books, 2003); Khaled Hosseini, *A Thousand Splendid Suns* (New York: Riverhead Books, 2007). A pair of novels that explore the Afghan and Afghan-American cultures. The novels offer insights into the experience of living in a culture other than one's birth culture.

Ildikó Lázár, Martina Huber-Kriegler, Denise Lussier, Gabriela S. Matei, and Christiane Peck (eds.), *Developing and Assessing Intercultural Communicative Competence: A Guide for Language Teachers and Teacher Educators* (Graz, Austria: Council of Europe, 2007). A European perspective that provides both the conceptual underpinnings and practical experiences for understanding intercultural competence. Also includes a CD-ROM with instructionally related activities.

Stephen W. Littlejohn and Karen A. Foss, *Theories of Human Communication*, 9th ed. (Belmont, CA: Thomson/Wadsworth, 2008). A comprehensive state-of-the-art summary for understanding various theories that pertain to intercultural communication.

Myron W. Lustig and Jolene Koester (eds.), *AmongUS: Essays on Identity, Belonging, and Intercultural Competence*, 2nd ed. (Boston: Allyn & Bacon,

2006). This collection of essays is written in the first person and documents the emotions and experiences of people living in a multicultural world.

Sherwyn P. Morreale, Brian H. Spitzberg, and J. Kevin Barge, *Human Communication: Motivation, Knowledge, and Skills,* 2nd ed. (Belmont, CA: Wadsworth, 2007). A basic communication textbook that also provides an intellectual foundation for understanding interpersonal communication competence.

Samuel Roll and Marc Irwin, *The Invisible Border: Latino Culture in America* (Boston: Intercultural Press, 2008). An example of a culture-specific investigation of one of the cultures comprising the United States. For those interested in understanding and bridging the cultural differences between Latinos and other U.S. Americans.

Brian H. Spitzberg and Gabrielle Chagnon, "Conceptualizing Intercultural Communication Competence," *The Sage Handbook of Intercultural Competence,* ed. Darla K. Deardorff (Thousand Oaks, CA: Sage, in press). An up-to-date summary of approaches to understanding intercultural communication competence.

For additional information about intercultural films and about Web sites for researching specific cultures, please turn to the Resources section at the back of this book.

CHAPTER 4

Cultural Patterns and Communication: Foundations

If you have had even limited contact with people from other cultures, you know that they differ in both obvious and subtle ways. An obvious cultural difference is in the food people eat, such as the ubiquitous hamburger, the U.S. offering to the world's palate. We identify pasta with Italy, stuffed grape leaves with Greece and Turkey, sushi with Japan, curry with India and Southeast Asia, and kimchee with Korea.

Another obvious difference between cultures is the clothing people wear. Walk down the streets near United Nations Plaza in New York City or in diplomatic areas of Washington, D.C., and you will see men wearing colorful African dashikis, women in graceful and flowing Indian saris, and men from Middle Eastern cultures with long robes and headdresses. Most television cable services now provide an array of shows that are set in various cultures. Watching those shows for even a short period of time can help to create an immediate awareness of some obvious differences between and among cultures.

Other cultural differences are more subtle and become apparent only after more extensive exposure. This chapter and the next are about those subtle, less visible differences that are taken for granted within a culture. In defining culture, we called the effects of these subtle differences *shared interpretations*. Shared interpretations lead to actions that are regarded as appropriate and effective behaviors within a culture. They are therefore very important, and they result from the culture's collective assumptions about what the world is, shared judgments about what it should be, widely held expectations about how people should behave, and predictable behavior patterns that are commonly shared. We are going to call these unseen but shared expectations *cultural patterns*.

It is extremely important that you understand differences in cultural patterns if you wish to develop competence in intercultural communication. Cultural patterns are the basis for interpreting the symbols used in communication. If the cultural patterns between people are sufficiently different, the symbols used in communicating will be interpreted differently and may be misunderstood—unless people are aware that no common set of behaviors is universally interpreted in the same way nor regarded with the same degree of favorability.

■ People from all cultures teach their children the norms for proper dress and behavior.

Defining Cultural Patterns

Shared beliefs, values, norms, and social practices that are stable over time and that lead to roughly similar behaviors across similar situations are known as cultural patterns. These cultural patterns affect perceptions of competence. Despite their importance in the development and maintenance of cultures, they cannot be seen, heard, or experienced directly. However, the consequences of cultural patterns—shared interpretations that are evident in what people say and do—are readily observable. Cultural patterns are primarily inside people, in their minds. They provide a way of thinking about the world, of orienting oneself to it. Therefore, cultural patterns are shared mental programs that govern specific behavior choices.

Cultural patterns provide the basic set of standards that guide thought and action. Some aspects of this mental programming are, of course, unique to each individual. Even within a culture, no two people are programmed identically, and these distinctive personality differences separate the members of a culture. In comparisons across cultures, some mental programs are essentially universal. A mother's concern for her newborn infant, for example, reflects a biological program that exists across all known cultures and is part of our common human experience.

In addition to those portions of our mental programs that are unique or universally held, there are those that are widely shared only by members of a particular group or culture. These collective programs can be understood only in the context of a particular culture, and they include such areas as the preferred degree of social equality, the importance of group harmony, the degree to which emotional displays are permitted, the value ascribed to assertiveness, and the like.

Cultural patterns are not so much consciously taught as unconsciously experienced as a by-product of day-to-day activities. Most core assumptions are programmed at a very early age and are reinforced continuously. Saudi Arabians, for example, are taught to admire courage, patience, honor, and group harmony. European Americans are trained to admire achievement, practicality, material comfort, freedom, and individuality.

Because of their importance in shaping judgments about intercultural competence, we will discuss cultural patterns in great detail through several approaches. We emphasize both what is similar about all cultural patterns and what is different among them. We begin by describing the basic components of all cultural patterns: beliefs, values, norms, and social practices. We then turn to characteristics of cultural patterns. Chapter 5 presents three systematic approaches, or taxonomies, to describe the ways in which cultures differ.

Components of Cultural Patterns

In Chapter 2, we offered a definition of culture as a learned set of shared interpretations about beliefs, values, norms, and social practices. At that point, however, we left these four key terms undefined. We now explain in some detail the nature of beliefs, values, norms, and social practices, which together constitute the components of cultural patterns.

CULTURE connections

We scatter the petals of the *zempasúchil* on our doorsteps, to help the dead find their way home, and put their photographs out so they can see they have come to the right house, and candles to see the way because if we do not, they will have to light their fingers and burn," Paola explained. "Also copal, incense, and flowers with a strong scent."

"And food with a strong aroma," André prompted her.

"Oh yes, and after the dead have eaten, that aroma will be gone because the dead will have taken away its spirit."

"To last them a whole year."

"And for the *angelitos*, the little children who died, we put out little things—little pieces of chocolate, Chiclets, peanuts, and of course *azúcar*—sugar birds and lambs. If we make *sopa*, or stew, it is mild for the children, not spicy."

"Families say they can hear the dishes clinking when the children are there," André broke in.

"And among the *campesinos*, the peasants, people put out brooms and tortilla presses for their daughters and spades and hoes for their sons so in the world they have gone to, they can continue the lives they had here." . . .

"On this day you visit homes where you knew the ones who died, and you bring offerings, and stay to eat with the family."

"You must do that. There are stories told about what happens to people who don't. Tell him."

"Yes, one man who did not believe all this, he went out drinking, all night long. When he walked home in the morning, he saw a crowd of dead people returning to their world, and his parents were there too. They were empty-handed. Others were taking back armfuls of offerings and his parents had only clay in their hands and it was burning. When he returned home, he fell ill and died."

"But the dead do not always like to go back. The *angelitos*, who come at midday on the thirty-first of October, have to leave on the first of November, at noon. Then the elders arrive and must return on the second. At three o'clock fireworks will be lit as a signal for them to leave. Also, a priest will walk through our town, ringing a bell and chanting. When the dead hear that, they leave for the panteón, and we go too to wash and clean and decorate the tombs, make them ready to receive them."

—Anita Desai

Beliefs

A **belief** is an idea that people assume to be true about the world. Beliefs, therefore, are a set of learned interpretations that form the basis for cultural members to decide what is and what is not logical and correct.

Beliefs can range from ideas that are central to a person's sense of self to those that are more peripheral. **Central beliefs** include the culture's fundamental teachings about what reality is and expectations about how the world works. Less central, but also important, are beliefs based on or derived from the teachings of those regarded as authorities. Parents, teachers, and other important elders transmit the culture's assumptions about the nature of the physical and interpersonal world. **Peripheral beliefs** refer to matters of personal taste. They contribute to each person's unique configuration of ideas and expectations within the larger cultural matrix.[1]

Discussing culturally shared beliefs is difficult because people are usually not conscious of them. Culturally shared beliefs are so fundamental to assumptions about what the world is like and how the world operates that they are typically unnoticed. We hope you will come to realize through this discussion of cultural beliefs that much of what you consider to be reality may, in fact, not be reality to people from other cultures. What you consider to be the important "givens" about the world, such as the nature of people and their relationships with one another, are based on your culturally shared beliefs, which have been transmitted to and learned by you and are not a description of some invariant, unchanging characteristic of the world.

A well-known example of a widely shared belief dates back to the time when Europeans believed that the earth was flat. That is, people "knew" that the earth was flat. Most people now "know" (believe) that the earth is basically round and would scoff at any suggestion that it is flat. Yet we still talk about Asia as "the East" and about Europe and the United States as "the West," even though California is due east of the major population centers in China.

Another example of a belief for many European Americans is that in "reality" there is a separation between the physical and spiritual worlds. If a teacher one day started kicking the doorsill at the front of the room, the students might begin to worry about the teacher's mental health. The students would probably not be concerned about the doorsill itself, nor would they be alarmed about the spirits who might reside there. Of course, you and they "know" that there are no spirits in doorsills. But people from Thailand and elsewhere "know" that spirits do indeed reside in inanimate objects such as doorsills, which is why doorsills should always be stepped over rather than on. In addition to their concern about the teacher, therefore, people from other cultures might conceivably worry about upsetting the spirits who dwell in the doorsill.

■ These Peruvian villagers have gathered to honor and pray for those who have died. Prayer is an activity that reflects aspects of one's culture.

Members of the European American culture see humans as separate from nature. Based on this set of beliefs about the world, European Americans have set out to control nature. From the viewpoint of the typical European American, a person who believes, as the typical Indian woman does, that she "catches colds and fevers from evil spirits that lurk in trees"[2] would be seen as strange. European Americans "know" that people do not become ill from spirits that live in trees. Yet, in the Indian culture, people "know" that human illness is caused by such spirits.

Values

Cultures differ not only in their beliefs but also in what they value. Values involve what a culture regards as good or bad, right or wrong, fair or unfair, just or unjust, beautiful or ugly, clean or dirty, valuable or worthless, appropriate or inappropriate, and kind or cruel.[3] Because values are the *desired* characteristics or goals of a culture, a culture's values do not necessarily describe its *actual* behaviors and characteristics. However, values are often offered as the explanation for the way in which people communicate. Thus, as Shalom Schwartz suggests, values serve as guiding principles in people's lives.[4]

From culture to culture, values differ in their valence and intensity. Valence refers to whether the value is seen as positive or negative. Intensity indicates the strength or importance of the value, or the degree to which the culture identifies the value as significant. For example, in some U.S. American cultures, the value of respect for elders is negatively valenced and held with a modest degree of intensity. Many U.S. Americans value youth rather than old age. In Korea, Japan, and Mexico, however, respect for elders is a positively valenced value, and it is very intensely held. It would be possible after studying any particular culture to determine its most important values and each value's valence and intensity.

CULTURE connections

In the compounds, people spent all their time with the group. As far as I can tell, none of my Afghan relatives was ever alone or ever wanted to be. And that's so different from my life today, here in the West. Because I write for a living, I spend most of my waking hours alone in my basement office. Oh, I jog, do errands, see people I know—but mostly, it's just a man and his thoughts in a blur of urban landscape. If I'm too much with other people, I need to balance it with some downtime. Most of the people I know are like this. We need solitude, because when we're alone, we're free from obligations, we don't need to put on a show, and we can hear our own thoughts.

My Afghan relatives achieved this same state by being with one another. Being at home with the group gave them the satisfactions we associate with solitude—ease, comfort, and the freedom to let down one's guard. The reason for this is hard to convey, but I'm going to try. Namely, our group self was just as real as our individual selves, perhaps more so.

—*Tamim Ansary*

Norms

Norms are the socially shared expectations of appropriate behaviors. When a person's behaviors violate the culture's norms, social sanctions are usually imposed. Like values, norms can vary within a culture in terms of their importance and intensity. Unlike values, however, norms may change over a period of time, whereas beliefs and values tend to be much more enduring.

Norms exist for a wide variety of behaviors. For example, the greeting behaviors of people within a culture are governed by norms. Similarly, good manners in a variety of situations are based on norms. Norms also exist to guide people's interactions and to indicate how to engage in conversation, what to talk about, and how to disengage from conversations. Because people are expected to behave according to their culture's norms, they therefore come to see their own norms as constituting the "right" way of communicating. Norms, then, are linked to the beliefs and values of a culture. Because they are evident through behaviors, norms can be readily inferred.

Social Practices

Social practices are the predictable behavior patterns that members of a culture typically follow. Thus, social practices are the outward manifestations of beliefs, values, and norms. In the United States, lunch is usually over by 1:30 p.m., gifts brought by dinner guests are usually opened in the presence of the guests, television watching dramatically increases during the annual Super Bowl, and children sleep alone or with other children. In Italy, lunch hasn't even begun by 1:30 p.m., and soccer is more popular than American football. In Malaysia, gifts are never opened in front of the giver; doing so is considered bad manners. In many Middle Eastern, Latin American, and Asian families, children routinely share beds with adult relatives.[5]

One type of social practice is informal and includes everyday tasks such as eating, sleeping, dressing, working, playing, and talking to others. Such behaviors are so predictable and commonplace within a culture that the subtle details about how they are accomplished may pass nearly unnoticed. For instance, cultures have social practices about eating with "good manners." Slurping one's food in Saudi Arabia and in many Asian cultures is the usual practice, and it is regarded favorably as an expression of satisfaction and appreciation for the quality of the cooking. But good manners in one culture may be bad manners in another; European Americans typically consider such sounds to be inappropriate.[6]

Another type of social practice is more formal and prescriptive. These include the rituals, ceremonies, and structured routines that are typically performed publicly and collectively: saluting the flag, praying in church, honoring the dead at funerals, getting married, and many other social practices. Of course, all members of a culture do not necessarily follow that culture's "typical" social practices; each person differs, in unique and significant ways, from the general cultural tendency to think and behave in particular ways. As William B. Gudykunst and Carmin M. Lee suggest, "Individuals in a culture generally are socialized in ways consistent with the cultural-level tendencies, but some individuals in every culture learn different tendencies."[7]

Characteristics of Cultural Patterns

In this section, we describe a set of similarities underlying all cultural patterns. In so doing, we draw heavily on the work of Kluckhohn and Strodtbeck and their theory of value orientations. Next, we elaborate on those ideas to provide a general overview of cultural patterns.

The Functions of Cultural Patterns

Florence Kluckhohn and Fred Strodtbeck wanted to make sense of the work of cultural anthropologists who, for many years, had described systematic variations both between and within cultures. That is, cultures clearly differed from one another, but within every culture there were individuals who varied from the cultural patterns most often associated with it.[8] To explain both these cultural-level and individual-level differences, Kluckhohn and Strodtbeck offered four conclusions about the functions of cultural patterns that apply to all cultures:

1. People in all cultures face common human problems for which they must find solutions.
2. The range of alternative solutions to a culture's problems is limited.
3. Within a given culture, there will be preferred solutions, which most people within the culture will select, but there will also be people who will choose other solutions.
4. Over time, the preferred solutions shape the culture's basic assumptions about beliefs, values, norms, and social practices—the cultural patterns.

The first conclusion, that all cultures face similar problems, is not just about everyday concerns such as "Do I have enough money to get through the month?" or "Will my parent overcome a serious illness?" Rather, as Edgar Schein suggests, the problems involve difficulties with external adaptation (how to survive) and internal integration (how to live together).[9] Kluckhohn and Strodtbeck describe five problems or orientations that each culture must address:

1. What is the human orientation to activity?
2. What is the relationship of humans to each other?
3. What is the nature of human beings?
4. What is the relationship of humans to the natural world?
5. What is the orientation of humans to time?

Each culture, in its own unique way, must provide answers to these questions in order to develop a coherent and consistent interpretation of the world. We will return to these questions, in modified form, in our discussion of cultural patterns.

Kluckhohn and Strodtbeck's second conclusion is that a culture's possible responses to these universal human problems are limited, as cultures must select their solutions from a range of available alternatives. Thus, a culture's orientation to the importance and value of activity can range from passive acceptance of the world (a "being" orientation), a preference for a gradual transformation of the human condition (a "being-in-becoming" orientation), or more direct intervention (a "doing" orientation). A culture's solution to how it should organize itself to deal with interpersonal relationships can vary along a

CULTURE connections

Jean Raymond's family had Haitian-style family reunions, complete with their own religious and cultural idiosyncrasies. My Jewish family get-togethers had their own traditions, with Sabbath candle lighting, challah, gefilte fish, and chopped liver, dances like the hora for the proper occasion.... Vodou sequined banners and paintings decorated our walls; drums and bamboo instruments adorned our living room as well as the menorah and we placed a proverbial tribute to the *lwa Legba* by the front door to welcome people alongside our Jewish mezuzah. I offered drops of rum to the spirits when I took a drink as routinely as I said Sabbath prayer on Friday nights, lit the Hanukkah candles, and fasted for the Jewish Day of Atonement on Yom Kippur.

I am no closer to understanding my relationship to the spiritual world now than I was when I first went to Haiti, but I have accepted the idea that I have one, even if I can't define it. Based on my experience with Vodou and my loyalty to my ancestors, I know firsthand that such energy exists. It's just that I've been slow to embrace it. Or explore it fully. Still, I haven't closed the door completely. I think that some day I may return to Souvenance, not as a journalist, or as the naïve *blan* that I was when I first went, but as a soul seeker who finally understands that the *lwas* can teach me things I can't learn anywhere else.

—Kathie Klarreich

continuum from hierarchical social organization ("linearity") to group identification ("collaterality" or collectivism) to individual autonomy ("individualism"). The available alternatives to the problem "What is the nature of human beings?" can range from "Humans are evil" to "Humans are a mixture of good and evil" to "Humans are good." A culture's response to the preferred relationship of humans to the natural world can range from a belief that "People are subjugated by nature" to "People live in harmony with nature" to "People master nature." Finally, the culture's preferred time orientation can emphasize events and experiences from the past, the present, or the future. Table 4.1 summarizes the Kluckhohn and Strodtbeck value orientation theory.

TABLE 4.1 **Kluckhohn and Strodtbeck's Value Orientations**

Orientation	Postulated Range of Variations		
Activity	Being	Being-in-becoming	Doing
Relationships	Linearity	Collaterality	Individualism
Human nature	Evil	Mixture of good and evil	Good
People-nature	Subjugation to nature	Harmony with nature	Mastery over nature
Time	Past	Present	Future

Source: Adapted from Florence R. Kluckhohn and Fred Strodtbeck, *Variations in Value Orientations* (Evanston, IL: Row, Peterson, 1960).

Kluckhohn and Strodtbeck's third conclusion is their answer to an apparent contradiction that scholars found when studying cultures. They argued that, within any culture, a preferred set of solutions will be chosen by most people. However, not all people from a culture will make exactly the same set of choices, and, in fact, some people from each culture will select other alternatives. For example, most people who are part of European American culture have a "doing" orientation, a veneration for the future, a belief in control over nature, a preference for individualism, and a belief that people are basically good and changeable. But clearly not everyone identified with the European American culture shares all of these beliefs.

The fourth conclusion by Kluckhohn and Strodtbeck explains how cultural patterns develop and are sustained. A problem that is regularly solved in a similar way creates an underlying premise or expectation about the preferred or appropriate way to accomplish a specific goal. Such preferences, chosen unconsciously, implicitly define the shared meanings of the culture. Over time, certain behaviors to solve particular problems become preferred, others permitted, and still others prohibited.

Kluckhohn and Strodtbeck's ideas have been very influential among intercultural communication scholars, and they form the foundation for our understanding of cultural patterns. In the following section, we extend their work to explain, in a general way, the variations in beliefs, values, norms, and social practices that are typically associated with cultural patterns. Chapter 5 extends this overview to focus on specific conceptual taxonomies that can be used to understand cultural differences.

An Overview of Cultural Patterns

Members of a culture generally have a preferred set of responses to the world. Imagine that, for each experience, there is a range of possible responses from which a culture selects its preferred response. In this section we draw on the ideas of Edward Stewart, Milton Bennett, John Condon, and Fathi Yousef, which extend the thoughts of Kluckhohn and Strodtbeck, in order to describe these alternative responses.[10] In so doing, we will compare and contrast the cultural patterns of different cultural groups and suggest their implications for the process of interpersonal communication. Comparing the patterns of different cultures can sometimes be tricky because a feature of one culture, when compared with another culture, may appear very different than it would when compared with a third culture. Kluckhohn and Strodtbeck's cultural orientations are especially useful because they describe a broad range of cultural patterns against which a particular culture can be understood.

The five major elements in Kluckhohn and Strodtbeck's description of cultural patterns address the manner in which a culture orients itself to activities, social relations, the self, the world, and the passage of time. Note that there are strong linkages among the various elements. As you read the descriptions in the sections that follow, try to recognize the preferred patterns of your culture. Also, focus on your own beliefs, values, norms, and social practices, as they may differ in certain respects from your culture's predominant pattern.

Activity Orientation   An **activity orientation** defines how the people of a culture view human actions and the expression of self through activities. This orientation provides answers to questions such as the following:

- Is it important to be engaged in activities in order to be a "good" member of one's culture?
- Can and should people change the circumstances of their lives?
- Is work very different from play?
- Which is more important, work or play?
- Is life a series of problems to be solved or simply a collection of events to be experienced?

To define their activity orientation, cultures usually choose a point on the being–becoming–doing continuum. "Being" is an activity orientation that values inaction and an acceptance of the status quo. African American and Greek cultures are usually regarded as "being" cultures. Another characterization of this orientation is a belief that all events are determined by fate and are therefore inevitable. Hindus from India often espouse this view.

A "becoming" orientation sees humans as evolving and changing; people with this orientation, including Native Americans and most South Americans, are predisposed to think of ways to change themselves as a means of changing the world.

"Doing" is the dominant characteristic of European Americans, who rarely question the assumption that it is important to get things done. Thus, European Americans often ask, "What do you do?" When they first meet someone, a common greeting is "Hi! How are you doing?" and Monday morning conversations between coworkers often center on what each person "did" over the weekend. Similarly, young children are asked what they want to be when they grow up (though what is actually meant is "What do you want to do when you grow up?"), and cultural heroes are those who do things. The "doing" culture is often the striving culture, in which people seek to change and control what is happening to them. The common adage "Where there's a will there's a way" captures the essence of this cultural pattern. When faced with adversity, for example, European Americans encourage one another to fight on, to work hard, and not to give up.

How a person measures success is also related to the activity orientation. In cultures with a "doing" orientation, activity is evaluated by scrutinizing a tangible product or by evaluating some observable action directed at others. In other words, activity should have a purpose or a goal. In the "being" and "becoming" cultures, activity is not necessarily connected to external products or actions; the contemplative monk or the great thinker is most valued. Thus the process of striving toward the goal is sometimes far more important than accomplishing it.

In "doing" cultures, work is seen as a separate activity from play and an end in itself. In the "being" and "becoming" cultures, work is a means to an end, and there is no clear-cut separation between work and play. For these individuals, social life spills over into their work life. When members of a "being" culture work in the environment of a "doing" culture, their behavior is often misinterpreted. A Latina employee described her conversation with a European American coworker who expressed anger that she spent so much "work" time on the telephone with family and friends. For the Latina, it was important to keep in contact with her friends and

■ Cultures with a "being" orientation value contemplative behaviors. In Thailand and Cambodia, all men are encouraged to serve as Buddhist monks, at least for a short period of time. These Cambodian monks are talking to a local woman.

family; for the European American, only work was done at work, and one's social and personal relationships were totally separated from the working environment. In a "doing" culture, employees who spend too much time chatting with their fellow employees may be reprimanded by a supervisor. In the "being" and "becoming" cultures, those in charge fully expect their employees to mix working and socializing. Along with the activity orientation of "doing" comes a problem–solution orientation. The preferred way of dealing with a difficulty is to see it as a challenge to be met or a problem to be solved. The world is viewed as something that ought to be changed in order to solve problems rather than as something that ought to be accepted as it is, with whatever characteristics it has.

In every culture, these preferences for particular orientations to activities shape the interpersonal communication patterns that will occur. In "doing" cultures, interpersonal communication is characterized by concerns about what people do and how they solve problems. There are expectations that people should be involved in activities, that work comes before play, and that people should sacrifice in other parts of their lives in order to meet their work responsibilities. In "being" cultures, interpersonal communication is characterized by being together rather than by accomplishing specific tasks, and there is generally greater balance between work and play. Figure 4.1 summarizes the alternative cultural orientations to activities.

1. How do people define activity?

doing ———————————————— becoming ———————————————— being

striving ——————————————————————————————— fatalistic

compulsive ——————————————————————————————— easygoing

2. How do people evaluate activity?

techniques ——————————————————————————————— goals

procedures ——————————————————————————————— ideals

3. How do people regard and handle work?

an end in itself ——————————————————————— a means to other ends

separate from play ——————————————————————— integrated with play

a challenge ——————————————————————————————— a burden

problem solving ——————————————————————— coping with situations

FIGURE 4.1   Activity orientations.

Social Relations Orientation   The social relations orientation describes how the people in a culture organize themselves and relate to one another. This orientation provides answers to questions such as the following:

- To what extent are some people in the culture considered better or superior to others?
- Can social superiority be obtained through birth, age, good deeds, or material achievement and success?
- Are formal, ritualized interaction sequences expected?
- In what ways does the culture's language require people to make social distinctions?
- What responsibilities and obligations do people have to their extended families, their neighbors, their employers or employees, and others?

A social relations orientation can range from one that emphasizes differences and social hierarchy to one that strives for equality and the absence of hierarchy. Many European Americans, for example, emphasize equality and evenness in their interpersonal relationships, even though certain groups have been treated in discriminatory and unequal ways. Equality as a value and belief is frequently expressed and is called on to justify people's actions. The phrase "We are all human, aren't we?" captures the essence of this cultural tenet. From within this cultural framework, distinctions based on age, gender, role, or occupation are discouraged. Conversely, other cultures, such as the Korean, emphasize status differences between individuals. Mexican American culture, drawing on its cultural roots in traditional Mexican values, also celebrates status differences and formalizes different ways of communicating with people depending on who they are and what their social characteristics happen to be.

One noticeable difference in social relations orientations is in the degree of importance a culture places on formality. In cultures that emphasize formality, people address others by appropriate titles, and highly prescriptive rules govern the interaction. Conversely, in cultures that stress equality, people believe that human relationships develop best when those involved can be informal with one another. Students from other cultures who study in the United States are usually taken aback by the seeming informality that exists between teachers and students. Many professors allow, even ask, students to call them by their first names, and students disagree with and challenge their teachers in front of the class. The quickness with which interpersonal relationships in the United States move to a first-name basis is mystifying to those from cultures where the personal form of address is used only for selected, special individuals. Many U.S. Americans who share aspects of both European American culture and another culture also express difficulty with this aspect of cultural behavior.

In cultures such as those of Japan, Korea, and China, individuals identify with only a few distinct groups, and the ties that bind people to these groups are so strong that group membership may endure for a lifetime. Examples of these relationships include nuclear and extended families, friends, neighbors, work groups, and social organizations. In contrast, European Americans typically belong to many groups throughout their lifetimes, and although the groups may be very important for a period of time, they are easily discarded when they are no longer needed. That is, voluntary and informal groups are meant to be important for brief periods of time, often serving a transitory purpose. In addition, it is accepted and even expected that European Americans often change jobs and companies. "Best friends" may only be best friends for brief periods.

Another important way in which social relations orientations can vary is how people define their social roles or their place in a culture. In some cultures, the family and the position into which a person is born determine a person's place. At the other extreme are cultures in which all people, regardless of family position, can achieve success and high status. Among African Americans and European Americans, for instance, there is a widespread belief that social and economic class should not predetermine a person's opportunities and choices. For example, consider the tale of Abraham Lincoln, a poor boy who went from a log cabin to the White House; or the books of Horatio Alger, the nineteenth century author who wrote numerous rags-to-riches stories of success and happiness that were achieved through hard work and perseverance; or the Sylvester Stallone hero in the movie *Rocky*, who went from journeyman boxer to heavyweight champion of the world; or *Working Girl* Tess McGill, the Melanie Griffith character who went from her entry-level job in the typing pool to a senior executive; or the saga of washed-up boxer Jim Braddock, played by Russell Crow in the movie *Cinderella Man*, who became a champion in the 1930s; or the heartwarming and true story of Chris Gardner, played by Will Smith in *The Pursuit of Happyness*, who overcame poverty and hardships to become a successful stockbroker and raise his son. In each of these examples, there is a common belief that people should not be restricted by the circumstances of their birth.

Cultural patterns can also prescribe appropriate behaviors for men and women. In some cultures, very specific behaviors are expected; other cultures allow more ambiguity in the expected roles of women and men.

A culture's social relations orientation affects the style of interpersonal communication that is most preferred. Cultures may emphasize indirectness, obliqueness, and ambiguity, which is the typical pattern for most Eastern European cultures and Mexican Americans, or they may emphasize directness and confrontation, which is the typical European American pattern.

The European American preference for "putting your cards on the table" and "telling it like it is" presupposes a world in which it is desirable to be explicit, direct, and specific about personal reactions and ideas, even at the expense of social discomfort on the part of the person

■ Some cultures believe that humans both can and should control the powerful forces of nature. Hoover Dam in Nevada represents one example of this worldview.

with whom one is interacting. For European Americans, good interpersonal communication skills include stating directly one's personal needs and reactions to the behaviors of others. Thus, if European Americans hear that others have complained about them, they would probably ask, "Why didn't they tell me directly if they have a problem with something that I have done?"

Contrast this approach to that of Asian cultures such as those in Japan, Korea, Thailand, and China, where saving face and maintaining interpersonal harmony are so highly valued that it would be catastrophic to confront another person directly and verbally express anger. The same values are usually preferred in India[11] and in many Eastern European cultures, where saying "no" might be regarded as offensive. A U.S. American scholar working in Hungary tells of asking his Hungarian colleague if he could borrow a particular book. Instead of saying "no," the Hungarian repeatedly provided other reasons why he couldn't loan the book at that specific moment: he was using it just now; his mother was sick; he needed the book to complete an essay before his mother died. The Hungarian's strong sense of connectedness to family and friends meant that it would not be polite to say "no" directly.[12]

The tendency to be verbally explicit in face-to-face interactions is related to a preference for direct interaction rather than interaction through intermediaries. Among European Americans there is a belief that, ideally, people should depend only on themselves to accomplish what needs to be done. Therefore, the notion of using intermediaries to accomplish either personal or professional business goals is not widely accepted.

Although African Americans prefer indirectness and ambiguity in conversations with fellow cultural members, they do not choose to use intermediaries in these conversations. In many cultures, however, the use of intermediaries is the preferred method of conducting business or passing on information.[13] Marriages are arranged, business deals are made, homes are purchased, and other major negotiations are all conducted through third parties. These third parties soften and interpret the messages of both sides, thereby shielding the parties from direct, and therefore risky and potentially embarrassing, transactions with each other. Similarly, among many cultures from southern Africa, such as Swaziland, there is a distinct preference for the use of intermediaries to deal with negotiations and conflict situations. Consider the experience of the director of an English program in Tunisia, a culture that depends on intermediaries. One of the Tunisian teachers had been consistently late to his morning classes. Rather than calling the teacher in and directly explaining the problem, the director asked the teacher's friend about the teacher's health and happiness. The director indicated that the teacher's late arrival for class might have been a sign that something was wrong. The friend then simply indirectly conveyed the director's concern to the late teacher, who was late no more.

A culture's social relations orientation also affects the sense of social reciprocity—that is, the underlying sense of obligation and responsibility between people. Some cultures prefer independence and a minimum number of obligations and responsibilities; alternatively, other cultures accept obligations and encourage dependence. The nature of the dependence is often related to the types of status and the degree of formality that exist between the individuals. Cultures that depend on hierarchy and formality to guide their social interactions are also likely to have both a formal means for fulfilling social obligations and clearly defined norms for expressing them. Figure 4.2 summarizes the alternative cultural orientations to social relations.

Self-Orientation   Self-orientation describes how people's identities are formed, whether the culture views the self as changeable, what motivates individual actions, and the kinds of people who are valued and respected. A culture's self-orientation provides answers to questions such as the following:

- Do people believe they have their own unique identities that separate them from others?
- Does the self reside in the individual or in the groups to which the individual belongs?
- What responsibilities does the individual have to others?
- What motivates people to behave as they do?
- Is it possible to respect a person who is judged "bad" in one part of life but is successful in another part of life?

1. How do people relate to others?

as equals ———————————————————————— hierarchical

informal ———————————————————————— formal

member of many groups ———————————— member of few groups

weak group identification ———————— strong group identification

2. How are roles defined and allocated?

achieved ———————————————————————— ascribed

gender roles similar ———————————— gender roles distinct

3. How do people communicate with others?

directly ———————————————————————— indirectly

no intermediaries ————————————————— intermediaries

4. What is the basis of social reciprocity?

independence ——————— interdependence ——————— dependence

autonomy ———————————————————————— obligation

FIGURE 4.2   **Social relations orientations.**

CULTURE connections

"Some men in safari suits came one day and grabbed the chest. Nobody was sure who they were or where they were planning to take the puppets. The abbot charged with their safekeeping was shown a government directive that the chest was to be moved for security reasons. When the abbot asked for details, they told him it was all confidential. There wasn't much he could do about it.

"And that's how the chest ended up in the archive department of the Ministry and why all hell broke loose. You see, the chest can't be opened by just anyone whenever they feel like it. The spirits of the puppets are incredibly powerful and amazingly temperamental. They were already—"

"How can puppets have spirits?" Civilai interrupted.

"What?"

"Puppets aren't people, and they aren't dead. So how—?"

"Ah, but the puppets are made of balsa, and before the wood to carve them is cut from the tree, the puppet-maker has to get permission from the tree spirits. The balsa is a gentle wood and spirits are plentiful in it. When they learn that the wood is going to be made into the image of a person, it's awfully tempting for the more nostalgic spirits to jump ship and settle in the form of the puppet. It's as if they've returned to their lost host.

—*Colin Cotterill*

For most European Americans, the emphasis on the individual self is so strong and so pervasive that it is almost impossible for them to comprehend a different point of view. Thus, many European Americans believe that the self is located solely within the individual, and the individual is definitely separate from others. From a very young age, children are encouraged to make their own decisions. Alternatively, cultures may define who people are only through their associations with others because an individual's self-definition may not be separate from that of the larger group. Consequently, there is a heightened sense of interdependence, and what happens to the group (family, work group, or social group) happens to the person. For example, Mary Jane Collier, Sidney Ribeau, and Michael Hecht found that Mexican Americans "place a great deal of emphasis on affiliation and relational solidarity."[14] The sense of being bonded or connected to others is very important to members of this cultural group. Vietnamese Americans have a similarly strong affiliation with their families.

The significance to intercultural communication of a culture's preferences for defining the self is evident in the statement of a Latina student describing her friendship with a second-generation Italian American woman, whose family has also maintained "traditional values."

> I think we are able to communicate so well because our cultural backgrounds are very similar. I have always been family-oriented and so has she. This not only allowed us to get along, but it allowed us to bring our families into our friendship. [For instance] a rule that the two of us had to live by up to this point has been that no matter how old we may get, as long as we are living at home we must ask our parents for permission to go out.

Related to self-orientation is the culture's view of whether people are changeable. Naturally, if a culture believes that people can change, it is likely to expect that human beings will strive to be "better," as the culture defines and describes what "better" means.

The source of motivation for human behavior is also part of a culture's self-orientation. Among African Americans and European Americans, individuals are motivated to achieve external success in the form of possessions, positions, and power. Self-orientation combines with the "doing" orientation to create a set of beliefs and values that place individuals in total control of their own fate. Individuals must set their own goals and identify the means necessary to achieve them. Consequently, failure is viewed as a lack of willpower and a disinclination to give the fullest individual effort. In this cultural framework, individuals regard it as necessary to rely on themselves rather than on others.

Another distinguishing feature of the cultural definition of self is whether the members of the culture believe that people are inherently bad, good, or some combination of these two. The Chinese, for example, believe people are inherently good, and they must therefore be protected from exposure to corrupting influences. Conversely, other cultures are influenced by religious tenets that regard humans as intrinsically bad. A related issue is whether the culture emphasizes duties or rights. One culture that expects their members to act because it is their duty to do so is the Japanese. In contrast, for European Americans, the concept of duties and obligations to others is not as powerful a motivator.

An additional part of self-orientation is the set of characteristics of those individuals who are valued and cherished. Cultures vary in their allegiance to the old or to the young, for example. Many cultures venerate their elders and view them as a source of wisdom and valuable life experience. Individuals in these cultures base decisions on the preferences and desires of their elders. Many Asian and Asian American cultures illustrate this preference. The value on youth typifies the European American culture, in which innovation and new ideas, rather than the wisdom of the past, are regarded as important. European Americans venerate the upstart, the innovator, and the person who tries something new. Figure 4.3 summarizes the alternative cultural orientations to the self.

World Orientation   Cultural patterns also tell people how to locate themselves in relation to the spiritual world, nature, and other living things. A world orientation provides answers to questions such as the following:

- Are human beings intrinsically good or evil?
- Are humans different from other animals and plants?
- Are people in control of, subjugated by, or living in harmony with the forces of nature?
- Do spirits of the dead inhabit and affect the human world?

In the African and African American worldview, human beings live in an interactive state with the natural and spiritual world. Daniel and Smitherman describe a fundamental tenet of the traditional African worldview as that of "a dynamic, hierarchical unity between God, man, and nature, with God serving as the head of the hierarchy."[15] In this view of the relationship between the spiritual and material world, humans are an integral part of nature. Thus, in the African and African American worldview, "One becomes a 'living witness' when he aligns himself with the forces of nature and instead of being a proselytized 'true believer' strives to live in harmony with the universe."[16] Native American groups, as well, clearly have a view of humans as living in harmony with nature.[17] Latino

1. How should people form their identities?

   by themselves ———————————————— with others

2. How changeable is the self?

   changeable ———————————————— unchangeable

   self-realization stressed ———————————————— self-realization not stressed

3. What is the source of motivation for the self?

   reliance on self ———————————————— reliance on others

   rights ———————————————— duties

4. What kind of person is valued and respected?

   young ———————————————— aged

   vigorous ———————————————— wise

   innovative ———————————————— prominent

   material attributes ———————————————— spiritual attributes

FIGURE 4.3 **Self-orientations.**

culture places a great value on spirituality but views humans as being subjugated to nature, with little power to control circumstances that influence their lives.[18] Asian Indians also have a worldview that humans are subjugated to nature.[19]

Most European Americans view humans as separate and distinct from nature and other forms of life. Because of the supremacy of the individual and the presumed uniqueness of each person, most European Americans regard nature as something to be manipulated and controlled in order to make human life better. Excellent examples of this cultural belief can be found in news reports whenever a natural disaster occurs in the United States. For instance, when Hurricane Katrina hit New Orleans and elsewhere along the Gulf Coast in August 2005 and nearly two thousand individuals died in the subsequent flooding, people were outraged that the flood protection and levee systems could be so unsafe. The assumption in these pronouncements was that the consequences of natural forces such as hurricanes could have been prevented simply by using better technology and by reinforcing the levees and other structures to withstand the forces of nature. Similarly, in August 2007, within a day of the collapse of a bridge that spanned the Mississippi River in Minneapolis, syndicated television news stations were broadcasting a headline that asked, "Deadly Bridge Collapse: Who's to Blame?"

The position that humans are separate and distinct from nature is also associated with a belief that disease, poverty, and adversity can be overcome to achieve health and wealth. In this cultural framework, the "natural" part of the human experience—illness, loss, even death—can be overcome, or at least postponed, by selecting the right courses of action and having the right kinds of attitudes.

The spiritual and physical worlds can be viewed as distinct or as one. Among European Americans there is generally a clear understanding that the physical world, of which humans are a part, is separate from the spiritual world. If people believe in a spiritual world, it exists apart from the everyday places where people live, work, and play.

1. What is the nature of humans in relation to the world?

   separate from nature ——————————————————integral part of nature

   humans modify nature ————————————————— humans adapt to nature

   health natural ———————————————————————— disease natural

   wealth expected ——————————————————————poverty expected

2. What is the world like?

   spiritual-physical dichotomy ————————————— spiritual-physical unity

   empirically understood ——————————————————— magically understood

   technically controlled ——————————————————spiritually controlled

FIGURE 4.4   **World orientations.**

Individuals who say they are psychic or who are mind readers are viewed with suspicion and curiosity. Those who have seen ghosts are questioned in an effort to find a more "logical" and "rational" explanation. In other cultural frameworks, however, it is "logical" and "rational" for spirits to live in both animate and inanimate objects.[20] Alternatives in cultural orientations to the world are summarized in Figure 4.4.

Time Orientation   The final aspect of cultural patterns concerns how people conceptualize time. Time orientation provides answers to questions such as the following:

- How should time be valued and understood?
- Is time a scarce resource, or is it unlimited?
- Is the desirable pace of life fast or slow?
- Is time linear or cyclical?

Some cultures choose to describe the future as most important, others emphasize the present, and still others emphasize the past. In Japanese and Chinese cultures, the anniversary of the death of a loved one is celebrated, illustrating the value these cultures place on the past. In contrast, Native Americans and Latinos are present-oriented. European Americans, of course, are future-oriented.

Most European Americans view time as a scarce and valuable commodity akin to money or other economic investments. They strive to "save time," "make time," "spend time," and "gain time." Events during a day are dictated by a schedule of activities, precisely defined and differentiated. Most cultures in Latin America bring an entirely different orientation to time, responding to individuals and circumstances rather than following a scheduled plan for the day. Similarly, Romanians also do not define punctuality as precisely as European Americans do. Thus, time is viewed within these cultural frames as endless and ongoing.

A culture's time orientation also suggests the pace of life. The fast, hectic pace of European Americans, governed by clocks, appointments, and schedules, has become so commonly accepted that it is almost a cliché. The pace of life in cultures such as India, Kenya, and Argentina and among African Americans is less hectic, more

1. How do people define time?

   future ——————————————— present ——————————————— past

   precisely measurable ————————————————————————— undifferentiated

   linear ——————————————————————————————— cyclical

2. How do people value time?

   scarce resource ——————————————————————— unlimited

   fast pace ————————————————————————— slow pace

FIGURE 4.5 **Time orientations.**

relaxed, and more comfortably paced. In African American culture, for example, orientations to time are driven less by a need to "get things done" and conform to external demands than by a sense of participation in events that create their own rhythm. As Jack Daniel and Geneva Smitherman suggest about time in African American culture,

> Being on time has to do with participating in the fulfillment of an activity that is vital to the sustenance of a basic rhythm, rather than with appearing on the scene at, say, "twelve o'clock sharp." The key is not to be "on time" but "in time."[21]

Alternatives in cultural orientations to time are summarized in Figure 4.5. In Chapter 8, the discussion of nonverbal communication codes also considers the influence of a culture's orientation toward time on aspects of communication.

A culture's underlying patterns consist of orientations to activity, social relations, the self, the world, and time. The interdependence among these aspects of culture is obvious from the preceding discussion. Kluckhohn and Strodtbeck provide a way to understand, rather than to judge, different cultural predispositions, and it demonstrates that there are different ways of defining the "real," "good," and "correct" ways to behave.

CULTURE connections

Diane and Blong met, as it happens, on the Fourth of July 1997 at one in the morning, "just after the fireworks." Diane can be as exact about times and dates as her husband is hypothetical and vague—apparently the Hmong do not pay much attention to dates and do not keep birth records, which makes tracing events in Blong's eventful life difficult. "But she remembers everything," Blong comments indulgently about Diane's precision, as though making room for a somewhat odd American obsession.

—Jessie Carroll Grearson and Lauren B. Smith

Cultural Patterns and Intercultural Competence

There is a strong relationship between the foundations of cultural patterns and intercultural competence. Remember that intercultural competence depends on knowledge, motivation, and actions, which occur in specific contexts with messages that are both appropriate and effective.

The patterns of a culture create the filter through which all verbal and nonverbal symbols are interpreted. Because all cultures have distinct beliefs, values, norms, and social practices, symbols do not have universal interpretations, nor will the interpretations have the same degree of favorability. Judgments of competence are strongly influenced by the underlying patterns of a person's cultural background. In every intercultural interaction, a cultural pattern that is different from one's own may be used to interpret one's messages. Every intercultural interaction, then, can be viewed as a puzzle or a mystery that needs to be solved.

How individuals define the relational context is always related to the mental programming that cultures provide. One person's definition of the relationship (e.g., friend) may not match that of the person with whom he or she interacts (e.g., fellow student), causing radically different expectations and interpretations of behaviors.

In solving the intercultural puzzle, it is critical to remember another valuable insight from Kluckhohn and Strodtbeck's foundational work. Although a culture (the collectivity of people) will make preferred choices about beliefs, values, norms, and social practices, not all cultural members will necessarily share all of those preferred choices, nor will they share them with the same degree of intensity. The immediate consequence of this conclusion for the development of intercultural competence is that every person represents the cultural group with which he or she identifies, but to a greater or lesser degree. A cultural pattern may be the preferred choice of most cultural members, but what can accurately be described for the culture in general cannot necessarily be assumed to be true for a specific individual. In simple terms, this principle translates into an important guideline for the development of intercultural competence: even though you may have culture-specific information, you can never assume that every person from that culture matches the profile of the typical cultural member.

Because cultural patterns describe what people perceive as their reality, what they view as desirable, how they should behave, and what they typically do, there are repercussions for the motivational component of intercultural competence. Recall that

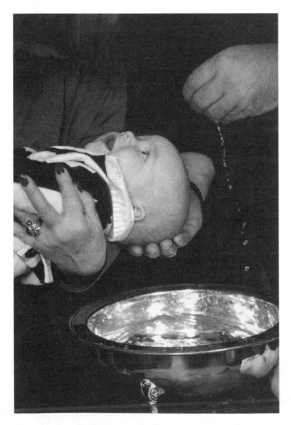

■ In the Baptism ceremony, Christians express their relationship to the spiritual world.

communicators' feelings in intercultural interactions affect their ability to be open to alternative interpretations. Yet if cultural patterns predispose people to a particular definition of what is real, good, and right, reactions to others as unreal, bad, or wrong may create psychological distance between interactants. When confronting a set of beliefs, values, norms, and social practices that are inconsistent with their own, many people will evaluate them negatively. Strong emotional reactions are often predictable; after all, these variations from other cultures challenge the basic view people have of their world. Nevertheless, other cultures' ways of believing and their preferred values are not crazy or wrong, just different.

Cultural patterns form the basis for what is considered to be communicatively appropriate and effective. Examples that illustrate how beliefs, values, norms, and social practices set the boundaries of appropriateness and effectiveness include such instances as speaking your mind, in contrast to being quiet; defending yourself against a criticism, in contrast to accepting it; confronting another person about a problem rather than indirectly letting her or him know of the concern; and emphasizing the differences in status in relationships, in contrast to emphasizing commonality. Simply knowing what is appropriate and what has worked to accomplish your personal objectives in your own culture may not, and in all likelihood will not, have similar results when you interact with culturally different others. Intercultural competence usually requires alternative choices for actions. Consequently, we recommend that, before acting, you should contemplate, draw on your culture-specific knowledge, and make behavioral choices that are appropriate for interacting with members of the other culture.

The patterns of a culture shape, but do not determine, the mental programming of its people. Because cultural patterns define how people see and define reality, they are a powerful emotional force in competent intercultural interaction.

CULTURE connections

For untold generations, the Kobuk Eskimos lived in balance with their world, and often they, not the animals they hunted, were the endangered species. If the land offered something, it was unquestioningly, thankfully accepted as a gift from a limitless storehouse, something that allowed The People to live. As long as they showed proper reverence by such rituals as slitting the dead animal's trachea—*nigiluq*—the animal spirit would escape and be reborn, to be hunted again. There was no burden of souls.

Clarence still practices *nigiluq*—believes, too, in the perpetual abundance it implies. Once after he'd returned from a spring hunt I asked him if he'd seen many caribou on the flats. With a rare, expansive smile he replied, "Lots. You could never finish 'em." Lllotttsss. He said the word as if it had ten letters, lips drawn back to bare tongue and teeth.

It's been twenty-five years since snow machines hit the country. Common sense says that all game populations have to be declining. Still, the best guess by both biologists and Eskimos is that wolves in the northwest arctic are actually increasing along with the caribou herd; you can find wolf trails and kill remains a few miles from most villages. The blue-white ocean of land seems vast enough, for now, to bear the pressure.

—*Nick Jans*

Summary

This chapter began the discussion about cultural patterns, which are invisible differences that characterize cultures. Beliefs, values, norms, and social practices are the ingredients of cultural patterns. Beliefs are ideas that people assume to be true about the world. Values are the desired characteristics of a culture. Norms are socially shared expectations of appropriate behaviors. Social practices, the final component of cultural patterns, are the predictable behavior patterns that people typically follow.

Cultural patterns are shared among a group of people, and they form the foundation for maintenance of cultures. They are stable over relatively long periods of time, and they lead most members of a culture to behave in roughly similar ways when they encounter similar situations.

Florence Kluckhohn and Fred Strodtbeck suggest that each culture selects a preferred set of choices to address common human issues. While not all people in the culture make exactly the same choices, the preferred solutions define the shared meanings of the culture.

Cultural patterns focus on the way cultures orient themselves to activities, social relations, the self, the world, and time. The activity orientation defines how people express themselves through activities and locate themselves on the being–becoming–doing continuum. The social relations orientation describes the preferred forms of interpersonal relationships within a culture. The self-orientation indicates the culture's conception of how people understand who they are in relation to others. The world orientation locates a culture in the physical and spiritual worlds. The time orientation directs a culture to value the past, present, or future.

For Discussion

1. How might individuals from *doing, being,* and *becoming* cultures engage in conflict in the workplace, in school, or in interpersonal relationships?
2. One person comes from a culture that believes "We're all humans, aren't we?" Another person comes from a culture that says "Status is everything." What might occur as these two individuals try to communicate with each other?

3. *Truth* or *lie, just* or *unjust, right* or *wrong,* and *good* or *bad* are all common human judgments of the actions of others. How does your awareness of cultural patterns affect your understanding of each of these sets of terms?
4. Using the five dimensions of cultural patterns described in this chapter, describe how you think each is displayed in your own culture.

For Further Reading

Ned Crouch, *Mexicans and Americans: Cracking the Cultural Code* (Yarmouth, ME: Nicholas Brealey Publishing, 2004). For those interested in understanding and bridging the cultural differences between Mexicans and U.S. Americans.

Martin J. Gannon and Associates, *Understanding Global Cultures: Metaphorical Journeys through 23 Nations, Clusters of Nations, and Continents,* 3rd ed. (Thousand Oaks, CA: Sage, 2004). An excellent guide to understanding the worldviews and perspectives of many cultures throughout the world.

Edward C. Stewart and Milton J. Bennett, *American Cultural Patterns,* rev. ed. (Yarmouth, ME: Intercultural Press, 1991). Provides a detailed description of European American cultural patterns, as well as some potential contrasts to the patterns of other cultures.

Craig Storti, *Americans at Work: A Guide to the Can-do People* (Yarmouth, ME: Intercultural Press, 2004). With a focus on understanding and explaining the cultural patterns of European Americans, which dominate the workplace in the United States, this book provides an excellent overview of European American cultural patterns.

For additional information about intercultural films and about Web sites for researching specific cultures, please turn to the Resources section at the back of this book.

CHAPTER 5

Cultural Patterns and Communication: Taxonomies

In the previous chapter, we provided an overview of the patterns that underlie all cultures. We described the nature of cultural patterns and the importance of beliefs, values, norms, and social practices in helping cultures to cope with problems. We now focus on specific conceptual taxonomies that are useful for understanding cultural differences.

We have chosen three different but related taxonomies to describe variations in cultural patterns. The first was developed by Edward Hall, who noted that cultures differ in the extent to which their primary message patterns are high context or low context. The second describes the ideas of Geert Hofstede, who identifies seven dimensions along which cultures vary. The third, by a group of researchers collectively known as the GLOBE team, incorporates many of the previously described ideas; the group identifies nine dimensions of culture and differentiates cultural *practices* (what people *actually* do) from cultural *values* (ideally, what people *should* do).

As you read the descriptions of cultural patterns by Hall, Hofstede, and the GLOBE researchers, we caution you to remember three points. First, there is nothing sacred about these approaches and the internal categories they employ. Each approach takes the whole of cultural patterns (beliefs, values, norms, and social practices) and divides them in different ways.

Second, the parts of each of the systems are interrelated. We begin the description of each system at an arbitrarily chosen point, presupposing other parts of the system that have not yet been described. Cultural patterns are understandable not in isolation but as a unique whole.

Finally, individual members of a culture may vary greatly from the pattern that is typical of that culture. Therefore, as you study these approaches to cultural patterns, we encourage you to make some judgments about how your own culture fits into the pattern. Then, as you place it within the pattern, also try to discern how you, as an individual, fit into the patterns described. Similarly, as you learn about other cultural patterns, please remember that a specific person may or may not be a typical representative of that culture. As you study your own cultural patterns and those of other cultures, you improve the knowledge component of intercultural competence.

CULTURE connections

"It is a matter of cultural sensitivity, I think," she said. "As an American, you are very direct. We Japanese are more polite; we discuss matters indirectly. It is our custom to communicate through mind-reading."

Alex protested. "But I'm not Japanese! How can I possibly be expected to read Japanese minds?" Or know her class rules, he thought.

"You must be patient. Most Japanese are not used to foreigners—we don't realize that Westerners don't think as we do. And, we are shy."

—*Sara Backer*

Hall's High- and Low-Context Cultural Taxonomy

Edward T. Hall, whose writings about the relationship between culture and communication are well known, organizes cultures by the amount of information implied by the setting or context of the communication itself, regardless of the specific words that are spoken.[1] Hall argues that every human being is faced with so many perceptual stimuli—sights, sounds, smells, tastes, and bodily sensations—that it is impossible to pay attention to them all. Therefore, one of the functions of culture is to provide a screen between the person and all of those stimuli to indicate what perceptions to notice and how to interpret them. Hall's approach is compatible with the other approaches discussed in this chapter. Where it differs is in the importance it places on the role of context.

According to Hall, cultures differ on a continuum that ranges from high to low context. High-context cultures prefer to use high-context messages in which most of the meaning is either implied by the physical setting or presumed to be part of the individual's internalized beliefs, values, norms, and social practices; very little is provided in the coded, explicit, transmitted part of the message. Examples of high-context cultures include Japanese, African American, Mexican, and Latino. Low-context cultures prefer to use low context messages, in which the majority of the information is vested in the explicit code. Low-context cultures include German, Swedish, European American, and English.

A simple example of high-context communication is interactions that take place in a long-term relationship between two people who are often able to interpret even the slightest gesture or the briefest comment. The message does not need to be stated explicitly because it is carried in the shared understandings about the relationship.

A simple example of low-context communication is now experienced by more and more people as they interact with computers. For computers to "understand" a message, every statement must be precise. Many computers will not accept or respond to instructions that do not have every space, period, letter, and number in precisely the right location. The message must be overt and very explicit.

Hall's description of high- and low-context cultures is based on the idea that some cultures have a preponderance of messages that are high context, others have messages that are mostly low context, and yet others have a mixture of both. Hall also describes other characteristics of high- and low-context cultures, which reveal the beliefs, values, norms, and social practices of the cultural system. These characteristics include the use of covert or overt messages, the importance of ingroups and outgroups, and the culture's orientation to time.

Use of Covert and Overt Messages

In a high-context culture such as that of Japan, meanings are internalized and there is a large emphasis on nonverbal codes. Hall describes messages in high-context cultures as almost preprogrammed, in which very little of the interpretation of the message is left to chance because people already know that, in the context of the current situation, the communicative behaviors will have a specific and particular message. In low-context cultures, people look for the meaning of others' behaviors in the messages that are plainly and explicitly coded. The details of the message are expressed precisely and specifically in the words that people use as they try to communicate with others.

Another way to think about the difference between high- and low-context cultures is to imagine something with which you are very familiar, such as repairing a car, cooking, sewing, or playing a particular sport. When you talk about that activity with someone else who is very familiar with it, you will probably be less explicit and instead use a more succinct set of verbal and nonverbal messages. You will talk in a verbal shorthand that does not require you to be specific and precise about every aspect of the ideas that you are expressing, because the others will know what you mean without their specific presentation. However, if you talk to someone who does not know very much about the activity, you will have to explain more, be more precise and specific, and provide more background information.

In a high-context culture, much more is taken for granted and assumed to be shared, and consequently the overwhelming preponderance of messages are coded in such a way that they do not need to be explicitly and verbally transmitted. Instead, the demands of the situation and the shared meanings among the interactants mean that the preferred interpretation of the messages is already known.

Consider, as an example of high-context messages, an event that occurred in Indonesia. A young couple met, fell in love, and wanted to marry. She was from a wealthy and well-connected family, whereas he was from a family of more modest means, but the

CULTURE connections

Like the rest of my family, I have no idea how old I am; I can only guess. A baby who is born in my country has little guarantee of being alive one year later, so the concept of tracking birthdays does not retain the same importance. When I was a child, we lived without artificial time constructions of schedules, clocks, and calendars. Instead, we lived by the seasons and the sun, planning our moves around our need for rain, planning our day around the span of daylight available. We told time by using the sun. If my shadow was on the west side, it was morning; when it moved directly underneath me, it was noon. When my shadow crossed to the other side, it was afternoon. As the day grew longer, so did my shadow—my cue to start heading home before dark.

When we got up in the morning, we decided what we'd do that day, then did that task the best we could until we finished or the sky grew too dark for us to see. There was no such notion of getting up and having your day all planned out for you. In New York, people frequently whip out their datebooks and ask, "Are you free for lunch on the fourteenth—or what about the fifteenth?" I respond with "Why don't you call me the day before you want to meet up?" No matter how many times I write down appointments, I can't get used to the idea. When I first came to London, I was mystified by the connection between people staring at their wrist, then crying, "I've got to dash!" I felt like everyone was rushing everywhere, every action was timed. In Africa there was no hurry, no stress. African time is very, very slow, very calm. If you say, "I'll see you tomorrow around noon," that means about four or five o'clock.

—Waris Dirie and Cathleen Miller

young couple did not regard this difference as a problem. So they shared their happy news with their respective families; shortly thereafter, the young man's parents were invited to the woman's home to socialize and to meet her parents. The social occasion was very cordial; the conversation was pleasant, and the two sets of parents were very gracious toward one another. At the appropriate time, the woman's parents served *nasi goring* (fried rice) and *rambutan* (star fruit), two foods that are very common in Indonesia. Finally, after an appropriate interval, the young man's parents thanked their hosts and left. Throughout the entire episode, the topic of the wedding was never broached. However, everyone knew that the wedding would never occur. After all, *nasi goring* doesn't go with *rambutan;* the high-context and face-saving message that the woman's parents communicated, and that the man's parents clearly understood, was that they disapproved of the marriage.

The difference between high-context and low-context cultural styles is illustrated in the following dialogue between a European American (low-context culture) and a Malaysian (high-context culture); the Malaysian's message is revealed only by implication. Both people in the dialogue teach at a community college in the United States, and the Malaysian's objective in this conversation is to have the European American drive him off campus for lunch because the Malaysian does not have a car.

■ A Japanese tea ceremony is an example of a high-context message. Nearly every movement, gesture, and action has significance to those who understand the "code" being used.

Malaysian:	Can I ask you a question?
European American:	Yes, of course.
Malaysian:	Do you know what time it is?
European American:	Yes, it's two o'clock.
Malaysian:	Might you have a little soup left in the pot?
European American:	What? I don't understand.
Malaysian:	(becoming more explicit since the colleague is not getting the point): I will be on campus teaching until nine o'clock tonight, a very long day for any person, let alone a hungry one!
European American:	(finally getting the point): Would you like me to drive you to a restaurant off campus so you can have lunch?
Malaysian:	What a very good idea you have!

Reactions in high-context cultures are likely to be reserved, whereas reactions in low-context cultures are frequently very explicit and readily observable. It is easy to understand why this is so. In high-context cultures, an important purpose in communicating is to promote and sustain harmony among the interactants. Unconstrained reactions could threaten the face or social esteem of others. In low-context cultures, however, an important purpose in communicating is to convey exact meaning. Explicit messages help to achieve this goal. If messages need to be explicit, so will people's reactions. Even when the message is understood, a person cannot assume that the meanings are clear in the absence of verbal messages coded specifically to provide feedback.

Importance of Ingroups and Outgroups

In high-context cultures, it is very easy to determine who is a member of the group and who is not. Because so much of the meaning of messages is embedded in the rules and rituals of situations, it is easy to tell who is acting according to those norms. As there are fixed and specific expectations for behaviors, deviations are easy to detect.

Another distinction concerns the emphasis placed on the individual in contrast to the group as a source of self-identity. In a high-context culture, the commitment between people is very strong and deep, and responsibility to others takes precedence over responsibility to oneself. Loyalties to families and the members of one's social and work groups are long-lasting and unchanging. This degree of loyalty differs from that found in a low-context culture, in which the bonds between people are very fragile and the extent of involvement and commitment to long-term relationships is lower.

Orientation to Time

The final distinguishable characteristic of high- and low-context cultures is their orientation to time. In the former, time is viewed as more open, less structured, more responsive to the immediate needs of people, and less subject to external goals and constraints. In low-context cultures, time is highly organized, in part because of the additional energy required to understand the messages of others. Low-context cultures are almost forced to pay more attention to time in order to complete the work of living with others.

As Table 5.1 indicates, Edward Hall's placement of cultures onto a continuum that is anchored by preferences for high-context messages and low-context messages offers a

TABLE 5.1   Characteristics of Low- and High-Context Cultures

High-Context Cultures	Low-Context Cultures
Covert and implicit	Overt and explicit
Messages internalized	Messages plainly coded
Much nonverbal coding	Details verbalized
Reactions reserved	Reactions on the surface
Distinct ingroups and outgroups	Flexible ingroups and outgroups
Strong interpersonal bonds	Fragile interpersonal bonds
Commitment high	Commitment low
Time open and flexible	Time highly organized

way to understand other variations in cultural patterns. A high-context culture chooses to use covert and implicit messages that rely heavily on nonverbal code systems. In a high-context culture, the group is very important, as are traditions, and members of the ingroup are easily recognized. Time is less structured and more responsive to people's needs. Low-context cultures are characterized by the opposite attributes: messages are explicit and dependent on verbal codes, group memberships change rapidly, innovation is valued, and time is highly structured.

Hofstede's Cultural Taxonomy

Geert Hofstede's impressive studies of cultural differences in value orientations offer another approach to understanding the range of cultural differences.[2] Hofstede's approach is based on the assertion that people carry mental programs, or "software of the mind," that are developed during childhood and are reinforced by their culture. These mental programs contain the ideas of a culture and are expressed through its dominant values. To identify the principal values of different cultures, Hofstede initially surveyed more than 100,000 IBM employees in seventy-one countries, and he has subsequently broadened his analysis to include many others.

Through theoretical reasoning and statistical analyses, Hofstede's early research identified five dimensions along which dominant patterns of a culture can be ordered: power distance, uncertainty avoidance, individualism versus collectivism, masculinity versus femininity, and long-term versus short-term orientation to time. Recently two additional dimensions have been added: indulgence versus restraint and monumentalism versus self-effacement. Hofstede's work provides an excellent synthesis of the relationships between cultural values and social behaviors.[3]

CULTURE connections

Ferhat Bey does not answer for a moment, his eyes fixed on the coals, then returns his attention to Kamil. He is painfully aware that Kamil has neglected to defer to him and assumes this is because Kamil is the son of a pasha and used to taking on airs. Still, in deference to his age, Kamil should speak less directly. One shows respect through formality, through indirection; there are necessary locutions within which questions and responses should be couched, muffled, like winter padding on a horse's hooves, so that the ring of fact on stone remains the prerogative of the elder, the teacher. What has he got to teach this upstart? thinks Ferhat Bey bitterly. He had failed and this brash young man will fail too.

"Who made up the household at that time?" Kamil asks.

The old man sighs and answers slowly, showing his displeasure at being interrogated. The young upstart should read the file; he had noted at least this much before he stopped writing.

—*Jenny White*

Power Distance

One of the basic concerns of all cultures is the issue of human inequality. Contrary to the claim in the U.S. Declaration of Independence that "all men are created equal," all people in a culture do not have equal levels of status or social power. Depending on the culture, some people might be regarded as superior to others because of their wealth, age, gender, education, physical strength, birth order, personal achievements, family background, occupation, or a wide variety of other characteristics.

Cultures also differ in the extent to which they view such status inequalities as good or bad, right or wrong, just or unjust, and fair or unfair. That is, all cultures have particular value orientations about the appropriateness or importance of status differences and social hierarchies. Thus power distance refers to the degree to which the culture believes that institutional and organizational power should be distributed unequally and the decisions of the power holders should be challenged or accepted.

Cultures that prefer small power distances—such as Austria, Denmark, Israel, and New Zealand—believe in the importance of minimizing social or class inequalities, questioning or challenging authority figures, reducing hierarchical organizational structures, and using power only for legitimate purposes. Conversely, cultures that prefer large power distances—such as those in Arab countries, Guatemala, Malaysia, and the Philippines—believe that each person has a rightful and protected place in the social order, that the actions of authorities should not be challenged or questioned, that hierarchy and inequality are appropriate and beneficial, and that those with social status have a right to use their power for whatever purposes and in whatever ways they deem desirable.

The consequences of the degree of power distance that a culture prefers are evident in family customs, the relationships between students and teachers, organizational practices, and in other areas of social life. Even the language systems in high power-distance cultures emphasize distinctions based on a social hierarchy.

Children raised in high power-distance cultures are expected to obey their parents without challenging or questioning them, while children raised in low power-distance cultures put less value on obedience and are taught to seek reasons or justifications for their parents' actions. Even the language of high power-distance cultures is more sensitive to hierarchical distinctions; Chinese and Korean languages, for instance, have separate terms for older brother, oldest brother, younger sister, youngest sister, and so on.

Students in high power-distance cultures are expected to comply with the wishes and requests of their teachers, and conformity is regarded very favorably. As a consequence, the curriculum in these cultures is likely to involve a great deal of rote learning, and students are discouraged from asking questions because questions might pose a threat to the teacher's authority. In low power-distance cultures, students regard their independence as very important, and they are less likely to conform to the expectations of teachers or other authorities. The educational system itself reinforces the low-power values by teaching students to ask questions, to solve problems creatively and uniquely, and to challenge the evidence leading to conclusions.

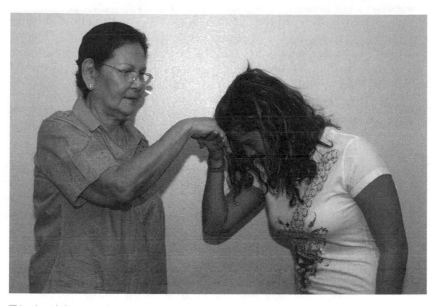

■ In the Philippines, large power distance is shown in this traditional gesture of greeting by a granddaughter to her grandmother.

In the business world, managers in high power-distance cultures are likely to prefer an autocratic or centralized decision-making style, whereas subordinates in these cultures expect and want to be closely supervised. Alternatively, managers in low power-distance cultures prefer a consultative or participative decision-making style, and their subordinates expect a great deal of autonomy and independence as they do their work.

European Americans tend to have a relatively low power distance, though it is by no means exceptionally low. However, when European Americans communicate with people from cultures that value a relatively large power distance, problems related to differences in expectations are likely. For example, European American exchange students in a South American or Asian culture sometimes have difficulty adapting to a world in which people are expected to do as they are told without questioning the reasons for the requests. Conversely, exchange students visiting the United States from high power-distance cultures sometimes feel uneasy because they expect their teachers to direct and supervise their work closely, but they may also have been taught that it would be rude and impolite to ask for the kinds of information that might allow them to be more successful.

Uncertainty Avoidance

Another concern of all cultures is how they will adapt to changes and cope with uncertainties. The future will always be unknown in some respects. This unpredictability and the resultant anxiety that inevitably occurs are basic in human experience.

Cultures differ in the extent to which they prefer and can tolerate ambiguity and, therefore, in the means they select for coping with change. Thus, all cultures differ in their perceived need to be changeable and adaptable. Hofstede refers to these variations as the uncertainty avoidance dimension, the extent to which the culture feels threatened by ambiguous, uncertain situations and tries to avoid them by establishing more structure.

At one extreme on this dimension are cultures such as those of Denmark, Jamaica, Ireland, and Singapore, which are all low in uncertainty avoidance and therefore have a high tolerance for uncertainty and ambiguity. They believe in minimizing the number of rules and rituals that govern social conduct and human behavior, in accepting and encouraging dissent among cultural members, in tolerating people who behave in ways that are considered socially deviant, and in taking risks and trying new things. Conversely, the cultures of Greece, Guatemala, Portugal, and Uruguay are among those that prefer to avoid uncertainty as a cultural value. They desire or even demand consensus about societal goals, and they do not like to tolerate dissent or allow deviation in the behaviors of cultural members. They try to ensure certainty and security through an extensive set of rules, regulations, and rituals.

Cultures must cope with the need to create a world that is more certain and predictable, and they do so by inventing rules and rituals to constrain human behaviors. Because members of high uncertainty-avoidance cultures tend to be worried about the future, they have high levels of anxiety and are highly resistant to change. They regard the uncertainties of life as a continuous threat that must be overcome. Consequently, these cultures develop many rules to control social behaviors, and they often adopt elaborate rituals and religious practices that have a precise form or sequence.

Members of low uncertainty-avoidance cultures tend to live day to day, and they are more willing to accept change and take risks. Conflict and competition are natural, dissent is acceptable, deviance is not threatening, and individual achievement is regarded as beneficial. Consequently, these cultures need few rules to control social behaviors, and they are unlikely to adopt religious rituals that require precise patterns of enactment.

Differences in level of uncertainty avoidance can result in unexpected problems in intercultural communication. For instance, European Americans tend to have a moderately low level of uncertainty avoidance. When these U.S. Americans communicate with someone from a high uncertainty-avoidance culture, such as those in Japan or France, they are likely to be seen as too nonconforming and unconventional, and they may view their Japanese or French counterparts as rigid and overly controlled. Conversely, when these U.S. Americans communicate with someone from an extremely low uncertainty-avoidance culture, such as the Irish or Swedes, they are likely to be viewed as too structured and uncompromising, whereas they may perceive their Irish or Swedish counterparts as too willing to accept dissent.

Individualism versus Collectivism

Another concern of all cultures, and a problem for which they must all find a solution, involves people's relationships to the larger social groups of which they are a part. People must live and interact together for the culture to survive. In doing so, they must develop a

CULTURE connections

All her life, in the Chinese way, April had tried to avoid conflict with her parents. She didn't want them to lose face by her marrying a Mexican American. But this correct Asian passivity was highly incorrect and even considered self-destructive in Western culture. Self-destructive didn't even exist in Asian thinking, for the self was not regarded as a separate entity.

Leslie Glass

way of relating that strikes a balance between showing concern for themselves and concern for others.

Cultures differ in the extent to which individual autonomy is regarded favorably or unfavorably. Thus, cultures vary in their tendency to encourage people to be unique and independent or conforming and interdependent. Hofstede refers to these variations as the individualism–collectivism dimension, the degree to which a culture relies on and has allegiance to the self or the group.

Highly individualistic cultures, such as the dominant cultures in Austria, Belgium, the Netherlands, and the United States, believe that people are only supposed to take care of themselves and perhaps their immediate families. In individualist cultures, the autonomy of the individual is paramount. Key words used to invoke this cultural pattern include *independence, privacy, self,* and the all-important *I.* Decisions are based on what is good for the individual, not for the group, because the person is the primary source of motivation. Similarly, a judgment about what is right or wrong can be made only from the point of view of each individual.

Cultures such as those in Guatemala, Indonesia, Pakistan, and West Africa value a collectivist orientation. They require an absolute loyalty to the group, though the relevant group might be as varied as the nuclear family, the extended family, a caste, or a jati (a subgrouping of a caste). In collectivist cultures, decisions that juxtapose the benefits to the individual and the benefits to the group are always based on what is best for the group, and the groups to which a person belongs are the most important social units. In turn, the group is expected to look out for and take care of its individual members. Consequently, collectivist cultures believe in obligations to the group, dependence of the individual on organizations and institutions, a "we" consciousness, and an emphasis on belonging.

Huge cultural differences can be explained by differences on the individualism–collectivism dimension. We have already noted that collectivistic cultures tend to be group-oriented. A related characteristic is that they typically impose a very large psychological distance between those who are members of their group (the ingroup) and those who are not (the outgroup). Ingroup members are required to have unquestioning loyalty, whereas outgroup members are regarded as almost inconsequential. Conversely, members of individualistic cultures do not perceive a large chasm between ingroup and outgroup members; ingroup members are not as close, but outgroup members are not as distant. Scholars such as Harry Triandis believe that the individualism–collectivism dimension is by far the most

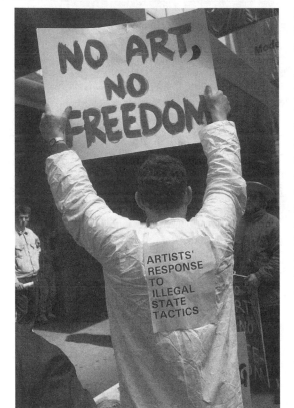

■ The preeminent status of the individual, and the individual's right to speak freely, are central characteristics of the cultural patterns of European Americans and others.

important attribute that distinguishes one culture from another[4]; thus, it has been extensively researched.

Individualist cultures train their members to speak out as a means of resolving difficulties. In classrooms, students from individualistic cultures are likely to ask questions of the teacher; students from collectivistic cultures are not. Similarly, people from individualistic cultures are more likely than those from collectivistic cultures to use confrontational strategies when dealing with interpersonal problems; those with a collectivistic orientation are likely to use avoidance, third party intermediaries, or other face-saving techniques. Indeed, a common maxim among European Americans, who are highly individualistic, is that "the squeaky wheel gets the grease" (suggesting that one should make noise in order to be rewarded); the corresponding maxim among the Japanese, who are somewhat collectivistic, is "the nail that sticks up gets pounded" (so one should always try to blend in).

Masculinity versus Femininity

A fourth concern of all cultures, and for which they must all find solutions, pertains to gender expectations and the extent to which people prefer achievement and assertiveness or nurturance and social support. Hofstede refers to these variations as the masculinity–femininity dimension. This dimension indicates the degree to which a culture values "masculine" behaviors, such as assertiveness and the acquisition of wealth, or "feminine" behaviors, such as caring for others and the quality of life.

At one extreme are masculine cultures such as those in Austria, Italy, Japan, and Mexico, which believe in achievement and ambition. In this view, people should be judged on their performance, and those who achieve have the right to display the material goods that they acquired. The people in masculine cultures also believe in ostentatious manliness, and very specific behaviors and products are associated with appropriate male behavior.

At the other extreme are feminine cultures such as those of Chile, Portugal, Sweden, and Thailand, which believe less in external achievements and shows of manliness and more in the importance of life choices that improve intrinsic aspects of the quality of life, such as service to others and sympathy for the unfortunate. People in these feminine cultures are also likely to prefer equality between the sexes, less

CULTURE connections

A powwow arena is a place for celebration by Native Indian people. It is an opportunity for Native Indian people from all parts of North America and Canada to share their music and their communal beliefs in the nature of life. As one powwow host stated before an initiation ceremony for a young girl, "This circle (the powwow arena) is the Creator's circle. It's a sacred place." For many Native Indian people, attending a powwow has the same characteristics as attending church. However, most Anglos usually cannot see the analogy. A "religious" service has different qualities for Anglos, and the celebratory atmosphere of powwows, as well as the presence of contests and vendors and grandstands, makes it difficult for many Anglos to recognize the sacred nature of what is occurring in front of them. Further, when Anglos behave inappropriately at powwows by being scantily clad or by walking into the arena to take pictures, few Native people will overtly criticize their actions. This is especially true when visitors are perceived as "guests." Numerous times I was encouraged to move ahead of Navajos when waiting in line for activities, told as they moved aside, "You're our guest." There may often be disapproving glances toward the Anglos, especially from the elderly Indians, but no direct confrontations. Except for children and some teenagers, most Native peoples at the powwows wear long pants or long skirts and do not expose their bodies unnecessarily.

—*Charles A. Braithwaite*

prescriptive role behaviors associated with each gender, and an acceptance of nurturing roles for both women and men.

Members of highly masculine cultures believe that men should be assertive and women should be nurturing. Sex roles are clearly differentiated, and sexual inequality is regarded as beneficial. The reverse is true for members of highly feminine cultures: men are far less interested in achievement, sex roles are far more fluid, and equality between the sexes is the norm.

Teachers in masculine cultures praise their best students because academic performance is rewarded highly. Similarly, male students in these masculine cultures strive to be competitive, visible, successful, and vocationally oriented. In feminine cultures, teachers rarely praise individual achievements and academic performance because social accommodation is more highly regarded. Male students try to cooperate with one another and develop a sense of solidarity, they try to behave modestly and properly, they select subjects because they are intrinsically interesting rather than vocationally rewarding, and friendliness is much more important than brilliance.

Long-Term versus Short-Term Time Orientation

A fifth concern of all cultures relates to its orientation to time. Hofstede has acknowledged that the four previously described dimensions have a Western bias, as they were

■ The *hejab,* or head scarf, is worn by many Muslim women as a statement of their cultural values.

developed by scholars from Europe or the United States who necessarily brought to their work an implicit set of assumptions and categories about the types of cultural values they would likely find. His time-orientation dimension is based on the work of Michael H. Bond, a Canadian who has lived in Asia for the past thirty years and who assembled a large team of researchers from Hong Kong and Taiwan to develop and administer a Chinese Value Survey to university students around the world.[5]

The time-orientation dimension refers to a person's point of reference about life and work. Cultures that promote a long-term orientation toward life admire persistence, thriftiness, and humility. Linguistic and social distinctions between elder and younger siblings are common, and deferred gratification of needs is widely accepted. Conversely, cultures with a short-term orientation toward changing events have an expectation of quick results following one's actions.[6] The Chinese, for example, typically have a long-term time orientation—note the tendency to mark time in year-long increments, as in the Year of the Dragon or the Year of the Dog—whereas Europeans typically have a short-term time orientation and aggregate time in month-long intervals (such as Aries, Gemini, Pisces, or Aquarius).

Indulgence versus Restraint

Recently Hofstede has included two additional dimensions to those previously described. Based on recent research, including ideas from Middle Eastern, Nordic, and Eastern European perspectives,[7] Hofstede has added the dimensions of indulgence versus restraint and monumentalism versus self-effacement.

The indulgence versus restraint dimension juxtaposes hedonism with self-discipline. Cultures high on indulgence encourage pleasure, enjoyment, spending, consumption, sexual gratification, and general merriment. Alternatively, cultures high on restraint encourage the control of such hedonistic gratifications, and the pleasures and enjoyment associated with leisure activities are discouraged.

Monumentalism versus Self-Effacement

The *monumentalism versus self-effacement* dimension juxtaposes stability with change. Cultures high on monumentalism encourage people to be like the monuments or statues that one commonly finds in parks or near government buildings: proud, unchangeable, upstanding, stable, and resolute. Alternatively, cultures high on self-effacement encourage humility, flexibility, adaptation to the situation, and feeling comfortable about life's paradoxes and inconsistencies. As Michael Minkov suggests, those from self-effacement cultures

> adapt relatively easily to foreign environments because their selves are fluid and flexible, are not overly proud of their cultural identity, and do not insist on retaining their cultural heritage. [Conversely,] people from monumentalist cultures may consider cultural adaptation a sort of treason, because they are more proud of who they are, and subscribe to the view that some self attributes, such as values and beliefs, must remain immutable. [For example,] it may be possible [for someone] to be a good meat-eating vegetarian Hindu, but there is no such thing as a decent pork-eating Muslim. A virtuous woman cannot believe in wearing a headscarf in Cairo while walking bareheaded in Paris. You must maintain the same kind of moral integrity and stability across all situations.[8]

Comparing Hofstede's Dimensions

Hofstede's foundational work has been widely cited and appropriately praised for its importance, clarity, straightforwardness, simplicity, and excellence. Each of Hofstede's dimensions provides insights into the influence of culture on the communication process. Table 5.2, which clusters the various cultures by geographic region, summarizes

TABLE 5.2 **Groupings on Hofstede's Dimensions**

Culture	Power Distance	Uncertainty Avoidance	Individualism–Collectivism	Masculinity–Femininity	Time Orientation
Anglo	**Low**	**Low**	**High**	**Medium**	**Low**
Australia	-108	-66	195	58	-53
Canada	-94	-79	154	10	-81
England	-113	-134	191	84	-74
Ireland	-145	-134	112	95	
New Zealand	-173	-75	149	42	-57
South Africa	-48	-75	91	68	
U.S.A.	-90	-87	200	63	-60
Latin Europe	**Medium**	**High**	**Medium to High**	**Low to High**	
France	39	82	116	-38	
Israel	-214	60	45	-16	
Italy	-44	35	137	105	
Malta	-16	124	66	-16	
Portugal	16	158	-67	-101	
Spain	-12	82	33	-43	

(Continued)

TABLE 5.2   (*Continued*)

Culture	Power Distance	Uncertainty Avoidance	Individualism– Collectivism	Masculinity– Femininity	Time Orientation
Nordic Europe	**Low**	**Low**	**High**	**Low**	
Denmark	-191	-184	129	-181	
Finland	-122	-32	83	-128	
Norway	-131	-70	108	-223	
Sweden	-131	-159	116	-239	-46
Germanic Europe	**Low**	**Medium**	**High**	**Low to High**	
Austria	-223	14	49	153	
Belgium	25	115	133	21	
Germany	-113	-7	99	84	-53
Luxembourg	-90	14	70	0	
Netherlands	-99	-58	154	-191	-7
Switzerland	-117	-37	104	105	
Eastern Europe	**Medium to High**	**Medium to High**	**Medium**	**Low to High**	**Low to Medium**
Bulgaria	48	77	-55	-53	
Czech Republic	-12	31	62	37	-117
Estonia	-90	-28	70	-106	
Greece	2	191	-34	37	
Hungary	-62	65	154	201	14
Poland	39	111	70	74	-50
Romania	140	98	-55	-43	
Russia	154	120	-17	-75	
Slovakia	204	-66	37	317	-29
Yugoslavia	76	90	-67	-154	
Latin America	**Medium**	**Medium to High**	**Low**	**Low to High**	
Argentina	-48	82	12	31	
Brazil	43	39	-22	-6	67
Chile	16	82	-84	-117	
Colombia	34	56	-126	74	
Costa Rica	-113	82	-118	-154	
Ecuador	85	1	-147	68	
Guatemala	163	145	-155	-69	
Jamaica	-67	-227	-17	95	
Mexico	99	65	-55	100	
Panama	163	82	-134	-32	
Peru	21	86	-113	-43	
El Salvador	30	115	-107	-53	

Culture	Power Distance	Uncertainty Avoidance	Individualism–Collectivism	Masculinity–Femininity	Time Orientation
Suriname	117	107	16	-69	
Trinidad	-58	-49	-113	42	
Uruguay	7	141	-30	-64	
Venezuela	99	39	-130	121	
Sub-Saharan Africa	**Medium**	**Low**	**Low**	**Medium**	**Low**
East Africa	21	-62	-67	-48	-74
West Africa	80	-53	-97	-22	-106
Middle East	**Medium to High**	**Medium**	**Medium**	**Medium**	
Arab countries	94	6	-22	15	
Morocco	48	6	12	15	
Turkey	30	77	-26	-27	
Southern Asia	**Medium to High**	**Low to Medium**	**Low**	**Medium**	**Low to High**
Bangladesh	94	28	-97	26	-22
India	80	-113	20	31	52
Indonesia	85	-79	-122	-22	
Iran	-7	-32	-9	-38	
Malaysia	204	-129	-72	0	
Pakistan	-21	14	-122	0	-163
Philippines	158	-96	-47	74	-96
Thailand	21	-11	-97	-85	35
Vietnam	48	-155	-97	-53	119
Confucian Asia	**Medium to High**	**Low to High**	**Low to Medium**	**Medium to High**	**High**
China	94	-155	-97	84	253
Hong Kong	39	-159	-76	37	176
Japan	-25	107	12	238	119
Singapore	66	-248	-97	-11	7
South Korea	2	77	-105	-59	102
Taiwan	-7	10	-109	-27	144

A large positive score means that the culture is high on that dimension. A large negative score means that the culture is low on that dimension. The average score is zero. Ratings are standardized scores, with the decimal point omitted.

Source: Based on data reported in Geert Hofstede, *Culture's Consequences: Comparing Values, Behaviors, Institutions, and Organizations across Nations*, 2nd ed. (Thousand Oaks, CA: Sage, 2001).

information for Hofstede's first five dimensions. Every culture, of course, forms an intricate and interrelated pattern; no one cultural dimension is sufficient to describe or understand this complexity. For each dimension in the table, we have also provided general descriptive labels (high, medium, low) to summarize the "typical" score of

those cultures within each geographic region. Note, however, that even cultures that are located very near others are not entirely similar; this range of scores underscores the importance of being cautious when making generalizations about cultures, even when they are within the same regions of the world (e.g., Latin America or the Middle East).

Cultures with similar configurations on Hofstede's dimensions would likely have similar communication patterns, and cultures that are very different from one another would probably behave dissimilarly. Hofstede's dimensions describe cultural expectations for a range of social behaviors: *power distance* refers to relationships with people higher or lower in rank, *uncertainty avoidance* to people's search for truth and certainty, *individualism–collectivism* to expected behaviors toward the group, *masculinity–femininity* to the expectations surrounding achievement and gender differences, *time orientation* to people's search for virtue and lasting ideals, *indulgence–restraint* to psychological impulse control, and *monumentalism–self-effacement* to pridefulness and adaptabillty.

■ Time management, productivity, and communication all depend on the patterns of one's culture to define their importance.

The GLOBE Cultural Taxonomy

A recent and very impressive study of differences in cultural patterns was conducted by Robert J. House and his team of more than 170 investigators.[9] This ongoing research effort is called Project GLOBE, which is an acronym for Global Leadership and Organizational Behavior Effectiveness. To date, the team has collected information from nearly 20,000 middle managers in 61 cultures. Individuals were asked to describe both the cultural *practices*—what is, or what people actually do—and the cultural *values*—what should be, or what is regarded as ideal—in their cultures.

The GLOBE research program builds on Hofstede's work and on that of Kluckhohn and Strodtbeck (which is described in the previous chapter). Nine dimensions are used to describe the dominant patterns of a culture: power distance, uncertainty avoidance, in-group collectivism, institutional collectivism, gender egalitarianism, assertiveness, performance orientation, future orientation, and humane orientation. The first six GLOBE dimensions are based on the work of Hofstede. The dimensions of power distance and uncertainty avoidance are identical in the two taxonomies. Hofstede's individualism–collectivism dimension has been separated into two GLOBE components: in-group collectivism and institutional collectivism.

Similarly, Hofstede's masculinity–femininity dimension has been divided into two components: gender egalitarianism and assertiveness. The remaining three GLOBE dimensions are based on the work of Kluckhohn and Strodtbeck. The GLOBE's performance orientation dimension relates to Kluckhohn and Strodtbeck's world-orientation dimension. The future orientation dimension is based on Kluckhohn and Strodtbeck's concept of time and the distinction among past-, present-, and future-oriented cultures. The GLOBE's humane orientation dimension is anchored in Kluckhohn and Strodtbeck's view of human nature, especially their distinction that cultures may regard humans on a continuum ranging from inherently "good" to inherently "bad." Table 5.3 provides the nine cultural dimensions studied in the

TABLE 5.3 GLOBE Dimensions and Cultural Characteristics

Dimension	Cultural Characteristics	Sample Items
Power Distance	The degree to which people believe that power should be stratified, unequally shared, and concentrated at higher levels of an organization or government.	Followers are (should be) expected to obey their leaders without question.
Uncertainty Avoidance	The extent to which people strive to avoid uncertainty by relying on social norms, rules, rituals, and bureaucratic practices to alleviate the unpredictability of future events.	Most people lead (should lead) highly structured lives with few unexpected events.
In-Group Collectivism	The degree to which people express pride, loyalty, and cohesiveness in their families.	Employees feel (should feel) great loyalty toward this organization.
Institutional Collectivism	The degree to which a culture's institutional practices encourage collective actions and the collective distribution of resources.	Leaders encourage (should encourage) group loyalty even if individual goals suffer.
Gender Egalitarianism	The extent to which people minimize gender role differences and gender discrimination while promoting gender equality.	Boys are encouraged (should be encouraged) more than girls to attain a higher education. (scored inversely)
Assertiveness	The degree to which people are assertive, confrontational, and aggressive in social relationships.	People are (should be) generally dominant in their relationships with each other.
Performance Orientation	The extent to which people encourage others to improve their task-oriented performance and excel.	Students are encouraged (should be encouraged) to strive for continuously improved performance.
Future Orientation	The degree to which people engage in future-oriented behaviors such as planning, investing in the future, and delaying gratification.	Most people live (should live) in the present rather than for the future. (scored inversely)
Humane Orientation	The degree to which people encourage others to be fair, altruistic, friendly, generous, caring, and kind.	Most people are (should be) generally very tolerant of mistakes.

Adapted from: Robert J. House, Paul J. Hanges, Mansour Javidan, Peter W. Dorfman, and Vipin Gupta (eds.), *Culture, Leadership, and Organizations: The GLOBE Study of 62 Societies* (Thousand Oaks, CA: Sage, 2004).

CULTURE connections

Balinese culture is one of the most methodical systems of social and religious organization on earth, a magnificent beehive of tasks and role and ceremonies. The Balinese are *lodged*, completely held, within an elaborate lattice of customs. A combination of several factors created this network but basically we can say that Bali is what happens when the lavish rituals of traditional Hinduism are superimposed over a vast rice-growing agricultural society that operates, by necessity, with elaborate communal cooperation. Rice terraces require an unbelievable amount of shared labor, maintenance and engineering in order to prosper, so each Balinese village has a *banjar*—a united organization of citizens who administer, through consensus, the village's political and economic and religious and agricultural decisions. In Bali, the collective is absolutely more important than the individual, or nobody eats.

—*Elizabeth Gilbert*

GLOBE research, their cultural characteristics, and sample items. The information in this table provides a useful reference guide to help you understand the GLOBE ideas more easily.

Power Distance

As Hofstede suggested, one of the basic concerns of all cultures is the issue of human inequality. Cultures differ in the extent to which they view status inequalities as desirable or undesirable. Thus *power distance* refers to the degree to which cultures believe that social and political power should be distributed disproportionately, shared unequally, and concentrated among a few top decision makers.

High power-distance cultures, such as those in France, Argentina, and Nigeria, believe it is very appropriate to have differences among social classes. Upward mobility ought to be limited, because people already occupy their correct places in the social hierarchy. The decisions of the powerful authorities should be met with unchallenged acceptance.

Conversely, low power-distance cultures like those in Australia, Denmark, and Albania believe it is important to minimize or even eliminate social class differences. Upward mobility is high, because an equal opportunity for each person is an overriding goal. Questioning and challenging the decisions of authorities is regarded as each person's duty and responsibility, as only through such challenges will social and political power be used well.

Uncertainty Avoidance

All cultures need to have some degree of predictability in their social worlds. While complete certainty can never be achieved, humans could not survive in a world of total and chaotic uncertainty. Thus cultures vary in the degree of predictability they prefer. These variations constitute the *uncertainty avoidance* dimension, which is the extent to which cultures feel threatened by the unpredictability of the future and therefore try to establish more structure in the form of rules, regulations, rituals, and mandatory practices.

Cultures such as those in Sweden, Switzerland, and China are relatively high on uncertainty avoidance. Therefore, they prefer to avoid uncertainty as a cultural value, desire or even demand consensus about societal goals, and do not tolerate dissent or allow deviation in the behaviors of cultural members. They try to ensure certainty and security through an extensive set of instructions about how one ought to behave. As a result, cultures that are high on uncertainty avoidance prefer to develop many ways to control people's social behaviors. These controls exist as formal regulations and as informal rules about acceptable conduct, and they also include elaborate rituals and religious practices that have a precise form or sequence.

Cultures such as those in Russia, Bolivia, and South Korea are relatively low on uncertainty avoidance. They, therefore, have a higher tolerance for uncertainty and ambiguity and are much more comfortable with the unpredictability of life. Consequently, rules and regulations are kept to a minimum, dissent is tolerated, and deviance is more likely to be regarded as peculiar or eccentric rather than as threatening.

In-Group Collectivism

The in-group collectivism dimension is similar to what Hofstede calls individualism–collectivism. Individualistic cultures have low in-group collectivism, whereas collectivistic cultures rate high on this dimension.

In-group collectivism reflects the degree to which people express pride, loyalty, and solidarity with their family or similar group. In cultures with high in-group collectivism, individuals take pride in and define their sense of self—quite literally, their sense of who they are—in terms of their family or similar group. That is, people's identities within collectivistic cultures are closely tied to their ingroups, and strong group memberships are both required and desired. As the African saying suggests, in collectivist cultures, "I am because we are." Representative cultures that are high on in-group collectivism include those in Georgia, Morocco, and the Philippines.

In individualistic cultures—those that are low on in-group collectivism—the independence and autonomy of the individual is an overriding feature. People's identities within individualistic cultures are separate from, and perhaps very distant from, those of the group. Group membership is often regarded as voluntary, and allegiance with one's ingroup—even with one's family—is not expected to be overly strong. Included in this category are such cultures as those in New Zealand, Finland, and the Netherlands.

Institutional Collectivism

Another aspect of the dimension that Hofstede called individualism–collectivism is concerned with the basis upon which decisions are made and the group's resources are allocated. The dimension of institutional collectivism represents the degree to which cultures support, value, and prefer to distribute rewards based on group versus individual interests.

In cultures that are high on institutional collectivism, decisions that juxtapose the benefits to the group with the benefits to the individual nearly always base the decision on what is best for the group. Thus, in cultures like those in Qatar and Japan, group activities are typically preferred to individual actions.

In cultures that are low on institutional collectivism, decisions are based on what is good for the individual, with little regard for the group. Because the person is the primary

CULTURE connections

"For you, it's all about how you stand out. Who is the smartest, the richest, the best. For us, it's all about blending in. Like the patches that make up a quilt. One by one, we're not much to look at. But put us together, and you've got something wonderful."

—Jodi Picoult

source of motivation, individual autonomy and actions tend to dominate. Thus, in Italy and Greece, decisions are based on individual merit rather than on collective involvement.

Gender Egalitarianism

If you carefully read the description of Hofstede's masculinity–femininity dimension, you will note that it combines two related attributes that, in the GLOBE project, have been separated into separate dimensions: a belief in equality between women and men and a preference for forceful assertiveness. The first of these attributes is called gender egalitarianism and is the extent to which a culture minimizes differences in gender expectations for men versus women.

Cultures such as those in Hungary and Poland, which are near the midpoint of the gender egalitarianism dimension, believe that gender equality is preferred, that men and women

■ Within Japanese culture, which is high on institutional collectivism, there is often a very strong identification with one's work group. Here, a group of Japanese businesspeople collectively share a group moment.

■ Gender egalitarianism, which minimizes differences among men and women, is evident in this conversation between two businesspeople.

should be treated in the same way, and that unequal treatment solely because of one's biological sex or gender constitutes discrimination and should not occur. Conversely, cultures like those in Austria and Egypt, which are low in gender egalitarianism, engage in unequal treatment of men and women. In this view, there are inherent differences between men and women, and these differences require dissimilar expectations and treatments. Rather than regarding these fundamental differences negatively, cultures that are low on gender egalitarianism view the divergence in gender roles and expectations as normal and natural.

Assertiveness

Another concern of all cultures, which also requires every culture to find a solution, pertains to the cultural preference for dominance and forcefulness or nurturance and social support. This assertiveness dimension describes the extent to which people value and prefer tough aggressiveness or tender nonaggressiveness.

Cultures high on the assertiveness dimension value strength, success, and taking the initiative. Competition is good, winning is desirable, and rewards should go to those who are victorious. People are encouraged to be competitive, visible, and successful. Representative cultures include those in Germany and Hong Kong.

Conversely, cultures low on the assertiveness dimension value modesty, tenderness, warm relationships, and cooperation. Competition is bad, a win–lose orientation is unacceptable, and rewards should be shared among all. Nurturance and social support are important, as are modesty, cooperation with others, and a sense of solidarity. Friendliness is much more important than brilliance. Typical of this orientation are the cultures in Kuwait and Thailand.

Performance Orientation

The degree to which a culture encourages and rewards people for their accomplishments is called the performance orientation dimension. Depending on the culture, some people might be regarded as superior to others because of who they are—the "correct" family background, age, gender, birth order, or school—whereas others may acquire status based on personal achievements such as the amount of education, success in business, physical strength, occupation, or a wide variety of other characteristics.

In high performance-oriented cultures, such as those in Canada and Singapore, status is based on what a person has accomplished. Schooling and education are critical to one's success, people are expected to demonstrate some initiative in work-related tasks, and expectations are high. Conversely, in low performance-oriented cultures, like those in Colombia and Guatemala, status is based on who you are. Attending the "right" school is important, as are family connections, seniority, loyalty, and tradition.

An important component of performance orientation is people's preferred relationship to the natural and spiritual world. As Kluckhohn and Strodtbeck suggested in the previous chapter, some cultures view nature as something to be conquered and controlled, others see themselves as living in harmony with nature, and still others view themselves as subjugated to nature.

High performance-oriented cultures assert their dominance over nature, and they try to shape the world to fit their needs. Getting the job done is far more important than maintaining effective relationships, for what really matters is the task-related results that show what someone has accomplished. People in high performance-oriented cultures value competitiveness, assertiveness, and achievement. In contrast, people in low performance-oriented cultures feel more controlled by nature and want to live in harmony with the natural and spiritual environment. Maintaining effective relationships is more important in such cultures than is getting the job done; what matters most are cooperation, integrity, and loyalty.

Another important distinction related to performance orientation is Edward Hall's concept of low-context versus high-context messages, which we discussed earlier. High performance-oriented cultures tend to be low-context; they prefer to use messages that are clear, explicit, and direct. They also have a monochronic approach to time; time is valuable and limited, events are sequential, and punctuality is preferred. Conversely, low performance-oriented cultures use high-context messages more often; their intent is to avoid direct confrontations and maintain harmony in their relationships.

Future Orientation

Locating one's world in time—and thereby giving structure, coherence, and significance to events—creates order and meaning in people's lives. The extent to which a culture plans for forthcoming events is the future orientation dimension. Related slightly to Hofstede's long-term dimension and very directly to Kluckhohn and Strodtbeck's ideas on time orientation (see Chapter 4), the future orientation dimension describes the degree to which cultures advocate long-term planning and deferred gratification or the deeply felt satisfaction that comes from experiencing the simple pleasures of the present moment.

Cultures differ, of course, in the extent to which they prefer to focus on the future rather than on the spontaneity of the present. Those high in future orientation, such as Iran and Hong Kong, believe that current pleasures are less important than future benefits, so they believe in planning, self-control, and activities that have a delayed impact. Cultures

CULTURE connections

"You don't understand," she said. "You think a woman feels bad if she's exchanged for cows or money. But if there's no exchange she feels worth nothing. I cost my husband *ten* cows. I had a good education from Irish nuns in Mbarara. I speak English and can run a business. My father spent money on me, why give me away for nothing? Our families keep accounts of what girls cost to feed and clothe and educate, that way they can show a daughter is valuable to a young man's family. You want a healthy, educated bride—OK, you pay for it!"

—Dervla Murphy

like those in Portugal and Venezuela are low in future orientation and thus prefer to enjoy fully the experiences currently under way; they like to live "in the moment" and are less constrained by doubts about the past or concerns about the future.

People from cultures that are high in future orientation want to save money and other resources. They believe in strategic planning, and they value economic success. People from cultures that are low in future orientation are more likely to spend now rather than save for later. They view material and spiritual achievements as opposing goals, and they prefer the latter.

Humane Orientation

The final GLOBE dimension, humane orientation, refers to the extent to which cultures encourage and reward their members for being benevolent and compassionate toward others or are concerned with self-interest and self-gratification.

Cultures high in humane orientation value expressions of kindness, generosity, caring, and compassion, and people who express social support for others are admired. Members of humane-oriented cultures are expected to help others financially and emotionally, to share information that others may need, to spend time with others, and to offer empathy and love. Representative cultures include Zambia and Indonesia.

Cultures low in humane orientation value comfort, pleasure, satisfaction, and personal enjoyment. People from low humane-orientation cultures are expected to confront personal problems by themselves, and they are concerned primarily with individual gratification. Typical of this orientation are the cultures of Spain and white South Africa.

Comparing the GLOBE Dimensions

As we suggested in Chapter 4, cultural patterns represent a universal social choice that must be made by each culture and that is learned from the family and throughout the social institutions of a culture: in the degree to which children are encouraged to have their own desires and motivations, in the solidarity and unity expected in the family, in the role models that are presented, and throughout the range of messages that are conveyed.

Table 5.4 provides information on each of the GLOBE *practices* for sixty-one countries. Table 5.5 provides this information for each of the GLOBE *values*. The regional

TABLE 5.4   Groupings on the GLOBE Dimensions: Actual Practices

Culture	Power Distance	Uncertainty Avoidance	In-Group Collectivism	Institutional Collectivism	Gender Egalitarianism	Assertiveness	Performance Orientation	Future Orientation	Humane Orientation
Anglo									
Australia	-1.02	0.38	-1.33	0.10	-1.61	0.35	0.52	0.65	0.39
Canada (English)	-0.84	0.69	-1.21	0.32	-0.81	-0.28	1.28	0.98	0.83
England	-0.06	0.81	-1.45	0.05	-0.89	0.00	0.93	-0.05	-0.78
Ireland	-0.06	0.23	-0.01	0.92	-2.13	-0.63	0.28	0.65	1.81
New Zealand	-0.67	0.98	-2.01	1.35	-2.10	-2.01	-0.82	1.56	0.48
South Africa (white)	-0.04	-0.12	-0.88	0.89	-1.96	1.23	0.61	0.03	-1.26
USA (white)	-0.70	-0.02	-1.22	-0.12	-1.78	1.10	0.65	0.98	0.16
Latin Europe									
France	1.18	0.44	-0.67	-0.12	-0.97	0.79	-0.24	0.83	-1.45
Israel	-1.05	-0.25	-0.61	0.51	-2.18	0.22	0.00	-0.05	0.02
Italy	0.59	-0.62	-0.28	-1.36	-2.04	-0.22	-1.30	-1.31	-0.97
Portugal	0.61	-0.42	0.49	-0.79	-0.91	-1.37	-0.30	-1.26	-0.38
Spain	0.80	-0.32	0.41	-0.96	-2.66	0.74	-0.74	-0.23	-1.62
Switzerland (French)	-0.74	1.36	-1.77	-0.07	-1.56	-1.87	0.91	0.38	-0.34
Nordic Europe									
Denmark	-3.02	1.76	-2.20	1.32	-0.19	-0.30	1.28	0.30	0.73
Finland	-0.67	1.43	-1.47	0.92	-1.75	-0.28	0.85	-0.73	-0.28
Sweden	-0.77	1.92	-2.03	2.33	-0.43	-2.12	1.17	-0.96	0.02
Germanic Europe									
Austria	-0.53	1.66	-0.41	0.12	-2.45	1.29	1.32	0.86	-0.78
Germany (prev. East)	0.85	1.66	-0.86	-1.65	-2.53	1.59	0.22	-0.03	-1.45
Germany (prev. West)	0.17	1.76	-1.54	-1.10	-2.42	1.10	0.91	0.38	-1.91
Netherlands	-2.50	0.89	-1.97	0.51	-1.35	0.46	1.65	0.55	-0.49
Switzerland	-0.65	2.01	-1.60	-0.45	-2.77	0.99	1.91	2.12	-1.03

Culture	Power Distance	Uncertainty Avoidance	In-Group Collectivism	Institutional Collectivism	Gender Egalitarianism	Assertiveness	Performance Orientation	Future Orientation	Humane Orientation
Eastern Europe									
Albania	-1.31	0.68	0.80	0.70	-0.78	2.03	0.02	1.79	1.14
Georgia	0.10	-1.10	1.42	-0.52	-1.21	0.08	-0.95	-0.55	0.18
Greece	0.52	-1.28	0.16	-2.40	-1.40	1.18	-0.97	-2.27	-1.57
Hungary	0.90	-1.73	0.14	-1.72	0.22	1.75	-1.39	-1.69	-1.55
Kazakhstan	0.31	-0.84	0.15	0.10	-0.43	0.85	-0.61	-1.33	-0.21
Poland	-0.18	-0.90	0.50	0.68	0.05	-0.25	-1.60	-0.53	-1.01
Russia	0.80	-2.13	0.65	0.60	0.19	-1.29	-2.10	-1.79	-0.32
Slovenia	0.36	-0.64	0.38	-0.28	-0.11	-0.41	-0.56	-1.11	-0.63
Latin America									
Argentina	1.08	-0.85	0.49	-1.41	-1.37	0.19	-1.67	-1.13	-0.21
Bolivia	-1.56	-1.35	0.44	-0.50	-1.21	-0.99	-0.52	-1.23	-0.09
Brazil	0.36	-0.93	0.04	-1.00	-1.86	0.13	-0.09	-0.15	-0.91
Colombia	0.90	-0.98	0.79	-1.05	-0.39	0.13	-1.26	-0.40	-0.78
Costa Rica	-1.02	-0.57	0.23	-0.76	-1.18	-1.10	-0.54	0.05	0.62
Ecuador	0.26	-0.80	0.90	-0.84	-2.50	-0.17	-0.24	0.25	1.17
El Salvador	1.18	-0.90	0.27	-1.29	-2.26	1.29	-0.11	-0.96	-0.80
Guatemala	0.99	-1.43	0.65	-1.32	-2.64	-0.72	-1.32	-0.73	-0.42
Mexico	0.10	0.03	0.76	-0.45	-0.97	0.82	0.04	0.00	-0.24
Venezuela	0.52	-1.20	0.52	-0.69	-1.02	0.49	-1.08	-1.96	0.33
Sub-Saharan Africa									
Namibia	0.26	0.06	-0.86	-0.28	-0.32	-0.66	-0.78	-1.08	-0.28
Nigeria	1.46	0.21	0.55	-0.26	-2.66	1.04	0.52	-0.45	0.02
South Africa (black)	-3.02	0.71	-0.08	0.34	-0.91	0.57	1.71	1.41	0.52
Zambia	0.31	-0.10	0.94	0.87	-3.07	-0.22	-0.50	0.15	2.38
Zimbabwe	1.15	-0.02	0.57	-0.31	-2.58	-0.25	-0.17	0.35	0.75

(Continued)

TABLE 5.4 (Continued)

Culture	Power Distance	Uncertainty Avoidance	In-Group Collectivism	Institutional Collectivism	Gender Egalitarianism	Assertiveness	Performance Orientation	Future Orientation	Humane Orientation
Middle East									
Egypt	-0.60	-0.17	0.67	0.60	-3.20	-0.66	0.02	0.43	1.33
Kuwait	-0.13	0.08	0.89	0.58	-3.82	-1.43	-1.28	-0.38	0.89
Morocco	2.25	-0.35	1.66	-0.16	-2.48	1.01	-1.28	0.53	0.89
Qatar	-0.30	0.16	-0.11	1.28	-0.38	0.66	0.50	-0.86	1.46
Turkey	0.92	-0.88	0.99	-0.52	-2.99	1.04	-0.24	-0.68	-0.32
Southern Asia									
India	0.69	-0.02	1.05	0.32	-2.96	-1.16	0.74	0.38	1.00
Indonesia	0.01	-0.40	0.72	0.05	-1.99	-0.80	0.02	0.10	1.25
Iran	0.59	-0.82	1.20	-0.88	-2.72	-0.30	-0.32	1.21	0.29
Malaysia	-0.02	1.03	0.49	0.87	-1.32	-0.77	1.58	0.60	1.63
Philippines	0.61	-0.45	1.65	0.29	-0.97	-0.39	0.65	0.28	2.15
Thailand	1.06	-0.39	0.75	-0.52	-1.75	-1.40	-0.91	-0.43	1.50
Confucian Asia									
China	-0.32	1.29	0.89	1.25	-2.56	-1.07	-0.22	0.88	0.56
Hong Kong	-0.51	0.26	0.23	-0.28	-1.43	1.43	0.39	1.76	-0.40
Japan	-0.16	-0.15	-0.71	2.26	-2.18	-1.54	0.95	0.30	0.43
Singapore	-0.44	1.91	0.67	1.56	-0.81	0.05	2.64	2.01	-1.26
South Korea	1.01	-1.02	0.53	2.28	-4.04	0.68	0.26	1.13	-0.59
Taiwan	0.01	-0.20	0.60	0.12	-2.91	-0.63	-0.43	0.43	-0.57

A large positive score means that the culture is high on that *practices* dimension. A large negative score means that the culture is low on that *practices* dimension. The average score is zero. Ratings are standardized scores, with the decimal point omitted. For the Gender Egalitarianism dimension, a large positive score means that the cultural practices are feminine. A large negative score means that the cultural practices are masculine. A score of zero indicates egalitarianism.

Source: Based on data reported in Robert J. House, Paul J. Hanges, Mansour Javidan, Peter W. Dorfman, and Vipin Gupta (eds.), *Culture, Leadership, and Organizations: The Globe Study of 62 Societies* (Thousand Oaks, CA: Sage, 2004).

TABLE 5.5 Groupings on the GLOBE Dimensions: Ideal Values

Culture	Power Distance	Uncertainty Avoidance	In-Group Collectivism	Institutional Collectivism	Gender Egalitarianism	Assertiveness	Performance Orientation	Future Orientation	Humane Orientation
Anglo									
Australia	0.13	-1.07	0.21	-0.68	2.16	-0.03	-0.85	-0.20	0.68
Canada (English)	-0.10	-1.44	0.81	-1.14	2.35	0.48	-0.36	0.59	0.94
England	0.19	-0.86	-0.35	-0.86	2.47	-0.19	-1.07	-0.17	0.02
Ireland	-0.07	-1.00	0.18	-0.30	2.41	0.24	-0.68	0.08	0.19
New Zealand	2.31	-0.87	2.39	-1.08	0.49	-0.44	0.97	0.86	-2.54
South Africa (white)	-0.28	0.06	0.65	-0.72	1.27	-0.21	0.39	0.83	0.99
USA (white)	0.33	-1.03	0.26	-1.14	2.24	0.74	-0.46	0.56	0.46
Latin Europe									
France	0.07	0.02	0.57	1.06	1.50	-0.68	-0.36	0.44	2.13
Israel	-0.05	-0.42	0.21	-0.94	1.50	-0.10	-0.61	-0.62	0.85
Italy	-0.77	-0.27	0.12	0.78	1.85	-0.01	1.00	0.35	0.68
Portugal	-1.03	-0.33	0.73	1.12	2.39	-0.38	-0.17	1.34	-0.51
Spain	-1.38	0.20	0.32	0.92	1.73	0.26	0.32	-0.47	1.16
Switzerland (French)	0.19	-1.31	-0.90	-0.86	1.46	-0.07	-1.70	0.08	0.85
Nordic Europe									
Denmark	0.07	-1.33	-0.48	-1.10	2.28	-0.66	-2.85	-1.04	0.10
Finland	-0.80	-1.28	-0.70	-1.26	0.99	0.12	-1.05	0.47	1.69
Sweden	-0.10	-1.68	1.01	-1.60	2.43	-0.33	-1.48	-0.47	0.99
Germanic Europe									
Austria	-0.86	-1.59	-1.12	-0.02	1.75	-1.53	-0.95	0.44	1.47
Germany (prev. East)	-0.13	-1.13	-1.26	-0.12	1.90	-0.90	-0.66	0.41	0.06
Germany (prev. West)	-0.57	-2.14	-1.37	0.16	1.88	-1.11	-1.58	0.17	0.15
Netherlands	-0.83	-2.27	-1.39	-0.38	2.09	-1.22	-1.05	-1.40	-1.00
Switzerland	-0.86	-2.40	-2.03	-0.10	1.94	-0.93	-1.73	0.08	0.50

(Continued)

TABLE 5.5 (Continued)

Culture	Power Distance	Uncertainty Avoidance	In-Group Collectivism	Institutional Collectivism	Gender Egalitarianism	Assertiveness	Performance Orientation	Future Orientation	Humane Orientation
Eastern Europe									
Albania	2.28	1.19	-1.26	-0.60	0.40	0.87	-0.19	-0.98	-0.38
Georgia	0.30	0.98	-0.04	-1.82	-0.57	0.78	0.12	-0.80	0.76
Greece	-1.01	0.74	-0.59	1.32	1.88	-1.31	-0.75	-0.44	-0.87
Hungary	-0.71	0.04	-0.37	-0.48	1.33	-0.72	0.49	0.02	0.24
Kazakhstan	1.20	-0.35	-0.65	-1.40	1.58	0.02	-1.09	-1.64	0.85
Poland	1.12	0.12	0.18	-1.04	1.10	0.11	-0.73	0.50	-0.56
Russia	-0.34	0.71	0.32	-1.70	0.38	-1.50	-0.05	-1.25	0.72
Slovenia	-0.48	0.58	0.10	-0.72	1.75	1.14	-0.19	1.37	-0.78
Latin America									
Argentina	-1.18	0.04	1.31	1.16	2.07	-0.87	0.68	1.19	0.68
Bolivia	1.96	0.10	0.90	0.72	1.58	-0.15	0.32	0.29	-1.57
Brazil	-1.12	0.58	-1.45	1.76	2.09	-1.38	0.46	0.53	1.12
Colombia	-2.02	0.56	1.59	1.28	2.11	-0.60	0.44	1.40	0.81
Costa Rica	-0.45	-0.09	1.12	0.88	1.35	0.33	-0.73	-0.17	-1.92
Ecuador	-1.27	0.85	0.37	1.34	1.25	-0.27	0.29	-0.01	-0.73
El Salvador	-0.16	1.11	2.33	1.82	1.39	-0.32	1.17	1.89	0.15
Guatemala	-1.12	0.40	1.28	0.98	1.12	-0.29	1.00	0.56	-0.73
Mexico	0.33	1.02	0.76	0.36	1.54	-0.06	0.88	0.62	-1.44
Venezuela	-1.30	1.02	1.37	1.30	1.73	-0.75	0.71	1.19	-0.51
Sub-Saharan Africa									
Namibia	-0.42	0.80	1.09	-0.72	0.53	0.12	1.51	1.34	-0.12
Nigeria	-0.13	1.57	-0.54	0.58	0.51	-0.90	1.31	0.95	1.25
South Africa (black)	2.66	0.25	-1.89	-0.88	0.55	-0.01	-0.73	-3.12	-1.57
Zambia	-0.89	0.06	0.26	0.00	0.66	0.83	0.97	0.86	0.46
Zimbabwe	-0.19	0.15	0.48	0.26	0.97	1.16	1.39	1.49	-1.04

Culture	Power Distance	Uncertainty Avoidance	In-Group Collectivism	Institutional Collectivism	Gender Egalitarianism	Assertiveness	Performance Orientation	Future Orientation	Humane Orientation
Middle East									
Egypt	1.47	1.18	-0.32	0.22	-1.73	-0.83	0.73	-0.17	-1.13
Kuwait	1.26	0.22	-0.68	0.82	-1.16	-0.10	0.58	0.23	-1.61
Morocco	1.09	1.84	0.98	1.20	0.15	-0.22	2.02	0.50	0.37
Qatar	1.44	0.30	-0.21	0.78	-1.31	-0.04	1.02	0.02	-0.56
Turkey	-0.95	0.06	0.26	1.04	1.06	-1.76	0.80	-1.70	0.41
Southern Asia									
India	-0.28	0.15	-0.98	-0.06	1.08	1.40	0.24	0.29	-0.65
Indonesia	-1.03	0.97	-0.01	0.88	-0.23	1.34	0.49	-0.68	-1.17
Iran	0.19	1.18	0.51	1.60	-0.53	1.75	0.83	0.38	0.81
Malaysia	0.68	0.40	0.48	0.26	-0.46	1.47	0.95	0.26	0.37
Philippines	-0.05	0.82	1.39	0.08	1.23	1.97	1.05	1.07	-0.29
Thailand	0.36	1.58	0.23	0.72	0.34	-0.53	1.70	-0.65	-1.83
Confucian Asia									
China	1.06	1.05	-1.62	-0.36	-0.68	2.42	-1.87	-0.86	-0.47
Hong Kong	1.47	-0.01	-1.56	-0.64	0.74	1.47	0.00	-0.95	-0.47
Japan	0.36	-0.50	-1.15	-1.50	0.70	3.02	-0.61	-2.37	-0.07
Singapore	0.89	-0.68	-0.48	-0.33	1.08	0.87	0.02	-0.71	1.60
South Korea	-0.54	0.06	-0.73	-1.63	0.46	-0.12	0.46	-2.12	0.76
Taiwan	0.10	1.10	-0.62	0.82	0.13	-1.38	-0.73	-0.65	-0.73

A large positive score means that the culture is high on that *values* dimension. A large negative score means that the culture is low on that *values* dimension. The average score is zero. Ratings are standardized scores, with the decimal point omitted. For the Gender Egalitarianism dimension, a large positive score means that the cultural ideal is feminine. A large negative score means that the cultural ideal is masculine. A score of zero indicates the cultural ideal is egalitarian.

Source: Based on data reported in Robert J. House, Paul J. Hanges, Mansour Javidan, Peter W. Dorfman, and Vipin Gupta (eds.), *Culture, Leadership, and Organizations: The Globe Study of 62 Societies* (Thousand Oaks, CA: Sage, 2004).

groupings of the countries in the table reflect the analytical work of the GLOBE research team, which supports the appropriateness of these clusters of nations. Thus the tables organize the countries in the GLOBE studies by geographic areas and provide their scores on the GLOBE dimensions. With the exception of the gender egalitarianism dimension, large positive scores mean that the culture is high on that dimension, and large negative scores mean that the culture is low on that dimension. The gender egalitarian dimension requires you to do a different kind of interpretation of the information, because a score close to zero indicates a gender egalitarian culture, and a large negative score represents a culture that is very masculine in its orientation.

The GLOBE research helps to clarify our understanding of cultural patterns in two ways. First, it separates cultural practices—the ways that people typically behave in everyday communication interactions—from cultural values, or what people regard as important and believe is ideal. One might expect, of course, that practices and values are similar, but they are not always so. Sometimes, when a culture's practices are "extreme" on a dimension, the preferred ideal is that it be less so. In Spain, for example, power distance is very high, but the "ideal" or preferred power distance is low. In Nordic European cultures, institutional collectivism is uniformly low, but the ideal is that it should be much higher. In China, in-group collectivism is high, but the preference is for it to be much lower. Throughout Germanic Europe, assertiveness is typically high, but people's ideal is that it should be lower. In Egypt and Kuwait, humane orientation is high, but people would like it to be lower. Thus, in many cultures and in many ways, there is a tension between what *is* and what *should be*.

Second, the GLOBE research helps to explain the complex nature of cultural patterns. By providing updated information on a wide range of cultures, by refining the distinctions that differentiate among cultures, and by revising and expanding the cultural dimensions that are relevant, this effort substantially increases our understanding of cultures and of intercultural communication. To provide just one example of the usefulness of the expanded GLOBE dimensions, consider the Japanese practices for institutional collectivism and for in-group collectivism. Whereas the Japanese are extremely high in institutional collectivism, they are somewhat below the average for in-group collectivism. That is, decisions in Japan are most often made, and resources among the Japanese are typically distributed, in a very collectivist fashion, but the collective group for the Japanese—that is, the group with which people identify most closely—is not necessarily the family but rather the organization, the nation, or some other social unit. New Zealanders, Swedes, and Danes, among others, have patterns on these dimensions that are similar to the Japanese; Greeks, Guatemalans, Colombians, and others have the opposite pattern.

Cultural Taxonomies and Intercultural Competence

The major lesson in this chapter is that cultures vary systematically in their choices about solutions to basic human problems. The taxonomies offer lenses through which cultural variations can be understood and appreciated, rather than negatively evaluated and disregarded. The categories in these taxonomies can help you to describe the fundamental aspects of cultures. As frames of reference, they provide mechanisms to understand all intercultural communication events. In any intercultural encounter, people may be communicating from very different perceptions of what is "reality," what is "good," and what is "correct" behavior. The competent intercultural communicator must recognize that cultural variations in addressing basic human issues such as social relations, emphasis on self or group, and preferences for verbal or nonverbal code usage will always be a factor in intercultural communication.

The taxonomies allow you to use culture-specific knowledge to improve intercultural competence. First, begin by seeking out information about the cultural patterns of those individuals with whom you engage in intercultural communication. To assist your understanding of the culture, select one of the taxonomies presented and seek information that allows you to create a profile of the culture's preferred choices. Libraries and the Internet are natural starting places for this kind of knowledge. So, too, are representatives of the culture. Engage them in conversation as you try to understand their culture. Most people welcome questions from a genuinely curious person. Be systematic in your search for information by using the categories thoroughly. Think about the interrelatedness of the various aspects of the culture's patterns.

Second, study the patterns of your own culture. Because you take your beliefs, values, norms, and social practices for granted, stepping outside of your cultural patterns by researching them is very useful. You might want to describe the preferences of your own culture by using one of the taxonomies.

The third step requires only a willingness to reflect on your personal preferences. Do your beliefs, values, norms, and social practices match those of the typical person in your culture? How do your choices coincide with and differ from the general cultural description?

Finally, mentally consider your own preferences by juxtaposing them with the description of the typical person from another culture. Note the similarities and differences in beliefs, values, norms, and social practices. Can you predict where misinterpretations may occur because of contrasting assumptions about what is important and good? For example, the European American who shares the culture's preference for directness would inevitably encounter difficulties in communication with a typical member of the Japanese culture or a typical Latino cultural member. Similarly, knowing that you value informality, and usually act accordingly, can help you to monitor your expressions when communicating with someone from a culture that prefers formality. Viewing time as linear often causes problems in communication with people from cultures with other orientations to time. Interpretations of behavior as "late," "inattentive," or "disrespectful," rather than just "different," can produce alternative ways of viewing the ticking of the clock.

Summary

This chapter discussed three important taxonomies that can be used to describe cultural variations. Edward Hall placed cultures on a continuum from high context to low context. High-context cultures prefer messages in which most of the meaning is either implied by the physical setting or is presumed to be part of the individual's internalized beliefs, values, norms, and social practices; low-context cultures prefer messages in which the information is contained within the explicit code.

Geert Hofstede described seven dimensions along which dominant patterns of a culture can be ordered: power distance, uncertainty avoidance, individualism–collectivism, masculinity–femininity, time orientation, indulgence–restraint, and monumentalism–self-effacement. The power-distance dimension assesses the degree to which the culture believes that institutional power should be distributed equally or unequally. The uncertainty avoidance dimension describes the extent to which cultures prefer and can tolerate ambiguity and change. The individualism–collectivism dimension describes the degree to which a culture relies on and has allegiance to the self or the group. The masculinity femininity dimension indicates the degree to which a culture values assertiveness and "manliness" or caring for others and the quality of life. The time-orientation dimension refers to a long-term versus short-term orientation toward life and work. The indulgence–restraint dimension contrasts pleasure-seeking with self-restraint. The monumentalism–self-effacement dimension compares prideful stability with humble adaptation.

The GLOBE researchers identified nine dimensions of culture and distinguished between cultural *practices* (what people actually do) and cultural *values* (what people should do). The power distance and uncertainty avoidance dimensions are similar to those that Hofstede described. In-group collectivism and institutional collectivism refine Hofstede's individualism–collectivism dimension; in-group collectivism is concerned with family loyalty, whereas societal collectivism refers to group-oriented actions.

Gender egalitarianism and assertiveness refine Hofstede's masculinity–femininity dimension; gender egalitarianism is about equality between men and women, while assertiveness is about social dominance. Performance orientation refers to task- or work-related accomplishments, future orientation is about preferences for delayed versus immediate gratifications, and humane orientation is concerned with fairness and generosity.

The ideas presented in this chapter and the previous one offer alternative lenses through which cultures can be understood and appreciated. Taken together, these two chapters provide multiple frames of reference that can be used to enhance your knowledge, motivations, and skills in intercultural communication.

For Discussion

1. What does Edward Hall mean when he refers to culture as a "screen" for its members?
2. Describe how each of Hofstede's dimensions of cultural patterns is displayed within your culture.
3. Does Hofstede's taxonomy coincide with your own intercultural experiences? Explain.
4. Consider the following two philosophical statements: "I think; therefore, I am" and "I am because we are." What do these two statements reveal about the underlying cultural values of those who use them?
5. Compare your own practices and values with the GLOBE's cultural practices and cultural values. In what ways are they the same? Different? What might this suggest about intercultural communication?

For Further Reading

Edward T. Hall, *Beyond Culture* (New York: Anchor Books, 1989). Describes, in great detail, the cultural variations among high- and low-context cultures.

Robert J. House, Paul J. Hanges, Mansour Javidan, Peter W. Dorfman, and Vipin Gupta (eds.), *Culture, Leadership, and Organizations: The GLOBE Study of 62 Societies* (Thousand Oaks, CA: Sage, 2004). A momentous work that presents ground-breaking research on the current practices and value dimensions that differ among cultures. Provides extensive quantitative evidence for cultural variations on the nine GLOBE dimensions.

Jagdeep S. Chhokar, Felix C. Brodbek, and Robert J. House (eds.), *Culture and Leadership across the World: The GLOBE Book of In-Depth Studies of 25 Societies* (Mahwah, NJ: Erlbaum, 2007). A companion to the earlier GLOBE book, this volume provides in-depth qualitative information about the dimensions of culture.

Bradley L. Kirkman, Kevin B. Lowe, and Cristina B. Gibson, "A Quarter Century of *Culture's Consequences*: A Review of Empirical Research Incorporating Hofstede's Cultural Values Framework," *Journal of International Business Studies* 37 (2006): 285–320. An overview on the extensive research on Hofstede's first five dimensions on which cultures can vary.

Craig Storti, *Americans at Work: A Guide to the Can-Do People* (Yarmouth, ME: Intercultural Press, 2004). A concise description of European American cultural patterns.

For additional information about intercultural films and about Web sites for researching specific cultures, please turn to the Resources section at the back of this book.

CHAPTER 6

Cultural Identity and Cultural Biases

In the previous two chapters, we emphasized the critical importance of cultural patterns in shaping the preferred ways to think, feel, and act in a variety of situations. An equally interesting and important question in the development of intercultural communication competence concerns how people come to identify themselves as belonging to a particular cultural group. For example, how and when does a child begin to think of herself as a Latina, Japanese American, or Japanese? When do adults who are born into one culture and living in another begin to think of their cultural identity as embracing parts of both their original culture and the later culture? Similarly, how are some people defined as "not members" of our cultural group? How and why do groups of people from one culture develop negative attitudes and actions toward other cultural groups?

The present chapter discusses some aspects of cultural identity that can have a very large effect on intercultural communication. We begin with a discussion of cultural

CULTURE connections

I'm a black + white + I don't know what else = both/neither/other, "half" transracially adopted, descendant of people I've never met. A freckled, brown-skinned, curly/straight/frizzy brown-haired (with some black, blond, and orange thrown in), German-American raised, Spanish-speaking gringa and multicolorful part-time expatriate. I'm mixed. What I *am* is *ME*.

—*Sara B. Busdiecker*

identity and the powerful ways in which one's self-concept as a member of a particular cultural group filters our interpretations of the world. Then we explore the nature of cultural biases, rooted in cultural identity, as we examine the effects of ethnocentrism, stereotyping, prejudice, discrimination, and racism on intercultural interactions.

Cultural Identity

As part of the socialization process, children learn to view themselves as members of particular groups. Children in all cultures, for example, are taught to identify with their families (even though, as Chapter 10 indicates, whom to include as part of one's "family" differs across cultures). As a child becomes a teenager and then an adult, the development of vocational and avocational interests creates new groups with which to identify. "Baseball player," "ballet dancer," or "scientist" may become important labels to describe the self.

Another feature of socialization is that people are taught about groups to which they do not belong, and they often learn that certain groups should be avoided. This tendency to identify as a member of some groups, called *ingroups,* and to distinguish these ingroups from *outgroups* is so prevalent in human thinking that it has been described as a universal human tendency.[1] Recent scholarship is investigating the role of new media in supporting or diminishing this human tendency to define others as either part of our own ingroup or as part of our outgroup.[2]

The Nature of Identity

Related to the distinction between ingroup and outgroup membership is the concept of one's *identity* or self-concept. An individual's self-concept is built on cultural, social, and personal identities.[3]

Cultural identity refers to one's sense of belonging to a particular culture or ethnic group. It is formed in a process that results from membership in a particular culture, and it involves learning about and accepting the traditions, heritage, language, religion, ancestry, aesthetics, thinking patterns, and social structures of a culture. That is, people internalize the beliefs, values, norms, and social practices of their culture and identify with that culture as part of their self-concept.

Social identity develops as a consequence of memberships in particular groups within one's culture.[4] The characteristics and concerns common to most members of such social groups shape the way individuals view their characteristics. The types of groups with which people identify can vary widely and might include perceived similarities due to age, gender, work, religion, ideology, social class, place (neighborhood, region, and nation), and common interests. For instance, those baseball players, ballet dancers, and scientists who strongly identify with their particular professions likely view themselves as "belonging" to "their" group of professionals, with whom they have similar traits and share similar concerns.

Finally, personal identity is based on people's unique characteristics, which may differ from those of others in their cultural and social groups. You may like cooking or chemistry, singing or sewing; you may play tennis or trombones, soccer or stereos; you may view yourself as studious or sociable, goofy or gracious; and most assuredly you have abilities, talents, quirks, and preferences that differ from those of others.

For ease and clarity, we have chosen to present aspects of a person's identity as separate categories. There is a great deal of interdependence, however, among these three aspects of identity. Characteristics of people's social identities will inevitably be linked to the preferences shaped by their cultural identities. Similarly, how people enact their unique interests will also be heavily influenced by their cultural identities. Thus, for example, a teenage girl's identity will likely be strongly linked to her culture's preferences for gendered role behaviors as well as to her social class and her personal characteristics and traits.[5]

◼ In this intercultural family, the child will draw upon the cultures of both of parents in forming her own cultural identity.

The Formation of Cultural Identity

Cultural identities often develop through a process involving three stages: unexamined cultural identity, cultural identity search, and cultural identity achievement.[6] During the unexamined cultural identity stage, one's cultural characteristics are taken for granted, and consequently there is little interest in exploring cultural issues. Young children, for instance, typically lack an awareness of cultural differences and the distinguishing characteristics that differentiate one culture from another. Teenagers and adults may not want to categorize themselves as belonging to any particular culture. Some people may not have explored the meanings and consequences of their cultural membership but may simply have accepted preconceived ideas about it that were obtained from parents, the community, the mass media, and others.

Consequently, some individuals may unquestioningly accept the prevailing stereotypes held by others and may internalize common stereotypes of their own culture and of themselves. Scholars have suggested that the cultural identities of many European Americans, in particular, have remained largely unexamined, a consequence of the power, centrality, and privilege that the European American cultural group has had in the United States.[7] As Judith Martin, Robert Krizek, Thomas Nakayama, and Lisa Bradford suggest,

> This lack of attention to white identity and self-labeling reflects the historical power held by Whites in the United States. That is, Whites as the privileged group take their identity as the norm or standard by which other groups are measured, and this identity is therefore invisible, even to the extent that many Whites do not consciously think about the profound effect being white has on their everyday lives.[8]

Cultural identity search involves a process of exploration and questioning about one's culture in order to learn more about it and to understand the implications of membership in that culture. By exploring the culture, individuals can learn about its strengths and may come to a point of acceptance both of their culture and of themselves. For some individuals, a turning point or crucial event precipitates this stage, whereas for others it just begins with a growing awareness and reinterpretation of everyday experiences. Common to this stage is an increased social and political awareness along with an increased desire to learn more about one's culture. Such learning may be characterized by an increased degree of talking with family and friends about cultural issues, independent reading of relevant sources, enrolling in appropriate courses, or increased attendance at cultural events such as festivals and museums. There may also be an emotional component to this stage, of varying intensity, which involves tension, anger, and perhaps even outrage directed toward other groups. These emotions may intensify as people become aware of and wrestle with the effects of discrimination on their present and future lives and the potential difficulties in attaining educational, career, and personal objectives.

CULTURE connections

If there is one universal experience commonly cited among those who have embraced a multiracial identity, it is the frequency with which we are asked the "What are you?" question. We are constantly called upon to either explain what others perceive as our ambiguous racial appearance, or to choose sides and declare an allegiance to one ethnic group over another. Meanwhile, those biracial people whose looks are more easily aligned with traditional, single-race categories do not face such interrogation to nearly the same degree. "I can't racially classify you, and it's bothering me," the questioners seem to be saying, "so tell me what you are so I can figure out which box to put you in and determine how to relate to you."

—*Elliott Lewis*

■ The use of the Menorah and related artifacts in the celebration of Chanukah helps this Jewish American family to strengthen their cultural identity.

Cultural identity achievement is characterized by a clear, confident acceptance of oneself and an internalization of one's cultural identity. Such acceptance can calmly and securely be used to guide one's future actions. People in this stage have developed ways of dealing with stereotypes and discrimination so that they do not internalize others' negative perceptions and are clear about the personal meanings of their culture. This outcome contributes to increased self-confidence and positive psychological adjustment. Table 6.1 provides sample comments from individuals in each of the three stages of cultural identity development.

Characteristics of Cultural Identity

Once formed, cultural identities provide an essential framework, organizing and interpreting our experiences of others. This is because cultural identities are central, dynamic, and multifaceted components of one's self-concept.

Cultural identities are central to a person's sense of self. Like gender and race, your culture is more "basic" because it is broadly influential and is linked to a great number of other aspects of your self-concept. These core aspects of your identity are likely to be important in most of your interactions with others. Most components of your identity, however, become important only when they are activated by specific circumstances. For many people, the experience of living in another culture or interacting with a person from a different culture triggers an awareness of their own cultural identities that they did not have before. When a component of your identity becomes conscious and important to you, or "activated," your experiences get filtered through that portion of your identity. Aspects of

TABLE 6.1	Stages in the Development of Cultural Identity	
Stage	**Sample Comments**	**Source of Comments**
Unexamined cultural identity	"My parents tell me about where they lived, but what do I care? I've never lived there."	Mexican American male
	"Why do I have to learn who was the first black woman to do this or that? I'm just not too interested."	African American female
	"I don't have a culture. I'm just an American."	European American male
Cultural identity search	"I think people should know what black people had to go through to get to where we are now."	African American female
	"There are a lot of non-Japanese people around me, and it gets pretty confusing to try and decide who I am."	Japanese American male
	"I want to know what we do and how our culture is different from others."	Mexican American female
Cultural identity achievement	"My culture is important, and I am proud of what I am. Japanese people have so much to offer."	Japanese American male
	"It used to be confusing to me, but it's clear now. I'm happy being black."	African American female

Source: Adapted from Jean S. Phinney, "A Three-Stage Model of Ethnic Identity Development in Adolescence," *Ethnic Identity: Formation and Transmission among Hispanics and Other Minorities,* ed. Martha E. Bernal and George P. Knight (Albany: State University of New York Press, 1993), 61–79.

one's cultural identity can be activated not only by direct experiences with others but also by the media reports, by artistic portrayals that have particular cultural themes, by musical performances (such as rap music) that are identified with specific cultural groups, and by a range of other personal and mass-mediated experiences.[9] Thus, if individuals from one's culture are frequently portrayed in popular films and television programs, this can provide a sense of legitimacy for the culture and can help to establish that the culture's members are attractive, desirable, and good. Conversely, the absence of such role models in the media can dampen one's identification with the culture and the individuals' perceptions that the culture is vital and vibrant. Because your cultural identity is likely to be central to your sense of self, most of your experiences are interpreted or "framed" by your cultural membership.

Because cultural identities are dynamic, your cultural identity—your sense of the culture to which you belong and who you are in light of this cultural membership—exists within a changing social context. Consequently, your identity is not static, fixed, and enduring; rather, it is dynamic and changes with your ongoing life experiences. In even the briefest encounter with people whose cultural backgrounds differ from your own, your sense of who you are *at that instant* may well be altered, at least in some small ways. Over time, as you adapt to various intercultural challenges, your cultural identity may be transformed into one that is substantially different from what it used to be.[10] The inaccurate belief that cultural identities are permanent, that "Once a Swedish American, always a Swedish

CULTURE connections

It amazed me that I never ceased to amaze them. I had never been a minority before. I felt large, ungainly, and pale. With my damp hair pulled back in a bun, I looked like Olive Oyl. And a little voice in my head kept whispering, "I can never fit in here." ...

Who am I without the tapestry of my family, friends, work, and possessions tightly woven around me? In the midst of so much hubbub, I felt entirely alone. Without my music, my food, my language, *my* obligations, I hardly knew who I was.

I felt like a button that had fallen off.

—Meg Wirth

American," ignores the possibility of profound changes that people may experience as a result of their intercultural contacts. Indeed, recent communication technologies have made it easier, and therefore more common, for those living within a "foreign" culture to maintain connections to their culture-of-origin—both those "back home" and others who, like themselves, are experiencing the changes and disconnections of living in a new culture.[11]

Cultural identities are also multifaceted. At any given moment, you have many "components" that make up your identity. For instance, a specific person may simultaneously view herself as a student, an employee, a friend, a woman, a Southerner, a daughter, a Methodist, a baby boomer, and more. Similarly, there are typically many facets or components to your cultural identity.

Many people incorrectly assume that an individual could, or perhaps should, identify with only one cultural group. However, as Young Yun Kim suggests,

> If someone sees himself or herself, or is seen by others, as a Mexican-American, then this person's identity is [commonly] viewed to exclude all other identities. This tendency to see cultural identity in an "all-or-none" and "either-or" manner glosses over the fact that many people's identities are not locked into a single, uncompromising category, but incorporate other identities as well.[12]

Given our increasingly multicultural world, in which people from many cultures coexist and in which the United States has become a country where individuals from many cultures live and interact, the multifaceted characteristic of cultural identity becomes even more important.[13]

Cultural Biases

In Chapter 2, we defined culture as a learned set of shared interpretations about beliefs, values, norms, and social practices that affect the behaviors of a relatively large group of people. We also pointed out that culture really exists in people's minds, but that the consequences of culture—the shared interpretations—can be seen in people's communication behaviors. Shared interpretations, which we have called cultural patterns, provide guidelines about how people should behave, and they indicate what to expect in interactions with others. In other words, a culture's shared interpretations create predictability and stability in people's lives. Cultural similarity allows people to reduce uncertainty and to know what to expect when interacting with others.

Interaction only within one's own culture produces a number of obvious benefits. Because the culture provides predictability, it reduces the threat of the unknown. When something or someone that is unknown or unpredictable enters a culture, the culture's beliefs, values, norms, and social practices tell people how to interpret and respond appropriately, thus reducing the perceived threat of the intrusion. Cultural patterns also allow for automatic responses to stimuli; in essence, cultural patterns save people time and energy.

Intercultural communication, by definition, means that people are interacting with at least one culturally different person. Consequently, the sense of security, comfort, and predictability that characterizes communication with culturally similar people is lost. The greater the degree of interculturalness, the greater the loss of predictability and certainty. Assurances about the accuracy of interpretations of verbal and nonverbal messages are lost.

Terms that are often used when communicating with culturally different people include *unknown, unpredictable, ambiguous, weird, mysterious, unexplained, exotic, unusual, unfamiliar, curious, novel, odd, outlandish,* and *strange.* As you read this list, consider how the choice of a particular word might also reflect a particular value. What characteristics, values, and knowledge allow individuals to respond more competently to the threat of dealing with cultural differences? What situations heighten the perception of threat among members of different cultural groups? To answer questions such as these, we need to explore how people make sense of information about others as they categorize or classify others in their social world.

Social Categorizing

Three features in the way all humans process information about others are important to your understanding of intercultural competence. First, as cognitive psychologists have repeatedly demonstrated, people impose a pattern on their world by organizing the stimuli that bombard their senses into conceptual categories. Every waking moment, people are presented with literally hundreds of different perceptual stimuli. Therefore, it becomes necessary to simplify the information by selecting, organizing, and reducing it to less complex forms. That is, to comprehend stimuli, people organize them into categories, groupings, and patterns. As a child, you might have completed a drawing by connecting numbered dots. Emerging from the lines was the figure of an animal or a familiar toy. Even though its complete form was not drawn, it was relatively easy to identify. This kind of recognition occurs simply because human beings have a tendency to organize perceptual cues to impose meaning, usually by using familiar, previous experiences.

Second, most people tend to think that other people perceive, evaluate, and reason about the world in the same way that they do. In other words, humans assume that other people with whom they interact are like themselves. Indeed, it is quite common for people to draw on their personal experiences to understand and evaluate the motivations of others. This common human tendency is sometimes called ethnocentrism.

Third, humans simplify the processing and organizing of information from the environment by identifying certain characteristics as belonging to certain categories of persons and events. For example, a child's experiences with several dogs that growled and snapped are likely to result in a future reaction to other dogs as if they will also growl and snap. The characteristics of particular events, persons, or objects, once experienced, are often assumed to be typical of similar events, persons, or objects. Though these assumptions are sometimes accurate, often they are not. Not all dogs necessarily growl and snap at young children. Nevertheless, information processing results in a simplification of the world, so that prior experiences are used as the basis for determining both the categories and the attributes of the events. This process is called stereotyping.

Please note that we are describing these human tendencies nonevaluatively. Their obvious advantage is that they allow people to respond efficiently to a variety of perceptual stimuli. Nevertheless, this organization and simplification can create some genuine obstacles to intercultural competence because they may lead to prejudice, discrimination, and racism.

Ethnocentrism

Twenty-five hundred years ago, the Greek historian Herodotus, whom Cicero called "The Father of History," related a story about Darius, the first monarch of the great Persian empire. Darius became king of Persia (now Iran) in 521 B.C., and he ruled a vast empire that, for a time, included most of the "known" world, including southeastern Europe, northern Africa, India, southern Russia, and the Middle East. Darius, so the story goes,

> sent for the Greeks at his court to ask them their price for devouring the corpses of their ancestors. They replied that no price would be high enough. Thereupon the Persian king summoned the representatives of an Indian tribe which habitually practiced the custom from which the Greeks shrank, and asked them through the interpreter, in the presence of the Greeks, at what price they would burn the corpses of

CULTURE connections

It was amazing that *gaijin* could not smell themselves, the *batakusai*—butter stink—they emanated from eating so much dairy. The odor overwhelmed Kenzo as he stepped through the security door of the American Embassy in Toranomon. The Marine guard, a massively built, pink-faced jarhead who was the offending source, handed him a visitor's pass, and Kenzo hurried off to the Consular Section, trying to suck in fresh air. Only there wasn't any fresh air in the nine-story building, just recycled air conditioning, which made his skin prickle and itch.

—*Don Lee*

their ancestors. The Indians cried aloud and besought the king not even to mention such a horror. From these circumstances the historian drew the following notable moral for human guidance: If all existing customs could somewhere be set before all men in order that they might select the most beautiful for themselves, every nation would choose out, after the most searching scrutiny, the customs they had already practiced.[14]

In the preceding passage, Herodotus described what is now called *ethnocentrism,* which is the notion that the beliefs, values, norms, and practices of one's own culture are superior to those of others.

All cultures teach their members the "preferred" ways to respond to the world, which are often labeled as "natural" or "appropriate." Thus, people generally perceive their own experiences, which are shaped by their own cultural forces, as natural, human, and universal.

Cultures also train their members to use the categories of their own cultural experiences when judging the experiences of people from other cultures. Our culture tells us that the way we were taught to behave is "right" or "correct," and those who do things differently are wrong. William G. Sumner, who first introduced the concept of ethnocentrism, defined it as "the view of things in which one's own group is the center of everything, and all others are scaled and rated with reference to it."[15] Sumner illustrates how ethnocentrism works in the following example:

> When Caribs were asked whence they came, they replied, "We alone are people." "Kiowa" means real or principal people. A Laplander is a "man" or "human being." The highest praise a Greenlander has for a European visiting the island is that the European by studying virtue and good manners from the Greenlanders soon will be as good as a Greenlander. Nature peoples call themselves "men" as a rule. All others are something else, but not men. The Jews divide all mankind into themselves and Gentiles—they being the "chosen people." The Greeks and Romans called outsiders "barbarians." Arabs considered themselves as the noblest nation and all others as barbarians. Russian books and newspapers talk about its civilizing mission, and so do the books and journals of France, Germany, and the United States. Each nation now regards itself as the leader of civilization, the best, the freest, and the wisest. All others are inferior.[16]

Ethnocentrism is a learned belief in cultural superiority. Because cultures teach people what the world is "really like" and what is "good," people consequently believe that the values of their culture are natural and correct. Thus, people from other cultures who do things differently are wrong. When combined with the natural human tendency to prefer what is typically experienced, ethnocentrism produces emotional reactions to cultural differences that reduce people's willingness to understand disparate cultural messages.

Ethnocentrism tends to highlight and exaggerate cultural differences. As an interesting instance of ethnocentrism, consider beliefs about body odor. Most U.S. Americans spend large sums of money each year to rid themselves of natural body odor. They then replace their natural odors with artificial ones as they apply deodorants, bath powders, shaving lotions, perfumes, hair sprays, shampoos, mousse, gels, toothpaste, mouthwash, and breath mints. Many U.S. Americans probably believe that they do not have an odor—even after they have routinely applied most, if not all, of the artificial ones in the preceding list. Yet the same individuals will react negatively to culturally different others who do not remove natural body odors and who refuse to apply artificial ones.

Another example of ethnocentrism concerns the way in which cultures teach people to discharge mucus from the nose. Most U.S. Americans purchase boxes of tissues and strategically place them at various points in their homes, offices, and cars so that they will be available for use when blowing their noses. In countries where paper products have historically been scarce and very expensive, people blow their noses onto the ground or the street. Pay attention to your reaction as you read this last statement. Most U.S. Americans, when learning about this behavior, react with a certain amount of disgust. But think about the U.S. practice of blowing one's nose into a tissue or handkerchief, which is then placed on the desk or into a pocket or purse. Now ask yourself which is really more disgusting—carrying around tissues with dried mucus in them or blowing the mucus onto the street? Described in this way, both practices have a certain element of repugnance, but because one's culture teaches that there is one preferred way, that custom is familiar and comfortable and the practices of other cultures are seen as wrong or distasteful.

Ethnocentrism can occur along all of the dimensions of cultural patterns discussed in the previous two chapters. People from individualistic cultures, for instance, find the idea that a person's self-concept is tied to a group to be unfathomable. To most U.S. Americans, the idea of an arranged marriage seems strange at best and a confining and reprehensible limitation on personal freedom at worst.

One area of behavior that quickly reveals ethnocentrism is personal hygiene. For example, U.S. Americans like to see themselves as the cleanest people on Earth. In the

◼ The U.S. American preoccupation with body odors can be seen on the shelves of many stores.

United States, bathrooms contain sinks, showers or bathtubs, and toilets, thus allowing the efficient use of water pipes. Given this arrangement, people bathe themselves in close proximity to the toilet, where they urinate and defecate. Described in this way, the cultural practices of the United States may seem unclean, peculiar, or even absurd. Why would people in a so-called modern society place two such contradictory functions next to each other? People from many other cultures, who consider the U.S. arrangement to be unclean and unhealthy, share that sentiment. Our point here is that what is familiar and comfortable inevitably seems the best, right, and natural way of doing things. Judgments about what is "right" or "natural" create emotional responses to cultural differences that may interfere with our ability to understand the symbols used by other cultures. For example, European Americans think it is "human nature" to orient oneself to the future and to want to improve one's material status in life. Individuals whose cultures have been influenced by alternative forces, resulting in contrary views, are often judged negatively and treated with derision.

To be a competent intercultural communicator, you must realize that you typically use the categories of your own culture to judge and interpret the behaviors of those who are culturally different from you. You must also be aware of your own emotional reactions to the sights, sounds, smells, and variations in message systems that you encounter when communicating with people from other cultures. The competent intercultural communicator does not necessarily suppress negative feelings but acknowledges their existence and seeks to minimize their effect on her or his communication. If you are reacting strongly to some aspect of another culture, seek out an explanation in the ethnocentric preferences that your culture has taught you.

Stereotyping

Journalist Walter Lippmann introduced the term *stereotyping* in 1922 to refer to a selection process that is used to organize and simplify perceptions of others.[17] Stereotypes are a form of generalization about some group of people. When people stereotype others, they take a category of people and make assertions about the characteristics of all people who belong to that category. The consequence of stereotyping is that the vast degree of differences that exists among the members of any one group may not be taken into account in the interpretation of messages.

To illustrate how stereotyping works, read the following list: college professors, surfers, Marxists, Democrats, bankers, New Yorkers, Californians. Probably, as you read each of these categories, it was relatively easy for you to associate particular characteristics and traits with each group. Now imagine that a person from one of these groups walked into the room and began a conversation with you. In all likelihood, you would associate the group's characteristics with that specific individual.

Your responses to this simple example illustrate what typically occurs when people are stereotyped. First, someone identifies an outgroup category—"they"—whose characteristics differ from those in one's own social ingroup. Next, the perceived dissimilarities between the groups are enlarged and accentuated, thereby creating differences that are clearer and more distinct. By making sharper and more pronounced boundaries between the groups, it becomes more difficult for individuals to move

■ The depiction of stereotypes in TV shows like *The Sopranos* and in the films of actors such as Jackie Chan underscores the links between media portrayals of various cultural groups and everyday prejudices.

from one group to another. Concurrently, an evaluative component is introduced, whereby the characteristics of the outgroup are negatively judged; that is, the outgroup is regarded as wrong, inferior, or stigmatized as a result of given characteristics. Finally, the group's characteristics are attributed to all people who belong to the group, so that a specific person is not treated as a unique individual but as a typical member of a category.

Categories that are used to form stereotypes about groups of people can vary widely, and they might include the following:

- Regions of the world (Asians, Arabs, South Americans, Africans)
- Countries (Kenya, Japan, China, France, Great Britain)
- Regions within countries (Northern Indians, Southern Indians, U.S. Midwesterners, U.S. Southerners)
- Cities (New Yorkers, Parisians, Londoners)
- Cultures (English, French, Latino, Russian, Serbian, Yoruba, Mestizo, Thai, Navajo)
- Race (African, Caucasian)

CULTURE connections

What had I been thinking? I woke up each morning hoping to feel a bit more French, more intimately connected to my family heritage in some incredibly dramatic and clear way, but I was always still just me, a California girl having great fun playing at being French. It was pure folly to have thought that my shiny new French passport would suddenly endow me with insight into the mysterious nuances of the French and their way of interpreting the world. I have never felt so glaringly American as I did that morning, sitting in that attic in the heart of Paris...

—*Christina Henry de Tessan*

- Religion (Muslim, Hindu, Buddhist, Jewish, Christian)
- Age (young, old, middle-aged, children, adults)
- Occupations (teacher, farmer, doctor, housekeeper, mechanic, architect, musician)
- Relational roles (mother, friend, father, sister, brother)
- Physical characteristics (short, tall, fat, skinny)
- Social class (wealthy, poor, middle class)

This list is by no means exhaustive. What it should illustrate is the enormous range of possibilities for classification and simplification. Consider your own stereotypes of people in these groups. Many may have been created by direct experience with only one or two people from a particular group. Others are probably based on secondhand information and opinions, output from the mass media, and general habits of thinking; they may even have been formed without any direct experience with individuals from the group. Yet many people are prepared to assume that their stereotypes are accurate representations of all members of specific groups.[18] Interestingly, stereotypes that are based on secondhand opinions — that is, stereotypes that are derived from the opinions of others or from the media—tend to be more extreme, less variable from one person to another, more uniformly applied to others, and more resistant to change than are stereotypes based on direct personal experiences and interactions.[19]

Stereotypes can be inaccurate in three ways.[20] First, as we have suggested, stereotypes often are assumed to apply to all or most of the members of a particular group or category, resulting in a tendency to ignore differences among the individual members of the group. This type of stereotyping error is called the *outgroup homogeneity effect* and results in a tendency to regard all members of a particular group as much more similar to one another than they actually are.[21] Arab Americans, for instance, complain that other U.S. Americans often hold undifferentiated stereotypes about members of their culture. Albert Mokhiber laments that

if there's problem in Libya we're all Libyans. If the problem is in Lebanon we're all Lebanese. If it happens to be Iran, which is not an Arab country, we're all Iranians. Conversely, Iranians were picked on during the Gulf War as being Arabs. Including one fellow who called in who was a Polynesian Jew. But he looked like what an Arab should look like, and he felt the wrath of anti-Arab discrimination. Nobody's really free from this. The old civil rights adage says that as long as the rights of one are in danger, we're all in danger. I think we need to break out of our ethnic ghetto mentality, all of us, from various backgrounds, and realize that we're in this stew together.[22]

A second form of stereotype inaccuracy occurs when the group average, as suggested by the stereotype, is simply wrong or inappropriately exaggerated. This type of inaccuracy occurs, for instance, when Germans are stereotypically regarded as being very efficient, or perhaps very rigid, when they may actually be less efficient or less rigid than the exaggerated perception of them would warrant.

A third form of stereotype inaccuracy occurs when the degree of error and exaggeration differs for positive and negative attributes. For instance, imagine that you have stereotyped a culture as being very efficient (a positive attribute) but also very rigid and inflexible in its business relationships (a negative attribute). If you tend to overestimate the prevalence and importance of the culture's positive characteristics, such as its degree of efficiency, while simultaneously ignoring or underestimating its rigidity and other negative characteristics, you would have a "positive valence inaccuracy." Conversely, a "negative valence inaccuracy" occurs if you exaggerate the negative attributes while ignoring or devaluing its positive ones. This latter condition, often called *prejudice*, will be discussed in greater detail later.

The problems associated with using stereotyping as a means of understanding individuals is best illustrated by identifying the groups to which you belong. Think about the characteristics that might be stereotypically assigned to those groups. Determine whether the characteristics apply to you or to others in your group. Some of them may be accurate descriptions; many, however, will be totally inaccurate, and you would resent being thought of in that way. Stereotypes distort or hide the individual. Ultimately, people may become blind to the actual characteristics of the group because not all stereotypes are accurate. Most are based on relatively minimal experiences with particular individuals.

Stereotype inaccuracy can lead to errors in interpretations and expectations about the behaviors of others. Interpretation errors occur because stereotypes are used not only to categorize specific individuals and events but also to judge them. That is, one potentially harmful consequence of stereotypes is that they provide inaccurate labels for a group of people, which are then used to interpret subsequent ambiguous events and experiences involving members of those groups. As Ziva Kunda and Bonnie Sherman-Williams note,

> Consider, for example, the unambiguous act of failing a test. Ethnic stereotypes may lead perceivers to attribute such failure to laziness if the actor is Asian but to low ability if the actor is Black. Thus stereotypes will affect judgments of the targets' ability even if subjects base these judgments only on the act, because the stereotypes will determine the meaning of the act.[23]

Because stereotypes are sometimes applied indiscriminately to members of a particular culture or social group, they can also lead to errors in one's expectations about the future behaviors of others. Stereotypes provide the bases for estimating, often inaccurately, what members of the stereotyped group are likely to do. Most disturbingly, stereotypes will likely persist even when members of the stereotyped group repeatedly behave in ways that disconfirm them. Once a stereotype has taken hold, members of the stereotyped group who behave in nonstereotypical ways will be expected to compensate in their future actions in order to "make up for" their atypical behavior. Even when some individuals from a stereotyped group repeatedly deviate from expectations, they may be regarded as exceptions or as atypical members of their group. Indeed, stereotypes may remain intact, or may even be strengthened, in the face of disconfirming experiences; those who hold the stereotypes often expect that the other members of the stereotyped social group will be even *more* likely to behave as the stereotype predicts, in order to "balance out" or compensate for the "unusual" instances that they experienced. That is, stereotypes encourage people to expect future behaviors that compensate for perceived inconsistencies and thus allow people to anticipate future events in a way that makes it unnecessary to revise their deeply held beliefs and values.[24]

The process underlying stereotyping is absolutely essential for human beings to function. Some categorization is necessary and normal. Indeed, there is survival value in the ability to make accurate generalizations about others, and stereotypes function as mental "energy-saving devices" to help make those generalizations efficiently.[25] However, stereotypes may also promote prejudice and discrimination directed toward members of cultures other than one's own. Intercultural competence requires an ability to move beyond stereotypes and to respond to the individual. Previous experiences should be used only as guidelines or suggested interpretations rather than as hard-and-fast categories. Judee Burgoon, Charles Berger, and Vincent Waldron suggest that mindfulness—that is, paying conscious attention to the nature and basis of one's stereotypes—can help to reduce stereotype inaccuracies and thereby decrease intercultural misunderstandings.[26]

Prejudice

Prejudice refers to negative attitudes toward other people that are based on faulty and inflexible stereotypes. Prejudiced attitudes include irrational feelings of dislike and even hatred for certain groups, biased perceptions and beliefs about the group members that are not based on direct experiences and firsthand knowledge, and a readiness to behave in negative and unjust ways toward members of the group. Gordon Allport, who first focused scholarly attention on prejudice, argued that prejudiced people ignore evidence that is inconsistent with their biased viewpoint, or they distort the evidence to fit their prejudices.[27]

The strong link between prejudice and stereotypes should be obvious. Prejudiced thinking is dependent on stereotypes and is a fairly normal phenomenon.[28] To be prejudiced toward a group of people sometimes makes it easier to respond to them. We are not condoning prejudice or the hostile and violent actions that may occur as a result of prejudice. We are suggesting that prejudice is a universal psychological process; all people have a propensity for prejudice toward others who are unlike themselves. For individuals to move beyond prejudicial attitudes and for societies to avoid basing social structures on their prejudices about groups of people, it is critical to recognize the prevalence of prejudicial thinking.

■ These spray-painted tombstones of Russian Jews in St. Petersburg illustrate the prejudice, discrimination, and racism (called "anti-Semitism" when referring to Jews) experienced by many cultural groups.

What functions does prejudice serve? We have already suggested that the thought process underlying prejudice includes the need to organize and simplify the world. Richard Brislin describes four additional benefits, or what he calls functions, of prejudice.[29] First, he suggests that prejudice satisfies a *utilitarian* or adjustment function. Displaying certain kinds of prejudice means that people receive rewards and avoid punishments. For example, if you express prejudicial statements about certain people, other people may like you more. It is also easier to simply dislike and be prejudiced toward members of other groups because they can then be dismissed without going through the effort necessary to adjust to them. Another function that prejudice serves is an *ego-defensive* one; it protects self-esteem.[30] If others say or do things that are inconsistent with the images we hold of ourselves, our sense of self may be deeply threatened, and we may try to maintain our self-esteem by scorning the sources of the message. So, for example, people who are unsuccessful in business may feel threatened by groups whose members are successful. Prejudice may function to protect one's self-image by denigrating or devaluing those who might make us feel less worthy.[31] Still another advantage of prejudicial attitudes is the *value-expressive* function. If people believe that their group has certain qualities that are unique, valuable, good, or in some way special, their prejudicial attitudes toward others is a way of expressing those values. Finally, Brislin describes the *knowledge function* as prejudicial attitudes that people hold because of their need to have the world neatly organized and boxed into categories. This function takes the normal human proclivity to organize the world to an extreme. The rigid application of categories and the prejudicial attitudes assigned to certain behaviors and beliefs provide security and increase predictability. Obviously, these functions cannot be neatly applied to all

CULTURE connections

Dawoud remembers an incident in fourth grade when one of the little girls got her lunch stolen, and he looked up to find the teacher singling him out. He saw her cold stare and her accusatory finger waving in his face, and he felt baffled and confused. "I was innocent, I didn't even get the connection. '*Me?*' I stammered. 'Are you talking to *me?*'" asked Dawoud in a sweat. Yes, she meant *him,* and he was to go down to the guidance office immediately. He was the culprit. There was no doubt in her mind. Dawoud rose up from his seat, walked the long march to the door amid the quiet stares of his classmates, and dutifully took himself to the guidance office, where the counselor interpreted his "acting out" as some kind of "mental problem" and gave him some "weird" tests "putting square pegs in round holes." In Dawoud's memory this is one story among many. "I'd get singled out. Much of the time I was in a conflicted state. There were strange things going on, but what do you say? I couldn't name what was happening, and I couldn't find the words or the courage to ask."

The following year, in fifth grade, he remembers that the class was writing a group play about Colonial America, and the play was to be written in verse. Dawoud loved the assignment and he leapt right into the middle of the work. "I *loved* writing poetry. It was a breeze for me. So I started knocking this stuff out." The teacher was gratified by the way her class pulled off the assignment so quickly and with such apparent ease and mature collaboration. She inquired of everyone how they had been so incredibly productive, and the children all pointed to Dawoud, who smiled back shyly. "I remember," says Dawoud with hurt in his eyes, "how her expression changed in that moment. The raised eyebrow, the amazement, the surprise." She must have applauded his inspired work and thanked him for his contribution. But the only thing that Dawoud can remember is her utter bafflement and *his* inner confusion. "The teacher was unable to reconcile my brightness with her stereotype of me. How could this black boy produce this verse? She seemed *tormented* by this. It was always this way in elementary school. At the same moment I'd receive these great commendations, I'd be sent off to the guidance counselor."

—*Sara Lawrence-Lightfoot*

instances of prejudice. Nor are people usually aware of the specific reasons for their prejudices. For each person, prejudicial attitudes may serve several functions.

Discrimination

Whereas *prejudice* refers to people's attitudes or mental representations, the term discrimination refers to the behavioral manifestations of that prejudice. Thus discrimination can be thought of as prejudice "in action."

Discrimination can occur in many forms. From the extremes of segregation and apartheid to biases in the availability of housing, employment, education, economic resources, personal safety, and legal protections, discrimination represents unequal treatment of certain individuals solely because of their membership in a particular group.

Teun van Dijk has conducted a series of studies of people's everyday conversations as they discussed different racial and cultural groups. Van Dijk concludes that, when individuals make prejudicial comments, tell jokes that belittle and dehumanize others, and share negative stereotypes about others, they are establishing and legitimizing the existence of their prejudices and are laying the "communication groundwork" that will make it acceptable for people to perform discriminatory acts.[32]

Often, biases and displays of discrimination are motivated not by direct hostility toward some other group but merely by a strong preference for, and loyalty to, one's own culture.[33] Thus, the formation of one's cultural identity, which we discussed earlier in this chapter, can sometimes lead to hostility, hate, and discrimination directed against nonmembers of that culture.

Racism

One obstacle to intercultural competence to which we want to give special attention is racism. Because racism often plays such a major role in the communication that occurs between people of different races or ethnic groups, it is particularly important to understand how and why it occurs.

The word racism itself can evoke very powerful emotional reactions, especially for those who have felt the oppression and exploitation that stems from racist attitudes and behaviors.

■ Racism is a force with which both individuals and social systems must grapple. This monument, in California's Manzanar War Relocation Center, stands as a reminder that about 120,000 Japanese American citizens were rounded up and placed in one of ten internment camps in the United States during World War II.

For members of the African American, Asian American, Native American, and Latino cultures, racism has created a social history shaped by prejudice and discrimination.[34] For individual members of these groups, racism has resulted in the pain of oppression. To those who are members of cultural groups that have had the power to oppress and exploit others, the term *racism* often evokes equally powerful thoughts and emotional reactions that deny responsibility for and participation in racist acts and thinking. In this section, we want to introduce some ideas about racism that illuminate the reactions of both those who have received racist communication and those who are seen as exhibiting it.

Robert Blauner has described racism as a tendency to categorize people who are culturally different in terms of their physical traits, such as skin color, hair color and texture, facial structure, and eye shape.[35] Dalmas Taylor offers a related approach that focuses on the behavioral components of racism. Taylor defines racism as the cumulative effects of individuals, institutions, and cultures that result in the oppression of ethnic minorities.[36] Taylor's approach is useful in that it recognizes that racism can occur at three distinct levels: individual, institutional, and cultural.

At the individual level, racism is conceptually very similar to prejudice. Individual racism involves beliefs, attitudes, and behaviors of a given person toward people of a different racial group.[37] Specific European Americans, for example, who believe that African Americans are somehow inferior, exemplify individual racism. Positive contact and interaction between members of the two groups can sometimes change these attitudes. Yet, as the preceding discussion of prejudice suggests, people with prejudicial beliefs about others often distort new information to fit their original prejudices.

At the institutional level, racism is the exclusion of certain people from equal participation in the society's institutions solely because of their race.[38] Institutional racism is built into such social structures as the government, schools, the media, and industry practices. It leads to certain patterns of behaviors and responses to specific racial or cultural groups that allow those groups to be systematically exploited and oppressed. For example, institutional racism has precluded both Jews and African Americans from attending certain public schools and universities, and at times it has restricted their participation in particular professions.[39] Repeated instances of institutional racism, which commonly appear in the popular media, can be especially difficult to overcome. By focusing on some topics or characteristics and not on others, the media often "prime" people's attention and thereby influence the interpretations and evaluations one makes of others. Such biased portrayals can be particularly salient when the media provide people's primary or only knowledge of particular cultures and their members. Consider, for example, Elizabeth Bird's insightful analysis of the ways in which Native Americans are marginalized by the popular media's portrayal of their sexuality:

> The representations we see are structured in predictable, gendered ways. Women are faceless, rather sexless squaws in minor roles, or sexy exotic princesses or maidens who desire White men. Men are either handsome young warriors, who desire White women, or safe sexless wise elders, who dispense ancient wisdom. Nowhere, in this iconography, do the male and female images meet. The world where American Indian men and women love, laugh, and couple *together* lurks far away in the shadows. These days, representations of American Indians are more accurate, in terms of costume, cultural detail, and the like than in the 1950s, when White actors darkened their skins to play American Indians. As far as suggesting an authentic, subjective American Indian experience, though, there has been little progress.[40]

As Bird concludes, current portrayals of Native Americans "may be more benign images than the squaw or the crazed savage, but they are equally unreal and, ultimately, equally dehumanizing."[41]

At the cultural level, racism denies the existence of the culture of a particular group[42]—for example, the denial that African Americans represent a unique and distinct culture that is separate from both European American culture and all African cultures. Cultural racism also involves the rejection by one group of the beliefs and values of another, such as the "negative evaluations by whites of black cultural values."[43]

Although *racism* is often used synonymously with *prejudice* and *discrimination,* the social attributes that distinguish it from these other terms are oppression and power. Oppression refers to "the systematic, institutionalized mistreatment of one group of people by another."[44] Thus, racism is the tendency by groups in control of institutional and cultural power to use it to keep members of groups who do not have access to the same kinds of power at a disadvantage. Racism oppresses entire groups of people, making it very difficult, and sometimes virtually impossible, for their members to have access to political, economic, and social power.[45]

Forms of racism vary in intensity and degree of expression, with some forms far more dangerous and detrimental to society than others. The most extreme form of racism is *old-fashioned racism.* Here, members of one group openly display obviously bigoted views about those from another group. Judgments of superiority and inferiority are common-place in this kind of racism, and there is a dehumanizing quality to it. African Americans and other cultural groups in the United States have often experienced this form of racism from other U.S. Americans.

Symbolic racism, which is sometimes called *modern racism,* is currently prevalent in the United States. In symbolic racism, members of a group with political and economic power believe that members of some other group threaten their traditional values, such as individu-alism and self-reliance. Fears that the outgroup will achieve economic or social success, with a simultaneous loss of economic or social status by the ingroup, typify this form of racism. In many parts of the United States, for instance, this type of racism has been directed toward Asians and Asian Americans who are accused of being too "pushy" because they have achieved economic success. Similarly, symbolic racism includes the expression of feelings that members of cultures such as African Americans and Mexican Americans are moving too fast in seeking social change, are too demanding of equality and social justice, are not playing by the "rules" established in previous generations, and simply do not deserve all that they have recently gained. Paradoxically, symbolic racists typically do not feel personally threat-ened by the successes of other cultures, but they fear for their core values and the continued maintenance of their political and economic power.[46]

Tokenism as a form of racism occurs when individuals do not perceive themselves as prejudiced because they make small concessions to, while holding basically negative attitudes toward, members of the other group. Tokenism is the practice of reverse discrimination, in which people go out of their way to favor a few members of another group in order to main-tain their own self-concepts as individuals who believe in equality for all. Such behaviors may increase a person's esteem, but they may also decrease the possibilities for more meaningful contributions to intercultural unity and progress.

Aversive racism, like tokenism, occurs when individuals who highly value fairness and equality among all racial and cultural groups nevertheless have negative beliefs and feelings about members of a particular race, often as a result of childhood socialization experiences. Individuals with such conflicting feelings may restrain their overt racist behaviors, but they may also avoid close contact with members of the other group and may express their underly-ing negative attitudes subtly, in ways that appear rational and that can be justified on the basis of some factor other than race or culture. Thus, the negativity of aversive racists "is more likely to be manifested in discomfort, uneasiness, fear, or avoidance of minorities rather than overt hostility."[47] An individual at work, for instance, may be polite but distant to a coworker from another culture but may avoid that person at a party they both happen to attend.

Genuine likes and dislikes may also operate as a form of racism. The cultural prac-tices of some groups of people can form the basis for a prejudicial attitude simply because the group displays behaviors that another group does not like. For example, individuals from cultures that are predominantly vegetarian may develop negative attitudes toward those who belong to cultures that eat meat.

Finally, the least alarming form of racism, and certainly one that everyone has experi-enced, is based on the degree of unfamiliarity with members of other groups. Simply re-sponding to unfamiliar people may create negative attitudes because of a lack of experience with the characteristics of their group. The others may look, smell, talk, or act differently, all of which can be a source of discomfort and can form the basis for prejudicial attitudes or racist actions.

Identity, Biases, and Intercultural Competence

In Chapters 4 and 5, we suggested that learning about the preferences that describe your own culture's patterns, in order to understand better your own beliefs, values, norms, and social practices, was an important step toward improving intercultural competence. The discussion of cultural identity in this chapter should serve to reinforce this guideline. A good place to begin is by describing your own cultural identity. Is this relatively easy for you to do? Have you always been aware of your cultural background, or have you experienced events that have caused you to search for an understanding of your cultural identity? Do you place your cultural identity primarily in one cultural group or in several cultural groups? How does your cultural identity shape your social and personal identity? Does your cultural identity result in a strong sense of others as either in or out of your cultural group? If so, were you taught to evaluate negatively those who are not part of your cultural group? Conversely, do you sometimes feel excluded from and evaluated negatively by people from cultures that differ from your own? The answers to these questions will help you to understand the possible consequences, both positive and negative, of your cultural identity as you communicate interculturally.

To improve your intercultural competence by building positive motivations, or emotional reactions, to intercultural interactions, take an honest inventory of the various ways in which you categorize other people. Can you identify your obvious ethnocentric attitudes about appearance, food, and social practices? Make a list of the stereotypes, both positive and negative, that you hold about the various cultural groups with which you regularly interact. Now identify those stereotypes that others might hold about your culture. By engaging in this kind of self-reflective process, you are becoming more aware of the ways in which your social categorizations detract from an ability to understand communication from culturally different others.

Ethnocentrism, stereotyping, prejudice, discrimination, and racism are so familiar and comfortable that overcoming them requires a commitment both to learning about

CULTURE connections

I am, again, on the line.

I've been drawn to it my entire life, beginning with frequent childhood jaunts across it to Tijuana and back—that leap from the monochrome suburban grids of Southern California to the Technicolor swirl of urban Baja California and back. I am an American today because of that line—and my parents' will to erase it with their desire. I return to it again and again because I am from both sides. So for me, son of a mother who emigrated from El Salvador and a Mexican American father who spent his own childhood leaping back and forth, the line is a sieve. And it is a brick wall. It defines me even as I defy it. It is a book without a clear beginning or end, and despite the fact that we refer to it as a "line," it is not even linear; to compare it to an actual book I'd have to invoke Cortázar's "Hopscotch." This line does and does not exist. It is a historical, political, economic and cultural fact. It is a laughable, puny, meaningless thing. It is a matter of life and death.

—*Rubén Martínez*

other cultures and to understanding one's own. A willingness to explore various cultural experiences without prejudgment is necessary. An ability to behave appropriately and effectively with culturally different others, without invoking prejudiced and stereotyped assumptions, is required. Although no one can completely overcome the obstacles to intercultural competence that naturally exist, the requisite knowledge, motivation, and skill can certainly help to minimize the negative effects of prejudice and discrimination.

The intercultural challenge for all of us now living in a world where interactions with people from different cultures are common features of daily life is to be willing to grapple with the consequences of prejudice, discrimination, and racism at the individual, social, and institutional levels. Because *prejudice* and *racism* are such emotionally charged concepts, it is sometimes very difficult to comment on their occurrence in our interactions with others. Individuals who believe that they have perceived discriminatory remarks and prejudicial actions often recognize that there may be substantial social costs associated with speaking out, and consequently they may sometimes be unwilling to risk the negative evaluations from their coworkers, fellow students, teachers, or service providers that would likely occur should they directly confront such biases and demand interactions that do not display them.[48] Conversely, those who do not regard themselves as having prejudiced or racist attitudes and who believe they never behave in discriminatory ways are horrified to learn that others might interpret their attitudes as prejudiced and their actions as discriminatory. Although discussions about prejudice, discrimination, and racism can lead to a better understanding of the interpersonal dynamics that arise as individuals seek to establish mutually respectful relationships, they can just as easily lead to greater divisions and hostilities between people. The challenge for interculturally competent communicators is to contend with the pressing but potentially inflammatory issues of prejudice and discrimination in a manner that is both appropriate and effective.

We are also challenged to function competently in a world that, increasingly, is characterized by multiple cultures inhabiting adjacent and often-overlapping terrain. The ability to adapt to these intercultural settings—to maintain positive, healthy relationships with people from cultures other than your own—is the hallmark of the interculturally competent individual.

Summary

This chapter began with a discussion of cultural identity. The cultures with which you identify affect your views about where you belong and whom you consider to be "us" and "them."

Next, we discussed the biases that impede the development of intercultural competence. Ethnocentrism, stereotyping, prejudice, discrimination, and racism occur because of the human need to organize and streamline the processing of information. When people assume that these "thinking shortcuts" are accurate representations, intercultural competence is impaired.

Cultural biases are based on normal human tendencies to view ourselves as members of a particular group and to view others as not belonging to that group. Status, power, and economic differences heavily influence all intercultural contacts. Cultural biases are a reminder that all relationships take place within a political, economic, social, and cultural context. The intercultural challenge for all of us, as we live in a world where interactions with people from different cultures are common features of daily life, is to be willing to grapple with the consequences of prejudice, discrimination, and racism at the individual, social, and institutional levels.

For Discussion

1. If people are born into one culture but raised in another, to which culture(s) do they belong?
2. What are the advantages and disadvantages for U.S. Americans who grow up with multiple cultural heritages?
3. What do people lose, and what do they gain, from having an ethnocentric perspective?
4. Is it possible for European Americans to be the recipients of any form of racism in the United States?
5. Why might less obvious or less alarming forms of racism be just as dangerous as old-fashioned or symbolic racism?

For Further Reading

Gordon W. Allport, *The Nature of Prejudice* (Cambridge, MA: Addison-Wesley, 1954). A classic work that established our understanding of the hows, whys, and nature of prejudice in human interaction.

Sapna Cheryan and Benoît Monin, "'Where Are You Really From?': Asian Americans and Identity Denial," *Journal of Personality and Social Psychology* 89 (2005): 717–730. Examines issues of identity, stereotyping, and discrimination of a U.S. cultural group.

Yoshihisa Kashima, Klaus Fiedler, and Peter Freytag (eds.), *Stereotype Dynamics: Language-Based Approaches to the Formation, Maintenance, and Transformation of Stereotypes* (New York: Erlbaum, 2008). Details how our stereotypes of others develop, persist, and (sometimes) change.

Todd D. Nelson, *The Psychology of Prejudice,* 2nd ed. (Boston: Allyn & Bacon, 2006). Provides a thorough understanding of the causes and consequences of stereotyping and prejudice and offers some approaches for reducing prejudice.

For additional information about intercultural films and about Web sites for researching specific cultures, please turn to the Resources section at the back of this book.

Verbal Intercultural Communication

KEY TERMS

In this chapter, we consider the effects of language systems on people's ability to communicate interculturally. In so doing, we explore the accuracy of a statement by the world-famous linguistic philosopher Ludwig Wittgenstein, who asserted that "the limits of my language are the limits of my world."

The Power of Language in Intercultural Communication

Consider the following examples, each of which illustrates the pivotal role of language in human interaction:

> A U.S. business executive is selected by her company for an important assignment in Belgium, not only because she has been very successful but also because she speaks French. She prepares her materials and presentation and sets off for Belgium with high expectations for landing a new contract for her firm. Once in Belgium, she learns that, although the individuals in the Belgian company certainly speak French, and there are even individuals who speak German or English, their first language and the preferred language for conducting their business is Flemish. Both the U.S. business executive and her company failed to consider that Belgium is a multicultural and multilingual country populated by Walloons who speak French and Flemings who speak Flemish.

> Vijay is a student from India who has just arrived in the United States to attend graduate school at a major university. Vijay began to learn English in primary school, and since his field of study is engineering, even his classes in the program leading to his bachelor's degree were conducted in English. Vijay considers himself to be proficient in the English language. Nevertheless, during his first week on campus, the language of those around him is bewildering. People seem to talk so fast that Vijay has difficulty differentiating one word from another. Even when he recognizes the words, he cannot quite understand what people mean by them. His dormitory roommate seemed to say, "I'll catch you later" when he left the room. The secretary in the departmental office tried to explain to him about his teaching assistantship and the students assigned to the classes he was helping to instruct. Her references to students who would attempt to "crash" the course were very puzzling to him. His new faculty advisor, sensing Vijay's anxiety about all of these new situations, told him to "hang loose" and "go with the flow." When Vijay inquired of another teaching assistant about the meaning of these words, the teaching assistant's only reaction was to shake his head and say, "Your advisor's from another time zone!" Needless to say, Vijay's bewilderment continued.

Language—whether it is English, French, Swahili, Flemish, Hindi, or one of the world's other numerous languages—is a taken-for-granted aspect of people's lives. Language is learned without conscious awareness. Children are capable of using their language competently before the age of formal schooling. Even during their school years, they learn the rules and words of the language and do not attend to how the language influences the way they think and perceive the world. It is usually only when people speak their language to those who do not understand it or when they struggle to become competent in another language that they recognize language's central role in the ability to function, to accomplish tasks, and, most important, to interact with others. It is only when the use of language no longer connects people to others or when individuals are denied the use of their language that they recognize its importance.

There is a set of circumstances involving communication with people from other cultural backgrounds in which awareness of language becomes paramount. Intercultural communication usually means interaction between people who speak different languages. Even when the individuals seem to be speaking the same language—a person from Spain interacting with someone from Venezuela, a French Canadian conversing with a French-speaking citizen of Belgium, or an Australian person visiting the United States—the differences in the specific dialects of the language and the different cultural

CULTURE connections

For the first time I fully understood what an isolating factor language can be. My own identity and ability to integrate into Brazil were founded in language and my capacity to communicate. I found a surprising side of me, so timid that it hamstrung my ability to interact. No one who knew me from home would ever guess I knew how to be shy, but here I had often frozen in embarrassment, swallowing words I could speak perfectly well moments earlier, creating a lonely cocoon of my own silence. Sometimes the hassle of attempting to communicate was so intimidating that I chose to hibernate in my apartment.

—Eliza Bonner

practices that govern language use can mystify those involved, and they can realistically be portrayed as two people who speak different languages.

In this chapter, we explore the nature of language and how verbal codes affect communication between people of different cultural backgrounds. Because this book is written in English and initially intended for publication and distribution in the United States, many of the examples and comparisons refer to characteristics of the English language as it is used in the United States. We begin with a discussion of the characteristics and rule systems that create verbal codes and the process of interpretation from one verbal code to another. We then turn to a discussion of the all-important topic of the relationship among language, culture, thought, and intercultural communication. As we consider this issue, we explore the Sapir–Whorf hypothesis of linguistic relativity and assess the scholarly evidence that has been amassed both in support of the hypothesis and in opposition to it. We also consider the importance of language in the identity of ethnic and cultural groups. The chapter concludes with a consideration of verbal codes and intercultural competence.

Definition of Verbal Codes

Discussions about the uniqueness of human beings usually center on people's capabilities to manipulate and understand symbols that allow interaction with others. In a discussion of the importance of language, Charles F. Hockett noted that language allows people to understand messages about many different topics from literally thousands of people. Language allows a person to talk with others, to understand or disagree with them, to make plans, to remember the past, to imagine future events, and to describe and evaluate objects and experiences that exist in some other location. Hockett also pointed out that language is taught to individuals by others and, thus, is transmitted from generation to generation in much the same way as culture. In other words, language is learned.[1]

Popular references to language often include not only spoken and written language but also "body language." However, we will discuss the latter topic in the next chapter on nonverbal codes. Here, we will concentrate on understanding the relationship of spoken and written language, or verbal codes, to intercultural communication competence.

The Features of Language

Verbal means "consisting of words." Therefore, a verbal code is a set of rules about the use of words in the creation of messages. Words can obviously be either spoken or written. Verbal codes, then, include both oral (spoken) language and non-oral (written) language.

Children first learn the oral form of a language. Parents do not expect two-year-olds to read the words on the pages of books. Instead, as parents speak aloud to a child, they identify or name objects in order to teach the child the relationship between the language and the objects or ideas the language represents. In contrast, learning a second language as an adolescent or adult often proceeds more formally, with a combination of oral and non-oral approaches. Students in a foreign language class are usually required to buy a textbook that contains written forms of the language, which then guide students in understanding both the oral and the written use of the words and phrases.

The concept of a written language is familiar to all students enrolled in U.S. college and university classes, as they all require at least reasonable proficiency in the non-oral form of the English language. Fewer and fewer languages exist only in oral form. When anthropologists and linguists discover a culture that has a unique oral language, they usually attempt to develop a written form of it in order to preserve it. Indeed, many Hmong who immigrated to the United States from their hill tribes in Southeast Asia have had to learn not only the new language of English but also, in many instances, the basic fact that verbal codes can be expressed in written form. Imagine the enormous task it must be not only to learn a second language but also first to understand that language can be written.

Our concern in this chapter is principally with the spoken verbal codes that are used in face-to-face intercultural communication. Nevertheless, because the written language also

■ Although English is spoken in many parts of the world, its use varies greatly. This sign of caution in a Shanghai shopping mall differs from the words you would find on an escalator in the United States.

CULTURE connections

It was my first year of school, my first days away from the private realm of our house and tongue. I thought English would be simply a version of our Korean. Like another kind of coat you could wear. I didn't know what a difference in language meant then. Or how my tongue would tie in the initial attempts, stiffen so, struggle like an animal booby-trapped and dying inside my head. Native speakers may not fully know this, but English is a scabrous mouthful. In Korean, there are no separate sounds for L and R, the sound is singular and without a baroque Spanish trill or roll. There is no B and V for us, no P and F. I always thought someone must have invented certain words to torture us. *Frivolous. Barbarian....*

I will always make bad errors of speech. I remind myself of my mother and father, fumbling in front of strangers. Lelia says there are certain mental pathways of speaking that can never be unlearned. Sometimes I'll say *riddle* for *little*, or *bent* for *vent*, though without any accent and so whoever's present just thinks I've momentarily lost my train of thought. But I always hear myself displacing the two languages, conflating them—maybe conflagrating them—for there's so much rubbing and friction, a fire always threatens to blow up between the tongues. Friction, affliction. In kindergarten, kids would call me "Marble Mouth" because I spoke in a garbled voice, my bound tongue wrenching itself to move in the right ways.

—Chang-rae Lee

influences the way the language is used orally, written verbal codes play a supporting role in our discussion, and some of our examples and illustrations draw on written expressions of verbal codes in intercultural communication.

An essential ingredient of both verbal and nonverbal codes is symbols. As you recall from Chapter 1, symbols are words, actions, or objects that stand for or represent a unit of meaning. The relationship between symbols and what they stand for is often highly arbitrary, particularly for verbal symbols.

Another critical ingredient of verbal codes is the system of rules that governs the composition and ordering of the symbols. Everyone has had to learn the rules of a language—how to spell, use correct grammar, and make appropriate vocabulary choices—and thereby gain enough mastery of the language to tell jokes, to poke fun, and to be sarcastic. Even more than differences in the symbols themselves, the variations in rules for ordering and using symbols produce the different languages people use.

Rule Systems in Verbal Codes

Five different but interrelated sets of rules combine to create a verbal code, or language. These parts, or components, of language are called phonology, morphology, semantics, syntactics, and pragmatics.

Phonology   When you listen to someone who speaks a language other than your own, you will often hear different (some might even say "strange") sounds. The basic sound units of a language are called phonemes, and the rules for combining phonemes constitute the phonology of a language. Examples of phonemes in English include the sounds you make when speaking, such as [k], [t], or [a].

The phonological rules of a language tell speakers which sounds to use and how to order them. For instance, the word *cat* has three phonemes: a hard [k] sound, the short [a] vowel, and the [t] sound. These same three sounds, or phonemes, can be rearranged to form other combinations: *act, tack,* or even *tka.* Of course, as someone who speaks and writes English, your knowledge of the rules for creating appropriate combinations of phonemes undoubtedly suggests to you that *tka* is improper. Interestingly, you know that *tka* is incorrect even though you probably cannot describe the rules that make it so.[2]

Languages have different numbers of phonemes. English, for example, depends on about forty-five phonemes. The number of phonemes in other languages ranges from as few as fifteen to as many as eighty-five.[3]

Mastery of another language requires practice in reproducing its sounds accurately. Sometimes it is difficult to hear the distinctions in the sounds made by those proficient in the language. Native U.S. English speakers often have difficulty in hearing phonemic distinctions in tonal languages, such as Chinese, that use different pitches for many sounds, which then represent different meanings. Even when the differences can be heard, the mouths and tongues of those learning another language are sometimes unable to produce these sounds. In intercultural communication, imperfect rendering of the phonology of a language—in other words, not speaking the sounds as native speakers do—can make it difficult to be understood accurately. Accents of second-language speakers, which we discuss in more detail later in this chapter, can sometimes provoke negative reactions in native speakers.

Morphology   Phonemes combine to form morphemes, which are the smallest units of meaning in a language. The 45 English phonemes can be used to generate more than 50 million morphemes! For instance, the word *comfort,* whose meaning refers to a state of ease and contentment, contains one morpheme. But the word *comforted* contains two morphemes: *comfort* and *-ed.* The latter is a suffix that means that the comforting action or activity happened in the past. Indeed, although all words contain at least one morpheme, some words (such as *uncomfortable,* which has three morphemes) can contain two or more. Note that morphemes refer only to meaning units. Though the word *comfort* contains smaller words such as *or* and *fort,* these other words are coincidental to the basic meaning of *comfort.* Morphemes, or meaning units in language, can also differ depending on the way they are pronounced. In Chinese, for instance, the word pronounced as "ma" can have four different meanings—mother, toad, horse, or scold—depending on the tone with which it is uttered.[4] Pronunciation errors can have very unintended meanings!

Semantics   As noted earlier, morphemes—either singly or in combination—are used to form words. The study of the meaning of words is called semantics. The most convenient and thorough source of information about the semantics of a language is the dictionary, which defines what a word means in a particular language. A more formal way of describing the study of semantics is to say that it is the study of the relationship between words and what they stand for or represent. You can see the semantics of a language in action when a baby is being taught to name the parts of the body. Someone skilled in the language points to and touches the baby's nose and simultaneously vocalizes the word *nose.* Essentially, the baby is being taught the vocabulary of a language. Competent communication in any language

■ Can you order from this menu in Italy?

requires knowledge of the words needed to express ideas. You have probably experienced the frustration of trying to describe an event but not being able to think of words that accurately convey the intended meaning. Part of what we are trying to accomplish with this book is to give you a vocabulary that can be used to understand and explain the nature of intercultural communication competence.

Communicating interculturally necessitates learning a new set of semantic rules. The baby who grows up where people speak Swahili does not learn to say *nose* when the protruding portion of the face is touched; instead, she or he is taught to say *pua*. For an English speaker to talk with a Swahili speaker about his or her nose, at least one of them must learn the word for nose in the other's language. When learning a second language, much time is devoted to learning the appropriate associations between the words and the specific objects, events, or feelings that the language system assigns to them. Even those whose intercultural communication occurs with people who speak the "same" language must learn at least some new vocabulary. The U.S. American visiting Great Britain will confront new meanings for words. For example, *boot* refers to the storage place in a car, or what the U.S.-English-speaking person would call the *trunk*. *Chips* to the British are *French fries* to the U.S. American. A *Band-Aid* in the United States is called a *plug* in Great Britain. As Winston Churchill so wryly suggested, the two countries are indeed "divided by a common language."

The discussion of semantics is incomplete without noting one other important distinction: the difference between the denotative and connotative meanings of words. Denotative meanings are the public, objective, and legal meanings of a word. Denotative meanings are those found in the dictionary or law books. In contrast, connotative meanings are personal, emotionally charged, private, and specific to a particular person.

As an illustration, consider a common classroom event known as a *test*. When used by a college professor who is speaking to a group of undergraduate students, *test* is a relatively easy word to define denotatively. It is a formal examination that is used to assess a person's degree of knowledge or skill. But the connotative meanings of *test* probably vary greatly from student to student; some react to the idea with panic, and others are blasé and casual. Whereas denotative meanings tell, in an abstract sense, what the words mean objectively, our interest in intercultural communication suggests that an understanding of the connotative meanings—the feelings and thoughts evoked in others as a result of the words used in the conversation—is critical to achieving intercultural competence.

As an example of the importance of connotative meanings, consider the experience reported by a Nigerian student who was attending a university in the United States. When working with a fellow male student who was African American, the Nigerian called to him by saying, "Hey, boy, come over here." To the Nigerian student, the term *boy* connotes a friendly and familiar relationship, is a common form of address in Nigeria, and is often used to convey a perception of a strong interpersonal bond. To the African American student, however, the term *boy* evokes images of racism, oppression, and an attempt to place him in an inferior social status. Fortunately, the two students were friends and were able to talk to each other to clarify how they each interpreted the Nigerian student's semantic choices; further misunderstandings were avoided. Often, however, such opportunities for clarification do not occur.

Another example is seen in the casual conversation of a U.S. American student and an Arab student. The former had heard a radio news story about the intelligence of pigs and was recounting the story as "fact" when the Arab student forcefully declared, "Pigs are dirty animals, and they are very dumb." The U.S. American student describes her reaction: "In my ignorance, I argued with him by telling him that it was true and had been scientifically proven." It was only later that she learned that as part of the religious beliefs of devout Muslims, pigs are believed to be unclean. Learning the connotative meanings of language is essential in achieving competence in another culture's verbal code.

Syntactics The fourth component of language is syntactics, the relationship of words to one another. When children are first learning how to combine words into phrases, they are being introduced to the syntactics of their language. Each language stipulates the correct way to arrange words. In English it is not acceptable to create a sentence such as the following: "On by the book desk door is the the." It is incorrect to place the preposition *by* immediately following the preposition *on*. Instead, each preposition must have an object, which results in phrases such as "on the desk" and "by the door." Similarly, articles such as *the* in a sentence are not to be presented one right after the other. Instead, the article is placed near the noun, which produces a sentence that includes "the book," "the door," and "the desk." The syntactics of English grammar suggest that the words in the preceding nonsense sentence might be rearranged to form the grammatically correct sentence "The book is on the desk by the door." The order of the words helps establish the meaning of the utterance.

Each language has a set of rules that govern the sequence of the words. To learn another language, you must learn those rules. The sentence "John has, to the store to buy some eggs, gone" is an incorrect example of English syntax but an accurate representation of German syntax.

Pragmatics The final component of all verbal codes is pragmatics, the effect of language on human perceptions and behaviors. The study of pragmatics focuses on how language is actually used. A pragmatic analysis of language goes beyond phonology, morphology, semantics, and syntactics. Instead, it considers how users of a particular language are able to understand the meanings of specific utterances in particular contexts. For example, some people regard the U.S. American greeting ritual that asks *"How are you?"* as insincere and perhaps even hypocritical. As an Israeli woman observed,

No matter if your kids are on drugs, your spouse is leaving you, and you just declared bankruptcy, you are expected to smile, and say, "Everything is great!" Why do Americans ask if they don't really want to know?[5]

CULTURE connections

When I was learning to read and speak the Tamil language I slowly came to realize that it had no word for "hope." When I questioned my Hindu teacher about this, he asked me in turn what I meant by hope. Does hope mean anything? Things will be what they will be.... This conversation helped me to realize that in English also the word "hope" often stands for nothing more than a desire for what may or may not be.

—*Lesslie Newbigin*

Of course, to U.S. Americans the frequently asked question *"How are you?"* is simply intended as a pleasant and polite greeting ritual and is not expected to be an inquiry into one's well-being.

By learning the pragmatics of language use, you understand how to participate in a conversation and you know how to sequence the sentences you speak as part of the conversation. Thus, when you are eating a meal with a group of people and somebody says, "Is there any salt?" you know that you should give the person the salt shaker rather than simply answering "yes."

To illustrate how the pragmatics of language use can affect intercultural communication, imagine yourself as a dinner guest in a Pakistani household. You have just eaten a delicious meal. You are relatively full but not so full that it would be impossible for you to eat more if it was considered socially appropriate to do so. Consider the following dialogue:

Hostess: I see that your plate is empty. Would you like some more curry?

You: No, thank you. It was delicious, but I'm quite full.

Hostess: Please, you must have some more to eat.

You: No, no thank you. I've really had enough. It was just great, but I can't eat another bite.

Hostess: Are you sure that you won't have any more? You really seemed to enjoy the brinjals. Let me put just a little bit more on your plate.

What is your next response? What is the socially appropriate answer? Is it considered socially inappropriate for a dinner guest not to accept a second helping of food? Or is the hostess pressing you to have another helping because, in her culture, your reply is not interpreted as a true negative response? Even if you knew Urdu, the language spoken in Pakistan, you would have to understand the pragmatics of language use to respond appropriately—in this instance, to say "no" at least three times.

The rules governing the pragmatics of a language are firmly embedded in the larger rules of the culture and are intimately associated with the cultural patterns discussed in Chapters 4 and 5. For example, cultures vary in the degree to which they encourage people to ask direct questions and to make direct statements. Imagine a student from the United States who speaks some Japanese and who subsequently goes to Japan as an exchange student. The U.S. American's culturally learned tendency is to deal with problems directly, and she may therefore confront her Japanese roommate about the latter's habits in order to "clear the air"

CULTURE connections

Barrett had one of those accents that used to make me feel very self-conscious about my own flat mid-America voice. Sneh sneh sneh, I say, snick snick snick; the sound scissors make shearing off thick hair. My father always managed to cover up his Englishness with a transatlantic patina, but without his actor's skill at mimicry my grasp of this new language has not been entirely successful. Even though I've learned to say knickers when I mean underpants, people still remark, 'Oh, you're *American*' every time I open my mouth. As if American is a synonym for no culture, no history, the wrong vocabulary. I pronounce flower with an er in it, God with an awe. Although inside me there's a different voice, refined and full of ironic insight, it always comes out *awe, er, um*, and instead of 'Absolutely!' I say 'You bet!' (a New World stress on the element of risk). In England, a less extreme landscape, people seem more sure of their footing. They're always saying 'Absolutely!' . . .

—*Leslie Forbes*

and establish an "open" relationship. Given the Japanese cultural preference for indirectness and face-saving behaviors, the U.S. American student's skill in Japanese does not extend to the pragmatics of language use. As Wen Shu Lee suggests, these differences in the pragmatic rule systems of languages also make it very difficult to tell a joke—or even to understand a joke—in a second language.[6] Humor requires a subtle knowledge of both the expected meanings of the words (semantics) and their intended effects (pragmatics).

Interpretation and Intercultural Communication

Translation can be defined as the use of verbal signs to understand the verbal signs of another language.[7] Translation usually refers to the transfer of written verbal codes between languages. Interpretation refers to the oral process of moving from one code to another. When heads of state meet, an interpreter accompanies them. The translator, in contrast to the interpreter, usually has more time to consider how she or he wants to phrase a particular passage in a text. Interpreters must make virtually immediate decisions about which words or phrases would best represent the meanings of the speaker.

The Role of Interpretation in Today's World   Issues surrounding the interpretation of verbal codes from one language to another are becoming more and more important for all of us. Such issues include whether the words or the ideas of the original should be conveyed, whether the translation should reflect the style of the original or that of the translator, and whether an interpreter should correct cultural mistakes.

In today's global marketplace, health care workers, teachers, government workers, and businesspeople of all types find that they are increasingly required to use professional interpreters to communicate verbally with their clients and, thus, fulfill their professional obligations.[8] Similarly, instructions for assembling consumer products that are sold in the United States but manufactured in another country often demonstrate the difficulty in moving from one language to another. Even though the words on the printed instruction sheet are in English, the instructions may not be correct or accurately interpreted.

Issues in interpretation, then, are very important. People involved in intercultural transactions must often depend on the services of multilingual individuals who can help to bridge the intercultural communication gap.

Types of Equivalence   If the goal in interpreting from one language to another is to represent the source language as closely as possible, a simpler way of describing the goal is with the term equivalence. Those concerned about developing a science of translation have described a number of different types of equivalence. Dynamic equivalence has been offered as one goal of good translation and interpretation.[9] Five kinds of equivalence must be considered in moving from one language to another: vocabulary, idiomatic, grammatical–syntactical, experiential, and conceptual equivalence.[10]

Vocabulary Equivalence   To establish vocabulary equivalence, the interpreter seeks a word in the target language that has the same meaning in the source language. This is sometimes very difficult to do. Perhaps the words spoken in the source language have no direct equivalents in the target language. For instance, in Igbo, a language spoken in Nigeria, there is no word for *window*. The word in Igbo that is used to represent a window, *mpio*, actually means "opening." Likewise, there is no word for *efficiency* in the Russian language, and the English phrase "A house is not a home" has no genuine vocabulary equivalent in some languages. Alternatively, there may be several words in the target language that have similar meanings to the word in the source language, so the interpreter must select the word that best fits the intended ideas. An interpreter will sometimes use a combination of words in the target language to approximate the original word, or the interpreter may offer several different words to help the listener understand the meaning of the original message.

■ This sign, which is in Chinese, Korean, Spanish, Vietnamese, Japanese, Tagalog, and English, reflects the many languages used by U.S. Americans.

Idiomatic Equivalence   An idiom is an expression that has a meaning contrary to the usual meaning of the words. Phrases such as "Eat your heart out," "It's raining cats and dogs," and "Eat humble pie" are all examples of idioms. Idioms are so much a part of language that people are rarely aware of using them. Think of the literal meaning of the following idiom: "I was so upset I could have died." Or consider the plight of a Malaysian student who described his befuddlement when his fellow students in the United States initiated conversations by asking, "What's up?" His instinctive reaction was to look up, but after doing so several times he realized that the question was an opening to conversation rather than a literal reference to something happening above him. Another example is the request a supervisor in a university media center made to a student assistant from India, who tended to take conversations and instructions literally. The supervisor instructed the assistant to "put this videotape on the television." The supervisor was later surprised to learn that the videotape was literally placed on top of the television, instead of being played for the class. The challenge for interpreters is to understand the intended meanings of idiomatic expressions and to translate them into the other language.

Grammatical–Syntactical Equivalence   The discussion later in this chapter about some of the variations among grammars highlights the problems in establishing equivalence in grammatical or syntactical rule systems. Quite simply, some languages make grammatical distinctions that others do not. For instance, when translating from the Hopi language into English, the interpreter has to make adjustments for the lack of verb tenses in Hopi because tense is a necessary characteristic of every English utterance.

Experiential Equivalence   Differing life experiences are another hurdle the interpreter must overcome. The words presented must have some meaning within the experiential framework of the person to whom the message is directed. If people have never seen a television, for instance, a translation of the phrase "I am going to stay home tonight and watch television" would have virtually no meaning to them. Similarly, although clocks are a common device for telling time and they govern the behaviors of most U.S. Americans, many people live in cultures in which there are no clocks and no words for this concept. Some Hmong people, upon moving to the United States, initially had difficulty with the everyday experience of telling time with a clock.

CULTURE connections

Arabic is a language fond of formal indirectness, and, during the first planning sessions of the Arab-language edition of "The Apprentice," the producers decided to replace "You're fired!"—Donald Trump's catchphrase of blunt humiliation—with a line that translates into English as "May God be kind to you."

—*Ian Parker*

Conceptual Equivalence   Conceptual equivalence takes us back to the discussions in Chapters 4 and 5 about cultural patterns being part of a person's definition of reality. Conversation with people with radically different cultural patterns requires making sense of the variety of concepts that each culture defines as real and good.

Language, Thought, Culture, and Intercultural Communication

Every language has its unique features and ways of allowing those who speak it to identify specific objects and experiences. These linguistic features, which distinguish each language from all others, affect how the speakers of the language perceive and experience the world. To understand the effects of language on intercultural communication, questions such as the following must be explored:

- How do initial experiences with language shape or influence the way in which a person thinks?
- Do the categories of a language—its words, grammar, and usage—influence how people think and behave?

More specifically, consider the following question:

- Does a person growing up in Saudi Arabia, who learns to speak and write Arabic, "see" and "experience" the world differently than does a person who grows up speaking and writing Tagalog in the Philippines?

Although many scholars have advanced ideas and theories about the relationships among language, thought, culture, and intercultural communication, the names most often associated with these issues are Benjamin Lee Whorf and Edward Sapir. Their theory is called linguistic relativity.

The Sapir–Whorf Hypothesis of Linguistic Relativity

Until the early part of the twentieth century, in western Europe and the United States, language was generally assumed to be a neutral medium that did not influence the way people experienced the world.[11] During that time, the answer to the preceding question would have been that, regardless of whether people grew up learning and speaking Arabic or Tagalog, they would experience the world similarly. The varying qualities of language would not have been expected to affect the people who spoke those languages. Language, from this point of view, was merely a vehicle by which ideas were presented, rather than a shaper of the very substance of those ideas.

In 1921, anthropologist Edward Sapir began to articulate an alternative view of language, asserting that language influenced or even determined the ways in which people thought.[12] Sapir's student, Benjamin Whorf, continued to develop Sapir's ideas through the 1940s. Together, their ideas became subsumed under several labels, including the theory of linguistic determinism, the theory of linguistic relativity, the Sapir–Whorf hypothesis, and the Whorfian hypothesis. The following quotation from Sapir is typical of their statements:

These school children in Pakistan are practicing their writing. The Sapir–Whorf hypothesis underscores the relationship between their language and their experiences in the world.

Human beings do not live in the objective world alone, nor alone in the world of social activity as ordinarily understood, but are very much at the mercy of the particular language which has become the medium of expression for their society. It is quite an illusion to imagine that one adjusts to reality essentially without the use of language and that language is merely an incidental means of solving specific problems of communication or reflection. The fact of the matter is that the "real world" is to a large extent unconsciously built up on the language habits of the group.... The worlds in which different societies [cultures] live are distinct worlds, not merely the same world with different labels attached.... We see and hear and otherwise experience very largely as we do because the language habits of our community predispose certain choices of interpretation.[13]

Our discussion of the Sapir–Whorf hypothesis is not intended to provide a precise rendering as articulated by Sapir and Whorf, which is virtually impossible to do. During the twenty years in which they formally presented their ideas to the scholarly community, their views shifted somewhat, and their writings include both "firmer," or more deterministic views of the relationship between language and thought, and "softer" views that describe language as merely influencing or shaping thought.

In the "firm," or deterministic, version of the hypothesis, language functions like a prison—once people learn a language, they are irrevocably affected by its particulars. Furthermore, it is never possible to translate effectively and successfully between languages, which makes competent intercultural communication an elusive goal.

The "softer" position is a less causal view of the nature of the language–thought relationship. In this version, language shapes how people think and experience their world, but this influence is not unceasing. Instead, it is possible for people from different initial language systems to learn words and categories sufficiently similar to their own so that communication can be accurate.

If substantial evidence had been found to support the firmer version of the Sapir–Whorf hypothesis, it would represent a dismal prognosis for competent intercultural communication. Because so few people grow up bilingually, it would be impossible to transcend the boundaries of their linguistic experiences. Fortunately, the weight of the scholarly evidence, which we summarize in the following section, debunks the notion that people's first language traps them inescapably in a particular pattern of thinking. Instead, evidence suggests that language plays a powerful role in *shaping* how people think and experience the world. Although the shaping properties of language are significant, linguistic equivalence can be established between people from different language systems.[14]

Sapir and Whorf's major contribution to the study of intercultural communication is that they called attention to the integral relationship among thought, culture, and language. In the following section, we discuss some of the differences in the vocabulary and grammar of languages and consider the extent to which these differences can be used as evidence to support the two positions of the Sapir–Whorf hypothesis. As you consider the following ideas, examine the properties of the languages you know. Are there specialized vocabularies or grammatical characteristics that shape how you think and experience the world as you use these languages?

Variations in Vocabulary   The best known example of vocabulary differences associated with the Sapir–Whorf hypothesis is the large number of words for snow in the Eskimo language. (The language is variously called Inuktitut in Canada, Inupit in Alaska, and Kalaallisut in Greenland.) Depending on whom you ask, there are from seven to fifty different words for snow in the Inuktitut language.[15] For example, there are words that differentiate falling snow (*gana*) and fully fallen snow (*akilukak*). The English language has fewer words for snow and no terms for many of the distinctions made by Eskimos. The issue raised by the Sapir–Whorf hypothesis is whether the person who grows up speaking Inuktitut actually perceives snow differently than does someone who grew up in Southern California and may only know snow by secondhand descriptions. More important, could the Southern Californian who lives with the Inupit in Alaska learn to differentiate all of the variations of snow and to use the specific Eskimo words appropriately? The firmer version of the Sapir–Whorf hypothesis suggests that linguistic differences are accompanied by perceptual differences, so that the English speaker looks at snow differently than does the Eskimo speaker.

Numerous other examples of languages have highly specialized vocabularies for particular features of the environment. For instance, in the South Sea islands, there are numerous words for coconut, which not only refer to the object of a coconut but also indicate how the coconut is being used or to a specific part of the coconut.[16] Similarly, in classical Arabic, thousands of words are used to refer to a camel.[17]

Another variation in vocabulary concerns the terms a language uses to identify and divide colors in the spectrum. For example, the Kamayura Indians of Brazil have a single word that refers to the colors that English speakers would call blue and green. The best translation of the word the Kamayuras use is "parakeet colored."[18] The Dani of West New Guinea divide all colors into only two words, which are roughly equivalent in English to "dark" and "light."[19] The important issue, however, is whether speakers of these languages are able to distinguish among the different colors when they see them or can experience only the colors suggested by the words available for them to use. Do the Kamayura Indians actually see blue and green as the same color because they use the same word to identify both? Or does their language simply identify colors differently than does English?

Do you think that you could learn to distinguish all of the variations of the object "snow" that are important to the Eskimos? Could you be taught to see all of the important characteristics of a camel or a coconut? Such questions are very important in accepting or rejecting the ideas presented in the firm and soft versions of the Sapir–Whorf hypothesis.

Researchers looking at the vocabulary variations in the color spectrum have generally found that, although a language may restrict how a color can be labeled verbally, people can still see and differentiate among particular colors. In other words, the Kamayura

CULTURE connections

Hindi	English Equivalent
baap or pitagi	Father
maa	Mother
baba or dada	Father's father
amma or dadi	Father's mother
nana	Mother's father
nani	Mother's mother
taaya	Father's elder brother or paternal cousin
taayi	Wife of father's elder brother or paternal cousin
chacha	Father's younger brother, or paternal cousin
chachi	Wife of father's younger brother, or paternal cousin
mama	Mother's brother
mami	Wife of mother's brother
booa	Father's sister
foofa	Husband of father's sister
mausi	Mother's sister
mausa	Husband of mother's sister
bahai	Brother, male paternal cousin
bhabhi	Brother's wife
bhatija	Brother's son
bhatiji	Brother's daughter
bahin	Sister, female paternal cousin
geja	Sister's husband
bhanja	Sister's son
bhangi	Sister's daughter
beta	Son
bahu	Son's wife, daughter-in-law
pota	Son's son
poti	Son's daughter
beti	Daughter or niece
daamaad	Daughter's husband
naati	Daughter's son
naatin	Daughter's daughter
soosar	Father-in-law
sasu	Mother-in-law
saala	Wife's brother
saali	Wife's sister
saadoo	Husband of wife's sister
nanad	Husband's sister
nandoi	Husband of husband's sister

(continued)

jaith	Husband's elder brother, or paternal cousin
jethani	Wife of husband's elder brother, or paternal cousin
dewar	Husband's younger brother, or paternal cousin
samdhi	Son/daughter-in-law's father
samdhan	Son/daughter-in-law's mother
derani	Wife of husband's younger brother, or paternal cousin

—Leigh Minturn

Indians can, in fact, see both blue and green, even though they use the same linguistic referent for both colors.[20] The evidence on color perception and vocabulary, then, does not support the deterministic version of the Sapir–Whorf hypothesis.

What about all those variations for snow, camels, and coconuts? Are they evidence to support the firm version of the Sapir–Whorf hypothesis? A starting point for addressing this issue is to consider how English speakers use other words along with essentially the one word English has for "particles of water vapor that, when frozen in the upper air, fall to earth as soft, white, crystalline flakes." English speakers are able to describe verbally many variations of snow by adding modifiers to the root word. People who live in areas with a lot of snow are quite familiar with *dry snow, heavy snow, slush,* and *dirty snow.* Skiers have a rich vocabulary to describe variations in snow on the slopes. It is possible, therefore, for a person who has facility in one language to approximate the categories of another language. The deterministic position of Sapir–Whorf, then, is difficult to support. Even Sapir and Whorf's own work can be used to argue against the deterministic interpretation of their position because, in presenting all of the Eskimo words for snow, Whorf provided their approximate English equivalents.

A better explanation for linguistic differences is that variations in the complexity and richness of a language's vocabulary reflect what is important to the people who speak that language. To an Eskimo, differentiating among varieties of snow is much more critical to survival and adaptation than it is to the Southern Californian, who may never see snow. Conversely, Southern Californians have numerous words to refer to four-wheeled motorized vehicles, which are very important objects in their environment. However, we are certain that differences in the words and concepts of a language do affect the ease with which a person can change from one language to another because there is a dynamic interrelationship among language, thought, and culture.

Variations in Linguistic Grammars   A rich illustration of the reciprocal relationship among language, thought, and culture can be found in the grammatical rules of different languages. In the following discussion, you will once again see how the patterns of a culture's beliefs, values, norms, and social practices, as discussed in Chapters 4 and 5, permeate all aspects of the culture. Because language shapes how its users organize the world, the patterns of a culture will be reflected in its language and vice versa.

Cultural Conceptions of Time   Whorf himself provided detailed descriptions of the Hopi language that illustrate how the grammar of a language is related to the perceptions of its users. Hopi do not linguistically refer to time as a fixed point or place but rather as a movement in the stream of life. The English language, in contrast, refers to time as a specific point that exists on a linear plane divided into past, present, and future. Hopi time is more like an ongoing process; the here and now (the present) will never actually arrive, but it will always be approaching. The Hopi language also has no tenses, so the people do not place events into the neat categories of past, present, and future that native speakers of English have come to expect. As Stephen Littlejohn has suggested, the consequences of these linguistic differences is that

> Hopi and SAE [Standard Average European] cultures will think about, perceive, and behave toward time differently. For example, the Hopi tend to engage in lengthy preparing activities. Experiences (getting prepared) tend to accumulate as time gets later. The emphasis is on the accumulated experience during the course of time, not on time as a point or location. In SAE cultures, with their spatial treatment of time, experiences are not accumulated in the same sense. Elaborate and lengthy preparations are not often found. The custom in SAE cultures is to record events (space-time analogy) such that what happened in the past is objectified in space (recorded).[21]

Because a culture's linguistic grammar shapes its experiences, the speakers of Hopi and English will experience time differently, and each may find it difficult to understand the view of time held by the other. Judgments about what is "natural," "right," or "common sense" will obviously vary and will be reinforced by the linguistic habits of each group.

Showing Respect and Social Hierarchy   Languages allow, and to a certain extent force, speakers to display respect for others. For instance, it is much easier to show respect in Spanish than it is in English. Consider the following sentences:

> ¿Sabe usted dónde está la profesora?
> Know you where is the professor? [Do you know where the professor is?]
> ¿Sabes dónde está la profesora?
> Know you where is the professor? [Do you know where the professor is?]

These distinctly different Spanish sentences are identical when translated into English. The sentences in Spanish reflect the differences in the level of respect that must be shown between the person speaking and the person being addressed. The pronoun *usted* is used in the first example to mark the speaker's question as particularly formal or polite. The *s* in *Sabes* in the second example marks the relationship between the speaker and the person being addressed as familiar or informal. In the actual practice of Spanish, a younger person would not use the informal grammatical construction to address an older person, just as an older person would not use the formal *usted* with a person who was much younger.

This example illustrates once again that the grammar of a language can at least encourage its users to construct their interactions with others in particular ways. When a language directs a speaker to make distinctions among the people with whom the speaker interacts, in this instance by showing linguistically a greater respect for some and not others, the language helps to remind its users of social distinctions and the behaviors that are appropriate to them. Thus, language professors who teach Spanish to English-speaking students often note that the English speaker is not behaving respectfully.

The degree to which a language demands specific words and grammatical structures to show the nature of the relationship between the communicators suggests how much a culture values differences between people. In the frameworks of the ideas presented in Chapters 4 and 5, Spanish-speaking cultures would be more likely to value a hierarchical social organization and a large power distance. Chinese, Japanese, and Korean languages also reflect the relative social status between the addresser and addressee. In Hindi, Korean, and other languages, there are specific words for older brother, older sister, younger brother, and younger sister, which remind all siblings of their relative order in the family and the norms or expectations appropriate to specific familial roles. Languages with grammatical and semantic features that make the speakers decide whether to show respect and social status to others are constant reminders of those characteristics of social interaction. In contrast, a language with few terms to show status and respect tends to minimize those status distinctions in the minds of the language's users.

Pronouns and Cultural Characteristics English is the only language that capitalizes the pronoun *I* in writing. English does not, however, capitalize the written form of the pronoun *you.* Is there a relationship between the individualism that characterizes most of

CULTURE connections

After five weeks of intense study, I panicked. I suddenly realized that I had not learned the Woleaian equivalent for "to have." How could I have overlooked something so basic? In English, you learn "to have" shortly after "to be." "Have" is the 11th most commonly used word in English; the concept is essential.

I had previously studied German and Spanish and knew that *haben* and *tener* held equally important places in those languages, respectively. I must have been doing a terribly inept job of learning Woleaian. What else had I missed?

Well, whatever else I'd missed, I hadn't missed "to have." It wasn't there to be missed. There are Woleaian equivalents for some of its uses, but not for the term itself. You cannot, in Woleaian, say "I have food," or "I have a car." You cannot "have" a wife, a good time, or a seat on an airplane. You cannot even "have" the flu. (The equivalent is "the flu saw me.")

Why do Woleaians lack a term so central to the other languages I knew? I have a theory. Language reveals culture, and Woleaian life is generally based on sharing, rather than owning. "To have," which is basically an ownership term, is simply not that important there.

In a society where food and many other things are automatically shared, "Is there breadfruit?" is a more reasonable question than "May I have some breadfruit?" The first is a standard question in Woleaian, the second cannot be said. Woleaians do have ways to denote ownership, of course. But sharing plays a larger role in their lives, and ownership plays a smaller role in their language.

Whatever the reason for the lack of "to have," there's no mystery behind the most common form of "hello" among Woleaians. *Butog mwongo!* (Come and eat!) expresses their hospitality, their love of food, and their love of sharing. It is not just a greeting, it is a genuine invitation—at any time of the day or night.

—*Jerry Miller*

the English-speaking countries and this feature of the English language? In contrast, consider that there are more than twelve words for *I* in Vietnamese, more than ten in Chinese, and more than one hundred in Japanese.[22] Does a language that demands a speaker to differentiate the self (the "I") from other features of the context (for example, other people or the type of event) shape the way speakers of that language think about themselves? If "I" exist, but "I" am able to identify myself linguistically only through reference to someone else, will "I" not have a different sense of myself than the English-speaking people who see themselves as entities existing apart from all others?[23]

As an example of the extreme contrasts that exist in the use and meanings of pronouns, consider the experiences of Michael Dorris, who lived in Tyonek, Alaska, an Athabaskan-speaking Native American community:

> Much of my time was spent in the study of the local language, linguistically related to Navajo and Apache but distinctly adapted to the subarctic environment. One of its most difficult features for an outsider to grasp was the practice of almost always speaking and thinking in a collective plural voice. The word for people, "dene," was used as a kind of "we"—the subject for virtually every predicate requiring a personal pronoun—and therefore any act became, at least in conception, a group experience.[24]

Imagine having been trained in the language that Dorris describes. Would speaking such a language result in people who think of themselves as part of a group rather than as individuals?[25] Alternatively, if you are from a culture that values individualism, would you have difficulty communicating in a language that requires you always to say *we* instead of *I*? If your cultural background is more group-oriented, would it be relatively easy for you to speak in a language that places you as part of a group?

Linguistic Relativity and Intercultural Communication The semantic and syntactic features of language are powerful shapers of the way people experience the physical and social world. Sapir and Whorf's assertions that language *determines* our reality have proved to be false. Language does not determine our ability to sense the physical world, nor does the language first learned create modes of thinking from which there is no escape. However, language shapes and influences our thoughts and behaviors. The vocabulary of a language reflects what you need to know to cope with the environment and the patterns of your culture. The semantics and syntactics of language gently nudge you to notice particular kinds of things in your world and to label them in particular ways. All of these components of language create habitual response patterns to the people, events, and messages that surround you. Your language intermingles with other aspects of your culture to reinforce the cultural patterns you are taught.

The influence of a particular language is something you can escape; it is possible to translate to or interact in a second language. But as the categories for coding or sorting the world are provided primarily by your language, you are predisposed to perceive the world in a particular way, and the reality you create is different from the reality created by those who use other languages with other categories.

When the categories of languages are vastly different, people will have trouble communicating with one another. Differences in language affect what is relatively easy to say and what seems virtually impossible to say. As Wilma M. Roger has suggested, "Language and the cultural values, reactions, and expectations of speakers of that language are subtly melded."[26]

We offer one final caution. For purposes of discussion, we have artificially separated vocabulary and grammar, as if language is simply an adding together of these two elements. In use, language is a dynamic and interrelated system that has a powerful effect on people's thoughts and actions. The living, breathing qualities of language as spoken and used, with all the attendant feelings, emotions, and experiences, are difficult to convey adequately in an introductory discussion such as this one.

Language and Intercultural Communication

The earlier sections of this chapter may have given the impression that language is stable and used consistently by all who speak it. However, even in a country that has predominantly only one language, there are great variations in the way the language is spoken (accents), and there are wide deviations in how words are used and what they mean. Among U.S. Americans who speak English, it is quite common to hear many different accents. It is also quite common to hear words, phrases, and colloquial expressions that are common to only one region of the country. Think of the many voices associated with the speaking of English in the United States. Do you have an auditory image of the way someone sounds who grew up in New York City? How about someone who grew up in Georgia? Wisconsin? Oregon? The regional variations in the ways English is spoken reflect differences in accents and dialects.

Increasingly, U.S. Americans speak many first languages other than English. As noted in Chapter 1, multiple language systems are represented in U.S. schools. Employers in businesses must now be conscious of the different languages of their workers. In addition, specialized linguistic structures develop for other functions within the context of a larger language. Because language differences are powerful factors that influence the relationships between ethnic and cultural groups who live next to and with each other in communities and countries, we will examine the variations among languages of groups of people who essentially share a common political union.[27] We begin by considering the role of language in maintaining the identity of a cultural group and in the relationship between cultural groups who share a common social system. We then talk about nonstandard versions of a language, including accents, dialects, and argot, and we explore their effects on communication with others.

Language, Ethnic Group Identity, and Dominance   Each person commonly identifies with many different social groups. For example, you probably think of yourself as part of a certain age grouping, as male or female, as married or unmarried, and as a college student or someone who is simply interested in learning about intercultural communication. You may also think of yourself as African American, German American, Vietnamese American, Latino, Navajo, or one of the many other cultural groups composing the population of the United States. You may also identify with a culture from outside of the United States.

Henri Tajfel argues that humans categorize themselves and others into different groups to simplify their understanding of people. When you think of someone as part of a particular social group, you associate that person with the values of that group.[28] In this section we are particularly concerned with the ways in which language is used to identify people in a group, either by the group members themselves or by outsiders from other groups. Some of the questions we are concerned with include the following: How important is language to the members of a culture? What is the role of language in the maintenance of a culture? Why do some languages survive over time while others do not? What role does language play in the relationship of one culture to another?

The importance that cultures attribute to language has been well established.[29] In fact, some would argue that the very heart of a culture is its language and that a culture dies if its language dies.[30] However, it is difficult to determine the exact degree of importance that language has for someone who identifies with a particular group because there are so many factors that affect the strength of that identification. For example, people are more likely to have a strong sense of ethnic and linguistic identity if members of other important cultural groups acknowledge their language in some way. In several states within the United States, for example, there have been heated legal battles to allow election ballots to be printed in languages other than English. Those advocating this option are actually fighting to gain official status and support for their languages.

A language will remain vital and strong if groups of people who live near one another use the language regularly. The sheer number of people who identify with a particular language and their distribution within a particular country or region have a definite effect on the vigor of the language. For people who are rarely able to speak the language of their culture, the centrality of the language and the cultural or ethnic identity that goes with it are certainly diminished. Their inability to use the language results in lost opportunities to express their identification with the culture that it symbolizes.

The extent to which a culture maintains a powerful sense of identification with a particular language is called perceived ethnolinguistic vitality, which refers to "the individual's subjective perception of the status, demographic characteristics, and institutional support of the language community."[31] Very high levels of perceived ethnolinguistic

■ Can you guess what this business in Vietnam is selling?

vitality mean that members of a culture will be unwilling to assimilate their linguistic behavior with other cultures that surround them.[32] Howard Giles, one of the foremost researchers in how languages are used in multilingual societies, concludes that there are likely to be intense pressures on cultural members to adopt the language of the larger social group and to discontinue the use of their own language when

1. the members of a culture lack a strong political, social, and economic status;
2. there are few members of the culture compared to the number of people in other groups in the community; and
3. institutional support to maintain their unique cultural heritage is weak.[33]

When multiple languages are spoken within one political boundary, there are inevitably political and social consequences. In the United States, for example, English has maintained itself as the primary language over a long period of time. Immigrants to the United States have historically been required to learn English in order to participate in the wider political and commercial aspects of the society. Schools offered classes only in English, television and radio programs were almost exclusively in English, and the work of government and business also required English. The English-only requirement has not been imposed without social consequences, however. In Micronesia, for example, where there are nine major languages and many dialects, people are demonstrably apprehensive about communicating with others when they must use English instead of their primary language.[34]

In recent years in the United States, there has been a change in the English-only pattern. Now in many areas of the country there are large numbers of people for whom English is not the primary language. As a consequence, teaching staffs are multilingual; government offices provide services to non-English speakers; and cable television has an extensive array of entertainment and news programming in Spanish, Chinese, Japanese, Arabic, and so on.

In some countries, formal political agreements acknowledge the role of multiple languages in the government and educational systems. Canada has two official languages: English and French. Belgium uses three: French, German, and Flemish. In Singapore, English, Mandarin, Malay, and Tamil are all official languages, and India has more than a dozen.

When India was established in 1948, one of the major problems concerned a national language. Although Hindi was the language spoken by the largest number of people, the overwhelming majority of the people did not speak it. India's solution to this problem was to identify sixteen national languages, thus formalizing in the constitution the right for government, schools, and commerce to operate in any of them. Even that solution has not quelled the fears of non-Hindi speakers that Hindi will predominate. In the mid-1950s, there was political agitation to redraw the internal state boundaries based on the languages spoken in particular regions. Even now, major political upheavals periodically occur in India over language issues.

Because language is such an integral part of most people's identities, a great deal of emotion is attached to political choices about language preferences. However, what is most central to intercultural competence is the way in which linguistic identification influences the interaction that occurs between members of different cultural groups. In interpersonal communication, language is used to discern ingroup and outgroup members. That is, language provides an obvious and highly accurate cue about whether people share each other's cultural background. If others speak as you do, you are likely to assume that they are similar to you in other important ways.

CULTURE connections

"Today my teacher said we got to learn 'proper' English, so we can study things like math and science. Ho, man! Kids got plenty angry. Everybody yelling. 'How we going talk to parents widdout Pidgin? Pidgin same as English.'"

She played with her fork, slightly embarrassed. "I raised my hand and said Pidgin is *not* the same as English. It's not an inferior kind of English. It's a *different* language than English. Like French, or Spanish. Like Hawaiian Mother Tongue. My teacher said that was a good point. So now I have to write a paper on it."

The family sat quiet, not understanding.

"So now...she punishing you?" Ben asked.

"No, Uncle. It's sort of an honor, and I get extra credit for the paper. She wants me to write about how it's important that we speak all three languages. Hawaiian, Pidgin, English, so we can keep up with the rest of the world. We going to be what she calls...trilingual."

—*Kiana Davenport*

Howard Giles has developed communication accommodation theory to explain why people in intercultural conversations may choose to *converge* or *diverge* their communication behaviors to that of others.[35] At times, interactants will converge their language use to that of their conversational partners by adapting their speech patterns to the behaviors of others. They do so when they desire to identify with others, appear similar to them, gain their approval, and facilitate the development of smooth and harmonious relationships. At other times, interactants' language use will diverge from their conversational partners and will thus accentuate their own cultural memberships, maintain their individuality, and underscore the differences between themselves and others. Giles suggests that the likelihood that people will adapt and accommodate to others depends on such factors as their knowledge of others' communication patterns, their motivations to converge or diverge, and their skills in altering their preferred repertoire of communication behaviors.

People also make a positive or negative evaluation about the language that others use. Generally speaking, there is a pecking order among languages that is usually buttressed and supported by the prevailing political order. Thus,

> In every society the differential power of particular social groups is reflected in language variation and in attitudes toward those variations. Typically, the dominant group promotes its patterns of language use as dialect or accents by minority group members reduce their opportunities for success in the society as a whole. Minority group members are often faced with difficult decisions regarding whether to gain social mobility by adopting the language patterns of the dominant group or to maintain their group identity by retaining their native speech style.[36]

In the United States, there has been a clear preference for English over the multiple other languages that people speak, and those who speak English are evaluated according to their various accents and dialects. African Americans, for instance, have often been judged negatively for their use of Black Standard English, which has grammatical forms that differ from those used in Standard American English.[37] In the next section, we discuss the consequences of these evaluations and the effects of alternative forms of language use on intercultural communication competence.

Alternative Versions of a Language   No language is spoken precisely the same way by all who use it. The sounds made when speaking English by someone from England, Australia, or Jamaica differ from the speech of English-speaking U.S. Americans. Even among those who share a similar language and reside in the same country, there are important variations in the way the language is spoken. These differences in language use include the way the words are pronounced, the meanings of particular words or phrases, and the patterns for arranging the words (grammar). Terms often associated with these alternative forms of a language include *dialect, accent, argot* (pronounced "are go"), and *jargon.*

Dialects   Dialects are versions of a language with distinctive vocabulary, grammar, and pronunciation that are spoken by particular groups of people or within particular regions. Dialects can play an important role in intercultural communication because they often trigger a judgment and evaluation of the speaker. Dialects are measured against a "standard" spoken version of the language. The term *standard* does not describe inherent or naturally occurring characteristics but, rather, historical circumstances. For example, among many U.S. Americans, Standard American English is often the preferred dialect and conveys power and dominance. But as John R. Edwards has suggested, "As a dialect, there is nothing intrinsic, either linguistically or esthetically, which gives Standard English special status."[38]

Occasionally, use of a nonstandard dialect may lead to more favorable evaluations of the speaker. Thus, a U.S. American may regard someone speaking English with a British accent as more "cultured" or "refined." However, most nonstandard dialects of English are frequently accorded less status and are often considered inappropriate or unacceptable in education, business, and government. For example, speakers of Spanish- or Appalachian-accented English, as well as those who speak Black Standard English, are sometimes unfairly assumed to be less reliable, less intelligent, and of lower status than those who speak Standard American English.[39]

One dialect frequently used in the United States has been variously called Black Standard English, Black English, African American Vernacular English,

■ A big challenge in learning a new language is to be understood clearly when speaking.

and Ebonics. Linguists have estimated that about 90 percent of the African American community uses Ebonics at least some of the time. Geneva Smitherman explains some of the linguistic forces that underlie Ebonics by providing an example of some African American women at a beauty shop, one of whom exclaims, "The Brotha be looking good; that's what got the Sista nose open!" According to Smitherman:

> In this statement, *Brotha* refers to an African American man, *looking good* refers to his style (not necessarily the same thing as physical beauty in Ebonics), *Sista* is an African American woman, and her passionate love for the Brotha is conveyed by the phrase *nose open* (the kind of passionate love that makes you vulnerable to exploitation). *Sista nose* is standard Ebonics grammar for denoting possession, indicated by adjacency/ context (rather than the /'s, s'/). The use of *be* means that the quality of *looking good* is not limited to the present moment but reflects the Brotha's past, present, and future essence. As in the case of Efik and other West African languages, aspect is important in the verb system of US Ebonics, conveyed by the use of the English verb *be* to denote a recurring, habitual state of affairs. (Contrast *He be looking good* with *He looking good,* which refers to the present moment only—certainly not the kind of *looking good* that opens the nose!). Note further that many Black writers and today's Hip Hop artists employ the spellings "Brotha" and "Sista" to convey a pronunciation pattern showing West African language influence, i.e., a vowel sound instead of an /r/ sound. The absence of the /r/ at the end of words like "Sista" parallels /r/ absence in many West African languages, many of which do not have the typical English /r/ sound. Also in these communities, kinship terms may be used when one is referring to other African people, whether they are biologically related or not.[40]

Like all dialects, Ebonics is not slang, sloppy speech, incorrect grammar, or broken English. Rather, it reflects an intersection of West African languages and European American English, which initially developed during the European slave trade and the enslavement of African peoples throughout the Americas and elsewhere.

Accents   Distinguishable marks of pronunciation are called *accents*. Accents are closely related to dialects. Research studies repeatedly demonstrate that speakers' accents are used as a cue to form impressions of them.[41] Those of you who speak English with an accent or in a nonstandard version may have experienced the negative reactions of others, and you know the harmful effects such judgments can have on intercultural communication. Studies repeatedly find that accented speech and dialects provoke stereotyped reactions in listeners, so that the speakers are usually perceived as having less status, prestige, and overall competence. Interestingly, these negative perceptions and stereotyped responses sometimes occur even when the listeners themselves use a nonstandard dialect.[42]

If you are a speaker of Standard American English, you speak English with an "acceptable" accent. Can you recall conversations with others whose dialect and accent did not match yours? In those conversations, did you make negative assessments of their character, intelligence, or goodwill? Such a response is fairly common. Negative judgments that are made about others simply on the basis of how they speak are obviously a formidable barrier to competence in intercultural communication. For example, an Iranian American woman describes the frustration and anger experienced by her father, a physician, and her mother, a nurse, when they attempted to communicate with others by telephone. Although both of her parents had immigrated to the United States many years before, they spoke English with a heavy accent. These educated people were consistently responded to as if they lacked intelligence simply because of their accent. Out of sheer frustration, they usually had their daughter, who spoke English with a U.S. accent, conduct whatever business needed to be accomplished on the telephone.

Jargon and Argot   Both jargon and argot are specialized forms of vocabulary. Jargon refers to a set of words or terms that are shared by those with a common profession or experience. For example, students at a particular university share a jargon related to

CULTURE connections

"I love your grandmother's accent," my high school friend told me after a visit to my house. I looked at her in confusion. "What accent?"

She assured me my grandmother spoke with an accent, although she wasn't sure what kind. I knew Grandma's parents had come from Norway, but it had never occurred to me that she had an accent. She just spoke like Grandma. The next time she came to our house, I tried to listen to her words more objectively. Sure enough, all those round, musical vowels of hers weren't just her unique way of talking; she had a Norwegian accent.

It made me wonder what else I hadn't realized about my relatives, just because I knew them too well to see them clearly. A few years later, my friend Sue gave me a clear reminder of how easy it can be to take things for granted.

Sue's husband, Daniel, had come to the United States from Kenya. They had met and married in Minnesota. When their son, Jeff, was born, they decided that Sue would speak to him in English and Daniel in Kikuyu, so that he would be bilingual right from the start. The plan worked well, and Jeff spoke both English and Kikuyu with ease from an early age.

When Jeff was seven years old, several members of Daniel's family came from Kenya for a visit. Sue and Daniel were thrilled. Wouldn't they be proud when Jeff conversed freely with his relatives in Kikuyu! They explained to Jeff that Daddy's family would be coming to stay with them, and Jeff eagerly helped them plan activities for the visitors. He seemed excited to have them come.

At the airport on the big day, Daniel greeted his family and introduced them to his wife. Then he proudly introduced his son in Kikuyu and waited for the conversation to begin. But as soon as the relatives started speaking to Jeff, he stared at them in surprise and clammed up. He wouldn't say a word to anyone in any language. Daniel's family tried to be polite, and Daniel assured them Jeff really did know how to talk, but the conversation on the way back to the house was a little strained, with Jeff remaining absolutely silent.

It wasn't until Daniel got everyone home and settled that he had a chance to talk with his son and find out what had upset him. Jeff had never met anyone else who spoke Kikuyu, only his dad. All his life Jeff had assumed that this was a special secret language between him and his father that no one else knew. And then all these strangers had shown up, speaking their private language! It had been a shock.

—*Sharon Huntington*

CULTURE connections

We were weaving between Spanish and English, all of us fluent in both. It was something I had to get more accustomed to now, living on the West Coast, where people wove their conversations between the two tongues as commonly as if they were one.

—*Marcos M. Villatoro*

general education requirements, registration techniques, add or drop procedures, activity fees, and so on. Members of a particular profession depend on a unique set of meanings for words that are understood only by other members of that profession. The shorthand code used by law-enforcement officers, lawyers, those in the medical profession, and even professors at colleges and universities are all instances of jargon.

Argot refers to a specialized language that is used by a large group within a culture to define the boundaries of their group from others who are in a more powerful position in society. As you might expect, argot is an important feature in the study of intercultural communication. Unlike jargon, argot is typically used to keep those who are not part of the group from understanding what members say to one another. The specialized language is used to keep those from the outside, usually seen as hostile, at bay.

Code Switching   Because of the many languages spoken in the United States, you will likely have many opportunities to hear and perhaps to participate in a form of language use called code switching. Code switching refers to the selection of the language to be used in a particular interaction by individuals who can speak multiple languages. The decision to use one language over another is often related to the setting in which the interaction occurs—a social, public, and formal setting versus a personal, private, and informal one. In his poignant exploration about speaking Spanish in an English-speaking world, Richard Rodriguez describes his attachment to the language associated with this latter setting.

> When I was a boy, things were different. The accent of *los gringos* was never pleasing nor was it hard to hear. Crowds at Safeway or at bus stops would be noisy with sound. And I would be forced to edge away from the chirping chatter above me....
>
> But then there was Spanish. *Español:* my family's language. *Español:* the language that seemed to me to be a private language. I'd hear strangers on the radio and in the Mexican Catholic church across town speaking in Spanish, but I couldn't really believe that Spanish was a public language, like English. Spanish speakers, rather, seemed related to me, for I sensed that we shared—through our language—the experience of feeling apart from *los gringos.*... Spanish seemed to me the language of home....
>
> A family member would say something to me and I would feel myself specially recognized. My parents would say something to me and I would feel embraced by the sounds of their words. Those sounds said: *I am speaking with ease in Spanish. I am addressing you in words I never use with* los gringos. *I recognize you as someone special, close, like no one outside. You belong with us. In the family.*[43]

A person's conversational partner is another important factor in code-switching decisions. Many African Americans, for instance, switch their linguistic codes based on the culture and gender of their conversational partners.[44]

The topic of conversation is another important influence on the choice of a linguistic code. One study found that Moroccans, for instance, would typically use French when discussing scientific or technological topics and Arabic when discussing cultural or religious ones. Interestingly, people's attitudes toward a particular topic were found to be consistent with the underlying beliefs, values, norms, and social practices of the culture whose language they choose to speak.[45]

Verbal Codes and Intercultural Competence

The link between knowledge of other verbal codes and intercultural competence is obvious. To speak another language proficiently requires an enormous amount of effort, energy, and time. The opportunity to study another language in your college curriculum is a choice we highly recommend to prepare you for a multicultural and multilingual world. Those world citizens with facility in a second or third language will be needed in every facet of society.

Many English speakers have a false sense of security because English is studied and spoken by so many people around the world. There is arrogance in this position that should be obvious because it places all of the responsibility for learning another language on the non-English speaker. Furthermore, even if two people from different cultures are using the verbal code system of one of the interactants, significant influences on their communication arise from their initial languages.

The multicultural nature of the United States and the interdependence of world cultures means that multiple cultures and multiple languages will be a standard feature of people's lives. Despite our strong recommendation that you learn and be tolerant of other languages, it is virtually impossible for anyone to be proficient in all of the verbal codes that might be encountered in intercultural communication. However, there are important ways to improve competence in adjusting to differences in verbal codes when communicating interculturally.

First, the study of at least one other language is extraordinarily useful in understanding the role of differences in verbal codes in intercultural communication. Genuine fluency in a second language demonstrates experientially all of the ways in which language embodies another culture. It also reveals the ways in which languages vary and how the nuances of language use influence the meanings of symbols. Even if you never become genuinely proficient in it, the study of another language teaches much about the culture of those who use it and the categories of experience the language can create. Furthermore, such study demonstrates, better than words written on a page or spoken in a lecture, the difficulty in gaining proficiency in another language and may lead to an appreciation of those who are struggling to communicate in second or third languages.

Short of becoming proficient in another language, learning about its grammatical features can help you understand the messages of the other person. Study the

CULTURE connections

We can't really know what a pleasure it is to run in our own language until we're forced to stumble in someone else's. It was a great relief when Khaderbhai spoke in English.

—Gregory David Roberts

connections between the features of a verbal code and the cultural patterns of those who use it. Even if you are going to communicate with people from another culture in your own first language, there is much that you can learn about the other person's language and the corresponding cultural patterns that can help you to behave appropriately and effectively.

Knowledge of another language is one component of the link between competence and verbal codes. Motivation, in the form of your emotional reactions and your intentions toward the culturally different others with whom you are communicating, is another critical component. Trying to get along in another language can be an exhilarating and very positive experience, but it can also be fatiguing and frustrating. The attempt to speak and understand a new verbal code requires energy and perseverance. Most second-language learners, when immersed in its cultural setting, report a substantial toll on their energy.

Functioning in a culture that speaks a language different from your own can be equally tiring and exasperating. Making yourself understood, getting around, obtaining food, and making purchases all require a great deal of effort. Recognizing the possibility of irritability and fatigue when functioning in an unfamiliar linguistic environment is an important prerequisite to intercultural competence. Without such knowledge, the communicator may well blame his or her personal feelings of discomfort on the cultures that are being experienced.

The motivation dimension also concerns your reactions to those who are attempting to speak your language. In the United States, for example, those who speak English often lack sympathy for and patience with those who do not. If English is your first language, notice those learning it and provide

■ Learning other languages is an important feature of intercultural competence.

whatever help you can. Respond patiently. If you do not understand, ask questions and clarify. Try making your verbal point in alternative ways by using different sets of words with approximately equivalent meanings. Speak slowly, but do not yell. Lack of skill in a new language is not caused by a hearing impairment. Be aware of the jargon in your speech, and provide a definition of it. Above all, to the best of your ability, withhold judgments and negative evaluations; instead, show respect for the enormous difficulties associated with learning a new language.

An additional emotional factor to monitor in promoting intercultural competence is your reaction to nonstandard versions of a language. The negative evaluations that nonstandard speech often triggers are a serious impediment to competence.

Competence in intercultural communication can be assisted by behaviors that indicate interest in the other person's verbal code. Even if you have never studied the language of those with whom you regularly interact, do attempt to learn and use appropriate words and phrases. Get a phrase book and a dictionary to learn standard comments or queries. Learn how to greet people and to acknowledge thanks. At the same time, recognize your own limitations and depend on a skilled interpreter when needed.

Intercultural competence requires knowledge, motivation, and actions that recognize the critical role of verbal codes in human interaction. Although learning another language is a very important goal, it is inevitable that you will need to communicate with others with whom you do not share a common verbal code.

Summary

In this chapter, we have explored the vital role of verbal codes in intercultural communication. The features of language and the five rule systems were discussed. Phonology, the rules for creating the sounds of language, and morphology, the rules for creating the meaning units in a language, were described briefly. The study of the meaning of words (semantics), the rules for ordering the words (syntactics), and the effects of language on human perceptions and behaviors (pragmatics) were also described. We then discussed the difficulties in establishing equivalence in the process of interpretation from one language to another.

The important relationships among language, thought, culture, and behavior were explored. The Sapir–Whorf hypothesis of linguistic relativity, which concerns the effects of language on people's thoughts and perceptions, was discussed. We noted that the firmer version of the hypothesis portrays language as the determiner of thought, and the softer version portrays language as a shaper of thought; variations in words and grammatical structures from one language to another provide important evidence in the debate on the Sapir–Whorf hypothesis; and that each language, with its own unique features, serves as a shaper rather than determiner of human thought, culture, and behavior.

Finally, variations in language use within a nation were considered. Language plays a central role in establishing and maintaining the identity of a particular culture. Language variations also foster a political hierarchy among cultures within a nation; nonstandard versions of a language, including accents, dialects, jargon, and argot, are often regarded less favorably than the standard version. The concept of code switching, and some factors that affect the selection of one language over another, were also discussed. The chapter concluded with a discussion of intercultural competence and verbal communication.

For Discussion

1. Based on the examples at the beginning of this chapter, what do you think Ludwig Wittgenstein meant when he said that "the limits of my language are the limits of my world"?
2. Is accurate translation and interpretation from one language to another possible? Explain.
3. What is the difference between a dialect and an accent? Between jargon and argot? Give an example of each of these terms.
4. If you speak more than one language (or language dialect), when is each of them used? That is, in what places, relationships, or settings do you use each of them?
5. If you could construct an ideal society, would it be one in which everyone spoke the same language? Or does a society in which people speak different languages offer greater advantages? Explain.

For Further Reading

Mark Abley, *Spoken Here: Travels Among Threatened Languages* (Boston: Houghton Mifflin, 2003). An examination of the fascinating subject of languages that have only a few native speakers remaining and the efforts that are being made to preserve these languages. It also looks at what is lost when a language dies, as well as the forces, from pop culture to global politics, that threaten to wipe out 90 percent of all languages by the end of the century.

John J. Gumperz and Stephen C. Levinson (eds.), *Rethinking Linguistic Relativity* (Cambridge: Cambridge University Press, 1996). A good source for additional information on the Sapir–Whorf hypothesis. A modern classic.

Steven Pinker, *The Stuff of Thought: Language as a Window into Human Nature* (New York: Viking, 2007). A very readable explanation of how our use of words in everyday life reveals our human nature.

Geneva Smitherman, *Word from the Mother: Language and African Americans* (New York: Routledge, 2006). Offers insights into the language use that helps to shape the culture and experiences of African Americans.

Eva Alcón Soler and Maria Pilar Safont Jordà (eds.), *Intercultural Language Use and Language Learning* (Dordrecht, Netherlands: Springer, 2007). Offers examples of the semantic, syntactic, and pragmatic issues that arise in teaching and using a foreign language.

Maryanne Wolf, *Proust and the Squid: The Story and Science of the Reading Brain* (New York: HarperCollins, 2007). An intriguing exploration of the ways the human brain adapts to be able to learn to read, with varying adaptations linked to alphabets and languages. A scholarly and engaging "good read" that will both inform and entertain with its prose.

For additional information about intercultural films and about Web sites for researching specific cultures, please turn to the Resources section at the back of this book.

CHAPTER 8

Nonverbal Intercultural Communication

KEY TERMS

Learning to communicate as a native member of a culture involves knowing both the verbal and the nonverbal code systems that are used. The verbal code system, which was considered in the last chapter, constitutes only a portion of the messages that people exchange when they communicate. In this chapter, we explain the types of messages that are often regarded as more foundational or more elemental to human communication. Taken together, these messages constitute the nonverbal communication system.

Definition of Nonverbal Codes

The importance of nonverbal codes in communication has been well established. Nonverbal communication is a multichanneled process that is usually performed spontaneously; it typically involves a subtle set of nonlinguistic behaviors that are often enacted subconsciously.[1] Nonverbal behaviors can become part of the communication process when someone intentionally tries to convey a message or when someone attributes meaning to the nonverbal behavior of another, whether or not the person intended to communicate a particular meaning.

An important caution related to the distinction between nonverbal and verbal communication must be made as you learn about nonverbal code systems. Though we describe the communication of nonverbal and verbal messages in separate chapters for explanatory convenience, it would be a mistake to assume that they are actually separate and independent communication systems.[2] In fact, they are inseparably linked together to form the code systems through which the members of a culture convey their beliefs, values, thoughts, feelings, and intentions to one another. As Sheila Ramsey suggests:

> Verbal and nonverbal behaviors are inextricably intertwined; speaking of one without the other is, as Birdwhistell says, like trying to study "noncardiac physiology." Whether in opposition or complementary to each other, both modes work to create the meaning of an interpersonal event. According to culturally prescribed codes, we use eye movement and contact to manage conversations and to regulate interactions; we follow rigid rules governing intra- and interpersonal touch, our bodies synchronously join in the rhythm of others in a group, and gestures modulate our speech. We must internalize all of this in order to become and remain fully functioning and socially appropriate members of any culture.[3]

Thus, our distinction between nonverbal and verbal messages is a convenient, but perhaps misleading, way to sensitize you to the communication exchanges within and between cultures.

Characteristics of Nonverbal Codes

Nonverbal communication messages function as a "silent language" and impart their meanings in subtle and covert ways.[4] People process nonverbal messages, both the sending and receiving of them, with less awareness than they process verbal messages. Contributing to the silent character of nonverbal messages is the fact that most of them are continuous and natural, and they tend to blur into one another. For example, raising one's hand to wave goodbye is a gesture made up of multiple muscular movements, yet it is interpreted as one continuous movement.

CULTURE connections

A patter of footsteps announced my first customer—a skinny little girl, maybe four years old, with long black hair and a runny nose. She regarded the strange *naluaqmiu* before her with alarm. When I smiled, she steadied herself and solemnly laid a grubby handful of change on the counter, still eyeing me warily. In my best storekeeper's voice, I asked her what she needed today.

Silence.

"Candy?" I prompted.

She didn't answer, but her eyes widened at the array behind the counter—cases of Milky Ways, Twizzlers, Drax Snax, LifeSavers, Garbage Can-dy—at least twenty varieties.

"Which one?"

More wide-eyed silence.

"This one?"…

"What about this one?"

Finally in exasperation I laid a Drax Snax and some Twizzlers on the counter and sorted out her change. With an expression of complete ecstasy the pretty little girl opened her mouth….

It took me a couple weeks to figure out that she'd been talking to me all along. The Inupiat are subtle, quiet people, and much of their communication hinges on nonverbal cues. Raising the eyebrows or widening the eyes means yes; a wrinkled nose is a negative. The poor girl had been shouting at me, "Yes! Yes! YES!" All these years later, I still recall that first simple failure to understand; it reminds me of all my failures since then, and of the distance that remains.

—*Nick Jans*

Unlike verbal communication systems, however, there are no dictionaries or formal sets of rules to provide a systematic list of the meanings of a culture's nonverbal code systems. The meanings of nonverbal messages are usually less precise than are those of verbal codes. It is difficult, for example, to define precisely the meaning of a raised eyebrow in a particular culture.

Skill in the use of nonverbal message systems has only recently begun to receive formal attention in the educational process, a reflection of the out-of-awareness character of nonverbal codes.

Relationship of Nonverbal to Verbal Communication

The relationship of nonverbal communication systems to the verbal message system can take a variety of forms. Nonverbal messages can be used to accent, complement, contradict, regulate, or substitute for the verbal message.

Nonverbal messages are often used to *accent* the verbal message by emphasizing a particular word or phrase, in much the same way as *italics* add emphasis to written messages. For instance, the sentence "He did it" takes on somewhat different meanings, depending on whether the subject (*He* did it), the verb (He *did* it), or the object of the verb (He did *it*) is emphasized.

Nonverbal messages that function to clarify, elaborate, explain, reinforce, and repeat the meaning of verbal messages *complement* the verbal message. Many U.S. Americans shake their heads up and down while saying yes to reinforce the verbal affirmation. Similarly, smiling while talking to someone helps to convey a generally pleasant tone and encourages a positive interpretation of the verbal message. Pointing forcefully at someone while saying "*He* did it!" helps to elaborate and underscore the verbal message.

Nonverbal messages can also *contradict* the verbal message. These contradictions could occur purposefully, as when you say yes while indicating no with a wink or a gesture; or they may be out of your conscious awareness, as when you say, "I'm not upset," while your facial expression and tone of voice indicate just the opposite. Contradictions between the verbal and nonverbal channels often indicate that something is amiss. Although the contradictory cues might indicate an attempt at deception, a less evaluative interpretation might simply be that the verbal message is not all that the person could convey. In intercultural communication, these apparent incongruities, when they occur, might serve as a cue that something is wrong.

When nonverbal messages help to maintain the back-and-forth sequencing of conversations, they function to *regulate* the interaction. Conversations are highly structured, with people typically taking turns at talking in a smooth and highly organized sequence. Speakers use nonverbal means to convey that they want the other person to talk or that they do not wish to be interrupted, just as listeners indicate when they wish to talk and when they prefer to continue listening. Looking behaviors, vocal inflections, gestures, and general cues of readiness or relaxation all help to signal a person's conversational intentions.

Finally, nonverbal messages that are used in place of the verbal ones function as a *substitute* for the verbal channel. They are used when the verbal channel is blocked or when people choose not to use it. Head nods, hand gestures, facial displays, body movements, and various forms of physical contact are often used as a substitute for the verbal message.

The specific nonverbal messages used to accent, complement, contradict, regulate, or substitute for the verbal messages will vary from culture to culture. In intercultural communication, difficulties in achieving competence in another verbal code are compounded by variations in the nonverbal codes that accompany the spoken word.

Cultural Universals in Nonverbal Communication

Charles Darwin believed that certain nonverbal displays were universal.[5] The shoulder shrug, for example, is used to convey such messages as "I can't do it," "I can't stop it from happening," "It wasn't my fault," "Be patient," and "I do not intend to resist." Michael Argyle has listed a number of characteristics of nonverbal communication that are universal across all cultures: (1) the same body parts are used for nonverbal expressions; (2) nonverbal channels are used to convey similar information, emotions, values, norms, and self-disclosing messages; (3) nonverbal messages accompany verbal communication and are used in art and ritual; (4) the motives for using the nonverbal channel, such as when speech is impossible, are similar across cultures; and (5) nonverbal messages are used to coordinate and control a range of contexts and relationships that are similar across cultures.[6]

Paul Ekman's research on facial expressions demonstrates the universality of many nonverbal emotional displays.[7] Ekman discovered three separate sets of facial muscles that operate independently and can be manipulated to form a variety of emotional expressions. These muscle sets include the forehead and brow; the eyes, eyelids, and base of the nose; and the cheeks, mouth, chin, and rest of the nose. The muscles in each of these facial regions are combined in a variety of unique patterns to display emotional states. For example, fear is indicated by a furrowed brow, raised eyebrows, wide-open eyes, creased or pinched base of the nose, taut cheeks, partially open mouth, and upturned upper lip. Because the ability to produce such emotional displays is consistent across cultures, there is probably a biological or genetic basis that allows these behaviors to be produced in all humans in a particular way.

Another universal aspect of nonverbal communication is the need to be territorial. Robert Ardrey, an ethologist, has concluded that territoriality is an innate, evolutionary characteristic that occurs in both animals and humans.[8] Humans from all cultures mark and claim certain spaces as their own.

Although some aspects of nonverbal code systems are universal, it is also clear that cultures choose to express emotions and territoriality in differing ways. These variations are of particular interest in intercultural communication.

Cultural Variations in Nonverbal Communication

Most forms of nonverbal communication can be interpreted only within the framework of the culture in which they occur. Cultures vary in their nonverbal behaviors in three ways. First, cultures differ in the specific repertoire of behaviors that are enacted. Movements, body positions, postures, vocal intonations, gestures, spatial requirements, and even dances and ritualized actions are specific to a particular culture.

Second, all cultures have display rules that govern when and under what circumstances various nonverbal expressions are required, preferred, permitted, or prohibited. Thus, children learn both how to communicate nonverbally and the appropriate display rules that govern their nonverbal expressions. Display rules indicate such things as how far apart people should stand while talking, whom to touch and where, the speed and timing of movements and gestures, when to look directly at others in a conversation and when to look away, whether loud talking and expansive gestures or quietness and controlled movements should be used, when to smile and when to frown, and the overall pacing of communication.

The norms for display rules vary greatly across cultures. For instance, Judith N. Martin, Mitchell R. Hammer, and Lisa Bradford found that Latinos and European Americans differ in their judgments about the importance of displaying behaviors that signal approachability (smiling, laughing, and pleasant facial expressions) and poise (nice appearance, appropriate conversational distance, and appropriate posture) in conversations. The differences are related to whether the interaction is viewed as primarily task oriented or socially oriented, and whether the conversational partners are from their own or from different cultural groups. Specifically, approachability and poise behaviors are most important for Latinos when working with other Latinos and when socializing with people from other cultures. In contrast, European Americans think it most important to display these behaviors only when socializing with another European American.[9]

■ Behaviors that are insignificant in one culture may be very meaningful in another. This man relaxes and shows the soles of his feet to visitors. In many cultures this would be regarded as an insult.

Such differences in display rules can cause discomfort and misinterpretations. For instance, a Vietnamese woman named Hoa is visiting her cousin in the United States. As Hoa arrives,

> her cousin Phuong and some of his American friends are waiting at the airport to greet her. Hoa and Phuong are both excited about their meeting because they have been separated for seven years. As soon as Hoa enters the passenger terminal, Phuong introduces her to his friends, Tom, Don, and Charles. Tom steps forward and hugs and kisses Hoa. She pushes him away and bursts into tears.[10]

The difference in when, where, and who it is acceptable to kiss was the source of the discomfort for Hoa; in her cultural display rules, it is an insult for a boy to hug and kiss a girl in public.

Display rules also indicate the intensity of the behavioral display that is acceptable. In showing grief or intense sadness, for instance, people from southern Mediterranean cultures may tend to exaggerate or amplify their displays, European Americans may try to remain calm and somewhat neutral, the British may understate their emotional displays by showing only a little of their inner feelings, and the Japanese and Thai may attempt to mask their sorrow completely by covering it with smiling and laughter.[11]

Third, cultures vary in the **interpretations**, or meanings, that are attributed to particular nonverbal behaviors. Three possible interpretations could be imposed on a given instance of nonverbal behavior: it is random, it is idiosyncratic, or it is shared.[12] An interpretation that the behavior is *random* means that it has no particular meaning to anyone. An *idiosyncratic* interpretation suggests that the behaviors are unique to special individuals or relationships, and they therefore have particular meanings only to these people. For example, family members often recognize that certain unique behaviors of a person signify a specific emotional state. Thus, a family member who tugs on her ear may indicate, to other family members, that she is about to explode in anger. The third interpretation is that the behaviors have *shared* meaning and significance, as when a group of people jointly attribute the same meaning to a particular nonverbal act.

However, cultures differ in what they regard as random, idiosyncratic, and shared. Thus, behaviors that are regarded as random in one culture may have shared significance in another. For example, John Condon and Fathi Yousef describe an incident in which a British professor in Cairo inadvertently showed the soles of his shoes to his class while leaning back in his chair; the Egyptian students were very insulted.[13] The professor's random behavior of leaning back and allowing the soles of his shoes to be seen was a nonverbal behavior with the shared meaning of insult in Egyptian culture. A female graduate student from Myanmar was similarly aghast at the disrespectful behavior of her U.S. American classmates, some of whom put their feet on empty desks, thus showing the soles of their shoes to the professor.[14] Such differences in how cultures define *random* can lead to problems in intercultural communication; if one culture defines a particular behavior as random, that behavior will probably be ignored when someone from a different culture uses it to communicate something.

Even nonverbal behaviors that have shared significance in each of two cultures may mean something very different to their members. As Ray Birdwhistell suggests, "A smile in one society portrays friendliness, in another embarrassment, and in still another may contain a warning that unless tension is reduced, hostility and attack will follow."[15] U.S. Americans typically associate the smile with happiness or friendliness. To the Japanese, the smile can convey a much wider range of emotions, including happiness, agreement, sadness, embarrassment, and disagreement. And though the Thais smile a lot, Koreans rarely smile and regard those who do as superficial.

Nonverbal repertoires, their corresponding display rules, and their preferred interpretations are not taught verbally. Rather, they are learned directly through observation and personal experience in a culture. Because they are frequently acquired outside of conscious awareness, they are rarely questioned or challenged by their users and are often noticed only when they are violated. In intercultural communication, therefore, misunderstandings often occur in the interpretations of nonverbal behaviors because different display rules create very different meanings about the appropriateness and effectiveness of particular interaction sequences. Consider, for instance, the following example:

> An American college student, while having a dinner party with a group of foreigners, learns that her favorite cousin has just died. She bites her lip, pulls herself up, and politely excuses herself from the group. The interpretation given to this behavior will vary with the culture of the observer. The Italian student thinks, "How insincere; she doesn't even cry." The Russian student thinks, "How unfriendly; she didn't care enough to share her grief with her friends." The fellow American student thinks, "How brave; she wanted to bear her burden by herself."[16]

As you can see, cultural variations in nonverbal communication alter the behaviors that are displayed, the meanings that are imposed on those behaviors, and the interpretations of the messages.

CULTURE connections

Smiling, I shook my head and offered Arthur a virulently pink bun that someone had forced on me. He took it in the Batswana manner, placing his left hand on his right forearm as a sign of politeness and murmured, 'Thank you, Rra'.

—Will Randall

Nonverbal Messages in Intercultural Communication

Messages are transmitted between people over some sort of channel. Unlike written or spoken words, however, nonverbal communication occurs in multiple channels simultaneously. Thus, several types of nonverbal messages can be generated by a single speaker at any given instant. When you "read" or observe the nonverbal behaviors of others, you might notice where they look, how they move, how they orient themselves in space and time, what they wear, and the characteristics of their voice. All of these nonverbal codes use particular channels or means of communicating messages, which are interpreted in a similar fashion by members of a given culture. We will discuss six types of nonverbal codes to demonstrate their importance in understanding how members of a culture attempt to understand, organize, and interpret the behaviors of others. We will consider body movements, space, touch, time, voice, and other nonverbal code systems.

Body Movements

The study of body movements, or body language, is known as kinesics. Kinesic behaviors include gestures, head movements, facial expressions, eye behaviors, and other physical displays that can be used to communicate. Of course, like all other forms of communication, no single type of behavior exists in isolation. Specific body movements can be understood only by taking the person's total behavior into account.

Paul Ekman and Wallace Friesen have suggested that there are five categories of kinesic behaviors: emblems, illustrators, affect displays, regulators, and adaptors.[17] We will consider each type of kinesic behavior in turn.

Emblems Emblems are nonverbal behaviors that have a direct verbal counterpart. Emblems that are familiar to most U.S. Americans include such gestures as the two-fingered peace symbol and arm waving to indicate hello or goodbye. Emblems are typically used as a substitute for the verbal channel, either by choice or when the verbal channel is blocked for some reason. Underwater divers, for example, have a rich vocabulary of kinesic behaviors that are used to communicate with their fellow divers. Similarly, a baseball coach uses kinesic signals to indicate a particular pitch or type of play, which is usually conveyed by an elaborate pattern of hand motions that involve touching the cap, chest, wrist, and other areas in a pattern known to the players.

■ The CEO of a major U.S. company gestures at a news conference. These illustrators accompany his talk and underscore the words he is using.

Emblems, like all verbal languages, are symbols that have been arbitrarily selected by the members of a culture to convey their intended meanings. For example, there is nothing peacelike in the peace symbol, which is a nonverbal emblem that can be displayed by extending the index and middle fingers upward from a clenched fist. Indeed, in other cultures the peace symbol has other meanings; Winston Churchill used the same symbol to indicate victory, and to many people in South American countries, it is regarded as an obscene gesture. The meanings of emblems are learned within a culture and, like verbal codes, are used consciously by the culture's members when they wish to convey specific ideas to others. Because emblems have to be learned to be understood, they are culture-specific.

Emblems can be a great source of misunderstanding in intercultural communication because the shared meanings for an emblem in one culture may be different in another. In many South Pacific islands, for instance, people raise their eyebrows to indicate "yes." Albanians and Bulgarians signal "yes" by shaking their heads from side to side, and they signal no by moving their heads up and down.[18] Similarly, in Turkey, to say "no" nonverbally, just

> nod your head up and back, raising your eyebrows at the same time. Or just raise your eyebrows; that's "no." ...
>
> By contrast, wagging your head from side to side doesn't mean "no" in Turkish; it means "I don't understand." So if a Turk asks you, "Are you looking for the bus to Ankara?" and you shake your head, he'll assume you don't understand English, and will probably ask you the same question again, this time in German.[19]

Sometimes these misunderstandings might be seen as very humorous if their consequences weren't so serious to the participants. A U.S. engineer, for example, unintentionally offended his German counterpart by giving the common U.S. gesture for "OK": hand up, thumb and forefinger held in a circle, to indicate that he had done

CULTURE connections

Mainland professors don't always understand that a Hawaiian student's reluctance to participate in class discussions, or the student's avoidance of eye contact (to show respect for an elder), does not signal lack of interest.

—*Joyce Mercer*

a good job. The German interpreted the gesture's meaning as a crude reference to a body orifice and walked off the job.[20]

Illustrators   Illustrators are nonverbal behaviors that are directly tied to, or accompany, the verbal message. They are used to emphasize, explain, and support a word or phrase. They literally illustrate and provide a visual representation of the verbal message. In saying "the huge mountain," for example, you may simultaneously lift your arms and move them in a large half-circle. Similarly, you may point your index finger to emphasize an important idea or use hand motions to convey directions to a particular address. Unlike emblems, however, none of these gestures has meaning in itself. Rather, the meaning depends on the verbal message it underscores.

Illustrators are less arbitrary than emblems, which makes them more likely to be universally understood. But differences in both the rules for displaying illustrators and in the interpretations of them can be sources of intercultural misunderstanding. In Asian cultures, for example, calling for a person or a taxi while waving an index finger is very inappropriate, akin to calling a dog. Likewise, beckoning someone with the palm facing body, fingers turned upward, can be offensive; Filipinos, Vietnamese, Mexicans, and others regard this gesture as disrespectful, because it is used to call those who are inferior in status.[21] Instead, the whole right hand is used, palm down, with the fingers together in a scooping motion toward the body. Similarly, punching the fist into the open palm as a display of strength may be misinterpreted as an obscene gesture whose meaning is similar to a Westerner's use of the middle finger extended from a closed fist.

Affect Displays   Affect displays are facial and body movements that show feelings and emotions. Expressions of happiness or surprise, for instance, are displayed by the face and convey a person's inner feelings. Though affect displays are shown primarily through the face, postures and other body displays can also convey an emotional state.

Many affect displays may be universally recognized. The research of Paul Ekman and his colleagues indicates that, regardless of culture, the primary emotional states include happiness, sadness, anger, fear, surprise, disgust, contempt, and interest.[22] In addition to these primary affect displays, there are about thirty affect blends, combinations of the primary emotions. Although recent evidence supports Ekman's view,[23] James A. Russell argues that more information is needed to prove that there are indeed universal interpretations of emotional displays. He suggests that the categories for interpreting affect displays may actually vary somewhat across cultures.[24]

CULTURE connections

When Dith Pran was asked what he would reply if asked if Khmers care less about the death of their loved ones than other people do, he said, "The only difference, maybe, is that with Cambodians, the grief leaves the face quickly, but it goes inside and stays there for a long time."

—Paul Opstad

■ The *wai* gesture is an emblem that is used throughout Thailand both as a greeting and to say goodbye.

Affect displays may be unconscious and unintentional, such as a startled look of surprise, a blush of embarrassment, or dilated pupils due to pleasure or interest. Or affect displays may be conscious and intentional, as when we purposely smile and look at another person to convey warmth and affection. Cultural norms often govern both the kind and amount of affect displays shown. The Chinese, for instance, typically have lower frequency, intensity, and duration of affect displays than their European counterparts.[25]

Regulators Regulators are nonverbal behaviors that help to synchronize the back-and-forth nature of conversations. This class of kinesic behaviors helps to control the flow and sequencing of communication and may include head nods, eye contact, postural shifts, back-channel signals (such as "Uh-huhm" or "Mmm-mmm"), and other turn-taking cues.

Regulators are used by speakers to indicate whether others should take a turn and by listeners to indicate whether they wish to speak or would prefer to continue listening. They also convey information about the preferred speed or pacing of conversations and the degree to which the other person is understood and believed.

Regardless of culture, taking turns is required in all conversations. Thus, for interpersonal communication to occur, talk sequences must be highly coordinated. Regulators are those subtle cues that allow people to maintain this high degree of coordination.

Regulators are culture-specific. For instance, people from high-context cultures such as Korea and Japan are especially concerned with meanings conveyed by the eyes. In an interesting study comparing the looking behaviors of African Americans and European Americans in a conversation, Marianne LaFrance and Clara Mayo found that there were many differences in the interpretations of turn-taking cues. European Americans tend to look directly into the eyes of the other person when they are the listeners, whereas African Americans prefer to look away. Unfortunately, to African Americans, such behaviors by European Americans may be regarded as invasive or confrontational when interest and involvement are intended. Conversely, the behaviors of African Americans could be regarded by European Americans as a sign of indifference or inattention when respect is intended. LaFrance and Mayo also found that, when African American speakers pause while simultaneously looking directly at their European American listeners, the listeners often interpret this as a signal to speak, only to find that the African American person is also speaking.[26]

Adaptors   Adaptors are personal body movements that occur as a reaction to an individual's physical or psychological state. Scratching an itch, fidgeting, tapping a pencil, and smoothing one's hair are all behaviors that fulfill some individualized need.

Adaptors are usually performed unintentionally, without conscious awareness. They seem to be more frequent under conditions of stress, impatience, enthusiasm, or nervousness, and they are often interpreted by others as a sign of discomfort, uneasiness, irritation, or other negative feelings.

Space

The use of space functions as an important communication system in all cultures. Cultures are organized in some spatial pattern, and that pattern can reveal the character of the people in that culture. Two important features of the way cultures use the space around them are the different needs for personal space and the messages that are used to indicate territoriality.

Cultural Differences in the Use of Personal Space   Wherever you go, whatever you do, you are surrounded at all moments by a personal space "bubble." Edward Hall, who coined the term proxemics to refer to the study of how people differ in their use of personal space, has suggested that people interact within four spatial zones or distance ranges: intimate, personal, social, and public.[27] These proxemic zones are characterized by differences in the ways that people relate to one another and in the behaviors that typify the communication that will probably occur in them. Table 8.1, which is based on Hall's observations of U.S. Americans, displays the differences from zone to zone in the types and intensity of sensory information that is received by those who are involved in a communication experience.

Personal space distances are culture specific. People from colder climates, for instance, typically use large physical distances when they communicate, whereas those from warm-weather climates prefer close distances. The personal space bubbles for northern Europeans are therefore large, and people expect others to keep their distance. The personal space bubbles for Europeans get smaller and smaller, however, as one travels south toward the Mediterranean. Indeed, the distance that is regarded as intimate in Germany, Scandinavia, and England overlaps with what is regarded as a normal conversational distance in France

TABLE 8.1   Zones of Spatial Difference Typical of European Americans

Spatial Distance Zone	Spatial Distance (in feet)	Usage	Other Characteristics
Intimate	0–1½	Loving; comforting; protecting; fighting	Minimal conversation; smell and feel of other; eye contact unlikely
Personal	1½–4	Conversations with intimates, friends, and acquaintances	Touch possible; much visual detail
Social	4–12	Impersonal and social gatherings	More formal tone; some visual detail lost; eye contact likely
Public	12–up	Lectures; concerts; plays; speeches; ceremonies; protection	Subtle details lost; only obvious attributes noticed

CULTURE connections

Umeeta has herself changed since she came to the United States, absorbed some elements of American-style interaction. "When I was in India recently," she says, "people would walk close to me, and I found myself moving away." Time is less elastic for her, too, than it once was. "Being in the United States has affected how I experience time. I wish I could spend more of it talking, sitting together with friends without a goal, never thinking about the hour. But I myself am on a schedule; work takes up too much of my life."

—Jessie Carroll Grearson and Lauren B. Smith

and the Mediterranean countries of Italy, Greece, and Spain. Thus, when an Italian and a Norwegian attempt to have a simple informal conversation, for example, the Italian tries to move closer—into his comfort zone for such conversations—whereas the Norwegian continually tries to move backward in an attempt to maintain the "correct" conversational distance. The resulting interaction, which might look like a slow-motion dance across the room, could be comical except that it results in negative evaluations on both sides; the Norwegian thinks his southern European counterpart is "too close for comfort," whereas the Italian regards his northern European neighbor as "too distant and aloof."

The habitual use of the culturally proper spacing distance is accompanied by a predictable level and kind of sensory information. For example, if the standard cultural spacing distance in a personal conversation with an acquaintance is about three feet, people will become accustomed to the sights, sounds, and smells of others that are usually acquired at that distance. For someone who is accustomed to a larger spacing distance, at three feet the voices will sound too loud, it might be possible to smell the other person's breath, the other person will seem too close and perhaps out of the "normal" focal range, and the habitual ways of holding the body may no longer work. Then, the culturally learned cues that are so helpful within one's culture can become a hindrance. One European American student, for instance, in commenting on a party that was attended by many Italians and Spaniards, exclaimed, "They would stand close enough that I could almost feel the air coming from their mouths." Similar reactions to intercultural encounters are very common. As Edward and Mildred Hall have suggested:

> Since most people don't think about personal distance as something that is culturally patterned, foreign spatial cues are almost inevitably misinterpreted. This can lead to bad feelings which are then projected onto the people from the other culture in a most personal way. When a foreigner appears aggressive and pushy, or remote and cold, it may mean only that her or his personal distance is different from yours.[28]

Cultural Differences in Territoriality   Do you have a favorite chair or classroom seat that you think "belongs" to you? Or do you have a room, or perhaps just a portion of a room, that you consider to be off limits to others? The need to protect and defend a particular spatial area is known as territoriality, a set of behaviors that people display to show that they "own" or have the right to control the use of a particular geographic area.

People mark their territories in a variety of ways. It can be done formally using actual barriers such as fences and signs that say "No Trespassing" or "Keep Off the Grass." Territories can also be marked informally by nonverbal markers such as clothing, books, and other personal items that indicate a person's intent to control or occupy a given area.

Cultural differences in territoriality can be exhibited in three ways. First, cultures can differ in the general degree of territoriality that its members tend to exhibit. Some cultures are far more territorial than others. For instance, as Hall and Hall point out in their comparison of Germans and French:

> People like the Germans are highly territorial; they barricade themselves behind heavy doors and soundproof walls to try to seal themselves from others in order to concentrate on their work. The French have a close personal distance and are not as territorial. They are tied to people and thrive on constant interaction and high-information flow to provide them the context they need.[29]

Second, cultures can differ in the range of possible places or spaces about which they are territorial. A comparison of European Americans with Germans, for example, reveals that both groups are highly territorial. Both have a strong tendency to establish areas that they consider to be their own. In Germany, however, this feeling of territoriality extends to "all possessions, including the automobile. If a German's car is touched, it is as though the individual himself has been touched."[30]

Finally, cultures can differ in the typical reactions exhibited in response to invasions or contaminations of their territory. Members of some cultures prefer to react by withdrawing or avoiding confrontations whenever possible. Others respond by insulating themselves from the possibility of territorial invasion, using barriers or other boundary markers. Still others react forcefully and vigorously in an attempt to defend their "turf" and their honor.

Touch

Touch is probably the most basic component of human communication. It is experienced long before we are able to see and speak, and it is a fundamental part of the human experience.

The Meanings of Touch   Stanley E. Jones and A. Elaine Yarbrough have identified five meanings of touch that are important in understanding the nature of intercultural communication.[31] Touch is often used to indicate **affect**, the expression of positive and negative feelings and emotions. Protection, reassurance, support, hatred, dislike, and disapproval are all conveyed through touch; hugging, stroking, kissing, slapping, hitting, and kicking are all ways in which these messages can be conveyed. Touch is also used as a sign of *playfulness*. Whether affectionately or aggressively, touch can be used to signal that the other's behavior should not be taken seriously. Touch is frequently used as a means of *control*. "Stay here," "Move over," and similar messages are communicated through touch. Touching for control may also indicate social dominance. High-status individuals in most Western countries, for instance, are more likely to touch than to be touched, whereas low-status individuals are likely to receive touching behaviors from their superiors.[32] Touching for *ritual* purposes occurs mainly on occasions involving introductions or departures. Shaking hands, clasping shoulders, hugging, and kissing the cheeks or lips are all forms of greeting rituals. Touching is also used in *task-related* activities. These touches may be as

■ Cultures differ in the use of touching and space. These African men from the Ivory Coast hold hands, which in many cultures is a commonly accepted behavior among male friends.

casual as a brief contact of hands when passing an object, or they may be as formal and prolonged as a physician taking a pulse at the wrist or neck.

Cultural Differences in Touch   Cultures differ in the overall amount of touching they prefer. People from high-contact cultures such as those in the Middle East, Latin America, and southern Europe touch each other in social conversations much more than do people from noncontact cultures such as Asia and northern Europe. These cultural differences can lead to difficulties in intercultural communication. Germans, Scandinavians, and Japanese, for example, may be perceived as cold and aloof by Brazilians and Italians, who in turn may be regarded as aggressive, pushy, and overly familiar by northern Europeans. As Edward and Mildred Hall have noted, "In northern Europe one does not touch others. Even the brushing of the overcoat sleeve used to elicit an apology."[33] A comparable difference was observed by Dean Barnlund, who found that U.S. American students reported being touched twice as much as did Japanese students.[34]

Cultures also differ in where people can be touched. In Thailand and Malaysia, for instance, the head should not be touched because it is considered to be sacred and the locus of a person's spiritual and intellectual powers. In the United States, the head is far more likely to be touched.[35]

Cultures vary in their expectations about who touches whom. In Japan, for instance, there are deeply held feelings against the touch of a stranger. These expectations are culture-specific, and even cultures that exist near one another can have very different norms. Among the Chinese, for instance, shaking hands among people of the opposite sex is perfectly acceptable; among many Malay, it is not. Indeed, for those who practice the Muslim religion, casual touching between members of the opposite sex is strictly forbidden. Both men and women have to cleanse themselves ritually before praying if they happen to make physical contact

CULTURE connections

"Do you find Chinese ways strange?" I looked at her closely.

Cynthia scrunched her nose up and twisted her lips. "Sometimes." She smiled. "I'm not sure why exactly. At first, it's just the language, I think, I couldn't understand the accents—it's not like school." ...

"And the way people move, squatting, and always bumping into each other on the sidewalk, the buses. Chinese people touch each other more. Women and women. Men and men. When you would come up to me and touch my arm, that surprised me at first."

"We're always bumping each other but we aren't like Americans. We touch the outside but never show our inside."

—*May-lee Chai*

with someone of the opposite sex. Holding hands, for example, or walking with an arm across someone's shoulder or around the waist, or even grabbing an elbow to help another cross the street, are all considered socially inappropriate behaviors between men and women. In some places there are legal restrictions against public displays of hugging and kissing, even among married couples. However, this social taboo refers only to opposite-sex touching; it is perfectly acceptable for two women to hold hands or for men to walk arm in arm. Many European Americans, of course, have the opposite reaction; they react negatively to same-sex touching (particularly among men) but usually do not mind opposite-sex touching.

Finally, cultures differ in the settings or occasions in which touch is acceptable. Business meetings, street conversations, and household settings all evoke different norms for what is considered appropriate. Cultures make distinctions between those settings that they regard as public and those considered private. Although some cultures regard touching between men and women as perfectly acceptable in public conversations, others think that such activities should occur only in the privacy of the home; to them, touch is a highly personal and sensitive activity that should not occur where others might see it.

Time

The study of time—how people use it, structure it, interpret it, and understand its passage—is called chronemics. We consider chronemics from two perspectives: time orientations and time systems.

Time Orientations   Time orientation refers to the value or importance the members of a culture place on the passage of time. In Chapter 1, we indicated that communication is a process, which means that people's behaviors must be understood as part of an ongoing stream of events that changes over a period of time. Chapters 4 and 5 suggested that members of a culture share a similar worldview about the nature of time. We also indicated that different cultures can have very different conceptions about the appropriate ways to comprehend events and experiences. Specifically, some cultures are predominantly past-oriented, others are present-oriented, and still others prefer a future-oriented worldview. As we briefly review these cultural orientations about time, take note of the amazing degree of interrelationship—in this case the link between a culture's nonverbal code system and its cultural patterns—that characterizes the various aspects of a culture.

Past-oriented cultures regard previous experiences and events as most important. These cultures place a primary emphasis on tradition and the wisdom passed down from older generations. Consequently, they show a great deal of deference and respect for parents and other elders, who are the links to these past sources of knowledge. Events are circular, as important patterns perpetually recur in the present; therefore, tried-and-true methods for overcoming obstacles and dealing with problems can be applied to current difficulties. Many aspects of the British, Chinese, and Native American experiences, for instance, can be understood only by reference to their reverence for traditions, past family experiences, or tribal customs. Consider this example of a past-oriented culture the Samburu, a nomadic tribe from northern Kenya that reveres its elders:

> The elders are an invaluable source of essential knowledge, and in an environment that by its very nature allows only a narrow margin for error, the oldest survivors must

CULTURE connections

Dtui had been sitting for an hour in front of the office of the politburo member. She hadn't made an appointment with Civilai. That wasn't a particularly Lao thing to do. Appointments were rarely kept. She knew he had to come to his office eventually, and much sooner than she'd expected she was proven right.

– Colin Cotterill

possess the most valuable knowledge of all. The elders know their environment intimately—every lie and twist of it. The land, the water, the vegetation; trees, shrubs, herbs—nutritious, medicinal, poisonous. They know each cow, and have a host of specific names for the distinctive shape and skin patterns of each animal in just the same way that Europeans distinguish within the general term flower, or tree.[36]

Present-oriented cultures regard current experiences as most important. These cultures place a major emphasis on spontaneity and immediacy and on experiencing each moment as fully as possible. Consequently, people do not participate in particular events or experiences because of some potential future gain; rather, they participate because of the immediate pleasure the activity provides. Present-oriented cultures typically believe that unseen and even unknown outside forces, such as fate or luck, control their lives. Cultures such as those in the Philippines and many Central and South American countries are usually present-oriented, and they have found ways to encourage a rich appreciation for the simple pleasures that arise in daily activities.

Future-oriented cultures believe that tomorrow—or some other moment in the future—is most important. Current activities are not accomplished and appreciated for their own sake but for the potential future benefits that might be obtained. For example, you go to school, study for your examinations, work hard, and delay or deny present rewards for the potential future gain that a rewarding career might provide. People from future-oriented cultures, which include many European Americans, believe that their fate is at least partially in their own hands and that they can control the consequences of their actions.

Time Systems   **Time systems** are the implicit cultural rules that are used to arrange sets of experiences in some meaningful way. There are three types of time systems: technical, formal, and informal.

Technical time systems are the precise, scientific measurements of time that are calculated in such units as nanoseconds. Typically, members of a culture do not use technical time systems because they are most applicable to specialized settings such as the research laboratory. Consequently, technical time systems are of little relevance to the common experiences that members of a culture share.

Formal time systems refer to the ways in which the members of a culture describe and comprehend units of time. Time units can vary greatly from culture to culture. Among many Native American cultures, for instance, time is segmented by the phases of the moon, the changing seasons, the rise and fall of the tides, or the movements of the sun. Similarly, when a Peruvian woman was asked for the distance to certain Inca ruins, she indicated their location by referring nonverbally to a position in the sky that represented the distance the sun would travel toward the horizon before the journey would be complete.[37] Among European Americans, the passage of time is segmented into seconds, minutes, hours, days, weeks, months, and years.

Time's passage may likewise be indicated by reference to significant events such as the birth of a royal son or an important victory in battle. Time intervals for particular events or activities may also be based on significant external events, such as the length of a day or the phases of the moon. Alternatively, time intervals may be more arbitrary, as in the length of a soccer game or the number of days in a week. These ways of representing the passage of time, however arbitrary, are the culture's formal time system. Sequences such as the months in the year are formally named and are explicitly taught to children and newcomers as an important part of the acculturation process.

The formal time system includes agreements among the members of a culture on such important issues as the extent to which time is regarded as valuable and tangible. European Americans, of course, typically regard time as a valuable, tangible commodity that is used or consumed to a greater or lesser degree.

Informal time systems refer to the assumptions cultures make about how time should be used or experienced. How long should you wait for someone who will be ready soon, in a minute, in a while, or shortly? When is the proper time to arrive for a 9:00 A.M. appointment or an 8:00 P.M. party? As a dinner guest, how long after your arrival would you expect the meal to be served? How long should you stay after the meal has been concluded? Cultures have unstated expectations about the timing and duration of such events. Although these expectations differ, depending on such factors as the occasion and the relative importance of those being met or visited, they are widely held and consistently imposed as the proper or appropriate way to conduct oneself as a competent member of the culture. In this regard, Edward Hall has reported:

> The time that it takes to reach an agreement or for someone to make up his mind operates within culturally defined limits. In the U.S. one has about four minutes in the business world to sell an idea. In Japan the well-known process of "nemawashi"—consensus building, without which nothing can happen—can take weeks or months. None of this four-minute sell.[38]

Perhaps the most important aspect of the culture's informal time system is the degree to which it is monochronic or polychronic.[39] A monochronic time system means that things should be done one at a time, and time is segmented into precise, small units. In a monochronic time system, time is viewed as a commodity; it is scheduled, managed, and arranged. European Americans, like members of other monochronic cultures, are very time-driven. Similarly, within Swiss-German culture, people will

■ Can you guess what this hand gesture means? In China, it represents the number "eight" and is commonly used.

often interpret tardiness as a personal insult.[40] The ubiquitous calendar or scheduler that many people carry, which tells them when, where, and with whom to engage in activities, is an apt symbol of a monochronic culture. An event is regarded as separate and distinct from all others and should receive the exclusive focus of attention it deserves. These events also have limits or boundaries, so that there are expected beginning and ending points that have been scheduled in advance. Thus people from monochronic cultures

> find it disconcerting to enter an office overseas with an appointment only to discover that other matters require the attention of the man we are to meet. Our ideal is to center the attention first on one thing and then move on to something else.[41]

A polychronic time system means that several things are being done at the same time. In Spain and among many Spanish-speaking cultures in Central and South America, for instance, relationships are far more important than schedules. Appointments will be quickly broken, schedules readily set aside, and deadlines unmet without guilt or apology when friends or family members require attention. Those who use polychronic time systems often schedule multiple appointments simultaneously, so keeping "on schedule" is an impossibility that was never really a goal. European Americans, of course, are upset when they are kept waiting for a scheduled appointment, particularly when they discover that they are the third of three appointments that have been scheduled at exactly the same hour.

Cultural Differences in Perceptions and Use of Time   Cultures differ in their time orientations and in the time systems they use to give order to experiences. Misunderstandings can occur between people who have different time orientations. For instance, someone from a present-oriented culture might view people from past-oriented cultures as too tied to tradition and people from future-oriented cultures as passionless slaves to efficiency and materialism. Alternatively, someone from a future-oriented culture might view those from present-oriented cultures as self-centered, hedonistic, inefficient, and foolish.[42] This natural tendency to view one's own practices as superior to all others is a common source of problems in intercultural communication.

Cultures also differ in the formal and informal time systems they use to determine how long an event should take, and even how long "long" is. Misinterpretations often occur when individuals from monochronic and polychronic cultures attempt to interact. Each usually views the other's responses to time "commitments" as disrespectful and unfriendly. Interculturally competent individuals, however, are typically aware of the time systems they are using to regulate their behaviors, and they are able to adapt their time orientations to the prevailing social and situational constraints. For example, participants at a board meeting of a Puerto Rican Community Center used European American references to time when they were focused on their work but employed "Puerto Rican time" when the goal was socializing.[43] Similarly, in some intercultural situations, the name of a culture will be added after a meeting time to designate if the time is to be regarded as fixed or flexible.[44]

Voice

Earlier in this chapter, we stated that nonverbal messages are often used to accent or underscore the verbal message by adding emphasis to particular words or phrases. Indeed, the many qualities of the voice itself, in addition to the actual meaning of the words, form the vocalic nonverbal communication system. Vocalics also include many nonspeech sounds, such as belching, laughing, and crying, and vocal "filler" sounds such as *uh, er, um,* and *uh-huh.*

Vocal versus Verbal Communication   Vocalic qualities include pitch (high to low), rate of talking (fast to slow), conversational rhythm (smooth to staccato), and volume (loud to soft). Because spoken (i.e., verbal) language always has some vocal elements, it is difficult to separate the meaning conveyed by the language from that conveyed by the vocalic components. However, if you can imagine that these words you are now reading are a transcript of a lecture we have given, you will be able to understand clearly the distinctions we are describing. Although our words—the language spoken—are here on the printed page, the vocalics are not. Are we speaking rapidly or slowly? How does our inflection change to emphasize a point or to signal a question? Are we yelling, whispering, drawling, or speaking with an accent? Do our voices indicate that we are tense, relaxed, strained, calm, bored, or excited? The answers to these types of questions are conveyed by the speaker's voice.

Cultural Differences in Vocal Communication   There are vast cultural differences in vocalic behaviors. For example, unlike English, many Asian languages are tonal. The same Chinese words when said with a different vocalic tone or pitch can have vastly different meanings. In addition to differences in tone or pitch, there are large cultural differences in the loudness and frequency of speaking. Latinos, for instance, perceive themselves as talking more loudly and more frequently than European Americans.[45]

The emotional meanings conveyed by the voice are usually taken for granted by native language users, but they can be the cause of considerable problems when they fail to conform to preconceived expectations. For instance, when a Saudi Arabian man is speaking in English, he will usually transfer his native intonation patterns without necessarily being aware that he has done so. In Arabic, the intonation pattern is such that many of the individual words in the sentence are stressed. Although a flat intonation pattern is used in declarative sentences, the intonation pattern for exclamatory sentences is much stronger and more emotional than that in English. The higher pitch of Arabic speakers also conveys a more emotional tone than that of English speakers. Consequently, differences in vocal characteristics may result in unwarranted negative impressions. The U.S. American may incorrectly perceive that the Saudi Arabian is excited or angry when in fact he is not. Questions by the Saudi that merely seek information may sound accusing. The monotonous tone of declarative sentences may be perceived as demonstrating apathy or a lack of interest. Vocal stress and intonation differences may be perceived as aggressive or abrasive when only polite conversation is intended. Conversely, the Saudi Arabian may incorrectly interpret certain behaviors of the U.S. American speaker as an expression of calmness and pleasantness when anger or annoyance is being conveyed. Similarly, a statement that seems to be a firm assertion to the U.S. American speaker may sound weak and doubtful to the Saudi Arabian.[46]

Other Nonverbal Code Systems

Many other nonverbal code systems are relevant to an understanding of intercultural communication because virtually everything we say, do, create, and wear can communicate messages about our culture and ourselves. These other codes include the chemical, dermal, physical, and artifactual systems that create a multichanneled set of nonverbal messages.

Chemical Code System   The interpretations made from chemically based body functions form the chemical code system. Chemical codes include natural body odor, tears, sweat, gas, household smells, and similar phenomena. People have distinct chemical code systems that are affected by their way of living, food preferences, habits, and environment. These differences are often used to make judgments or interpretations about members of a culture. For instance, most meat-eating Westerners have a distinct body odor that may be unpleasant to cultures that do not consume red meat. Similarly, many hotels in Malaysia have posted signs that say "No Durians" to discourage their guests from bringing in the pungent, sweet-tasting fruit that many consider to be a delicacy. Among many Arabic-speaking cultures, attempts to mask body odors with perfumes is considered an insult; for both Arabs and Filipinos, smelling another person's breath is so favorably regarded that close spatial distances in conversations are used to obtain it.

Dermal Code System   The short-term changes in skin texture or sensitivity that result from physical or psychological reactions to the environment form the dermal code system. Dermal codes include blushing, blanching, goose flesh, and related experiences. Particularly in high-context cultures, subtle changes in skin tonalities may be carefully observed to obtain the information needed to act appropriately.

CULTURE connections

No discovery pleased me more, on that first excursion from the city, than the full translation of the famous Indian head-wiggle. The weeks I'd spent in Bombay with Prabaker had taught me that the shaking or wiggling of the head from side to side—that most characteristic of Indian expressive gestures—was the equivalent of a forward nod of the head, meaning *Yes.* I'd also discerned the subtler senses of *I agree with you,* and *Yes, I would like that.* What I learned, on the train, was that a universal message attached to the gesture, when it was used as a greeting, which made it uniquely useful.

Most of those who entered the open carriage greeted the other seated or standing men with a little wiggle of the head. The gesture always drew a reciprocal wag of the head from at least one, and sometimes several of the passengers. I watched it happen at station after station, knowing that the newcomers couldn't be indicating *Yes,* or *I agree with you* with the head-wiggle because nothing had been said, and there was no exchange other than the gesture itself. Gradually, I realised that the wiggle of the head was a signal to others that carried an amiable and disarming message: *I'm a peaceful man. I don't mean any harm.*

Moved by admiration and no small envy for the marvellous gesture, I resolved to try it myself. The train stopped at a small rural station. A stranger joined our group in the carriage. When our eyes met for the first time, I gave the little wiggle of my head, and a smile. The result was astounding. The man beamed a smile at me so huge that it was half the brilliance of Prabaker's own, and set to such energetic head waggling in return that I was, at first, a little alarmed. By journey's end, however, I'd had enough practice to perform the movement as casually as others in the carriage did, and to convey the gentle message of the gesture. It was the first truly Indian expression my body learned, and it was the beginning of a transformation that has ruled my life, in all the long years since that journey of crowded hearts.

—*Gregory David Roberts*

Physical Code System   The relatively unchanging aspects of the body form the physical code system: weight, body shape, facial features, skin color, eye color, hair, characteristics that denote age and gender, and similar features. Indeed, the cultural standards for beauty vary greatly, as can expectations about how people should look.

Artifactual Code System   The creations that people make, use, or wear are the artifactual code system. These aspects of material culture include the tools, clothing, buildings, furnishings, jewelry, lighting, and color schemes that are common to the members of a culture. Clothing styles, cosmetics, and body ornamentations, for instance, are used to fulfill the culture's needs for modesty, self-expression, or privacy. Differences in privacy needs, in particular, are often indicated by such features as closed doors in the United States, sound-proofed doors in Germany, tree-lined barriers at property lines in England, or paper-thin walls in Japan.

Synchrony of Nonverbal Communication Codes

Cultures train their members to synchronize the various nonverbal behaviors to form a response pattern that typifies the expected behaviors in that culture. Subtle variations in the response patterns are clearly noticed, even when they differ by only a few thousandths of a second. William Condon, who describes himself as "a white, middle-class male," suggests that interactional synchrony is learned from birth and occurs within a fraction of a second. Condon compares the differences in the speech and gestures of African Americans and European Americans:

> If I say the word "because" both my hands may extend exactly together. In Black behavior, however, the right hand may begin to extend with the "be" portion slightly ahead of the left hand and the left hand will extend rapidly across the "cause" portion. This creates the syncopation, mentioned before, which can appear anywhere in the body. A person moves in the rhythm and timing of his or her culture, and this rhythm is in the whole body.... It may be that those having different cultural rhythms are unable to really "synch-in" fully with each other.... I think that infants from the first moments of life and even in the womb are getting the rhythm and structure and style of sound, the rhythms of their culture, so that they imprint to them and the rhythms become part of their very being.[47]

CULTURE connections

Nepalis do not knock before they enter closed doors as it is assumed one will always be decently covered. I suppress a wave of indignation when someone bursts in unannounced. This whole experience is a challenge to the right of privacy we assume at home. In Nepal the need to be alone would be culturally aberrant and usually physically impossible. I think with some amusement now of the festering family argument that occasionally resurfaced because each of my sons felt entitled to a room of his own.

—*Barbara J. Scot*

Behavioral synchrony in the use of nonverbal codes can be found in virtually all cultures. Not only must an individual's many behaviors be coordinated appropriately, they must also mesh properly with the words and movements of the other interactants. Coordination in Japanese bowing behaviors, for example, requires an adaptation to the status relationships of the participants; the inferior must begin the bow, and the superior decides when the bow is complete. If the participants are of equal status, they must begin and end their bows simultaneously. This is not as easy as it seems. As one Japanese man relates:

> Perfect synchrony is absolutely essential to bowing. Whenever an American tries to bow to me, I often feel extremely awkward and uncomfortable because I simply cannot synchronize bowing with him or her....bowing occurs in a flash of a second, before you have time to think. And both parties must know precisely when to start bowing, how deep, how long to stay in the bowed position, and when to bring their heads up.[48]

Similar degrees of coordination and synchrony can be found in most everyday activities. Sensitivity to these different nonverbal codes can help you to become more interculturally competent.

Nonverbal Communication and Intercultural Competence

The rules and norms that govern most nonverbal communication behaviors are both culture-specific and outside of conscious awareness. That is, although members of a culture know and follow their culture's expectations, they probably learned the norms for proper nonverbal expressiveness very early in childhood, and these norms may never have been articulated verbally.[49] Sometimes, therefore, the only way you will know that a cultural norm exists is when you break it!

An important consequence of this out-of-awareness aspect is that members of a culture use their norms to determine appropriate nonverbal behaviors and then make negative judgments about others' feelings, motives, intentions, and even their attractiveness if these norms are violated.[50] Often the violations will be inaccurately attributed to aspects of personality, attitudes, or intelligence rather than to a mismatch between learned nonverbal codes. U.S. Americans, for instance, highly value positive nonverbal displays and typically regard someone who smiles as more intelligent than someone who does not; the Japanese, however, whose cultural norms value constraint in nonverbal expressiveness, do

CULTURE connections

By then, I was used to the averted gaze of devout Muslim men, and it seemed normal to me to be conversing with someone whose eyes were focused on a floor tile an inch in front of my shoe. He was considering whether to let me meet his wife.

—*Geraldine Brooles*

■ These two Korean businesswomen illustrate several kinds of nonverbal messages. Notice the meanings that you attribute to their gestures, facial expressions, body postures, clothing, and the distance they stand from one another.

not equate expressiveness with intelligence.[51] The very nature of nonverbal behaviors makes inaccurate judgments difficult to recognize and correct.

The following suggestions will help you use your knowledge of nonverbal communication to improve your intercultural competence. These suggestions are designed to help you notice, interpret, and use nonverbal communication behaviors to function more appropriately and more effectively in intercultural encounters.

Researchers have been known to take weeks or even months to analyze the delicate interaction rhythms involved in a single conversation. Of course, most people do not have the luxury of a month to analyze someone's comments before responding. However, the knowledge that the patterns of behavior will probably be very complex will help sensitize you to them and may encourage you to notice more details.

No set of behaviors is universally correct, so the "right" behaviors can never be described in a catalog or list. Rather, the proper behaviors are those that are appropriate and effective in the context of the culture, setting, and occasion. What is right in one set of circumstances may be totally wrong in another. Although it is useful to gather culture-specific information about appropriate nonverbal behaviors, even this knowledge should be approached as relative because prescriptions of "right" behavior rarely identify all of the situational characteristics that cultural natives "know."

By monitoring your emotional reactions to differences in nonverbal behaviors, you can be alert to the interpretations you are making and therefore to the possibility of alternative meanings. Strong visceral responses to differences in smell, body movement, and personal spacing are quite common in intercultural communication. Knowledge that these might occur, followed by care in the interpretation of meanings, is critical.

Skillful interpretation includes observation of general tendencies. Focus on what members of the other culture prefer and the ways in which they typically behave. How, when, and with whom do they gesture, move, look, and touch? How are time and space used to define and maintain social relationships? It is much harder to pay attention to these general tendencies than you might think because, in all likelihood, you have not had much practice in consciously looking for patterns in the commonplace, taken-for-granted activities through which cultural effects are displayed. Nevertheless, it is possible, with practice, to improve your observation skills.

Even after making observations, be tentative in your interpretations and generalizations. You could be wrong. You will be far more successful in making sense of others' behaviors if you avoid the premature closure that comes with assuming you know for certain what something means. Think of your explanations as tentative working hypotheses rather than as unchanging facts.

Next, look for exceptions to your generalizations. These exceptions are very important because they help you recognize that no one individual, regardless of the thoroughness and accuracy with which you have come to understand a culture, will exactly fit the useful generalizations you have formed. The exceptions that you note can help you limit the scope of your generalizations and recognize the boundaries beyond which your judgments may simply not apply. Maybe your interpretations apply only to men, or students, or government officials, or strangers, or the elderly, or potential customers. Maybe your evaluations of the way time and space are structured apply only to business settings, or among those whose status is equal, or with particular people like yourself. Though it is necessary to make useful generalizations to get along in another culture, it is equally necessary to recognize the limits of these generalizations.

Finally, practice to improve your ability in observing, evaluating, and behaving in appropriate and effective ways. Practice increases your skills in recognizing specific patterns to people's behaviors, in correctly interpreting the meanings and likely consequences of those behaviors, and in selecting responses that are both appropriate and effective. Like all skills, your level of intercultural competence will improve with practice. Of course, the best form of practice is one that closely approximates the situations in which you will have to use the skills you are trying to acquire. Therefore, we encourage you to seek out and willingly engage in intercultural communication experiences.

Summary

Although there is some evidence that certain nonverbal communication tendencies are common to all humans, cultures vary greatly in the repertoire of behaviors and circumstances in which nonverbal exchanges occur. A smile, a head nod, and eye contact may all have different meanings in different cultures.

This chapter considered the important nonverbal code systems used to supplement, reinforce, or substitute the verbal code systems. Nonverbal code systems are the silent language of communication. They are less precise and less consciously used and interpreted than verbal code systems, but they can have powerful effects on perceptions of and interpretations about others. The nonverbal code systems relating to body movements, space, touch, time, voice, and other nonverbal code systems were each described. Finally, the interrelationship of these nonverbal code systems with one another and with the verbal code system was explored.

For Discussion

1. What are some examples of cultural universals? Can you think of examples from your personal experiences that either confirm or contradict the idea of cultural universals?
2. It is widely believed by many that "a smile is universally understood." Do you agree with this statement? Why or why not.
3. Touch is one of the most fundamental parts of the human experience. But cultural differences in the norms for touching can cause problems in intercultural interactions. Provide examples of your touching norms that you believe differ for people from cultures other than your own.
4. We know that cultures use and value time differently. What kinds of judgments might be made of those who use time differently from the ways that your culture does?
5. Each culture socializes its members to speak at its "preferred" rate and volume. Can you think of instances when you have made judgments about others because they spoke louder or softer, or faster or slower, than you wanted? If so, what were the evaluations you made? Were these judgments connected to cultural differences in vocal communication?
6. What are some of the ways that U.S. Americans have been taught (or have unconsciously learned) to synchronize their nonverbal behaviors?

For Further Reading

Edward T. Hall, *The Hidden Dimension* (New York: Anchor Books, 1990). An exploration of the variations in the use of space across cultures and how that use reflects cultural values and establishes rules for interactions. A classic book that was influential in the study of nonverbal communication across cultures.

Mark L. Knapp and Judith A. Hall, *Nonverbal Communication in Human Interaction*, 6th ed. (Belmont, CA: Thomson/Wadsworth, 2006). Offers the basic perspectives and literature on nonverbal communication. Focuses on the people, behaviors, environments, and messages that affect communication.

Dale Leathers and Michael H. Eaves, *Successful Nonverbal Communication: Principles and Applications*, 4th ed. (Boston: Allyn & Bacon, 2008). A very readable introduction to the topic of nonverbal communication. This is a useful summary because it is current and links well to other key concepts presented in Intercultural Competence.

David Matsumoto, "Culture and Nonverbal Behavior," *The Sage Handbook of Nonverbal Communication*, ed. Valerie Manusov and Miles L. Patterson (Thousand Oaks, CA: Sage, 2006). A scholarly summary that explores the universal and culturally specific displays and expressions of nonverbal behaviors.

For additional information about intercultural films and about Web sites for researching specific cultures, please turn to the Resources section at the back of this book.

CHAPTER 9

The Effects of Code Usage in Intercultural Communication

KEY TERMS

Practical, everyday communication experiences—greeting a friend, buying something from a shopkeeper, asking directions, or describing a common experience—require messages to be organized in a meaningful way. Cultures differ, however, in the patterns that are preferred for organizing ideas and communicating them to others. These differences affect what people regard as logical, rational, and a basis for sound reasoning and conclusions.

This chapter focuses on the consequences for intercultural communication of differences in the way cultures use verbal and nonverbal communication. Do people in particular cultures have distinctive preferences for what, where, when, and with whom to speak? Are there differences in what are regarded as the ideal ways to organize ideas and present them to others? What constitutes appropriate forms of reasoning, evidence, and proof in a discussion or argument? Is proof accomplished with a statistic, an experience, an expert's testimony, or a link between some aspect of the problem and the emotions of the listener? What is considered "rational" and "logical"? In short, how do conversations differ because of the differences in culture, language, and nonverbal codes?

Competent intercultural communication requires more than just an accurate rendition of the verbal and nonverbal codes that others use. The "logic" of how those codes are organized and used must also be understood.

This chapter begins by considering alternative preferences for the organization of messages. Next we discuss cultural variations in persuasive communication. Finally, differences in the structure of conversations are presented as another way in which code systems influence intercultural competence.

Preferences in the Organization of Messages

Cultures have distinct preferences for organizing ideas and presenting them in writing and in public speeches. Consider what you have been taught in English composition courses as the "correct" way to structure an essay, or recall the organizational patterns you have used to structure the content of a speech. The premise underlying our discussion is that cultures provide preferred ways for people to organize and convey thoughts and feelings. These preferences influence the ways people communicate and the choices they make to arrange ideas in specific patterns.

In this section, we first describe the organizational features of the English language as it is used in the United States. We then explore the organizational features associated with other languages used in particular cultures.

Organizational Preferences in the Use of U.S. English

For most cultures, the correct use of language is most easily observed when the language is formally taught in the school system. English is a standard feature of the U.S. high school curriculum, and English composition is a requirement for virtually all U.S. college students. The development of oral communication skills, which usually includes training in public speaking, is also a common requirement for many college students. In both written and oral communication courses, users of U.S. English explicitly learn rules that govern how ideas are to be presented. Indeed, the features that characterize a well-organized essay in U.S. English are very similar to the features of a well-organized public speech.

The structure of a good essay or speech in U.S. English requires the development of a specific theme. A thesis statement, which is the central organizing idea of the speech or essay, is the foundation on which speakers or writers develop their speech or essay. Ideally, thesis statements are clear and specific; speakers and writers must present their

CULTURE connections

After listening to C. J. for three years, I felt somewhat prepared to carry on conversations the Asian way. No linear progression. Catching the point of their stories, whether C. J. 's or Phourim's, was like capturing fireflies. In talking with Phourim, I had no expectation of going in a straight line from point A to point B and the purpose of the discussion.

—Patricia Harrington

ideas in a straightforward and unambiguous manner. Often, the thesis statement is provided in the opening paragraph of an essay or in the beginning of a speech.

The paragraph is the fundamental organizational unit of written English. Paragraphs are composed of sentences and should express a single idea. A straightforward presentation of the main idea typically appears as the topic sentence of the paragraph, and it is often located at or near the beginning of the paragraph.[1]

There are other rules that guide how paragraphs are combined into an essay or main points into a speech. Generally, correct organization in U.S. English means that writers or speakers clearly state their thesis at the beginning and provide the audience with an overview of their main points. As the key to good organization, students are taught to outline the main points of the essay or speech by subordinating supporting ideas to the main ideas. In fact, most teachers give students explicit instructions to help them learn to organize properly.

In U.S. English there is also a preferred way to develop the main points. If a speaker is talking about scuba diving, with main points on equipment and safety tips, he or she is expected to develop the point on equipment by talking only about equipment. Safety tips should not be mentioned in the midst of the discussion about equipment. If the speaker gave examples related to safety tips in the middle of the discussion on equipment, listeners (or readers) trained in the preferences embedded in U.S. English would become confused and would think the speaker was disorganized. A teacher would probably comment on the organizational deficiencies and might lower the student's grade because the speech does not match the expected form of a well-organized speech.

The organizational pattern preferred in the formal use of U.S. English can best be described as linear. This pattern can be visualized as a series of steps or progressions that move in a straight line toward a particular goal or idea. Thus, the preferred organizational pattern forms a series of "bridges," where each idea is linked to the next.

Organizational Preferences in Other Languages and Cultures

Some years ago, Robert Kaplan systematically began to study the preferred organizational patterns of nonnative speakers of English. In an article that is usually credited with launching a specialization called contrastive rhetoric, Kaplan characterized the preferences for the organization of paragraphs among people from different language and cultural groups.[2] Scholars such as Ulla Connor have extended Kaplan's work to look at the patterns of cultural differences when writing language.[3]

■ Los Angeles mayor Antonio Villaraigosa uses his persuasive skills to convince his audience. Cultures differ in the evidence and arguments they regard as persuasive.

The practical consequences of language use on the organization of ideas are often obvious to teachers of English as a second language (ESL). Even after nonnative English speakers have mastered the vocabulary and grammar of the English language, they are unlikely to write an essay in what is considered "correct" English form. In fact, because of the particular style for the organization and presentation of ideas, ESL teachers can often identify the native language of a writer even when the essay is written in English.

One important difference in organizational structure concerns languages that are speaker-responsible versus those that are listener-responsible. In English, which is a speaker-responsible language, the speaker is expected to provide the structure and, therefore, much of the specific meaning of the statements.[4] Because the speaker tells the listener exactly what is going to be talked about and what the speaker wants the listener to know, prior knowledge of the speaker's intent is not necessary. In Japanese, which is a listener-responsible language, speakers need to indicate only indirectly what they are discussing and what they want the listener to know when the conversation is over. The listener is forced to construct the meaning, and usually does so, based on shared knowledge between the speaker and the listener.

The U.S. English concepts of thesis statements and paragraph topic sentences have no real equivalents in many languages. Studies of Japanese, Korean, Thai, and Chinese language use indicate that, in these languages, the thesis statement is often buried in the passage.[5] Thus, for example, the preferred structure

CULTURE connections

A form of traditional Malagasy oratory, *kabary* is based on the unhurried telling of ancestral proverbs, metaphors, and riddles, frequently in a dialogue using call and response.

Originally used in public gatherings and political assemblies of a pre-literate era, the form has since evolved and been popularized, but it has kept its specific rules. Today, despite the rising literacy rate and the familiarity with different manners of speech, *kabary* is still considered necessary for communication during ritual events, and is also used widely in regular, day-to-day talk.

—*Danna Harman*

of a Japanese paragraph is often called a "gyre" or a series of "stepping stones" that depend on indirection and implication to connect ideas and provide the main points.[6] The rules for language use in Japan mean that speakers may not tell the listener the specific point being conveyed; rather, the topic is circled delicately to imply its domain.[7]

Imagine the consequences of an intercultural interaction between a Japanese person and a U.S. American. What might happen if one of them is able to speak in the other's language and is sufficiently skilled to convey meaning linguistically but is not adept at the logic of the language? The Japanese person is likely to think that the U.S. American is rude and aggressive. Conversely, the U.S. American is likely to think that the Japanese person is confusing and imprecise. Both people in this intercultural interaction are likely to feel dissatisfied, confused, and uncomfortable.

The nonlinear structure of Japanese language use also characterizes Hindi, one of India's national languages. In Hindi, one does not typically develop just one unified thought or idea; rather, the preferred style contains digressions and includes related material.[8] When using English, speakers of Hindi exhibit the characteristics of the Hindi organizational style and provide many minor contextual points before advancing the thesis.[9]

How do you think U.S. teachers of English would grade an assignment that was written in English by a native Hindi speaker? We can easily imagine the comments about the lack of organization and the poor development of the ideas. Because the Indian writing and speaking conventions have an obvious preference for nonlinearity, they are likely to be perceived, from a U.S. perspective, as illogical.

Chinese discourse styles are similar to those of Hindi English. Rather than relying on a preview statement to orient the listener to the discourse's overall direction, the Chinese rely heavily on contextual cues. Chinese speech also tends to use single words such as *because, as,* and *so* to replace whole clause connectives, such as "in view of the fact that," "to begin with," or "in conclusion," that are commonly used in English.[10]

Cultural patterns interact with code systems to create expectations about what is considered the proper or the logical way to organize the presentation of ideas. What is considered the right way to organize ideas within one culture may be regarded in another as some combination of illogical, disorganized, unclear, confusing, imprecise, rude, discourteous, aggressive, and ineffective.[11] In intercultural communication, people make judgments about the appropriateness and effectiveness of others' thoughts, and these assumptions about the "right" way to communicate may vary greatly and may lead to misunderstandings.

CULTURE connections

The American style of learning is to ask questions, discuss the theory and then go do it and ask more questions. The Japanese style is to observe the master, not ask questions and then get your hands dirty at the very beginning. If you ask questions, it can suggest that the master didn't do his job properly. The different styles can cause problems.

—*Sacramento Bee*

Cultural Variations in Persuasion

Persuasion involves the use of symbols to influence others. Persuasion may occur in formal, public settings, such as when a candidate for political office tries to win votes through speeches and advertisements. On many occasions, persuasive messages are mediated through television, video, film, photographs, and even music and art. More commonly, persuasion occurs in everyday interactions between people. Our daily conversations include attempts to influence others to accept our ideas, agree with our preferences, or engage in behaviors that we want. In other words, we all take part in persuasion on a regular basis. For example, you might try to convince your roommate to clean the apartment. Or perhaps you want your coworkers to increase their involvement in your work group's project. You might even attempt to persuade your professor to give you an extension on the due date for your term paper.

Persuasion in Intercultural Encounters

In today's multicultural world, many of our persuasive encounters will likely involve culturally heterogeneous individuals. An African American salesperson may have her territory expanded to include Australia and finds that her primary contact there is Chinese. A European American college student may need to negotiate a desired absence from class with a Latino professor. Japanese tourists in South Africa may want room service even though the service is shut down for the night. An Indian manager for a major international bank may have employees reporting to him who are Bengali, New Zealanders, Swiss, British, and Chinese. All of these communicative situations require knowledge and skill in using the appropriate means of persuasion; whereas members of some cultures genuinely enjoy the persuasive or argumentative encounter, many others shun such confrontations.[12]

The effective use of verbal and nonverbal codes to persuade another varies greatly from culture to culture. For instance, there are differences in *what* cultures consider to be acceptable evidence, in *who* can be regarded as an authority, in *how* evidence is used to create persuasive arguments, and in *when* ideas are accepted as reasonable. These preferred ways to persuade others are called the culture's persuasive style. When people from diverse cultures communicate, the differences in their persuasive styles are often very evident.

The word *logical* is often used to describe the preferred persuasive style of a culture. Logic and rationality seem to be invoked as though there were some firm "truth" somewhere that simply has to be discovered and used in order to be convincing. We agree with James F. Hamill, however, that "because logic has cultural aspects, an understanding of social life requires an understanding of how people think in their own cultural context."[13] In fact, Stephen Toulmin, a leading philosopher who studies human reasoning, claims that what people call "rationality" varies from culture to culture and from time to time.[14] A phrase that sums up these variations is ethno-logics or alternative logics.

Persuasion involves an interaction between a speaker and his or her audience, in which the speaker intends to have the audience accept a point of view or a conclusion. Persuasion usually involves evidence, establishing "logical" connections between the pieces of evidence, and ordering the evidence into a meaningful arrangement—all of which is used to persuade the audience to accept the speaker's point of view or conclusion. In each of these elements of persuasion, there are substantial variations from culture to culture. In the following sections, we describe some of these variations.[15]

Cultural Differences in What Is Acceptable as Evidence

Evidence is what a persuader offers to those she or he is trying to persuade. In any given persuasive situation, we have available to us a myriad of sensory information or ideas. For example, suppose that students are trying to persuade a teacher to give an extension on a paper's due date. There have probably been numerous events that students could select as evidence. Maybe many students had been ill for a day, or perhaps the teacher had been sick. Or perhaps during one critical lecture, the noise of construction workers just outside the classroom made it difficult to pay attention to the discussion. Any of these events might be used as evidence to support the conclusion that the paper's due date ought to be postponed. An idea or experience does not become evidence, however, until it is selected for use in the persuasive interaction. What we choose from among all of the available cues is highly influenced by our culture.

There are no universally accepted standards about what constitutes evidence or about how evidence should be used in support of claims or conclusions. In many cultures, people use parables or stories as a form of evidence. But the contents of those stories, and their use in support of claims, differ widely. Devout Muslims and Christians, for example, may use stories from the Koran or the Bible as a powerful form of evidence; the story is offered, the lesson from the story is summarized, and the evidence is regarded as conclusive. In other cultures, the story itself must be scrutinized to determine how illustrative it is compared with other possibilities. Native American stories, for instance, rarely provide a deductive conclusion; consistent with a cultural value of indirectness, the story may simply end with "That's how it was" and expect the listeners to infer the relationship between the story and the current circumstances.[16] For Kenyans, persuasive messages depend on narratives and personal stories as supporting evidence in speeches.[17] Similarly, cultures influenced by Confucianism often rely on metaphors and analogies as persuasive evidence.[18]

CULTURE connections

When grandmama died in 1940 at eighty-three, our whole household held its breath. She had promised us a sign of her leaving, final proof that her life had ended well. My parents knew that without any clear sign, our own family fortunes could be altered, threatened. Stepmother looked every day into the small cluttered room the ancient lady had occupied. Nothing was touched; nothing changed. Father, thinking that a sign should appear in Grandmama's garden, looked at the frost-killed shoots and cringed: *No, that could not be it.*

My two older teenage brothers and my sister, Liang, were embarrassed by my parents' behaviour. What would white people in Vancouver think of us? We were Canadians now, *Chinese-Canadians*, a hyphenated reality that our parents could never accept. So it seemed, for different reasons, we were all holding our breath, waiting for *something.*

—*Wayson Choy*

The European American culture prefers physical evidence and eyewitness testimony, and members of that culture see "facts" as the supreme kind of evidence. Popular mysteries on television or in best-selling books weave their tales by giving clues through the appearance of physical evidence or facts—a button that is torn off a sleeve, a record of calls made from one person's telephone to another, or a bankbook that shows regular deposits or withdrawals. From all of these pieces of evidence, human behavior and motivation are regarded as apparent. In some cultures, however, physical evidence is discounted because no connection is seen between those pieces of the physical world and human actions. People from cultures that view the physical world as indicative of human motivation have difficulty understanding this point of view.

The use of expert testimony in the persuasive process also varies greatly from one culture to another. In certain African cultures, the words of a witness would be discounted or even totally disregarded because people believe that, if you speak up about seeing something, you must have a particular agenda in mind; in other words, no one is regarded as objective. In the Chinese legal system, the primary purpose of testimony is not to gather information but to persuade the court while shaming the defendant into confessing.[19] The U.S. legal system, however, depends on the testimony of others; witnesses to traffic accidents, for example, are called to give testimony concerning the behavior of the drivers involved in the accident. Teachers of adults who are learning English indicate that these students may not understand the relative weight or authority to give to a scholarly presentation in a journal or academic work versus opinions found in an editorial column of a newspaper or magazine.[20]

■ To persuade potential employers, this woman is arranging the evidence on her resume. Evidence, logic, and reasoning are all shaped by one's cultural background.

Cultural Differences in Styles of Persuasion

Perhaps the best way to understand what a culture might regard as logical or reasonable is to refer to the culture's dominant patterns, which we discussed in Chapters 4 and 5. Cultural patterns supply the underlying assumptions that people within a culture use to determine what is "correct" and reasonable, and they therefore provide the persuader's justification for linking the evidence to the conclusions desired from the audience.[21] These differences in the ways people prefer to arrange the evidence, assumptions, and claims constitute the culture's persuasive style.[22]

Much of the tradition of persuasion and rhetoric among European Americans is influenced by the rhetoric of Aristotle, who emphasized the separation of logic and reason from emotion. This Aristotelian perspective is also common to the rhetorical traditions of many European cultures, but it is antithetical to good rhetorical practices in numerous other cultures.[23]

Thai, Arab, and Chinese discourse all have rhetorical traditions that emphasize the importance of emotion in assessing the truthfulness of a situation. Thus an examination of persuasive letters written by native Thai speakers and native English speakers found that the Thai used a combination of logical arguments, emotional pleas, and requests based on the speaker's *ethos* (credibility, character, and appeal to others), while the English speakers depended almost solely on logical arguments.[24] Similarly, a comparison of newspaper editorials from the United States (in English) to those from Saudi Arabia (in Arabic) found substantial differences in the persuasive techniques employed; though the editorials from both cultures made strong assertions, the persuasive appeals in the U.S. editorials were direct and explicit, whereas the Saudi editorials used implied arguments and indirect language that provided an opportunity to disagree without requiring the reader to concede the disagreement.[25] Likewise U.S. Americans tend to vary their phrasing and utilize alternate ways of saying the same thing during business negotiations, while the Chinese typically just restate their position repeatedly without changing it publicly before first consulting privately among themselves.[26]

Lakota speakers may offer stories that are related to their persuasive point, but the persuader may not make explicit the link to the conclusion.[27] Likewise, Latin American speakers may use passive sentence constructions and descriptions to lead others to a conclusion that is not stated specifically.[28] Mexicans, among others, are sometimes very emotional and dramatic, and they may subordinate the goal of accuracy to one involving pleasantness. Thus, when a U.S. American asks a Mexican shopkeeper a question, the shopkeeper may be concerned less with the correctness of details than with the maintenance of a harmonious relationship.[29]

Even seemingly "objective" reporting of news may convey a subtle persuasive message. Japanese newspapers and television news shows, for example, routinely refer to Japanese adults by their family name plus *san*, the latter word being an address term denoting respect or honor. As Daniel Dolan suggests, however, "this respect is *conditional*, because in most instances of reporting about a person associated with criminal activity, mass media reporters will publicly divest an individual of the personal address term *san* and in its place use *yogisha* [suspect], *hikoku* [accused], or family name alone. The effect is to banish the person, at least temporarily, from functioning citizenry."[30]

CULTURE connections

About "English only": Let me tell you a little story that happened in Houston, Texas, just before I became a national best-selling author. I met this young woman at the University of Houston. She looked like she was part Black, part White, and part American Indian. She was stunningly beautiful, with huge greenish eyes. She spoke Spanish. I asked her where she was from. She said Panama. I asked how she liked the United States. She said she didn't, and that as soon as she graduated she wanted to return to Panama. I asked why. She told me that she'd had a boyfriend for four years. "And the other day he said 'I think I love you,' so I dropped him as fast as I could. My God," she added, "after four years he was still thinking about our love. I can't stand to be around people who are always thinking so much."

I laughed. I could see her point completely, because in Spanish you'd never say, "I think I love you," especially after four years. That would be an insult. You'd say, "I feel love for you so deeply that when I just think of you, I start to tremble and feel my heart flutter." Why? Because Spanish is a feeling-based language that comes first from the heart, just as English is a thinking-based language that comes first from the head. And Yaqui, Navajo, and the fifty-seven dialects of Oaxacan are ever-changing languages that come first from the soul, then go to the heart, and lastly to the brain.

—*Victor Villaseñor*

We would like to elaborate on the idea of persuasive style because, like many of the other characteristics of a culture, it is an important cultural attribute that is taken for granted within a culture but affects communication between cultures. As we have cautioned elsewhere, not every person in a culture will select the culture's preferred style. Rather, we are describing a cultural tendency, a choice or preference that most people in the culture will select most of the time.

Barbara Johnstone describes three general strategies of persuasion that can form a culture's preferred style: the quasilogical, presentational, and analogical.[31] Each of these styles depends on different kinds of evidence, organizational patterns, and conclusions. As you read the descriptions of these styles, try to imagine what a persuasive encounter would be like and what might happen if others preferred a different persuasive style.

Quasilogical Style   The preferred style for members of many Western cultures is the quasilogical style. In this style, the preference is to use objective statistics and testimony from expert witnesses as evidence. The evidence is then connected to the conclusion in a way that resembles formal logic. In formal logic, once the listener accepts or believes the individual pieces of evidence, the conclusions follow "logically" and must also be accepted. In the quasilogical style, the speaker or persuader will connect the evidence to the persuasive conclusion by using such words as *thus, hence,* and *therefore.* The form or arrangement of the ideas is very important.

The dominance of the quasilogical style for English speakers is underscored by advice given to students of English as a second language: "English-speaking readers are convinced by facts, statistics, and illustrations in arguments; they move from generalizations to specific examples and expect explicit links between main topics and subtopics; and they value originality."[32] The underlying assumption of this style is that, if the idea is "true," it simply needs to be presented in a logical way so that its truthfulness becomes apparent to all. Those who prefer the quasilogical style assume that it is possible to discover what is true or false and right or wrong about a particular experience. In other words, they believe that events can be objectively established and verified.

Presentational Style   The presentational style emphasizes and appeals to the emotional aspects of persuasion. In this style, it is understood that people, rather than the idea itself, are what make an idea persuasive. That is, ideas themselves are not inherently persuasive; what makes them compelling is how they are presented to others. Thus, an immutable truth does not exist, and there are no clear rights or wrongs to be discovered.

In the presentational style, the persuader uses language to create an emotional response. The rhythmic qualities of words and the ability of words to move the hearer visually and auditorily are fundamental to this style of persuasion. You have probably read poetry or literature that stimulated a strong emotional reaction. Those who use a presentational style persuade in the same way. By the use of words, the ideas of the speaker become so vivid and real that the persuasive idea almost becomes embedded in the consciousness of the listener. The language of this style of persuasion is filled with sensory words that induce the listener to *look, see, hear, feel,* and ultimately *believe.*

CULTURE connections

Native American people hesitate to tell anyone directly what they *should* do. With many Native American people, it is not customary to say, "You must not do that." A story indirectly says to children, "You may act this way, but look at the consequences." ...

There are cultural storytelling conventions in Native American tradition that vary sharply from European American tradition and which may account, in part, for the observed powerful effects of the telling of *lesson* stories: (1) while European heroes are praised for succeeding, Native American heroes are honored for their attempt, even if they fail; (2) when animals talk in European stories, they usually imitate human characteristics and failures, but when they talk in Native American stories, it is because they are respected as equals in the natural world, with wisdom to share; (3) many characters are not given names, underlining the universality of human experience over situation-specific events; (4) nonverbal communication through gesture and voice is given an equal rather than a supplementary role in oral tales, which may appear verbally lean; and (5) the spirit world and the physical world exist side by side and are so close that it is possible to move back and forth between the two without effort....

Consistent with an appreciation for indirect teaching, a Native American lesson story is told without further explication of meaning and contains no surprise endings, shocks, or ironic twists. To an analytical mind a lesson story may seem to have no deductive conclusion, ending only with the teller saying something like, "That's how it was." Tellers do not lift out the "moral" of the story for the listener or offer the accepted point of view, which might be consistent with the linear and discursive nature of traditional American education.

—Sunwolf

Analogical Style   The analogical style seeks to establish an idea (a conclusion) and to persuade the listener by providing an analogy, a story, or a parable in which there is either an implicit or explicit lesson to be learned. The storybook pattern that begins "Once upon a time" is one example of this style, as are the sermons of many ministers and preachers. An assumption underlying the analogical style is that the collective experience of groups of people—the culture—is persuasive, rather than the ideas themselves or the characteristics of a dynamic individual. Historical precedent takes on great importance because what convinces is a persuader's ability to choose the right historical story to demonstrate the point. In the analogical style, skill in persuasion is associated with the discovery and narration of the appropriate story—a story that captures the essence of what the persuader wants the listeners to know.

Persuasive encounters involving people with different stylistic preferences may result in neither person being persuaded by the other. To a person with a cultural preference for a quasilogical style, the presentational style will appear emotional and intuitive, and the analogical style will appear irrelevant. To those using the presentational style, the quasilogical style will appear dull, insignificant, and unrelated to the real issues. To those using the analogical style, the quasilogical style will seem blunt and unappealing.

An interesting example of the clash in preferences for persuasive styles is described by Donal Carbaugh:

> I have heard several Russian speakers in public who were asked questions of fact yet responded with impassioned, even artful expressions of an image of the good, presenting a moral tale of an ideal world as it should be. Russians likewise heard many Americans stating—sometimes in great detail—troubling truths, rather than expressing common virtues or the shared fiber of a strong moral life. In fact, as a result in part of conversing in these distinctive cultural ways, Russians are often led to portray Americans as soul-less or immoral, too willing to spill the discreditable trust and unable to state any shared morality; Americans in turn are often led to portray Russians as not fully reasonable, as unable

■ Both this Peruvian woman (left) and Dutch woman (right) use a sales pitch to influence shoppers. People the world over depend on persuasion to transform interested customers into purchasing customers.

CULTURE connections

The black [American] culture is characterized by an oral tradition. Knowledge, attitudes, ideas, notions are traditionally transmitted orally, not through the written word. It is not unusual, then, that the natural leader among black people would be one with exceptional oratorical skills. He must be able to talk, to speak—to preach. In the black religious tradition, the successful black preacher is an expert orator. His role involves more, however. His relationship with his parishioners is reciprocal; he talks to them, and they talk back to him. That is expected. In many church circles this talk-back during a sermon is a firm measure of the preacher's effectiveness.

—*Charles V. Hamilton*

to answer basic questions of fact, too willing in public to be passionate, too righteous, to the point of being illogical.[33]

Behind the misunderstandings that Carbaugh describes is a Russian preference for the presentational style and a European American preference for the quasilogical style.

Cultural Variations in the Structure of Conversations

All conversations differ on a number of important dimensions: how long one talks; the nature of the relationship between the conversants; the kinds of topics discussed; the way information is presented; how signals are given to indicate interest and involvement; and even whether conversation is regarded as a useful, important, and necessary means of communicating. In this section, we explore some of the differences in the way cultures shape the use of codes to create conversations. Our usual caution applies: when cultural tendencies are described, remember that not all members of the culture will necessarily reflect these characteristics.

Value of Talk and Silence

The importance given to words varies greatly from one culture to the next. Among African Americans and European Americans, for example, words are considered very important. In informal conversations between friends, individuals often "give my word" to assure the truth of their statement. In the legal setting, people swear that their words constitute "the truth, the whole truth, and nothing but the truth." Legal obligations are contracted with formal documents to which people affix their signatures—another set of words. The spoken word is seen as a reflection of a person's inner thoughts. Even the theories of communication that are presented in most books about communication—including this one—are highly influenced by underlying assumptions that give words the ability to represent thoughts. In this characteristically Western approach to communication, people need words to communicate accurately and completely with one another. Conversely, silence is often taken by many Western Europeans and European Americans to convey a range of negative experiences—awkwardness, embarrassment, hostility, uninterest, disapproval, shyness, an unwillingness to communicate, a lack of verbal skills, or an expression of interpersonal incompatibility.[34]

Some cultures are very hesitant about the value of words. Asian cultures, such as those of Japan, Korea, and China, as well as southern African cultures, such as those of Swaziland, Zambia, and Lesotho, have quite a different evaluation of words and talking. They all place much more emphasis on the value of silence, on the unspoken meaning or intentions, and on saying as little as is necessary.[35] Because of a combination of historical and cultural forces, spoken words in these cultures are sometimes viewed with some suspicion and disregard. Taoist sayings such as "One who speaks does not know" and "To be always talking is against nature" convey this distrust of talking and wordiness.[36]

Cultures influenced by Confucian and Buddhist values frequently disparage spoken communication. In Japan, the term *haragei* (wordless communication) describes the cultural preference to communicate without using language. Donald Klopf elaborates on this Japanese penchant:

> The desire not to speak is the most significant aspect or feature of Japanese language life. The Japanese hate to hear someone make excuses for his or her mistakes or failures. They do not like long and complicated explanations. Consequently, the less talkative person is preferred and is more popular than the talkative one, other conditions being equal. If one has to say something normally, it is said in as few words as possible.[37]

In Korea, the strong religious and cultural influence of Confucian values has devalued oral communication and made written communication highly regarded. June Ock Yum, in an interesting exploration of the relationship between Korean philosophy and communication, says, "Where the written communication was dominant, spoken words were underrated as being apt to run on and on, to be mean and low. To read was the profession of scholars, to speak the act of menials."[38] Buddhism, also a major influence on Korean thought, teaches, "True communication is believed to occur only when one speaks without the mouth and when one hears without the ears."[39]

Such cultural preferences for silence over talkativeness are not confined to those who have been influenced by Confucian and Buddhist values. In Swaziland, for example, people are suspicious of those who talk excessively. As Peter Nwosu has observed:

> The Swazis are quick to attribute motives when a person during negotiations is very pushy, engages in too much self-praise, or acts like he or she knows everything. "People who talk a lot are not welcome; be calm, but not too calm that they suspect you are up to some mischief," remarks an official of the Swazi Embassy in Washington, D.C. Indeed, there is such a thin line between talkativeness and calmness that it is difficult for a foreigner to understand when one is being "too talkative" or "too calm."[40]

People from Finland are also less willing than European Americans to talk, even among close friends.[41] Donal Carbaugh describes a visit that he and his wife had with some Finnish friends, who asked,

> "When you are with your friends in the United States, do you talk most all of the time?" My wife and I looked at each other, nodded, and smiled, while I responded: "Well, uhm, yes, pretty much." Liisa (Finnish friend) said: "How do you do that? That must be exhausting! We all laughed as my wife and I admitted, "Yeah, at times, it can be."[42]

CULTURE connections

When she calls out to Ashoke, she doesn't say his name. Ashima never thinks of her husband's name when she thinks of her husband, even though she knows perfectly well what it is. She has adopted his surname but refuses, for propriety's sake, to utter his first. It's not the type of thing Bengali wives do. Like a kiss or caress in a Hindi movie, a husband's name is something intimate and therefore unspoken, cleverly patched over. And so, instead of saying Ashoke's name, she utters the interrogative that has come to replace it, which translates roughly as "Are you listening to me?"

—Jhumpa Lahiri

The consequences of these differences in preferences for talking are illustrated by a Japanese American student and an African American student who became roommates. Over a period of a few weeks, the African American student sought social interaction and conversation with his Japanese American roommate, who seemed to become less and less willing to converse. The African American student interpreted this reticence as an indication of dislike and disinterest rather than as an indication of cultural differences in conversational preferences. Finally, he decided to move to a different room, because he felt too uncomfortable with the silence to remain.

There are also different cultural preferences for silence and the place of silence in conversations. Keith Basso describes a number of interpersonal communication experiences in which members of the Apache tribe prefer silence, whereas non–Native Americans might prefer to talk a lot: meetings between strangers, the initial stages of a courtship, an individual returning home to relatives and friends after a long absence, a person verbally expressing anger, someone being sad, and during a curing ceremony.[43] Basso gives this assessment of the value placed on introductions:

> The Western Apache do not feel compelled to "introduce" persons who are unknown to each other. Eventually, it is assumed, strangers will begin to speak. However, this is a decision that is properly left to the individuals involved, and no attempt is made to hasten it. Outside help in the form of introductions or other verbal routines is viewed as presumptuous and unnecessary.
>
> Strangers who are quick to launch into conversations are frequently eyed with undisguised suspicion. A typical reaction to such individuals is that they "want something," that is, their willingness to violate convention is attributed to some urgent need which is likely to result in requests for money, labor, or transportation.[44]

In sum, the fundamental value and role of talk as a tool for conversation vary from culture to culture.

Rules for Conversations

Cultures provide an implicit set of rules to govern interaction. Verbal and nonverbal codes come with a set of cultural prescriptions that determine how they should be used. In this section, we explore some of the ways in which conversational structures can vary from one culture to another. In Chapter 11, we also consider some aspects of conversational structures that are particularly relevant to the development of intercultural relationships.

Some of the ways in which conversational rules can vary are illustrated in the following questions:

- How do you know when it is your turn to talk in a conversation?
- When you talk to a person you have never met before, how do you know what topics are acceptable for you to discuss?
- In a conversation, must your comments be directly related to those that come before?
- When you are upset about a grade, how do you determine the approach to take in a conversation with the teacher or even *if* you should have a conversation with the teacher?
- When you approach your employer to ask for a raise, how do you decide what to say?
- If you want someone to do something for you, do you ask for it directly, or do you mention it to others and hope that they will tell the first person what it is that you want?
- If you decide to ask for something directly, do you go straight to the point and say, "This is what I need from you," or do you hint at what you want and expect the other person to understand?
- When you speak, do you use grand language filled with images, metaphors, and stories, or do you simply and succinctly present the relevant information?

Cultural preferences would produce many different answers to these questions. For example, European Americans signal a desire to speak in a conversation by leaning forward a small degree, slightly opening their mouth, and establishing eye contact. In another culture, those same sets of symbols could be totally disregarded because they have no meaning, or they could mean something totally different (for example, respectful listening). Acceptable topics of conversations for two U.S. American students meeting in a class might include their majors, current interests, and where they work. Those same topics in some other cultures—particularly if there happens to be a high unemployment rate—might be regarded as too personal for casual conversations, but discussions about religious beliefs and family history might seem perfectly acceptable. Though European Americans expect comments in a conversation to be related to previous ones, Japanese express their views without necessarily responding to what the other has said.[45]

William Gudykunst and Stella Ting-Toomey describe cultural variations in conversational style along four dimensions: direct–indirect, elaborate–succinct, personal–contextual, and instrumental–affective.[46] Cultures that prefer a direct style, such as European Americans, use verbal messages that are explicit in revealing the speaker's true intentions and desires. In contrast, those that prefer an indirect style will veil the speaker's true wants and needs with ambiguous statements. African Americans and Koreans, for example, prefer an indirect style, as do the Japanese, for whom interactions are governed in part by a desire to avoid saying "no" directly.

Cultural conversational styles also differ on a dimension of elaborate to succinct. The elaborate style, which is found in most Arab and Latino cultures, results in the frequent use of metaphors, proverbs, and other figurative language. The expressiveness of this style

■ Like all exchanges, this conversation is governed by a complex set of rules about who talks to whom, for how long, and on what topics. Yet the participants are unlikely to be consciously aware of these rules until someone breaks them.

contrasts with the succinct style, in which people give precisely the amount of information necessary. In the succinct style, there is a preference for understatement and long pauses, as in Japanese American, Native American, and Chinese American cultures.

In cultures that prefer a personal style, in contrast to those that prefer a contextual style, there is an emphasis on conversations in which the individual, as a unique human being, is the center of action. This style is also characterized by more informality and less status-oriented talk. In the contextual style, the emphasis is on the social roles that people have in relationships with others. Japanese, Chinese, and Indian cultures all emphasize the social role or the interpersonal community in which a particular person is embedded. The style is very formal and heightens awareness of status differences by accentuating them.

In the instrumental style, communication is goal-oriented and depends on explicit verbal messages. Affective styles are more emotional and require sensitivity to the underlying meanings in both the verbal and nonverbal code systems. Min-Sun Kim suggests that this goal-oriented style, which is characterized by a heightened concern for "getting the job done," is preferred by people from individualistic cultures, whereas the affective style, which is concerned with the feelings and emotions of others, typifies people from collectivistic cultures.[47] Thomas Kochman has articulated some of the differences in conversational styles between European Americans and African Americans:

> The differing potencies of black and white public presentations are a regular cause of communicative conflict. Black presentations are emotionally intense, dynamic, and demonstrative; white presentations are more modest and emotionally restrained.[48]

Melanie Booth-Butterfield and Felecia Jordan similarly found that African American females were more expressive, more involved with one another, more animated, and more at ease than were their European American counterparts, who appeared more formal and restrained.[49] Because of these differences in conversational style, an African American and a European American may judge each other negatively.

Sometimes a cultural style that differs substantially from one's own can be so unfamiliar that it can seem chaotic—except, of course, that it works. A U.S. American working in Budapest described a meeting of his Hungarian colleagues as a group of people "sitting around a table shouting at each other, interrupting, not seeming to listen when others were speaking, but then suddenly reaching a decision which seemed to satisfy everyone."[50]

Ronald Scollon and Suzanne Wong-Scollon, who have studied the Athabaskan, a cultural group of native peoples in Alaska and northern Canada, describe similar problems in intercultural communication:

> When an Athabaskan and a speaker of English talk to each other, it is very likely that the English speaker will speak first. . . . The Athabaskan will feel it is important to know the relationship between the two speakers before speaking. The English speaker will feel talking is the best way to establish a relationship. While the Athabaskan is waiting to see what will happen between them, the English speaker will begin speaking, usually asking questions of fact, to find out what will happen. Only where there is a longstanding relationship and a deep understanding between the two speakers is it likely that the Athabaskan will initiate the conversation.[51]

Regulating conversations is also problematic for the English speaker and an Athabaskan because the latter uses a longer pause—about a half second longer—between turns. The effects of this slightly longer pause would be comical if the consequences for intercultural communication were not so serious.

> When an English speaker pauses, he waits for the regular length of time (around one second or less), that is, *his* regular length of time, and if the Athabaskan does not say anything, the English speaker feels he is free to go on and say anything else he likes. At the same time the Athabaskan has been waiting his regular length of time before coming in. He does not want to interrupt the English speaker. This length of time we think is around one and one-half seconds. It is just enough longer that by the time the Athabaskan is ready to speak the English speaker is already speaking again. So the Athabaskan waits again for the next pause. Again, the English speaker begins just enough before the Athabaskan was going to speak. The net result is that the Athabaskan can never get a word in edgewise (an apt metaphor in this case), while the English speaker goes on and on.[52]

CULTURE connections

The language rolled over and around me. I thought at first that it was loneliness that drove these elderly people to fill the air with stories, to tell a story again rather than let the conversation die, but I soon learned that this was a national trait. Serbs hate silence. The presence of another person provides an irresistible opportunity to talk. As a language teacher, I recognized and appreciated the ways in which the most casual acquaintances abetted my efforts to speak.

—Deryn P. Verity

CULTURE connections

What's confusing to English speakers about Athabaskans

They do not speak

They keep silent

They avoid situations of talking

They only want to talk to close acquaintances

They play down their own abilities

They act as if they expect things to be given to them

They deny planning

They avoid direct questions

They never start a conversation

They talk off the topic

They never say anything about themselves

They are slow to take a turn in talking

They ask questions in unusual places

They talk with a flat tone of voice

They are too indirect, inexplicit

They don't make sense

They just leave without saying anything

What's confusing to Athabaskans about English speakers

They talk too much

They always talk first

They talk to strangers or people they don't know

They think they can predict the future

They brag about themselves

They don't help people even when they can

They always talk about what is going to happen later

They ask too many questions

They always Interrupt

They only talk about what they are Interested in

They don't give others a chance to talk

They are always getting excited when they talk

They aren't careful when they talk about things or people

—*Ronald Scollon and Suzanne Wong-Scollon*

These very real differences in the nature of conversations play a critical role in intercultural communication. The ultimate result is often a negative judgment of other people rather than a recognition that the variability in cultural preferences is creating the difficulties.

Effects of Code Usage on Intercultural Competence

Developing competence in the practical, everyday use of verbal and nonverbal codes is undoubtedly a major challenge for the intercultural communicator. But simply knowing the syntactic rules of other code systems is not sufficient to be able to use those code systems well.

The most important knowledge you can take away from this chapter is the realization that people from other cultures may organize their ideas, persuade others, and structure their conversations in a manner that differs from yours. You should attempt, to the greatest extent possible, to understand your own preferences for using verbal and nonverbal codes to accomplish practical goals. If you can, mentally set aside your beliefs and the accompanying evaluative labels. Instead, recognize that your belief system and the verbal and nonverbal symbols that are used to represent it were taught to you by your culture and constitute only one among many ways of understanding the world and accomplishing one's personal objectives.

Differences in the ways people prefer to communicate can affect their ability to interact competently in an intercultural encounter. Look for differences in the ways that people from other cultures choose to accomplish their interpersonal objectives. Look for alternative logics. Approach the unfamiliar as a puzzle to be solved rather than as something to be feared or dismissed as illogical, irrational, or wrong. Much can be learned about the effects of code usage by observing others. If your approach is not successful, notice how members of the culture accomplish their objectives.

Summary

The chapter described the effects on intercultural communication of cultural differences in the way verbal and nonverbal codes are used. These differences affect how people attempt to understand messages, organize ideas, persuade others, and engage in discussions and conversations.

We began with a discussion of differences in cultural preferences for organizing and arranging messages, and we contrasted the organizational preferences of U.S. English, which are typically linear, with those of other languages and cultures.

Cultural variations in persuasion and argumentation were considered next. We emphasized that appropriate forms of evidence, reasoning, and rationality are all culturally based and can affect intercultural communication. Indeed, there are major differences in persuasive styles that are taken for granted within a culture but that affect the communication between cultures.

Cultural variations also exist in the structure of conversations. The importance given to talk and silence, the social rules and interaction styles that are used in conversations, and even the cues used to regulate the back-and-forth sequencing of conversations can all create problems for intercultural communicators.

Finally, we noted that differences in the way people prefer to communicate can affect the ability to behave appropriately and effectively in intercultural encounters. These cultural preferences typically operate outside of awareness and may lead to judgments that others are "wrong" or "incorrect" when they are merely different.

For Discussion

1. What does it mean to learn the "logic" of a language?
2. In what ways does the U.S. legal system reflect the European American view of argumentation and persuasion?
3. Does your culture value a particular style of persuasion? Do your own preferred ways of persuading others reflect your culture's style of persuasion?
4. What does silence communicate to you? How is your culture's use of silence connected to Hall's cultural patterns of low and high context?
5. Members of some cultures will invariably say "yes" even though, given the situation and their true feelings, the answer is most likely "no." How do you explain this phenomenon?

For Further Reading

Donal Carbaugh, *Cultures in Conversation* (Mahwah, NJ: Erlbaum, 2005). Illustrates, through several in-depth studies of cultures, how human conversation or "talk" is embedded in one's culture.

Ulla Connor, Ed Nagelhout, and William V. Rozycki (eds.), *Contrastive Rhetoric: Reaching to Intercultural Rhetoric* (Philadelphia: John Benjamins, 2008). With its focus on contrastive rhetoric, this book explores and explains the importance of intercultural communication across a broad array of cultures and rhetorical texts.

Richard D. Rieke, Malcolm O. Sillars, and Tarla Rai Peterson, *Argumentation and Critical Decision Making*, 7th ed. (Boston: Allyn & Bacon, 2009). A text on argumentation and critical thinking. Use the framework we provide in this chapter to read and evaluate the cultural framework embedded within their recommended use of evidence, argument, and reasoning.

Andrea Rocci, "Pragmatic Inference and Argumentation in Intercultural Communication," *Intercultural Pragmatics* 3–4 (2006): 409–422. While highly theoretical, this article provides a useful examination of the elements of arguments and conclusions. It provides a conceptual framework to help learn about variations across cultural traditions.

Ron Scollon and Suzanne Wong-Scollon, *Intercultural Communication: A Discourse Approach*, 2nd ed. (Malden, MA: Blackwell, 2001). Offers numerous examples of the relationships between a person's language, thinking, and logical actions. Explores how language and culture provide a preferred structure to conversations. A modern classic in intercultural communication.

For additional information about intercultural films and about Web sites for researching specific cultures, please turn to the Resources section at the back of this book.

CHAPTER 10

Intercultural Competence in Interpersonal Relationships

KEY TERMS

All relationships imply connections. When you are in an interpersonal relationship, you are connected—in a very important sense, you are bound together—with another person in some substantial way. Of course, the nature of these ties is rarely physical. Rather, in interpersonal relationships, you are connected to others by virtue of your shared experiences, interpretations, perceptions, and goals.

Cultural Variations in Interpersonal Relationships

In Chapter 2, we indicated that communication is interpersonal as long as it involves a small number of participants who can interact directly with one another and who therefore have the ability to adapt their messages specifically for one another. Of course, different patterns of interpersonal communication are likely to occur with different types of interpersonal relationships. We believe it is useful to characterize the various types of interpersonal relationships by the kinds of social connections the participants share.

Types of Interpersonal Relationships

Some interpersonal connections occur because of blood or marriage. Others exist because of overlapping or interdependent objectives and goals. Still others bind people together because of common experiences that help to create a perception of "we-ness." However, all interpersonal relationships have as their common characteristic a strong connection among the individuals.

The number of interpersonal relationships that you have throughout your life is probably very large. Some of these relationships are complex and involved, whereas others are simple and casual; some are brief and spontaneous, while others may last a lifetime. Some of these relationships, we hope, have involved people from different cultures.

Interpersonal relationships between people from different cultures can be difficult to understand and describe because of the contrasts in culturally based expectations about the nature of interpersonal communication. However, regardless of the cultures involved or the circumstances surrounding the relationship's formation, there is always some sort of bond or social connection that links or ties the people to one another. The participants may be strangers, acquaintances, friends, romantic partners, or family or kinship members. Each relationship carries with it certain expectations for appropriate behaviors that are anchored within specific cultures. People in an intercultural relationship, then, may define their experiences very differently and may have dissimilar expectations; for example, a stranger to someone from one culture may be called a friend by someone from another culture.

Strangers   You will undoubtedly talk to many thousands of people in your lifetime, and most of them will be strangers to you. But what exactly is a stranger? Certainly, a stranger is someone whom you do not know and who is therefore unfamiliar to you. But is someone always a stranger the first time you meet? How about the second time, or the third? What about the people you talked with several times, although the conversation was restricted to the task of seating you in a restaurant or pricing your groceries, so names were never actually exchanged? Are these people strangers to you? Your answers to these questions, like so many of the ideas described in this book, depend on what you have been taught by your culture.

In the United States, for instance, the social walls that are erected between strangers may not be as thick and impenetrable as they are in some collectivistic cultures. European Americans, who are often fiercely individualistic as a cultural group, may not have developed the strong ingroup bonds that would promote separation from outsiders. Among the Greeks, however, who hold collectivistic values, the word for "non-Greek" translates as "stranger."

Even in the United States, the distinction between stranger and nonstranger is an important one; young children are often taught to be afraid of people they do not know. Compare, however, a U.S. American's reaction toward a stranger with that of a Korean in a similar situation. In Korea, which is a family-dominated collectivist culture, a stranger is anyone to whom you have not been formally introduced. Strangers in Korea are "nonpersons" to whom the rules of politeness and social etiquette simply do not apply. Thus, Koreans may jostle you on the street without apologizing or, perhaps, even noticing. However, once you have been introduced to a Korean, or the Korean anticipates in other ways that he or she may have an ongoing interpersonal relationship with you, elaborate politeness rituals are required.

Acquaintances   An acquaintance is someone you know, but only casually. Therefore, interactions tend to be on a superficial level. The social bonds that link acquaintances are very slight. Acquaintances will typically engage in social politeness rituals, such as greeting one another when first meeting or exchanging small talk on topics generally viewed as more impersonal such as the weather, hobbies, fashions, and sports. But acquaintances do not

CULTURE connections

An equally perplexing experience for me was the reaction of most U.S. Americans to my family background. I come from a fairly large extended family with some history of polygyny. Polygyny is the union between a man and two or more wives. (Polygamy, a more general term, refers to marriage among several spouses, including a man who marries more than one wife or a woman who marries more than one husband.) Polygyny is an accepted and respected marriage form in traditional Igbo society. My father, Chief Clement Muoghalu Nwosu, had two wives. My paternal grandfather, Chief Ezekwesili Nwosu, was married to four. My great grandfather, Chief Odoji, who also married four wives, was the chief priest and custodian of traditional religion in my town, Umudioka town, a small rural community in Anambra State of the Federal Republic of Nigeria....

The traditional economic structure in Igbo society dictated this familial arrangement whereby a man would have more than one spouse and produce several children, who would then assist him with farm work, which is regarded as the fiber and glue of economic life in traditional Igbo society. Each wife and her own children live in a separate home built by the husband. Each wife is responsible for the upkeep of her immediate family, with support from her husband.

—*Peter O. Nwosu*

◼ These Italian men share a friendly moment of conversation. In every culture, expectations about social behaviors are influenced by a set of rules.

typically confide in one another about personal problems or discuss private concerns. Of course, the topics appropriate for small talk, which do not include personal and private issues, will differ from one culture to another. Among European Americans, it is perfectly appropriate to ask a male acquaintance about his wife; in the United Arab Emirates, it would be a major breach of social etiquette to do so. In New Zealand, it is appropriate to talk about national and international politics; in Pakistan, these and similar topics should be avoided. In Austria, discussions about money and religion are typically sidestepped; elsewhere, acquaintances may well be asked "personal" questions about their income and family background.

Friends   As with many of the other terms that describe interpersonal relationships, *friend* is a common expression that refers to many different types of relationships. "Good friends," "close friends," and "just friends" are all commonly used expressions among U.S. Americans. Generally speaking, a friend is someone you know well, someone you like, and someone with whom you feel a close personal bond. A friendship usually includes higher levels of intimacy, self-disclosure, involvement, and intensity than does acquaintanceship. In many ways, friends can be thought of as close acquaintances.

Unlike kinships, friendships are voluntary, even though many friendships start because the participants have been thrust together in some way. Because they are voluntary, friendships usually occur between people who see themselves as similar in some important ways and who belong to the same social class.

European American friendships tend to be very compartmentalized because they are based on a shared activity, event, or experience. The European American can study with one friend, play racquetball with another, and go to the movies with a third. As suggested in Chapter 4, this pattern occurs because European Americans typically classify people according to what they do or have achieved rather than who they are. Relations among European Americans are therefore fragmented, and they view themselves and others as a composite of distinct interests.

The Thai are likely to react more to the other person as a whole and will avoid forming friendships with those whose values and behaviors are in some way deemed undesirable.[1] Unlike friendships in the United States, in Thailand a friend is accepted completely or not at all; a person cannot disapprove of some aspect of another's political beliefs or personal life and still consider her or him to be a friend. Similarly, the Chinese typically have fewer friends than European Americans do, but Chinese friends expect one another to be involved in all aspects of their lives and to spend much of their free time together. Friends are expected to anticipate others' needs and to provide unsolicited advice about what to do. These differing expectations can cause serious problems as a Chinese and a European American embark on the development of what each sees as a "friendship."[2]

John Condon has noted that the language people use to describe their interpersonal relationships often reflects the underlying cultural values about their meaning and importance. Thus, Condon says, friendships among European Americans are expressed by terms such as *friends, allies,* and *neighbors,* all of which reflect an individualistic cultural value. However, among African Americans and some Southern whites, closeness between friends is expressed by such terms as *brother, sister,* or *cousin,* suggesting a collectivist cultural value. Mexican terms for relationships, like the cultural values they represent, are similar to those of African Americans. Thus, when European Americans and Mexicans speak of close friendships, the former will probably use a word such as *partner,* which suggests a voluntary association, whereas Mexicans may use a word such as *brother* or *sister,* which suggests a lasting bond that is beyond the control of any one person.[3]

As interpersonal relationships move from initial acquaintance to close friendship, five types of changes in perceptions and behaviors will probably occur. First, friends interact more frequently; they talk to each other more often, for longer periods of time, and in more varied settings than acquaintances do. Second, the increased frequency of interactions means that friends will have more knowledge about and shared experiences with each other than will acquaintances, and this unique common ground will probably develop into a private communication code to refer to ideas, objects, and experiences that are exclusive to the relationship. Third, the increased knowledge of the other person's motives and typical behaviors means that there is an increased ability to predict a friend's reactions to common situations. The powerful need to reduce uncertainty in the initial stages of relationships, which we discuss in greater detail later in this chapter, suggests that acquaintanceships are unlikely to progress to friendships without the ability to predict the others' intentions and expectations. Fourth, the sense of "we-ness" increases among friends. Friends often feel that their increased investment of time and emotional commitment to the relationship creates a

CULTURE connections

She saw Mma Seeonyana standing outside her front door, a brown paper bag in her hand. As she parked the tiny white van at the edge of the road, she noticed the older woman watching her. This was another good sign. It was a traditional Botswana pursuit to watch other people and wonder what they were up to; this modern habit of indifference to others was very hard to understand. If you watched people, then it was a sign that you cared about them, that you were not treating them as complete strangers. Again, it was all a question of manners.

—*Alexander McCall Smith*

sense of interdependence, so that individual goals and interests are affected by and linked to each person's satisfaction with the relationship. Finally, close friendships are characterized by a heightened sense of caring, commitment, trust, and emotional attachment to the other person, so that the people in a friendship view it as something special and unique.[4]

Intercultural friendships can vary in a variety of ways: whom a person selects as a friend, how long a friendship lasts, the prerogatives and responsibilities of being a friend, the number of friends that a person prefers to have, and even how long a relationship must develop before it becomes a friendship. African American friends, for instance, expect to be able to confront and criticize one another, sometimes in a loud and argumentative manner.[5] Latinos, Asian Americans, and African Americans feel that it takes them, on the average, about a year for an acquaintanceship to develop into a close friendship, whereas European Americans feel that it takes only a few months.[6] For intercultural friendships to be successful, therefore, they may require an informal agreement between the friends about each of these aspects for the people involved to have shared expectations about appropriate behaviors.

Romantic Partners   The diversity of cultural norms that govern romantic relationships is an excellent example of the wide range of cultural expectations. Consider, for instance, the enormous differences in cultural beliefs, values, norms, and social practices about love, romance, dating, and marriage.

Among European Americans, dating usually occurs for romance and companionship. A dating relationship is not viewed as a serious commitment that will necessarily, or even probably, lead to an engagement. If they choose to do so, couples will marry because

■ Friendships are often based on common interests and experiences, as these bicyclists know. Sometimes, however, differences in cultural patterns may cause difficulties in managing interpersonal relationships.

of love and affection for each other. Although family members may be consulted before a final decision is made, the choice to marry is made almost exclusively by the couples themselves.

In Argentina and Spain, dating is taken more seriously. Indeed, dating the same person more than twice may mean that the relationship will lead to an engagement and, ultimately, marriage. Yet engagements in these Spanish-speaking cultures typically last a long time and may extend over a period of years, as couples work, save money, and prepare themselves financially for marriage.

In contrast, casual dating relationships and similar opportunities for romantic expression among unmarried individuals are still quite rare in India; marriages there are usually arranged by parents, typically with the consent of the couple. So when a European American couple—friends of the bride's family—was invited to a wedding in India, they brought their 14-year-old daughter. The day before the wedding, at the bride's home, a group of girls was seated tightly on a large bed in the parents' bedroom. Except for the European American, all the girls were Indian. Their conversation was raucous and rambling. As it turned to the topic of marriage—as such conversations often do at a wedding—the Indian girls chattered away about whom they hoped their parents might pick to be their husbands. Taken aback by the notion of an arranged marriage, the European American girl asserted her individualism, declared that *she* would find her *own* husband, and announced that she would make these choices without *any* intervention from her parents. The Indian girls initially reacted quizzically to this strange pronouncement; then, as its implications slowly sank in, they displayed looks of puzzlement, astonishment, concern, and finally fear. One of the girls asked, "Aren't your parents even going to help you?" To the Indian girls, it was unfathomable that they would have to select their life-partners without the help of parents and other elders.

Similar patterns of familial involvement can also be found in Muslim cultures, where marriage imposes great obligations and responsibilities on the families of the couple. In Algeria, for instance, a marriage is seen as an important link between families, not individuals; consequently, the selection of a spouse may require the approval of the entire extended family. In Indonesia, the opportunities for men and women to be together, particularly in unchaperoned settings, are much more restricted.

In both India and Algeria, romantic love is believed to be something that develops after marriage, not before. Even in Colombia, where, because of changes in customs and cultural practices, arranged marriages are no longer fashionable, the decision to get married requires family approval. Yet research by Stanley Gaines on the nature of intercultural romantic relationships found a great deal of similarity in the communication across cultures.[7]

Family   Family or kinship relationships are also characterized by large cultural variations. Particularly important to the development of intercultural relationships are these factors: how the family is defined, or who is considered to be a member of the family; the formality of roles and behavioral expectations for particular family members; and the importance of the family in social relationships and personal decisions.

Among European Americans, and even among members of most European cultures, family life is primarily confined to interactions among the mother, father, and children. Households usually include just these family members, though the extended family unit also includes grandparents, aunts, uncles, and cousins. Though the amount and quality of interaction among extended family members will vary greatly from family to family, members of the extended family rarely live together in the same household or take an active part in the day-to-day lives of the nuclear family members.

Family relationships in other cultures can be quite different. Among Latinos, for instance, the extended family is very important.[8] Similarly, in India the extended family dominates; grandparents, aunts, uncles, and many other relatives may live together in one household. Families in India include people who would be called second or third cousins in the European American family, and the unmarried siblings of those who have become family members through marriage may also be included in the household. These "family members" would rarely be defined as such in the typical European American family. Among Native Americans, family refers to all members of the clan.[9] No particular pattern of family relationships can be said to typify the world's cultures. Many Arab families, for instance, include multiple generations of the male line. Often three generations—grandparents, married sons and their wives, and unmarried children—will live together under one roof. Among certain cultural groups in Ghana, however, just the opposite pattern can be found; families have a matrilineal organization, and the family inheritance is passed down through the wife's family rather than the husband's.

Expected role behaviors and responsibilities also vary among cultures. In Argentina, family roles are very clearly defined by social custom; the wife is expected to raise the children, manage the household, and show deference to the husband. In India, the oldest male son has specific family and religious obligations that are not requirements for other sons in the same family. Languages sometimes reflect these specialized roles. In China, for example,

[a] sister-in-law is called by various names, depending on whether she is the older brother's wife, the younger brother's wife, or the wife's sister. Aunts, uncles, and cousins are named in the same way. Thus, a father's sister is "ku," a mother's sister is "yi," an uncle's wife is "shen," and so on.[10]

Families also differ in their influence over a person's social networks and decision making. In some cultures, the family is the primary means through which a person's social life is maintained. In others, such as among European Americans, families are almost peripheral to the social networks that are established. In the more collectivist cultures such as Japan, Korea, and China, families play a pivotal role in making decisions for children, including the choice of university, profession, and even marital partner. In contrast, in individualistic cultures, where children are taught from their earliest years to make their own decisions, a characteristic of "good parenting" is to allow children to "learn for themselves" the consequences of their own actions.

The increasing number of people creating intercultural families, in which husband and wife represent different cultural backgrounds, poses new challenges for family communication. Often, the children in these families are raised in an intercultural household that is characterized by some blending of the original cultures. Differences in the expectations of appropriate social roles—of wife and husband, son and daughter, older and younger child, or husband's parents and wife's parents—require a knowledge of and sensitivity to the varying influences of culture on family communication.

■ Because culture influences expectations about appropriate and effective behaviors, intercultural families may need to pay more attention to the negotiation of their relationship rules.

Dimensions of Interpersonal Relationships

People throughout the world use at least three primary dimensions to interpret interpersonal communication messages: control, affiliation, and activation.[11]

Control   Control involves status or social dominance. We have control to the extent that we have the power and prestige to influence the events around us. Depending on the culture, control can be communicated by a variety of behaviors, including touching, looking, talking, and the use of space. Supervisors, for instance, are more likely to touch their subordinates than vice versa. In many cultures, excessive looking behaviors are viewed as attempts to "stare down" the other person and are usually seen as an effort to exert interactional control. Similarly, high-power individuals seek and are usually given

CULTURE connections

I remember asking a twenty-year-old student in economics at Delhi University…if she loved the childhood friend her parents had decided she should marry. "That's a very difficult question," she answered. "I don't know. This whole concept of love is very alien to us. We're more practical. I don't see stars, I don't hear little bells. But he's a very nice guy, and I think I'm going to enjoy spending my life with him. Is that love?" She shrugged.

—Elisabeth Bumiller

more personal space and a larger territory to control than their low-power counterparts. Of course, many of these same behaviors, when used in a different context, could also indicate other aspects of the interpersonal relationship. Excessive eye contact, for example, might not be an indication of power; it may merely mean that the two individuals are deeply in love. Usually, however, there are other situational cues that can be used to help interpret the behaviors correctly.

Control is often conveyed by the specific names or titles used to address another person. Do you address physicians, teachers, and friends by their first names, or do you say *Doctor, Professor,* or *Mr.* or *Ms.*? In Malaysia and many other places, personal names are rarely used among adults because such use might imply that the other person has little social status. Instead,

> a shortened form or a pet name is often used if a kin term is not appropriate. This is to avoid showing disrespect, since it is understood that the more familiar the form of address to a person, the more socially junior or unimportant he must be regarded.[12]

In cultures that are very attuned to status differences among people, such as Japan, Korea, and Indonesia, the language system requires distinctions based on people's degree of social dominance. In Indonesia, for instance,

> the Balinese speak a language which reflects their caste, a tiered system where (like the Javanese) at each level their choice of words is governed by the social relationship between the two people having a conversation.[13]

Intercultural communication is often characterized by an increased tendency to *mis*interpret nonverbal control and status cues. In both the United States and Germany, for instance, private offices on the top floors and at the corners of most major businesses are reserved for the highest-ranking officials and executives; in France, executives typically prefer an office that is centrally located, in the middle of their subordinates if possible, in order to stay informed and to control the flow of activities. Thus, the French may infer that the Germans are too isolated and the Germans that the French are too easily interrupted to manage their respective organizations well.

CULTURE connections

To exit a marriage in Bali leaves a person alone and unprotected in ways that are almost impossible for a Westerner to imagine. The Balinese family unit, enclosed within the walls of a family compound, is merely everything—four generations of siblings, cousins, parents, grandparents and children all living together in a series of small bungalows surrounding the family temple, taking care of each other from birth to death. The family compound is the source of strength, financial security, health care, day care, education and—most important to the Balinese—spiritual connection.

The family compound is so vital that the Balinese think of it as a single, living person. The population of a Balinese village is traditionally counted not by the number of individuals, but by the number of compounds. The compound is a self-sustaining universe. So you don't leave it.

—*Elizabeth Gilbert*

Affiliation   Members of a culture use affiliation to interpret the degree of friendliness, liking, social warmth, or immediacy that is being communicated. Affiliation is an evaluative component that indicates a person's willingness to approach or avoid others. Albert Mehrabian suggests that we approach those people and things we like and we avoid or move away from those we do not like.[14] Consequently, affiliative behaviors are those that convey a sense of closeness, communicate interpersonal warmth and accessibility, and encourage others to approach.

Affiliation can be expressed through eye contact, open body stances, leaning forward, close physical proximity, touching, smiling, a friendly tone of voice, and other communication behaviors. Edward Hall has called those cultures that display a high degree of affiliation "high-contact" cultures; those that display a low level are called "low-contact" cultures.[15]

Compared with low-contact cultures, members of high-contact cultures tend to stand closer, touch more, and have fewer barriers, such as desks and doors, to separate themselves from others. High-contact cultures, which are generally located in warmer climates, include many of the cultures in South America, Latin America, southern Europe, and the Mediterranean region; most Arab cultures; and Indonesia. Low-contact cultures, which tend to be located in colder climates, include the Japanese, Chinese, U.S. Americans, Canadians, and northern Europeans. One explanation for these climate-related differences is that the harshness of cold-weather climates forces people to live and work closely with one another in order to survive, and some cultures have compensated for this forced togetherness by developing norms that encourage greater distance and privacy.[16]

Activation   Activation refers to the ways people react to the world around them. Some people seem very quick, excitable, energetic, and lively; others value calmness, peacefulness, and a sense of inner control. Your perception of the degree of activity that another person exhibits is used to evaluate that person as fast or slow, active or inactive, swift or sluggish, relaxed or tense, and spirited or deliberate.

Cultures differ in what they consider acceptable and appropriate levels of activation in a conversation. For instance, among many of the black tribes of southern Africa, loud talking is considered inappropriate. Similarly, among Malaysians,

> too much talk and forcefulness on the part of an adult speaker is disapproved.... A terse, harmonious delivery is admired.... The same values—of evenness and restraint—hold for Malay interpersonal relations generally. Thus Malay village conversation makes little use of paralinguistic devices such as facial expression, body movement, and speech tone.... Malays are not highly emotive people.[17]

Thais, like Malays, often dampen or moderate their level of responsiveness. As John Feig suggests,

> Thais have a tendency to neutralize all emotions; even in a very happy moment, there is always the underlying feeling: I don't want to be too happy now or I might be correspondingly sad later; too much laughter today may lead to too many tears tomorrow.[18]

Iranians tend to have the opposite reaction, as they are often very emotionally expressive in their conversations. Particularly when angry, a man's conversation may consist of behaviors such as "turning red, invoking religious oaths, proclaiming his injustices for all to hear, and allowing himself to be held back."[19]

European Americans are probably near the midpoint of this dimension. Compared to the Japanese, for instance, European Americans tend to be fairly active and expressive in their conversations. As Harvey Taylor suggested:

> An American's forehead and eyebrows are constantly in motion as he speaks, and these motions express the inner feelings behind the words. The "blank," nearly motionless Japanese forehead reveals very little of the Japanese person's inner feelings to the American (but not necessarily to the Japanese). Therefore the American feels that the Japanese is not really interested in the conversation or (worse yet) that the Japanese is hiding the truth.[20]

Compared to Jordanians, Iranians, African Americans, and Latinos, however, European Americans are passive and reserved in conversational expressiveness.

It is useful once again to remind you that all beliefs, values, norms, and social practices lie on a continuum. How a particular characteristic is displayed or perceived in a specific culture is interpreted against the culture with which it is being compared. Thus it is possible for an African American to seem very active and emotionally expressive to the Japanese but quite calm and emotionally inexpressive to the Kuwaitis.

Dynamics of Interpersonal Relationships

Interpersonal relationships are dynamic. That is, they are continually changing, as they are pushed and pulled by the ongoing tugs of past experiences, present circumstances, and future expectations.

One useful way to think about relational dynamics is to view people in interpersonal relationships as continually attempting to maintain their balance amidst changing circumstances. To illustrate, imagine that you and your partner are attempting to do a common dance routine such as a country line dance, a tango, or a waltz. Now imagine that you are dancing aboard a ship at sea: the floor rises and falls to the pulsing of the waves; uneven electrical power makes the music speed up and slow down; and your partner wants to add graceful variations to the typical sequence of steps. Your efforts to stay "in rhythm" and coordinate your movements with the music and with your partner are analogous to the adaptations that people must continually make to the ongoing dynamics of interpersonal relationships.

Leslie Baxter suggests that the changing dynamics in interpersonal relationships are due to people's attempts to maintain a sense of "balance" among opposing and seemingly contradictory needs. These basic contradictions in relationships, called "dialectics," create ongoing tensions that affect the way people connect to one another.[21] Three dialectics have been identified as important in interpersonal relationships: autonomy–connection, novelty–predictability, and openness–closedness. Each of the dialectics has corresponding cultural-level components.

The autonomy–connection dialectic is perhaps the most central source of tensions in interpersonal relationships. Individuals inevitably vary, at different moments of their interpersonal relationships, in the extent to which they want a sense of separation from others (autonomy) and a feeling of attachment to others (connection). Note the word *and* in the previous sentence; both types of interpersonal needs, though they may seem contradictory, occur simultaneously. As we implied in our discussions of individualism–collectivism in Chapter 5, a culture teaches its members both the "correct" range of autonomy and connection

CULTURE connections

I was in Mexico a couple of years ago and worked quite closely with a Mexican colleague who was very helpful. Now he is working here in New York on a six-month placement, but we are not working on the same project. He seems to be having some problems getting authorization for some of our systems, but I have a target to meet and if I spend time helping him I'm going to end up behind schedule myself. He also expects us to lunch together most days, but I usually just have a sandwich at my desk, and he wants to make arrangements for after work when I have other things to do. He needs to learn to stand on his own two feet.

—From a letter to Gwyneth Olofsson

and how these should be expressed when communicating with others. Thus, while the general level of autonomy desired by someone from an individualistic culture may be relatively high, one's specific needs for autonomy and connection will vary across time and relationships.

The novelty–predictability dialectic relates to people's desire for change and stability in their interpersonal relationships. All relationships require moments of novelty and excitement, or they will be emotionally dead. They also require a sense of predictability, or they will be chaotic. The novelty–predictability dialectic refers to the dynamic tensions between these opposing needs. The cultural dimension of uncertainty avoidance provides a way of understanding the general range of novelty and predictability that people desire. At specific moments within each relationship, however, individuals can vary in their preferences for novelty and predictability.

The openness–closedness dialectic relates to people's desire to share or withhold personal information. To some extent, openness and self-disclosure are necessary to establish and maintain relational closeness and intimacy. However, privacy is an equally important need; the desire to establish and maintain boundaries is basic to the human condition. For instance, a person may be open to interpersonal contact at certain moments, or with specific individuals, or about certain topics. There will also be times when that person may want to shut the office door or find another way to lessen the degree of interpersonal contact. The openness–closedness dialectic operates not only within a relationship but also in decisions about the public presentation of the relationship to others. Individuals in interpersonal relationships must continually negotiate what kinds of information about their relationship they want to reveal or withhold from others. Several cultural dimensions may affect openness–closedness. Collectivist cultures, for instance, with their tightly knit ingroups and relatively large social distances from outgroups, typically encourage openness within the ingroup and closedness to outgroup members. Alternatively, cultures that value large power distances may expect openness within interpersonal relationships to be asymmetric, such that those relatively lower in social status are expected to share personal information with their superiors.

Each of these relational dialectics, and others as well, contributes to a dynamically changing set of circumstances that affect what people expect, want, and communicate in interpersonal relationships. As the following section explains, how people in interpersonal relationships maintain an appropriate balance among these dialectics relates to their maintenance of face.

The Maintenance of Face in Interpersonal Relationships

A very important concept for understanding interpersonal communication among people from different cultures is that of face, or the public expression of the inner self. Erving Goffman defined face as the favorable social impression that a person wants others to have of him or her.[22] Face therefore involves a claim for respect and dignity from others.

The definition of *face* suggests that it has three important characteristics. First, face is *social*. This means that face is not what an individual thinks of himself or herself but rather how that person wants others to regard his or her worth. Face therefore refers to the public or social image of an individual that is held by others. Face, then, always occurs in a relational setting. Because it is social, one can only gain or lose face through actions that are known to others. The most heroic deeds, or the most bestial ones, do not affect a person's face if they are done in complete anonymity. Nor can face be claimed independent of the social perceptions of others. For instance, the statement "No matter what my teachers think of me, I know I am a good student" is not a statement about face. Because face has a social component, a claim for face would occur only when the student conveys to others the idea that teachers should acknowledge her or his status as a good student. In this sense, the concept of *face* is only meaningful when considered in relation to others in the social network.[23] Consequently, it differs from such psychological concepts as self-esteem or pride, which can be claimed for oneself independently of others and can be increased or decreased either individually or socially.

Second, face is an *impression,* which may or may not be shared by all, that may differ from a person's self-image. People's claims for face, therefore, are not requests to know what others actually think about them; instead, they are solicitations from others of favorable expressions about them. To maintain face, people want others to act toward them with respect, regardless of their "real" thoughts and impressions. Thus, face maintenance involves an expectation that people will act as though the others are appreciated and admired.

Third, face refers only to the *favorable* social attributes that people want others to acknowledge. Unfavorable attributes, of course, are not what others are expected to admire. However, cultures may differ in the behaviors that are highly valued, and they may have very different expectations, or norms, for what are considered to be desirable face behaviors.

Types of Face Needs

Penelope Brown and Stephen Levinson extended Goffman's ideas by proposing a universal model of social politeness.[24] They pointed out that, regardless of their culture, all people have face and a desire to maintain and even gain more of it. Face is maintained through the use of various politeness rituals in social interactions, as people try to balance the competing goals of task efficiency and relationship harmony.[25] Tae-Seop Lim suggests that

CULTURE connections

It turned out that Baba had had no cash on him for the oranges. He'd written Mr. Nguyen a check and Mr. Nguyen had asked for an ID. "He wants to see my license," Baba bellowed in Farsi. "Almost two years we've bought his damn fruits and put money in his pocket and the son of a dog wants to see my license!"

"Baba, it's not personal," I said, smiling at the Nguyens. "They're supposed to ask for an ID."

"I don't want you here," Mr. Nguyen said, stepping in front of his wife. He was pointing at Baba with his cane. He turned to me. "You're nice young man but your father, he's crazy. Not welcome anymore."

"Does he think I'm a thief?" Baba said, his voice rising. People had gathered outside. They were staring. "What kind of a country is this? No one trusts anybody!"

"I call police," Mrs. Nguyen said, poking out her face. "You get out or I call police."

"Please, Mrs. Nguyen, don't call the police. I'll take him home. Just don't call the police, okay? Please?"

"Yes, you take him home. Good idea," Mr. Nguyen said. His eyes, behind his wire-rimmed bifocals, never left Baba. I led Baba through the doors. He kicked a magazine on his way out. After I'd made him promise he wouldn't go back in, I returned to the store and apologized to the Nguyens. Told them my father was going through a difficult time. I gave Mrs. Nguyen our telephone number and address, and told her to get an estimate for the damages. "Please call me as soon as you know. I'll pay for everything, Mrs. Nguyen. I'm so sorry." Mrs. Nguyen took the sheet of paper from me and nodded. I saw her hands were shaking more than usual, and that made me angry at Baba, his causing an old woman to shake like that.

"My father is still adjusting to life in America," I said, by way of explanation.

I wanted to tell them that, in Kabul, we snapped a tree branch and used it as a credit card. Hassan and I would take the wooden stick to the bread maker. He'd carve notches on our stick with his knife, one notch for each loaf of *naan* he'd pull for us from the *tandoor*'s roaring flames. At the end of the month, my father paid him for the number of notches on the stick. That was it. No questions. No ID.

—*Khaled Hosseini*

there are three kinds of face needs: the need for control, the need for approval, and the need for admiration.[26] We now describe these three universal face needs.

The Need for Control Control face is concerned with individual requirements for freedom and personal authority. It is related to people's need for others to acknowledge their individual autonomy and self-sufficiency. As Lim suggests, it involves people's

> image that they are in control of their own fate, that is, they have the virtues of a full-fledged, mature, and responsible adult. This type of face includes such values as "independent," "in control of self," "initiative," "mature," "composed," "reliable," and "self-sufficient." When persons claim these values for themselves, they want to be self-governed and free from others' interference, control, or imposition.[27]

The claim for control face, in other words, is embodied in the desire to have freedom of action.

The Need for Approval   Approval face is concerned with individual requirements for affiliation and social contact. It is related to people's need for others to acknowledge their friendliness and honesty. This type of face is similar to what the Chinese call *lien*,[28] or the integrity of moral character, the loss of which makes it impossible for a person to function appropriately within a social group. As Hsien Chin Hu relates,

> A simple case of *lien*-losing is afforded by the experience of an American traveler in the interior of China. In a little village she had made a deal with a peasant to use his donkey for transportation. On the day agreed upon the owner appeared only to declare that his donkey was not available, the lady would have to wait one day. Yet he would not allow her to hire another animal, because she had consented to use his ass. They argued back and forth first in the inn, then in the courtyard; a crowd gathered around them, as each stated his point of view over and over again. No comment was made, but some of the older people shook their heads and muttered something, the peasant getting more and more excited all the time trying to prove his right. Finally he turned and left the place without any more arguments, and the American was free to hire another beast. The man had felt the disapproval of the group. The condemnation of his community of his attempt to take advantage of the plight of the traveler made him feel he had "lost *lien*."[29]

Lien is maintained by acting with good *jen*, the Chinese term for "man." As Francis Hsu explains:

> When the Chinese say of so-and-so "*ta pu shih jen*" (he is not *jen*), they do not mean that this person is not a human animal; instead they mean that his behavior in relation to other human beings is not acceptable."[30]

Hsu regards the term *jen* as similar in meaning to the Yiddish term *mensh*, which refers to a good human being who is kind, generous, decent, and upright. Such an individual should therefore be admired for his or her noble character. As Leo Rosten says of this term,

> It is hard to convey the special sense of respect, dignity, approbation, that can be conveyed by calling someone "a real *mensh*."...The most withering comment one might make on someone's character or conduct is: "He is not (did not act like) a *mensh*."...The key to being "a real *mensh*" is nothing less than—character: rectitude, dignity, a sense of what is right, responsible, decorous. Many a poor man, many an ignorant man, is a *mensh*.[31]

Thus, approval face reflects the desire to be treated with respect and dignity.

The Need for Admiration   Admiration face is concerned with individual needs for displays of respect from others. It is related to people's need for others to acknowledge their talents and accomplishments. This type of face is similar to what the Chinese call *mien-tzu*, or prestige acquired through success and social standing. One's *mien-tzu*

> is built up through high position, wealth, power, ability, through cleverly establishing social ties to a number of prominent people, as well as through avoidance of acts that would cause unfavorable comment....All persons growing up in any community have the same claim to *lien*, an honest, decent "face"; but their *mien-tzu* will differ with the status of the family, personal ties, ego's ability to impress people, etc.[32]

Thus, admiration face involves the need for others to acknowledge a person's success, capabilities, reputation, and accomplishments.

Facework and Interpersonal Communication

The term facework refers to the actions people take to deal with their own and others' face needs. Everyday actions that impose on another, such as requests, warnings, compliments, criticisms, apologies, and even praise, may jeopardize the face of one or more participants in a communicative act. Ordinarily, say Brown and Levinson,

> people cooperate (and assume each other's cooperation) in maintaining face in interaction, such cooperation being based on the mutual vulnerability of face. That is, normally everyone's face depends on everyone else's being maintained, and since people can be expected to defend their faces if threatened, and in defending their own to threaten others' faces, it is in general in every participant's best interest to maintain each others' face.[33]

The degree to which a given set of actions may pose a potential threat to one or more aspects of people's face depends on three characteristics of the relationship.[34] First, the potential for face threats is associated with the control dimension of interpersonal communication. Relationships in which there are large power or status differences among the participants have a great potential for people's actions to be interpreted as face-threatening. Within a large organization, for instance, a verbal disagreement between a manager and her employees will have a greater potential to be perceived as face-threatening than will an identical disagreement among employees who are equal in seniority and status.

Second, face-threat potential is associated with the affiliation dimension of interpersonal communication. That is, relationships in which participants have a large social distance, and therefore less social familiarity, have a great potential for actions to be perceived as face-threatening. Thus, very close family members may say things to one another that they would not tolerate from more distant acquaintances. Relationships where strangers have no formal connection to one another but are, for example, simply waiting in line at the train station, the taxi stand, or the bank, may sometimes be seen as an exception to this general principle.[35] As Ron Scollon and Suzie Wong-Scollon suggest, "Westerners often are struck with the contrast they see between the highly polite and deferential Asians they meet in their business, educational, and governmental contacts and the rude, pushy, and aggressive Asians they meet on the subways of Asia's major cities."[36] At many train stations in the People's Republic of China, for example,

> people are not in the midst of members of their own community, so the drive to preserve face and act with proper behavior is much lower. Passengers usually wait in waiting rooms until the attendant moves a barrier and they can cross the area between them and the train. The competition is quite fierce as passengers rush toward the train with their luggage, and they have little regard for the safety of other passengers. Often, fellow travelers are injured by luggage, knocked to the ground, or even pushed between the platform and the train, where they fall to the tracks.[37]

Third, face-threat potential is related to culture-specific evaluations that people make. That is, cultures may make unique assessments about the degree to which particular actions are inherently threatening to a person's face. Thus, certain actions within one culture may be regarded as face-threatening, whereas those same actions in another culture may be regarded as perfectly acceptable. In certain cultures, for instance, passing someone a bowl of soup with only one hand, or with one particular hand, may be regarded as an insult and therefore a threat to face; in other cultures, however, those same actions are perfectly acceptable.

CULTURE connections

She was jolted by the ringing of her phone. It was Chen. There was traffic noise in the background.

"Where are you, Chief Inspector Chen?"

"On my way home. I had a call from Party Secretary Li. He invites you to a Beijing Opera performance this evening."

"Does Mr. Li want to discuss the Wen case with me?"

"I'm not sure about that. The invitation is to demonstrate our bureau's attention to the case, and to you, our distinguished American guest."

"Isn't it enough to assign you to me?" she said.

"Well, in China, Li's invitation gives more face."

"Giving face—I've heard only about losing face."

"If you are a somebody, you give face by making a friendly gesture."

"I see, like your visit to Gu. So I have no choice?"

"Well, if you say no, Party Secretary Li will lose face. The bureau will, too—including me."

"Oh no! Yours is one face I have to save." She laughed. "What shall I wear to the Beijing Opera?"

"Beijing Opera is not like Western opera. You don't have to dress formally, but if you do—"

"Then I'm giving face, too."

"Exactly. Shall I pick you up at the hotel?"

—Qiu Xiaolong

Stella Ting-Toomey[38] and Min-Sun Kim[39] both suggest that cultural differences in individualism–collectivism affect the facework behaviors that people are likely to use. In individualist cultures, concerns about message clarity and preserving one's own face are more important than maintaining the face of others, because tasks are more important than relationships, and individual autonomy must be preserved. Consequently, direct, dominating, and controlling face-negotiation strategies are common, and there is a low degree of sensitivity to the face-threatening capabilities of particular messages. Conversely, in collectivist cultures, the mutual preservation of face is extremely important, because it is vital that people be approved and admired by others. Therefore, indirect, obliging, and smoothing face-negotiation strategies are common, direct confrontations between people are avoided, concern for the feelings of others is heightened, and ordinary communication messages are seen as having a great face-threatening potential.

Facework and Intercultural Communication

Competent facework, which lessens the potential for specific actions to be regarded as face-threatening, encompasses a wide variety of communication behaviors. These behaviors may include apologies, excessive politeness, the narration of justifications or excuses, displays of deference and submission, the use of intermediaries or other avoidance strategies, claims of common ground or the intention to act cooperatively, or the use of implication or indirect speech. The specific facework strategies a person uses, however, are shaped and modified by his or her culture. For instance, the Japanese and U.S. Americans have very different reactions when they realize that they have committed a face-threatening act and would like to restore the other's face. The Japanese prefer to adapt their messages to the social status of their interaction partners and provide an appropriate apology. They want to repair the damage, if possible, but without providing reasons that explain or justify their original error. Conversely, U.S. Americans would prefer to adapt their messages to the nature of the provocation and provide verbal justifications for their initial actions. They may use humor or aggression to divert attention from their actions but do not apologize for their original error.[40]

As another example of culture-specific differences in facework behaviors, consider the comments that are commonly appended to the report cards of high school students in the United States and in China. In the United States, evaluations of high school students include specific statements about students' strengths and weaknesses. In China, however, the high school report cards that are issued at the end of each semester never criticize the students directly; rather, teachers use indirect language and say "I wish that you would make more progress in such areas as..." in order to save face while conveying his or her evaluations.[41]

Facework is a central and enduring feature of all interpersonal relationships. Facework is concerned with the communication activities that help to create, maintain, and sustain the connections between people. As Robyn Penman says:

> Facework is not something we do some of the time, it is something that we unavoidably do all the time—it is the core of our social selves. That it is called face and facework is curious but not critical here. What is critical is that the mechanism the label stands [for] seems to be as enduring as human social existence. In the very act of communicating with others we are inevitably commenting on the other and our relationship with them. And in that commenting we are maintaining or changing the identity of the other in relationship to us.[42]

Improving Intercultural Relationships

Competent interpersonal relationships among people from different cultures do not happen by accident. They occur as a result of the knowledge and perceptions people have about one another, their motivations to engage in meaningful interactions, and their ability to communicate in ways that are regarded as appropriate and effective. To improve these interpersonal relationships, then, it is necessary to learn about and thereby reduce anxiety and uncertainty about people from other cultures, to share oneself with those people, and to handle the inevitable differences in perceptions and expectations that will occur.

Learning about People from Other Cultures

The need to know, to understand, and to make sense of the world is a fundamental necessity of life. Without a world that is somewhat predictable and that can be interpreted in a sensible and meaningful way, humankind would not survive.

CULTURE connections

Like many other newcomers to the Anglo world, I was struck by the elasticity of the English concept of 'friend', which could be applied to a wide range of relationships, from deep and close, to quite casual and superficial. This was in stark contrast to the Polish words *przyjaciel* (male) and *przyjaciólka* (female), which could only stand for exceptionally close and intimate relationships. What struck me even more was the importance of the concept embodied in the Polish word *koledzy* (female counterpart *koleżanki*) as a basic conceptual category defining human relations – quite unlike the relatively marginal concept encoded in the English word *colleague*, relevant only to professional elites. It became clear to me that concepts such as *'koledzy'* (*'koleżanki'*) and *'przyjaciele'* (*przyjaciótki*) (plural) organised the social universe quite differently from concepts such as 'friends'.

—Anna Wierzbicka

We have already suggested in Chapter 5 that both individuals and cultures can differ in their need to reduce uncertainty and in the extent to which they can tolerate ambiguity and, therefore, in the means they select to adapt to the world. The human need to learn about others, to make sense of their actions, and to understand their beliefs, values, and behaviors has typically been studied under the general label of uncertainty reduction theory.[43] This theory explains the likelihood that people will seek out additional information about one another, but it deals primarily with the knowledge component of communication competence. William B. Gudykunst has recently revised uncertainty reduction theory and renamed it anxiety/uncertainty management theory.[44] It now focuses more clearly on intercultural communication, incorporates the emotional or motivational component of intercultural competence, and emphasizes ways to cope with or manage the inherent tensions and anxieties that inevitably occur in many intercultural encounters. In the sections that follow, we describe the components, causes, and consequences of uncertainty management behaviors and some strategies for reducing uncertainty in interpersonal relationships among people from different cultures.

Components of Uncertainty and Anxiety Management Some degree of unpredictability exists in all interpersonal relationships, but it is typically much higher in intercultural interactions. There are two broad components involved in the management of uncertainty behaviors: uncertainty and anxiety. Uncertainty refers to the extent to which a person lacks the knowledge, information, and ability to understand and predict the intentions and behaviors of another. Anxiety refers to an individual's degree of emotional tension and her or his inability to cope with change, to live with stress, and to contend with vague and imprecise information.

Uncertainty and anxiety are influenced by culture. In Chapter 5, when we discussed Hofstede's value dimensions, we suggested that cultures differ in the extent to which they prefer or can cope with uncertainty. It should now be obvious that Hofstede's uncertainty avoidance dimension is related to what is here being referred to as anxiety/uncertainty management.

■ Competent intercultural communication often leads to a reduction in uncertainty and anxiety in intercultural interactions.

Causes of Uncertainty and Anxiety   Three conditions are related to uncertainty and anxiety management behaviors. These are your expectations about future interactions with other people, the incentive value or potential rewards that relationships with other people may have for you, and the degree to which other people exhibit behaviors that deviate from or do not match your expectations.

The first condition is your expectations about future interactions with another person. If you believe that you are very likely to interact with some person on future occasions, the degree to which you can live with ambiguity and insufficient information about that person will be low, and your need for more knowledge about that person will be high. Conversely, if you do not expect to see and talk with someone again, you will be more willing to remain uncertain about her or his motives and intentions, your anxiety level will be relatively low, and you will therefore not attempt to seek out any additional information. This person will continue to be a stranger. Anxiety/uncertainty management theory suggests that sojourners and immigrants who know they will be interacting in a new culture for a long period of time will be more likely to try to reduce their uncertainty about how and why people behave than will a tourist or temporary visitor.

The second condition, incentive value, refers to the perceived likelihood that the other person can fulfill various needs that you have, give you some of the resources that you want, or provide you with certain rewards that you desire. If a person's incentive value is high—that is, if the other person has the potential to be very rewarding to you—your need to find out more about that person will be correspondingly high. As you might expect, a high incentive value also increases the degree to which a person will be preferred or viewed as interpersonally attractive. Of course, the needs or rewards that people might want vary widely; the incentive value of a given person is related to his or her ability to

CULTURE connections

Neither that evening nor at virtually any other point during my travels did the Kurds I met ask me any personal questions—not even whether I was married or had children. To have done so, one Kurdish woman explained to me, would have been considered rude.

—Christiane Bird

provide such benefits as status, affection, information, services, goods, money, or some combination of these resources.[45]

One form of incentive value that has been widely investigated is the perceived similarity of the other person. The similarity–attraction hypothesis suggests that we like and are attracted to those whom we regard as comparable to ourselves in ways that we regard as important. Conversely, we are unlikely to be attracted to those who are very different from us. This hypothesis implies that, at least in the initial stages of intercultural encounters, the dissimilarities created by cultural differences may inhibit the development of new interpersonal relationships.

The third condition is the degree of deviance that the other person exhibits. Deviant behaviors are those that are not typically expected because they are inconsistent with the common norms that govern particular social situations. When a person acts deviantly, both your level of anxiety and your degree of uncertainty about that person increase, because he or she is far less predictable to you. Conversely, when a person conforms to your expectations by behaving in a predictable way, your level of anxiety and your degree of uncertainty about that person decrease. A person who behaves in deviant and unexpected ways is often disliked and is regarded as interpersonally unattractive, whereas one who conforms to others' expectations and is therefore predictable is often most liked and preferred. In intercultural communication, it is extremely likely that the other person will behave "deviantly" or differently from what you might expect. Thus, uncertainty about people from other cultures will typically be high, as will the level of anxiety and tension that you experience.

Consequences of Uncertainty and Anxiety Management   Because intercultural communication involves people from dissimilar cultures, each person's behaviors are likely to violate the others' expectations and create uncertainty and anxiety. Consequently, there is always the possibility that fear, distrust, and similar negative emotions may prevail. Often, but not always, the negative emotions can be overcome, and positive outcomes can result.

Judee Burgoon has developed expectancy violations theory to explain when deviations from expectations will be regarded as positive or as negative.[46] All behaviors that differ from expectations will increase the degree of uncertainty in an interaction. Burgoon suggests that how a person interprets and reacts to the deviations of another depends on how favorably that person is perceived. If the other person is perceived positively, violations of your expectation that increase interaction involvement will be seen as favorable, whereas violations of expectations that decrease interaction involvement will be viewed as unfavorable. To illustrate, imagine that you are having a conversation with someone who is standing closer to you than you would expect. This is clearly a violation of your expectations, but how would you likely react to this situation? Burgoon suggests that, if the person is positively valenced—because, for example, you regard the person as physically attractive—then you may view the violation and the other person favorably, whereas if the other person is negatively valenced, then you will regard the violation and the other person unfavorably and may attempt to back away or escape. Conversely, imagine that your conversation is with someone who is standing farther away than your typical or expected interaction distance. If the person is positively valenced, you may attempt to compensate for the violation by moving closer, whereas if the person is negatively valenced, you will likely attribute negative connotations—he or she is aloof, cold—to the person.

The positive consequences of anxiety and uncertainty management behaviors that are applicable to intercultural communication can be grouped under two general labels: informational consequences and emotional consequences. *Informational consequences* result from the additional knowledge that has been gained about other people, including facts or inferences about their culture; increased accuracy in the judgments made about their beliefs, values, norms, and social practices; and an increased degree of confidence that they are being perceived accurately.

Emotional consequences may include increased levels of self-disclosure, heightened interpersonal attraction, increases in intimacy behaviors, more frequent nonverbal displays of positive emotions, and an increased likelihood that future intercultural contacts will be regarded as favorable. Of course, these positive outcomes all presume that the reduction in anxiety and uncertainty about another person will result in an increase in positive communicator valence, which is not necessarily so. Unfortunately, as Gudykunst suggests, negative perceptions in intercultural encounters frequently occur because people are not *mindful*—focused, aware, open to new information, and tolerant of differences. This allows our cultural assumptions to remain unchallenged. As we have seen, the perception that a person is acting in a deviant way (as defined by one's own cultural expectations) will often lead to decreased satisfaction with the encounter.

Strategies for Reducing Uncertainty and Anxiety To behave both appropriately and effectively in an intercultural encounter, you must make an accurate assessment about many kinds of information: the individual characteristics of the person with whom you interact, the social episodes that are typical of the particular setting and occasion, the specific roles that are being played within the episode, the rules of interaction that govern what people can say and do, the setting or context within which the interaction occurs, and the cultural patterns that influence what is regarded as appropriate and effective. Thus, uncertainty is not reduced for its own sake, but occurs every day for strategic purposes. As Charles R. Berger suggested:

> To interact in a relatively smooth, coordinated, and understandable manner, one must be able both to predict how one's interaction partner is likely to behave, and, based on these predictions, to select from one's own repertoire those responses that will optimize outcomes in the encounter.[47]

There are three general types of strategies—passive, active, and interactive—that can be used to gain information about other people and thus reduce one's level of uncertainty and degree of anxiety. *Passive* strategies involve quiet and surreptitious observation of another person to learn how he or she behaves. *Active* strategies include efforts to obtain information about another person by asking others or structuring the environment to place the person in a situation that provides the needed information. *Interactive* strategies involve actually conversing with the other person in an attempt to gather the needed information. As you might expect, there are large cultural differences in the preferred strategies that are used to reduce uncertainty and manage anxiety in intercultural encounters. For example, European Americans are more likely than their Japanese counterparts to use active strategies such as asking questions and self-disclosing as a way to obtain information about another person, whereas the Japanese are more likely to use passive strategies.[48]

Sharing Oneself with People from Other Cultures

The human tendency to reveal personal information about oneself and to explain one's inner experiences and private thoughts is called self-disclosure. Self-disclosure occurs among people of all cultures, but there are tremendous cultural differences in the breadth, depth, valence, timing, and targets of self-disclosing events.

The *breadth* of self-disclosing information refers to the range of topics that are revealed, and European Americans tend to self-disclose about more topics than do members of most other cultures. For example, Tsukasa Nishida found that European Americans discussed a much wider range of topics that were related to the self (such as health and personality) with strangers than did Japanese; also, Japanese had far more self-related topics than did European Americans that they would never discuss with others.[49] Ghanaians tend to self-disclose about family and background matters, whereas U.S. Americans self-disclose about career concerns.[50] In contrast,

> Chinese culture takes a conservative stand on self-disclosure. For a Chinese, self-centered speech would be considered boastful and pretentious. Chinese tend to scorn those who often talk about themselves and doubt their motives when they do so. Chinese seem to prefer talking about external matters, such as world events. For Americans, self-disclosure is a strategy to make various types of relationships work; for Chinese, it is a gift shared only with the most intimate relatives and friends.[51]

The *depth* of the self-disclosing information refers to the degree of "personalness" about oneself that is revealed. Self-disclosure can reveal superficial aspects ("I like broccoli") or very private thoughts and feelings ("I'm afraid of my father"). Of the many cultures that have been studied, European Americans are among the most revealing self-disclosers. European Americans disclose more than African Americans, who in turn disclose more than Mexican Americans.[52] European Americans also disclose more than the British,[53] French,[54] Germans, Japanese,[55] and Puerto Ricans.[56]

Valence refers to whether the self-disclosure is positive or negative, and thus favorable or unfavorable. Not only do European Americans disclose more about themselves than do members of many other cultures but they are also more likely to provide negatively valenced information. Compared to many Asian cultures, for example, European Americans are far less concerned with issues of "face" and are therefore more inclined to share information that may not portray them in the most favorable way.

Timing refers to when the self-disclosure occurs in the course of the relationship. For European Americans, self-disclosure in new relationships is generally high because the participants share information about themselves that the others do not know. A person's name, hometown, employment or educational affiliations, and personal interests are all likely to be shared in initial interactions. As the relationship progresses, the amount of self-disclosure diminishes because the participants have already learned what they need to know to interact appropriately and effectively. Only if the relationship becomes more personal and intimate will the amount of self-disclosure again begin to increase. But the timing of the self-disclosure process can be very different in other cultures. For example, Native Americans typically reveal very little about themselves initially because they believe that too much self-disclosure at that stage is inappropriate. A similar pattern may be found among members of Asian cultures.

Target refers to the person to whom self-disclosing information is given. Among European Americans, spouses are usually the targets of a great deal of self-disclosure, and mutual self-disclosure is widely regarded as contributing to an ideal and satisfactory marriage.[57] The breadth and depth of self-disclosure among other European American family members are of much lesser degree. Other cultures have different patterns. Among the Igbos of Nigeria, for instance, age is used to determine the appropriate degree of self-disclosure among interactants, younger interactants being expected to self-disclose far more than their older counterparts. As a cultural norm, when elder Igbos are in an initial encounter with someone who is younger, they have the right to inquire about the young person's background, parents, hometown, and similar information that may ultimately lead to contact with distant relatives or old friends.

Handling Differences in Intercultural Relationships

Conflict in interpersonal relationships is a major nemesis for most people. Add the complications of different cultural backgrounds, and problems in managing conflict can become

CULTURE connections

I was doing everything wrong when I visited Paris. I would walk down the Champ Elysées smiling and greeting people, as if I were in St. Louis. In shops, I said I wanted this or that, and I was ignored. When Parisians refused to help me with a problem, I went away meekly.

Pretty soon, I figured the clichés about the mean, arrogant French were true....

[I've since learned that] the French smile at people they know, not at strangers. Shopkeepers expect a little small talk, and all you need to start getting along in France are five magic words: *"Excusez-moi de vous déranger"* ("Excuse me for bothering you").

Bombs may fall or the house may catch fire...but the French people will not shorten this formality by so much as a syllable.

—*Susan Spano*

even more severe. Stella Ting-Toomey and John Oetzel's work provides some direction for managing intercultural conflict.[58]

Ting-Toomey and Oetzel use the distinction between collectivism and individualism, which is discussed more fully in Chapter 5. Briefly, in collectivist cultures, interpersonal bonds are relatively enduring, and there are distinct ingroups and outgroups. Collectivist cultures are often very traditional. In individualistic cultures, the bonds between people are more fragile, and because people belong to many different groups that often change, membership in ingroups and outgroups is very flexible. Individualistic cultures are therefore often characterized by rapid innovation and change.

Conflict may involve either task or instrumental issues. Task issues are concerned with how to do something or how to achieve a specific goal, whereas instrumental issues are concerned with personal or relationship problems, such as hostility toward another person. The distinction therefore focuses on conflict about ideas versus conflict about people.

Ting-Toomey and Oetzel believe that people in collectivistic and individualistic cultures typically define and respond to conflict differently. In collectivistic cultures, people are more likely to merge task and instrumental concerns, and conflict is therefore likely to be seen as personal. To shout and scream publicly, thus displaying the conflict to others, threatens everyone's face to such an extreme degree that such behavior is usually avoided at all costs. In contrast, people from individualistic cultures are more likely to separate the task and the instrumental dimensions. Thus, they are able to express their agitation and anger (perhaps including shouting and strong nonverbal actions) about an issue and then joke and socialize with the other person once

■ Issues of disclosure, conflict resolution, and face maintenance affect all interpersonal relationships. These businesspeople confer informally about their work.

the disagreement is over. It is almost as if once the conflict is resolved, it is completely forgotten.

Because there is a great deal of volatility and variability in people's behaviors in individualistic cultures, there is often considerable potential for conflict. Because people are encouraged to be unique, their behaviors are not as predictable as they would be in collectivistic cultures. Also, because expectations are individually based rather than group-centered, there is always the possibility that the behavior of any one person will violate the expectations of another, possibly producing conflict.

Cultures also shape attitudes toward conflict. In collectivistic cultures, which value indirectness and ambiguity, conflicts and confrontations are typically avoided. Thus, rather than trying to resolve the problem directly, people in collectivistic cultures will attempt to maintain the external smoothness of the relationship. In individualistic cultures, which are also more likely to be "doing" or activity-oriented cultures, people's approach to conflict will be action-oriented. That is, the conflict precipitates actions, and the conflict is explicitly revealed and named.[59]

A very important concept for understanding how people from different cultures handle conflict is that of face, which we discussed earlier in this chapter. In conflicts, in particular, face is very likely to be threatened, and all participants are vulnerable to the face-threatening acts that can occur.

The actions of people in conflict can include attempts to save face for themselves, others, or all participants. Members of collectivistic cultures are likely to deal with face threats such as conflicts by selecting strategies that smooth over their disagreements and allow them to maintain the face of both parties, that is, mutual face-saving. As Ringo Ma suggests, however, such strategies do not simply ignore the conflicting issues; after all, conflicts do get resolved in high-context cultures. Rather, nonconfrontational alternatives are used to resolve differences. Often, for instance, a friend of those involved in the conflict, or an elderly person respected by all, will function as an unofficial intermediary who attempts to preserve the face of each person and the relationship by preventing rejection and embarrassment.[60] Members of individualistic cultures, conversely, are likely to deal with face threats in a direct, controlling way. It is important to their sense of self to maintain their own face, to take charge, to direct the course of action, and in so doing to protect their own dignity and self-respect even at the expense of others.[61]

Imagine a scene involving two employees assigned to an important and high-tension project. Perhaps they are operating under serious time constraints, or perhaps the lives of many people depend on their success. Inevitably, disagreements about how to approach the assignment, as well as the specifics of the assignment itself, are likely to occur. Now assume that one employee is from a collectivistic culture such as Korea and the other is from an individualistic culture such as England. The difficulties inherent in completing their assignment will probably be increased by the great differences in their approaches to the problems that will arise. Each person's attempt to maintain face may induce the other to make negative judgments and evaluations. Each person's attempt to cope with the conflict and accomplish the task may produce even more conflict.[62] As Ting-Toomey and Oetzel suggest, these differences will need to be addressed before the work can be accomplished successfully.

CULTURE connections

Presented by the couples as an often unresolvable problem was the loss of place, culture and family that resulted from one partner's leaving his or her home of origin. The immigrant partner in the couple almost invariably expressed a longing for his or her own landscape and climate, and a deep sadness about the distance from extended family members. Other topics that frequently arose were loss of religion and language. While many couples were originally optimistic about importing religion and language from their native lands, they found that the United States exerted a pressure to assimilate that was very difficult to resist. As a result, these essential elements of culture were preserved only through great effort, if at all. For example, while Hueping Chin has managed to teach her son to speak Chinese fluently, as he grows older, their dialogue in Chinese sometimes falters in the face of new topics: "How does the space shuttle work? I find it hard to explain that to him in Chinese." The words of Jat Aluwalia capture the sense of regret that some felt: "I admit defeat; I guess the sense of being Indian ends with me."

— Jessie Carroll Grearson and Lauren B. Smith

Interpersonal Relationships and Intercultural Competence

Intercultural competence in interpersonal relationships requires knowledge, motivation, and skill in using verbal and nonverbal codes, as described in previous chapters. In addition, it requires behaviors that are appropriate and effective for the different types and dimensions of interpersonal relationships described in this chapter.

Competence in intercultural relationships requires that you understand the meanings attributed to particular types of interpersonal relationships. Whom should you consider to be a stranger, an acquaintance, a friend, or a family member? What expectations should you have for people in these categories? What clues do people from other cultures offer about their expectations for you? Your expectations about the nature of interpersonal relationships affect how you assign meaning to other people's behaviors.

Your willingness to understand the face needs of people from other cultures and to behave appropriately to preserve and enhance their sense of face is critical to your intercultural competence. Always consider a person's need to maintain a favorable face in her or his interactions with others. Perceptions of autonomy, approval, and respect by others are important, but you must meet these face needs with facework that is appropriate to the other's cultural beliefs.

Your expectations about self-disclosure, obtaining information about others, and handling disagreements will not, in all likelihood, be the same as those of people from other cultures. Competence in developing and maintaining intercultural relationships requires knowledge of differences, a willingness to consider and try alternatives, and the skill to enact alternative relational dynamics.

Summary

People in an intercultural relationship may have very different expectations about the preferred nature of their social interactions. The types of interpersonal relationships, including those among strangers, acquaintances, friends, romantic partners, and family members, may also vary greatly across cultures.

Interpersonal relationships can be interpreted along the three dimensions of control, affiliation, and activation. The control dimension provides interpretations about status or social dominance. The affiliation dimension indicates the degree of friendliness, liking, and social warmth that is being communicated. The activation dimension is concerned with interpersonal responsiveness.

The concept of face refers to the positive social impressions that people want to have and would like others to acknowledge. Face includes the need for autonomy or individual freedom of action, approval or inclusion in social groups, and admiration or respect from others because of one's accomplishments. The need for facework depends on the control and affiliation dimensions of interpersonal communication and on culture-specific judgments about the extent to which certain actions inherently threaten one's face.

To improve intercultural relationships, you must learn about people from other cultures and thereby reduce the degree of uncertainty. Sharing yourself in appropriate ways with people from other cultures and learning to use culturally sensitive ways to handle the differences and disagreements that may arise are additional ways to improve intercultural relationships.

For Discussion

1. What is a friend to you? What do you expect of your friends?
2. What is meant by the concept of "face"? Have you ever experienced a loss of face?
3. Describe the relationship among the following terms: *face, face maintenance, facework, embarrassment, truthfulness, dishonesty, fear,* and *withdrawal.*
4. Why do anxiety and uncertainty management play a particularly powerful role in intercultural communication?
5. Do differences in what we categorize as "public" and "private" information hold any consequences for the development of a relationship?
6. How do you think email, text messaging, and other forms of Internet communication have affected the development of intercultural relationships?

For Further Reading

Rosemary Breger and Rosanna Hill (eds.), *Cross-Cultural Marriage: Identity and Choice* (New York: Berg, 1998). Contributions in this volume explore the personal experiences of those in intercultural marriages, as well as placing the positive and negative issues that emerge in such marriages in social, legal, and psychological contexts.

Kathy Domenici and Stephen W. Littlejohn, *Facework: Bridging Theory and Practice* (Thousand Oaks, CA: Sage, 2006). Thoroughly researched and very practical, this book on face and facework in interpersonal communication is an excellent sourcebook. A useful balance between conceptual and the applied ideas.

Laura K. Guerrero, Peter A. Andersen, and Walid A. Afifi, *Close Encounters: Communication in Relationships,* 2nd ed. (Thousand Oaks, CA: Sage, 2007). An intermediate-level textbook, it provides an excellent and readable summary of current theory and research. Explains and explores the theories that dominate the study of interpersonal communication.

Min-Sun Kim, *Non-Western Perspectives on Human Communication: Implications for Theory and Practice* (Thousand Oaks, CA: Sage, 2002). A useful and very readable compendium that takes a non-U.S. view of interpersonal communication theories and practices.

John G. Oetzel and Stella Ting-Toomey (eds.), *The Sage Handbook of Conflict Communication: Integrating Theory, Research, and Practice* (Thousand Oaks, CA: Sage, 2006). Provides a comprehensive overview of theory and research on conflict in a variety of human communication settings. Includes a substantial section on conflict in intercultural communication.

Julia T. Wood, *Interpersonal Communication: Everyday Encounters,* 5th ed. (Belmont, CA: Thomson/ Wadsworth, 2007). A presentation of the fundamentals of interpersonal communication that parallels some of the major topics in this textbook.

For additional information about intercultural films and about Web sites for researching specific cultures, please turn to the Resources section at the back of this book.

11 Episodes, Contexts, and Intercultural Interactions

There is a repetitiveness to everyday communication experiences that helps to make them understandable and predictable. The recurring features of these common events, which we call social episodes, allow you to anticipate what people may do, what will likely happen, and what variations from the expected sequence of events could mean.

Social Episodes in Intercultural Relationships

People undertake intercultural relationships in predictable ways. In this section, we describe how communication experiences are grouped into common events. Our point is that people's interactions are structured by their participation in events that are quite predictable and routine.

The Nature of Social Episodes

Think about how your daily life is structured. If you are like most people, there is a great deal of predictability in what you do each day and even with whom you do it. If you are attending a college or university, much of your life is taken up with such activities as attending class, studying, talking with a classmate in the cafeteria, working at a job, going shopping, meeting a friend after work, attending a party, and eating dinner. These are the kinds of structures in your life that we refer to as social episodes—that is, interaction sequences that are repeated over and over again. Not only do these social episodes recur, but their structure is also very predictable. The individuals who participate in these episodes generally know what to expect from others and what others expect from them. It is almost as if there were an unwritten script that tells you roughly what to say, whom to say it to, and how to say it.

Take the example of going to class. You probably attend class in a room filled with chairs, or tables with chairs, that face the front of the room. When you take a seat, you put your notebooks and other texts on the floor or under the desk. You keep your chair oriented in the way all the other chairs are oriented. The room is arranged so that you can look at the teacher, and there is a clearly marked space in the front of the room for the teacher to stand or sit. When you enter the classroom, you never consider taking that spot. You expect the teacher, when she or he walks into the room, to do so. You do not expect the teacher to walk into the room and take the chair next to you.

If you get to class early enough, you might engage in small talk with another student. There are fairly predictable topics you might discuss, depending on how well you know each other. You probably talk about the class, whether you have done the reading, how your work is going, and the assignments. You might talk about the teacher and analyze his or her strengths and weaknesses. You might talk about the weather, the latest sports scores, or other common topics.

You expect the teacher to give a lecture or in some other way provide a sense of structure for the class. You take notes if the teacher gives a lecture, trying to summarize the key points. If you talk to a classmate while the teacher is lecturing, you whisper rather than talk in a loud voice. If the teacher did not enact the behaviors you expect for the person playing the part of "teacher," you might complain about it to others. Similarly, if one of your fellow classmates did not follow the expected behaviors for "being a student," you might think there was something wrong.

The purpose of this extended example is to underscore our point that much of what people do is made up of social episodes, which are repetitive, predictable, and routine behaviors that form the structure of their interactions with others. These social episodes provide information about how to interpret the verbal and nonverbal symbols of the interactants. The meanings of the symbols are understood because of the context in which they are given. Because those who participate in a social episode usually have the same understanding about what is to take place, they usually know how to behave, what to say, and how to interpret the actions and intentions of others.

In social episodes that include intercultural interactions, however, those involved may—and in all likelihood will—have very different expectations and interpretations about people's behaviors and intentions. As the interaction becomes more and more ambiguous, the expected behaviors that pattern the social episode also become more unpredictable and problematic. Though your culture teaches you to interpret the meanings and

CULTURE connections

Doris would get irritated at things that were even less intelligible to me—when the chauffeur opened the car door for her, for instance. The chauffeur was then specifically instructed not to open the door for her, but he often forgot or else thought the instruction too bizarre to be abided by. And so she would get angry again, directing her words at her husband but intending them, I thought, for all of us. At home the thing that had her fleeing from the lunch table was the way my mother would press her to have a bit of this or a bit more of that, a gesture, to us, of common courtesy. We kept explaining to Doris that Mother did not mean any harm by it, that she thought she was just being hospitable and polite, and that Doris should just ignore it. And we kept telling my mother to stop, not to urge her to eat anything, and my mother would restrain herself for a time and then forget and lapse once more into offering her some dish. I did not understand then why it was so irritating to be pressed to eat, but I understand it somewhat more now. I returned to Egypt on a visit after a long absence and found myself snapping at my hosts for continually urging me to eat, particularly as I was watching my weight and, faced with the feasts with which tables are habitually laid among both the barely comfortable and the well-to-do, I was having a hard enough time of it as it was.

—*Leila Ahmad*

behaviors in social episodes in particular ways, other cultures may provide their members with very different interpretations of these same experiences.

Components of Social Episodes

There are five components of social episodes, each of which influences intercultural communication: cultural patterns, social roles, rules of interaction, interaction scenes, and interaction contexts.

Cultural Patterns   Cultural patterns are shared judgments about what the world is and what it should be, and widely held expectations about how people should behave. The patterns of a culture's beliefs and values, described in Chapters 4 and 5, permeate the ways in which members of a culture think about their world.

Cultural patterns are like tinted glasses that color everything people see and to which they respond. The episodes that are used to structure people's lives—attending class, eating dinner, playing with a friend, going to work, talking with a salesperson—are certainly common to many cultures. But the interpretations that are imposed on these behaviors vary greatly, depending on the cultural patterns that serve as the lens through which the social episodes are viewed. Tamar Katriel, for example, describes a common episode in middle-class Israeli life called *mesibot kiturim,* or "griping party." She argues that, while these griping parties might occur in other cultures, they are particularly important in Israel and reflect a communally oriented cultural pattern.[1]

Joseph Forgas and Michael Bond found that Hong Kong Chinese and Australian students, although leading superficially very similar lives—going to classes, studying, and so on—perceived various social episodes very differently. The perceptions of the Chinese students reflected values and cultural patterns associated with that culture's emphasis on community, the collective good, and acceptance of authority. The Australian students saw the same episodes in terms of self-confidence, competition, and the pleasure they might receive from the interactions in which they participated.[2]

Social Roles   A social role is a set of expected behaviors associated with people in a particular position. Common roles that exist in most cultures include student, mother, father, brother, sister, boss, friend, service person, employee, sales clerk, teacher, manager, soldier, woman, man, and mail carrier. The role that you take in a particular social episode strongly suggests to you the way in which you should act. If you are participating in an episode of a boss giving an employee a performance review, you would expect to behave very differently if you were the employee rather than the boss. If another person is upset about the comments of a coworker, your response would be influenced by the particular role you play in relationship to the upset person. Are you in the role of friend, relative, or employer? Your answer to the question will definitely affect how you respond to the person's concerns. In many episodes, you play clearly defined roles that give you guidance about what you should say to the other person and even how you should say it. Furthermore, the role you are playing is matched by the roles of others in the episode. You have expectations for yourself based on your roles, and you also have expectations for others based on their roles

■ This Vietnamese wedding illustrates the components of social episodes: cultural patterns, social roles, rules of interaction, interaction scenes, and interaction contexts.

CULTURE connections

Many outsiders do not understand the simple differences in culture and lifestyle in France…or the French way of thinking. They invariably go home with stories of those quaint little Frenchies. Those who are able to adjust are changed forever and usually choose to stay, or to return when possible.

The pace of life in France is different. For me, used to a rather hectic American day, it was a relief when I slowed down and actually enjoyed my life in the French style. I had been the person who ate a peanut butter and jelly sandwich over the keyboard. I never had time to cook; my family survived on take-out, fast food, Boston Chicken and lamb chops on Sunday nights. Suddenly meals and social life were the most important parts of my day. Yes, more important than my work. In France they were the anchors to a day and to a lifetime. In the United States, we rarely made time for our friends and the people we cared most about—and they understood this, or said they did, because they were in the same jam. In France nothing was more important.

In France people sat at table for three hours (or longer), ate slowly and had real conversations. This contrasted with an eat-and-run American pattern or even the "independent dinners" we had in our family because everyone had different activities and different needs. Other than Thanksgiving, Jewish holiday feast dinners and a few dinners out with friends, I don't remember sitting at table for much more than an hour in the United States…or having discussions about politics and philosophy.

People in France made less money than those in the United States but still lived better—partly because of this slower pace of life, partly because of the cultural importance of a good meal (with good wine, *bien sûr*) and partly because, with less discretionary income, priorities were better defined. If a French person had to choose between new clothes or a concert ticket, the concert ticket usually won out.

—*Suzy Gershman*

The expectations for appropriate behavior for the roles of student and teacher are quite apparent in the example at the beginning of this section. However, appropriate behaviors for these roles will vary greatly among cultures. In many Asian cultures, it is not acceptable to ask a teacher questions or to whisper to another student. Students are expected to stand up when the teacher enters the room and again when the teacher leaves the room. The students would never call a teacher by his or her first name but only by a formal title.

The role of friends also varies greatly from culture to culture. As discussed in Chapter 10, European Americans have a tendency to call a lot of people "friends," and they often separate their friends into different categories based on where the friendship is established. They might have friends at work, friends from their neighborhoods, and friends from clubs or organizations to which they belong. Many of these friendships are fairly transitory and might last only as long as people work for the same organization or live in the same neighborhood. When the place in which the friendship is conducted is no longer shared in common, the friendship no longer exists in any active sense. In many other cultures, people may have fewer friends, but these friendships are often maintained for longer periods of time.

The importance of this discussion to your participation in intercultural communication should be obvious. Even though you may think you are fulfilling a particular role (such as that of student, friend, house guest, or customer), the expectations of the role may vary widely between your culture and the culture in which you are interacting. There are also sets of rules that generally govern the interactions among people in an episode. Some of these rules are related to specific roles, but others are simply norms or guides to govern behavior.

Rules of Interaction   Rules of interaction provide a predictable pattern or structure to social episodes and give relationships a sense of coherence.[3] Rules of interaction are not written down somewhere, nor are they typically shared verbally. Instead, they operate at the level of unwritten, unspoken expectations. Most of the time, people are not even consciously aware of the rules that govern a social episode until they are broken. Think about the various kinds of rules, for example, that govern the interactions at a wedding. In addition to the various roles (bride, groom, parents, bridesmaids, groomsmen, and guests), there are a host of rules embedded in the different types of weddings that occur. A wedding invitation from a U.S. American couple that is engraved on heavy linen paper and announces a candlelight ceremony at dusk suggests something about the rules governing what a guest should wear and how a guest should act. In contrast, a photocopied invitation on colored paper announcing that pizza and beer will be served following the ceremony suggests a very different set of rules. Often, in weddings between people from different cultures, a portion of the "rules of interaction" from each culture is enacted. During such intercultural marriages, the rules that are typically unspoken may have been verbalized and negotiated, as the ceremony tries to honor and appreciate both cultural heritages.[4]

Rules of interaction include such diverse aspects as what to wear, what is acceptable to talk about, the sequence of events, and the artifacts that are part of the event. B. Aubrey Fisher stated:

> Virtually every social relationship has rules to determine what is appropriate and what is inappropriate for that relationship. For some relationships, the most important rules can be found in a larger social context. Meet someone at a church social, and you will probably conform to rules appropriate to interpersonal communication in a church. For other relationships, the important rules are created during the process of interaction. After you get to know someone, you are more likely to be innovative and to do something "different."[5]

CULTURE connections

Everyone watched the chef lift a large fish out of the bowl. The fish had been sedated by partial freezing, but curled its body from side to side, attempting a slow-motion escape. First, the chef attached the fish to a cutting board with a skewer right below the eye, and another in the midpoint of the tail. Then, with a thin, sharp knife like a scalpel, he carefully cut diagonal slices in the fish's side. Alex could see the fish gasping through its gills and felt sick.

… The guests applauded as the chef removed the first slice and placed it on a small dish for Alex, the guest of honor.

He had to eat this.

He understood the need to accept cultural differences. He was a guest required to participate in the customs of his host. Yet knowing this didn't change the fish back into a fish again.

—*Sara Backer*

In France, for instance, you would never talk about your work at a dinner party, even if all of the people there were in some way connected to the same place of work. Among most U.S. American businesspeople, however, it is commonplace to expect talk about business at a dinner table. An invitation to a dinner party can mean that immediately upon arrival, you will be given the meal and only after you have eaten will you sit and talk leisurely with your hosts; or the invitation may mean that you must spend a substantial period of time before a meal is served in having drinks and talking with your hosts. Do you bring gifts such as flowers, wine, or candy? If so, are there particular artifacts that are taboo, such as wine or other forms of alcohol in Saudi Arabia or chrysanthemums in Italy (which are only given at a funeral)? If you are offered something to eat or drink, must it be accepted because to do otherwise would be considered an insult? (Yes, for Azerbaijanis, among others.)[6]

Even the definition of what constitutes a "meal" can vary from culture to culture. One such example is of Doug, who is invited to dinner in the home of a Nepalese woman named Sangita and her husband, Lopsang.

> She (Sangita) ushers Doug into a lower-level room of their two-story home and invites him to sit on a bench among several that surround a large coffee table. Soon, Sangita and her son, Rinji, begin bringing down food: buffalo, chicken, lentil pancakes. After about one and one-half hours of eating and talking, Doug thanks Sangita and rises to leave.
>
> In disbelief, Sangita asks, "Where are you going? We haven't had dinner yet." Doug is astounded until Sangita explains, "These were just snacks. From now on you should know that if you haven't had the rice, you haven't eaten yet!"[7]

The three ascend the stairs to the upper level of the house where Sangita's husband greets them before a dinner table set with rice, vegetables, buffalo jelly, and dal (lentil stew). As Doug learned, the rules of interaction provide culture-specific instructions about what should and should not occur in particular social episodes.

Interaction Scenes   Interaction scenes are made up of the recurring, repetitive topics that people talk about in social conversations. Most conversations are organized around these ritualized and routinized scenes, which are the chunks of conversational behavior adapted to the particular circumstances.

Kathy Kellermann describes a standard set of interaction scenes that are commonly used by college students in U.S. universities when engaged in informal conversations. As Figure 11.1 indicates, Kellermann's research suggests that interaction scenes are organized into subsets, so that the scenes in subset 1 come before those in subset 2, and so on; however, within a particular subset, no specific order of scenes exists. Consequently, an informal conversation among acquaintances might include such topics as a ritualized greeting ("Hello!"), a reference to the other person's health ("How are you?"), a reference to the present situation, a discussion of the weather, a comment on people known in common, other common interests, a positive evaluation of the other person ("Nice to see you again!"), a reason for terminating the conversation ("I'm late for a meeting"), and finally a good-bye sequence.[8] Notice that certain scenes are part of more than one subset; these scenes function as a bridge to link the subsets together and thus help the conversation to flow from idea to idea.

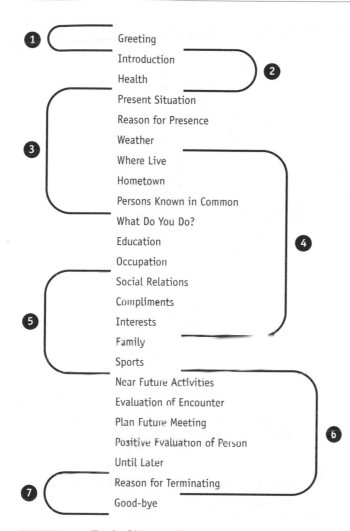

FIGURE 11.1   Typical interaction scenes.

Source: Kathy Kellermann, "The Conversation MOP: II. Progression through Scenes in Discourse," *Human Communication Research, 17* (1991), 388.

Conversations among people from other cultures have a similar structure. That is, a standard set of scenes or topics is used to initiate and maintain conversations, and the conversations flow from beginning to end in a more-or-less predictable pattern, which is typically understood and followed by the interactants. However, there are important differences in the ways the conversations of people from other cultures are organized and sequenced, including the types of topics discussed and the amount of time given to each one.

The actual topics in an interaction scene can vary widely from one culture to another. In Hong Kong, for instance, conversations among males often include inquiries about the other person's health and business affairs. In Denmark or the French portion of Belgium, questions about people's incomes are to be avoided. In Algeria, topics such as

CULTURE connections

On the way, Susan gave me a quick course in Vietnamese table manners. She said, "Don't leave your chopsticks sticking up in the rice bowl. That's a sign of death, like the joss sticks in the bowls in cemeteries and family altars. Also, everything is passed on platters. You have to try everything that's passed to you. If you empty a glass of wine or beer, they automatically refill it. Leave half a glass if you don't want any more."

"Sounds like South Boston."

"Listen up. The Vietnamese don't belch like the Chinese do to show they enjoyed the meal. They consider that crude, as we do."

"I don't consider belching crude. But then, I don't belong to the Junior League."

— Nelson DeMille

the weather, health, or the latest news are acceptable, but one would almost never inquire about female family members. In Ecuador and Chile, it is appropriate, almost obligatory, to inquire politely about the other person's family. Among Africans, a person is expected to inquire first about a person's well-being before making a request.

The amount of time, and therefore the extent of detail, that is given to each conversational topic may also vary from one culture to another. For example, an Asian colleague who was working in the United States was asked one Monday morning, "What did you do over the weekend?" He began on Friday evening and listed every event that had taken place over the past two days. It was far more information than his polite U.S. American colleague wanted to know, and she spread the word around the office: "Never ask what he did on his time off!"[9] It is well known that European Americans like to get down to business in their conversations and will typically avoid elaborate sequences of small talk. Social and business conversations among the Saudis and Kuwaitis, on the other hand, will include far more elaborate greeting rituals, some phrases actually being repeated several times before the conversation moves on to subsequent sequences. Similarly, when Africans meet, they typically inquire extensively about the health and welfare of each other's parents, relatives, and family members. Although the Japanese do not typically repeat words or phrases, they also prefer to spend considerably more time in the "getting to know you" phase of social conversations.

Difficulties can arise in intercultural interactions when the participants differ in their expectations. At a predominantly African American university in Washington, D.C., for example, an encounter took place between an African American student; African students from Tanzania, Nigeria, and Kenya; and Caribbean students from Jamaica, Trinidad, and Tobago. The African American student, who did not share the others' expectations about the need for elaborate greeting rituals before making a simple request, walked into the graduate assistant's office to inquire about the time. "Hi! Does anyone know what time it is?" he asked, without any formal greetings. No one responded. After a few moments, he repeated his question, apparently frustrated. The African and Caribbean students looked up but continued with their work without responding. At this point the Nigerian student, who realized that the problems were due to incompatible expectations, responded to the

CULTURE connections

Simi and Vivek enter a little pavilion and sit with the *pundit*. Everyone ignores the actual ceremony, except we foreigners. After a lot more chanting, ululating, conch-blowing and feet-touching, Simi and Vivek are tied together to circle a sacred fire seven times. Each circle is accompanied by its own mantra—mostly all to protect the husband. Vivek places red powder on Simi's central hair parting to mark her as a married woman, and we surround them and throw red rose petals.

—Sarah Macdonald

first student's question. The student thanked him and left the room. When the African American had gone, the other students wondered aloud why the Nigerian had answered the question. "He has no respect," one of them remarked. "How could he walk into the room and ask about the time without greeting anyone?" another argued. Interestingly, both the African American and the other students were simply attempting to conform to their own expectations about the appropriate behaviors in an interaction scene involving strangers who are making requests.

Interaction Contexts   Interaction contexts are the settings or situations within which social episodes occur. Contexts impose a "frame" or reference point around communication experiences by helping people to determine what specific actions should mean, what behaviors are to be expected, and how to act appropriately and effectively in a particular interaction.

Contexts for Intercultural Communication

U.S. Americans are increasingly being asked to participate in social episodes within three specific contexts that we would like to highlight: health care, education, and business. Each provides an important and recurring meeting ground where people from many cultures converge and interact. We now describe in greater detail the particular importance and challenge of these three contexts.

The Health Care Context

In Chapter 1 we indicated that the need for intercultural competence arises, in part, because of the increased cultural mixing that has occurred across national boundaries and within the United States itself. The health care context affects doctors, nurses, counselors, and health care workers, as well as patients, families, communities, and cultural groups. Within the health care setting, there are often multiple cultures represented among those who are the medical providers, others who work in the setting, and still others who benefit from the services provided.[10] The consequences to human life and suffering from a lack of intercultural competence in the health care context should be obvious.

CULTURE connections

I gave birth in a Manila hospital to the son we had planned to call Martin, who died a few hours later. For me, the death of my baby was something that should not have happened, unthinkable, unbearable. But for the gentle Filipina nurses, the loss was sad but part of life, bound to happen from time to time. Their sympathy was firmly mixed with a cheerful certainty that I would be back next year with another one—as so many women are in the Philippines, whether the infant lives or dies.

It was our good fortune that my time in the village had allowed me to observe and compare responses to death. On the afternoon of Martin's birth, I described to Barkev the way Filipinos would express their sympathy. Don't expect to be left alone, I said, and don't expect people tactfully to avoid the subject. Expect friends to seek us out and to show their concern by asking specific factual questions. Rather than a euphemistic handling of the event and a denial of the ordinary course of life, we should be ready for the opposite. An American colleague of my husband might shake hands, nod his head sadly, perhaps murmuring, "We were so sorry to hear," and beat a swift retreat; a Filipino friend would say, "It was so sad that your baby died. Did you see him? Who did he look like? Was he baptized? How much did he weigh? How long were you in labor?"

Stereotypes often conceal their opposites. In other contexts Filipinos describe Americans as "brutally frank," while Americans find Filipinos frustratingly indirect and evasive. Yet in the handling of death, Filipinos behave in a manner which Americans might characterize as "brutally frank" and seem to go out of their way to evoke the expression of emotion, while Americans can only be called euphemistic and indirect, going to great lengths to avoid emotional outbreaks.

—*Mary Catherine Bateson*

Communication scholars have begun to study the specific characteristics of the intercultural health care context in an effort to improve communication competence.[11] Similarly, health care professionals have responded to the intercultural imperative by including courses that are designed to increase intercultural communication skills within their professional training and development programs. In fact, health care professionals are increasingly educated and trained with the goal of improving their intercultural competence. The elements of intercultural competence on which we focus— one's knowledge, motivations, and skilled actions—are repeatedly identified as essential to the health care professional seeking to provide the best health care.[12] The nursing profession, for instance, has developed a specialization in "transcultural nursing" and has a well-established professional organization, the Transcultural Nursing Society.[13] Textbooks, training materials, and studies of the competence of students and faculty alike are now common within nursing education settings, and courses in transcultural nursing are standard offerings in many nursing degree programs.[14] Resource materials are now available to assist all health care providers as they interact with people representing a range of cultural backgrounds.[15] Indeed, as a prerequisite to their certification, many health care providers are asked to demonstrate their competence in interacting with diverse cultural groups.[16] This increased emphasis on intercultural competence extends to mental health professionals,[17] speech language therapists,[18] and even occupational therapists.[19]

■ A multicultural medical team meets to discuss their patients' needs

Culture's Influence on the Health Care Context   Cultural patterns provide the lenses through which people come to understand their world. All participants in the health care context—the providers, the patients, their families, and the larger social world—draw from their own cultural patterns and expectations about what constitutes appropriate and effective medical care. These cultural patterns often lead to very clear expectations about the right and wrong ways to treat illnesses and help people—expectations that are not necessarily shared by those from other cultures. While scholars have offered several ways to conceptualize the systematic relationship of cultural patterns to health care, there is a remarkable similarity among their presentations. Three general approaches characterize beliefs about health that cultures might adopt to explain issues of illness and wellness: magico-religious or personalistic, holistic or naturalistic, and biomedical or Western.[20] These three approaches bear a strong resemblance to elements in the cultural patterns we described in Chapters 4 and 5.

In the magico-religious or personalistic approach, health and illness are closely linked to supernatural forces. Mystical powers, typically outside of human control, cause health and illness. A person's health is therefore at the mercy of these powerful forces for good or evil. Sometimes illnesses occur because of transgressions or improper actions; the restoration of health is thus a gift, or even a reward, for proper conduct. Within this approach, health and illness are usually seen as anchored in or related to the whole community rather than to a specific individual. The actions of one person, then, can dramatically affect others. Treatments for illnesses within this framework are directed toward soothing or removing problematic supernatural forces rather than toward changing something organic within the individual. Healers, who are best equipped to deal with both the spiritual and the physical worlds, perform such treatments. Some African cultures, for example, believe that demons and evil spirits cause illness.[21] Many Asian cultures also believe in the supernatural as an important source of illness.[22] Within the United States, cultural groups with many members who share such beliefs include various Latino and African American cultures.

In the **holistic or naturalistic approach**, humans desire to maintain a sense of harmony with the forces of nature. Illness is explained in systemic terms and occurs when organs in the body (such as the heart, spleen, lungs, liver, and kidneys) are out of balance with some aspect of nature. There is thus a great emphasis on the prevention of illness by maintaining a sense of balance and good health. Good health, however, means more than just an individual's biological functioning. Rather, it includes her or his relationship to the larger social, political, and environmental circumstances. Some diseases, for instance, are thought to be caused by external climatic elements such as wind, cold, heat, dampness, and dryness. Native Americans, for example, often define health in terms of a person's relationship to nature; health occurs if a person is in harmony with nature, whereas sickness occurs because a principle of nature has been violated. As Richard Dana suggests, "healing the cultural self for American Indians and Alaska Natives must be holistic to encompass mind, body, and spirit."[23] A common distinction within this approach is contrasting of both foods and diseases as either hot or cold. The classification of a disease as hot or as cold links it both to a diagnosis and to a treatment.[24] The ancient Chinese principle of yin and yang captures the essence of this distinction; everything in the universe is either positive or negative, cold or hot, light or dark, male or female, plus or minus, and so on, and people should have a harmonious balance between these opposing forces in their approach to all of life's issues.

In the **biomedical or Western approach**, people are thought to be controlled by biochemical forces. Consequently, objective, physical data are sought. Good health is achieved by knowing which biochemical reactions to set in motion. Disease occurs when a part of the body breaks down, resulting in illness or injury. Doctors and nurses, who fix the biochemical problem affecting the "broken part," thus making the body healthy again, provide treatments. This approach is closely linked to European American cultural patterns and has had a major influence on the development of the health care system in the United States. Indeed, the biomedical approach is so dominant within the United States that it is sometimes very difficult for individuals—providers and patients alike—to act competently in and adapt themselves to alternative cultural patterns.[25]

Often these approaches to health and health care will collide in an intercultural encounter. An example of the collision of the magico-religious approach with the Western approach occurred in a sixth-grade classroom when the teacher saw red marks on the neck and forehead of a Vietnamese student. The teacher suspected abuse, but the marks were caused by the student's parents, who had treated the student's cold by dipping a coin into oil and rubbing very hard until the coin turned the skin red. The parents believed that internal bad winds caused illness, and, by bringing the winds to the surface, a person can be healed of colds and upper respiratory problems. People from many Asian cultures hold similar beliefs.

Such health care clashes, often due to differing cultural patterns, highlight the impact of cultural differences on health care practices. An emergency room nurse, for example, took a call from a teenager whose father cut himself with an electric hedge trimmer and was bleeding heavily. Following a typical emergency room triage protocol, the nurse asked what the family was doing to treat the wound and learned that this Iranian family was treating it with honey, which they believed had the power to heal. After the family arrived at the emergency room, the nurse was surprised to see that the wound had already begun to close, and the bleeding had stopped.[26]

Family and Gender Roles in the Health Care Context The role of the individual patient, in contrast to the role of the family, is an important difference in the functioning of health care systems. The health care system in the United States typically focuses solely on the individual patient as the source of the medical problems in need of a cure. Yet many cultures in the United States are more collectivist and group-oriented, and this difference can be the basis for serious problems and misunderstandings. Cultures that value the community or the extended family, for instance, may influence people's willingness to keep important health care appointments. Navajo women, for example, who often give priority to family members' needs, have been known to forgo clinic appointments when someone from the extended family stops in to visit and ask for help.[27] Likewise, competent treatment for Latino patients may require the involvement and agreement of other family members, not just the patient.[28]

The responsibilities of family members in the health care context differ widely across cultures. Among the Amish communities in the United States, for example, the family includes a large, extended group, with adult members of the extended family having obligations and responsibilities to children other than their own biological ones. Hospital rules that give rights and responsibilities only to members of the immediate family pose challenges when an Amish child is hospitalized. The large number of people who expect to make lengthy visits to the child may prove difficult for the medical staff.[29] Similarly, when suggesting health care intervention strategies for Pacific Islanders and Hawaiians, experts recommend focusing on the entire family, rather than on just the identified patient, in order to be effective.[30]

In many cultures, health care providers are expected to talk about the nature of the illness and its prognosis with family members but not with the patient. It is the family members, not the patient, who are expected to make decisions about the nature of treatment.[31] Of course, intercultural difficulties may occur when the family's ideas about the appropriate course of treatment differ from those of the medical staff. A Latino teenager, for example, was hospitalized on an oncology unit. Problems occurred when his family took him home for a day but did not follow the medical rules for such visits. He ate forbidden foods, did not return to the hospital at the specified time, and generally did not follow other aspects of his treatment. The medical team was upset with the family because the patient suffered a setback. The parents, however, knew that their son had only a limited time to live and wanted him to be with his family and enjoy what little time he had.[32]

Many cultures have strong expectations about modesty, and expectations about bodily displays for women can make the medical examination itself a source of intercultural difficulties. In some cultures, for instance, role requirements governing appropriate behaviors for women do not permit undressing for an examination by male physicians or nurses. Among many Latina women, for example, there are strong social taboos against showing the body to others; disrobing for a medical examination may be embarrassing and difficult.[33] Similarly, Latina women are uncomfortable revealing personal information in the presence of sons and daughters who may accompany them to the medical appointment.

Cultural differences in the role requirements that restrict interaction between women and men may also require that the medical caregivers be sensitive to important differences in needs and expectations. For example, ten-year-old Ahmed was hospitalized with complications from an appendectomy, and his mother had planned to stay all night with him in his hospital room. She became very distressed when Patrick, another boy, was brought into the room as a patient; Patrick's father also wanted to stay with his son, but the appropriate role behavior for Ahmed's mother precludes interactions with men outside of her family. Fortunately, the hospital staff was sensitive to the cultural issues; they recognized the importance of the problem and moved Ahmed to a private room.[34]

Conversational Structures, Language, and Nonverbal Communication   Because of different interaction rules, the medical interview between caregiver and patient can be another source of intercultural communication problems. Latinos and Arabs, for example, may engage in extensive small talk before indicating their reasons for the medical interview. Interviews with Native Americans may be punctuated with extensive periods of silence. Medical interviewers may consider such small talk or silence a "waste of time" rather than a vital component of the person's cultural pattern that affects his or her comfort level and willingness to proceed with the interview.[35] Similarly, direct and explicit discussions with many Asians and Asian Americans may pose serious threats to their face, and the use of indirection or other face-saving strategies may be preferred.[36]

In many cultures, doctors are perceived as authority figures with whom one must agree in the face-to-face medical interview. A patient may know that he or she will not be able to follow a proposed treatment plan but may be reluctant to respond to the doctor in a way that might appear to be a challenge to the doctor's authority.[37] Similarly, individuals from cultures that see health care workers as authority figures will be reluctant to initiate interaction and ask questions.[38] Patients from individualistic and low-context cultures, for instance, often feel that it is very important to communicate verbally with their physicians, and they are therefore very motivated to do so. Conversely, patients from collectivistic and high-context cultures may be much more apprehensive about participation as a patient in their medical care, and they may therefore avoid conversing with their physicians during medical interviews.[39] Latinos, for example, may not want to provide direct answers to questions posed by the health care provider.[40]

A common challenge often arises because patients and medical care workers do not even speak the same language. Large urban hospitals and health care offices reflect the increasing multilingual characteristics of the United States. Interpreters often play a key role in allowing health care workers to communicate with patients.[41] Health care education programs offer nurses, doctors, and other health care professionals many pathways to improve their ability to interact with patients who primarily speak other languages.[42]

Ambiguities in the use of language can present additional difficulties in diagnosing and treating illnesses. Idiomatic language in the health care context can create misunderstandings, such as when a nurse indicated to a Chinese-born physician that a patient had "cold feet" about an upcoming surgery and the physician, seeking to rule out circulatory problems, ordered vascular tests.[43] Or consider the case of a nurse or pharmacist who instructs a patient to "take three pills a day at mealtime" and expects that the patient will take one pill at each of three meals. Patients who come from cultures that do not separate their day into three major mealtimes may instead take all three pills simultaneously at the

■ Because health care may require the display of and access to one's body in ways that are private and personal, cultural expectations about what behaviors are permitted or prohibited are particularly important in such settings.

one large meal that is eaten every day.[44] A misunderstanding with very serious ramifications happened to a nonnative speaker of English who had signed a consent form for a tubal ligation, or "having her tubes tied." The woman thought that "tied" meant that the procedure could be reversed should she later decide to have more children. Only the skilled intervention of an interculturally competent health care worker, who understood the ambiguity in the language and clearly explained to the woman the consequences of her decision, prevented a medical procedure that was not wanted.[45]

It is not just ambiguities in understanding and in translating the English language that challenges health care workers. The Spanish language, for example, which is used by several U.S. cultures, has many words and grammatical constructions that vary from one cultural group to another.[46] Such cases highlight problems of intercultural misunderstandings and the implications for "informed consent" in the intercultural health care context.

Nonverbal communication can also pose unique challenges in the health care context. Eye contact, for example, can have a multitude of meanings. Consider an interaction between a European American health care professional and a Nigerian patient. To the European American, direct eye contact is expected; when not given, individuals are often regarded as untrustworthy and disrespectful. To the Nigerian, who comes from a large power-distance culture, direct eye contact may be avoided to show respect. Similarly, the appropriate use of touch varies widely across cultures, and, therefore, health care professionals must adjust the use of touch as healing to be appropriate to the cultures of their patients. European Americans will touch the head of a child as a sign of friendliness, yet for some Southeast Asians such a gesture would be understood as an insult, since the head is the locus of one's soul.[47] Similar difficulties in the health care setting can arise for other aspects of nonverbal communication. As you reflect on these differences, you will understand the importance of intercultural competence.

The effective treatment of a patient's pain by the health care professional requires an ability to interpret the patient's nonverbal and verbal symbols so that a culturally appropriate medical intervention can occur. In many cultures, for instance, individuals are taught to be more stoic and circumspect in verbally identifying the severity of their pain. In other cultures, there is an expectation that one will use very emotional and dramatic terms to describe one's experience of pain.[48]

Intercultural Competence in the Health Care Context   Health care professionals assume a special responsibility in assuring that they understand their patients in order to treat them effectively. This responsibility requires a willingness to attempt to understand the cultural patterns—the beliefs, values, and interaction norms—of their patients. There are excellent reference books now available to health care professionals in which the general characteristics of various cultures are presented. However, in the health care context, as in all others, you must remember that each individual may or may not share the preferences of her or his cultural group.

The Educational Context

The U.S. educational system—from kindergarten to college and on through graduate school—increasingly requires competent intercultural communication skills from all of its participants. Because of the culturally diverse student populations throughout the U.S. educational system, people must give increased attention to the factors that students, parents, teachers, administrators, other educational professionals, and ordinary citizens face when challenged to communicate in the educational context.

Culture's Influence on the Educational Context   All participants in the educational context—teachers, students, parents, school administrators, and other staff—bring their cultures' beliefs, values, norms, and social practices with them. Differences in cultural backgrounds may produce developmental variations in children's cognitive, physical, and motor abilities, as well as in their language, social, and emotional maturity.[49]

Communication within a classroom, in the playground of an elementary school, or within a college dormitory is typically governed by a set of rules based within one cultural group. In the United States, the dominance of the patterns associated with the European American culture pervade the educational system, setting the expectations for teachers, administrators, and students about how to behave and learn effectively and appropriately.[50] Yet, for most teachers in U.S. schools, it is an everyday occurrence to have students who come from cultural backgrounds other than their own. The demographic profiles of students in U.S. schools routinely identify many who speak different languages at home and who come from a large range of cultures. As a student in high school, or now in college, we

CULTURE connections

Similarly, and perhaps not surprisingly, both my graduate students and many undergraduates in Rwanda and in Graz also struggled to find a voice in my classes, since most had encountered only traditional lectures in the past. I succeeded in getting them to express opinions contrary to the textbooks or ones even simply questioning my own assertions only by breaking them into small groups and assigning them a sort of "devil's advocacy" role that they found unusual and at first very uncomfortable (though one they soon approached with enthusiasm). Upon returning to the States, I noted again how our students are far more active participants in the classroom and are far less reticent at challenging the perspectives of their teachers and peers. While our students' knowledge base vis-à-vis world events may be thin in comparison to their European and African counterparts, their ability to engage critically with each other, with popular culture, and with the latest trends in technology and identity-political issues is much sharper.

—*Donald E. Hall*

The intercultural nature of classrooms, from elementary school through college, requires educators to adapt their approaches to teaching and learning.

anticipate that you may have already experienced classrooms of people from diverse cultural backgrounds. Alternatively, you may be a parent interacting within your children's school system. Students in intercultural communication classes may be preparing to teach in elementary or high schools. As the statistics presented in Chapter 1 demonstrate, many current teachers, and certainly most future teachers, will work in a setting that demands the knowledge, motivations, and skills of a competent intercultural communicator. In the words of Janet Bennett and Riikka Salonen, the U.S. campus today is "culturally complicated."[51]

For many students, attending school can itself be an intercultural experience. Elvira, for example, is a junior Filipina American student who, on a daily basis, crosses the cultural boundary from her Filipino home to her U.S. American high school. Although she attends regularly and receives very high grades, she is concerned that the school experiences cut her off from her sister and friends. Sonia, similarly, is a Mexican American high school student who is very popular with her Latina friends but consistently feels like an outsider at school. This makes it very difficult for her to be academically and socially successful in the educational context.[52]

Scholars in communication and education have begun to document the many ways that cultural differences can lead to dissimilarities in interpretations and expectations about competent behaviors for students and teachers. Problematic issues include differences in expectations concerning such classroom behaviors as the rules for participation and turn taking, discipline and control, and even pedagogical approaches such as lectures, group learning, and self-paced work. Intercultural problems also arise when parents and other family members attempt to communicate with various officials representing the school.

The Role of the Teacher   Recall from Chapter 4 that cultures differ in the ways they choose to define activities, social relations, the self, the world, and the passage of time. All of these choices can influence preferences for how students and teachers relate to each other in the classroom.[53]

Teachers have a unique and powerful influence on student interactions in the classroom and beyond. Consequently, classroom teachers have a potent effect on how well students from different cultures learn. Teachers come to the classroom carrying with them both their unique personality characteristics and the influences of their culture. Increasingly, scholars and practitioners in the United States and throughout the world are recognizing the unique challenges of multicultural classrooms, and substantial attention is now being given to ways that teachers can be more effective and appropriate—that is, more competent—in their adaptations to the learning styles that characterize the range of their students' cultures.

Teachers, then, have a particular responsibility to demonstrate intercultural communication competence. Often the first step for teachers is to become aware of cultural differences and then adapt when and how they approach their students. For example, an African American teacher of French, in what had been a predominantly European American East Coast suburban high school, described his experiences in teaching a changing, more multicultural student body:

> When I first found myself teaching classes of mostly black kids, I went home frustrated every night because I knew I wasn't getting through to them, and they were giving me a hard time. It only started getting better when I finally figured out that I had to reexamine everything I was doing.[54]

This teacher began by being aware of cultural differences and then changing his approach to teaching.[55] Students training to become teachers in the elementary and secondary schools in the United States now are routinely required to take courses to learn how to adapt their classroom teaching in ways that maximize learning for culturally diverse students.[56]

Those who prefer a more hierarchical relationship between individuals will structure the relationship between student and teacher with greater status differences. German instructors, for example, tend to be more formal, aloof, and socially distant than their U.S. counterparts.[57] Similarly, within many Asian and Asian American cultures, teachers are highly revered and respected. Students and parents would not openly and directly question the authority and statements of a teacher. Consider, for example, the types of communication messages and the proper role behaviors of students and teachers in Chinese classrooms. If you are familiar with U.S. classrooms, compare your experiences with the following:

> Students who are late for class should get the teacher's permission to enter the classroom. Even in college, students have to sit quietly in rows that face the teacher, listen attentively, and take careful notes. Students must also raise their hands and stand at attention when they answer or want to ask questions. Not raising a hand is a violation of classroom rules, and not standing up is a violation of the reverence rule.[58]

As this description conveys, the Chinese classroom is characterized by a high degree of formality. Many people from cultures with similar preferences for formality are shocked to find European American teachers with their penchant for informality. Many U.S. professors, for instance, encourage students to call them by their first names; while many students prefer such informality, some feel uncomfortable because it suggests disrespect.

Even a teacher's seemingly inconsequential personal preference has the potential to create discomfort among students and their parents, often without the teacher even knowing about it. One such example is of a woman who was considered one of the best English teachers in her school but who used red ink to address her notes of encouragement to the students. For Koreans, particularly Buddhists, the teacher's "insignificant" preference to write the students' names in red ink created enormous distress, because a Buddhist only writes people's names in red at their death or at the anniversary of their death.[59]

Classroom Interaction   Cultural characteristics also influence what is appropriate and effective communication within the classroom. That is, culture shapes what is considered to be desirable and undesirable classroom behaviors. From the expectations for students interacting with their teachers, to the manner in which they relate with one another, to the language and topics considered appropriate for teachers and students to discuss, to the overall structure of interaction within a classroom—culture affects perceptions of competent classroom interaction.

Students from collectivistic cultures are generally more accepting of messages about appropriate classroom behaviors and will comply with teachers' requests about classroom management.[60] Even the nature of teachers' persuasive messages differs across cultures. Chinese college teachers, for instance, appeal to the group in gaining student compliance, whereas European American teachers, with a cultural preference for individualism, stress the benefit to the specific student.[61] Within the classroom, the treatment of personal property is also influenced by the culture of the students, with "personal" items such as toys, books, and clothing perceived very differently in individualistic and in collectivistic cultures.[62]

Classroom discussion and participation also vary greatly across cultures. Donal Carbaugh, who studies how culture is displayed in people's conversations, makes a comparison between European American expectations for classroom interaction and those of the Blackfeet, one of the Native American tribes in the United States. These differences are displayed in Table 11.1. It is easy to imagine a classroom with a European American teacher and students from both cultures; the European American students would, in all likelihood, feel much more comfortable and would thus have a better learning experience.[63] Similarly, many Native American and Asian American students are unwilling to volunteer, speak out, or raise problems or concerns unless the teacher specifically calls on them by name. Korean students, for instance, are often unwilling to talk with their teachers even when the teachers have incorrectly calculated the students' scores on an exam.[64] Questions for clarification are rarely asked of the teacher directly; to do so might be regarded as a challenge to the teacher's authority and could threaten her or his face should the answer not be known.

Students from many cultures who go to school in the United States sometimes find it difficult to adapt to the verbal style expected of them. Conversely, when U.S. students study overseas, they often experience similar difficulties in understanding the cultural

TABLE 11.1   Blackfeet and European American Communication in a Classroom Setting

	Blackfeet	European American
Primary Mode	Silence	Speaking
Cultural Premise	Listener-active, interconnected	Speaker-active, constructive
Secondary Mode	Verbal speaking	Silence
Social Position	Differences by gender and age	Commonality, equality
Typical Speaker	Elder male	Citizen
Cultural Persona	Relational connection	Unique individual
Values	Nature, heritage, modesty, stability	Upward mobility, change, progress

Source: Adapted from Donal Carbaugh, *Cultures in Conversation* (Mahwah, NJ: Erlbaum, 2005), 92.

expectations related to the educational context.[65] Yet a willingness to speak in class is a communication characteristic highly valued by European American teachers and students, whose cultural framework celebrates individual achievement and responsibility. To students from cultures that emphasize the collective good and the maintenance of face, however, such behaviors in the classroom are too competitive, as they disrupt the group's harmony and separate people from one another. Native American fifth- and sixth-graders, for example, perceived their high-verbal teachers to have less competence in their oral delivery of messages.[66] Similarly, African American children, whose culture emphasizes the development of verbal skills and expressiveness, are often affected in their classroom interactions with their European American teachers:

> In both verbal and nonverbal language, they [African American children] are more theatrical, show greater emotion, and demonstrate faster responses and higher energy.... African-American speakers are more animated, more persuasive, and more active in the communication process. They often are perceived as confrontational because of this style. On the other hand, the school, and most Anglo-American teachers, are more oriented toward a passive style, which gives the impression that the communicator is somewhat detached, literal, and legalistic in use of the language. Most African-American students find this style distancing and dissuasive.[67]

Another example of cultural consequences on the learning environment can be seen in the research of Steven T. Mortenson, who found that, while both Chinese and U.S. American students responded to academic failure in similar ways, the Chinese students were less likely to express their concerns about academic failure to others and instead were more likely to experience physical illnesses.[68]

■ This typical elementary school classroom depicts the intercultural character of many schools across the United States.

Turn taking within the classroom is also governed by cultural expectations. Watch how teachers in your various classes regulate the flow of conversations and contributions. A teacher has a particular set of expectations about who speaks in the classroom as well as when and how to speak. Is it acceptable for students to talk among themselves? How loudly can they talk to each other? How long can private conversations continue before the teacher asks for them to stop? How do students get permission to speak in class? All of these classroom behaviors, which are crucial to how teachers evaluate their students and how students evaluate teachers and classroom environments, are grounded in cultural expectations.

Cultural patterns directly affect preferred ways to learn in the classroom. Think for a moment about the classroom experiences you have had. Did they encourage students to work cooperatively in groups? Or were classroom activities designed to encourage students to work alone, succeeding or failing on their individual merits? Latino children, whose culture teaches the importance of family and group identities, are more likely to value cooperativeness than competitiveness.[69] Because Native American cultural patterns emphasize the group, harmony with nature, and circularity, children from that culture often respond better to learning approaches that are noncompetitive, holistic, and cooperative.[70] European American children, in contrast, often prefer learning approaches that emphasize competition, discrete categories for information, and individual achievement.

Families and the Educational System   Another key set of relationships in which competent intercultural communication is essential is in the interaction of parents, and sometimes other family members, with school personnel, including teachers, administrators, and others. Consider the following examples of how parents from different cultural backgrounds with children in kindergarten classrooms interacted with their children and the classroom:

> In Ms. Nelson's kindergarten classroom, some of the Chinese-American mothers come to school every day at lunch time. They bring hot lunches and hand-feed their five year old children. In another kindergarten classroom, Mexican American mothers walk their children to school. When the bell rings they enter the classrooms with their children. They walk the children to their tables and help them take off their jackets. They hang their children's jackets and book bags on the hooks, generally located in the back of the room, before leaving the classroom. When parent-teacher conferences were held in early October, a European-American mother proudly told her child's teacher that Elizabeth could tie her own shoes when she was four years old.[71]

The range of differences in parental involvement with their children at this grade level indicates the wide range of meanings and expectations that parents from different cultures can have of teachers in one school and one classroom.

Because the value of education differs from one culture to another, the importance of a student's success in school will also vary. For Thais and Filipinos, for instance, education affects the entire family's status and social standing. By excelling in school, therefore, children bring honor to their families while preparing for future successes that will further enhance the family stature. Education is thus a family concern, rather than an individual achievement.[72]

Even the need for the customary parent–teacher conferences may not make much sense to parents from cultures in which there is no expectation that parents will play an active role in decisions about their children's education.[73] Many Middle Eastern parents, for instance, expect their children will do well in school. Thus, when the children actually do well, there is generally less overt praise or material reward than is common in the United States; children are doing what is expected of them. However, when children do not do well, parents may present a variety of attitudes including denial, blaming the school, blaming the child, and feeling ashamed.[74]

Similar expectations exist among many Asian and Asian American parents. A teacher's request for a routine conference, for example, may be met with a sense of skepticism or a deep concern that a disobedient child may have dishonored the family. Because of face-saving needs, the parents may even assume that the exact nature of this problem will not be stated explicitly but must be discerned through a clever analysis and interpretation of the teacher's subtle clues. The teacher's bland statements that their child behaves well are therefore regarded as merely a social politeness. Not wanting to heap unlimited praise on the child for fear of setting false expectations, the teacher may unwittingly provide the parents with just the sort of high-context hints and generalities about the child's faults and weaknesses that they will interpret as an indication of a deeper and more difficult problem in need of correction.

A poignant example of the consequences of differing cultural expectations, complicated by linguistic difficulties, is the story of Magdalena, a Mexican immigrant mother, and her son Fabian. Because Fabian was not behaving appropriately in the school, the school officials asked Magdalena to have Fabian evaluated by a professional. Concerned about Fabian and wanting to be responsive to the school's request, Magdalena took Fabian to see their family doctor. As the situation at the school became more negative, the teachers and administrators believed that Magdalena was ignoring the seriousness of the

CULTURE connections

In high school, I tried to emulate the five-paragraph essay. I was in honors and AP classes and always got A's, but I was never totally proficient like the other students in their writing. Grammar and usage was natural for them, but not for me. Remember, my first language was Spanish. I spoke Spanish at home to my parents and siblings, so I intermixed my sentence structures and rhetorical patterns. Oftentimes they'd see this as a deficiency. I wanted to go on tangents and use imagery, like my father did when he told his cuentos y historias. I wanted to incorporate my oral skills from my culture into the written text, but was not allowed to do so. I emulated this plastic voice until I went to college. And even then, only a select few teachers encouraged this form of writing.

This writing was the personal narrative. I learned to use personal narrative in my essays and short stories and incorporated personal narrative characteristics in my poetry. I had never been given this freedom. I had never been validated in this way. I wish I had been allowed to use personal narrative from day one of my second shot at first grade. I know I would be a more effective writer today.

—*Maria J. Estrada*

problem and was not responding to their request. Ultimately, Fabian was expelled from school.[75] As Jerry McClelland and Chen Chen conclude:

> The combination of the school's instructions, the interpreter's translation, and her comprehension of the message resulted in Magdalena not understanding that a counselor's report, rather than a physician's report, was being requested. Given the Mexican culture in which she grew up, Magdalena was puzzled by the message to have Fabian checked. Magdalena said that in Mexico, if there is a problem with a child, the teacher and parent talk to each other and do not bring in a third person to give an opinion.[76]

Intercultural Competence in the Educational Context   The challenge to develop one's intercultural competence and fulfill the promise that cultural diversity brings to the educational context is aptly summarized by Josina Macau. She suggests that creating a constructive learning environment in an age of cultural diversity requires that people be sensitive to different and sometimes competing experiences.[77]

The intercultural challenges of communicating in a different language, which we described in Chapters 7 and 9, are also prominent within the educational context. Increasingly, schools in the United States are finding it advantageous to translate the letters that are sent home to parents, so that immigrant parents are better able to learn about key school issues and events. Even then, the unique features of each language, the presence of colloquialisms, and the use of specialized terminology still present barriers for parents whose primary language is not U.S. English.[78]

The starting point for developing intercultural competence in the educational context is to understand one's own cultural background. It is particularly important that teachers and administrators recognize their culture's influence on expectations about how classrooms should operate and how students should behave. The stakes for developing intercultural competence in education are very high. Although the following example focuses on Native Americans, it is equally true of students from a variety of cultural backgrounds. It illustrates the importance of the educational context and the potential for both permanent and harmful consequences as a result of interactions within that context.

> When many young Native American children enter the classroom, they frequently find themselves in foreign environments where familiar words, values, and lifestyles are absent. As the classroom activities and language become increasingly different from the familiar home environment, the students suffer a loss of self-confidence and self-esteem, a loss that is sometimes irreparable.[79]

The Business Context

The business context is increasingly intercultural. Just as those working in or receiving services from the health care and educational contexts must look to the development of competent intercultural communication, intercultural competence in our work lives is a critical asset.[80] Commerce and trade are global and affect us daily. Indeed, bookstores now regularly stock reference materials that provide insights into specific cultures and suggest some of the dos and don'ts of conducting business with individuals from those cultures.[81] Just look at your possessions and you will see ample evidence of the products that have crossed national and cultural boundaries. People, however, are the key ingredients in the intercultural business world.

Throughout most of your working life, you will likely be within an intercultural business context; some of your customers, coworkers, supervisors, and subordinates will come from cultures that differ from your own. Many organizations today include people who were born in one country, educated in another, and working in yet another. Many projects—by architects, engineers, business people, medical personnel, financial managers, and others—are done in one country during their daytime and electronically transmitted across the globe for work during the daytime of another culture's workforce. Intercultural communication in the business context is also increased by the availability of easy, fast, and inexpensive communication. Employees of multinational business organizations are now able to conduct their work using email, chat boards, and verbal interaction over various Internet services. Similarly, most of the major cities in the world can be reached within a day or two; these technological innovations make communication quick and sometimes inexpensive, but they also can be potentially problematic because of intercultural differences.

Many businesspeople are inadequately prepared for an intercultural assignment; in one study, for instance, up to 20 percent of U.S. managers on temporary international assignments failed to adjust adequately and returned home prematurely.[82] The underlying problem, experts agree, is top management's ethnocentricity and its corresponding failure to provide adequate preparation and rewards for these intercultural assignments.[83] A compounding problem is that, too often, graduates from U.S. universities lack the "basic skills they need to be globally competent professionals."[84] Consequently, some U.S.-based multinational firms are hesitant to send these employees abroad, preferring instead to use U.S.-trained international students or in-country locals who have international experience.

Culture's Influence on the Business Context   The discussion of cultural patterns in Chapters 4 and 5 is particularly useful in understanding culture's influence on the business context. Differences in cultural patterns create widely dissimilar expectations for how a business is structured and what is considered appropriate and effective—and therefore successful—communication within that business. Chapter 5 described the GLOBE research on the dimensions of cultural patterns, which directly apply to business organizations around the world. The GLOBE researchers developed their empirically based conclusions by surveying people who work in organizations, thus giving us great insight into the expectations for behavior in the world's businesses. While all of the dimensions described are useful for understanding issues in the intercultural business context, our discussion will highlight differences in business practices that are related to in-group collectivism, which is commonly described as the individualism–collectivism dimension.

Cultural variations in people's relationships to their organizations are important in understanding the intercultural business context. Is the critical unit of analysis and of human action the individual or the group? Specific areas of intercultural business that are associated with variations in individualism–collectivism include the following:

- *Who speaks for the organization?* In organizations within individualistic cultures, a single person may represent a company in its negotiations. In collectivistic cultures, a group of representatives would likely be involved in negotiations.

■ Work settings are increasingly culturally diverse, providing opportunities to improve intercultural competence.

■ *Who decides for the organization?* Organizations within individualistic cultures likely empower their negotiators to make decisions that are binding on the company. Such decisions are often made rapidly and without consultation from the home office once the negotiations have begun. Organizations within collectivistic cultures often require extensive consultations among the delegation members and with the home office at each step in the negotiation process, as no single individual has the exclusive power for decision making.

■ *What motivates people to work?* Do people work because they are motivated by the possibility of individual rewards, as is common in individualistic cultures, or is group support and solidarity with one's colleagues a primary motivator? Reward systems to encourage employees' best efforts vary widely. In Mexico, for instance, though the individual is valued, rewards for independent actions and individual achievements that are successful with U.S. Americans may not be strong motivators. Thus, production contests and "employee of the month" designations to encourage Mexican employees are often unsuccessful.[85]

■ *What is the basis for business relationships?* In collectivistic cultures, it is vital that businesspeople establish cordial interpersonal relationships and maintain them over time. The assumption that it is possible to have a brief social exchange that will produce the degree of understanding necessary to establish a business agreement is simply incorrect. In many African cultures, for example, friendship takes precedence over business. Similarly, most Middle Easterners extend their preference for sociability to business meetings, where schedules are looser and the first encounter is only for getting acquainted and not for business.[86] A similar regard for establishing social relationships as a prelude to doing business is also common in China and Korea.[87] Indeed, the very notion of trustworthiness differs across intercultural business relationships, with individualistic cultures often emphasizing personal integrity in judging another's trustworthiness while collectivistic cultures emphasize one's commitment to the group or the organization.[88]

In Korea, the most important concept when doing business, and indeed the most important concern for all Korean interpersonal relationships, is that of *kibun*. *Kibun* refers to an individual's personal harmony, pleasurable inner feelings, positive state of mind, sense of pride, and dignity. In Korean relationships, keeping *kibun* in good order takes precedence over virtually all other considerations. In the business context, people must maintain a harmonious atmosphere that enhances the *kibun* of all, for to damage people's *kibun* may irreparably damage interpersonal relationships and create lifelong enemies.[89] Koreans believe that maintaining *kibun* is more important than attaining immediate goals, accomplishing task-related objectives, or telling the absolute truth. That is,

> *Kibun* enters into every aspect of Korean life. Knowing how to judge the state of other people's *kibun*, how to avoid hurting it, and keeping your own *kibun* in a satisfactory state are important skills.... For example, a Korean's *kibun* is damaged when his subordinate does not show proper respect, that is, by not bowing soon enough, not using honorific words, not contacting the superior within an appropriate period of time, or worse, handing something to him with the left hand. Most of these rules of etiquette are well known to Koreans, and while they are often difficult or cumbersome to remember, they must be heeded to avoid hurting *kibun*.[90]

Another scholar-practitioner who has studied the impact of cultural patterns on communication competence in the intercultural workforce is Fons Trompenaars.[91] After many years of studying companies around the globe, Trompenaars identified the cultural dimension of universalism–particularism as especially useful in understanding how business practices vary because of culture. Universalistic cultures prefer to make business decisions based on a consistent application of rules, whereas particularistic cultures choose instead to adapt the rules to specific circumstances and relationships. William B. Gudykunst and Yuko Matsumoto indicate that universalism–particularism is related to the individualism–collectivism dimension. They suggest that businesspeople from individualistic cultures tend to be universalistic and apply the same value standards to all, whereas those from collectivistic cultures tend to be particularistic and apply different value standards to ingroups and outgroups.[92] Some features of the impact of this variation on the conduct of international business include the following:

- *What is the meaning of a contract?* Someone from a universalistic culture may view the signed contract as binding on all, whereas someone from a particularistic culture may view the contract as valid only if the circumstances remain unchanged, which may include whether the person who signed the contract is still part of his or her company. For example, the Chinese concept of legal or contractual agreements differs from the U.S. concept. In the United States, of course, a business contract is binding and should be implemented precisely as agreed. In China, however, contracts are regarded more as statements of intent rather than as promises of performance. Therefore, they are binding only if the circumstances and conditions that were in effect when the contract was signed are still present when the contract should be implemented.[93]
- *Are job evaluations conducted uniformly or adapted to specific individuals?* Within universalistic cultures, all individuals in similar jobs are evaluated using

standardized criteria. Within particularistic cultures, the performance criteria depend upon people's relationships with others and their standing within the organization.

■ *Are corporate office directives typically heeded or circumvented?* In universalistic cultures, directives from corporate headquarters are valued and are heeded throughout the organization. In particularistic cultures, such directives are often ignored or circumvented because they don't apply to the particular circumstances of a specific subsidiary or branch office.

Just as in the educational and health care contexts, every element of the business context can be influenced by culture. In the remainder of this section, we first consider the important functions of business negotiations and conducting business deals. We next focus on the interpersonal work environment of intercultural teams. Finally, we look at cultural differences in conversational structure, in language, and in nonverbal communication that influence the business context. Though we separate these topics for ease of discussion, we do want to remind you that, in actual communication in the business context, their impact on culture forms an interconnected whole that can not be understood as a set of unrelated parts.

Business Negotiation and Deal Making   In the business context, the core activity of much intercultural communication involves conducting negotiations to make a business deal. These interactions occur on behalf of large multinational corporations that are discussing multibillion dollar contracts, to the small business owners who want something manufactured in another country, to salespeople who are selling products to people who are culturally different from themselves.

■ Conducting business among intercultural teams can be both challenging and rewarding.

Cultures differ in the preferred flow or pacing of business negotiations. In the initial stages of a negotiation, for example, German business managers may ask numerous questions about technical details. In Scandinavia, there is a great deal of initial frankness and a desire to get right down to business. Among the French, however, the early emphasis is on laying out all aspects of the potential deal. In contrast, many Italian and Asian managers may use these same initial stages to get to know the other person by talking about subjects other than the business deal. Likewise, preliminaries in Spain may take several days.[94] Similarly, problems often characterize Mexican and U.S. American negotiations, which arise from a greater emphasis on relational concerns by Mexican negotiators and on task behaviors by U.S. negotiators.[95] Many Africans also want a friendship to be established before doing business.[96]

In the United States and in other Western countries, where individual achievement is valued, advancements occur because of one's accomplishments, there is a shorter-term and results-oriented approach to negotiating, and a high priority is placed on getting the job done and accomplishing task-related objectives. Interpersonal communication is typically direct, confrontational, face-to-face, and informal. Negotiating teams are willing to make decisions and concessions in the public negotiation setting, where individuals within the team may disagree publicly with one another. One individual is usually given the authority to make decisions that are binding on all.[97] Romanians, though, prefer a negotiation style that is indirect and does not address issues straightforwardly. For Romanians, U.S. Americans often appear too confrontational and aggressive.[98] Among the Japanese, however, who value group loyalty and age, advancement is based on seniority, there is a longer term approach to negotiating, and the formation and nurturance of longer lasting business relationships are extremely important. Interpersonal communication is likely to be indirect, conciliatory in tone, and formal. Often an intermediary is used, the real decision making occurs privately and away from the actual negotiations, the negotiating teams make group decisions, and all team members are expected to present a united front. Such differences may lead to difficulties and to failure for the unwary. Consider the attempts of a U.S. businessman trying to negotiate an important deal in India:

> Joel, in his frustration, tried to speed up matters, as a lot more issues had to be addressed, but the Indians felt that he was only interested in finalizing and implementing the deal. They also began to question his intelligence, abilities, and sincerity. His informal way of addressing them also made them uncomfortable and not respected. All in all, they didn't really trust him or the deal he was proposing.[99]

Table 11.2 provides additional examples of some of the key differences in ways of thinking and in expectations for business negotiations across five cultures.

Cultural differences in business practices are also evident in the use of interpersonal relationships for strategic purposes. In Colombia and other Latin American countries, for example, achieving objectives by using interpersonal connections to obtain jobs, contracts, supplies, and other contacts—that is, giving and receiving personal favors to create an interdependent network of relationships—is regarded very positively.[100] Similar customs exist in India and elsewhere. While not as widespread throughout the multicultural U.S. workplace, such practices as providing emotional support to fellow workers, and thereby building informal social networks that can be used strategically to circumvent the bureaucracy, is a common practice.[101]

TABLE 11.2	**Business negotiation in five countries**				
Dimension	Finland	India	Mexico	Turkey	United States
Goal: contract or relationship		Business in India is personal, establish relationships	Mexicans seek long-term relationships	Establish relationships before negotiating	Establish rapport quickly; then move to negotiating
Attitude: win/lose or win/win			Mexicans have a win-win attitude		Look for mutual gains, whenever possible
Personal style: informal or formal		Negotiations follow formal procedures, but the atmosphere is friendly and relaxed	Established etiquette must be followed		Americans do not like formality or rituals in business interaction
Communication: direct or indirect	Finns are direct	"No" is harsh. Evasive refusals are common and more polite	Mexican negotiators may seem indirect and avoid saying "no"	Politeness is important	Be direct and to the point
Time sensitivity: high or low	Finns begin business right away, without small talk. It is not appropriate to be late	Indians conduct business at a leisurely pace. "Time-is-money" is an alien concept	The business atmosphere is easy going	Do not expect to get right down to business. The pace of meetings and negotiations is slow	US negotiators expect quick decisions and solutions
Emotionalism: high or low	Use objective facts, rather than subjective feelings. Serious and reserved	Facts are less persuasive than feelings	Truth is based on feelings. Emotional arguments are more effective than logic	Turks show emotion. Feelings carry more weight than objective facts	Subjective feelings are not considered "facts." Points are made by accumulating facts
Team organization: one leader or consensus	Individuals are responsible for decisions	Decisions will be made at the top	Authority is vested in a few at the top. Mexicans prefer consensus		Individuals with relevant knowledge and skills make decisions
Risk taking: high or low		Indians take risks	Mexicans avoid risk	Turks take risks	

Source: Lynn E. Metcalf, Allan Bird, Mahesh Shankarmahesh, Zeynep Aycan, Jorma Larimo, and Di'dimo Dewar Valdelamar, "Cultural Tendencies in Negotiation: A Comparison of Finland, India, Mexico, Turkey, and the United States," *Journal of World Business* 41 (2006): 382–394.

CULTURE connections

From the U.K. about South Korea:

I work for a company that has a subsidiary in Korea, so I go there quite frequently on business. I have a good relationship with a highly esteemed Korean manager who has worked for us for many years. We now need to find a local firm to supply a component, and this manager has strongly recommended his brother's company. I am rather wary about this and feel that this manager has put me in an awkward position. I don't want to lay myself open to accusations of favoritism or even corruption. Anyway, I am going to put the job out to bid, but feel that by doing so I am risking creating ill feeling within my own company.

In South Korea loyalty to one's family is a duty, and your manager would be failing in his duty if he did not try to help his brother win the order. On the other hand, he appears to be a loyal member of your company too, and may genuinely feel that his brother's company is likely to be your best supplier. Certainly personal relationships can facilitate business wherever in the world you find yourself, and in Eastern Asia knowledge of someone's background and family is seen as providing a form of guarantee of their personal commitment to your business. Naturally you should listen to what other companies have to offer, but be prepared to spend time in discussions with the company your manager recommended. It would be silly to exclude the best contender because of an exaggerated sense of fairness, and certainly most Indians, East Asians, and Latin Americans would find such a decision totally incomprehensible.

—*From a letter to Gwyneth Olofsson*

The importance and value of social hierarchy and face maintenance is illustrated by many Chinese businesses. Chinese businesspeople will likely have to check with their superiors before making any real decisions. In Chinese organizations, superiors are expected to participate in many decisions that U.S. managers might routinely delegate to subordinates. The Chinese process of consulting the next higher level in the hierarchy often continues up the bureaucratic ladder to the very top of the organization. Thus, the autonomy that is expected and rewarded in the United States may be regarded as insubordination in China.[102] Likewise, while decisions to approve or reject specific requests or proposals may be communicated clearly by Chinese managers, justifications for such decisions are often vague or omitted in an effort to protect the face of the employees. In a business negotiation involving Chinese and U.S. Americans, therefore, attempts by the U.S. team to insist on explanations for Chinese decisions may communicate a lack of respect and a failure to acknowledge the Chinese attempts at face maintenance.

Intercultural competence is required for successful business transactions within the intercultural United States. Consider the circumstances of Ms. Youngson, the head of a corporate sales division, who sent her sales representatives to the Chinese and Korean merchants in her city. She had a competent sales crew, she thought, but they were remarkably unsuccessful. Finally, out of desperation, she sent her team to a training workshop designed to help them understand the needs of Asian customers. They discovered numerous cultural errors in their sales approach, including the most grievous error of focusing on the business of the sale too quickly, rather than going through steps to establish a trusting relationship. The sales representatives also learned not to sit unless they were invited to do so, and they were trained not to put their materials on the desk or even to lean on it.[103]

Even when negotiations have been successful, cultural variations in common social practices can cause problems. Consider the experience of Richard, who works for a U.S. company that ships refrigerated containers to Asia. Richard's company uses a yellow marker to indicate that the product has passed inspection. This makes Chinese customers suspicious of the quality of the products, since Chinese manufacturers use yellow to signify a defective product.[104]

Conversational Structure, Language, and Nonverbal Communication We began this chapter by describing the many social episodes that form much of the social interaction of our lives. The business context has many social episodes enacted with rules derived from various aspects of culture. Something seemingly as simple as the exchange of business cards can set the tone for subsequent business relationships. Many U.S. businesspeople simply take the business cards offered to them and, after a perfunctory glance, tuck them away; in most Asian cultures, however, the exchange of business cards requires a more involved ritual in which the cards are examined carefully upon their receipt.

The ease of international telecommunications brings businesspeople from around the globe into interactions using the common communication episode of "making an introductory telephone call." Yet something as straightforward as the protocol for a common telephone call is shaped by the many differences that one's culture creates. Variations in the purposes of telephone calls, their degree of formality, the expectations about appropriate opening and closing remarks, and the anticipated length of the conversation all present intricate choices for achieving intercultural communication competence.[105] In India, for example, call center workers have had to receive extensive intercultural training to deal with irate U.S. callers. The U.S. Americans

> often wanted a better deal or an impossibly swift resolution, and were aggressive and sometimes abrasive about saying so. The Indians responded according to their deepest natures: They were silent when they didn't understand, and they often committed to more than they could deliver. They would tell the Americans that someone would get back to them tomorrow to check on their problems, and no one would.[106]

As part of their training, the Indian workers watched *Friends* and *Ally McBeal* to get an initial grounding in U.S. interaction patterns. Then they were taught how to begin conversations, how to end them, how to express empathy, and—however unnatural it might feel—how to be assertive.

Many books are now available to help people navigate a world in which intercultural business contacts are increasing because of modern communication technologies such as fax machines, emails, and telephone conversations. These books provide specific tips on conducting business in the intercultural business context.[107]

How language is used in business contexts is also highly influenced by culture. There is, for example, much more formality used by French-speaking Canadians than by English-speaking Canadians.[108] Mexican businesspeople are likely to use persuasive arguments that, from the perspective of many U.S. Americans, may seem "overly dramatic."[109] Differences in role expectations and in the rules for interactions between Japanese and U.S. American businesspeople are not confined to meetings that take place in Japan, nor are they limited to negotiations among teams from different organizations. Young Yun Kim and Sheryl Paulk found that communication problems and misunderstandings occurred within a Japanese-owned company in the United States because of the Japanese preference for indirectness and the U.S. American preference for directness.[110] Indonesians similarly prefer a high level of indirectness in business contexts.[111]

Specific aspects of differences in nonverbal communication also pose challenges in the business context. The United States, England, China, France, Japan, and Germany all operate with an expectation of punctuality. In Germany, being even two or three minutes late is considered insulting.[112]

Nonverbal behaviors such as smiling, head nodding, and silence also differ across cultures, and competent business practices require an understanding of these distinctions. As Roong Sriussadapron describes,

> When an expatriate supervisor assigned a task to a Thai local employee, the Thai employee smiled, nodded his head, and said nothing. The expatriate supervisor thought that his assignment would be accomplished by his Thai subordinate without any problem while his Thai subordinate had made no commitment. In fact, he only acknowledged that he would try his best and keep working with no deadline unless he was clearly notified.... Culturally speaking, Thais usually do not refuse someone immediately when they are asked to do something. Thai employees rarely voice refusal to work, especially with their supervisors, even though they feel unwilling, unable, or unavailable.[113]

Touching, conversational distances, and eye contact also vary in their appropriate use. In India, men routinely hold hands as a sign of friendship and not of sexual interest; this challenges U.S. American and European managers, who interpret the nonverbal behavior quite differently.[114] Eye contact with Saudi Arabians can also become problematic for those from the United States or from some European cultures, because the Saudis do not engage in direct eye contact but rather sit much closer to those with whom they are interacting.[115]

Even the seating arrangements and protocol during many business negotiations are highly prescribed. Among the Japanese, tables are never round in such business settings, and the expression "head of the table" is meaningless. Contrary to the usual practice in the United States, the power seat is not necessarily occupied by the most senior person present. Rather, whoever is most knowledgeable about the specific discussion topic takes the power seat and is designated as the company's official spokesperson for this aspect of the negotiations. At the conclusion of the business meeting, ritualistic thank-you's are uttered while all are still seated, both sides arise simultaneously and begin bowing, and the power person from the host company is expected to stay with the "guests" until they are outside the premises and are able to depart.[116]

Intercultural Teams   The reality of the workforce and how business is conducted globally in today's world means that many individuals now work in intercultural teams. This puts a premium on those individuals who have the knowledge, motivation, and skills to become interculturally competent. Individuals now work with others from multiple cultural backgrounds. Sometimes those teams are within their own business organization and located within one office or geographic space, while, at other times, the members of their work teams are spread across the globe in different countries and different time zones. Supervisors increasingly have teams of people who are from different cultures and who work in different countries. One of the challenges for intercultural communication in today's business context is developing intercultural competence in multicultural teams. Consider, for example, managing differences seemingly as small as preferences for email versus chat and discussion boards within intercultural teams. In one study of U.S. students and German students, Elizabeth Gareis found that the U.S. students preferred email, while the German students preferred discussion boards.[117]

Intercultural teams must accomplish their tasks and work objectives, at times despite the absence of a common language with which to communicate. A recent study of intercultural teams within European organizations documents the importance of intercultural competence in language use. The findings suggest that team members often switch from one language to another in their attempts to be understood, that they pay extra attention to clarifying their ideas and explaining their thoughts as a means of reducing linguistic misunderstandings, and that English was the language most often used by these intercultural teams.[118]

Corinne Rosenberg describes a "culturally challenged" work team of a U.S. multinational corporation that was located in Europe, serviced a geographic area that included parts of Africa and the Middle East, and reported to supervisors and colleagues in the United States. These work teams were replete with cultural misunderstandings and ineffective intercultural communication. Managers of these teams who were involved in email exchanges and conference calls ignored the reality of time-zone differences. Cultural differences in communication style also contributed to the team's ineffectiveness. British members, whose style was less direct and more reticent, felt undervalued. To adjust to the multicultural team environment, these British team members had to learn to adapt their communication style without feeling that they had given up their own cultural mannerisms.[119]

Work roles also differ across cultures. Among the Japanese, work roles are an extension of the family hierarchy. That is,

> presidents are "family heads," executives "wise uncles," managers "hard-working big brothers," workers "obedient and loyal children." American workers employed in Japanese-managed companies do not see themselves as "loyal and obedient children" and instead hold traditional American values of individualism, competitiveness, and social mobility.[120]

Another area in which cultural differences affect the business context is in gender expectations. Cultures differ in their prescriptive roles for men and women, and in many cultures women are unlikely to have managerial or supervisory positions in business. Women from the United States may have to make careful adjustments to be interculturally competent in the business setting.[121]

Expectations about the "proper" way to conduct employee performance appraisals and provide a rationale for judgments and actions are another source of cultural differences. For example, Chinese managers do not provide their subordinates with the detailed performance appraisals that are customary in many U.S. firms. Feedback on failures and mistakes is often withheld, which allows subordinates to save face and maintain their sense of esteem for future tasks within the organization.[122] Philip Harris, Robert Moran, and Sarah Moran describe some important differences in the way one conducts competent performance appraisals in the United States, Saudi Arabia, and Japan. In the United States, performance appraisals are meant to be objective and are given in a direct style, typically in writing, and the employee is often expected to provide a written rebuttal. In Saudi Arabia, the interpersonal relationship is the basis for the appraisal; the appraisal is given indirectly and is not put in writing, but a Saudi will retreat if there is negativity implied. In Japan, the basis of the appraisal is a combination of objective and subjective; it is presented in writing, includes a high degree of formality but with criticisms very subtly presented, and it is rare for the employee to disagree.

Intercultural Competence in the Business Context   What kinds of knowledge, motivations, and skills constitute "competence" in the business context? The very nature of competence itself may differ across cultures. That is, cultures often can hold fundamentally different expectations about how competence ought to be displayed. Compare, for example, the organizations with which you are familiar to the typical Thai organization. In Thai companies, people are perceived as communicatively competent only if they know how to avoid conflict with others, can control their emotional displays (both positive and negative), can use polite forms of address when talking to others, and can demonstrate respect, tactfulness, and modesty in their behaviors.[123]

CULTURE connections

When you are walking down the road in Bali and you pass a stranger, the very first question he or she will ask you is, "Where are you going?" The second question is, "Where are you coming from?" To a Westerner, this can seem like a rather invasive inquiry from a perfect stranger, but they're just trying to get an orientation on you, trying to insert you into the grid for the purposes of security and comfort. If you tell them that you don't know where you're going, or that you're just wandering about randomly, you might instigate a bit of distress in the heart of your new Balinese friend. It's far better to pick some kind of specific direction—*anywhere*—just so everybody feels better.

The third question a Balinese will almost certainly ask you is, "Are you married?" Again, it's a positioning and orienting inquiry. It's necessary for them to know this, to make sure that you are completely in order in your life. They really want you to say yes. It's such a relief to them when you say yes. If you're single, it's better not to say so directly. And I really recommend that you not mention your divorce at all, if you happen to have had one. It just makes the Balinese so worried. The only thing your solitude proves to them is your perilous dislocation from the grid. If you are a single woman traveling through Bali and somebody asks you, "Are you married?" the best possible answer is: "Not yet." This is a polite way of saying, "No," while indicating your optimistic intentions to get that taken care of just as soon as you can.

Even if you are eighty years old, or a lesbian, or a strident feminist, or a nun, or an eighty-year-old strident feminist lesbian nun who has never been married and never intends to get married, the politest possible answer is still: "Not yet."

—*Elizabeth Gilbert*

As the workforce has become more culturally diverse, scholars and practitioners have tried to provide managers and their employees with the tools to work together successfully. Many managers now receive ongoing training about diversity issues, and company employees are often given similar opportunities to improve their knowledge, motivation, and skills. Most people recognize that the cultural heterogeneity of the workforce brings with it special challenges and opportunities, both for companies and for the individuals who work in them.[124] Work teams that are culturally diverse, for example, are often more innovative and creative than are culturally homogeneous work groups,[125] but only if the team can use its differences to its advantage.[126] Percy W. Thomas bluntly summarizes the challenge to us all:

> Twenty years of studying, teaching, and seeking to understand human reactions to differences of all sorts has led me to three conclusions: (1) People lack the communication skills, sensitivity, understanding, flexibility, and trust necessary to establish effective relationships; (2) many reactions to people who are culturally, racially, ethnically, and sexually different are based on irrational fears and nonsensical stereotypes; and (3) people do not know how to deal with their irrational fears, attitudes, beliefs, and behaviors as they relate to inappropriate and counterproductive responses to diversity.[127]

The stakes for businesses are very high. Companies can lose the valuable talent of good employees when cultural differences affect their work negatively. Employees themselves experience their work environments in such a way as to affect their own mental well-being. As Thomas says:

> Companies lose millions of dollars "chasing the wind" by settling employee grievances, EEO complaints, and expensive class-action suits, and furthermore, they lose their competitive edge in the marketplace. The costs that stem from maintaining a culturally insensitive environment can be staggering. Many studies show that employee dissatisfaction costs the company large sums of money. Increased use of sick leave, high absenteeism, and simple anomie among workers are often indicators of a culturally insensitive environment.[128]

Charles R. Bantz describes the lessons he learned from working in a multicultural research team engaged in a long-term project spanning several years and several continents. Bantz recommends that increased attention and effort in four key areas would be most useful: gathering information about the multiple perspectives that will inevitably be present; maintaining flexibility and a willingness to adapt to differing situations, issues, and needs; building social relationships as well as task cohesion; and clearly identifying and emphasizing mutual long-term goals.[129]

CULTURE connections

During the evenings, Majed and his family often entertained guests, who almost always dropped by unannounced, as is the Kurdish custom. Guests often stopped by during the day as well, and at least one woman of the house was always expected to be home to receive them, with tea, fruit, and candy at the ready.

—*Christiane Bird*

Episodes, Contexts, and Intercultural Competence

Recall from Chapter 3 that interaction contexts are a component of intercultural competence related to the associations between two people interacting in specific settings. The discussion in this chapter on social episodes and interaction contexts elaborates on these important ideas. Just as a picture hung on the wall has a frame around it, each intercultural encounter is surrounded or defined by a cultural frame. Competence in intercultural communication requires understanding the nature of this cultural frame.

People frame their intercultural encounters by the definitions or labels they give to particular social episodes. The activities in which you interact are chunked or grouped into social episodes that are influenced by your cultural patterns, roles, rules, interaction scenes, and interaction contexts. Someone else may take a social episode that to you is "small talk with a classmate" as "an offer of friendship." What is to you a businesslike episode of "letting off steam with a coworker about one of her mildly irritating habits" may be viewed as a "public humiliation." Do not assume that what you regard as appropriate social roles and sensible rules of interaction will necessarily be comfortable or even acceptable to another.

Summary

Social episodes are the repetitive, predictable, and routine behaviors that form the structure of one's interactions with others. Social episodes are made up of cultural patterns, social roles, rules of interaction, interaction scenes, and interaction contexts. People frame intercultural interactions by the expectations they have for particular social episodes.

Three specific social contexts—health care, education, and business—have become prominent meeting grounds where people from many cultures converge and interact. Each context was described in some detail to illustrate the importance of intercultural competence in everyday experiences.

For Discussion

1. What are social episodes? When, if ever, are people affected by them?
2. What are interaction contexts? How does culture affect interaction contexts?
3. Describe an intercultural encounter you have had in the health care, education, or business context. What issues or concerns surfaced as a result of this intercultural encounter? How did you deal with these concerns?
4. What actions can people take to be more interculturally competent in everyday contexts?

For Further Reading

Richard Brislin, *Working with Cultural Differences: Dealing Effectively with Diversity in the Workplace* (Westport, CT: Praeger, 2008). An up-to-date presentation of ideas and information. Provides an interdisciplinary summary of theories and their application.

Madonna G. Constantine and Derald Wing Sue (eds.), *Addressing Racism: Facilitating Cultural Competence in Mental Health and Educational Settings* (Hoboken, NJ: Wiley, 2006). This excellent compilation of research looks very specifically at the health and educational contexts and examines the interplay among cultural differences, prejudice, racism, and human interaction.

Bonnie M. Davis, *How to Teach Students Who Don't Look Like You: Culturally Relevant Teaching Strategies* (Thousand Oaks, CA: Corwin/Sage, 2006). A practical guide for teachers working in intercultural classrooms. Contains specific suggestions for effective and appropriate intercultural teaching.

Anne Fadiman, *The Spirit Catches You and You Fall Down: A Hmong Child, Her American Doctors, and the Collision of Two Cultures* (New York: Farrar, Straus, and Giroux, 1997). A case study of one Hmong family's experiences within the U.S. health care system. Illustrates the dramatic differences in expectations of competent health care within the two cultural frameworks.

Evelyne Glaser, Manuela Guilherme, María del Carmen Méndez García, and Terry Mughan (eds.), *Icopromo–Intercultural Competence for Professional Mobility* (Strasbourg: Council of Europe, 2007). Reports of several research projects conducted to understand intercultural competence in professional business contexts. Includes a CD-ROM that reports on research and offers a practical set of exercises to improve competence in the work setting.

Robert T. Moran, Philip R. Harris, and Sarah V. Moran, *Managing Cultural Differences: Global Leadership Strategies for the 21st Century,* 7th ed. (Boston: Butterworth-Heinemann, 2007). A compendium of how various business functions are influenced by cultural differences.

Larry D. Purnell and Betty J. Paulanka, *Guide to Culturally Competent Health Care* (Philadelphia: F. A. Davis, 2005). An excellent guide to the effects of beliefs, values, norms, and social practices on expectations of appropriate and effective communication within the health care setting.

For additional information about intercultural films and about Web sites for researching specific cultures, please turn to the Resources section at the back of this book.

CHAPTER 12

The Potential for Intercultural Competence

KEY TERMS

It should be clear by now that we are personally committed to understanding the dynamics of culture and its effects on interpersonal communication. William Shakespeare suggested that the world is a stage filled with actors and actresses, but they come from different cultures and they need to coordinate their scripts and actions to accomplish their collective purposes. The image of a multicultural society is one that we firmly believe will characterize most people's lives in the twenty-first century. Intercultural communication will become far more commonplace in people's day-to-day activities, and the communication skills that lead to the development of intercultural competence will be a necessary part of people's personal and professional lives.

It should also be clear that intercultural communication is a complex and challenging activity. Intercultural competence, although certainly attainable in varying degrees, will elude everyone in at least some intercultural interactions. Nevertheless, we hope that, in addition to the challenges of intercultural interaction, this book also reminds you of the joys of discovery that can occur when interacting with people whose culture differs from your own.

In this closing chapter, we turn our attention to some final thoughts about enhancing your intercultural competence. First we look at intercultural contacts and explore what makes them more likely to be beneficial. Next we discuss some critical ethical issues that affect intercultural interactions. Following this, we offer a point of view about certain events that have been particularly newsworthy. By focusing on these events, we offer a glimpse into the ways that enormously powerful events and experiences can shape an entire generation's intercultural interactions—that is, how members of that generation are likely to perceive and engage people from other cultures. We also look at the apparent dichotomies that seem to shape individuals and nations in today's world. We conclude with an expression of optimism about the future of intercultural communication and with a renewed awareness of the need for a lifelong commitment to improving our multicultural world.

Intercultural Contact

Many people believe that creating the opportunity for personal contact fosters positive attitudes toward members of other groups. Indeed, this assumption provides the rationale for numerous international exchange programs for high school and college students. There are also international "sister city" programs, wherein a U.S. city pairs itself with a city in another country and encourages the residents of both cities to visit with and stay in one another's homes. Sometimes, of course, intercultural contact does overcome the obstacles of cultural distance, and positive attitudes between those involved do result.

Unfortunately, there is a great deal of historical and contemporary evidence to suggest that contact between members of different cultures does not always lead to good feelings. In fact, under many circumstances, such contact only reinforces negative attitudes or may even change a neutral attitude into a negative one. For instance, tourists in other countries are sometimes repelled by the inhabitants, and immigrants to the United States have not always been accepted by the communities into which they have settled. In some communities and among some people, there is still much prejudice and negative feeling between European Americans and African Americans. The factors that lead to cordial and courteous interactions among people from different cultural groups are very complicated. One factor, that of access to and control of institutional and economic power, strongly influences attitudes between members of different cultures.

Dominance and Subordination between Groups

Not all groups within a nation or region have equal access to sources of institutional and economic power. When cultures share the same political, geographic, and economic landscapes, some form of a status hierarchy often develops. Groups of people who are distinguished by

■ Intercultural contacts do not always lead to positive feelings among the participants. The sign in this store window, which protests U.S. immigration policies, illustrates the tensions that can occur in some intercultural encounters.

their religious, political, cultural, or ethnic identity often struggle among themselves for dominance and control of the available economic and political resources. The cultural group that has primary access to institutional and economic power is often characterized as the dominant culture.

Internationally, there have been numerous instances of genocide, "ethnic cleansing," civil wars that pit one cultural group against another, and numerous outbreaks of violence between members of cultural groups sharing the same territory. In the United States, racial tensions between African Americans and European Americans have resulted in numerous incidents. Immigrants from various parts of the world have experienced open hostility, and sometimes violent reactions, from people who live in areas where they have settled. When these kinds of competitive tensions characterize the political and economic setting in which individuals from differing cultures interact, intercultural communication is obviously affected.

Scholars have given considerable attention to the influence of dominant and subordinate group membership on interpersonal and intercultural communication processes.[1] The results of their investigations suggest that there is a very interesting set of relationships among the factors that affect these interactions. For instance, members of dominant cultures will often devalue the language styles of subordinate cultural members and judge the "correctness" of their use of preferred speech patterns. In some cases, members of subordinate cultures will try to accommodate or adapt their speech to that of the dominant culture. In other circumstances, they will very deliberately emphasize their group's unique speech characteristics when they are in the presence of people from the dominant culture.

As we will discuss in Chapter 9, special forms of language are often used to signal identification among members of the subordinate group and to indicate a lack of submission to the dominant group. Similarly, members of the dominant group are likely to retain the special characteristics of their language, including preferences for certain words, accents, and linguistic patterns, and may therefore devalue the linguistic patterns of others. For example, there are instances in which European Americans have devalued the use of Black Standard English.[2]

Members of the dominant group also have much greater access to public and mass communication channels. They may be excessively influential in determining the conversational topics that are regarded as socially relevant, the societal issues that are deemed important enough to be worthy of public attention, and the "proper" language for expressing one's views in social discussions. As muted group theory suggests, individuals who do not belong to the dominant group are often silenced by a lack of opportunities to

CULTURE connections

When you have been a refugee, abandoned all your loves and belongings, your memories become your belongings. Images of the past, snippets of old conversations, furnish the world within your mind. When you have nothing left to guard, you guard your memories. You guard them with silence. You do not draw your treasures into the light, lest exposure soften their sharp—sad or gay—details (the best lesson I ever learned from visiting museums). Remembering becomes not simply a preoccupation but a full-time occupation. What you once witnessed is the story that brought journalists to your doorstep, but they left without the scoop. What you once witnessed is what scholars sought in the archives but did not find. What you once witnessed is what biographers intended to write. But how much can biographers do if the witnesses are silent?

—*Roya Hakakian*

express their experiences, perceptions, and worldviews. Essentially, the power of the dominant group's communication may function to silence or "mute" the voices of subordinate group members. To have their concerns recognized publicly, subordinate group members may be obliged to use the language and communication styles of the dominant group. Although muted group theory was initially applied to women's marginalized voices,[3] it has also been applied to cultural groups.[4] Mark Orbe, for example, describes African American males as a muted group, since their talking patterns and worldview are not part of the dominant group's norms in the United States.[5] By addressing the ways in which groups are marginalized, muted group theory allows us to understand the basic concerns of nondominant voices and encourages a more equitable world where no voices are silenced.

Attitudes among Cultural Members

The naïve view of intercultural contact—that any intercultural contact is likely to be beneficial—has been proven repeatedly to be incorrect. But what, then, are the conditions under which intercultural contacts might turn out to be favorable? What do we know about the attitudes that form when people have frequent intercultural contacts with one another?

In his classic study on the contact hypothesis, Yehuda Amir describes four conditions that are likely to lead to positive attitudes as a result of intercultural communication. Interestingly, each of these conditions affects the motivational component of intercultural competence. The first condition is that there must be support from the top. That is, if the high-status individuals—those who are in charge or who are recognized as authority figures—support the intercultural contact, it is more likely to lead to a positive outcome.

The second condition for positive intercultural interactions is that those involved have a personal stake in the outcome. This means that the individuals involved have something to gain if they are successful—or something to lose if they are unsuccessful—that makes them regard the interactions as personal. If someone is personally invested in the outcome of the interaction, there is increased motivation to do well and make it thrive.

The third condition affecting the likelihood that intercultural interactions will be regarded as positive is that the actual intercultural contacts are viewed as pleasing and constructive. Interactions that are enjoyable make people feel good about their experiences and increases the prospects for further intercultural contacts.

The fourth condition that Amir says will likely lead to favorable attitudes as a consequence of intercultural interactions is related to the perceived outcome of the interaction. When all parties have the potential to be effective—that is, when the members of both cultures either have common goals or view the interaction as allowing them to achieve their own individual goals—then successful cooperation is possible, and the interactants are very likely to perceive the intercultural contact as having the potential to be beneficial.[6]

Additional investigations suggest that four more factors also affect attitudes and outcomes. One is the *strength of identification* that the members of a culture have for their cultural group. Do the individuals in an encounter think of the person with whom they are interacting as a unique individual, or do they view that person primarily as a representative of a different cultural group? Similarly, do the interactants view themselves as unique individuals or as representatives of particular cultural groups? One study finds that the outcomes of intercultural encounters depend on the extent to which cultural identities are seen as an important component of people's interpersonal identities.[7] Identification with their culture increases if they have a relatively high status within the group, as well as if the bonds to their culture are strong and all their friends and social networks are associated with it.

Intercultural communication outcomes are also affected by the degree of *perceived threat*. If the members of a culture believe that certain fundamental aspects of their cultural identity—such as their language and special characteristics—are threatened, they are likely to increase their identification with their culture, and intercultural contacts are less likely to be favorable. Even groups that are in the majority sometimes see the presence of people from other cultures as threatening. For example, consider the perceived threat and consequent reactions of U.S. Americans to immigrants who are willing to work for a lower wage.

Another factor is the degree of *typicality* with which the other interactants are viewed. That is, participants in intercultural encounters make a judgment about the degree to which specific individuals are typical or atypical of their culture, which in turn influences the positive or negative character of their attitudes. More important, typicality affects the likelihood that experiences with one member of a culture are generalized to other members of that culture.[8] For example, if someone is viewed as unique and unrepresentative of the typical members of a culture, a positive experience with that individual will not necessarily result in positive attitudes toward other people from the same cultural group.

The nature of the interactants' *cultural stereotypes* is another factor in intercultural contacts. Miles Hewstone and Howard Giles propose that these stereotypes are used as filters to assess the behaviors of members of other groups.[9] They also suggest that, if a person does not conform to the cultural stereotype in some important way, that person is dismissed as atypical. Consequently, negative stereotypes toward the culture can persist even when there are positive and favorable interactions with a member of the culture.

Outcomes of Intercultural Contact

Both fictional and nonfictional accounts of intercultural contacts are replete with references to individual and cultural changes. References are made to people who "go native" and who seem to adjust or adapt to life in the new culture. References are also made to those who retain their own cultural identity by using only their original language and by living in cultural ghettos. During the height of the British Empire in India, for example, many British officials and their families tried to re-create the British lifestyle in India, in a climate not conducive to tuxedos and fancy dresses, with layers and layers of slips and decorative fabrics.

It is generally accepted that intercultural communication creates stress for most individuals. In intercultural communication, the certainty of one's own cultural framework is gone, and there is a great deal of uncertainty about what other code systems mean. Individuals who engage in intercultural contacts for extended periods of time will respond to the stress in different ways. Most will find themselves incorporating at least some behaviors from the new culture into their own repertoire. Some take on the characteristics, the norms, and even the values and beliefs of another culture willingly and easily. Others resist the new culture and retain their old ways, sometimes choosing to spend time in enclaves populated only by others like themselves. Still others simply find the problems of adjusting to a new culture to be intolerable, and they leave if they can.

People's reactions also change over time. That is, the initial reactions of acceptance or rejection often shift as increased intercultural contacts produce different kinds of outcomes. Such changes in the way people react to intercultural contacts are called *adaptation*.

Adaptation   Words such as *assimilation, adjustment, acculturation,* and even *coping* are used to describe how individuals respond to their experiences in other cultures. Many of these terms refer to how people from one culture react to prolonged contact with those from another. Over

CULTURE connections

We loved living in Mexico, but ultimately tired of being outsiders. The downside of a culture rooted in family clans is that friends aren't as integral. Annalena's classmates rarely invited her home to play because there they played with their cousins. We had genuinely warm, but stubbornly superficial relationships with our neighbors. While it was possible for us to feel gloriously swept away by the splendor of saint's day celebrations, these holidays would never belong to us. And because most of the expatriates we met were either cantina-hopping college students or cocktail party-hopping retirees, we didn't fit in with the foreigners either....

But we've been home five months now, and I'm not sure we belong in California anymore either. We're struggling to reconcile the Mexican sky that now fills our hearts with the daily grind of a more or less upwardly mobile life. I find myself willfully spacing out, trying to slow down the pace, trying to hold onto the sense that time is simply time, not money. Perhaps we've become permanent expatriates—neither fish nor fowl, forever lost no matter our location. But this fluidity also means that we're now like mermaids and centaurs—magic creatures who always know there's another way.

—*Gina Hyams*

Intercultural adaptations are made both by the host culture and by the sojourners. As this photo illustrates, many Irish grocery stores now carry traditional Polish food items, since sojourners from other cultures often long for the familiar tastes from home.

the years, different emotional overtones have been attached to these terms. To some people, for instance, *assimilation* is a negative outcome; to others, it is positive. Some consider *adjustment* to be "good," whereas for others it is "bad."

We offer an approach that allows you to make your own value judgment about what constitutes the right kind of outcome. We believe that competent adjustment to another culture will vary greatly from situation to situation and from person to person. We have used the broader term of *adaptation* to characterize these adjustments because it subsumes various forms of cultural or individual adaptation.

> *Adaptation is the process by which people establish and maintain relatively stable, helpful, and mutually shared relationships with others upon relocating to an unfamiliar cultural setting.*[10]

Note that this definition suggests that, when individuals adapt to another culture, they must learn how to "fit" themselves into it. Again, remember that different individuals and different groups will make the fit in different ways.

Adaptation includes physical, biological, and social changes. Physical changes occur because people are confronted with new physical stimuli—they eat different food, drink different water, live in different climates, and reside in different kinds of housing. When people are exposed to a new culture, they may undergo actual physical or biological changes. People deal with new viruses and bacteria; new foods cause new reactions and perhaps even new allergies. Prolonged contact between groups results in intermarriage, and the children of these marriages are born with a mixture of the genetic features of the people involved. Social relationships change with the introduction of new people. Outgroups may become bonded with the ingroups, for example, in opposition to the new outgroup members. Such changes may also cause individuals to define themselves in new and different ways.[11]

Alternatively, the culture itself might change because of the influences of people from other cultures. The French, for example, have raised concerns about the effects of the English language on their own language and culture. Traditional societies have sometimes expressed this distress about the Westernization or urbanization of their cultures.

Culture Shock versus Adaptation Sustained intercultural contact that requires total immersion in another culture may produce a phenomenon that has sometimes been called culture shock. Anthropologist Kalvero Oberg, who provided an early elaboration of the term, describes some of the reasons it occurs:

> Culture shock is precipitated by the anxiety that results from losing all our familiar signs and symbols of social intercourse. These signs or cues include the thousand and one ways in which we orient ourselves to the situations of daily life: when to shake hands and what to say when we meet people, when and how to give tips, how to give orders to servants, how to make purchases, when to accept and when to refuse invitations, when to take statements seriously and when not. Now these cues, which may be words, gestures, facial expressions, customs, or norms, are acquired by all of us in the course of growing up and are as much a part of our culture as the language we speak or the beliefs we accept. All of us depend for our peace of mind and our efficiency on hundreds of these cues, most of which we are not consciously aware.[12]

That is, culture shock is said to occur when people must deal with a barrage of new perceptual stimuli that are difficult to interpret because the cultural context has changed. Things taken for granted at home require virtually constant monitoring in the new culture to assure some degree of understanding. The loss of predictability, coupled with the fatigue that results from the need to stay consciously focused on what would normally be taken for granted, produces the negative responses associated with culture shock. These can include

> excessive washing of the hands; excessive concern over drinking water, food, dishes, and bedding; fear of physical contact with attendants or servants; the absent-minded, faraway stare (sometimes called the "tropical stare"); a feeling of helplessness and a desire for dependence on long-term residents of one's own nationality; fits of anger over delays and other minor frustrations; delay and outright refusal to learn the language of the host country; excessive fear of being cheated, robbed, or injured; great concern over minor pains and eruptions of the skin; and finally, that terrible longing to be home, to be able to have a good cup of coffee and a piece of apple pie, to walk into that corner drugstore, to visit one's relatives, and in general, to talk to people who really make sense.[13]

An interesting consequence of the many new information technologies is that those residing far from their homeland, in an unfamiliar cultural environment, can now communicate more easily and more often with friends and family back home. Similarly, the new media provide the ability to have virtual interactions with others from one's culture—via email, listservs, chat groups, blogs, Internet-based video and phone conversations, and instant messages—who are also living in the "foreign" land and are experiencing comparable difficulties and a lack of predictability that living in a new culture brings. Such exchanges, for example, can provide an opportunity to describe one's feelings of alienation and homesickness while adjusting to a new culture, thus reducing the stresses and strains of the adaptation.

Often associated with culture shock are the U-curve and W-curve hypotheses of cultural adaptation. In the U-curve hypothesis, the initial intercultural contacts are characterized by a positive, almost euphoric, emotional response. As fatigue mounts and culture shock sets in, however, the individual's responses are more and more negative, until finally a low point is reached. Then, gradually, the individual develops a more positive attitude and the new culture seems less foreign, until a positive emotional response once again occurs.

The U-curve hypothesis has been extended to the W-curve, which includes the person's responses to her or his own culture upon return.[14] It posits that a second wave of culture shock, which is similar to the first and has been called re-entry shock, may occur when the

CULTURE connections

And Fuling was a frightening place because the people had seen so few outsiders. If I ate at a restaurant or bought something from a store, a crowd would quickly gather, often as many as thirty people spilling out into the street. Most of the attention was innocent curiosity, but it made the embarrassment of my bad Chinese all the worse—I'd try to communicate with the owner, and people would laugh and talk among themselves, and in my nervousness I would speak even worse Mandarin. When I walked down the street, people constantly turned and shouted at me. Often they screamed *waiguoren* or *laowai,* both of which simply meant "foreigner." Again, these phrases often weren't intentionally insulting, but intentions mattered less and less with every day that these words were screamed at me. Another favorite was "hello," a meaningless, mocking version of the word that was strung out into a long "hah-loooo!" This word was so closely associated with foreigners that sometimes the people used it instead of *waiguoren*—they'd say, "Look, here come two hellos!" And often in Fuling they shouted other less innocent terms—*yangguizi,* or "foreign devil"; *da bizi,* "big nose"—although it wasn't until later that I understood what these phrases meant.

The stresses piled up every time I went into town: the confusion and embarrassment of the language, the shouts and stares, the mocking calls. It was even worse for Adam, who was tall and blond; at least I had the advantage of being dark-haired and only slightly bigger than the locals.

—*Peter Hessler*

individual returns home and must readapt to the once taken-for-granted practices that can no longer be followed without question. Some returnees to the United States, for instance, have difficulties with the pace of life, the relative affluence around them, and the seemingly superficial values espoused by the mass media. Others are frustrated when their colleagues and friends seem uninterested in their intercultural experiences, which may have changed them profoundly, but instead want simply to fill them in on "what they missed." Such re-entry problems, of course, are not confined to U.S. Americans who have been to another culture.[15] Japanese school-age children who returned from living in English-speaking countries, for instance, have identified readjustment problems because of their differences from their peers, the precise expectations for their behaviors in school, their reduced proficiency in the Japanese language, and their interpersonal styles.[16] One girl had to dye her hair black because it had lightened from the sun. Another had to remind herself continually, "I shouldn't be different from others; I should do the same as others in doing anything."[17]

Though initially regarded as plausible, the U-curve and the W-curve hypotheses do not provide sufficiently accurate descriptions of the adaptation process. They do not account, for instance, for those whose experiences remain favorable, for those who fail to adapt and return home prematurely, or for those whose level of discomfort changes little during the adaptation period. Rather, there seem to be a variety of possible adaptation patterns that individuals could experience, depending on their particular circumstances. The pattern of adaptation varies widely from one individual to the next, and therefore no single pattern can be said to characterize the typical adaptation process.[18]

The term *culture shock* can now be seen to describe a pattern in which the individual has severe negative reactions on contact with another culture. Such extreme responses, however, in which the person's knowledge, motivation, and skills are initially insufficient to cope with the strangeness of a new culture, are among many likely reactions. We therefore prefer the more general term adaptation to refer to the pattern of accommodation and acculturation that results from people's contact experiences with another culture. As many theorists have suggested, it is through adaptation that personal transformation from cultural contact takes place.[19]

The Adaptation Process   Efforts to describe the adaptation process suggest a more complex set of patterns than the U-curve and the W-curve hypotheses provide. Daniel J. Kealey found that the U-curve was an accurate description of the adaptation process for only about 10 percent of the individuals he studied; the majority experienced little change (30 percent remained highly satisfied, 10 percent stayed moderately satisfied, and 15 percent maintained a low level of satisfaction throughout); and another 35 percent had an extremely low level of satisfaction initially but improved continuously for the duration of their intercultural assignment.[20] Interestingly, many in this latter group, which experienced the most severe adjustment stress, eventually became the most competent in their ability to function in another culture.

There is also ample evidence to suggest that the adaptation process has multiple dimensions or factors associated with it.[21] For example, Mitchell R. Hammer, William B. Gudykunst, and Richard L. Wiseman have suggested that intercultural effectiveness consists of three such dimensions: the ability to deal with psychological stress, skill in communicating with others both effectively and appropriately, and proficiency in establishing interpersonal relationships.[22] Colleen Ward and her colleagues have identified just two dimensions of adaptation: psychological and sociocultural. The former is similar to Hammer and his colleagues' first dimension, and the latter seems to combine the remaining two.[23] Similarly, Guo-Ming Chen found that communicator adaptability and interaction with others were major positive contributors to international students' ability to cope with adjustment difficulties in the United States.[24]

Despite such distinctions, however, the adaptation process has usually been viewed as a single "package" of related features that all follow the same trajectory of change for a given individual. However, distinct patterns of change likely characterize each dimension of adaptation. Thus, for instance, the time it takes to adjust to the pace of life in an unfamiliar culture may be very different from the rate of adaptation to the culture's expectations regarding the use of indirection in language.

Types of Adaptation   Answers to two important questions shape the response of individuals and groups to prolonged intercultural contact, thus producing different outcomes. The first concern is whether it is considered important to maintain one's cultural identity and to display its characteristics. The second concern involves whether people believe it is important to maintain relationships with their outgroups.[25]

Assimilation occurs when it is deemed relatively unimportant to maintain one's original cultural identity but it is important to establish and maintain relationships with other cultures. The metaphor of the United States as a melting pot, which envisions many cultures giving up their individual characteristics to build the new, homogenized cultural identity of the United States, illustrates the choice described in Figure 12.1 (on page 322) as assimilation. Assimilation means taking on the new culture's beliefs, values, norms, and social practices.

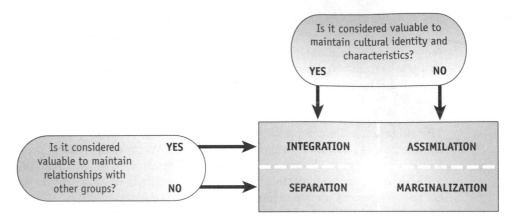

FIGURE 12.1   Forms of acculturation.

Source: John W. Berry, Uichol Kim, and Pawel Boski, "Psychological Acculturation of Immigrants," *Cross-Cultural Adaptation: Current Approaches,* ed. Young Yun Kim and William B. Gudykunst (Newbury Park, CA: Sage, 1988).

When an individual or group retains its original cultural identity while seeking to maintain harmonious relationships with other cultures, integration occurs. Countries such as Switzerland, Belgium, and Canada, with their multilingual and multicultural populations, are good examples. Integration produces distinguishable cultural groups that work cooperatively to ensure that the society and the individuals continue to function well. Both integration and assimilation promote harmony and result in an appropriate fit of individuals and groups to the larger culture.

When individuals or groups do not want to maintain positive relationships with members of other groups, the outcomes are starkly different. If a culture does not want positive relationships with another culture and if it also wishes to retain its cultural characteristics, separation may result. If the separation occurs because the more politically and economically powerful culture does not want the intercultural contact, the result of the forced separation is called segregation. The history of the United States provides numerous examples of segregation in its treatment of African Americans. If, however, a nondominant group chooses not to participate in the larger society in order to retain its own way of life, the separation is called seclusion. The Amish are a good example of this choice.

When individuals or groups neither retain their cultural heritage nor maintain positive contacts with the other groups, marginalization occurs. This form of adaptation is characterized by confusion and alienation. The choices of marginalization and separation are reactions against other cultures. The fit these outcomes achieve in the adaptation process is based on battling against, rather than working with, the other cultures in the social environment.[26]

For purposes of simplification, Figure 12.1 suggests that each of the questions must be answered as wholly "yes" or "no." In reality, however, people could choose a variety of points between these two extremes. The French, for example, while certainly not isolationists, have raised concerns about the effects of the English language on their own language and culture. Similarly, traditional societies have sometimes been distressed about the Westernization or urbanization of their cultures while simultaneously expressing a desire for increased contact and trade.

Obviously, not all individuals acculturate similarly. Some find the daily challenges of responding to another culture to be too stressful and overwhelming. If possible, such individuals will choose to return to their culture of origin; if they cannot do so, various kinds of maladaptive adjustments, or even mental illnesses, can occur.

At the opposite extreme, and of particular interest to us, are those individuals who move easily among many cultures. Such people generally have a profound respect for many varied points of view and are able to understand others and to communicate appropriately and effectively with people from a variety of cultures. Such individuals are able to project a sense of self that transcends any particular cultural group.

Young Yun Kim uses the term intercultural personhood to describe the progression by which individuals move beyond the thoughts, feelings, and behaviors of their initial cultural framework to incorporate other cultural realities. She describes the process as

> a special kind of mindset that promises greater fitness in our increasingly intercultural world. Intercultural personhood represents a continuous struggle of searching for the authenticity in self and others within and across cultural groups. It is a way of existence that transcends the perimeters of a particular tradition, and one that is capable of embracing and incorporating seemingly divergent cultural elements into one's own

CULTURE connections

There are other ways in which Ashoke and Ashima give in. Though Ashima continues to wear nothing but saris and sandals from Bata, Ashoke, accustomed to wearing tailor-made pants and shirts all his life, learns to buy ready-made. He trades in fountain pens for ballpoints, Wilkinson blades and his boar-bristled shaving brush for Bic razors bought six to a pack. Though he is now a tenured full professor, he stops wearing jackets and ties to the university. Given that there is a clock everywhere he turns, at the side of his bed, over the stove where he prepares tea, in the car he drives to work, on the wall opposite his desk, he stops wearing a wristwatch, resigning his Favre Leuba to the depths of his sock drawer. In the supermarket they let Gogol fill the cart with items that he and Sonia, but not they, consume: individually wrapped slices of cheese, mayonnaise, tuna fish, hot dogs. For Gogol's lunches they stand at the deli to buy cold cuts, and in the mornings Ashima makes sandwiches with bologna or roast beef. At his insistence, she concedes and makes him an American dinner once a week as a treat, Shake 'n Bake chicken or Hamburger Helper prepared with ground lamb.

Still, they do what they can. They make a point of driving into Cambridge with the children when the Apu Trilogy plays at the Orson Welles, or when there is a Kathakali dance performance or a sitar recital at Memorial Hall. When Gogol is in the third grade, they send him to Bengali language and culture lessons every other Saturday, held in the home of one of their friends. For when Ashima and Ashoke close their eyes it never fails to unsettle them, that their children sound just like Americans, expertly conversing in a language that still at times confounds them, in accents they are accustomed not to trust.

—*Jhumpa Lahiri*

unique worldview. The process of becoming intercultural affirms creative courage and resourcefulness of humans because it requires discovering new symbols and new patterns of life.[27]

Interculturally competent communicators integrate a wide array of culture-general knowledge into their behavioral repertoires, and they are able to apply that knowledge to the specific cultures with which they interact. They are also able to respond emotionally and behaviorally with a wide range of choices in order to act appropriately and effectively within the constraints of each situation. They have typically had extensive intercultural communication experiences, and they have learned to adjust to alternative patterns of thinking and behaving.

The Ethics of Intercultural Competence

Those who attempt to achieve intercultural competence must face a number of ethical dilemmas. It is imperative to explore the following issues to become aware of the choices that are made all too often without due consideration and reflection.

There are three key ethical dilemmas. The first is summarized in the adage "When in Rome, do as the Romans do." The second asks if it is possible to judge a particular belief, value, norm, or social practice as morally reprehensible. If so, when and under what circumstances? Stated in a slightly different way, if all cultures have differing beliefs, values, norms, and social practices, does that mean there are no true rights and wrongs? The third dilemma relates to the consequences of intercultural contacts. Are they necessarily positive for individuals and their societies? In other words, should all intercultural contacts be encouraged?

CULTURE connections

In a world composed of a few hundred nations, thousands of groups speaking thousands of languages, and more than 6 billion inhabitants, what is a reasonable goal? Clearly, we can no longer simply draw a curtain or build a wall that isolates groups from one another indefinitely. We homo sapiens must somehow learn how to inhabit neighboring places—and the same planet—without hating one another, without lusting to injure or kill one another, without acting on xenophobic inclinations even if our own group might emerge triumphant in the short run. Often the desideratum *tolerance* is invoked, and it may be the case that it is all that we can aspire to. Wordsmiths of a more optimistic temperament opt for romantic language; on the eve of World War II, poet W. H. Auden declared, "We must love one another or die."[2]

I prefer the concept of respect. Rather than ignoring differences, being inflamed by them, or seeking to annihilate them through love or hate, I call on human beings to accept the differences, learn to live with them, and value those who belong to other cohorts.

—*Howard Gardner*

When in Rome …

A fundamental issue confronting those who are in the midst of another culture is a decision about how much they should change their behaviors to fit the beliefs, values, norms, and social practices of those with whom they interact. Whose responsibility is it to attempt to take into account cultural differences in communication? Is it the responsibility of the visitors, newcomers, or sojourners to adjust their behaviors to the cultural framework of the host culture, or should members of the host culture adjust their communication and make allowances for the newcomers and strangers? Because English predominates in the United States, are all those who live in the United States required to use English? To what extent must individuals adapt their cultural beliefs, values, norms, and social practices to the dominant cultural patterns?

The old saying "When in Rome, do as the Romans do," which clearly places the responsibility for change on the newcomer, offers a great deal of wisdom, but it cannot be followed in all circumstances. In most cases, behaviors that conform to cultural expectations show respect for the other culture and its ways. Conformity with common cultural practices also allows the newcomer to interact with and to meet people from the host culture on some kind of genuine basis. Respecting differences in nonverbal and verbal codes means that the ethical intercultural communicator takes responsibility for learning as much about these codes as is possible and reasonable. Naturally, what is possible and reasonable will vary, depending on a range of circumstances. Sometimes, wholesale adoption of new cultural practices by a group of newcomers may be seen as disrespectful and can upset those from the host culture. In the past, for example, U.S. and European students visiting India wore Indian clothes, didn't wear shoes, and lived in very poor circumstances. Many Indians regarded this "conforming" behavior as insulting and disrespectful of their cultures. The visitor to a culture cannot simply adopt the beliefs and practices of a new culture without also risking being perceived as insincere and superficial.

Sometimes it is difficult for people to change their behaviors to match cultural patterns that contradict their own beliefs and values. For example, many U.S. American women, who were taught to value freedom and equality, may find it difficult to respond positively to cultural practices that require women to wear veils in public and to use male drivers or chaperones. The ethical dilemma that intercultural communicators face is the decision about how far to go in adapting their behaviors to another culture. Should people engage in behaviors that they regard as personally wrong or difficult? At what point do people lose their own sense of self, their cultural identities, and their moral integrity? At what point does the adoption of new cultural behaviors offend and insult others? One of the challenges and delights of intercultural communication is in discovering the boundaries and touchstones of one's own moral perspective while simultaneously learning to display respect for other ways of dealing with human problems.

Another perspective from which to explore the ethical issues embedded in the adage is that of the "Romans." A common point of view, often expressed by U.S. Americans about those who have recently immigrated to the United States or who still retain many of the underlying patterns of their own culture, is that since these people now live in the United States, they should adjust to its cultural ways. The same comments are often made about students from other countries who come to the United States to study.

We ask you to consider the experiences of those people who immigrate to or study in another country. Perhaps you are such a person. Or perhaps your parents or grandparents did so. Not all immigrants or students have freely chosen the country where they now reside. Large numbers of people migrate from one country to another because political, military, and economic upheavals in their own country make living and learning there nearly impossible. For many, the choice to leave is juxtaposed against a choice to die, to starve, or to be politically censored. We also ask you to consider how difficult it must be for people to give up their culture. Remember how fundamental your cultural framework is, how it provides the logic for your behavior and your view of the world. How easy would it be for you if you were forced into new modes of behavior? Adjustment to another culture is difficult.

Are Cultural Values Relative or Universal?

A second ethical issue confronting the intercultural communicator is whether it is ever acceptable to judge the people of a culture when their behaviors are based on a radically different set of beliefs, values, norms, and social practices. Are there any values that transcend the boundaries of cultural differences? Are there any universally right or wrong values?

A culturally relativistic point of view suggests that every culture has its own set of values and that judgments can be made only within the context of the particular culture. Most people do not completely subscribe to this view, partly because it would lead to a lack of any firm beliefs and values on which to build a sense of self-identity.

David Kale argues that there are two values that transcend all cultures. First, the human spirit requires that all people must struggle to improve their world and to maintain their own sense of dignity, always within the context of their own particular culture. Thus, Kale suggests that "the guiding principle of any universal code of intercultural communication, therefore, should be to protect the worth and dignity of the human spirit."[28] The second universal value is a world at peace. Thus, all ethical codes must recognize the importance of working toward a world in which people can live at peace with themselves and one another.[29]

Ethical intercultural communicators continually struggle with the dilemmas presented by differences in cultural values. The tensions inherent in seeking to be tolerant of differences while holding firmly to one's own critical cultural values must

CULTURE connections

Mr. Malchode moved then to sit beside me. Quietly he said, "I don't mean to insult, but for your own sake you should know as a white you're intruding here. This is *our* place. It's not a zoo for tourists to see how 'natives' live. Even now we can't drink in a Messina hotel bar—the prices are trebled to keep us out. But you take it for granted you can come and drink here—you're white, so you can drink wherever you choose. Do you know enough about South Africa to understand what I say?"

—*Dervla Murphy*

always be reconciled. Kale's suggestions for responding ethically to cultural differences in values are excellent starting points for the internal dialogue that all competent intercultural communicators must conduct.

Do the Ends Justify the Means?

The final ethical dilemma we wish to raise concerns these questions: Should all intercultural contacts be encouraged? Are the outcomes of intercultural contacts positive? Are all circumstances appropriate for intercultural contact? In short, do the ends justify the means?

We have been shamelessly enthusiastic about the potential benefits and delights of intercultural interaction. Nevertheless, certain outcomes may not necessarily be justified by the means used to obtain them. Tourism, for example, can sometimes create an ethical dilemma. Although it often provides economic benefits for those living in the tourist destination and allows people from one culture to learn about another, it can also produce serious negative consequences. In some popular tourist destinations, for instance, the tourists actually outnumber the native population, and tourists may consume natural resources at a greater rate than they can be replaced. At the centuries-old archeological site of Cambodia's Angkor Wat, recent tourist increases—including a 27 percent boost in international visitors for 2006 alone—now use so much water from underground wells that the foundations of the famous temples are sinking, literally undermining the attractions those tourists came to experience.[50]

Sometimes, the prospect of increased economic development, and the tourist revenues they can generate, will alter the traditional relationships of a group of people to their land and property. About a generation ago, on Indonesia's island of Bali, Dutch multinational corporations began buying from the locals on Kuta Beach their prime but undeveloped land.

Rapid transportation allows many tourists to experience the wonders of previous civilizations, such as those at Cambodia's Angkor Wat (left) and Peru's Machu Picchu (right). Such World Heritage locations dramatically illustrate the ethical dilemma of balancing the positive outcomes of tourism with the practical realities of site destruction.

CULTURE connections

It's true that there are televisions, cola cans, and other nonessentials at the dump, but how can we begrudge the Inupiat the same excesses and comforts we enjoy? Life is bleak enough in the arctic winters as it is; the suicide rate in the Alaskan bush is the highest in the nation. But ask one of the elders if the old ways were better, or if they were enough.

> Back then, too hard. Always working. People always dying. Too much funeral. Now I have sixteen grandchildren, and all living. *Aarigaa*—that's good.

The Inupiat have always lived in the present, in a way many whites find inexplicable. You have to think what an archeologist a thousand years from now would make of what this latest version of arctic man has left behind. The Denbigh Flint people, the Old Whaling tradition, and the others took what they needed from the land, and most of it returned in due time, without a trace. There was no such thing as littering. Space age plastics and aluminum are another story. They don't go away.

This fact is slowly sinking in with the *Napaaqtugmiut*. Out on the river, many heave their empty pop cans overboard casually, or even with unmistakable gusto, as if the act of littering affirms their dominance over the land or signifies a ritual marking of territory. Some hunters leave trash out in the middle of nowhere, where it flutters in the wind year after year. They leave empty gas cans, laugh and call them "trail markers" if you ask why. I've often found myself sneaking along behind companions, surreptitiously picking up their cans and plastic, embarrassed when I'm discovered. I can never bring myself to ask them not to drop their trash by the trail, as they always have. Who am I to impose my own standards?

Other Eskimos, though, pick up candy wrappers and keep their fish camps clean. Most litter is swept seaward by high water, or lost in the vast ocean of land.

What we call trash is a matter of opinion. I was walking in the hills with an older Noatak man, far up a small, nameless valley. The mountains loomed over us on both sides, looking as they must have a thousand years ago. Following the creek bed, we came on a few rusted cans marking an old camp. Someone had stopped here, maybe twenty years before.

"*Aarigaa*," said my friend. "Now it doesn't seem so lonely."

—*Nick Jans*

The corporations then built huge tourist hotels and a massive tourist industry, which now rivals that of Hawai'i. Unfortunately, the former locals had to move to less-desirable places, and they now use the revenues from the sale of their land to buy motorbikes, on which they commute to the hotels and tourist venues in order to work as low-paid employees.

As an ethical intercultural communicator, some of the following questions must be confronted:

- Is it ethical to go to another country, for whatever reason, if you are naive and unprepared for cultural contact?
- Should intercultural contacts be encouraged for those who speak no language but their own?
- Should those who are prejudiced seek out intercultural contacts?

- Is it ethical to send missionaries to other countries?
- Is it acceptable to provide medical assistance to help a culture resist a disease, when in providing the assistance you may destroy the very infrastructure and nature of the indigenous culture?
- Is it justifiable for the sojourner from one culture to encourage a person from another culture to disregard his or her own cultural values?

There are no simple answers to any of these questions, but the competent intercultural communicator must confront these ethical dilemmas.

Ethics—Your Choices

We have offered few specific answers to these ethical dilemmas because every person must provide his or her own response. In the context of your own experiences and your own intercultural interactions, you must resolve the ethical dilemmas that will inevitably occur in your life. Kale provides four principles to guide you as you develop your own personal code of ethics. Ethical communicators should do the following:

- Address people of other cultures with the same respect that the communicators would like to receive themselves.
- Try to describe the world as they perceive it as accurately as possible.
- Encourage people of other cultures to express themselves in their unique natures.
- Strive for identification with people of other cultures.

The Perils and Prospects for Intercultural Competence

Today's world is buffeted by an enormously powerful set of forces. Some of these forces are not unique to this era but have existed at other times throughout the history of the world. Some, however, are wholly new, and they cause profound and, to some extent at least, unpredictable changes. The changes are set in motion by the speed with which global capital, information, goods, and the people who would trade in them can move across borders and throughout the world. Indeed, we are living through, yet do not fully understand, an unprecedented series of revolutions in communications, transportation, and technologies, which impose instantaneous interconnectedness upon most of the world's nations, their cultures, and their economies.

Impact of National and International Events on Intercultural Communication

Consider the following examples, each of which is drawn from the history of the United States and has had profound consequences throughout the world. As you reflect upon them, identify for yourself how these events were first shaped by global forces and, in turn, helped to shape subsequent global events.

October 24, 1929: A Thursday in early fall, and the day when the Roaring Twenties abruptly ended. The U.S. stock market crashed, a decade of unbelievable prosperity ended, and the Great Depression rapidly followed. Within three years, U.S. stock prices lost nearly 90 percent of their value, banks and other financial institutions collapsed, factories and businesses failed, unemployment soared by 700 percent, and ordinary working people were destitute, having lost both their jobs and their accumulated savings. Hunger was widespread, breadlines were commonplace, and medical care and durable goods were unaffordable. U.S. Americans of a certain age have been forever seared by these events, and their collective experiences have figured prominently in the subsequent financial, political, social, and vocational choices that were made.

December 7, 1941: A Sunday that, for many elderly U.S. Americans, will always be remembered as a day of infamy. The surprise was complete. The assault came that morning in two waves—the first at 7:53, the second an hour later. By ten o'clock it was over; more than 350 airplanes broke off the attack and left Oahu for their carriers, which returned them to Japan. Pearl Harbor, home of the U.S. Pacific Fleet, had been crippled: more than 2,000 dead, thousands more injured, eight battleships damaged or destroyed, and nearly 200 planes ruined. In the wake of this attack, both patriotism and fear followed; as the United States was drawn into World War II, courageous men and women marched off to defend their homeland and their loved ones, bravely facing death and the unfathomable horrors of war. Many who remained in the United States shared a newfound pride; U.S. flags were prominently displayed, slogans and posters to encourage patriotism were seemingly everywhere, and a desire to contribute to the national effort was palpable. Sadly, however, some U.S. Americans became the targets of unbridled fear, including those loyal U.S. citizens of Japanese ancestry who were required to abandon most of their belongings and were forced into detention camps for several years.

November 22, 1963: A warm Friday afternoon in Dallas. With an enthusiastic crowd cheering, President John F. Kennedy's motorcade passed through the streets in an open car. Suddenly at least three shots rang out, and the president was hit twice: in the base of

CULTURE connections

Mma Ramotswe had been thinking a great deal recently about how people might be fitted in. The world was a large place, and one might have thought that there was enough room for everybody. But it seemed that this was not so. There were many people who were unhappy, and wanted to move. Often they wished to come to the more fortunate countries—such as Botswana—in order to make more of their lives. That was understandable, and yet there were those who did not want them. This is our place, they said; you are not welcome.

It was so easy to think like that. People wanted to protect themselves from those they did not know. Others were different; they talked different languages and wore different clothes. Many people did not want them living close to them, just because of these differences. And yet, they were people, were they not? They thought the same way, and had the same hopes as anybody else did. They were our brothers and sisters, whichever way you looked at it, and you could not turn a brother or sister away.

—Alexander McCall Smith

the neck and squarely in the head. By 1:00 P.M.—less than an hour later—he was declared dead at the age of forty-six. In remarks prepared for delivery later that day, Kennedy had intended to say,

> In a world of complex and continuing problems, in a world full of frustrations and irritations, America's leadership must be guided by the lights of learning and reason or else those who confuse rhetoric with reality and the plausible with the possible will gain the popular ascendancy with their seemingly swift and simple solutions to every world problem.[31]

Three days later, leaders from more than 90 nations attended Kennedy's funeral; a million people lined the route as a horse-drawn caisson bore his body to St. Matthew's Cathedral for a requiem mass. Then, as more than a hundred million people watched on television, the president was buried in Arlington National Cemetery, where an eternal flame still marks his grave. Now, some forty years later, U.S. Americans of a certain age remember vividly the tragedy of that assassination.

January 28, 1986: A cold Tuesday morning in Florida. At 11:38, a rocket left its launching pad for a seven-day mission. The countdown hadn't exactly gone smoothly, with weather and equipment problems plaguing the launch, but after seven delays spanning five days, liftoff finally occurred. From classrooms across the nation, excited schoolchildren watched the live coverage of the shuttle's launch. They were eagerly following the successes of Christa McAuliffe, the first "teacher in space," who was to speak to them the following day in a live telecast. Just 73 seconds into the flight, the unimaginable happened: the space shuttle *Challenger* exploded in a fiery blast, instantly killing all seven crew members. The United States was stunned and shaken. The State of the Union address, scheduled for delivery by President Ronald Reagan that evening, was postponed. In its place, the president delivered a short but moving tribute to the fallen astronauts; three days later, a sorrowful nation participated via television in a memorial service in Houston, as the United States mourned the "*Challenger* Seven." Ask U.S. Americans of a certain age—particularly those who were schoolchildren then—and they will tell you that they vividly remember the day the *Challenger* exploded; nearly two decades later, many can recall precisely where they were and what they were doing when they learned of the disaster.

September 11, 2001: A clear Tuesday morning, with a hint of fall in the air. Abruptly, at 8:50 A.M., a hijacked commercial airplane smashed into the northern tower of New York's World Trade Center. Twenty-four minutes later, another hijacked plane struck the southern tower. Twenty-four minutes after that, at 9:38, a third hijacked plane struck the Pentagon, a portion of which collapsed. Pandemonium ensued. Within the hour, these jet-fueled fireballs had caused both of the 110-story towers of the World Trade Center to collapse. Fears of additional attacks were widespread: the Sears Tower in Chicago was evacuated, an antiterrorism division was mobilized in Los Angeles, and Seattle's Space Needle was closed. Air traffic was halted, financial markets were shut down, troops were mobilized, life was more uncertain, U.S. flags were everywhere, patriotism was admired, and donations soared. And Arab Americans—indeed, U.S. Americans from many cultures, as well as countless peace-loving Muslims throughout the world—were a bit more fearful for the safety of their children.

What sense should we make of these experiences, particularly the most recent of them? Each of these experiences, and many others we could provide from around the world, creates an indelible memory for certain U.S. Americans, who then pass on the

CULTURE connections

Our efforts to counter hatred, intolerance, and indifference must continue simultaneously at individual and structural levels. We must try to influence for good the minds and hearts of individual people through dialogue and confidence building. These efforts must be reinforced by our efforts to create just structures in society to support the ongoing work of negotiations in the human community. Only then will we have a chance to negate the terrible consequences of the tremendous conflicts facing humankind today.

—*Nelson Mandela*

lessons learned from them. Each of these events fundamentally alters the basic and often unquestioned understandings that people have of their social world, and it raises issues such as the following:

- What does my culture and nation represent to others? That is, from the perspective of others who view us differently than we view ourselves, what does my culture and nation stand for?
- What are the beliefs, values, norms, and social practices that seem to guide my culture's actions?
- In what ways am I interconnected with other cultures and economies in the world?
- To what extent should I trust people who seem different from me? To what extent must I trust people who seem different from me, as a prerequisite for our mutual survival?

Events such as those described above have profound effects on many individuals, who subsequently shape the understandings of others in the generations that follow. The September 11 terrorist attacks, for example, continue to test the very fabric of the United States as a multicultural nation. Fears and uncertainties have encouraged people to evaluate others negatively based solely on such attributes as their physical appearance,

CULTURE connections

There is a deep need to educate Americans on the importance of understanding other cultures and of the important role culture plays on the national agenda … [In the words of] Cellist Yo-Yo Ma: "A Senegalese poet said, 'In the end we will conserve only what we love. We will love only what we understand. And we will understand only what we are taught.' We must learn about other cultures in order to understand, in order to love and in order to conserve our common world heritage."

—*Final Report from the White House Conference on Culture and Diplomacy* choice of religious observance, culture of origin, and the like. But they have also created a healthy reevaluation of national priorities, the values inherent in a multicultural nation, and the means to achieve these goals.

Forces That Pull Us Together and Apart

There are two powerful yet opposing forces that are tugging on the United States and its many cultures. Indeed, these forces are not exclusive to the United States; they affect every nation and culture on earth, often in significant ways.

The opposing forces could variously be described as engagement versus isolationism, globalism versus nationalism, secularism versus spiritualism, consumerism versus fundamentalism, or capitalism versus tribalism. That is, intercultural relationships among cultural groups throughout the world are simultaneously being pushed together and wrenched apart. Though the terminology to describe these potent forces may vary, and their influential consequences may fluctuate widely across cultures and regions of the world, they nevertheless provide us with powerful lenses through which to view the changing interrelationships among the world's cultures.

One such force—promoting engagement, globalism, secularism, and capitalism—is nurtured and sustained by the economic interdependence of today's world. Economic interdependence, in turn, is linked to the rapid communications systems that now connect people virtually in real time, as events are displayed instantaneously through a variety of powerful technological innovations—television, film, videos, music, and the Internet. Transportation systems, as well, can quickly take people from one part of the globe to another. Almost anywhere one travels, there will be familiar signs of the interdependent global economy: television shows such as *Star Search*, *CSI*, and *American Idol* have burgeoning international audiences; film and musical performers, from rap to salsa to classical, from Kanye West to Avril Lavigne to the St. Petersburg Opera, are known internationally; and MTV is seen globally, with local shows adapting the U.S. format by tailoring it to their audiences' sensibilities. One can hear Peruvian musicians on a corner in Brussels, Beatles tunes in an elevator in Malaysia, reggae music on the streets of Guatemala City, and African rhythms at a park in San Francisco. In many parts of the world, the music played on the radio stations could be described, at least in part, as global and not representative of that country's musical traditions.

Closely related to mass media's impact is the speed of communications that now link much of the world. Events that occur in one country are displayed, within minutes, to people thousands of miles away. As a consequence, events in one part of the world have dramatic consequences in others. International telephone usage is on the rise; the Internet has drastically reduced the cost for such calls, and it has made it much easier to communicate over long distances.

Added to all of these forces is the stark reality of global economic interdependence. There are obvious signs of this "sharing" of the world's economy. The now-familiar KFC, Pizza Hut, and McDonald's fast-food outlets are seemingly everywhere; Fords, Toyotas, and Volkswagens are driven the world over; and consumer products by Coca Cola, Sony, Nestle, and Bayer are marketed internationally. The world traveler could easily assume, incorrectly, that similarities in consumer products and media messages result from or will lead to a homogenization of world cultures.

A counterpoint to these forces for globalization is another, and equally powerful, set of constraints. These alternative influences—for isolationism, nationalism, spiritualism, and tribalism—derive from a desire to preserve, protect, and defend what is seen as unique but threatened: the culture's language, religion, values, or way of life. As an example of these forces, consider the frequent desires expressed among members of a culture to protect its language from the intrusions of other languages; France, for example, is very vigilant about keeping non-French words from the national language. Similarly, people may elect to safeguard their economies from foreign products; they may do this formally—with protectionist tariffs on goods from other nations, particularly if the foreign goods compete favorably with those locally grown or manufactured—or informally, by common consent—witness the dearth of Japanese-manufactured automobiles in Detroit, where major U.S. automakers are located. Cultures and nations may also attempt to protect their people from the deleterious effects of the beliefs, values, norms, and social practices imposed on them from the "outside," which might negatively influence people's behaviors. Prohibitions of certain imported films, or videos of artistic performances, frequently occur in many places.

There is no doubt that these two sets of forces are powerful and dynamic, and they will likely shape much of the human experience in the twenty-first century. Discussions about these countervailing forces often come down to asking which forces are stronger: those promoting globalization and homogenization or those that encourage cultures to maintain their distinctiveness and unique ways of living?

We believe that what is missing from most discussions about the relative strengths of these forces is an understanding of the effects of culture on the human communication process. While these forces simultaneously push us together and pull us apart, what hasn't been acknowledged is that humans still bring their cultural backgrounds to their interpretations of these global events and symbols, which then shape the ways they make sense of them. That is, McDonald's arches, Jackie Chan's films, Jay-Z's music videos, Internet chatroom messages, and acts of "humanitarianism" are all interpreted and analyzed through individuals' differing cultural and national structures.

The patina of familiarity and commonality does not necessarily produce a shared understanding of the nature of everyday events. In Chapter 1, we discussed the important distinction between understanding and agreement in communication outcomes. The goal of living in a multicultural world, therefore, may sometimes mean that we must attempt to achieve understanding while recognizing that agreement may not always be likely, or even possible. Perhaps, however, we can sometimes "agree to disagree," with respect, civility, and caring. Intergroup tensions have characterized human interaction since the beginning of time, and they are not likely to abate soon. Stereotyping, we have suggested, is a natural and inevitable human tendency to categorize groups of others and thereby make the world more predictable. Our challenge is to assess individuals on their own merits, rather than merely as members of groups or nations, while simultaneously recognizing that humans typically identify, and often react to their worlds, as members of a culture.

Cultures and their symbolic systems also can change over time. No culture is static. Even cultures that have minimal contact with the outside world are affected by changing ecological conditions and events, which in turn change how they experience and understand their own familiar world.

■ These college graduates must live in a multicultural world that demands competent intercultural skills.

We suggest that both the forces promoting globalization and those encouraging individuation are mediated by the cultural patterns—the beliefs, values, norms, and social practices—of all peoples. Even identical messages, therefore, are interpreted differently by those whose codes and cultures differ. Even identical media, such as Internet discussion groups, can encourage an understanding of oneself and others or they can promote alienation and foster hate. In short, as Charles Ess and Fay Sudweeks suggest, a genuinely intercultural global village is an alternative to the polarizing options of "Jihad" and "McWorld."[32] Thus, while we recognize the far-reaching effects of technological, societal, and economic forces, we must also remember that one's culture provides the meaning systems by which all messages are experienced and interpreted.

Concluding Remarks

We began this book with a sense of optimism but also with a deep concern about the pressing need for intercultural communication competence. Here in the twenty-first century, such competence is an essential attribute for personal survival, professional success, national harmony, and international peace. The challenge of living in a multicultural world is the need to transcend the unpredictability of intercultural interactions, to cope with the accompanying fears that such interactions often engender, and to feel joy and comfort in the discovery of cultural variability.

Our focus has been on the interpersonal hurdles—the person-to-person problems—that arise in coping with the realities of cultural diversity. We commend and encourage all who have struggled to adjust to the multicultural nature of the human landscape. Inclusion

■ The challenge of leading an intercultural nation requires an unprecedented understanding of intercultural communication competence.

of others is the means to a better future, so we should be "widening our circle"[33] by acknowledging and celebrating cultural differences in all aspects of our lives.

The need for an intercultural mentality to match our multicultural world, the difficulties inherent in the quest of such a goal, the excitement of the challenges, and the rewards of the successes are summarized in the words of Troy Duster:

> There is no longer a single racial or ethnic group with an overwhelming numerical and political majority. Pluralism is the reality, with no one group a dominant force. This is completely new; we are grappling with a phenomenon that is both puzzling and alarming, fraught with tensions and hostilities, and yet simultaneously brimming with potential and crackling with new energy. Consequently, we swing between hope and concern, optimism and pessimism about the prospects for social life among people from differing racial and cultural groups.[34]

We urge you to view this book and each intercultural experience as steps in a lifelong commitment to competence in intercultural communication. Intercultural competence is, in many ways, an art rather than a science. Our hope is that you will use your artistic talents to make the world a better place in which people from all cultures can live and thrive.

CULTURE connections

It is always interesting to see something from another person's point of view, particularly if that person is very different from oneself. It broadens the horizons.

—*Nury Vittachi*

Summary

When one cultural group lives near other cultural groups, various forms of adaptation occur. The desire to maintain both an identification with the culture of origin and positive relationships with

other cultures influences the type of adaptation that is experienced. An intercultural transformation occurs when people are able to move beyond the limits of their own cultural experiences to incorporate the perspectives of other cultures into their own interpersonal interactions.

Ethical issues in the development of intercultural competence concern questions about whose responsibility it is to adjust to a different culture, issues about right and wrong, and the degree to which all intercultural contacts should be encouraged. Global forces, which bring people together, are met with equally strong forces that pull people apart. Always, however, people bring to every communicative interaction understandings that are filtered and framed by their own cultural patterns. Thus, one must interpret intercultural experiences within the context of national and international events.

For Discussion

1. Are there historical examples in the United States of some groups dominating and subordinating other cultural groups? Are there contemporary examples?
2. What responsibility does a visitor from another culture have to the host culture's ways of living, thinking, and communicating? For example, should people visiting from another culture accept or engage in behaviors they find ethically wrong but which the host culture sanctions as ethically correct?
3. What are some of the advantages and problems with cultural relativism?
4. Are there universal values that you believe are found in every culture? Explain.
5. What can we do—what can you do—to make the world a place where many cultures thrive?

For Further Reading

Donal Carbaugh, "Cultural Discourse Analysis: Communication Practices and Intercultural Encounters," *Journal of Intercultural Communication Research* 36 (2007): 167–182. Offers a framework that allows for a cultural analysis of communication. Though very theoretical, it provides a very understandable examination of intercultural encounters.

Cathy N. Davidson, *36 Views of Mount Fuji: On Finding Myself in Japan* (New York: Plume, 1993). A well-written narrative that documents the adaptation of a European American woman to life in Japan, as well as describing her readjustments upon returning to her culture of origin.

Jane Jackson, *Language, Identity and Study Abroad: Sociocultural Perspectives* (Oakville, CT: Equinox, 2008). Both a guide to international study experiences and an analysis of how these cultural experiences, if done well, can help one to develop an appreciation for people from other cultures.

Ann Kelleher and Laura Klein, *Global Perspectives: A Handbook for Understanding Global Issues*, 3rd ed. (Upper Saddle River, NJ: Prentice Hall, 2009). A broad presentation of salient ways to understand global issues. Focuses on ecological, economic, political, psychological, and sociological perspectives.

Young Yun Kim, *Becoming Intercultural: An Integrative Theory of Communication and Cross-Cultural Adaptation* (Thousand Oaks, CA: Sage, 2001). Provides a framework for understanding the experience of individuals who move (either physically or psychologically) from one cultural setting to another.

Dan Landis, Janet M. Bennett, and Milton J. Bennett (eds.), *Handbook of Intercultural Training*, 3rd ed. (Thousand Oaks, CA: Sage, 2004). A useful compendium of ideas for helping others to improve their intercultural competence. Translates current theories of intercultural communication into practical techniques for training others.

For additional information about intercultural films and about Web sites for researching specific cultures, please turn to the Resources section at the back of this book.

Resources

Information about cultures and about intercultural communication can come from many different sources. In addition to the resource materials within each chapter, we provide here a list of many resources that you can use to increase your culture-specific knowledge about the beliefs, values, norms, and social practices of many cultures.

Intercultural Films

Here are some suggestions for films you might want to view. Many of these films may be available at your local video rental store. In addition, many schools have audiovisual departments that might carry some of these titles.

Each of the film titles is followed (in parentheses) by the culture(s) portrayed. Typically, the central characters in the films are from the indicated cultures, and the action of the film's story is usually set in those cultures as well.

As we have mentioned at numerous places throughout this book, a word of caution is warranted. The characters in these films, like all other individuals you might experience, are not perfect representations of their cultures. While some of the revealed beliefs, values, norms, and social practices may be "typical" of a majority of members of the portrayed cultures, others may be common only to a few cultural members, and some characteristics will undoubtedly be unique to the individuals in the films. We caution you, therefore, to guard against the presumption that *any* depiction of cultural members will be a completely accurate one.

In our judgment, each of the listed films portrays the members of a culture with complexity and integrity. Omitted from this list are Hollywood blockbuster films such as *Dances with Wolves, The Joy Luck Club, The Kite Runner,* and *Schindler's List.* Although such films are often excellent (and, as is true with these four examples, are often must-see films), they are likely to be better known than those we list here. Our listing is by no means complete, but it does contain some of our favorites. Enjoy!

Babette's Feast (Danish)
The Barbarian Invasion (French Canadian)
Before the Rains (Asian Indian)
Bella (Latino)
Beyond Rangoon (Burmese)
Blue Kite (Chinese)

Bread and Chocolate (Swiss, Italian)
Bride and Prejudice (Asian Indian)
Children of Heaven (Iranian)
Cinema Paradiso (Italian)
The Circle (Iranian)
City of God (Brazilian)

Crash (various U.S. American)
Cry, The Beloved Country (South African)
Daughter from Danang (Vietnamese)
Eat Drink Man Woman (Chinese)
The Edge of America (Native American)
El Norte (Guatemalan, European American)
Eureka (Japanese)
Europa Europa (European)
The Gods Must Be Crazy (Sho Bushmen)
Good Bye Lenin (German)
A Great Wall (Chinese, Chinese-American)
Higher Learning (African American)
Il Postino (The Postman) (Italian)
Indochine (Vietnamese)
King of Masks (Chinese)
Kundun (Tibetan)
The Last Emperor (Chinese)
Like Water for Chocolate (Mexican)
Little Buddha (Tibetan)
To Live (Chinese)
The Makioka Sisters (Japanese)
Maria Full of Grace (Colombian)
Mediterraneo (Italian, Greek)
Mi Familia (Latino)

Mississippi Massala (African American, Indian American)
Mongolian Ping Pong (Mongolian)
My Favorite Season (French)
My Life as a Dog (Swedish)
My Sassy Girl (Yeopgijeogin geunyeo) (Korean)
Picture Bride (Japanese)
Pushing Hands (Chinese, Chinese American)
Raise the Red Lantern (Chinese)
Red Firecracker, Green Firecracker (Chinese)
The Road Home (Chinese)
The Scent of Green Papaya (Vietnamese)
Shall We Dance? (Japanese)
Soul Food (African American)
Spring, Summer, Fall, Winter ... and Spring (Korean)
The Story of Qui Ju (Chinese)
Tortilla Soup (Latino)
The Vertical Ray of the Sun (Vietnamese)
A Walk in the Clouds (Latino)
Water (Asian Indian)
The Way Home (Korean)
Witness (Amish)

Online Resources

General Online Search Engines

Alta Vista http://www.altavista.com/
AOL http://www.aol.com/
Ask http://www.ask.com/
Excite http://www.excite.com/
Go http://go.com/
Google http://www.google.com/
Hotbot http://www.hotbot.com/
Info http://www.info.com/
Live Search http://www.ndparking.com/livesearch.com
Lycos http://www.lycos.com/
MetaCrawler http://www.metacrawler.com/
MetaSearch http://metasearch.com/
MSN http://www.msn.com/
Northern Light http://www.nlsearch.com/
Search http://www.search.com/
WebCrawler http://www.webcrawler.com/
Yahoo http://www.yahoo.com/

Web sites about Multiple Countries and Their Cultures

Arab Net   http://www.arab.net/ Links to information about the geography, history, and culture of more than 20 countries in or near the Middle East.

Latin America   http://lanic.utexas.edu/subject/countries.html Links to information about more than 40 countries in Central and South America.

Library of Congress Country Studies   http://lcweb2.loc.gov/frd/cs The Library of Congress provides in-depth information about the culture, geography, and history of more than 100 countries around the world, from Albania to Zaire.

Lonely Planet: Travel Guides   http://www.lonelyplanet.com/destinations Where in the world do you want to go? The Lonely Planet series of travel guides provides information about many of the world's countries and cultures.

Rough Guides: Travel Guides   http://www.roughguides.com/ The Rough Guide series of travel guides provides an alternative set of information about many of the world's countries and cultures.

World Factbook   http://www.odci.gov/cia/publications/factbook/index.html Information on the geography, people, government, and other information for hundreds of countries.

Web sites about Specific Countries and Their Cultures

Albania   http://www.albanian.com/
Angola   http://www.angola.org/
Australia   http://www.csu.edu.au/australia/
Azerbaijan   http://www.friends-partners.org/oldfriends/azerbaijan/index.html
Bangladesh   http://www.virtualbangladesh.com/
Belgium   http://belgium.fgov.be/
Belize Government Page   http://www.belize.gov.bz/
Belize Online   http://www.belize.com/
Cambodia   http://www.cambodia.org/
Canada   http://canada.gc.ca/
Cape Verde   http://www.umassd.edu/specialprograms/caboverde/capeverdean.html
China, Republic of (Taiwan)   http://www.gio.gov.tw/
Denmark   http://www.denmarkemb.org/
Estonia: Country Guide   http://www.ciesin.ee/ESTCG/
Estonia: Institute of Baltic Studies   http://www.ibs.ee/
Finland   http://virtual.finland.fi/
France: French Ministry of Foreign Affairs   http://www.france.diplomatie.fr/index.gb.html
Georgia   http://www.parliament.ge/
Germany   http://www.germany-info.org
Ghana   http://www.ghanaweb.com
Guyana   http://www.guyana.org/
Hungary   http://www.fsz.bme.hu/hungary/homepage.html
Iceland   http://www.whatson.is/
Iran: Iranian Cultural Information Center   http://persia.org/
Iraq   http://www.iraqfoundation.org/
Ireland: Central Statistics Office   http://www.cso.ie/

Ireland, Northern   http://www.interknowledge.com/northern-ireland/index.html
Italy: Dolce Vita   http://www.dolcevita.com/
Italy: Embassy in U.S.   http://www.italyemb.org/
Jamaica   http://www.jamaicans.com/
Japan: Information Network   http://www.jinjapan.org/
Jewish: Judaism 101   http://www.jewfaq.org/
Jewish: Resources   http://shamash.org/trb/judaism.html
Kurdistan   http://www.xs4all.nl/~tank/kurdish/htdocs/index.html
Libya   http://ourworld.compuserve.com/homepages/dr_ibrahim_ighneiwa/
Mexico: Reference Desk   http://lanic.utexas.edu/la/Mexico/
Nepal   http://www.info-nepal.com/
Netherlands   http://www.nbt.nl/
New Zealand   http://nz.com/
Norway   http://www.norway.org/
Papua New Guinea   http://www.niugini.com/
Scotland   http://members.aol.com/sconemac/index.html
Singapore: Government   http://www.gov.sg/
Singapore: InfoMap   http://www.sg/
South Africa   http://www.polity.org.za/
Spain   http://www.docuweb.ca/SiSpain/english/index.html
Sweden   http://www.sverigeturism.se/smorgasbord/
Tunisia   http://www.tunisiaonline.com/
Turkey   http://www.turkey.org/
United Kingdom: Travel Guide   http://www.uktravel.com/index.html
United Kingdom: UK Online   http://www.open.gov.uk/
USA, African American: Black Network   http://www.netnoir.com
USA, Asian American: Asian American Net   http://www.asianamerican.net/
USA, Hawaiian   http://www.hawaii-nation.org/
USA, Latino: Hispanic Online   http://www.hispaniconline.com/
USA, Native Americans   http://www.indians.org/welker/nations1.htm
USA, Native Americans, Lakota   http://puffin.creighton.edu/lakota/index.html
USA, Native Americans, Seneca   http://www.sni.org/

Notes

Chapter 1

1. U.S. Census Bureau, "Annual Estimates of the Population by Sex, Race, and Hispanic Origin for the United States: April 1, 2000 to July 1, 2007," May 1, 2008, accessed July 1, 2008, from http://www.census.gov/popest/national/asrh/NC-EST2007-srh.html; U.S. Census Bureau, 2004, "Race and Hispanic Origin in 2005," accessed July 1, 2008, from http://www.census. gov/population/pop-profile/dynamic/RACEHO.pdf. See also: U.S. Census Bureau, Population Estimates Program, Tables DP1-2006, T3-2006, T4-2006, and T5-2006.

2. Projections based on information from Jeffrey Passel and D'Vera Cohn, "U.S. Population Projections: 2005–2050," Pew Research Center, February 11, 2008. Accessed July 1, 2008, from http://pewresearch.org/pubs/729/united-states-population-projections; U.S. Census Bureau, "Projected Population of the United States, by Race and Hispanic Origin: 2000 to 2050," accessed July 1, 2008, from http://www.census.gov/ipc/www/usinterimproj/.

3. William A. Henry III, "Beyond the Melting Pot," *Time*, April 9, 1990, 28.

4. U.S. Census Bureau, 2004, "U.S. Interim Projections by Age, Sex, Race, and Hispanic Origin," accessed December 17, 2007, from http://www.census.gov/ipc/www/usinterimproj/.

5. Lisa Friedman, "Immigrants and Their Kids May Produce 63% of Growth," *Los Angeles Daily News*, August 31, 2007, 4.

6. Angela Brittingham, "The Foreign-Born Population in the United States: Population Characteristics," U.S. Bureau of the Census, August 2000. See also: "Coming to America: A Profile of the Nation's Foreign Born," U.S. Census Bureau, August 2000.

7. Randolph E. Schmid, "Nearly 1 in 10 U.S. Residents Born Abroad, Report Says," *Sacramento Bee*, September 19, 1999, A7.

8. U.S. Census Bureau, 2008, "The Foreign-Born Population in 2004," accessed July 1, 2008, from http://www.census.gov/population/pop-profile/dynamic/ForeignBorn.pdf.

9. U.S. Census Bureau, 2004, "Race and Hispanic Origin in 2005," accessed July 1, 2008, from http://www.census.gov/population/pop-profile/dynamic/RACEHO.pdf.

10. Hyon B. Shin with Rosalind Bruno, "Language Use and English-Speaking Ability: 2000," U.S. Census Bureau, October 2003. Accessed July 3, 2008, from http://www.census.gov/prod/2003pubs/c2kbr-29.pdf.

11. U.S. Census Bureau, 2008, "The Foreign-Born Population in 2004," accessed July 1, 2008, from http://www.census.gov/population/pop-profile/dynamic/Foreign-Born.pdf. See also: U.S. Census Bureau, 2004, "The Foreign-Born Population in the United States: 2003," accessed July 1, 2008, from http://www.census.gov/prod/2004pubs/p20-551.pdf; U.S. Census Bureau, 2006 American Community Survey, Table S0502 (Selected Characteristics of the Foreign-Born Population by Period of Entry into the United States).

12. U.S. Census Bureau, 2006 American Community Survey, Table S0501 (Selected Characteristics of the Native and Foreign-Born Populations).

13. Antonia Pantoja and Wilhelmina Perry, "Cultural Pluralism: A Goal to Be Realized," *Voices from the Battlefront*, ed. Marta Moreno Vega and Cheryll Y. Greene (Trenton, NJ: Africa World Press, 1993), 136.

14. "Classrooms of Babel," *Newsweek*, February 11, 1991, 56–57.

15. Leanna Stiefel, Amy Ellen Schwartz, and Dylan Conger, "Language Proficiency and Home Languages of Students in New York City Elementary and Middle Schools," New York University: Taub Urban Research Center, February 2003.

16. David Ferrell and Robert Lee Hotz, "Ethnic Pockets Amid a Vast Fabric of English," *Los Angeles Times*, January 23, 2000, A1, A16–18.

17. U.S. Department of Education, National Center for Education Statistics, 2008, "Digest of Education Statistics, 2007 (NCES 2008-022)," Tables 179, 196, 197, 198. Accessed July 3, 2008, from http://nces.ed.gov/fastfacts/display.asp?id=98.

18. Juliana Barbassa, "More Foreign Students Attending U.S. Schools," *Los Angeles Daily News*, December 8, 2007, A9; *Open Doors 2007* (New York: Institute for International Education, 2007).

19. *Open Doors 2007* (New York: Institute for International Education, 2007).

20. Marshall McLuhan, *The Gutenberg Galaxy: The Making of Typographic Man* (Toronto: University of Toronto Press, 1962).

21. Richard W. Fisher, "Globalization's Impact on U.S. Growth and Inflation." Remarks before the Dallas, TX State Assembly, May 22, 2006. Accessed December 17, 2007, from http://www.dallasfed.org/news/speeches/fisher/2006/fs060522.cfm.

22. Fisher.

23. Vinnie Mirchandani, "Globalization and Technology," *Deal Architect*, July 8, 2007. Accessed December 17, 2007, from http://dealarchitect.typepad.com/deal_architect/globalization_and_technology/index.html.

24. Rob Baedeker, "Where Americans Visit Most," Forbes Traveler.com, November 1, 2007. Accessed December 19, 2007, from http://www.forbestraveler.com/best-lists/countries-americans-visit-story.html.

25. Thomas L. Friedman, *The World Is Flat: A Brief History of the Twenty-First Century*, further updated and expanded ed. (New York: Picador, 2007). To trace the development of Friedman's ideas, see also: Thomas L. Friedman, *The Lexus and the Olive Tree* (New York: Farrar, Straus, & Giroux, 1999).

26. U.S. Census Bureau and U.S. Bureau of Economic Analysis, *U.S. International Trade in Goods and Services: Annual Revision for 2006* (Washington, DC, June 8, 2007).

27. Fisher.

28. U.S. Census Bureau, *Asian Owned Firms: 2002* (Washington, DC: August, 2006).

29. Jim Hopkins, "African American Women Step Up in Business World," *USAToday*, August 24, 2006. Accessed December 18, 2007, from http://www.usatoday.com/money/smallbusiness/2006-08-24-women-biz-usat_x.htm.

30. HispanicBusiness.com, "Hispanic-Owned Businesses: Growth Projections to 2012." Accessed July 2, 2008 from http://www.hispanicbusiness.com/news/2008/4/11/hispanicowned_businesses_growth_projections_to_2012.htm.

31. Robert Shuter, "The Centrality of Culture," *Southern Communication Journal* 55 (1990): 241.

32. President's Commission on Foreign Language and International Studies (Washington, DC: Department of Health, Education and Welfare, 1979), 1.

33. David Holthouse and Mark Potok, "The Year in Hate," *Intelligence Report* 129 (Southern Poverty Law Center, 2008). Accessed July 2, 2008, from http://www.splcenter.org/intel/intelreport/article.jsp?aid=886.

34. Infoplease, "Summary of Hate Crime Statistics, 2002," accessed October 15, 2004, from http://www.infoplease.com/ipa/A0004885.html.

35. "Hate Crimes: From Sea to Shining Sea," *Esquire*, May 21, 2008. Accessed July 3, 2008, from http://www.esquire.com/features/hate-crime-0608.

36. David Crary, "Hate Crimes Linked to Immigration Debate," *Associated Press*, March 10, 2008. Accessed July 2, 2008, from http://www.commondreams.org/archive/2008/03/10/7587/; "Man Faces Charges over Nooses on Truck at Jena March," *CNN.com*, January 24, 2008. Accessed July 2, 2008, from http://www.cnn.com/2008/CRIME/01/24/jena.indictment/index.html.

37. Shaya Tayefe Mohajer, "Hate-Crime Charge Added in W.Va. Kidnap-Assault Case," *The Washington Post*, February 7, 2008, A07. Accessed June 29, 2008, from http://www.washingtonpost.com/wp-dyn/content/article/2008/02/06/AR2008020604208.html.

38. Sarah Garland, "Black, Jewish Leaders Target Hate Crimes," *The New York Sun*, January 7, 2008. Accessed July 3, 2008, from http://www.nysun.com/new-york/black-jewish-leaders-target-hate-crimes/68994/.

39. Alexandra Marks, "After 'hate-crime' melee, calm eludes Quaker school," *The Christian Science Monitor*, January 29, 2007. Accessed July 1, 2008, from http://www.csmonitor.com/2007/0129/p02s01-ussc.html.

40. Julia Kitlinski-Hong, "Asian Americans Remain Vigilant Against Hate Crimes," *New America Media*, July 12, 2007. Accessed July 3, 2008, from http://news.newamericamedia.org/news/view_article.html?article_id=fb6e6f8adfc2a362319644eef783b649.

41. Catharine R. Stimpson, "A Conversation, Not a Monologue," *Chronicle of Higher Education*, March 16, 1994, B1.

42. See Frank E. X. Dance, "The 'Concept' of Communication," *Journal of Communication* 20 (1970): 201–10; Frank E. X. Dance and Carl E. Larson, *The Functions of Human Communication* (New York: Holt, Rinehart and Winston, 1976), Appendix A.

43. Dance.

44. Dance and Larson.

45. Claude E. Shannon and Warren Weaver, *The Mathematical Theory of Communication* (Urbana: University of Illinois Press, 1949).

46. Interactional models include David K. Berlo, *The Process of Communication* (New York: Holt, Rinehart and Winston, 1960); Wilbur Schramm, *The Process and Effects of Mass Communication* (Urbana: University of Illinois Press, 1954); and Bruce H. Westley and Malcolm S. MacLean, Jr., "A Conceptual Model for Communication Research," *Journalism Quarterly* 34 (1957): 31–38.

47. Dean Barnlund, *Interpersonal Communication: Survey and Studies* (Boston: Houghton Mifflin, 1968), 512.

48. Donald W. Klopf, *Intercultural Encounters: The Fundamentals of Intercultural Communications* (Englewood, CO: Morton, 1987), 23–24.

49. John C. Condon, *Good Neighbors: Communicating with the Mexicans* (Yarmouth, ME: Intercultural Press, 1985), 34.

50. Quoted in Frank Bures, "A New Accent on Diversity," *Christian Science Monitor*, November 6, 2002, pp. 11–15. See also: Richard Rodriguez, *Brown: The Last Discovery of America* (New York: Viking, 2002).

Chapter 2

1. Alfred L. Kroeber and Clyde Kluckhohn, *Culture: A Critical Review of Concepts and Definitions* (Cambridge, MA: Harvard University Press, 1952).
2. Mary Jane Collier and Milt Thomas, "Cultural Identity: An Interpretive Approach," *Theories in Intercultural Communication*, ed. Young Yun Kim and William B. Gudykunst (Newbury Park, CA: Sage, 1988), 103.
3. See, for example, Maurice Berger, *White Lies: Race and the Myths of Whiteness*, 1st ed. (New York: Farrar, Straus, Giroux, 1999); Karen Brodkin, *How Jews Became White Folks and What That Says About Race in America* (New Brunswick, NJ: Rutgers University Press, 2000); Paul D. Buchanan, *Race Relations in the United States: A Chronology, 1896-2005* (Jefferson, NC: McFarland & Co., 2005); Eric L. Goldstein, *The Price of Whiteness: Jews, Race, and American Identity* (Princeton: Princeton University Press, 2006); Laura E. Gómez, *Manifest Destinies: The Making of the Mexican American Race* (New York: New York University, 2007); Noel Ignatiev, *How the Irish Became White* (New York: Routledge, 1996); David R. Roediger, *Working toward Whiteness: How America's Immigrants Became White: The Strange Journey from Ellis Island to the Suburbs* (New York: Basic Books, 2005); David R. Roediger, *The Wages of Whiteness: Race and the Making of the American Working Class*, Haymarket Series Rev. ed. (New York: Verso, 2007); Karen Elaine Rosenblum and Toni-Michelle Travis, *The Meaning of Difference: American Constructions of Race, Sex and Gender, Social Class, Sexual Orientation, and Disability*, 5th ed. (New York: McGraw-Hill, 2008).
4. Brodkin, 74. See also Gómez, *Manifest Destinies: The Making of the Mexican American Race*.
5. For an elaboration of this idea, see Brodkin; Richard Delgado and Jeanne Stefancic (eds.), *Critical White Studies: Looking Behind the Mirror* (Philadelphia: Temple University Press, 1997); Marc Edelman, "Devil, Not-Quite-White, Rootless Cosmopolitan: Tsuris in Latin America, the Bronx, and the USSR," *Composing Ethnography: Alternative Forms of Qualitative Writing*, ed. Carolyn Ellis and Arthur Bochner (Walnut Creek, CA: Altamira Press, 1996); Ruth Frankenberg, *White Women, Race Matters: The Social Construction of Whiteness* (Minneapolis: University of Minnesota Press, 1993); Ian F. Haney Lopez, *White by Law: The Legal Construction of Race* (New York: New York University Press, 1996); Noel Ignatiev, *How the Irish Became White* (Cambridge, MA: Harvard University Press, 1995); Rosenblum and Travis, *The Meaning of Difference: American Constructions of Race, Sex and Gender, Social Class, Sexual Orientation, and Disability;* David Stowe, "Uncolored People: The Rise of Whiteness Studies," *Lingua Franca* 6 (1996): 68–77.
6. Thierry Devos and Mahzarin R. Banaji, "American = White?" *Journal of Personality and Social Psychology* 88 (2005): 447–466.
7. Myron W. Lustig, "WSCA 2005 Presidential Address: Toward a Well-Functioning Intercultural Nation," *Western Journal of Communication* 69 (2005): 377–379.
8. Gustav Ichheiser, *Appearances and Realities: Misunderstanding in Human Relations* (San Francisco: Jossey-Bass, 1970), 8.
9. David McCullough, 1994 Commencement Address at the University of Pittsburgh, quoted in *Chronicle of Higher Education,* June 8, 1994, B2.
10. Geert Hofstede, *Culture's Consequences: International Differences in Work-Related Values* (Beverly Hills, CA: Sage, 1980).
11. Peter A. Andersen, "Cues of Culture: The Basis of Intercultural Differences in Nonverbal Communication," *Intercultural Communication: A Reader*, 8th ed., ed. Larry A. Samovar and Richard E. Porter (Belmont, CA: Wadsworth, 1997), 244–256; Edward T. Hall, *The Hidden Dimension* (New York: Doubleday, 1966); Miles L. Patterson, *Nonverbal Behavior: A Functional Perspective* (New York: Springer-Verlag, 1983); Carol Zinner Dolphin, "Variables in the Use of Personal Space in Intercultural Transactions," *Intercultural Communication: A Reader*, 8th ed., ed. Larry A. Samovar and Richard E. Porter (Belmont, CA: Wadsworth, 1997), 266–276.
12. Peter A. Andersen, Myron W. Lustig, and Janis F. Andersen, "Changes in Latitude, Changes in Attitude: The Relationship Between Climate and Interpersonal Communication Predispositions," *Communication Quarterly* 38 (1990): 291–311.
13. Charlotte Evans, "Barbed Wire, the Cutting Edge in Fencing," *Smithsonian* 22 (4) (July 1991): 72–78, 80, 82–83.
14. Henry Chu, "Ancient Hindu Blessings a Mouse Click Away," *Los Angeles Times,* December 24, 2007, A3.
15. See Clayton Jones, "Cultural Crosscurrents Buffet the Orient," *Christian Science Monitor*, December 8, 1993, 11, 13; Sheila Tefft, "Satellite Broadcasts Create Stir Among Asian Regimes," *Christian Science Monitor*, December 8, 1993, 12–13.
16. George A. Barnett and Meihua Lee, "Issues in Intercultural Communication Research," *Cross-Cultural and Intercultural Communication*, ed. William B. Gudykunst (Thousand Oaks, CA: Sage, 2003), 268.
17. James W. Chesebro, "Communication, Values, and Popular Television Series – a Twenty-Five Year Assessment and Final Conclusions," *Communication Quarterly* 51 (2003): 367–418.
18. Chesebro, 395-396, 398.
19. Daniel L. Hartl and Andrew G. Clark, *Principles of Population Genetics*, 4th ed. (Sunderland, MA: Sinauer Associates, 2007).

20. Sandra Scarr, A. J. Pakstis, S. H. Katz, and W. B. Barker, "Absence of Relationship between Degree of White Ancestry and Intellectual Skills within a Black Population," *Human Genetics* 39 (1977): 69–86; Sandra Scarr and Richard A. Weinberg, "I.Q. Test Performance of Black Children Adopted by White Families," *American Psychologist* 31 (1976): 726–739; Richard A. Weinberg, Sandra Scarr, and Irwin D. Waldman, "The Minnesota Transracial Adoption Study: A Follow-up of IQ Test Performance at Adolescence," *Intelligence* 16 (1992): 117–135. See also: Thomas J. Bouchard, Jr., David T. Lykken, Matthew McGue, Nancy Segal, and Auke Tellegen, "Sources of Human Physiological Differences: The Minnesota Study of Twins Reared Apart," *Science* 250 (1990): 223–228.

21. Michael Winkelman, *Ethnic Relations in the U.S.: A Sociohistorical Cultural Systems Approach* (Minneapolis: West, 1993), 67–68.

22. Cary Quan Gelernter, "Racial Realities," *Seattle Times/Post-Intelligencer*, January 15, 1989, K1. Reprinted in *Ethnic Groups*, vol. 4., ed. Eleanor Goldstein (Boca Raton, FL: Social Issues Resources Ser., 1994), art. no. 83.

23. Alan R. Rogers and Lynn B. Jorde, "Genetic Evidence on Modern Human Origins," *Human Biology* 67 (1995): 1–36; Linda Vigilant, Mark Stoneking, Henry Harpending, Kristen Hawkes, and Allan C. Wilson, "African Populations and the Evolution of Human Mitochondrial DNA," *Science* 253 (1991): 1503–1507; Nicholas Wade, *Before the Dawn: Recovering the Lost History of Our Ancestors* (New York: Penguin, 2006).

24. Wade.

25. Lundy Braun, "Race and Genetics—Reifying Human Difference: The Debate on Genetics, Race, and Health," *International Journal of Health Services* 36 (2006): 557–574; Eddie L. Hoover, "There Is No Scientific Rationale for Race-Based Research," *Journal of the National Medical Association* 99 (2007): 690–692; Race, Ethnicity, and Genetics Working Group, "The Use of Racial, Ethnic, and Ancestral Categories in Human Genetics Research," *American Journal of Human Genetics* 77 (2005): 519–532.

26. Troy Duster, "The Molecular Reinscription of Race: Unanticipated Issues in Biotechnology and Forensic Science," *Patterns of Prejudice* 40 (2006): 427–441; Reanne Frank, "What to Make of It? The (Re)Emergence of a Biological Conceptualization of Race in Health Disparities Research," *Social Science & Medicine* 64 (2007): 1977–1983.

27. Luigi Luca Cavalli-Sforza, "Human Evolution and Its Relevance for Genetic Epidemiology," *Annual Review of Genomics and Human Genetics* 8 (2007): 1–15.

28. Cavalli-Sforza, 13–14.

29. Charmaine D. M. Royal and Georgia M. Dunston, "Changing the Paradigm from 'Race' to Human Genome Variation," *Nature Genetics* 36 (2004): S5–S7.

30. For discussions of race and ethnicity as social and political distinctions rather than as a genetic one, see Linda Martín Alcoff and Eduardo Mendieta (eds.), *Identities: Race, Class, Gender, and Nationality* (Malden, MA: Blackwell, 2003); John D. Buenker and Lorman A. Ratner (eds.), *Multiculturalism in the United States: A Comparative Guide to Acculturation and Ethnicity* (Westport, CT: Greenwood, 2005); Rodney D. Coates (ed.), *Race and Ethnicity: Across Time, Space, and Discipline* (Boston: Brill, 2004); Stephanie Cole and Alison M. Parker (eds.), *Beyond Black & White: Race, Ethnicity, and Gender in the U.S. South and Southwest* (Arlington, TX: Texas A&M University Press, 2004); Steve Fenton, *Ethnicity* (Cambridge: Polity Press, 2003); Joan Ferrante and Prince Brown (eds.), *The Social Construction of Race and Ethnicity in the United States*, 2nd ed. (Upper Saddle River, NJ: Prentice Hall, 2001); Nancy Foner and George M. Fredrickson (eds.), *Not Just Black and White: Historical and Contemporary Perspectives on Immigration, Race, and Ethnicity in the United States* (New York: Russell Sage Foundation, 2004); David Theo Goldberg and John Solomos (eds.), *A Companion to Racial and Ethnic Studies* (Malden, MA: Blackwell, 2002); Harry Goulbourne (ed.), *Race and Ethnicity: Critical Concepts in Sociology* (New York: Routledge, 2001); Yasmin Gunaratnam, *Researching Race and Ethnicity: Methods, Knowledge, and Power* (Thousand Oaks, CA: Sage, 2003); Joseph F. Healey, *Diversity and Society: Race, Ethnicity and Gender* (Thousand Oaks, CA: Pine Forge Press, 2004); Joseph F. Healey and Eileen O'Brien (eds.), *Race, Ethnicity, and Gender: Selected Readings* (Thousand Oaks, CA: Pine Forge Press, 2004); Caroline Knowles, *Race and Social Analysis* (Thousand Oaks, CA: Sage, 2003); Maria Krysan and Amanda Lewis (eds.), *The Changing Terrain of Race and Ethnicity* (New York: Russell Sage Foundation, 2004); Jennifer Lee and Min Zhou (eds.), *Asian American Youth: Culture, Identity, and Ethnicity* (New York: Routledge, 2004); Peter Osborne and Stella Sandford (eds.), *Philosophies of Race and Ethnicity* (New York: Continuum, 2002); Raymond Scupin (ed.), *Race and Ethnicity: An Anthropological Focus on the United States and the World* (Upper Saddle River, NJ: Prentice Hall, 2003); Miri Song, *Choosing Ethnic Identity* (Malden, MA: Blackwell, 2003); Paul Spickard (ed.), *Race and Nation: Ethnic Systems in the Modern World* (New York: Routledge, 2004).

31. Audrey Smedley and Brian D. Smedley, "Race as Biology Is Fiction, Racism as a Social Problem Is Real: Anthropological and Historical Perspectives on the Social Construction of Race," *American Psychologist* 60 (2005): 16–26.

32. Marshall R. Singer, *Intercultural Communication: A Perceptual Approach* (Englewood Cliffs, NJ: Prentice Hall, 1987).

33. Jared Diamond, *Guns, Germs, and Steel: The Fates of Human Societies* (New York: W. W. Norton, 1999).

34. Diamond, 92.

35. The idea that the degree of heterogeneity among participants distinguishes intercultural from intracultural communication, and thereby results in a continuum of "interculturalness" of the communication, was first introduced by L. E. Sarbaugh, *Intercultural Communication* (Rochelle Park, NJ: Hayden, 1979).

36. For a more detailed discussion of the relationships among these terms, see Molefi Kete Asante and William B. Gudykunst (eds.), *Handbook of Intercultural Communication* (Newbury Park, CA: Sage, 1989), 7–13.

Chapter 3

1. The melting pot metaphor for U.S. cultural diversity was popularized by Israel Zangwell's play of 1908, *The Melting Pot*. The idea was anticipated more than 100 years earlier in Crèvecoeur's description of America: "Here individuals of all nations are melted into a new race of men, whose labors and posterity will one day cause great changes in the world." See J. Hector St. John Crèvecoeur, *Letter from an American Farmer* (New York: Albert and Charles Boni, 1782/1925), 55; Israel Zangwell, *The Melting Pot. Drama in Four Acts* (New York: Arno Press, 1908/1975). For an updated view of the melting pot metaphor, see Tamar Jacoby (ed.), *Reinventing the Melting Pot: The New Immigrants and What It Means to Be American* (New York: Basic Books, 2004).

2. Judith N. Martin, Robert L. Krizek, Thomas K. Nakayama, and Lisa Bradford, "Exploring Whiteness: A Study of Self Labels for White Americans," *Communication Quarterly* 44 (1996): 125–144; Thomas K. Nakayama and Robert L. Krizek, "Whiteness: A Strategic Rhetoric," *Quarterly Journal of Speech* 81 (1995): 291–309.

3. See Rodolfo O. de la Garza, Louis DeSipio, F. Chris Garcia, John Garcia, and Angelo Falcon, *Latino Voices: Mexican, Puerto Rican, & Cuban Perspectives on American Politics* (Boulder, CO: Westview Press, 1992).

4. James Diego Vigil, *From Indians to Chicanos: The Dynamics of Mexican American Culture* (Prospect Heights, IL: Waveland Press, 1980), 1.

5. Mark Z. Barabak, "Differences Found Among U.S. Hispanics," *San Diego Union*, August 30, 1991, A2.

6. Juan L. Gonzales, Jr., *Racial and Ethnic Groups in America* (Dubuque, IA: Kendall/Hunt, 1990), 199.

7. Earl Shorris, "The Latino vs. Hispanic Controversy," *San Diego Union-Tribune*, October 29, 1992, B11. See also Earl Shorris, *Latinos: A Biography of the People* (New York: Norton, 1992); Earl Shorris, "Latinos: The Complexity of Identity," *Report on the Americas* 26 (1992): 19–26.

8. Michael L. Hecht and Sidney Ribeau, "Sociocultural Roots of Ethnic Identity: A Look at Black America," *Journal of Black Studies* 21 (1991): 501–513.

9. For a discussion of the concept of communication competence, see Michael Byram, Adam Nichols, and David Stevens, *Developing Intercultural Competence in Practice* (New York: Multilingual Matters, 2001); Daniel J. Canary and Brian H. Spitzberg, "A Model of Competence Perceptions of Conflict Strategies," *Human Communication Research* 15 (1989): 630–649; Daniel J. Canary and Brian H. Spitzberg, "Attribution Biases and Associations between Conflict Strategies and Competence Outcomes," *Communication Monographs* 57 (1990): 139–151; Robert L. Duran and Brian H. Spitzberg, "Toward the Development and Validation of a Measure of Cognitive Communication Competence," *Communication Quarterly* 43 (1995): 259–275; DeWan Gibson and Mei Zhong, "Intercultural Communication Competence in the Healthcare Context," *International Journal of Intercultural Relations* 29 (2005): 621–634; David A. Griffith, "The Role of Communication Competencies in International Business Relationship Development," *Journal of World Business* 37 (2002): 256–265; Christopher Hajek and Howard Giles, "New Directions in Intercultural Communication Competence: The Process Model," *Handbook of Communication and Social Interaction Skills*, ed. John O. Greene and Brant R. Burleson (Mahwah, NJ: Lawrence Erlbaum, 2003), 935–957; Mitchell R. Hammer, "The Intercultural Conflict Style Inventory: A Conceptual Framework and Measure of Intercultural Conflict Resolution Approaches," *International Journal of Intercultural Relations* 2 (2005): 675–695; Mitchell R. Hammer, Milton J. Bennett, and Richard L. Wiseman, "Measuring Intercultural Sensitivity: The Intercultural Development Inventory," *International Journal of Intercultural Relations* 27 (2003): 421–443; Paige Johnson, A. Elizabeth Lindsey, and Walter R. Zakahi, "Anglo American, Hispanic American, Chilean, Mexican, and Spanish Perceptions of Competent Communication in Initial Interaction," *Communication Research Reports* 18 (2001): 36–43; Shelley D. Lane, *Interpersonal Communication: Competence and Contexts* (Boston: Pearson/Allyn & Bacon, 2008); Myron W. Lustig and Brian H. Spitzberg, "Methodological Issues in the Study of Intercultural Communication Competence," *Intercultural Communication Competence*, ed. Richard L. Wiseman and Jolene Koester (Newbury Park, CA: Sage, 1993) 153–167; Charles Pavitt, "The Ideal Communicator as the Basis for Competence Judgments of Self and Friend," *Communication Reports* 3 (1990): 9–14; Stefanie Rathje, "Intercultural Competence: The Status and Future of a Controversial Concept," *Language and Intercultural Communication* 7 (2007): 254–266; Brian H. Spitzberg, "Issues in the Development of a Theory of Interpersonal Competence in the Intercultural Context,"

International Journal of Intercultural Relations 13 (1989): 241–268; Brian H. Spitzberg, "An Examination of Trait Measures of Interpersonal Competence," *Communication Reports* 4 (1991): 22–29; Brian H. Spitzberg, "The Dialectics of (In)competence," *Journal of Social and Personal Relationships* 10 (1993): 137–158; Brian H. Spitzberg, "The Dark Side of (In)Competence," *The Dark Side of Interpersonal Communication*, ed. William R. Cupach and Brian H. Spitzberg (Hillsdale, NJ: Erlbaum, 1994): 25–49; Brian H. Spitzberg, "Intimate Violence," *Competence in Interpersonal Conflict*, ed. William R. Cupach and Daniel J. Canary (New York: McGraw-Hill; 1997): 174–201; Brian H. Spitzberg and Claire C. Brunner, "Toward a Theoretical Integration of Context and Competence Research," *Western Journal of Speech Communication* 56 (1991): 28–46; Brian H. Spitzberg and Gabrielle Chagnon, "Conceptualizing Intercultural Communication Competence," *The Sage Handbook of Intercultural Competence*, ed. Darla K. Deardorff (Thousand Oaks, CA: Sage, in press); Brian H. Spitzberg and William R. Cupach, *Interpersonal Communication Competence* (Beverly Hills, CA: Sage, 1984); Brian H. Spitzberg and William R. Cupach, *Handbook of Interpersonal Competence Research* (New York: Springer-Verlag, 1989); Brian H. Spitzberg and William R. Cupach, "Interpersonal Skills," *Handbook of Interpersonal Communication* (3rd ed.), ed. Mark L. Knapp and John R. Daly (Newbury Park, CA: Sage, 2002), 564–611; Brian H. Spitzberg and William R. Cupach (eds.), *The Dark Side of Interpersonal Communication*, 2nd ed. (Mahwah, NJ: Lawrence Erlbaum Associates, 2007); Stella Ting-Toomey, "Researching Intercultural Conflict Competence," *Journal of International Communication* 13 (2007): 7–30; Yu-Wen Ying, "Variation in Acculturative Stressors over Time: A Study of Taiwanese Students in the United States," *International Journal of Intercultural Relations* 29 (2005): 59–71.

10. Brian H. Spitzberg, "Communication Competence: Measures of Perceived Effectiveness," *A Handbook for the Study of Human Communication*, ed. Charles H. Tardy (Norwood, NJ: Ablex, 1988), 67–105.

11. William R. Cupach and T. Todd Imahori, "Identity Management Theory: Communication Competence in Intercultural Episodes and Relationships," *Intercultural Communication Competence*, ed. Richard L. Wiseman and Jolene Koester (Newbury Park, CA: Sage, 1993), 112–131; T. Todd Imahori and Mary L. Lanigan, "Relational Model of Intercultural Communication Competence," *International Journal of Intercultural Relations* 13 (1989): 269–286.

12. Fathi S. Yousef, "Human Resource Management: Aspects of Intercultural Relations in U.S. Organizations," *Intercultural Communication: A Reader*, 5th ed., ed. Larry A. Samovar and Richard E. Porter (Belmont, CA: Wadsworth, 1988), 175–182.

13. Ann Neville Miller, "An Exploration of Kenyan Public Speaking Patterns with Implications for the American Introductory Public Speaking Course," *Communication Education* 51 (2002): 168–182.

14. Jolene Koester and Margaret Olebe, "The Behavioral Assessment Scale for Intercultural Communication Effectiveness," *International Journal of Intercultural Relations* 12 (1988): 233–246; Margaret Olebe and Jolene Koester, "Exploring the Cross-Cultural Equivalence of the Behavioral Assessment Scale for Intercultural Communication," *International Journal of Intercultural Relations* 13 (1989): 333–347.

15. Brent D. Ruben, "Assessing Communication Competency for Intercultural Adaptation," *Group and Organization Studies* 1 (1976): 334–354; Brent D. Ruben, Lawrence R. Askling, and Daniel J. Kealey, "Cross-Cultural Effectiveness," *Overview of Intercultural Training, Education, and Research, Vol. I: Theory*, ed. David S. Hoopes, Paul B. Pedersen, and George W. Renwick (Washington, DC: Society for Intercultural Education, Training and Research, 1977), 92–105; Brent D. Ruben and Daniel J. Kealey, "Behavioral Assessment of Communication Competency and the Prediction of Cross-Cultural Adaptation," *International Journal of Intercultural Relations* 3 (1979): 15–48.

Chapter 4

1. Milton Rokeach, *Beliefs, Attitudes, and Values: A Theory of Organization and Change* (San Francisco: Jossey-Bass, 1969).

2. Elisabeth Bumiller, *May You Be the Mother of a Hundred Sons* (New York: Fawcett Columbine, 1990), 11.

3. Milton Rokeach, *The Nature of Human Values* (New York: Free Press, 1973); Milton Rokeach, "Value Theory and Communication Research: Review and Commentary," *Communication Yearbook* 3, ed. Dan Nimmo (New Brunswick, NJ: Transaction, 1979), 7–28.

4. Shalom H. Schwartz, "Universals in the Content and Structure of Values: Theoretical Advances and Empirical Tests in 20 Countries," *Advances in Experimental Social Psychology*, vol. 25, ed. Mark P. Zanna (San Diego: Academic Press, 1992), 1–65; Shalom H. Schwartz, "Are There Universal Aspects in the Structure and Content of Values?" *Journal of Social Issues* 50 (1994): 19–45; Shalom H. Schwartz and Anat Bardi, "Value Hierarchies across Cultures: Taking a Similarities Perspective," *Journal of Cross-Cultural Psychology* 32 (2001): 268–290; Shalom H. Schwartz, Gila Melech, Arielle Lehmann, Steven Burgess, Mari Harris, and Vicki Owens, "Extending the Cross-Cultural Validity of the Theory of Basic Human Values with a Different Method of Measurement," *Journal of Cross-Cultural Psychology* 32 (2001): 519–542; Shalom H. Schwartz and Tammy Rubel, "Sex

Differences in Value Priorities: Cross-Cultural and Multimethod Studies," *Journal of Personality and Social Psychology* 89 (2005): 1010–1028; Shalom H. Schwartz and Lilach Sagiv, "Identifying Culture-Specifics in the Content and Structure of Values," *Journal of Cross-Cultural Psychology* 26 (1995): 92–116; Shalom H. Schwartz, Markku Verasalo, Avishai Antonovsky, and Lilach Sagiv, "Value Priorities and Social Desirability: Much Substance, Some Style," *British Journal of Social Psychology* 36 (1997): 3–18; Naomi Struch, Shalom H. Schwartz, and Willem A. van der Kloot, "Meanings of Basic Values for Women and Men: A Cross-Cultural Analysis," *Personality and Social Psychology Bulletin* 28 (2002): 16–28.

5. Norine Dresser, *Multicultural Manners: Essential Rules of Etiquette for the 21st Century*, rev. ed. (Hoboken, NJ: Wiley, 2005) 30.

6. Dresser, 91.

7. William B. Gudykunst and Carmen M. Lee, "Cross-Cultural Theories," *Cross-Cultural and Intercultural Communication*, ed. William B. Gudykunst (Thousand Oaks, CA: Sage, 2003), 12.

8. Florence Rockwood Kluckhohn and Fred L. Strodtbeck, *Variations in Value Orientations* (Evanston, IL: Row, Peterson, 1960).

9. Edgar H. Schein, *Organizational Culture and Leadership* 2nd ed. (San Francisco: Jossey-Bass, 1992).

10. Our primary sources for this section include John C. Condon and Fathi Yousef, *An Introduction to Intercultural Communication* (Indianapolis: Bobbs-Merrill, 1975); Edward C. Stewart, *American Cultural Patterns: A Cross-Cultural Perspective* (Pittsburgh: Regional Council for International Education, 1971); Edward C. Stewart and Milton J. Bennett, *American Cultural Patterns: A Cross-Cultural Perspective*, rev. ed. (Yarmouth, ME: Intercultural Press, 1991). Excellent resources with thorough descriptions of the cultural patterns of U.S. American cultural groups include Don C. Locke, *Increasing Multicultural Understanding: A Comprehensive Model* (Newbury Park, CA: Sage, 1992); Eleanor W. Lynch and Marci J. Hanson, *Developing Cross-Cultural Competence: A Guide for Working with Young Children and Their Families* (Baltimore: Paul Brookes, 1992); and Esther Wanning, *Culture Shock: USA* (Singapore: Times Books International, 1991).

11. Rajesh Kumar and Anand Kumar Sethi, *Doing Business in India: A Guide for Western Managers* (New York: Palgrave Macmillan, 2005).

12. Yale Richmond, *From Da to Yes: Understanding the East Europeans* (Yarmouth, ME: Intercultural Press, 1995) 110.

13. See, for example, Ringo Ma, "The Role of Unofficial Intermediaries in Interpersonal Conflicts in the Chinese Culture," *Communication Quarterly* 40 (1992): 269–278.

14. Mary Jane Collier, Sidney A. Ribeau, and Michael L. Hecht, "Intracultural Communication Rules and Outcomes Within Three Domestic Cultures," *International Journal of Intercultural Relations* 10 (1986): 452. Also see Mary Jane Collier, "A Comparison of Conversations Among and Between Domestic Cultural Groups: How Intra- and Intercultural Competencies Vary," *Communication Quarterly* 36 (1988): 122–144.

15. Jack L. Daniel and Geneva Smitherman, "How I Got Over: Communication Dynamics in the Black Community," *Quarterly Journal of Speech* 62 (1976): 29.

16. Daniel and Smitherman, 31.

17. Jamake Highwater, *The Primal Mind* (New York: New American Library, 1981).

18. Melvin Delgado, "Hispanic Cultural Values: Implications for Groups," *Small Group Behavior* 12 (1981): 75.

19. Kumar and Sethi, 60.

20. Daniel and Smitherman, 29.

21. Daniel and Smitherman, 32.

Chapter 5

1. Edward T. Hall, *Beyond Culture* (Garden City, NY: Anchor, 1977).

2. Geert Hofstede, *Culture's Consequences: Comparing Values, Behaviors, Institutions, and Organizations across Nations*, 2nd ed. (Thousand Oaks, CA: Sage, 2001); Geert Hofstede, *Cultures and Orga-nizations: Software of the Mind* (London: Mc Graw-Hill, 1991).

3. Denise Rotondo Fernandez, Dawn S. Carlson, Lee P. Stepina, and Joel D. Nicholson, "Hofstede's Country Classification 25 Years Later," *Journal of Social Psychology* 137 (1997): 43–54; Bradley L. Kirkman, Kevin B. Lowe, and Cristina B. Gibson, "A Quarter Century of *Culture's Consequences*: A Review of Empirical Research Incorporating Hofstede's Cultural Values Framework," *Journal of International Business Studies* 37 (2006): 285–320.

4. See Harry C. Triandis, *The Analysis of Subjective Culture* (New York: Wiley, 1972); C. Harry Hui and Harry C. Triandis, "Individualism-Collectivism: A Study of Cross-Cultural Researchers," *Journal of Cross-Cultural Psychology* 17 (1986): 225–248.

5. Data from twenty-two countries are reported in: Chinese Culture Connection, "Chinese Values and the Search for Culture-Free Dimensions of Culture," *Journal of Cross-Cultural Psychology* 18 (1987): 143–164. Data on the People's Republic of China, which were added to the survey after the initial publication of results, can be found in Geert Hofstede, *Cultures and Organizations: Software of the Mind* (London: McGraw-Hill, 1991), 166. Data for the remaining four countries are from subsequent studies conducted by various researchers and reported in Hofstede, *Culture's Consequences*.

6. Hofstede, *Cultures and Organizations*, 164–166; *Culture's Consequences*, 360.

7. Geert Hofstede and Gert Jan Hofstede, *Cultures and Organizations: Software of the Mind*, Revised and Expanded 2nd ed. (New York: McGraw Hill, 2005); Geert Hofstede, Gert Jan Hofstede, Michael Minkov, and Henk Vinken, "VSM 08: Values Survey Module 2008 Manual," 2008. Accessed June 17, 2008, from http://feweb.uvt.nl/center/hofstede/ManualVSM08.doc; Geert Hofstede, Gert Jan Hofstede, Michael Minkov, and Henk Vinken, "VSM 08: Values Survey Module 2008 Questionnaire, English Language Version," 2008. Accessed June 17, 2008, from http://www.geerthofstede.nl/; Geert Hofstede, Gert Jan Hofstede, Michael Minkov, and Henk Vinken, "Announcing a New Version of the Values Survey Module: The VSM 08," 2008. Accessed June 17, 2008, from http://feweb.uvt.nl/center/hofstede/VSM08.html; Ronald Inglehart (ed.), *Human Values and Social Change: Findings from the Values Surveys* (Boston: Brill, 2003); Ronald Inglehart, Miguel Basañez, Jaime Díez-Medrano, Loek Halman, and Ruud Luijkx, *Human Beliefs and Values: A Cross-Cultural Sourcebook Based on the 1999-2002 Values Surveys* (Mexico: Siglo XXI Editores, 2004); Ronald Inglehart, Miguel Basañez, and Alejandro Moreno, *Human Values and Beliefs: A Cross-Cultural Sourcebook. Findings from the 1990-1993 World Values Survey* (Ann Arbor: University of Michigan Press, 1998); Ronald Inglehart and Pippa Norris, *Rising Tide: Gender Equality and Cultural Change around the World* (Cambridge: Cambridge University Press, 2003); Michael Minkov, "Monumentalism Versus Flexumility," 2007. Accessed June 18, 2008, from http://www.sietar-europa.org/congress2007/files/congress 2007_paper_Michael_Minkov.doc; Michael Minkov, *What Makes Us Different and Similar: A New Interpretation of the World Values Survey and Other Cross-Cultural Data* (Bulgaria: Klasika y Stil, 2007); Peter B. Smith, "Book Review: Michael Minkov, What Makes Us Different and Similar: A New Interpretation of the World Values Survey and Other Cross-Cultural Data," *International Journal of Cross Cultural Management* 8 (2008): 110–112.

8. Minkov 20.

9. Our discussion of the GLOBE research is based on the following: Neal Ashkanasy, Vipin Gupta, Melinda S. Mayfield, and Edwin Trevor-Roberts, "Future Orientation," *Culture, Leadership, and Organizations: The GLOBE Study of 62 Societies*, ed. Robert J. House, Paul J. Hanges, Mansour Javidan, Peter W. Dorfman, and Vipin Gupta (Thousand Oaks, CA: Sage, 2004), 282–342; Neal M. Ashkanasy, Edwin Trevor-Roberts, and Louise Earnshaw, "The Anglo Cluster: Legacy of the British Empire," *Journal of World Business* 37 (2002): 28–39; Gyula Bakacsi, Takács Sándor, Karácsonyi András, and Imrek Viktor, "Eastern European Cluster: Tradition and Transition," *Journal of*

World Business 37 (2002): 69–80; Dale Carl, Vipin Gupta, and Mansour Javidan, "Power Distance," *Culture, Leadership, and Organizations: The GLOBE Study of 62 Societies*, ed. Robert J. House, Paul J. Hanges, Mansour Javidan, Peter W. Dorfman, and Vipin Gupta (Thousand Oaks, CA: Sage, 2004), 513–563; Mary Sully De Luque and Mansour Javidan, "Uncertainty Avoidance," *Culture, Leadership, and Organizations: The GLOBE Study of 62 Societies*, ed. Robert J. House, Paul J. Hanges, Mansour Javidan, Peter W. Dorfman, and Vipin Gupta (Thousand Oaks, CA: Sage, 2004), 602–653; Deanne N. Den Hartog, "Assertiveness," *Culture, Leadership, and Organizations: The GLOBE Study of 62 Societies*, ed. Robert J. House, Paul J. Hanges, Mansour Javidan, Peter W. Dorfman, and Vipin Gupta (Thousand Oaks, CA: Sage, 2004), 395–436; P. Christopher Earley, "Leading Cultural Research in the Future: A Matter of Paradigms and Taste," *Journal of International Business Studies* 37 (2006): 922–931; Cynthia G. Emrich, Florence L. Denmark, and Deanne N. Den Hartog, "Cross-Cultural Differences in Gender Egalitarianism," *Culture, Leadership, and Organizations: The GLOBE Study of 62 Societies*, ed. Robert J. House, Paul J. Hanges, Mansour Javidan, Peter W. Dorfman, and Vipin Gupta (Thousand Oaks, CA: Sage, 2004), 343–394; Michele J. Gelfand, Dharm P. S. Bhawuk, Lisa Hisae Nishii, and David J. Bechtold, "Individualism and Collectivism," *Culture, Leadership, and Organizations: The GLOBE Study of 62 Societies*, ed. Robert J. House, Paul J. Hanges, Mansour Javidan, Peter W. Dorfman, and Vipin Gupta (Thousand Oaks, CA: Sage, 2004), 437–512; Vipin Gupta and Paul J. Hanges, "Regional and Climate Clustering of Societal Cultures," *Culture, Leadership, and Organizations: The GLOBE Study of 62 Societies*, ed. Robert J. House, Paul J. Hanges, Mansour Javidan, Peter W. Dorfman, and Vipin Gupta (Thousand Oaks, CA: Sage, 2004), 178–218; Vipin Gupta, Paul J. Hanges, and Peter Dorfman, "Cultural Clusters: Methodology and Findings," *Journal of World Business* 37 (2002): 11–15; Vipin Gupta, Gita Surie, Mansour Javidan, and Jagdeep Chhokar, "Southern Asia Cluster: Where the Old Meets the New?" *Journal of World Business* 37 (2002): 16–27; Paul J. Hanges and Marcus W. Dickson, "Agitation over Aggregation: Clarifying the Development of and the Nature of the GLOBE Scales," *Leadership Quarterly* 17 (2006): 522–536; Paul J. Hanges, Marcus W. Dickson, and Mina T. Sipe, "Rationale for GLOBE Statistical Analyses," *Culture, Leadership, and Organizations: The GLOBE Study of 62 Societies*, ed. Robert J. House, Paul J. Hanges, Mansour Javidan, Peter W. Dorfman, and Vipin Gupta (Thousand Oaks, CA: Sage, 2004), 219–233; Paul J. Hanges, Julie S. Lyon, and Peter W. Dorfman, "Managing a Multinational Team: Lessons from Project Globe," *Advances in International Management* 18 (2005): 337–360; Geert Hofstede, "What Did GLOBE Really Measure? Researchers' Minds Versus Respondents' Minds," *Journal of International*

Business Studies 37 (2006): 882–896; Robert J. House, Mansour Javidan, Paul Hanges, and Peter Dorfman, "Understanding Cultures and Implicit Leadership Theories across the Globe: An Introduction to Project GLOBE," *Journal of World Business* 37 (2002): 3–10; Robert J. House, Paul J. Hanges, Mansour Javidan, Peter W. Dorfman, and Vipin Gupta (eds.), *Culture, Leadership, and Organizations: The GLOBE Study of 62 Societies* (Thousand Oaks, CA: Sage, 2004); Robert J. House and Mansour Javidan, "Overview of GLOBE," *Culture, Leadership, and Organizations: The GLOBE Study of 62 Societies*, ed. Robert J. House, Paul J. Hanges, Mansour Javidan, Peter W. Dorfman, and Vipin Gupta (Thousand Oaks, CA: Sage, 2004), 9–28; Jon P. Howell, José DelaCerda, Sandra M. Martínez, Leonel Prieto, J. Arnoldo Bautista, Juan Ortiz, Peter Dorfman, and Maria J. Méndez, "Leadership and Culture in Mexico," *Journal of World Business* 42 (2007): 449–462; Mansour Javidan, "Performance Orientation," *Culture, Leadership, and Organizations: The GLOBE Study of 62 Societies*, ed. Robert J. House, Paul J. Hanges, Mansour Javidan, Peter W. Dorfman, and Vipin Gupta (Thousand Oaks, CA: Sage, 2004), 239–281; Mansour Javidan and Markus Hauser, "The Linkage between GLOBE Findings and Other Cross-Cultural Information," *Culture, Leadership, and Organizations: The GLOBE Study of 62 Societies*, ed. Robert J. House, Paul J. Hanges, Mansour Javidan, Peter W. Dorfman, and Vipin Gupta (Thousand Oaks, CA: Sage, 2004), 102–121; Mansour Javidan and Robert J. House, "Leadership and Cultures around the World: Findings from GLOBE: An Introduction to the Special Issue," *Journal of World Business* 37 (2002): 1–2; Mansour Javidan, Robert J. House, and Peter W. Dorfman, "A Nontechnical Summary of GLOBE Findings," *Culture, Leadership, and Organizations: The GLOBE Study of 62 Societies*, ed. Robert J. House, Paul J. Hanges, Mansour Javidan, Peter W. Dorfman, and Vipin Gupta (Thousand Oaks, CA: Sage, 2004), 29–48; Mansour Javidan, Robert J. House, Peter W. Dorfman, Paul J. Hange, and Mary Sully de Luque, "Conceptualizing and Measuring Cultures and Their Consequences: A Comparative Review of Globe's and Hofstede's Approaches," *Journal of International Business Studies* 37 (2006): 897–914; Jorge Correia Jesuino, "Latin Europe Cluster: From South to North," *Journal of World Business* 37 (2002): 81–89; Hayat Kabasakal and Muzaffer Bodur, "Arabic Cluster: A Bridge between East and West," *Journal of World Business* 37 (2002): 40–54; Hayat Kabasakal and Muzaffer Bodur, "Humane Orientation in Societies, Organizations, and Leader Attributes," *Culture, Leadership, and Organizations: The GLOBE Study of 62 Societies*, ed. Robert J. House, Paul J. Hanges, Mansour Javidan, Peter W. Dorfman, and Vipin Gupta (Thousand Oaks, CA: Sage, 2004), 564–601; Mark F. Peterson and Stephanie L. Castro, "Measurement Metrics at Aggregate Levels of Analysis: Implications for Organization Culture Research and the GLOBE Project,"

Leadership Quarterly 17 (2006): 506–521; Peter B. Smith, "When Elephants Fight, the Grass Gets Trampled: The GLOBE and Hofstede Projects," *Journal of International Business Studies* 37 (2006): 915–921; Erna Szabo, Felix C. Brodbeck, Deanne N. Den Hartog, Gerhard Reber, Jürgen Weiblere, and Rolf Wunderer, "The Germanic Europe Cluster: Where Employees Have a Voice," *Journal of World Business* 37 (2002): 55–68.

Chapter 6

1. Marilyn Brewer and Donald T. Campbell, *Ethnocentrism and Intergroup Attitudes* (New York: Wiley, 1976).

2. Osei Appiah, "Effects of Ethnic Identification on Web Browsers' Attitudes toward and Navigational Patterns on Race-Targeted Sites," *Communication Research* 31 (2004): 312–337; Danette Ifert Johnson, "Music Videos and National Identity on Post-Soviet Kazakhstan," *Qualitative Research Reports in Communication* 7 (2006): 9–14; Dana E. Mastro, "A Social Identity Approach to Understanding the Impact of Television Messages," *Communication Monographs* 70 (2003): 98–113; Andrew F. Wood and Matthew J. Smith, *Online Communication: Linking Technology, Identity, and Culture*, 2nd ed. (Mahwah, NJ: Lawrence Erlbaum, 2005).

3. Our labels are analogous to Triandis's tripartite distinction among one's collective self, public self, and private self. See: Harry C. Triandis, "The Self and Social Behavior in Differing Cultural Contexts," *Psychological Review* 96 (1989): 506–520. See also: Henri Tajfel, *Differentiation between Social Groups* (London: Academic Press, 1978); Henri Tajfel, *Human Groups and Social Categories: Studies in Social Psychology* (Cambridge: Cambridge University Press, 1981).

4. Julia T. Wood uses the term "social diversity" to refer to differences among people because of age, gender, sexual orientation, and the like. See: Julia T. Wood, "Celebrating Diversity in the Communication Field," *Communication Studies* 49 (1998): 172–178.

5. See, for example, Amanda J. Godley, "Literacy Learning as Gendered Identity Work," *Communication Education* 52 (2003): 273–285; Radha S. Hegde and Barbara Dicicco-Bloom, "Working Identities: South Asian Nurses and the Transnational Negotiations of Race and Gender," *Communication Quarterly* 50 (2002): 90–95; Patricia S. Parker, "Negotiating Identity in Raced and Gendered Workplace Interactions: The Use of Strategic Communication by African American Women Senior Executives within Dominant Culture Organizations," *Communication Quarterly* 50 (2002): 251–268; Saskia Witteborn, "Of Being an Arab Woman before and after September 11: The Enactment of Communal Identities in Talk," *Howard Journal of Communications* 15 (2004): 83–98.

6. Our discussion of the stages of cultural identity draws heavily upon the works of Jean S. Phinney, particularly Jean S. Phinney, "Ethnic Identity in Adolescents and Adults: Review of Research," *Psychological Bulletin* 108 (1990): 499–514; Jean S. Phinney, "Ethnic Identity and Self-Esteem: A Review and Integration," *Hispanic Journal of Behavioral Sciences* 13 (1991): 193–208; Jean S. Phinney, "A Three-Stage Model of Ethnic Identity Development in Adolescence," *Ethnic Identity: Formation and Transmission among Hispanics and Other Minorities*, ed. Martha E. Bernal and George P. Knight (Albany: State University of New York Press, 1993), 61–79; Jean S. Phinney, "Ethic Identity and Acculturation," *Acculturation: Advances in Theory, Measurement, and Applied Research*, ed. Kevin M. Chun, Pamela Balls Organista, and Gerardo Marín (Washington, DC: American Psychological Association, 2003), 63–81; Jean S. Phinney, "Ethnic Identity Exploration in Emerging Adulthood," *Emerging Adults in America: Coming of Age in the 21st Century*, ed. Jeffery Jensen Arnett and Jennifer Lynn Tanner (Washington, DC: American Psychological Association, 2006), 117–134; Jean S. Phinney and Anthony D. Ong, "Conceptualization and Measurement of Ethnic Identity: Current Status and Future Directions," *Journal of Counseling Psychology* 54 (2007): 271–281.

7. See, for example, Daniel Bernardi (ed.), *The Persistence of Whiteness: Race and Contemporary Hollywood Cinema* (New York: Routledge, 2007); Nyla R. Branscombe, Michael T. Schmitt, and Kristin Schiffhauer, "Racial Attitudes in Response to Thoughts of White Privilege," *European Journal of Social Psychology* 37 (2007): 203–215; Michael K. Brown, Martin Carnoy, Elliott Currie, Troy Duster, David B. Oppenheimer, Marjorie M. Shultz, and David Wellman, *Whitewashing Race: The Myth of a Color-Blind Society* (Berkeley: University of California Press, 2003); Leda Cooks, "Pedagogy, Performance, and Positionality: Teaching About Whiteness in Interracial Communication," *Communication Education* 52 (2003): 245–257; Thierry Devos and Mahzarin R. Banaji, "American = White?," *Journal of Personality and Social Psychology* 88 (2005): 447–466; Steve Garner, *Whiteness: An Introduction* (New York: Routledge, 2007); Robert Jensen, *The Heart of Whiteness: Confronting Race, Racism, and White Privilege* (San Francisco: City Lights, 2005); Frances E. Kendall, *Understanding White Privilege: Creating Pathways to Authentic Relationships across Race* (New York: Routledge, 2006); Eric D. Knowles and Kaiping Peng, "White Selves: Conceptualizing and Measuring a Dominant-Group Identity," *Journal of Personality and Social Psychology* 89 (2005): 223–241; George Lipsitz, *The Possessive Investment in Whiteness: How White People Profit from Identity Politics*, Revised and Expanded ed. (Philadelphia: Temple University Press, 2006); Judith N. Martin and Olga Idriss

Davis, "Conceptual Foundations for Teaching About Whiteness in Intercultural Communication Courses," *Communication Education* 50 (2001): 298–313; Ann Neville Miller and Tina M. Harris, "Communicating to Develop White Racial Identity in an Interracial Communication Class," *Communication Education* 54 (2005): 223–242; Nelson M. Rodriguez and Leila E. Villaverde (eds.), *Dismantling White Privilege: Pedagogy, Politics, and Whiteness* (New York: P. Lang, 2000); David R. Roediger, *Working toward Whiteness: How America's Immigrants Became White: The Strange Journey from Ellis Island to the Suburbs* (New York: Basic Books, 2005); David R. Roediger, *The Wages of Whiteness: Race and the Making of the American Working Class*, Revised ed. (New York: Verso, 2007); Karen Elaine Rosenblum and Toni-Michelle Travis (eds.), *The Meaning of Difference: American Constructions of Race, Sex and Gender, Social Class, Sexual Orientation, and Disability*, 5th ed. (New York: McGraw-Hill, 2008); Shelly Tochluk, *Witnessing Whiteness: First Steps toward an Antiracist Practice and Culture* (Lanham, MD: Rowman & Littlefield Education, 2008); John T. Warren, "Doing Whiteness: On the Performative Dimensions of Race in the Classroom," *Communication Education* 50 (2001): 91–108; John T. Warren and Kathy Hytten, "The Faces of Whiteness: Pitfalls and the Critical Democrat," *Communication Education* 53 (2004): 321–339.

8. Judith N. Martin, Robert L. Krizek, Thomas K. Nakayama, and Lisa Bradford, "Exploring Whiteness: A Study of Self Labels for White Americans," *Communication Quarterly* 44 (1996): 125–144. See also: Thomas K. Nakayama and Robert L. Krizek, "Whiteness: A Strategic Rhetoric," *Quarterly Journal of Speech* 81 (1995): 291–309.

9. Fernando P. Delgado, "Chicano Ideology Revisited: Rap Music and the (Re)Articulation of Chicanismo," *Western Journal of Communication* 62 (1998): 95–113; Fernando P. Delgado, "All Along the Border: Kid Frost and the Performance of Brown Masculinity," *Text and Performance Quarterly* 20 (2000): 388–401; Danette Ifert Johnson, "Music Videos and National Identity on Post-Soviet Kazakhstan"; Dana E. Mastro, "A Social Identity Approach to Understanding the Impact of Television Messages."

10. For interesting research on identity change among Asian Indians and Chinese Americans, see, respectively, Jean Bacon, "Constructing Collective Ethnic Identities: The Case of Second Generation Asian Indians," *Qualitative Sociology* 22 (1999): 141–160; Zhuojun Joyce Chen, "Chinese-American Children's Ethnic Identity: Measurement and Implications," *Communication Studies* 51 (2000): 74–95. For an analysis of the shifting identities of European Americans, see Ronald L. Jackson, II, and Katherine Simpson, "White Positionalities and Cultural Contracts: Critiquing Entitlement, Theorizing, and Exploring the Negotiation of White

Identities," *Ferment in the Intercultural Field*, ed. William J. Starosta and Guo-Ming Chen (Thousand Oaks, CA: Sage, 2003), 177–210.

11. Radhika Gajjala, "Interrogating Identities: Composing Other Cyberspaces," *Intercultural Alliances: Critical Transformation*, ed. Mary Jane Collier (Thousand Oaks, CA: Sage, 2003), 167–188.

12. Young Yun Kim, "Identity Development: From Cultural to Intercultural," *Interaction and Identity*, ed. Hartmut B. Mokros (New Brunswick, NJ: Transaction, 1996), 350.

13. Katherine Grace Hendrix, Ronald L. Jackson, and Jennifer R. Warren, "Shifting Academic Landscapes: Exploring Co-Identities, Identity Negotiation, and Critical Progressive Pedagogy," *Communication Education* 52 (2003): 177–190; S. Lily Mendoza, Rona T. Halualani, and Jolanta A. Drzewiecka, "Moving the Discourse on Identities in Intercultural Communication: Structure, Culture, and Resignifications," *Communication Quarterly* 50 (2002): 312–327; Kristin Moss and William V. Faux II, "The Enactment of Cultural Identity in Student Conversations on Intercultural Topics," *Howard Journal of Communications* 17 (2006): 21–37; Patricia S. Parker, "Negotiating Identity in Raced and Gendered Workplace Interactions"; Karen Elaine Rosenblum and Toni-Michelle Travis (eds.), *The Meaning of Difference: American Constructions of Race, Sex and Gender, Social Class, Sexual Orientation, and Disability*, 5th ed. (New York: McGraw-Hill, 2008).

14. Theodor Gomperz, *Greek Thinkers: A History of Ancient Philosophy*, Vol. 1 (trans. L. Magnus) (New York: Scribner's, 1901), 403–404.

15. William G. Sumner, *Folkways* (Boston: Ginn, 1940), 27.

16. Sumner.

17. Walter Lippmann, *Public Opinion* (New York: Harcourt, Brace, 1922), 25.

18. Marilynn B. Brewer, "When Stereotypes Lead to Stereotyping: The Use of Stereotypes in Person Perception," *Stereotypes and Stereotyping*, ed. C. Neil Macrae, Charles Stangor, and Miles Hewstone (New York: Guilford, 1996), 254–275; Diane M. Mackie, David L. Hamilton, Joshua Susskind, and Francine Rosselli, "Social Psychological Foundations of Stereotype Formation," *Stereotypes and Stereotyping*, ed. C. Neil Macrae, Charles Stangor, and Miles Hewstone (New York: Guilford, 1996), 41–78; Charles Stangor and Mark Schaller, "Stereotypes as Individual and Collective Representations," *Stereotypes and Stereotyping*, ed. C. Neil Macrae, Charles Stangor, and Miles Hewstone (New York: Guilford, 1996), 3–37.

19. Micah S. Thompson, Charles M. Judd, and Bernadette Park, "The Consequences of Communicating Social Stereotypes," *Journal of Experimental Social Psychology* 36 (2000): 567–599; Vincent Y. Yzerbyt, Alastair Coull, and Steve J. Rocher, "Fencing Off the Deviant: The Role of Cognitive Resources in the Maintenance of Stereotypes,"

Journal of Personality and Social Psychology 77(3) (1999): 449–462.

20. See Charles M. Judd and Bernadette Park, "Definition and Assessment of Accuracy in Social Stereotypes," *Psychological Review* 100 (1993): 109–128; Carey S. Ryan, Bernadette Park, and Charles M. Judd, "Assessing Stereotype Accuracy: Implications for Understanding the Stereotyping Process," *Stereotypes and Stereotyping*, ed. C. Neil Macrae, Charles Stangor, and Miles Hewstone (New York: Guilford, 1996), 121–157.

21. Marilynn B. Brewer, "Social Identity, Distinctiveness, and In-Group Homogeneity," *Social Cognition* 11 (1993): 150–164; Klaus Fiedler and Eva Walther, *Stereotyping as Inductive Hypothesis* (New York: Psychology Press, 2004); Bonnie L. Haines, *Bigger Than the Box: The Effects of Labeling* (Oacoma, SD: Unlimited Achievement Books, 2004); E. E. Jones, G. C. Wood, and G. A. Quattrone, "Perceived Variability of Personal Characteristics in In-Groups and Out-Groups: The Role of Knowledge and Evaluation," *Personality and Social Psychology Bulletin* 7 (1981): 523–528; John T. Jost and Brenda Major (eds.), *The Psychology of Legitimacy: Emerging Perspectives on Ideology, Justice, and Intergroup Relations* (New York: Cambridge University Press, 2001); Charles M. Judd and Bernadette Park, "Out-Group Homogeneity: Judgments of Variability at the Individual and Group Levels," *Journal of Personality and Social Psychology* 54 (1988): 778–788; Paul Martin Lester and Susan Dente Ross (eds.), *Images that Injure: Pictorial Stereotypes in the Media*, 2nd ed. (Westport, CT: Praeger, 2003); Toni Lester (ed.), *Gender Nonconformity, Race, and Sexuality: Charting the Connections* (Madison: University of Wisconsin Press, 2002); P. W. Linville and E. E. Jones, "Polarized Appraisals of Out-Group Members," *Journal of Personality and Social Psychology* 38 (1980): 689–703; Craig McGarty, Vincent Y. Yzerbyt, and Russell Spears (eds.) *Stereotypes as Explanations: The Formation of Meaningful Beliefs about Social Groups* (New York: Cambridge University Press, 2002); Brian Mullen and L. Hu, "Perceptions of Ingroup and Outgroup Variability: A Meta-Analytic Integration," *Basic and Applied Social Psychology* 10 (1989): 233–252; Thomas M. Ostrom, Sandra L. Carpenter, Constantine Sedikides, and Fan Li, "Differential Processing of In-Group and Out-Group Information," *Journal of Personality and Social Psychology* 64 (1993): 21–34; Michael Pickering, *Stereotyping: The Politics of Representation* (New York: Palgrave, 2001); David J. Schneider, *The Psychology of Stereotyping* (New York: Guilford, 2004).

22. David Barsamian, "Albert Mokhiber: Cultural Images, Politics, and Arab Americans," *Z Magazine*, May 1993, 46–50. Reprinted in *Ethnic Groups*, vol. 4, ed. Eleanor Goldstein (Boca Raton, FL: Social Issues Resources Ser., 1994), art. no. 73.

23. Ziva Kunda and Bonnie Sherman-Williams, "Stereotypes and the Construal of Individuating Information," *Personality and Social Psychology Bulletin* 19 (1993): 97.

24. John J. Seta and Catherine E. Seta, "Stereotypes and the Generation of Compensatory and Noncompensatory Expectancies of Group Members," *Personality and Social Psychology Bulletin* 19 (1993): 722–731.

25. C. Neil Macrae, Alan B. Milne, and Galen V. Bodenhausen, "Stereotypes as Energy-Saving Devices: A Peek Inside the Cognitive Toolbox," *Journal of Personality and Social Psychology* 66 (1994): 37–47.

26. Judee K. Burgoon, Charles R. Berger, and Vincent Waldron, "Mindfulness and Interpersonal Communication," *Journal of Social Issues* 56 (2000): 105–127.

27. Gordon W. Allport, *The Nature of Prejudice* (New York: Macmillan, 1954).

28. John F. Dovidio, John C. Brigham, Blair T. Johnson, and Samuel L. Gaertner, "Stereotyping, Prejudice, and Discrimination: A Closer Look," *Stereotypes and Stereotyping*, ed. C. Neil Macrae, Charles Stangor, and Miles Hewstone (New York: Guilford, 1996), 276–319.

29. Richard W. Brislin, *Cross-Cultural Encounters: Face-to-Face Interaction* (New York: Pergamon Press, 1981), 42–49.

30. For a recent test of the ego-defensive functions of attitudes, see Maria Knight Lapinski and Franklin Boster, "Modeling the Ego Defensive Function of Attitudes," *Communication Monographs* 68 (2001): 314–324.

31. Steven Fein and Steven J. Spencer, "Prejudice as Self-Image Maintenance: Affirming the Self Through Derogating Others," *Journal of Personality and Social Psychology* 73 (1997): 31–44.

32. Teun A. van Dijk, *Communicating Racism: Ethnic Prejudice in Thought and Talk* (Newbury Park, CA: Sage, 1987).

33. Marilynn B. Brewer, "The Psychology of Prejudice: Ingroup Love or Outgroup Hate?" *Journal of Social Issues* 55 (1999): 429–444. See also: Marilynn B. Brewer and Wendi L. Gardner, "Who Is This 'We'? Levels of Collective Identity and Self Representations," *Journal of Personality and Social Psychology* 71 (1996): 83–93.

34. For a discussion of the causes and consequences of some forms of racism, see Joe R. Feagin and Hernán Vera, *White Racism: The Basics* (New York: Routledge, 1995).

35. Robert Blauner, *Racial Oppression in America* (New York: Harper and Row, 1972), 112.

36. Dalmas A. Taylor, "Race Prejudice, Discrimination, and Racism," *Social Psychology*, ed. A. Kahn, E. Donnerstein, and M. Donnerstein (Dubuque, IA: Wm. C. Brown, 1984); cited in Phyllis A. Katz and Dalmas A. Taylor, "Introduction," *Eliminating Racism: Profiles in Controversy*, ed. Phyllis A. Katz and Dalmas A. Taylor (New York: Plenum, 1988), 6.

37. Katz and Taylor, 7.

38. Blauner.

39. James M. Jones, "Racism in Black and White: A Bicultural Model of Reaction and Evolution," *Eliminating Racism: Profiles in Controversy*, ed. Phyllis A. Katz and Dalmas A. Taylor (New York: Plenum, 1988), 130–131.

40. S. Elizabeth Bird, "Gendered Construction of the American Indian in Popular Media," *Journal of Communication* 49 (1999): 78.

41. Bird, 80. See also: Richard Morris, "Educating Savages," *Quarterly Journal of Speech* 83 (1997): 152–171.

42. Jones, 118–126.

43. Katz and Taylor, 7.

44. Jenny Yamoto, "Something about the Subject Makes It Hard to Name," *Race, Class, and Gender in the United States: An Integrated Study*, 2nd ed., ed. Paula S. Rothenberg (New York: St. Martin's Press, 1992), 58.

45. For discussions of racism and prejudice, see Linda Jacobs Altman, *Racism and Ethnic Bias: Everybody's Problem* (Berkeley Heights, NJ: Enslow, 2001); Joseph F. Aponte and Laura R. Johnson, "The Impact of Culture on the Intervention and Treatment of Ethnic Populations," *Psychological Intervention and Cultural Diversity*, 2nd ed., ed. Joseph F. Aponte and Julian Wohl (Boston: Allyn & Bacon, 2000), 18–39; Martha Augoustinos and Katherine J. Reynolds (eds.), *Understanding Prejudice, Racism, and Social Conflict* (Thousand Oaks, CA: Sage, 2001); Michael D. Barber, *Equality and Diversity: Phenomenological Investigations of Prejudice and Discrimination* (Amherst, NY: Humanity Books, 2001); Benjamin P. Bowser, Gale S. Auletta, and Terry Jones, *Confronting Diversity Issues on Campus* (Newbury Park, CA: Sage, 1994); Bernard Boxill (ed.), *Race and Racism* (New York: Oxford University Press, 2001); John C. Brigham, "College Students' Racial Attitudes," *Journal of Applied Social Psychology* 23 (1993): 1933–1967; Richard W. Brislin, "Prejudice and Intergroup Communication," *Intergroup Communication*, ed. William B. Gudykunst (London: Arnold, 1986), 74–85; Brislin (1981): 42–49; Charles E. Case, Andrew M. Greeley, and Stephan Fuchs, "Social Determinants of Racial Prejudice," *Sociological Perspectives* 32 (1989): 469–483; Farhad Dalal, "Insides and Outsides: A Review of Psychoanalytic Renderings of Difference, Racism, and Prejudice," *Psychoanalytic Studies* 3 (2001): 43–66; Samuel L. Gaertner and John F. Dovidio, "The Aversive Form of Racism," *Prejudice, Discrimination and Racism: Theory and Research*, ed. John F. Dovidio and Samuel L. Gaertner (New York: Academic Press, 1986), 61–89; Ellen J. Goldner and Safiya Henderson-Holmes (eds.), *Racing and (E)Racing Language: Living with the Color of Our Words* (Syracuse, NY: Syracuse University Press, 2001); Harry Goulbourne (ed.), *Race and Ethnicity: Critical Concepts in Sociology* (New York: Routledge, 2001); Edgar Jones, "Prejudicial Beliefs: Their Nature and Expression," *Racism and Mental Health: Prejudice*

and Suffering, ed. Kamaldeep Bhui (Philadelphia: Jessica Kingsley, 2002), 26–34; David Milner, "Racial Prejudice," *Intergroup Behavior*, ed. John C. Turner and Howard Giles (Chicago: University of Chicago Press, 1981), 102–143; Scott Plous (ed.), *Understanding Prejudice and Discrimination* (Boston: McGraw-Hill, 2003); Peter Ratcliffe, *The Politics of Social Science Research: Race, Ethnicity, and Social Change* (New York: Palgrave, 2001); Albert Ramirez, "Racism toward Hispanics: The Culturally Monolithic Society," *Eliminating Racism: Profiles in Controversy*, ed. Phyllis A. Katz and Dalmas A. Taylor (New York: Plenum, 1988), 137–157; Paula S. Rothenberg (ed.), *Race, Class, and Gender in the United States: An Integrated Study*, 5th ed. (New York: W. H. Freeman, 2001); James R. Samuel, *The Roots of Racism* (New York: Vantage, 2001); David O. Sears, "Symbolic Racism," *Eliminating Racism: Profiles in Controversy*, ed. Phyllis A. Katz and Dalmas A. Taylor (New York: Plenum, 1988), 53–84; Key Sun, "Two Types of Prejudice and Their Causes," *American Psychologist* 48 (1993): 1152–1153; Nicholas J. Ucci, *The Structure of Racism: Insights into Developing a New Language for Socio-Historical Inquiry* (Centereach, NY: Cybergraphic Fine Art, 2001); Ian Vine, "Inclusive Fitness and the Self-System: The Roles of Human Nature and Socio-cultural Processes in Intergroup Discrimination," *The Sociobiology of Ethnocentrism: Evolutionary Dimensions of Xenophobia, Discrimination, Racism, and Nationalism*, ed. Vernon Reynolds, Vincent Falger, and Ian Vine (London: Croom Helm, 1987), 60–80; Bernd Wittenbrink, Charles M. Judd, and Bernadette Park, "Evidence for Racial Prejudice at the Implicit Level and Its Relationship with Questionnaire Measures," *Journal of Personality and Social Psychology* 72 (1997): 262–274.

46. Jacqueline N. Sawires and M. Jean Peacock, "Symbolic Racism and Voting Behavior on Proposition 209," *Journal of Applied Social Psychology* 30 (2000): 2092–2099.

47. Brigham, 1934.

48. Cheryl R. Kaiser and Carol T. Miller, "Stop Complaining! The Social Costs of Making Attributions to Discrimination," *Personality and Social Psychology Bulletin* 27 (2001): 254–263.

Chapter 7

1. Charles F. Hockett, "The Origin of Speech," *Human Communication: Language and Its Psychobiological Bases* (Readings from Scientific American) (San Francisco: Freeman, 1982), 5–12.

2. No, it isn't just that tka begins with two consonant sounds. Spring begins with three such sounds. For an interesting discussion of the rules of language, see Steven Pinker, *The Language Instinct: How the Mind Creates Language* (New York: HarperCollins, 1994).

3. Roger Brown, *Social Psychology* (New York: Free Press, 1965); quoted in Donald W. Klopf, *Intercultural Encounters: The Fundamentals of Intercultural Communication* (Englewood, CO: Morton, 1987), 137.

4. Wen Shu Lee, "In the Names of Chinese Women," *Quarterly Journal of Speech* 84 (1998): 283–302.

5. Jeanette S. Martin and Lillian H. Chaney, *Global Business Etiquette: A Guide to International Communication and Customs* (Westport, CT: Praeger, 2006) 25.

6. Wen Shu Lee, "On Not Missing the Boat: A Processual Method for Inter/cultural Understanding of Idioms and Lifeworld," *Journal of Applied Communication Research* 22 (1994): 141–161.

7. Christiane F. Gonzalez, "Translation," *Handbook of International and Intercultural Communication*, ed. Molefi Kete Asante and William B. Gudykunst (Newbury Park, CA: Sage, 1989), 484.

8. For an example of the kinds of translation problems that occur in organizations with a multilingual workforce, see Stephen E. Banks and Anna Banks, "Translation as Problematic Discourse in Organizations," *Journal of Applied Communication Research* 19 (1991): 223–241. See also Henriette W. Langdon, *The Interpreter Translator Process in the Educational Setting* (Sacramento, CA: Resources in Special Education, California State University with the California Department of Education, 1994).

9. Eugene A. Nida, *Toward a Science of Translating* (Leiden, Netherlands: E. J. Brill, 1964).

10. Lee Sechrest, Todd L. Fay, and S. M. Zaidi, "Problems of Translation in Cross-Cultural Communication," *Intercultural Communication: A Reader*, 5th ed., ed. Larry A. Samovar and Richard E. Porter (Belmont, CA: Wadsworth, 1988), 253–262.

11. There is some evidence that, as early as the fifteenth century, an Asian scholar named Bhartvhari, in a work titled *Vahyapidan*, argued that speech patterns are determined by social contexts.

12. Edward Sapir, *Language: An Introduction to the Study of Speech* (New York: Harcourt Brace, 1921).

13. Edward Sapir; quoted in Benjamin Lee Whorf, "The Relation of Habitual Thought and Behavior to Language," *Language, Thought, and Reality: Selected Writings of Benjamin Lee Whorf*, ed. J. B. Carroll (Cambridge, MA: MIT Press, 1939/1956), 134.

14. For a thorough summary and discussion of the experimental research in psychology investigating the validity of the linguistic determinism hypothesis, see John J. Gumperz and Stephen C. Levison (eds.), *Rethinking Linguistic Relativity* (Cambridge: Cambridge University Press, 1996); Curtis Hardin and Mahzarin R. Banaji, "The Influence of Language on Thought," *Social Cognition* 11 (1993): 277–308; Earl Hunt and Franca Agnoli, "The Whorfian Hypothesis: A Cognitive Psychology Perspective," *Psychological Review* 98 (1991): 377–389.

15. Whorf suggested there may be about 7 words for *snow*, though the actual number is closer to 12. Over time and numerous retellings of this example, however, the number of words claimed to represent forms of snow has increased dramatically, typically to the 17 to 23 range; the *New York Times* once cavalierly referred to 100 different words. See Geoffrey K. Pullum, *The Great Eskimo Vocabulary Hoax, and Other Irreverent Essays on the Study of Language* (Chicago: University of Chicago Press, 1991); "The Melting of a Mighty Myth," *Newsweek*, July 22, 1991, 63.

16. Richard W. Brislin, Kenneth Cushner, Craig Cherrie, and Mahealani Yong, *Intercultural Interactions: A Practical Guide* (Beverly Hills, CA: Sage, 1986), 276.

17. John C. Condon and Fathi S. Yousef, *An Introduction to Intercultural Communication* (Yarmouth, ME: Intercultural Press, 1975), 182.

18. Michael Cole and Sylvia Scribner, *Culture and Thought: A Psychological Introduction* (New York: Wiley, 1974), 2.

19. Eleanor Rosch Heider and Donald C. Olivier, "The Structure of the Color Space in Naming and Memory for Two Languages," *Cognitive Psychology* 3 (1972): 337–354.

20. For a more complete discussion of the evidence on variations in vocabulary of the color spectrum, see Cole and Scribner, 45–50; Thomas M. Steinfatt, "Linguistic Relativity: Toward a Broader View," *Language, Communication, and Culture: Current Directions*, ed. Stella Ting-Toomey and Felipe Korzenny (Newbury Park, CA: Sage, 1989), 35–75.

21. Stephen W. Littlejohn, *Theories of Human Communication*, 4th ed. (Belmont, CA: Wadsworth, 1992), 209.

22. Li-Rong Lilly Cheng, *Assessing Asian Language Performance: Guidelines for Evaluating Limited-English-Language Proficient Students* (Rockville, MD: Aspen, 1987), 8.

23. For an interesting discussion of the difficulties that Mandarin speakers might have in using English pronouns appropriately, see Stephen P. Banks, "Power Pronouns and Intercultural Understanding," *Language, Communication, and Culture: Current Directions*, ed. Stella Ting-Toomey and Felipe Korzenny (Newbury Park, CA: Sage, 1989), 180–198.

24. Michael Dorris, *The Broken Cord* (New York: Harper and Row, 1989), 2.

25. See Earl Hunt and Franca Agnoli, "The Whorfian Hypothesis: A Cognitive Psychology Perspective," *Psychological Review* 98 (1991): 377–389.

26. Wilma M. Roger, *National Foreign Language Center Occasional Papers* (Washington, DC: Johns Hopkins University Press, February 1989).

27. Studies of the relationship of language and intercultural communication are often conducted under the rubric of "intergroup behavior" or "intergroup communication." See, for example, John C. Turner and Howard Giles (eds.), *Intergroup Behavior* (Chicago: University of Chicago Press, 1981).

28. Henri Tajfel, "Social Categorization, Social Identity, and Social Comparison," *Differentiation Between Social Groups*, ed. Henri Tajfel (London: Academic Press, 1978).

29. Aaron Castelan Cargile and Howard Giles, "Language Attitudes Toward Varieties of English: An American-Japanese Context," *Journal of Applied Communication Research* 26 (1998): 336–356; Howard Giles and Patricia Johnson, "The Role of Language in Ethnic Group Relations," *Intergroup Behavior*, ed. John C. Turner and Howard Giles (Chicago: University of Chicago Press, 1981), 199–243.

30. Joshua A. Fishman, "Language and Ethnicity," *Language, Ethnicity, and Intergroup Relations*, ed. Howard Giles (London: Academic Press, 1977), 15–58.

31. William B. Gudykunst, "Cultural Variability in Ethnolinguistic Identity," *Language, Communication, and Culture: Current Directions*, ed. Stella Ting-Toomey and Felipe Korzenney (Newbury Park, CA: Sage, 1989), 223.

32. Réal Allard and Rodrique Landry, "Subjective Ethnolinguistic Vitality Viewed as a Belief System," *Journal of Multilingual and Multicultural Development* 7 (1986): 1–12. For a review of the vitality framework, see Jake Harwood, Howard Giles, and Richard Y. Bourhis, "The Genesis of Vitality Theory: Historical Patterns and Discourse Dimensions," *International Journal of the Sociology of Language* 108 (1994): 167–206.

33. Howard Giles and Arlene Franklyn-Stokes, "Communicator Characteristics," *Handbook of International and Intercultural Communication*, ed. Molefi Kete Asante and William B. Gudykunst (Newbury Park, CA: Sage, 1989), 117–144.

34. Nancy F. Burroughs and Vicki Marie, "Communication Orientations of Micronesian and American Students," *Communication Research Reports* 7 (1990): 139–146.

35. Jennifer Fortman, "Adolescent Language and Communication from an Intergroup Perspective," *Journal of Language & Social Psychology* 22 (2003): 104–111; Cynthia Gallois, Howard Giles, Elizabeth Jones, Aaron C. Cargile, and Hiroshi Ota, "Accommodating Intercultural Encounters: Elaborations and Extensions," *Intercultural Communication Theory*, ed. Richard L. Wiseman (Thousand Oaks, CA: Sage, 1995), 115–147; Howard Giles and Nikolas Coupland, *Language: Contexts and Consequences* (Pacific Grove, CA: Brooks/Cole, 1991); Howard Giles and Kimberly A. Noels, "Communication Accommodation in Intercultural Encounters," *Readings in Cultural Contexts*, ed. Judith N. Martin, Thomas K. Nakayama, and Lisa A. Flores (Mountain View, CA: Mayfield, 1998), 139–149; Howard Giles and Patricia Johnson, "Ethnolinguistic Identity Theory: A Social Psychological Approach to Language Maintenance," *International Journal of the Sociology of*

Language 68 (1987): 66–99; Howard Giles, Anthony Mulac, James J. Bradac, and Patricia Johnson, "Speech Accommodation Theory: The Next Decade and Beyond," *Communication Yearbook 10*, ed. Margaret McLaughlin (Newbury Park, CA: Sage, 1987), 13–48; Bettina Heinz, "Backchannel Responses as Strategic Responses in Bilingual Speakers' Conversations," *Journal of Pragmatics* 35 (2003): 1113–1142; Han Z. Li, "Cooperative and Intrusive Interruptions in Inter- and Intracultural Dyadic Discourse," *Journal of Language & Social Psychology* 20 (2001): 259–284; Hung Ng Sik and John Anping He, "Code-switching in Tri-generational Family Conversations among Chinese Immigrants in New Zealand," *Journal of Language & Social Psychology* 23 (2004): 28–48.

36. Ellen Bouchard Ryan, Howard Giles, and Richard J. Sebastian, "An Integrative Perspective for the Study of Attitudes Toward Language Variation," *Attitudes toward Language Variation: Social and Applied Contexts*, ed. Ellen Bouchard Ryan and Howard Giles (London: Arnold, 1982), 1.

37. Michael L. Hecht, Mary Jane Collier, and Sidney Ribeau, *African American Communication: Ethnic Identity and Cultural Interpretation* (Newbury Park, CA: Sage, 1993), 84–89.

38. John R. Edwards, *Language Attitudes and Their Implications Among English Speakers*, ed. Ellen Bouchard Ryan and Howard Giles (London: Arnold, 1982), 22.

39. Hope Bock and James H. Pitts, "The Effect of Three Levels of Black Dialect on Perceived Speaker Image," *Speech Teacher* 24 (1975): 218– 225; James J. Bradac, "Language Attitudes and Impression Formation," *Handbook of Language and Social Psychology*, ed. Howard Giles and W. Peter Robinson (Chichester, England: Wiley, 1990), 387–412.

40. Geneva Smitherman, *Talkin That Talk: Language, Culture, and Education in African America* (New York: Routledge, 2000), 21–22.

41. For an excellent summary of research on the effect of accent and dialect variations among ethnic groups, see Giles and Franklyn-Stokes. See also: Diane M. Badzinski, "The Impact of Accent and Status on Information Recall and Perception Information," *Communication* 5 (1992): 99–106.

42. Edwards, 22–27.

43. Richard Rodriguez, *Hunger of Memory: The Education of Richard Rodriguez* (Toronto: Bantam Books, 1982), 14–16. Italics in original.

44. Hecht, Collier, and Ribeau 90; U. Dagmar Scheu, "Cultural Constraints in Bilinguals' Codeswitching," *International Journal of Intercultural Relations* 24 (2000): 131–150.

45. Abdelala Bentahila, *Language Attitudes among Arabic-French Bilinguals in Morocco* (London: Multilingual Matters, 1983), 27–65.

Chapter 8

1. Peter A. Andersen, "Consciousness, Cognition, and Communication," *Western Journal of Speech Communication* 50 (1986): 87–101; Peter A. Andersen, John P. Garrison, and Janis F. Andersen, "Implications of a Neurophysiological Approach for the Study of Nonverbal Communication," *Human Communication Research* 6 (1979): 74–89.

2. Albert E. Scheflen, "On Communication Processes," *Nonverbal Behavior: Applications and Cross-Cultural Implications*, ed. Aaron Wolfgang (New York: Academic Press, 1979), 1–16.

3. Sheila J. Ramsey, "Nonverbal Behavior: An Intercultural Perspective," *Handbook of Intercultural Communication*, ed. Molefi Kete Asante, Eileen Newmark, and Cecil A. Blake (Beverly Hills, CA: Sage, 1979), 111.

4. Edward T. Hall, *The Silent Language* (Garden City, NY: Doubleday, 1959).

5. Charles Darwin, *The Expression of Emotions in Man and Animals* (New York: Appleton, 1872).

6. Michael Argyle, *Bodily Communication* (New York: International Universities Press, 1975), 95.

7. Paul Ekman and Wallace V. Friesen, "Constants across Cultures in the Face and Emotion," *Journal of Personality and Social Psychology* 17 (1971): 124–129; Paul Ekman and Wallace V. Friesen, *Unmasking the Face* (Englewood Cliffs, NJ: Prentice-Hall, 1975); Alan J. Fridlund, Paul Ekman, and Harriet Oster, "Facial Expressions of Emotion: Review of Literature, 1970–1983," *Nonverbal Behavior and Communication*, 2nd ed., ed. Aron W. Siegman and Stanley Feldstein (Hillsdale, NJ: Erlbaum, 1987), 143–224.

8. Robert Ardrey, *The Territorial Imperative: A Personal Inquiry into the Animal Origins of Property and Nations* (New York: Atheneum, 1966).

9. Judith N. Martin, Mitchell R. Hammer, and Lisa Bradford, "The Influence of Cultural and Situational Contexts on Hispanic and Non-Hispanic Communication Competence Behaviors," *Communication Quarterly* 42 (1994): 160–179.

10. Norine Dresser, *Multicultural Manners: Essential Rules of Etiquette for the 21st Century*, rev ed. (Hoboken, NJ: Wiley, 2005), 15.

11. Robert G. Harper, Arthur N. Wiens, and Joseph D. Matarazzo, *Nonverbal Communication: The State of the Art* (New York: Wiley, 1978).

12. Sharon Ruhly, *Intercultural Communication*, 2nd ed. (Chicago: Science Research Associates, 1982), 23–26.

13. John C. Condon and Fathi S. Yousef, *Intercultural Communication* (Indianapolis: Bobbs-Merrill, 1975), 122.

14. Dresser, 56.

15. Ray Birdwhistell, *Kinesics and Context: Essays on Body Motion Communication* (Philadelphia: University of Pennsylvania, 1970), 34.

16. Joseph A. DeVito, *Messages: Building Interpersonal Communication Skills* (New York: Harper and Row, 1990), 218.

17. Paul Ekman and Wallace V. Friesen, "The Repertoire of Nonverbal Behavior: Categories, Origins, Usage, and Coding," *Semiotica* 1 (1969): 49–98.

18. Dresser, 11–12.

19. Tom Brosnahan and Pat Yale, *Turkey: A Lonely Planet Travel Survival Kit*, 5th ed. (Victoria, Australia: Lonely Planet, 1996), 27.

20. Jeanette S. Martin and Lillian H. Chaney, *Global Business Etiquette: A Guide to International Communication and Customs* (Westport, CT: Praeger, 2006), 52.

21. Martin and Chaney.

22. Paul Ekman, Wallace V. Friesen, and Phoebe Ellsworth, *Emotion in the Human Face: Guidelines for Research and an Integration of Findings* (New York: Pergamon Press, 1972).

23. See Klaus R. Scherer and Harald G. Wallbott, "Evidence for Universality and Cultural Variation of Differential Emotion Response Patterning," *Journal of Personality and Social Psychology* 66 (1994): 310–328.

24. James A. Russell, "Is There Universal Recognition of Emotion from Facial Expression? A Review of the Cross-Cultural Studies," *Psychological Bulletin* 115 (1994): 102–141; James A. Russell, "Culture and the Categorization of Emotion," *Psychological Bulletin* 110 (1991): 426–450.

25. Michael Harris Bond, "Emotions and Their Expressions in Chinese Culture," *Journal of Nonverbal Behavior* 17 (1993): 245–262.

26. Marianne LaFrance and Clara Mayo, "Racial Differences in Gaze Behavior During Conversations: Two Systematic Observational Studies," *Journal of Personality and Social Psychology* 33 (1976): 547–552.

27. Edward T. Hall, *The Hidden Dimension* (Garden City, NY: Doubleday, 1966).

28. Edward T. Hall and Mildred Reed Hall, *Understanding Cultural Differences* (Yarmouth, ME: Intercultural Press, 1990), 12.

29. Hall and Hall, 180.

30. Hall and Hall, 10.

31. Stanley E. Jones and A. Elaine Yarbrough, "A Naturalistic Study of the Meanings of Touch," *Communication Monographs* 52 (1985): 19–56.

32. Nancy M. Henley, *Body Politics: Power, Sex, and Nonverbal Communication* (Englewood Cliffs, NJ: Prentice-Hall, 1977).

33. Hall and Hall, 11.

34. Dean Barnlund, "Communication Styles in Two Cultures: Japan and the United States," *Organizational Behavior in Face-to-Face Interaction*, ed. Adam Kendon, Richard M. Harris, and Mary Ritchie Key (The Hague: Mouton, 1975), 427–456.

35. Sidney M. Jourard, "An Exploratory Study of Body Accessibility," *British Journal of Social and Clinical Psychology* 5 (1966): 221–231.

36. John Reader, *Man on Earth* (New York: Harper and Row, 1988), 91. Reader's ideas are based on Paul Spencer, *The Samburu: A Study in Gerontocracy in a Nomadic Tribe* (London: Routledge and Kegan Paul, 1968).

37. Reader, 163.

38. Edward T. Hall, "The Hidden Dimensions of Time and Space in Today's World," *Cross-Cultural Perspectives in Nonverbal Communication*, ed. Fernando Poyatos (Toronto: C. J. Hogrefe, 1988), 151.

39. Hall, *The Silent Language*.

40. Jane Engle, "Punctuailty: Some Cultures Are Wound Tighter than Others," *Los Angeles Times*, December 11, 2005, I3.

41. Hall, *The Silent Language*, 178.

42. Alexander Gonzalez and Philip G. Zimbardo, "Time in Perspective," *Psychology Today* 19 (March 1985): 20–26.

43. Trudy Milburn, "Enacting 'Puerto Rican Time' in the United States," *Constituting Cultural Difference through Discourse*, ed. Mary Jane Collier (Thousand Oaks, CA: Sage, 2001), 47–76.

44. Martin and Chaney, 37.

45. Rosita Daskel Albert and Gayle L. Nelson, "Hispanic/Anglo-American Differences in Attributions to Paralinguistic Behavior," *International Journal of Intercultural Relations* 17 (1993): 19–40.

46. Mara B. Adelman and Myron W. Lustig, "Intercultural Communication Problems as Perceived by Saudi Arabian and American Managers," *International Journal of Intercultural Relations* 5 (1981): 349–364; Myron W. Lustig, "Cultural and Communication Patterns of Saudi Arabians," *Intercultural Communication: A Reader*, 5th ed., ed. Larry A. Samovar and Richard E. Porter (Belmont, CA: Wadsworth, 1988), 101–103.

47. William S. Condon, "Cultural Microrhythms," *Interaction Rhythms: Periodicity in Communicative Behavior*, ed. Martha Davis (New York: Human Sciences Press, 1982), 66.

48. Befu 1975; as quoted in Sheila J. Ramsey, "Nonverbal Behavior," 118.

49. Holley S. Hodgins and Richard Koestner, "The Origins of Nonverbal Sensitivity," *Personality and Social Psychology Bulletin* 19 (1993): 466–473.

50. Anna-Marie Dew and Colleen Ward, "The Effects of Ethnicity and Culturally Congruent and Incongruent Nonverbal Behaviors on Interpersonal Attraction," *Journal of Applied Social Psychology* 23 (1993): 1376–1389.

51. David Matsumoto and Tsutomu Kudoh, "American-Japanese Cultural Differences in Attributions of Personality Based on Smiles," *Journal of Nonverbal Behavior* 17 (1993): 231–243. See also Ann Bainbridge Frymier,

Donald W. Klopf, and Satoshi Ishii, "Affect Orientation: Japanese Compared to Americans," *Communication Research Reports* 7 (1990): 63–66; Donald W. Klopf, "Japanese Communication Practices: Recent Comparative Research," *Communication Quarterly* 39 (1991): 130–143.

Chapter 9

1. Laurie G. Kirszer and Stephen R. Mandell, *The Brief Wadsworth Handbook*, 5th ed. (Boston: Wadsworth, 2006); Laurie G. Kirszer and Stephen R. Mandell, *The Concise Wadsworth Handbook*, 2nd ed. (Boston: Wadsworth, 2008); Laurie G. Kirszer and Stephen R. Mandell, *The Pocket Wadsworth Handbook*, 4th ed. (Boston: Wadsworth, 2008); Laurie G. Kirszer and Stephen R. Mandell, *The Wadsworth Handbook*, 8th ed. (Boston: Wadsworth, 2008).

2. Robert B. Kaplan, "Cultural Thought Patterns in Inter-Cultural Education," *Language Learning: A Journal of Applied Linguistics* 16 (1966): 1–20.

3. See, for example, Ulla Connor, "New Directions in Contrastive Rhetoric," *TESOL Quarterly* 36 (2002): 493–510; Ulla Connor, *Contrastive Rhetoric: Cross-Cultural Aspects of Second Language Writing* (Cambridge: Cambridge University Press, 1996).

4. John Hinds, "Reader versus Writer Responsibility: A New Typology," *Writing Across Languages: Analysis of L2 Written Text*, ed. Ulla Connor and Robert B. Kaplan (Reading, MA: Addison-Wesley, 1987), 141–152.

5. Connor, *Contrastive Rhetoric*.

6. Satoshi Ishii, "Thought Patterns as Modes of Rhetoric: The United States and Japan," *Intercultural Communication: A Reader*, 4th ed., ed. Larry A. Samovar and Richard E. Porter (Belmont, CA: Wadsworth, 1985), 97–102.

7. David Cahill, "The Myth of the 'Turn' in Contrastive Rhetoric," *Written Communication* 20 (2003): 170–194.

8. Yamuna Kachru, "Writers in Hindi and English," *Writing Across Languages and Cultures: Issues in Contrastive Rhetoric*, ed. Alan C. Purvis (Newbury Park, CA: Sage, 1988), 109–137.

9. Arpita Misra, "Discovering Connections," *Language and Social Identity*, ed. John L. Gumperz (Cambridge: Cambridge University Press, 1982), 57–71.

10. Linda Wai Ling Young, "Inscrutability Revisited," *Language and Social Identity*, ed. John L. Gumperz (Cambridge: Cambridge University Press, 1982), 72–84.

11. Keiko Hirose, "Pursuing the Complexity of the Relationship between L1 and L2 Writing," *Journal of Second Language Writing* 15 (2006): 142–146; Yunxia Zhu, "Understanding Sociocognitive Space of Written Discourse: Implications for Teaching Business Writing to Chinese Students," *IRAL: International Review of Applied Linguistics in Language Teaching* 44 (2006): 265–285.

12. Donald G. Ellis and Ifat Maoz, "Cross-Cultural Argument Interactions between Israeli-Jews and Palestinians," *Journal of Applied Communication Research* 30 (2002): 181–194; M. Sean Limon and Betty H. La France, "Communication Traits and Leadership Emergence: Examining the Impact of Argumentativeness, Communication Apprehension, and Verbal Aggressiveness in Work Groups," *Southern Communication Journal* 70 (2005): 123–133; Ringo Ma, "The Role of Unofficial Intermediaries in Interpersonal Conflicts in the Chinese Culture," *Communication Quarterly* 40 (1992): 269–278; Alicia M. Prunty, Donald W. Klopf, and Satoshi Ishii, "Argumentativeness: Japanese and American Tendencies to Approach and Avoid Conflict," *Communication Research Reports* 7 (1990): 75–79; Judith Sanders, Robert Gass, Richard Wiseman, and Jon Bruschke, "Ethnic Comparison and Measurement of Argumentativeness, Verbal Aggressiveness, and Need for Cognition," *Communication Reports* 5 (1992): 50–56; Sunwolf, "The Pedagogical and Persuasive Effects of Native American Lesson Stories, Sufi Wisdom Tales, and African Dilemma Tales," *Howard Journal of Communications* 10 (1999): 47–71; Shinobu Suzuki and Andrew S. Rancer, "Argumentativeness and Verbal Aggressiveness: Testing for Conceptual and Measurement Equivalence across Cultures," *Communication Monographs* 61 (1994): 256–279; Lynn H. Turner and Robert Shuter, "African American and European American Women's Visions of Workplace Conflict: A Metaphorical Analysis," *Howard Journal of Communications* 15 (2004): 169–183.

13. James F. Hamill, *Ethno-Logic: The Anthropology of Human Reasoning* (Urbana: University of Illinois Press, 1990), 23.

14. Stephen Toulmin, *Human Understanding, Volume I: The Collective Use and Evolution of Concepts* (Princeton, NJ: Princeton University Press, 1972).

15. For a thorough discussion about the relationship between cultural patterns and argumentation, see Andrea Rocci, "Pragmatic Inference and Argumentation in Intercultural Communication," *Intercultural Pragmatics* 3–4 (2006): 409–422.

16. Sunwolf.

17. Ann Neville Miller, "An Exploration of Kenyan Public Speaking Patterns with Implications for the American Introductory Public Speaking Course," *Communication Education* 51 (2002): 168–182.

18. Xiaosui Xiao, "From the Hierarchical *Ren* to Egalitarianism: A Case of Cross-Cultural Rhetorical Mediation," *Quarterly Journal of Speech* 82 (1996): 38–54.

19. Yanrong Chang, "Courtroom Questioning as a Culturally Situated Persuasive Genre of Talk," *Discourse & Society* 15 (2004): 705–722.

20. Robert B. Kaplan, "Foreword: What in the World Is Contrastive Rhetoric?" *Contrastive Rhetoric Revisited*

and Redefined, ed. Clayann Gillima Panetta (Mahwah, NJ: Erlbaum, 2001), vii–xx.

21. For a detailed discussion of cultural variability in argumentation, see Rocci.

22. Barbara Johnstone, "Linguistic Strategies for Persuasive Discourse," *Language, Communication, and Culture: Current Directions*, ed. Stella Ting-Toomey and Felipe Korzenny (Newbury Park, CA: Sage, 1989), 139–156.

23. Robert Shuter, "The Culture of Rhetoric," *Rhetoric in Intercultural Contexts*, ed. Alberto Gonzalez and Dolores V. Tanno (Thousands Oaks, CA: Sage, 2000), 12–13.

24. Ora-Ong Chakorn, "Persuasive and Politeness Strategies in Cross-Cultural Letters of Request in the Thai Business Context," *Journal of Asian Pacific Communication* 16 (2006): 3–46.

25. Abdulrahman M. Alhudhaif, *A Speech Act Approach to Persuasion in American and Arabic Editorials*, Diss. Purdue University, 2006. Dissertation Abstracts International, 66A, 10, Apr, 3623.

26. Angela Eagan and Rebecca Weiner, *Culture Shock! China: A Survival Guide to Customs and Etiquette* (Tarrytown, NY: Marshall Cavendish, 2007); Kathy Flower, *Culture Smart! China: A Quick Guide to Customs and Etiquette* (Portland, OR: Graphic Arts Books, 2003); Stanley B. Lubman, "Negotiations in China: Observations of a Lawyer Communicating with China," *Communicating with China*, ed. Robert A. Kapp (Chicago: Intercultural Press, 1983); Stanley B. Lubman (ed.), *China's Legal Reforms* (Oxford: Oxford University Press, 1996); Stuart Strother and Barbara Strother, *Living Abroad in China* (Berkeley, CA: Avalon Travel Publishing, 2006); Hu Wenzhong and Cornelius L. Grove, *Encountering the Chinese: A Guide for Americans* (Yarmouth, ME: Intercultural Press, 1991).

27. Anne Bliss, "Rhetorical Structures for Multilingual and Multicultural Students," *Contrastive Rhetoric Revisited and Redefined*, ed. Clayann Gilliam Panetta (Mahwah, NJ: Erlbaum, 2001).

28. Bliss.

29. John C. Condon, *Good Neighbors: Communicating with the Mexicans* (Yarmouth, ME: Intercultural Press, 1985).

30. Daniel Dolan, "Conditional Respect and Criminal Identity: The Use of Personal Address Terms in Japanese Mass Media," *Western Journal of Communication* 64 (1998): 459–473.

31. Johnstone.

32. Connor, *Contrastive Rhetoric*, 167.

33. Donal Carbaugh, *Cultures in Conversation* (Mahwah, NJ: Erlbaum, 2005), 19.

34. Howard Giles, Nikolas Coupland, and John Wiemann, "'Talk Is Cheap...' but 'My Word Is My Bond': Beliefs about Talk," *Sociolinguistics Today: International Perspectives*, ed. Kingsley Bolton and Helen Kwok (New York: Routledge, 1992), 218–243.

35. D. Lawrence Kincaid, "Communication East and West: Points of Departure," *Communication Theory: Eastern and Western Perspectives*, ed. D. Lawrence Kincaid (San Diego: Academic Press, 1987), 337.

36. Giles, Coupland, and Wiemann.

37. Donald W. Klopf, *Intercultural Encounters: The Fundamentals of Intercultural Communication*, 2nd ed. (Englewood Cliffs, NJ: Morgan, 1991), 181.

38. June Ock Yum, "Korean Philosophy and Communication," *Communication Theory: Eastern and Western Perspectives*, ed. D. Lawrence Kincaid (San Diego: Academic Press, 1987), 79.

39. Yum, 83.

40. Peter Nwosu, "Negotiating with the Swazis," *Howard Journal of Communication* 1 (1988): 148.

41. Aino Sallinen-Kuparinen, James C. McCroskey, and Virginia P. Richmond, "Willingness to Communicate, Communication Apprehension, Introversion, and Self-Reported Communication Competence: Finnish and American Comparisons," *Communication Research Reports* 8 (1991): 55–64.

42. Carbaugh, xxi.

43. Keith H. Basso, "'To Give Up on Words' Silence in Western Apache Culture," *Cultural Communication and Intercultural Contact*, ed. Donal L. Carbaugh (Hillsdale, NJ: Erlbaum, 1990), 303–320.

44. Basso, 308.

45. Klopf.

46. William B. Gudykunst and Stella Ting-Toomey, *Culture and Interpersonal Communication* (Newbury Park, CA: Sage, 1988), 99–116.

47. Sherry L. Beaumont and Shannon L. Wagner, "Adolescent-Parent Verbal Conflict: The Roles of Conversational Styles and Disgust Emotions," *Journal of Language & Social Psychology* 23 (2004): 338–368; Deborah A. Cai, Steven R. Wilson, and Laura E. Drake, "Culture in the Context of Intercultural Negotiation: Individualism–Collectivism and Paths to Integrative Agreements," *Human Communication Research* 26 (2000): 591–607; Min-Sun Kim, "Culture-Based Interactive Constraints in Explaining Intercultural Strategic Competence," *Intercultural Communication Competence*, ed. Richard L. Wiseman and Jolene Koester (Newbury Park, CA: Sage, 1993), 132–150; Min-Sun Kim, "Cross-Cultural Comparisons of the Perceived Importance of Conversational Constraints," *Human Communication Research* 21 (1994): 128–151; Min-Sun Kim, "Toward a Theory of Conversational Constraints: Focusing on Individual-Level Dimensions of Culture," *Intercultural Communication Theory*, ed. Richard L. Wiseman (Thousand Oaks, CA: Sage, 1995), 148–169; Min-Sun Kim and Mary Bresnahan, "Cognitive Basis of Gender Communication: A Cross-Cultural Investigation of Perceived Constraints in Requesting," *Communication Quarterly* 44 (1996): 53–69; Min-Sun Kim, John E. Hunter, Akira Miyahara, Ann-Marie

Horvath, Mary Bresnahan, and Hye-Jin Yoon, "Individual- vs. Culture-Level Dimensions of Individualism and Collectivism: Effects on Preferred Conversational Styles," *Communication Monographs* 63 (1996): 29–49; Min-Sun Kim, Renee Storm Klingle, William F. Sharkey; Hee Sun Park, David H. Smith, and Deborah Cai, "A Test of a Cultural Model of Patients' Motivation for Verbal Communication in Patient-Doctor Interactions," *Communication Monographs* 67 (2000): 262–283; Min-Sun Kim and William F. Sharkey, "Independent and Interdependent Construals of Self: Explaining Cultural Patterns of Interpersonal Communication in Multi-Cultural Organizational Settings," *Communication Quarterly* 43 (1995): 20–38; Min-Sun Kim, William F. Sharkey, and Theodore M. Singelis, "The Relationship of Individuals' Self-Construals and Perceived Importance of Interactive Constraints," *International Journal of Intercultural Relations* 18 (1994): 117–140; Min-Sun Kim, Ho-Chang Shin, and Deborah Cai, "Cultural Influences on the Preferred Forms of Requesting and Re-Requesting," *Communication Monographs* 65 (1998): 47–66; Min-Sun Kim and Steven R. Wilson, "A Cross-Cultural Comparison of Implicit Theories of Requesting," *Communication Monographs* 61 (1994): 210–235; Akira Miyahara, Min-Sun Kim, Ho-Chang Shin, and Kak Yoon, "Conflict Resolution Styles Among Collectivist Cultures: A Comparison between Japanese and Koreans," *International Journal of Intercultural Relations* 22 (1998): 505–525.

48. Thomas Kochman, "Force Fields in Black and White," *Cultural Communication and Intercultural Contact*, ed. Donal Carbaugh (Hillsdale, NJ: Erlbaum, 1990), 193–194.

49. Melanie Booth-Butterfield and Felecia Jordan, "Communication Adaptation Among Racially Homogeneous and Heterogeneous Groups," *Southern Communication Journal* 54 (1989): 265.

50. Yale Richmond, *From Da to Yes: Understanding the East Europeans* (Yarmouth, ME: Intercultural Press, 1995), 118.

51. Ronald Scollon and Suzanne Wong-Scollon, "Athabaskan-English Interethnic Communication," *Cultural Communication and Intercultural Contact*, ed. Donal Carbaugh (Hillsdale, NJ: Erlbaum, 1990), 270.

52. Scollon and Wong-Scollon, 273.

Chapter 10

1. John Paul Feig, *A Common Core: Thais and Americans*, rev. Elizabeth Mortlock (Yarmouth, ME: Intercultural Press, 1989), 50.

2. Hu Wenzhong and Cornelius L. Grove, *Encountering the Chinese: A Guide for Americans*, 2nd ed. (Yarmouth, ME: Intercultural Press, 1991).

3. John C. Condon, *Good Neighbors: Communicating with the Mexicans* (Yarmouth, ME: Intercultural Press, 1985).

4. Mary Jane Collier and Elirea Bornman, "Core Symbols in South African Intercultural Friendships," *International Journal of Intercultural Relations* 23 (1999): 133–156; Daniel Perlman and Beverley Fehr, "The Development of Intimate Relationships," *Intimate Relationships: Development, Dynamics, and Deterioration*, ed. Daniel Perlman and Steven Duck (Newbury Park, CA: Sage, 1987), 13–42.

5. Michael L. Hecht, Mary Jane Collier, and Sidney A. Ribeau, *African American Communication: Ethnic Identity and Cultural Interpretation* (Newbury Park, CA: Sage, 1993).

6. Mary Jane Collier, "Cultural Background and the Culture of Friendships: Normative Patterns," paper presented at the annual conference of the International Communication Association, San Francisco, May 1989. See also: Mary Jane Collier, "Conflict Competence within African, Mexican, and Anglo American Friendships," *Cross-Cultural Interpersonal Communication*, ed. Stella Ting-Toomey and Felipe Korzenny (Newbury Park, CA: Sage, 1991), 132–154.

7. Stanley O. Gaines, Jr., "Communalism and the Reciprocity of Affection and Respect among Interethnic Married Couples," *Journal of Black Studies* 27 (1997): 352–364; Stanley O. Gaines, Jr., et al., "Patterns of Attachment and Responses to Accommodative Dilemmas Among Interethnic/Interracial Couples," *Journal of Social and Personal Relationships* 16 (1999): 275–285; Stanley O. Gaines, Jr., et al., "Links between Race/Ethnicity and Cultural Values as Mediated by Racial/Ethnic Identity and Moderated by Gender," *Journal of Personality and Social Psychology* 72 (1997): 1460–1476; Stanley O. Gaines, Jr., with Raymond Buriel, James H. Liu, and Diana I. Ríos, *Culture, Ethnicity, and Personal Relationship Processes* (New York: Routledge, 1997). See also: Stella D. Garcia and Semilla M. Rivera, "Perceptions of Hispanic and African-American Couples at the Friendship or Engagement Stage of a Relationship," *Journal of Social and Personal Relationships* 16 (1999): 65–86; Regan A. R. Gurung and Tenor Duong, "Mixing and Matching: Assessing the Concomitants of Mixed-Ethnic Relationships," *Journal of Social and Personal Relationships* 16 (1999): 639–657; John McFadden, "Intercultural Marriage and Family: Beyond the Racial Divide," *Family Journal* 9 (2001): 39–42.

8. Irene I. Blea, *Toward a Chicano Social Science* (New York: Praeger, 1988); Richard Lewis, Jr., George Yancy, and Siri S. Bletzer, "Racial and Nonracial Factors That Influence Spouse Choice in Black/White Marriages," *Journal of Black Studies* 28 (1997): 60–78.

9. Don C. Locke, *Increasing Multicultural Understanding: A Comprehensive Model* (Newbury Park, CA: Sage, 1992), 55.

10. Lin Yutang, *The Chinese Way of Life* (New York: World, 1972), 78.

11. We have synthesized a variety of sources to provide this generalization.

12. William D. Wilder, *Communication, Social Structure and Development in Rural Malaysia: A Study of Kampung Kuala Bera* (London: Athlone Press, 1982), 107.

13. Joe Cummings, Susan Forsyth, John Noble, Alan Samagalski, and Tony Wheelan, *Indonesia: A Travel Survival Guide* (Berkeley, CA: Lonely Planet Publications, 1990), 321.

14. Albert Mehrabian, *Silent Messages* (Belmont, CA: Wadsworth, 1971).

15. Edward T. Hall, *The Hidden Dimension* (Garden City, NY: Doubleday, 1966).

16. Peter A. Andersen, Myron W. Lustig, and Janis F. Andersen, "Changes in Latitude, Changes in Attitude: The Relationship Between Climate and Interpersonal Communication Predispositions," *Communication Quarterly* 38 (1990): 291–311.

17. Wilder, 105.

18. Feig, 41.

19. William O. Beeman, *Language, Status, and Power in Iran* (Bloomington: Indiana University Press, 1986), 86.

20. Harvey Taylor, "Misunderstood Japanese Nonverbal Communication," *Gengo Seikatsu* (Language Life), 1974; quoted in Helmut Morsbach, "The Importance of Silence and Stillness in Japanese Nonverbal Communication: A Cross-Cultural Approach," *Cross-Cultural Perspectives in Nonverbal Communication,* ed. Fernando Poyatos (Toronto: C. J. Hogrefe, 1988), 206.

21. We rely primarily on Leslie A. Baxter, "A Dialectical Perspective on Communication Strategies in Relationship Development," *Handbook of Personal Relationships: Theory, Research, and Interventions,* ed. Stephen W. Duck (New York: Wiley, 1988), 257–273; Leslie A. Baxter, "Dialectical Contradictions in Relationship Development," *Journal of Social and Personal Relationships* 7 (1990): 69–88; Leslie A. Baxter and Barbara M. Montgomery, *Relating: Dialogues and Dialectics* (New York: Guilford Press, 1996). See also: Irwin Altman, "Dialectics, Physical Environments, and Personal Relationships," *Communication Monographs* 60 (1993): 26–34; Irwin Altman, Anne Vinsel, and Barbara B. Brown, "Dialectic Conceptions in Social Psychology: An Application to Social Penetration and Privacy Regulation," *Advances in Experimental Social Psychology,* vol. 14, ed. Leonard Berkowitz (New York: Academic Press, 1981), 107–160; Carl W. Backman, "The Self: A Dialectical Approach," *Advances in Experimental Social Psychology,* vol. 21, ed. Leonard Berkowitz (New York: Academic Press, 1988), 229–260; Daena Goldsmith, "A Dialectic Perspective on the Expression of Autonomy and Connection in Romantic Relationships," *Western Journal of Speech Communication* 54 (1990): 537–556; Angela Hoppe-Nagao and Stella Ting-Toomey, "Relational Dialectics and Management Strategies in Marital Couples," *The Southern Communication Journal* 67 (2002): 142–159.

22. See Erving Goffman, *Interaction Ritual: Essays on Face-to-Face Behavior* (Garden City, NY: Anchor Books, 1967).

23. David Yau-fai Ho, "On the Concept of Face," *American Journal of Sociology* 81 (1976): 867–884.

24. Penelope Brown and Stephen Levinson, "Universals in Language Use: Politeness Phenomena," *Questions and Politeness: Strategies in Social Interaction,* ed. Esther N. Goody (Cambridge: Cambridge University Press, 1978), 56–289; Penelope Brown and Stephen Levinson, *Politeness: Some Universals in Language Use* (Cambridge: Cambridge University Press, 1987). Though Brown and Levinson's ideas have been criticized on several points, the portions of their ideas expressed here are generally accepted. For a summary of the criticisms, see Karen Tracy and Sheryl Baratz, "The Case for Case Studies of Facework," *The Challenge of Facework: Cross-Cultural and Interpersonal Issues,* ed. Stella Ting-Toomey (Albany: State University of New York Press, 1994), 287–305.

25. Greg Leichty and James L. Applegate, "Social Cognitive and Situational Influences on the Use of Face-Saving Persuasive Strategies," *Human Communication Research* 17 (1991): 451–484.

26. We have modified Lim's terminology and concepts somewhat but draw on his overall conception. See Tae-Seop Lim, "Politeness Behavior in Social Influence Situations," *Seeking Compliance: The Production of Interpersonal Influence Messages,* ed. James Price Dillard (Scottsdale, AZ: Gorsuch Scarisbrick, 1990), 75–86; Tae-Seop Lim, "Facework and Interpersonal Relationships," *The Challenge of Facework: Cross-Cultural and Interpersonal Issues,* ed. Stella Ting-Toomey (Albany: State University of New York Press, 1994), 209–229; Tae-Seop Lim and John Waite Bowers, "Facework: Solidarity, Approbation, and Tact," *Human Communication Research* 17 (1991): 415–450.

27. Lim, 211.

28. The Wade–Giles system for the Romanization of Chinese words is used, rather than the newer *pin-yin* system, in order to maintain consistency with the terms used in the quotes by Hu and by Hsu. Terms that the Wade–Giles system would render as *lien* and *mien-tzu* are written in the *pin-yin* system as, respectively, *lian* and *mian zi*.

29. Hsien Chin Hu, "The Chinese Concepts of 'Face,'" *American Anthropologist* 46 (1944): 45–64.

30. Francis L. K. Hsu, "The Self in Cross-Cultural Perspective," *Culture and Self: Asian and Western Perspectives,* ed. Anthony J. Marsella, George DeVos, and Francis L. K. Hsu (New York: Tavistock, 1985), 33.

31. Leo Rosten, *The Joys of Yiddish* (New York: McGraw-Hill, 1968), 234.

32. Hu, 61–62.
33. Brown and Levinson, 66.
34. Brown and Levinson; see also: Robert T. Craig, Karen Tracy, and Frances Spisak, "The Discourse of Requests: Assessment of a Politeness Approach," *Human Communication Research* 12 (1986): 437–468.
35. Ron Scollon and Suzie Wong-Scollon, "Face Parameters in East-West Discourse," *The Challenge of Facework: Cross-Cultural and Interpersonal Issues,* ed. Stella Ting-Toomey (Albany: State University of New York Press, 1994), 133–157.
36. Scollon and Wong-Scollon, 137.
37. Lijuan Stahl, "Face-Negotiation," unpublished manuscript (San Diego: San Diego State University, 1993), 12–13.
38. See Jared R. Curhan, Margaret A. Neale, and Lee Ross, "Dynamic Valuation: Preference Changes in the Context of Face-to-Face Negotiation," *Journal of Experimental Social Psychology* 40 (2004): 142–151; John G. Oetzel, "The Effects of Ethnicity and Self-Construals on Self-Reported Conflict Styles," *Communication Reports,* 11 (1998): 133–144; John G. Oetzel, "The Influence of Situational Features on Perceived Conflict Styles and Self-Construals in Work Groups," *International Journal of Intercultural Relations,* 23 (1999): 679–695; John G. Oetzel and Stella Ting-Toomey, "Face Concerns in Interpersonal Conflict: A Cross-Cultural Empirical Test of the Face Negotiation Theory," *Communication Research* 30 (2003): 599–624; John G. Oetzel, Stella Ting-Toomey, Tomoko Masumoto, Yumiko Yokochi, Xiaohui Pan, Jiro Takai, and Richard Wilcox, "Face and Facework in Conflict: A Cross-Cultural Comparison of China, Germany, Japan, and the United States," *Communication Monographs* 68 (2001): 235–258; Stella Ting-Toomey, "Toward a Theory of Conflict and Culture," *Communication, Culture, and Organizational Processes,* ed. William B. Gudykunst, Lea P. Stewart, and Stella Ting-Toomey (Beverly Hills, CA: Sage, 1985), 71–86; Stella Ting-Toomey, "Intercultural Conflict Styles: A Face-Negotiation Theory," *Theories in Intercultural Communication,* ed. Young Yun Kim and William B. Gudykunst (Newbury Park, CA: Sage, 1988), 213–235; Stella Ting-Toomey, "Intergroup Diplomatic Communication: A Face-Negotiation Perspective," *Communicating for Peace,* ed. Felipe Korzenny and Stella Ting-Toomey (Newbury Park: Sage, 1990), 75–95; Stella Ting-Toomey, "Intercultural Conflict Competence," *Competence in Interpersonal Conflict,* ed. William R. Cupach and Daniel J. Canary (New York: McGraw-Hill, 1997), 120–147; Stella Ting-Toomey and Beth-Ann Cocroft, "Face and Facework: Theoretical and Research Issues," *The Challenge of Facework: Cross-Cultural and Interpersonal Issues,* ed. Stella Ting-Toomey (Albany: State University of New York Press, 1994), 307–340; Stella Ting-Toomey and John G. Oetzel, *Managing Intercultural Conflict Effectively* (Thousand Oaks, CA: Sage, 2001).
39. Min-Sun Kim, "Culture-Based Interactive Constraints in Explaining Intercultural Strategic Competence," *Intercultural Communication Competence,* ed. Richard L. Wiseman and Jolene Koester (Newbury Park, CA: Sage, 1993), 132–150; Min-Sun Kim, "Cross-Cultural Comparisons of the Perceived Importance of Conversational Constraints," *Human Communication Research* 21 (1994): 128–151; Min-Sun Kim, "Toward a Theory of Conversational Constraints: Focusing on Individual-Level Dimensions of Culture," *Intercultural Communication Theory,* ed. Richard L. Wiseman (Thousand Oaks, CA: Sage, 1995), 148–169; Min-Sun Kim, John E. Hunter, Akira Miyahara, Ann-Marie Horvath, Mary Bresnahan, and Hye-Jin Yoon, "Individual- vs. Culture-Level Dimensions of Individualism and Collectivism: Effects on Preferred Conversational Styles," *Communication Monographs* 63 (1996): 29–49; Min-Sun Kim and William F. Sharkey, "Independent and Interdependent Construals of Self: Explaining Cultural Patterns of Interpersonal Communication in Multi-Cultural Organizational Settings," *Communication Quarterly* 43 (1995): 20–38; Min-Sun Kim, William F. Sharkey, and Theodore M. Singelis, "The Relationship of Individuals' Self-Construals and Perceived Importance of Interactive Constraints," *International Journal of Intercultural Relations* 18 (1994): 117–140; Min-Sun Kim and Steven R. Wilson, "A Cross-Cultural Comparison of Implicit Theories of Requesting," *Communication Monographs* 61 (1994): 210–235; Akira Miyahara, Min-Sun Kim, Ho-Chang Shin, and Kak Yoon, "Conflict Resolution Styles Among 'Collectivist' Cultures: A Comparison between Japanese and Koreans," *International Journal of Intercultural Relations* 22 (1998): 505–525.
40. Dean C. Barnlund, "Apologies: Japanese and American Styles," *International Journal of Intercultural Relations* 14 (1990): 193–206; William R. Cupach and T. Todd Imahori, "Managing Social Predicaments Created by Others: A Comparison of Japanese and American Facework," *Western Journal of Communication* 57 (1993): 431–444; William R. Cupach and T. Todd Imahori, "A Cross-Cultural Comparison of the Interpretation and Management of Face: U.S. American and Japanese Responses to Embarrassing Predicaments," *International Journal of Intercultural Relations* 18 (1994): 193–219; Naoki Nomura and Dean Barnlund, "Patterns of Interpersonal Criticism in Japan and the United States," *International Journal of Intercultural Relations* 7 (1983): 1–18; Kiyoko Sueda and Richard L. Wiseman, "Embarrassment Remediation in Japan and the United States," *International Journal of Intercultural Relations* 16 (1992): 159–173.
41. Stahl, 14.
42. Robyn Penman, "Facework in Communication: Conceptual and Moral Challenges," *The Challenge of Facework: Cross-Cultural and Interpersonal Issues,* ed. Stella

Ting-Toomey (Albany: State University of New York Press, 1994), 21.

43. For an elaboration of uncertainty reduction theory, see Walid A. Afifi and Laura K. Guerrero, "Motivations Underlying Topic Avoidance in Close Relationships," *Balancing the Secrets of Private Disclosures,* ed. Sandra Petronio (Mahwah, NJ: Erlbaum, 2000), 165–179; Charles R. Berger, "Communicating Under Uncertainty," *Interpersonal Processes: New Directions in Communication Research,* ed. Michael E. Roloff and Gerald R. Miller (Newbury Park, CA: Sage, 1987), 39–62; Charles R. Berger and James J. Bradac, *Language and Social Knowledge: Uncertainty in Interpersonal Relations* (London: Arnold, 1982); Charles R. Berger and Richard J. Calabrese, "Some Explorations in Initial Interaction and Beyond: Toward a Developmental Theory of Interpersonal Communication," *Human Communication Research* 1 (1975): 99–112; James J. Bradac, "Theory Comparison: Uncertainty Reduction, Problematic Integration, Uncertainty Management, and Other Curious Constructs," *Journal of Communication* 51 (2001): 456–476; Glen W. Clatterbuck, "Attributional Confidence and Uncertainty in Initial Interaction," *Human Communication Research* 5 (1979): 147–157; William Douglas, "Uncertainty, Information-Seeking, and Liking During Initial Interaction," *Western Journal of Speech Communication* 54 (1990): 66–81; Daena J. Goldsmith, "A Normative Approach to the Study of Uncertainty and Communication," *Journal of Communication* 51 (2001): 514–533; William B. Gudykunst, "The Influence of Cultural Similarity, Type of Relationship, and Self-Monitoring on Uncertainty Reduction Processes," *Communication Monographs* 52 (1985): 203–217; William B. Gudykunst, Elizabeth Chua, and Alisa J. Gray, "Cultural Dissimilarities and Uncertainty Reduction Processes," *Communication Yearbook* 10, ed. Margaret McLaughlin (Beverly Hills, CA: Sage, 1984): 456–469; William B. Gudykunst and Tsukasa Nishida, "Individual and Cultural Influences on Uncertainty Reduction," *Communication Monographs* 51 (1984): 23–36; William B. Gudykunst, Seung-Mock Yang, and Tsukasa Nishida, "A Cross-Cultural Test of Uncertainty Reduction Theory: Comparisons of Acquaintances, Friends, and Dating Relationships in Japan, Korea, and the United States," *Human Communication Research* 11 (1985): 407–455; Jolanda Jetten, Michael A. Hogg, and Barbara-Ann Mullin, "In-Group Variability and Motivation to Reduce Subjective Uncertainty," *Group Dynamics* 4 (2000): 184–198; Kathy Kellermann and Rodney Reynolds, "When Ignorance Is Bliss: The Role of Motivation to Reduce Uncertainty in Uncertainty Reduction Theory," *Human Communication Research* 17 (1990): 5–75; Leanne K. Knobloch and Denise Haunani Solomon, "Information Seeking beyond Initial Interaction: Negotiating Relational Uncertainty within Close Relationships," *Human Communication Research* 28 (2002): 243–257; Angela Y. Lee, "The Mere Exposure Effect: An Uncertainty Reduction Explanation Revisited," *Personality & Social Psychology Bulletin* 27 (2001): 1255–1266; James W. Neuliep and Erica L. Grohskopf, "Uncertainty Reduction and Communication Satisfaction during Initial Interaction: An Initial Test and Replication of a New Axiom," *Communication Reports* 13 (2000): 67–77; Sally Planalp and James M. Honeycutt, "Events That Increase Uncertainty in Personal Relationships," *Human Communication Research* 11 (1985): 593–604; Sally Planalp, Diane K. Rutherford, and James M. Honeycutt, "Events That Increase Uncertainty in Personal Relationships II: Replication and Extension," *Human Communication Research* 14 (1988): 516–547; Michael Sunnafrank, "Predicted Outcome Value during Initial Interactions: A Reformulation of Uncertainty Reduction Theory," *Human Communication Research* 13 (1986): 3–33; Thomas C. Taveggia and Lourdes Santos Nieves Gibboney, "Cross Cultural Adjustment: A Test of Uncertainty Reduction Principle," *International Journal of Cross Cultural Management* 1 (2001): 153–171.

44. William B. Gudykunst, "Toward a Theory of Effective Interpersonal and Intergroup Communication: An Anxiety/Uncertainty Management (AUM) Perspective," *Intercultural Communication Competence,* ed. Richard L. Wiseman and Jolene Koester (Newbury Park, CA: Sage, 1994), 33–71; William B. Gudykunst, "Anxiety/Uncertainty Management Theory: Current Status," *Intercultural Communication Theory,* ed. Richard L. Wiseman (Thousand Oaks, CA: Sage, 1995), 8–58; William B. Gudykunst, "Intercultural Communication Theories," *Handbook of International and Intercultural Communication,* 2nd ed., ed. William B. Gudykunst and Bella Mody (Thousand Oaks, CA: Sage, 2002), 183–205; William B. Gudykunst and Carmen M. Lee, "Cross-Cultural Communication Theories," *Handbook of International and Intercultural Communication,* 2nd ed., ed. William B. Gudykunst and Bella Mody (Thousand Oaks, CA: Sage, 2002), 25–50; William B. Gudykunst and Tsukasa Nishida, "Anxiety, Uncertainty, and Perceived Effectiveness of Communication across Relationships and Cultures," *International Journal of Intercultural Relations* 25 (2001): 55–71; Kimberly N. Hubbert, William B. Gudykunst, and Sherrie L. Guerrero, "Intergroup Communication Over Time," *International Journal of Intercultural Relations* 23 (1999): 13–46; Craig R. Hullett and Kim Witte, "Predicting Intercultural Adaptation and Isolation: Using the Extended Parallel Process Model to Test Anxiety/Uncertainty Management Theory," *International Journal of Intercultural Relations* 25 (2001): 125–139; Walter G. Stephan, Cookie White Stephan, and William B. Gudykunst, "Anxiety in Intergroup Relations: A

Comparison of Anxiety/Uncertainty Management Theory and Integrated Threat Theory," *International Journal of Intercultural Relations* 23 (1999): 613–628.

45. Edna B. Foa and Uriel G. Foa, "Resource Theory: Interpersonal Behavior as Exchange," *Social Exchange: Advances in Theory and Research*, ed. Kenneth Gergen, Martin S. Greenberg, and Richard H. Willis (New York: Plenum Press, 1980), 77–101.

46. Judee K. Burgoon, "Nonverbal Violation of Expectations," *Nonverbal Interaction*, ed. John M. Wiemann and Randall P. Harrison (Beverly Hills, CA: Sage, 1983), 77–111; Judee K. Burgoon, "Interpersonal Expectations, Expectancy Violations, and Emotional Communication," *Journal of Language and Social Psychology* 12 (1993): 30–48; Judee K. Burgoon, "Cross-Cultural and Intercultural Applications of Expectancy Violations Theory," *Intercultural Communication Theory*, ed. Richard I. Wiseman (Thousand Oaks, CA: Sage, 1995), 194–214.

47. Berger, 41.

48. William B. Gudykunst and Tsukasa Nishida, "Individual and Cultural Influences on Uncertainty Reduction," *Communication Monographs* 51 (1984): 23–36. See also: Kevin Avruch, "Type I and Type II Errors in Culturally Sensitive Conflict Resolution Practice," *Conflict Resolution Quarterly* 20 (2003): 351–371; Michelle LeBaron, *Bridging Cultural Conflicts: A New Approach for a Changing World* (San Francisco, CA: Jossey-Bass, 2003); Dieter Senghaas, *The Clash within Civilizations: Coming to Terms with Cultural Conflicts* (New York: Routledge, 2002); Stella Ting-Toomey and John G. Oetzel, *Managing Intercultural Conflict Effectively* (Thousand Oaks, CA: Sage, 2001); Catherine H. Tinsley, "How Negotiators Get to Yes: Predicting the Constellation of Strategies Used across Cultures to Negotiate Conflict," *Journal of Applied Psychology* 86 (2001): 583–593.

49. Tsukasa Nishida, "Sequence Patterns of Self-Disclosure Among Japanese and North American Students," paper presented at the Conference on Communication in Japan and the United States, Fullerton, CA, March 1991.

50. Judith A. Sanders, Richard L. Wiseman, and S. Irene Matz, "A Cross-Cultural Comparison of Uncertainty Reduction Theory: The Cases of Ghana and the United States," paper presented at the annual conference of the International Communication Association, San Francisco, May 1989.

51. Changsheng Xi, "Individualism and Collectivism in American and Chinese Societies," *Our Voices: Essays in Culture, Ethnicity, and Communication*, ed. Alberto González, Marsha Houston, and Victoria Chen (Los Angeles: Roxbury, 1994), 155.

52. Robert Littlefield, "Self-Disclosure Among Some Negro, White, and Mexican-American Adolescents," *Journal of Counseling Psychology* 21 (1974): 133–136.

53. Sidney Jourard, "Self-Disclosure Patterns in British and American College Females," *Journal of Social Psychology* 54 (1961): 315–320.

54. Stella Ting-Toomey, "Intimacy Expressions in Three Cultures: France, Japan, and the United States," *International Journal of Intercultural Relations* 15 (1991): 29–46.

55. Dean Barnlund, *Public and Private Self in Japan and the United States: Communicative Styles of Two Cultures* (Tokyo: Simul Press, 1975); Ting-Toomey, "Intimacy Expressions."

56. Sidney Jourard, *Self-Disclosure: An Experimental Analysis of the Transparent Self* (New York: Wiley, 1971).

57. George Levinger and David J. Senn, "Disclosure of Feelings in Marriage," *Merrill Palmer Quarterly* 13 (1987): 237–249.

58. See Stella Ting-Toomey and John G. Oetzel, *Managing Intercultural Conflict Effectively* (Thousand Oaks, CA: Sage, 2001); Stella Ting-Toomey and John G. Oetzel, "Cross-Cultural Face Concerns and Conflict Styles: Current Status and Future Directions," *Handbook of International and Intercultural Communication*, 2nd ed., ed. William B. Gudykunst and Bella Mody (Thousand Oaks, CA: Sage, 2002): 143–163. Our discussion of managing conflict also draws on a number of works, including John G. Oetzel, "The Effects of Self-Construals and Ethnicity on Self-Reported Conflict Styles," *Communication Reports* 11 (1998): 133–144; John G. Oetzel, "The Influence of Situational Features on Perceived Conflict Styles and Self-Construals in Work Groups," *International Journal of Intercultural Relations* 23 (1999): 679–695; John Oetzel, Stella Ting-Toomey, Tomoko Masumoto, Yumiko Yokochi, Xiaohui Pan, Jiro Takai, and Richard Wilcox, "Face and Facework in Conflict: A Cross-Cultural Comparison of China, Germany, Japan, and the United States," *Communication Monographs* 68 (2001): 235–258; Stella Ting-Toomey, "Managing Conflict in Intimate Intercultural Relationships," *Conflict in Personal Relationships*, ed. Dudley D. Cahn (Hillsdale, NJ: Erlbaum, 1994), 47–77; Stella Ting-Toomey, Kimberlie K. Yee-Jung, Robin B. Shapiro, Wintilo Garcia, Trina J. Wright, and John G. Oetzel, "Ethnic/Cultural Identity Salience and Conflict Styles in Four US Ethnic Groups," *International Journal of Intercultural Relations* 24 (2000): 47–81; Ting-Toomey, "Conflict and Culture"; Stella Ting-Toomey, "Conflict Styles in Black and White Subjective Cultures," *Current Research in Interethnic Communication*, ed. Young Yun Kim (Beverly Hills, CA: Sage, 1986); Ting-Toomey, "Face Negotiation Theory" (see note 38).

59. Deborah A. Cai, Steven R. Wilson, and Laura E. Drake, "Culture in the Context of Intercultural Negotiation: Individualism-Collectivism and Paths to Integrative Agreements," *Human Communication Research* 26 (2000):

591–617; Ge Gao, "An Initial Analysis of the Effects of Face and Concern for 'Other' in Chinese Interpersonal Communication," *International Journal of Intercultural Relations* 22 (1998): 467–482.

60. Ringo Ma, "The Role of Unofficial Intermediaries in Interpersonal Conflicts in the Chinese Culture," *Communication Quarterly* 40 (1992): 269–278.

61. Ting-Toomey, "Face Negotiation Theory" (see note 38).

62. Susan Cross and Robert Rosenthal, "Three Models of Conflict Resolution: Effects on Intergroup Expectancies and Attitudes," *Journal of Social Issues* 55(3) (1999): 561–580.

Chapter 11

1. Tamar Katriel, *Communal Webs: Communication and Culture in Contemporary Israel* (Albany: State University of New York Press, 1991), 35–49.

2. Joseph P. Forgas and Michael H. Bond, "Cultural Influences on the Perception of Interaction Episodes," *Journal of Cross-Cultural Psychology* 11 (1985): 75–88.

3. Robert T. Craig and Karen Tracy, *Conversational Coherence: Form, Structure, and Strategy* (Beverly Hills, CA: Sage, 1983); Susan B. Shimanoff, *Communication Rules: Theory and Research* (Beverly Hills, CA: Sage, 1980).

4. Wendy Leeds-Hurwitz, "Intercultural Weddings and the Simultaneous Display of Multiple Identities," *Communicating Ethnic & Cultural Identity,* ed. Mary Fong and Rueyling Chuang (Lanham, MD: Rowman & Littlefield, 2004), 135–148.

5. B. Aubrey Fisher, *Interpersonal Communication: Pragmatics of Human Relationships* (New York: Random House, 1987), 59.

6. Norine Dresser, *Multicultural Manners: Essential Rules of Etiquette for the 21st Century,* Revised ed. (Hoboken, NJ: Wiley, 2005), 72.

7. Dresser, 76.

8. Kellermann calls these interaction scenes "Memory Organization Packets" (MOPs). Our description of her research is based on the following: Kathy Kellermann, "The Conversation MOP II: Progression Through Scenes in Discourse," *Human Communication Research* 17 (1991): 385–414; Kathy Kellermann, "The Conversation MOP: A Model of Pliable Behavior," *The Cognitive Bases of Interpersonal Communication,* ed. Dean E. Hewes (Hillsdale, NJ: Erlbaum, 1995); Kathy Kellerman and Tae-Seop Lim, "The Conversation MOP III: Timing of Scenes in Discourse," *Journal of Personality and Psychology* 54 (1990): 1163–1179.

9. Jeanette S. Martin and Lillian H. Chaney, *Global Business Etiquette: A Guide to International Communication and Customs* (Westport, CT: Praeger, 2006), 24.

10. See, for example, David T. Cowan and Ian Norman, "Cultural Competence in Nursing: New Meanings," *Journal of Transcultural Nursing,* 17 (2006): 82–88.

11. See Linda C. Lederman, *Beyond These Walls: Readings in Health Communication* (New York: Oxford University Press, 2008); Bernard Moss, *Communication Skills for Health and Social Care* (Thousand Oaks, CA: Sage, 2007); Renata Schiavo, *Health Communication: From Theory to Practice* (San Francisco: Jossey-Bass, 2007); Kevin B. Wright, Lisa Sparks, and Dan O'Hair, *Health Communication in the 21st Century* (Malden, MA: Blackwell, 2008); Heather M. Zoller and Mohan J. Dutta, *Emerging Perspectives in Health Communication: Meaning, Culture, and Power* (New York: Routledge, 2008).

12. See for example, Barbara Broome, "Culture 101," *Urologic Nursing* 26 (2006): 486–489; Cathleen A. Collins, Shawn I. Decker, and Karen A. Esquibel, "Definitions of Health: Comparison of Hispanic and African-American Elders," *Journal of Multicultural Nursing & Health* 12 (2006): 14–19; Y. S. Kim-Godwin, P. N. Clarke, and L. Barton, "A Model for the Delivery of Culturally Competent Community Care," *Journal of Advanced Nursing* 35 (2001): 918–925; Susan Kleiman, "Discovering Cultural Aspects of Nurse-Patient Relationships," *Journal of Cultural Diversity* 13 (2006): 83–86; Isveti Markova and Barbara Broome, "Effective Communication and Delivery of Culturally Competent Health Care," *Urologic Nursing* 27 (2007): 239–241; Mary Sobralske and Janet Katz, "Culturally Competent Care of Patients with Acute Chest Pain," *Journal of the American Academy of Nurse Practitioners* 17 (2005): 324–329; Vasso Vydelingum, "Nurses' Experiences of Caring for South Asian Minority Ethnic Patients in a General Hospital in England," *Nursing Inquiry* 13 (2006): 23–32; Yu Xu and Ruth Davidhizar, "Intercultural Communication in Nursing Education: When Asian Students and American Faculty Converge," *Journal of Nursing Education* 44 (2005): 209–215.

13. For a detailed discussion of professional opportunities in transcultural nursing, see Margaret M. Andrews, "Cultural Perspectives on Nursing in the 21st Century," *Journal of Professional Nursing* 8 (1992): 7–15.

14. See, for example, Joyceen S. Boyle and Margaret M. Andrews, *Transcultural Concepts in Nursing Care,* 2nd ed. (Philadelphia: Lippincott, 1995); Barbara Broome and Teena McGuinness, "A CRASH Course in Cultural Competence for Nurses," *Urologic Nursing* 27 (2007): 292–295; Nancy Campbell-Heider, Karol Pohlman Rejman, Tammy Austin-Ketch, Kay Sackett, Thomas Hugh Feeley, and Nancy C. Wilk, "Measuring Cultural Competence in a Family Nurse Practitioner Curriculum," *Journal of Multicultural Nursing & Health* 12 (2006): 23–24; Susan M. Dobson, *Transcultural Nursing: A Contemporary Imperative* (London: Scutari Press, 1991); Geri-Ann Galanti, *Caring for Patients from Different Cultures: Case Studies from American Hospitals,* 2nd ed. (Philadelphia: University of Pennsylvania Press, 1991);

Joyce Newman Giger and Ruth Elaine Davidhizar (eds.), *Transcultural Nursing: Assessment and Intervention*, 2nd ed. (St. Louis: Mosby Year Book, 1995); Suzan Kardong-Edgren, "Cultural Competence of Baccalaureate Nursing Faculty," *Journal of Nursing Education* 46 (2007): 360–366; Janice M. Morse (ed.), *Issues in Cross-Cultural Nursing* (New York: Churchill Livingstone, 1988); Janice M. Morse (ed.), *Cross-Cultural Nursing: Anthropological Approaches to Nursing Research* (Philadelphia: Gordon and Breach, 1989); Cheryl L. Reynolds and Madeleine Leininger; *Cultural Care Diversity and Universality Theory* (Newbury Park, CA: Sage, 1993); Jean Uhl (ed.), *Application of Cultural Concepts to Nursing Care: Proceedings of the Ninth Annual Transcultural Nursing Conference*, Scottsdale, AZ, September 1993 (Salt Lake City: Transcultural Nursing Society, 1984); Megan J. Wood and Marsha Atkins, "Immersion in Another Culture: One Strategy for Increasing Cultural Competency," *Journal of Cultural Diversity* 13 (2006): 50–54.

15. See, for example, Larry D. Purnell and Betty J. Paulanka, *Transcultural Health Care: A Culturally Competent Approach* (Philadelphia: F. A. Davis, 1998).

16. Kathryn Hopkins Kavanagh and Patricia H. Kennedy, *Promoting Cultural Diversity Strategies for Health Care Professionals* (Newbury Park, CA: Sage, 1992), 28.

17. See, for example, Madonna G. Constantine and Derald Wing Sue (eds.), *Strategies for Building Multicultural Competence in Mental Health and Educational Settings* (Hoboken, NJ: Wiley, 2005); George Henderson, Dorscine Spigner-Littles, and Virginia Hall Milhouse, *A Practitioner's Guide to Understanding Indigenous and Foreign Cultures: An Analysis of Relationships between Ethnicity, Social Class and Therapeutic Intervention Strategies*, 3rd ed. (Springfield, IL: Charles C Thomas, 2006); June L. Leishman, "Culturally Sensitive Mental Health Care: A Module for 21st Century Education and Practice," *International Journal of Psychiatric Nursing Research* 11 (2006): 1310–1321; Jane S. Mahoney, Elizabeth Carlson, and Joan C. Engebretson, "A Framework for Cultural Competence in Advanced Practice Psychiatric and Mental Health Education," *Perspectives in Psychiatric Care* 42 (2006): 227–233.

18. Sharon E. Kummerer and Norma A. Lopez-Reyna, "The Role of Mexican Immigrant Mothers' Beliefs on Parental Involvement in Speech–Language Therapy," *Communication Disorders Quarterly* 27 (2006): 83–94.

19. See, for example, Lucinda Dale, Raeanne Albin, Shelley Kapolka-Ullom, Annjanette Lange, Megan McCan, Kacey Quaderer, and Nikki Shaffer, "The Meaning of Work in the U.S. for Two Latino Immigrants from Colombia and Mexico," *Work* 25 (2005) 187–196.

20. Boyle and Andrews, 26–36; Kim Witte and Kelly Morrison, "Intercultural and Cross-Cultural Health Communication," *Intercultural Communication Theory*, ed. Richard L. Wiseman (Thousand Oaks, CA: Sage, 1995), 221–222.

21. Rachel E. Spector, *Cultural Diversity in Health and Illness*, 4th ed. (Norwalk, CT: Appleton-Lange, 1996), 193.

22. Sam Chan, "Families with Asian Roots," *Developing Cross-Cultural Competence: A Guide for Working with Young Children and Their Families*, ed. Eleanor W. Lynch and Marci J. Hanson (Baltimore: Paul Brookes, 1992), 223.

23. Richard H. Dana, "The Cultural Self as Locus for Assessment and Intervention with American Indians/Alaska Natives," *Journal of Multicultural Counseling and Development* 28 (2000): 66–82.

24. Chan, 222.

25. For a discussion of these issues, see D. Patricia Gray and Debra J. Thomas, "Critical Reflections on Culture in Nursing," *Journal of Cultural Diversity* 13 (2006): 76–82; Kavanagh and Kennedy, 22–24.

26. The examples here and in the preceding paragraph are adapted from Norine Dresser, *Multicultural Manners: Essential Rules of Etiquette for the 21st Century*, Revised ed. (Hoboken, NJ: Wiley, 2005).

27. Ursula M. Wilson, "Nursing Care of American Indian Patients," *Ethnic Nursing Care: A Multicultural Approach*, ed. Modesta Soberano Orque, Bobbie Bloch, and Lidia S. Ahumada Monroy (St. Louis: Mosby, 1983), 277.

28. Joan Kuipers, "Mexican Americans," *Transcultural Nursing: Assessment and Intervention*, 2nd ed., ed. Joyce Newman Giger and Ruth Elaine Davidhizar (St. Louis: Mosby Year Book, 1995), 205–234.

29. Boyle and Andrews, 151–155.

30. Noreen Mokuau and Pemerika Tauili'ili, "Families with Native Hawaiian and Pacific Island Roots," *Developing Cross-Cultural Competence: A Guide for Working with Young Children and Their Families*, ed. Eleanor W. Lynch and Marci J. Hanson (Baltimore: Paul Brookes, 1992), 313.

31. Witte and Morrison, 224.

32. Kavanagh and Kennedy, 37. See also: Kuipers.

33. See Kuipers, 209 and 212.

34. Adapted from Dresser, 146.

35. Kuipers, 209. See also: Kavanagh and Kennedy; Wilson, 277.

36. Chan, 241.

37. Witte and Morrison, 227.

38. See, for example, Joan Luckmann, *Transcultural Communication in Health Care* (Albany, NY: Delmar-Thomson Learning, 2000), 61.

39. Min-Sun Kim, Renee Storm Klingle, William F. Sharkey, Hee Sun Park, David H. Smith, and Deborah Cai, "A Test of a Cultural Model of Patients' Motivation for Verbal Communication in Patient-Doctor Interactions," *Communication Monographs* 67 (2000): 262–283.

40. Nilda Chong, *The Latino Patient: A Cultural Guide for Health Care Providers* (Yarmouth, ME: Intercultural Press, 2002).

41. See, for example, R. E. Nailon, "Nurses Concerns and Practices with Using Interpreters in the Care of Latino Patients in the Emergency Department," *Journal of Transcultural Nursing* 17 (2006): 119–128.

42. See, for example, Roxanne Amerson and Shelley Burgins, "Hablamos Español: Crossing Communication Barriers with the Latino Population," *Journal of Nursing* 44 (2005): 241–243.

43. Susan Raye Moffitt and Mimi Jenko, "Transcultural Nursing Principles: An Application to Hospice Care," *Journal of Hospice and Palliative Nursing* 8 (2006): 172–180.

44. Boyle and Andrews, 55.

45. Haffner, "Translation Is Not Enough: Interpreting in a Medical Setting," *Western Journal of Medicine* 157 (1992): 255–260.

46. Luckmann, 191.

47. Susan Raye Moffitt and Mimi Jenko, "Transcultural Nursing Principles: An Application to Hospice Care," *Journal of Hospice and Palliative Nursing* 8 (2006): 172–180.

48. For an excellent summary of cultural variations in what is regarded as the appropriate verbal and nonverbal means to express pain, see Mary Sobralske and Janet Katz, "Culturally Competent Care of Patients with Acute Chest Pain," *Journal of the American Academy of Nurse Practitioners*, 17 (2005): 324–329.

49. Jeffrey Trawick-Smith, *Early Childhood Development: A Multicultural Perspective*, 2nd ed. (Upper Saddle River, NJ: Merrill, 2000).

50. Lisa Delpit, *Other People's Children: Cultural Conflict in the Classroom* (New York: New Press, 1995); C. Raeff, Patricia M. Greenfield, and Blanca Quiroz, "Conceptualizing Interpersonal Relationships in the Cultural Contexts of Individualism and Collectivism," *Variability in the Social Construction of the Child*, ed. S. Harkness, C. Raeff, and C. Super, *New Directions in Child Development*, no. 87 (San Francisco: Jossey-Bass, 2000); Rosa Hernandez Sheets, *Diversity Pedagogy: Examining the Role of Culture in the Teaching-Learning Process* (Boston: Pearson, 2005).

51. Janet Bennett and Riikka Salonen, "Intercultural Communication and the New American Campus," *Change* March/April (2007): 46.

52. Patricia Phelan, Ann Locke Davidson, and Hanh Cao Yu, "Students' Multiple Worlds: Navigating the Borders of Family, Peer, and School Cultures," *Renegotiating Cultural Diversity in American Schools*, ed. Patricia Phelan and Ann Locke Davidson (New York: College Press, 1993), 52–88.

53. For an interesting ethnographic description of how Navajo philosophy permeates curriculum and classroom behaviors in a Navajo community college, see Charles A. Braithwaite, "Sa'ah Naagháí Bik'eh Hózhóón: An Ethnography of Navajo Educational Communication Practices," *Communication Education* 46 (1997): 219–233.

54. Gary R. Howard, "As Diversity Grows, So Must We," *Educational Leadership* 64 (2007): 16–22.

55. In an interesting study of teachers from rural, urban, and suburban schools across the Midwestern geographic region of the United States, Jennifer Mahon found that teachers had a tendency to minimize the cultural differences that were present among their students. See Jennifer Mahon, "Under the Invisibility Cloak? Teacher Understanding of Cultural Difference," *Intercultural Education* 17 (2006): 391–405.

56. Bonnie M. Davis, *How to Teach Students Who Don't Look Like You: Culturally Relevant Teaching Strategies* (Thousand Oaks, CA: Corwin Press, 2006); Carlos J. Ovando, Mary Carol Combs, and Virginia P. Collier, *Bilingual and ESL Classrooms: Teaching in Multicultural Contexts*, 4th ed. (Boston: McGraw Hill, 2006); Kikanza Nuri Robins, Randall B. Lindsey, Delores B. Lindsey, and Raymond D. Terrell, *Culturally Proficient Instruction: A Guide for People Who Teach*, 2nd ed. (Thousand Oaks, CA: Corwin Press, 2006); Teresa A. Wasonga, "Multicultural Education Knowledgebase, Attitudes and Preparedness for Diversity," *International Journal of Educational Management* 29 (2005): 67–74.

57. K. David Roach and Paul R. Byrne, "A Cross-Cultural Comparison of Instructor Communication in American and German Classrooms," *Communication Education* 50 (2001): 1–14.

58. Shuming Lu, "Culture and Compliance Gaining in the Classroom: A Preliminary Investigation of Chinese College Teachers' Use of Behavior Alteration Techniques," *Communication Education* 46 (1997): 20–21.

59. Norine Dresser, *Multicultural Manners: Essential Rules of Etiquette for the 21st Century*, Revised ed. (Hoboken, NJ: Wiley, 2005), 64.

60. Cristy Lee, Timothy Levine, and Ronald Cambra, "Resisting Compliance in the Multicultural Classroom," *Communication Education* 46 (1997): 29–43; Lu, 10–28.

61. Lu, 24–25.

62. Elise Trumbull, Carrie Rothstein-Fisch, Patricia M. Greenfield, and Blanca Quiroz, *Bridging Cultures between Home and School: A Guide for Teachers* (Mahwah, NJ: Erlbaum, 2001), 10.

63. Donal Carbaugh, *Cultures in Conversation* (Mahwah, NJ: Erlbaum, 2005).

64. Eunkyong L. Yook and Rosita Albert, "Perceptions of the Appropriateness of Negotiation in Education Settings: A Cross-Cultural Comparison among Koreans and Americans," *Communication Education* 47 (1998): 18–29.

65. Jolene Koester and Myron W. Lustig, "Communication Curricula in the Multicultural University," *Communication Education* 40 (1991): 250–254.

66. Paul David Bolls, Alex Tan, and Erica Austin, "An Exploratory Comparison of Native American and Caucasian Students' Attitudes toward Teacher Communicative

Behavior and toward School," *Communication Education* 46 (1997): 198–202. See also: Paul David Bolls and Alex Tan, "Communication Anxiety and Teacher Communication Competence Among Native American and Caucasian Students," *Communication Research Reports* 13 (1996): 205–213.

67. Barbara J. Shade and Clara A. New, "Cultural Influences on Learning: Teaching Implications," *Multicultural Education: Issues and Perspectives,* 2nd ed., ed. James A. Banks and Cherry A. McGee Banks (Boston: Allyn & Bacon, 1993), 320.

68. Steven T. Mortenson, "Cultural Differences and Similarities in Seeking Social Support as a Response to Academic Failure: A Comparison of American and Chinese College Students," *Communication Education* 55 (2006): 127–146.

69. Maria E. Zuniga, "Families with Latino Roots," *Developing Cross-Cultural Competence: A Guide for Working with Young Children and Their Families,* ed. Eleanor W. Lynch and Marci J. Hanson (Baltimore: Paul Brookes, 1992), 151–179.

70. Jennie R. Joe and Randi Suzanne Malach, "Families with Native American Roots," *Developing Cross-Cultural Competence: A Guide for Working with Young Children and Their Families,* ed. Eleanor W. Lynch and Marci J. Hanson (Baltimore: Paul Brookes, 1992), 108; Cornel Pewewardy, "Toward Defining a Culturally Responsive Pedagogy for American Indian Children: The American Indian Magnet School," *Multicultural Education for the Twenty-First Century, Proceedings of the Second Annual Meeting, National Association for Multicultural Education, February 13–16th, 1992,* ed. Carl A. Grant (Morristown, NJ: Paramount, 1992), 218.

71. Rosa Hernández Sheets, *Diversity Pedagogy: Examining the Role of Culture in the Teaching-Learning Process* (Boston: Pearson, 2005), 4.

72. See Sam Chan, "Families with Pilipino Roots," *Developing Cross-Cultural Competence: A Guide for Working with Young Children and Their Families,* ed. Eleanor W. Lynch and Marci J. Hanson (Baltimore: Paul Brookes, 1992), 276.

73. Leonard Davidman with Patricia T. Davidman, *Teaching with a Multicultural Perspective: A Practical Guide* (New York: Longman, 1994), 43; Trumbull, Rothstein-Fisch, Greenfield, and Quiroz, 55–74.

74. Virginia Shirin Sharifzadeh, "Families with Middle Eastern Roots," *Developing Cross-Cultural Competence: A Guide for Working with Young Children and Their Families,* ed. Eleanor W. Lynch and Marci J. Hanson (Baltimore: Paul Brookes, 1992), 341.

75. Jerry McClelland and Chen Chen, "Standing up for a Son: School Experiences of a Mexican Immigrant Mother," *Hispanic Journal of Behavioral Science* 19 (1997): 281–300.

76. McClelland and Chen, 291.

77. Josina Macau, *Embracing Diversity in the Classroom: Communication Ethics in an Age of Diversity,* ed. Josina Makau and Ronald C. Arnett (Urbana: University of Illinois Press, 1997), 48–67.

78. Andrea Sobel and Eileen Gale Kugler, *Educational Leadership* 64 (2007): 62–66.

79. Joe and Malach, 109.

80. See, for example, James Calvert Scott, "Developing Cultural Fluency: The Goal of International Business Communication Instruction in the 21st Century," *Journal of Education for Business* 74 (1999): 140–143.

81. See, for example, Abel Adekola and Bruno S. Sergi, *Global Business Management: A Cross-Cultural Perspective* (Burlington, VT: Ashgate, 2007); Daniel Altman, *Connected: 24 Hours in the Global Economy* (New York: Farrar, Straus and Giroux, 2007); Elizabeth Kathleen Briody and Robert T. Trotter, *Partnering for Organizational Performance: Collaboration and Culture in the Global Workplace* (Lanham, MA: Rowman & Littlefield, 2008); George Cairns, *International Business* (Thousand Oaks, CA: Sage, 2008); Penny Carté and Chris J. Fox, *Bridging the Culture Gap: A Practical Guide to International Business Communication,* 2nd ed. (Philadelphia: Kogan Page, 2008); John D. Daniels and Jeffrey A. Krug, *International Business and Globalization* (Thousand Oaks, CA: Sage, 2007); John D. Daniels, Lee H. Radebaugh, and Daniel P. Sullivan, *International Business: Environments and Operations,* 12th ed. (Upper Saddle River, NJ: Pearson Prentice Hall, 2009); Jeremy Haft, *All the Tea in China: How to Buy, Sell, and Make Money on the Mainland* (New York: Portfolio, 2007); Charles W. L. Hill, *International Business: Competing in the Global Marketplace,* 6th ed. (Boston: McGraw-Hill/Irwin, 2007); Jorma Larimo, *Contemporary Euromarketing: Entry and Operational Decision Making* (Binghamton, NY: International Business Press, 2007); Andrea Mandel-Campbell, *Why Mexicans Don't Drink Molson: Rescuing Canadian Business from the Suds of Global Obscurity* (Vancouver: Douglas & McIntyre, 2007); Dorothy McCormick, Patrick O. Alila, and Mary Omosa, *Business in Kenya: Institutions and Interactions* (Nairobi: University of Nairobi Press, 2007); William Hernández Requejo and John L. Graham, *Global Negotiation: The New Rules* (New York: Palgrave Macmillan, 2008); Carl Rodrigues, *International Management: A Cultural Approach,* 3rd ed. (Thousand Oaks, CA: Sage, 2008); Alan M. Rugman, *The Oxford Handbook of International Business,* 2nd ed. (New York: Oxford University Press, 2008); Oded Shenkar and Yadong Luo, *International Business,* 2nd ed. (Thousand Oaks, CA: Sage, 2008); Gabriele Suder, *International Business* (Thousand Oaks, CA: Sage, 2008); Xiaowen Tian, *Managing International Business in China* (New York: Cambridge University Press, 2007); Yonggui Wang and Richard Li-Hua, *Marketing Competences and Strategic Flexibility in China* (New York: Palgrave

Macmillan, 2007); Frederick F. Wherry, *Global Markets and Local Crafts: Thailand and Costa Rica Compared* (Baltimore: Johns Hopkins University Press, 2008); Stephen White, *Media, Culture and Society in Putin's Russia* (New York: Palgrave Macmillan, 2008); John Yabs, *International Business Operations in Kenya*, 2nd ed. (Nairobi: Lelax Global Ltd., 2007); George S. Yip and Audrey J. M. Bink, *Managing Global Customers: An Integrated Approach* (New York: Oxford University Press, 2007).

82. Rosalie L. Tung, "Expatriate Assignments: Enhancing Success and Minimizing Failure," *Academy of Management Executive* 1 (1987): 117–126.

83. Gary Oddou and Mark Mendenhall, "Expatriate Performance Appraisal: Problems and Solutions," *International Human Resource Management*, ed. Mark Mendenhall and Gary Oddou (Boston: PWS-Kent, 1991), 364–374; Rosalie Tung and Edwin L. Miller, "Managing in the Twenty-First Century: The Need for Global Orientation," *Management International Review* 30 (1990): 5–18.

84. Henry Kaufmann and Thomas S. Johnson, "Basic Training for the Global Marketplace," *Chief Executive*, July/August (2006): 26.

85. Philip R. Harris and Robert T. Moran, *Managing Cultural Differences*, 3rd ed. (Houston: Gulf, 1991).

86. Harris and Moran.

87. Boye Lafayette De Mente, *How to Do Business with the Japanese*, 2nd ed. (Lincolnwood, IL: NTC Business Books, 1993); Christopher Engholm, *When Business East Meets Business West: The Guide to Practice and Protocol in the Pacific Rim* (New York: Wiley, 1991).

88. Masami Nishishiba and David Ritchie, "The Concept of Trustworthiness: A Cross-Cultural Comparison Between Japanese and U.S. Business People," *Journal of Applied Communication Research* 28 (2000): 347–367.

89. Harris and Moran, 418.

90. Sonja Vegdahl Hur and Ben Seunghwa Hur, *Culture Shock! Korea* (Singapore: Times Books International, 1988), 34.

91. Fons Trompenaars, *Riding the Waves of Culture: Understanding Diversity in Global Business* (New York: Irwin, 1994); Fons Trompenaars and Charles Hampden-Turner, *Managing People across Cultures* (Chichester, England: Capstone, 2004); Fons Trompenaars and Peter Prud'Homme, *Managing Change across Corporate Cultures* (Chichester, England: Capstone, 2004); Fons Trompenaars and Peter Woolliams, *Business across Cultures* (Chichester, England: Capstone, 2003); Fons Trompenaars and Peter Woolliams, *Marketing across Cultures* (Chichester, England: Capstone, 2004).

92. William B. Gudykunst and Yuko Matsumoto, "Cross-Cultural Variability of Communication in Personal Relationships," *Communication in Personal Relationships Across Cultures*, ed. William B. Gudykunst, Stella Ting-Toomey, and Tsukasa Nishida (Thousand Oaks: Sage, 1996), 19–56.

93. Cindy P. Lindsay and Bobby L. Dempsey, "Ten Painfully Learned Lessons about Working in China: The Insights of Two American Behavioral Scientists," *Journal of Applied Behavioral Science* 19 (1983): 265–276.

94. Alex Blackwell, "Negotiating in Europe," *Hemispheres*, July 1994, 43.

95. Jo Ann G. Heydenfeldt, "The Influence of Individualism/Collectivism on Mexican and US Business Negotiation," *International Journal of Intercultural Relations*, 24 (2000): 383–407.

96. Philip R. Harris, Robert T. Moran, and Sarah V. Moran, *Managing Cultural Differences: Global Leadership Strategies for the 21st Century*, 6th ed. (Oxford, UK: Elsevier, 2004).

97. Alan Goldman, "Communication in Japanese Multinational Organizations," *Communicating in Multinational Organizations*, ed. Richard L. Wiseman and Robert Shuter (Thousand Oaks, CA: Sage, 1994), 49–59.

98. Yale Richmond, *From Da to Yes: Understanding the East Europeans* (Yarmouth, ME: Intercultural Press, 1995), 138.

99. Rajesh Kumar and Anand Kumar Sethi, *Doing Business in India: A Guide for Western Managers* (New York: Palgrave Macmillan, 2005): 104–105.

100. Lecia Archer and Kristine L. Fitch, "Communication in Latin American Multinational Organizations," *Communicating in Multinational Organizations*, ed. Richard L. Wiseman and Robert Shuter (Thousand Oaks, CA: Sage, 1994), 75–93.

101. Myria Watkins Allen, Patricia Amason, and Susan Holmes, "Social Support, Hispanic Emotional Acculturative Stress and Gender," *Communication Studies* 49 (1998): 139–157; Patricia Amason, Myria Watkins Allen, and Susan A. Holmes, "Social Support and Acculturative Stress in the Multicultural Workplace," *Journal of Applied Communication Research* 27 (1999): 310–334.

102. Lindsay and Dempsey.

103. Norine Dresser, *Multicultural Manners: Essential Rules of Etiquette for the 21st Century*, Revised ed. (Hoboken, NJ: Wiley, 2005), 156.

104. Dresser, 68.

105. Farid Elashmawi and Philip R. Harris, *Multicultural Management 2000: Essential Cultural Insights for Global Business Success* (Houston: Gulf, 1998), 118–125.

106. David Streitfeld, "A Crash Course on Irate Calls," *Los Angeles Times*, August 2, 2004, A1, A8. See also: Paul Davies, *What's This India Business? Offshore Outsourcing, and the Global Services Revolution* (Yarmouth, ME: Nicholas Brealey International, 2004).

107. See, for example, Jeanette S. Martin and Lillian H. Chaney, *Global Business Etiquette: A Guide to International Communication and Customs* (Westport, CT: Praeger, 2006) 155–158.

108. Philip R. Harris, Robert T. Moran, and Sarah V. Moran, *Managing Cultural Differences: Global Leadership Strategies for the 21st Century*, 6th ed. (Oxford, UK: Elsevier, 2004), 295.

109. Harris, Moran, and Moran, 323.

110. Young Yun Kim and Sheryl Paulk, "Interpersonal Challenges and Personal Adjustments: A Qualitative Analysis of the Experiences of American and Japanese Co-Workers," *Communicating in Multinational Organizations*, ed. Richard L. Wiseman and Robert Shuter (Thousand Oaks, CA: Sage, 1994), 117–140. See also: Alan E. Omens, Stephen R. Jenner, and James R. Beatty, "Intercultural Perceptions in United States Subsidiaries of Japanese Companies," *International Journal of Intercultural Relations* 11 (1987): 249–264; David W. Shwalb, Barbara J. Shwalb, Delwyn L. Harnisch, Martin L. Maehr, and Kiyoshi Akabane, "Personal Investment in Japan and the U.S.A.: A Study of Worker Motivation," *International Journal of Intercultural Relations* 16 (1992): 107–124.

111. Harris, Moran, and Moran, 381.

112. Lillian H. Chaney and Jeanette S. Martin, *Intercultural Business Communication*, 3rd ed. (Upper Saddle River, NJ: Pearson, 2004), 127.

113. Roong Sriussadapron, "Managing International Business Communication Problems at Work: A Pilot Study in Foreign Companies in Thailand," *Cross Cultural Management: An International Journal* 13 (2006): 330–344.

114. Rajesh Kumar and Anand Kumar Sethi, *Doing Business in India: A Guide for Western Managers* (New York: Palgrave Macmillan, 2005), 110.

115. Harris, Moran, and Moran, 43.

116. Richard H. Reeves-Ellington, "Using Cultural Skills for Cooperative Advantage in Japan," *Human Organization* 52 (1993): 203–215.

117. Elizabeth Gareis, "Virtual Teams: A Comparison of Online Communication Channels," *Journal of Language for International Business* 17 (2006): 6–21.

118. Evelyne Glaser and Manuela Guilherme, "Intercultural Competence for Multicultural Teams: A Qualitative Study," *Intercultural Competence for Professional Mobility [CD]*, ed. Evelyne Glaser, Manuela Guilherme, María del Carmen Méndez García, and Terry Mughan (Strasbourg: Council of Europe Publishing, 2007), 1–19.

119. Corinne Rosenberg, "EMEA-US Culture Clash: Resolving Diversity Issues through Reflective Evaluated Action Learning," *Industrial and Commercial Training* 37 (2005): 304–308.

120. William I. Gordon, "Organizational Imperatives and Cultural Modifiers," *Business Horizons* 27 (1984): 81.

121. See, for example, Christalyn Branner and Tracey Wilson, *Doing Business with Japanese Men: A Woman's Handbook* (Berkeley, CA: Stone Bridge Press, 1993).

122. Harris, Moran, and Moran, 43.

123. Nongluck Sriussadaporn-Charoenngam and Fredric M Jablin, "An Exploratory Study of Communication Competence in Thai Organizations," *Journal of Business Communication* 36 (1999): 382–418.

124. See, for example, Monir H. Tayeb, *The Management of a Multicultural Workforce* (New York: Wiley, 1996); R. Roosevelt Thomas, Jr., *Redefining Diversity* (New York: AMACOM, 1996); Lewis Brown Griggs and Lente Louise Louw (eds.), *Valuing Diversity* (New York: McGraw-Hill, 1995).

125. Steven H. Cady and Joanie Valentine, "Team Innovation and Perceptions of Consideration: What Difference Does Diversity Make?" *Small Group Research* 30 (1999): 730–750. See also: Georges Buzaglo and Susan A. Wheelan, "Facilitating Work Team Effectiveness: Case Studies from Central America," *Small Group Research* 30 (1999): 108–129; Graeme L Harrison, Jill L. McKinnon, Anne Wu, and Chee W. Chow, "Cultural Influences on Adaptation to Fluid Workgroups and Teams," *Journal of International Business Studies* 31 (2000): 489–505.

126. Lisa Millhous, "The Experience of Culture in Multicultural Groups: Case Studies of Russian-American Collaboration in Business," *Small Group Research* 30(3) (1999): 280–308.

127. Percy W. Thomas, "A Cultural Rapport Model," *Valuing Diversity*, ed. Lewis Brown Griggs and Lente Louise Louw (New York: McGraw-Hill, 1995), 136–137.

128. Thomas, 137.

129. Charles R. Bantz, "Cultural Diversity and Group Cross-Cultural Team Research," *Journal of Applied Communication Research* 21 (1993): 1–20.

Chapter 12

1. For summaries of these studies, see William B. Gudykunst (ed.), *Intergroup Communication* (London: Arnold, 1986); Ellen Bouchard Ryan and Howard Giles (eds.), *Attitudes toward Language Variation: Social and Applied Contexts* (London: Arnold, 1982).

2. Cynthia Gallois, Arlene Franklyn-Stokes, Howard Giles, and Nikolas Coupland, "Communication Accommodation in Intercultural Encounters," *Theories in Intercultural Communication*, ed. Young Yun Kim and William B. Gudykunst (Newbury Park, CA: Sage, 1988), 157–188.

3. Marsha Houston and Cheris Kramarae, "Speaking from Silence: Methods of Silencing and Resistance," *Discourse & Society* 2 (1991): 387–399; Cheris Kramarae, *Women and Men Speaking* (Rowley, MA: Newbury House, 1981).

4. Mary M. Meares, John G. Oetzel, Annette Torres, Denise Derkacs, and Tamar Ginossar, "Employee Mistreatment and Muted Voices in the Culturally Diverse Workplace," *Journal of Applied Communication Research* 32 (2004): 4–27.

5. Mark P. Orbe, "'Remember, It's Always Whites' Ball': Descriptions of African American Male Communication," *Communication Quarterly* 42 (1994): 287–300.

6. Yehuda Amir, "Contact Hypothesis in Ethnic Relations," *Psychological Bulletin* 71 (1969): 319–343.

7. Gallois et al.

8. Miles Hewstone and Rupert Brown, "Contact Is Not Enough: An Intergroup Perspective on the 'Contact Hypothesis,'" *Contact and Conflict in Intergroup Encounters*, ed. Miles Hewstone and Rupert Brown (Oxford: Blackwell, 1986), 1–44.

9. Miles Hewstone and Howard Giles, "Social Groups and Social Stereotypes in Intergroup Communication: A Review and Model of Intergroup Communication Breakdown," *Intergroup Communication*, ed. William B. Gudykunst (London: Arnold, 1986), 10–26.

10. The definition is modified from one proposed by Young Yun Kim. See Young Yun Kim, "Adapting to an Unfamiliar Culture," *Handbook of International and Intercultural Communication*, 2nd ed., ed. William B. Gudykunst and Bella Mody (Thousand Oaks, CA: Sage, 2002), 260; Young Yun Kim, *Becoming Intercultural: An Integrative Theory of Communication and Cross-Cultural Adaptation* (Thousand Oaks, CA: Sage, 2001), 31; Young Yun Kim, "Adapting to a New Culture: An Integrative Communication Theory," *Theorizing about Intercultural Communication*, ed. William B. Gudykunst (Thousand Oaks, CA: Sage, 2005), 375–400.

11. John W. Berry, Uichol Kim, and Pawel Boski, "Psychological Acculturation of Immigrants," *Cross-Cultural Adaptation: Current Approaches*, ed. Young Yun Kim and William B. Gudykunst (Newbury Park, CA: Sage, 1988).

12. Kalvero Oberg, "Cultural Shock: Adjustment to New Cultural Environments," *Practical Anthropology* 7 (1960): 176.

13. Oberg.

14. D. Bhugra, "Migration and Depression," *Acta Psychiatrica Scandinavica* 108 (2003): 67–72; Michael Brein and Kenneth H. David, "Intercultural Communication and the Adjustment of the Sojourner," *Psychological Bulletin* 76 (1971): 215–230; Kevin F. Gaw, "Reverse Culture Shock in Students Returning from Overseas," *International Journal of Intercultural Relations* 24 (2000): 83–104; J. Gullahorn and J. E. Gullahorn, "An Extension of the U-Curve Hypothesis," *Journal of Social Issues* 14 (1963): 33–47; Daniel J. Kealey, "A Study of Cross-Cultural Effectiveness: Theoretical Issues, Practical Applications," *International Journal of Intercultural Relations* 13 (1989): 387–428; Otto Klineberg and W. Frank Hull, *At a Foreign University: An International Study of Adaptation and Coping* (New York: Praeger, 1979); Jolene Koester, "Communication and the Intercultural Reentry: A Course Proposal," *Communication Education* 23 (1984): 251–256; Judith N. Martin, "The Intercultural Reentry: Conceptualizations and Suggestions for Future Research," *International Journal of Intercultural Relations* 8 (1984): 115–134; Craig Storti, *The Art of Coming Home* (Yarmouth, ME: Intercultural Press, 2001); Ching Wan, "The Psychology of Culture Shock," *Asian Journal of Social Psychology* 7 (2004): 233–234; Colleen Ward, Stephen Bochner, and Adrian Furnham, *The Psychology of Culture Shock*, 2nd ed. (New York: Routledge, 2001).

15. See, for instance, Sarah Brabant, C. Eddie Palmer, and Robert Gramling, "Returning Home: An Empirical Investigation of Cross-Cultural Reentry," *International Journal of Intercultural Relations* 14 (1990): 387–404.

16. Walter Enloe and Philip Lewin, "Issues of Integration Abroad and Readjustment to Japan of Japanese Returnees," *International Journal of Intercultural Relations* 11 (1987): 223–248; Louise H. Kidder, "Requirements for Being 'Japanese': Stories of Returnees," *International Journal of Intercultural Relations* 16 (1992): 383–393.

17. Enloe and Lewin, 235.

18. Nancy Adler, "Re-Entry: Managing Cross-Cultural Transitions," *Group and Organization Studies* 6 (1981): 341–356; Austin Church, "Sojourner Adjustment," *Psychological Bulletin* 91 (1982): 540–572; Dennison Nash, "The Course of Sojourner Adaptation: A New Test of the U-Curve Hypothesis," *Human Organization* 50 (1991): 283–286.

19. See, for example, Young Yun Kim and Brent D. Ruben, "Intercultural Transformation: A Systems Theory," *Theories in Intercultural Communication*, ed. Young Yun Kim and William B. Gudykunst (Newbury Park, CA: Sage, 1988), 299–321.

20. Daniel J. Kealey, "A Study of Cross-Cultural Effectiveness: Theoretical Issues, Practical Applications," *International Journal of Intercultural Relations* 13 (1989): 387–428.

21. Andrew G. Ryder, Lynn E. Alden, and Delroy L. Paulhus, "Is Acculturation Unidimensional or Bidimensional? A Head-to-Head Comparison in the Prediction of Personality, Self-Identity, and Adjustment," *Journal of Personality and Social Psychology* 79 (2000): 49–65.

22. Mitchell R. Hammer, William B. Gudykunst, and Richard L. Wiseman, "Dimensions of Intercultural Effectiveness: An Exploratory Study," *International Journal of Intercultural Relations* 2 (1978): 382–393.

23. See Colleen Ward and Antony Kennedy, "Locus of Control, Mood Disturbance, and Social Difficulty During Cross-Cultural Transitions," *International Journal of Intercultural Relations* 2 (1992): 175–194; Colleen Ward and Antony Kennedy, "Acculturation and Cross-Cultural Adaptation of British Residents in Hong Kong," *Journal of Social Psychology* 133 (1993): 395–397; Colleen Ward and Antony Kennedy, "The Measurement of Sociocultural Adaptation," *International Journal of Intercultural Relations* 23 (1999): 659–677; Colleen Ward and Wendy Searle, "The Impact of Value Discrepancies and Cultural Identity on Psychological and Sociological Adjustment of Sojourners," *International Journal of Intercultural Relations* 15 (1991): 209–225.

24. Guo-Ming Chen, "Communication Adaptability and Interaction Involvement as Predictors of Cross-Cultural Adjustment," *Communication Research Reports* 9 (1992): 33–41.
25. Berry, Kim, and Boski, 66.
26. Berry, Kim, and Boski, 71.
27. Kim and Ruben, 313–314.
28. David W. Kale, "Ethics in Intercultural Communication," *Intercultural Communication: A Reader*, 6th ed., ed. Larry A. Samovar and Richard E. Porter (Belmont, CA: Wadsworth, 1991), 423.
29. Kale.
30. Ker Munthit, "Cambodia Tourism Boom a Mixed Blessing," *Desert News* (Salt Lake City), December 3, 2006, online edition; Dante Ramos, "Touring the Tragic Kingdom," *Boston Globe*, October 28, 2007, online edition.
31. John F. Kennedy, "Remarks Prepared for Delivery at the Trade Mart in Dallas," November 22, 1963. Accessed online July 6, 2008, from http://www. jfklibrary.org/Historical+Resources/Archives/Reference+Desk/Speeches/JFK/003POF03TradeMart11221963.htm.
32. Charles Ess and Fay Sudweeks, *Culture, Technology, and Communication: Towards an Intercultural Global Village* (Albany: State University of New York Press, 2001). See also: Radhika Gajjala, "Interrogating Identities: Composing Other Cyberspaces," *Intercultural Alliances: Critical Transformation*, ed. Mary Jane Collier (Thousand Oaks, CA: Sage, 2003), 167–188.
33. Myron W. Lustig (Primary Program Planner), "Widening Our Circle," Conference theme for the annual convention of the Western States Communication Association (Albuquerque, 2004).
34. Troy Duster, "Understanding Self-Segregation on the Campus," *Chronicle of Higher Education*, September 25, 1991, B2.

Text Credits

p. 4: Data gathered from Bureau of the Census, 2008; www.adherents.com; and www.about.com.

p. 7: Reprinted with the permission of Simon & Schuster, Inc. from *Translations of Beauty* by Mia Yun. Copyright © 2004 by Mia Yun. All rights reserved.

p. 11: Deon Meyer, *Dead at Daybreak*. New York: Little, Brown, 2000, p. 150.

p. 15: Reprinted with permission of *Hispanic Outlook Magazine*. Visit our Web site at www.HispanicOutlook.com.

p. 18: Nina Mehta, "From Here to Poland," *Half and Half: Writers on Growing Up Biracial and Bicultural,* ed. Claudine Chiawei O'Hearn (New York: Pantheon Books, 1998), 219.

p. 20: Lewis, Elliott, "The Clorox Complex," pp 77–78. From *Fade: My Journeys in Multiracial America*. New York: Carroll & Graf Publishers, 2006. Copyright © 2006 by Elliott Lewis. Reprinted by permission of Basic/Carroll & Graff, a member of Perseus Books Group.

p. 21: Martin Luther King, Jr.

p. 22: Leila Ahmad, *A Border Passage: From Cairo to America—A Woman's Journey*. New York: Penguin Books, 1999, pp. 25–26.

p. 26: Myron W. Lustig, "Culture's Core," *Western Journal of Communication,* 60(4), Fall 1996, pp. 415–416.

p. 28: From "The Cab Driver's Daughter," by Waheeda Samady, in *Snapshots: This Afghan American Life,* ed. Tamim Ansary and Yalda Asmatey, Kajakai Press, San Francisco, 2008. Reprinted with permission from the author.

p. 30: Meri Nana-Ama Danquah, "Life as an Alien," in *Half and Half: Writers on Growing Up Biracial and Bicultural,* ed. Claudine Chiawei O'Hearn (New York: Pantheon Books, 1998), 99, 104–105, 106.

p. 31: From *American Chica* by Marie Arana, copyright © 2001 by Marie Arana. Used by permission of Dial Press/Dell Publishing, a division of Random House, Inc.

p. 32: Lionel Trilling, *The Liberal Imagination: Essays on Literature and Society.* New York: Viking, 1950, p. 203.

p. 35: Dana Stabenow, *A Grave Denied*. New York: St. Martin's Press, 2003, p. 33.

p. 40: Christiane Bird, *A Thousand Sighs, A Thousand Revolts*. New York: Random House, 2005, p. 13.

p. 43: From *West of Kabul, East of New York: An Afghan American Story* by Tamim Ansary. Copyright © 2002 by Tamim Ansary. Used with permission from Macmillan Publishers.

p. 53: Caroline Hwang, "The Good Daughter." *Newsweek,* September 21, 1998, p. 16.

p. 55: Toni Morrison, commencement Speech, May 28, 2004, Wellesley College (http://www.wellesley.edu/PublicAffairs/Commencement/2004/morrison.html, retrieved June 7, 2004).

pp. 58–59: Fariss Samarrai, "All American-American," *The Christian Science Monitor,* July 3, 2001, 22. Reprinted with permission from the author.

p. 62: Nicole Krauss, *The History of Love*. New York: W.W. Norton & Co., 2005, pp. 95–97

p. 64: Richard Rodriguez, "'Blaxicans' and Other Reinvented Americans," *Chronicles of Higher Education*, September 12, 2003, B11.

p. 68: From "First, the Blanket," by Kate Baldus. In *Expat: Women's True Tales of Life Abroad,* edited by Christina Henry de Tessan. Copyright © 2002 by Christina Henry de Tessan. Reprinted by permission of Seal Press, a member of Perseus Books Group.

p. 71: "Minority Students Face Identity Issue" by Jose Antonio Vargas. Dec. 8, 2003, p. A1. © San Francisco Chronicle. Reprinted by permission.

p. 74: From *Madame Dread* by Kathie Klarreich. New York: Nation Books, 2005, pp. 28–29. Copyright © 2005 by Kathie Klarreich. Reprinted by permission of Nation Books, a member of Perseus Books Group.

p. 76: Thurgood Marshall, spoken at Independence Hall in Philadelphia. July 4, 1992.

p. 78: Jessica Adler, "Our Actions and Outlook Spoke for Us," *The Christian Science Monitor,* May 2, 2002, 18–19. Reprinted by permission.

p. 86: Excerpt from *The Zigzag Way: A Novel* by Anita Desai. Reprinted by permission of Houghton Mifflin Harcourt Publishing Company. All rights reserved.

p. 88: From *West of Kabul, East of New York: An Afghan American Story* by Tamim Ansary. Copyright © 2002 by Tamim Ansary. Used with permission from Macmillan Publishers.

p. 91: From *Madame Dread* by Kathie Klarreich. New York: Nation Books, 2005. Copyright © 2005 by Kathie Klarreich. Reprinted by permission of Nation Books, a member of Perseus Books Group.

p. 99: Excerpt from *Thirty-Three Teeth* by Colin Cotterill, © 2005 by Colin Cotterill, published by permission of Soho Press, Inc.

p. 103: Jessie Carroll Grearson and Lauren B. Smith, *Love in a Global Village*. Iowa City: University of Iowa Press, 2001, pp. 69–70. Reprinted with permission.

p. 105: Nick Jans, *The Last Light Breaking: Living among Alaska's Inupiat Eskimos*. Seattle: Alaska Northwest Books, 1993, pp. 105–106. Reprinted with permission.

p. 108: From *American Fuji* by Sara Backer, copyright © 2001 by Sara Backer. Used by permission of Marion Wood Books, an imprint of G. P. Putnam, a division of Penguin Group (USA) Inc.

p. 110: Waris Dirie and Cathleen Miller, *Desert Flower*. New York: William Morrow and Company, 1998, p. 25.

p. 113: From *The Sultan's Seal* by Jenny White. Copyright © 2006 by Jenny White. Used by permission of W. W. Norton & Company, Inc.

p. 117: Leslie Glass, *The Silent Bride*. New York: Onyx, 2002, p. 212.

p. 119: From Myron W. Lustig & Jolene Koester, *AmongUs: Essays on Identity, Belonging, and Intercultural Competence*, 2/e. Published by Allyn & Bacon, Boston, MA. Copyright © 2006 by Pearson Education. Adapted by permission of the publisher.

p. 126: "Indonesia," from *Eat, Pray, Love* by Elizabeth Gilbert, copyright © 2006 by Elizabeth Gilbert. Used by permission of Viking Penguin, a division of Penguin Group (USA) Inc., and Bloomsbury Publishing, Plc.

p. 128: Jodi Picoult, *Plain Truth*. New York: Washington Square Press, 2000, p. 128.

p. 131: Dervla Murphy, *The Ukimwi Road: From Kenya to Zimbabwe*. Woodstock, NY: Overlook Press, 1993, p. 128.

p. 142: Excerpt from *What Are You: Voices of Mixed-Race Young People* by Pearl Fuyo Gaskins. Copyright © 1999 by Pearl Fuyo Gaskins. Reprinted by permission of Henry Holt and Company, LLC. Reproduced with permission of Blackwell Publishing, Ltd.

p. 144: From *Fade: My Journeys in Multiracial America*. Copyright © 2006 by Elliott Lewis. Reprinted by permission of Basic/Carroll & Graff, a member of Perseus Books Group.

p. 147: From "Muddy Waters in Borneo," by Meg Wirth. In *Expat: Women's True Tales of Life Abroad*, edited by Christina Henry de Tessan. Copyright © 2002 by Christina Henry de Tessan. Reprinted by permission of Seal Press, a member of Perseus Books Group.

p. 149: From *Country of Origin: A Novel* by Don Lee. Copyright © 2004 by Don Lee. Used by permission of W. W. Norton & Company, Inc.

p. 154: From "Living the Dream in Paris" by Christina Henry de Tessan. In *Expat: Women's True Tales of Life Abroad*, edited by Christina Henry de Tessan. Copyright © 2002 by Christina Henry de Tessan. Reprinted by permission of Seal Press, a member of Perseus Books Group.

p. 158: From *Respect: An Exploration* by Sara Lawrence-Lightfoot. New York: Basic Books, 2000, p. 140.

p. 162: Excerpt from Rubén Martínez, "The Crossing." *West Magazine*: June 25, 2006, p. 21.

p. 167: From "Saudades" by Eliza Bonner. In *Expat: Women's True Tales of Life Abroad*, edited by Christina Henry de Tessan. Copyright © 2002 by Christina Henry de Tessan. Reprinted by permission of Seal Press, a member of Perseus Books Group.

p. 169: Chang-rae Lee, *Native Speaker*. New York: Riverhead Books, 1995, pp. 233–234.

p. 173: Lesslie Newbigin, *The Gospel in a Pluralistic Society*, Grand Rapids: W. B. Eerdman, 1989, p. 101.

p. 174: Leslie Forbes, *Fish, Blood and Bone*. New York: Farrar, Straus and Giroux, 2001, p. 25.

p. 176: Ian Parker. "The Mirage." *The New Yorker*, Oct. 17, 2005. Reprinted with permission from Ian Parker.

pp. 180–181: Leigh Minturn, *Sita's Daughters: Coming Out of Purdah*. New York: Oxford University Press, 1993.

p. 183: Jerry Miller, "A Language of Sharing and Poetic Pictures," *The Christian Science Monitor*, November 20, 2000, 22. Reprinted by permission.

p. 188: From *House of Many Gods* by Kiana Davenport, copyright © 2006 by Kiana Davenport. Used by permission of Ballantine Books, a division of Random House, Inc.

p. 191: Sharon Huntington, "The Secret Language of Parents," *The Christian Science Monitor*, July 28, 1997, 17. Reprinted by permission.

p. 192: Marcos M. Villatoro, *A Venom Beneath the Skin*. New York: Dell, 2005, p. 164.

p. 194: Gregory David Roberts, *Shantaram*. New York: St. Martin's Griffin, 2003, p. 287.

p. 199: Nick Jans, *The Last Light Breaking: Living among Alaska's Inupiat Eskimos*. Seattle: Alaska Northwest Books, 1993, pp. 34–35. Reprinted by permission.

p. 204: Will Randall, *Botswana Time*. London: Abucus, 2005, p. 116.

p. 205: Joyce Mercer, "Native Hawaiians Push to Extend and Deepen University Diversity," *Chronicle of Higher Education*, August 3, 1994, A28.

p. 206: Paul Opstad, "Some Considerations in Counseling Cambodians," *Intercultural Network News*, 1(4), July/August 1990, 2.

p. 209: Jessie Carroll Grearson and Lauren B. Smith, *Love in a Global Village.* Iowa City: University of Iowa Press, 2001, pp. 36–37. Reprinted by permission.

p. 211: May-lee Chai, *My Lucky Face.* New York: Soho Press, pp. 112–113.

p. 213: Excerpt from *Thirty-Three Teeth* by Colin Cotterill, © 2005 by Colin Cotterill, published by permission of Soho Press, Inc.

p. 217: Gregory David Roberts, *Shantaram.* New York: St. Martin's Griffin, 2003, pp. 106–107.

p. 218: Barbara J. Scot, *The Violet Shyness of Their Eyes.* Corvalis, OR: Calyx Books, 1993, p. 34.

p. 219: Geraldine Brooles, *Nine Parts of Desire: The Hidden World of Islamic Women.* New York: Doubleday, 1994, pp. 226–227.

p. 225: Patricia Harrington, *Death Stalks the Khmer.* Baltimore: AmErica House, 2000, p. 28.

p. 226: Danna Harman, "In Kabary, the Point is to Avoid the Point." Reproduced with permission from the May 9, 2002 issue of *The Christian Science Monitor* (www.csmonitor.com). © 2002 The Christian Science Monitor. All rights reserved.

p. 227: From *Sacramento Bee*, 6/2/91, p. A18.

p. 229: *The Jade Peony* by Wayson Choy is published in the U.S. by Other Press and in Canada 1995 by Douglas & McIntyre, Ltd. Reprinted by permission of the author and publisher.

p. 232: Pages 314–315 from *Burro Genius: A Memoir* by Victor Villaseñor. Copyright © 2004 by Victor Villaseñor. Reprinted by permission of HarperCollins Publishers.

p. 233: Sunwolf, "The Pedagogical and Persuasive Effects of Native American Lesson Stories, Sufi Wisdom Tales and African Dilemma Tales," *The Howard Journal of Communication,* 10 (1999): 47–71.

p. 235: Charles V. Hamilton, *The Black Preacher in America* (New York: William Morrow, 1972), 42, quoted in Nolefi Kete Asante, *The Afrocentric Idea* (Philadelphia: Temple University Press, 1987), 47.

p. 237: Excerpts from *The Namesake* by Jhumpa Lahiri. Copyright © 2003 by Jhumpa Lahiri. Reprinted by permission of Houghton Mifflin Harcourt Publishing Company. All rights reserved.

p. 240: From "The Long Conversation" by Deryn P. Verity. In *Expat: Women's True Tales of Life Abroad,* edited by Christina Henry de Tessan. Copyright © 2002 by Christina Henry de Tessan. Reprinted by permission of Seal Press, a member of Perseus Books Group.

p. 241: "Athabaskan-English Interethnic Communication" by Ronald Scollon and Suzanne-Wong Scollon in *Cultural Communication and Intercultural Contact,* edited by Donal Carbaugh, p. 284. Copyright © 1981 by Taylor & Francis Group LLC – Books. Reproduced with permission of Taylor & Francis Group LLC – Books in the formats Textbook and Other book via Copyright Clearance Center.

p. 246: From Myron W. Lustig & Jolene Koester, *AmongUs: Essays on Identity, Belonging, and Intercultural Competence,* 2/e. Published by Allyn & Bacon, Boston, MA. Copyright © 2006 by Pearson Education. Adapted by permission of the publisher.

p. 248: Alexander McCall Smith, *The Full Cupboard of Life.* New York: Anchor, 2003, p. 110.

p. 252: Elisabeth Bumiller, *May You Be the Mother of a Hundred Sons.* (New York: Fawcett Columbine, 1990), 8.

p. 253: "Indonesia," from *Eat, Pray, Love* by Elizabeth Gilbert, copyright © 2006 by Elizabeth Gilbert. Used by permission of Viking Penguin, a division of Penguin Group (USA) Inc., and Bloomsbury Publishing, Plc.

p. 256: From *When in Rome or Rio or Riyadh: Cultural Q & A's for Successful Business Behavior Around the World* by Gwyneth Olofsson, copyright © 2004 by Gwyneth Olofsson, p. 277. Used by permission of Intercultural Press, Inc.

p. 258: From *The Kite Runner* by Khaled Hosseini, copyright © 2003 by Khaled Hosseini. Used by permission of Riverhead Books, an imprint of Penguin Group (USA) Inc.

p. 261: Excerpt from *A Loyal Character Dancer*, copyright © 2002 by Qiu Xiaolong, reprinted by permission of Soho Press, Inc.

p. 263: Anna Wierzbicka, "The Double Life of a Bilingual," in *Working at the Interface of Cultures,* edited by Michael Bond. London: Routledge, 1997, p. 117.

p. 265: From Christiane Bird, *A Thousand Sighs, A Thousand Revolts.* New York: Random House, 2005, p. 44.

p. 268: "Five Magic Words Help Ease the Way" by Susan Spano from *Los Angeles Times,* 5/9/04, pp. L6–7.

p. 271: Jessie Carroll Grearson and Lauren B. Smith, *Love in a Global Village.* Iowa City: University of Iowa Press, 2001, pp. xviii–xix. Reprinted with permission.

p. 276: Leila Ahmad, *A Border Passage: From Cairo to America— A Woman's Journey.* New York: Penguin Books, 1999, p. 161.

p. 278: From *C'est La Vie* by Suzy Gershman, copyright © 2004 by Suzy Gershman. Used by permission of Viking Penguin, a division of Penguin Group (USA) Inc.

p. 279: From *American Fuji* by Sara Backer, copyright © 2001 by Sara Backer. Used by permission of Marion Wood Books, an imprint of G. P. Putnam, a division of Penguin Group (USA) Inc.

p. 282: Nelson DeMille, *Up Country.* New York: Warner Books, 2002, p. 419.

p. 283: Sarah Macdonald, *Holy Cow: An Indian Adventure.* New York: Broadway Books, 2003, p. 63.

p. 284: Pages 18–19 from *Peripheral Visions* by Mary Catherine Bateson. Copyright © Mary Catherine Bateson. Reprinted by permission of HarperCollins Publishers.

p. 290: Donald E. Hall, *The Academic Community: A Manual for Change.* Columbus: The Ohio State University Press, 2007, pp. 42–43.

p. 296: Maria J. Estrada, "Personal Narrative as a Route to Voice," *Hispanic Outlook,* November 19, 1999, 36–37.

p. 304: From *When in Rome or Rio or Riyadh: Cultural Q & A's for Successful Business Behavior Around the World* by Gwyneth Olofsson, copyright © 2004 by Gwyneth Olofsson, p. 302. Used by permission of Intercultural Press, Inc.

p. 308: "Indonesia," from *Eat, Pray, Love* by Elizabeth Gilbert, copyright © 2006 by Elizabeth Gilbert. Used by permission of Viking Penguin, a division of Penguin Group (USA) Inc., and Bloomsbury Publishing, Plc.

p. 309: From Christiane Bird, *A Thousand Sighs, A Thousand Revolts.* New York: Random House, 2005, p. 34.

p. 315: Roya Hakakian, *Journey from the Land of No.* New York: Three Rivers Press, 2004, p. 14.

p. 317: From "Before and After Mexico" by Gina Hyams. In *Expat: Women's True Tales of Life Abroad,* edited by Christina Henry de Tessan. Copyright © 2002 by Christina Henry de Tessan. Reprinted by permission of Seal Press, a member of Perseus Books Group.

p. 320: Peter Hessler, *River Town: Two Years on the Yangtze.* New York: Perennial, 2001, p. 65.

p. 323: Excerpts from *The Namesake* by Jhumpa Lahiri. Copyright © 2003 by Jhumpa Lahiri. Reprinted by permission of Houghton Mifflin Harcourt Publishing Company. All rights reserved.

p. 324: Howard Gardner, *Five Minds for the Future.* Boston: Harvard Business School Press, 2007, pp. 106–107.

p. 326: Dervla Murphy, *South from the Limpopo.* Woodstock, NY: The Overlook Press, 1997, p. 14.

p. 328: Nick Jans, *The Last Light Breaking: Living among Alaska's Inupiat Eskimos.* Seattle: Alaska Northwest Books, 1993, pp. 121–122. Reprinted with permission.

p. 330: Alexander McCall Smith, *The Full Cupboard of Life.* New York: Anchor, 2003, p. 27.

p. 332: Nelson Mandela.

p. 332: Final report from the White House Conference on Culture and Diplomacy, November 28, 2000.

p. 336: Nury Vittachi, *The Feng Shui Detective.* Hong Kong: Chameleon Press, 2000, 310.

Author Index

Subject Index